YVES SAINT LAURENT

A BIOGRAPHY

YVES SAINT LAURENT

LAURENCE BENAÏM

TRANSLATED FROM THE FRENCH BY KATE DEIMLING

Rizzoli
ex libris

First published in the United States of America in 2019
by Rizzoli Ex Libris, an imprint of
Rizzoli International Publications, Inc.
300 Park Avenue South
New York, NY 10010
www.rizzoliusa.com

2019 2020 2021 2022 / 10 9 8 7 6 5 4 3 2 1

Distributed in the U.S. trade by Random House, New York

Printed in the United States

ISBN: 978-0-8478-6339-6

Library of Congress Control Number: 2018951394

Front cover photograph: Horst P. Horst / Vogue © Condé Nast Publications, Inc.

Mural by Atelier Mériguet-Carrère, home of Yves Saint Laurent
and Pierre Bergé, Deauville, Normandy.

Yves Saint Laurent by Laurence Benaïm © Èditions Grasset & Fasquelle, 2002

To Rachel and Herman Frajder

"My weapon is the way I see my era."
YVES SAINT LAURENT

"Is there not some danger in pretending to be dead?"
MOLIÈRE, *The Imaginary Invalid*, ACT III, SCENE 17

"'We are Lion,' he said, 'and lions in the desert
are sometimes depressed. You think they're
screwed and then suddenly they wake up and…'
And he imitated the MGM lion's roar."
JEAN-JACQUES SCHUHL, *Ingrid Caven*

CONTENTS

PREFACE

At 5 Avenue Marceau, there were many kinds of silence: the silence of lines; the cream-colored silence of the toiles, or test garments; the soft, round silence of the workshops; the silence of hands; the cold, stony silence of waiting, when he wasn't there; the happy silence of a smile glimpsed in a mirror; and the silence of beauty, a love story between the models and him. And then the silence of fear and doubt, which haunted him.

I first encountered Yves Saint Laurent as a designer in 1986, and a year later we had the chance to meet in person. This biography was first published in 1993 and new editions came out in 2002, when Yves Saint Laurent closed his fashion house, and again in 2010. He once told me, "You know my life much better than I do." Clearly, this isn't true. Writing the life of this man during his lifetime meant refusing to fall into certain traps. I never tried to avoid his dark areas, but I emphasized the light inside that made him so different. Others chose to follow him elsewhere. While he identified with many different characters, primarily Proust's Swann, Yves Saint Laurent exists as an irreducible individual, beyond himself and beyond the body that he let collapse, crumple, thicken, and decay, the body that he abandoned and subjected to all kinds of violence—drugs, rehab, and uncontrolled loneliness.

In 2018, ten years after his death, Yves Saint Laurent is still isolated. He was the man who understood women with a glance before even meeting them. He became their way of seeing the world. He was surely the first to express desire in all its facets in his designs, from domination to submission, without the old erotic clichés. With him, everything stemmed from sincerity as well as artifice, flowing from his passion-red heart. Red for Yves Saint Laurent was not the red carpet with women draped in black who all look alike, smoothed out and standardized. It was the velvet curtain of the theater of night; it was poppy kisses that leave marks everywhere—on cheeks, on champagne glasses, in the imagination. It was parties without selfies where everyone was a potential double of Yves. He was hero and heroine, an angel-demon, unique, of all centuries and all sexes. His was a kingdom of phantoms of freedom, excitement, chimeras, shadowy caresses, divine cuff bracelets from old movies, and the giddy celebrations of the damned. Yves Saint Laurent remains the sui generis designer for things that happen behind closed doors, mysterious parties, women who practice the aloof art of seduction. He read into the hearts of redheads, and his chaste goddesses with boyish busts are the same ones that he sketched as a teenager in Oran, dreaming of these creatures with "violent makeup" who appeared at Dior from 1958 to 1960. His wild beasts, his serpents, with eyes the color of the abyss.

He belonged to the nameless people of exile. He was both an asteroid and the core of an old comet, a supernova that shifted the perception of the solar system of fashion. From Chanel's beloved sun and Dior's star-talisman, Yves Saint Laurent created a ball of fire. He is the meteor that continues to light up the galaxy long after his death. For me, that is his supreme strength: he was not just the spiritual son of Chanel and Dior, of time and the moment, of style and fashion. He invented a universal language, a way of seeing and of revealing personalities that he stripped down while dressing them—images of women who were mothers, sisters, lovers.

What remains of the glory that the pale young man from Oran was able to maintain for half a century, in fire and passion, with Pierre Bergé as his mentor? The giant has been somewhat diminished since revelations and confessions have sought to tear away everything that he had desperately tried to preserve: the honor of a couturier. His strength was to defend himself with what he had created, with the love that he continued to project, and with the boldness of not belonging to any caste. The more the cameras focus on the bedroom of the deceased, the more he scoffs at his predators, upstages his followers, and inspires virtue. He answers for himself, engaging in battle whatever the cost may be. The dresses have souls that gain strength from the ravages of time: they stand up straight, and never give up. That day, his dog Moujik ate the tapes from my tape recorder.

Writing is not just remembering, but also telling, observing, looking, and bearing witness to what is eternally there: a mystery that resists all attempts to box it in, all guided tours, all biopics, and all eyes riveted on this body of which he was the sorcerer's apprentice. In order to escape himself—in order to create by going beyond himself—this Saint was the combined radiance of Yves and Laurent. An infernal threesome. A lesson in grace. With his glorious blacks and his drunken blue-greens, he sketched personalities, shredding the earthly ideal expressed by Théophile Gautier: "No matter what we do, happiness is white and pink; we can hardly depict it differently. Soft colors are its birthright. It has on its palette only sea green, sky blue, and straw yellow."[1] Instead of these pastel snapshots, Yves Saint Laurent preferred the danger, chasms, and magic of his imaginary journeys.

The empire that he built with Pierre Bergé arose in a whirlwind of exhilaration. With the soul of a couturier, he designed for the soul and the skin, eliminating fashion's bland prettiness. He freed fashion of its conventions, ceremonies, and fussiness. For him, the line of a dress was primarily a look, a necessity—an expression that was enhanced by a bold accessory, by the interplay of colors, the combination of materials, and the dramatic reinvention of the self, never stiff or constrained. No crinolines and no geometry. He was the first one to get it. Maison Christian Dior still has assistants' sketches with annotations by the twenty-two-year-old Yves Saint Laurent: "This isn't a wide skirt but a sheath!" We can sense his presence—infuriated, obsessive, swearing silently, inserting dashes, crossing out the design called Metamorphosis and adding a disgusted "oh!" When revising the Armide design, he commented, "Not so many gathers, it looks like a parcel!" YSL had no more patience for the almost-good-enough than he did for himself. Paris is now merely the shadow of the city that he made his capital and his perfume.

Saint Laurent is Kahina singing "I Will Survive." Being there, to defend himself, and to defend a profession. Drawing the line against fuss and bother, the too small, narrowmindedness, and boredom. Defying the taboos of the bourgeoisie, whom he put through the wringer. Ten years after his death, Yves Saint Laurent has never been so inspiring. He vibrates and dances, as free as his sketches. Behind his bars, the lion roars, anxious and unpredictable. Yves Saint Laurent's clothes always seem younger than those who look at them and remember them. Jackets with protruding shoulders. Cloches in white piqué fabric at a rakish angle on the head. Impressions of ties, bodice belts, bouquets of artificial flowers, silver fox, feathered birds, rhinestone stars, fiery lips. With the first fashion show in 1962, the launch of Rive Gauche in 1966, and the famous Liberation collection in 1971, Yves Saint Laurent expressed "the consistently aesthetic experience of the world" in his designs.[2] He is about standing out, disturbing, and creating a strange beauty that overwhelms everything in its path. As predatory as Andy Warhol, he never stopped re-creating and imposing his elective affinities—his kaleidoscope of quotations, affiliations, and addictions—on the runways of the world.

There remain phantoms, presences, superstitions, memories, the impudent Vilaine Lulu, and all those who worked with him, their eyes still brimming with tears. In Paris, some people see him as a magician or a medium. At 5 Avenue Marceau, in the large conference room, his portrait by Irving Penn is still there, observing the world from behind the hand that he used like a domino mask. In Marrakesh, taxi drivers say they remember him, as well as "Monsieur Majorelle." Mirages. He died before his light. It keeps him awake. There is the untouchable beauty of the Orpheus in mousseline, and there is the street that inspired him and that he clothed, but the street, more faithless, no longer remembers him. Or barely. Yet where would it be without him? Without his androgynous peacoats, his trench coats, this male wardrobe that he turned into a series of essential women's items? He turned pants, which women were forbidden to wear at French companies until 1968, into a classic. The memory of Yves Saint Laurent is recharged like a battery of paradoxes. His sense of extremes. His velvet Lady Macbeths. His Eves in Rive Gauche safari jackets, nude under their Le Smokings. He is in the museum along with his icons. He is on the outside with everything that his name signifies: freedom to be, to move, to invent one's life. To trace it out the way one designs a dream in front of a mirror. Finding liberation from the little darts of existence, its false pleats, everything that stands in the way of a look.

YVES SAINT LAURENT

1 / BITTERSWEET ORAN

The women of Oran, Algeria, had only one concern: definitively out-flirting the women of Algiers. They sparkled with merriment and wit out at the casino, at teas, or at intimate dinners in neighboring villas. The naval officers preferred Oran to Algiers: the girls were prettier. In Algiers, the seat of government offices, people socialized in small groups, played bridge, and went to bed at nine o'clock. But Oran was on Spanish time. People from Oran considered people from Algiers cold and inhospitable; people from Algiers considered people from Oran vulgar and mocked their pronunciation: "Are you from *Oron?*"

Shaped like an amphitheater opening up to the Mediterranean, at the base of Murdjadjo, the city sat on a low, marshy plain between the two slopes of the ravine that gave it its name: Ourahan. In its eagerness to build and make money, the city developed haphazardly. In Oran, men made business deals and women had beautiful children. The husbands made a lot of money; the wives spent it. Cosmopolitan and radiant, Oran hunkered down into its castes. The only way to escape them was to leave. At the top of the pyramid were the colonists, wealthy from agriculture, and the notables, who advertised for French live-in servants. Then there were the "minor Frenchmen": bureaucrats, teachers, professors. Jews and Spaniards completed the mosaic of Europeans. The Arabs were in the majority, but they weren't seen, except in the morning, when, after unloading the boats, they came back in groups of five or six and walked across the city toward the *village nègre*, the Arab neighborhood. Their strong bodies, tanned from work, glistened in the sunshine. Here, on the Saint-Michel plateau, lived the Mathieu-Saint-Laurent family.

Descended from Pierre Mathieu de Metz (born in 1640), the Mathieu-Saint-Laurents came from an Alsatian family of magistrates that had fled Colmar, France, in 1870 to escape the Germans. Their name was originally Mathieu de Heidolsheim. Yves's grandmother was a close friend of the sculptor Bartholdi and posed for him in front of the Schwendi Fountain in Colmar (her bust is in the municipal museum). His grandfather, Marie-Jules-Henri, established himself in Oran as a lawyer after studying Latin. Instead of land or farms, the family owned a twelve-room mansion, mahogany furniture in the Egyptian Revival style, and a living room presided over by an ancestral portrait of Joseph Ignace Mathieu, Baron of Mauvière, the man who drew up the marriage contract between Napoleon and Joséphine de Beauharnais. They referred to the painting as "a gift from the emperor" or "the David."

Under a partly cloudy sky, Yves Henri Donat Mathieu-Saint-Laurent was born on August 1, 1936, at the Jarsaillon clinic. It was the 214th day of the year, the feast day of Saint Hope. That was a fitting coincidence, since, as Yves's mother, Lucienne, recalled, "My husband's family had just lost a son following a wasp sting. Yves was like a gift from God!" They went all the way to Algiers to buy him a crib. Baptized on August 25, he would be followed by two sisters: Michèle in 1942 and Brigitte in 1945.

In the summer of 1936, Oran—as well as Algeria—was a happy place. People perused the newspaper at outdoor cafés. The August 1 issue of *L'Echo d'Oran* enthusiastically reported that the Führer had inaugurated the Olympic Games in Berlin as Dr. Goebbels hailed the flame of peace. So what if requisitioned ocean liners landed in Oran with refugees from the Spanish cities of Alicante and Valencia? Oran had other things on its mind.

Entertainment, for example: after dinner, there were concerts by the Orchestre Lamoureux, theater productions by the Galas Karsenty, and evenings at the Canastel casino. Boastful Oran residents considered their theater "the most famous stage, along with the Capitole in Toulouse," according to Lucienne. These performances were the place to be for the local elite. Oran was also the city of a thousand movie theaters. For a few cents, you could go to the Plaza, the Roxy, the Eden, the Idéal, the Régina, or other big movie theaters, sit in plush red seats, and look the stars right in their eyes. *L'Echo d'Oran*'s movie critic usually found the plot "exciting," the dialogue "witty," and the rhythm "frenzied," especially at the end, when the star and her partner would kiss and make up.

That year, Yvonne Printemps and Pierre Fresnay starred in *La Dame aux Camélias*, Marlene Dietrich glowed in her swan-down stole in *Desire* as the enchanting Madeleine de Beaupré, who drank tea from a crystal cup and was given pale yellow roses. *L'Echo d'Oran* soon recommended mousseline dresses and "fun, new" little Tyrolean prints. Another idol of the silver screen, Danielle Darrieux, whirled amorously with Charles Boyer in *Mayerling*. The women of Oran were already waltzing Vienna-style and dreaming of an impossible love at the imperial court with a handsome Crown Prince Rudolf in a braided uniform to whom they'd say, "Take me away!"

With a black crepe dress that fetchingly revealed her shoulders, Lucienne Mathieu-Saint-Laurent, Yves's mother, looked like Danielle Darrieux in *Mademoiselle ma Mère*. Her hairstyle and fluttering eyelashes were just like those of Darrieux, a big-name star whom all the women envied. Her emerald eyes were brought out by a thin pencil line in place of her eyebrows.

Lucienne's background was like something out of a novel: née Wilbaux, she was born to a Spanish mother from Sidi Bel Abbès and a Belgian father who was an engineer for coal mines in the Ouenza area at the northeastern tip of Algeria, Lucienne was raised by her mother's sister, Renée, a very wealthy widow whose deceased husband, Emile Cayla, was a music-loving architect. This aunt had furniture by Majorelle and Gallé, and early on she gave Lucienne a taste "for jewelry, dresses, everything." Lucienne grew up living a double life. She was unhappy as a boarding school student at Lycée Stéphane Gsell for girls, but went to her first ball in 1930, spent her summers in grand style in Paris with her cousins Henri and Pierre, and had already enjoyed the silken elegance of the Hôtel Royal in Evian. The Caylas stayed at the Impérial Palace in Annecy and the Martinez in Cannes, places where one had to dress for dinner. A shadowy Spanish chauffeur in uniform drove the Bugatti: "He was known for having affairs with his female customers."

The Lucienne of 1936 carefully filled the porcelain candy dishes with a natural gift for luxury. She wasn't one of those thrifty women who were driven by a sense of duty and family, who found black lingerie vulgar and considered actresses trashy. Frivolous and flirtatious, she had the manners of a lady. All her affection for the colonists' wives was expressed in a smile—a smile that judged but didn't prevent her from succumbing to the charms of these very rich, very beautiful, and very dark-haired women: "You have to see these women in Rio Salado swimming with their huge diamond rings." Although Lucienne did lose her engagement ring, it didn't happen at the beach.

Her husband worked a great deal, and traveled. Charles Mathieu-Saint-Laurent had a good position, and his neighbors considered him distinguished. He was in charge of an insurance company and managed a chain of cinemas in Morocco, Tunisia, and Algeria, which meant that his children could go to the movies for free. Imposing and athletic, he was a handsome man who took life as it came, tackling its challenges skillfully. Like his father, he did his *baccalauréat* at Oran's Lycée Lamoricière. At age nineteen, he studied law in Marseille and came back to Oran for summers with his uncle, a doctor for the city opera. Like so many other couples, Charles Mathieu-Saint-Laurent and Lucienne Wilbaux met on the Boulevard Seguin. "He was very handsome and six years older," Lucienne recalled. "He always wore a bowler hat and a white raincoat. There was a tea with dancing. He invited me. We were married on July 4, 1935."

The Mathieu-Saint-Laurents had French servants. Angèle did the cooking. Marie handled the heavy cleaning. The concierge took in the laundry (the washtub was in the courtyard). Only the gardener was Arab. The neighbors heard from Bartolo the delivery man that Madame regularly ordered cases of champagne. She liked to give parties and the crème de la crème were invited: the mayor, the prefect, the deputy prefect, important wine merchants, lawyers, industrialists, cheese wholesalers, etc. The Mathieu-Saint-Laurents loved to go out, especially Lucienne. At night, she said, they went "from one beautiful affair to the next." The best receptions were given by Madame Berthouin-Maraval, from an old wealthy Oran family. The president of the Association Amicale des Arts Africains, she also headed the charitable organizations the Beehive and the Drop of Milk. She gave parties in her Villa Eugénie amidst chinoiserie and gilded angels. She had flown across the Sahara and written poetry collections, *Land of Light* and *The Songs of the Hoggar Mountains*. She was an extremely wealthy eccentric who could be seen on Sundays at the Place d'Armes giving out Red Cross badges, wearing a black mousseline dress and a hat "as if she's going to the races," as people commented. "Proper" women whispered that she was the bishop's mistress. Lucienne didn't care about any of that. She was mostly concerned about her own clothing. What would she wear to the Admiralty, the yacht club, the tennis club, to dance the romantic rumba as the scent of Guerlain's Vol de Nuit wafted through the air and the sound of Tino Rossi's voice rose from the phonograph: "*Sous les étoiles d'argent…une mélodie monte vers le firmament. Dans la nuit, écoutez les mandolines…écoutez ces voix divines.*"

Yves grew up in the midst of laughter, sunshine, and secrets that gleamed dangerously in the eyes of an inscrutable mother. He was the boy king and had everything: stuffed animals, cars, tricycles, shows of *Snow White and the Seven Dwarfs*. At Little Vichy, a park with pebble paths along the promenade by the pond, the older children rode donkeys while the little ones made sand castles. Yves was dressed like a fancy sailor, with white pants and sandals. He learned quickly what was expected of him. He played the role of child with an admirable sense of caprice. "No, you don't look good in that," he told his Aunt Renée. She changed her outfit three times to make him happy.

The house at 11 Rue Stora was a house of women. In its rooms were vases of zinnias and all the merriment in the world. The neighbors remembered Lucienne's laughter, how it spilled out like a pearl necklace tumbling down a pink marble staircase. In the morning, she put on "something simple" to go look at the fruit at the market and came back with her arms full of flowers. Angèle had made lunch. In the afternoon, she ran errands in town. A rather snobbish sister-in-law sometimes held teas that she reluctantly attended. She walked down the Boulevard Seguin in her beautiful green dress. She was crazy about the vivid cotton fabric that she bought at the large fabric store, Michel, their local version of Bouchara in Paris. "Splendid," the neighbors commented as they drank their *agua limón* at Korsia. The mood of Yves's childhood was set by a flirtatious mother and a fanciful grandmother who wrote poetic letters, sang in churches, and hadn't forgotten she was once a great beauty. And Angèle's round beignets were a delicious afternoon snack.

From June to September, the Mathieu-Saint-Laurents stayed in their villa in Trouville. Just like Bouisseville, Clairefontaine, and Saint-Roch, Trouville was a beach for Oran's *grande bourgeoisie*. It was a question of caste. The more modest families settled for a cabin in Aïn el-Franine or had picnics on the beach and got annoyed at the traffic jams on the coastal road when they returned home on Sunday evenings. The Arabs didn't go to the beach. In Trouville, the Mathieu-Saint-Laurents got together with friends. The adults played canasta, gossiped in the sun, and had grilled tomatoes and lamb chops for lunch under the veranda. The children swam in the morning. The waves curled. When the bell rang, they'd come back barefoot, their eyes stinging from saltwater. The ground, stripped away by the hot dry wind called the sirocco, burned their feet. Parents always said the wind made them tired. Well-behaved children ate sole and took naps. On quiet days, they went swimming in the afternoon.

Yves's closest friend was named Simone Tronc. Her parents were married the same day as the Mathieu-Saint-Laurents and they also lived on the Saint-Michel plateau. Simone was born on June 30, 1936, and she and Yves were twins at heart. Their houses in Trouville were next door to each other, and every afternoon at four o'clock she came out to call him to the fence. One summer followed another single-file, like the stories of Séraphin that beautiful Irène Ayasse, a family friend nicknamed "la Golondrina," told in the shade. "Oh, I'm so sick of all these kids making such a racket that my head feels like a kettledrum." Their interests evolved. Simone remembered a "wonderful thing": an old raft from the American army, half ripped open. "We played with it all the time. There were also large abandoned buoys. We loved the big waves. The idea was to let yourself be carried and pretend you were drowning. We called it 'taxi.' That was when we were learning to swim."

In Oran, different spheres existed side by side but never mixed. Yves Mathieu-Saint-Laurent grew up in a separate world, a privileged fairytale existence removed from local and international events. On July 3, 1940, during the Mers-el-Kébir affair, when the British bombed the French fleet, the Mathieu-Saint-Laurents were in the cellar. Yves was not quite four years old. This was one of the few disturbing events to mar his family's happy life. Yet despite appearances, their laid-back, prosperous city was raging with anti-Semitism. On May 1, fighting broke out between fascists and Jews at the Café Riche. Members of the Croix-de-Feu marched down Rue d'Arzew with swastikas pinned to their jackets: "Down with the Jews now, let's hang them by their noses." And, of course, in 1940 the Crémieux decree granting French citizenship to Jews was abolished with great zeal. In fact, the yacht club that the Mathieu-Saint-Laurents belonged to had always unofficially banned Jews. It is interesting that much later Yves Saint Laurent would identify with Marcel Proust's Swann and point out that the character was Jewish.

Although Yves was attached to his hometown like a true son of the Mediterranean, his unusual, almost feminine sensibility inculcated in him—perhaps through these episodes—a hatred for bourgeois people who lived with fake Louis XV furniture, bought cream puffs at the Epi d'Or, and regularly went to Vichy to treat their livers. Their intolerance was accompanied by a determined focus on their own happiness.

Through his attraction to the marginalized, Yves discovered what made him different. As a teenager in Oran, he copied down a poem by Jacques Prévert decrying "the yellow star of cruel human stupidity" that throws its shadow on "the most beautiful rose of the Rue des Rosiers." "Her name was Sarah / or Rachel / and her father was a hatmaker / or a furrier / and he really loved salted herring." The narrative of the poem, which takes place in Paris, in the Jewish quarter of the Marais, ends this way: "But never more will she open the window / the door of a sealed train car / has closed over her once and for all…" though the sun "continues its course" and tries "to forget these things."

*

In Oran, the mosquitoes disappeared after the Americans arrived. The war left few memories in Oran: square white bread, cans of corned beef, and chewing gum with long-lasting flavor. And then the first bottles of Coca-Cola. "We saw red and white cases! They were iceboxes. From then on, life on the beach changed," recalled Simone. Naturally, she drank her first Coke at the Mathieu-Saint-Laurent house. "At Yves's house, everything was allowed." But for the poorer French citizens of Oran, the war meant grape sugar, cake with rolled oats, Jerusalem artichokes, sweet potatoes, and overcoats worn inside out as dressing gowns. Their children wore shoes with articulated soles. They thought of France, dreaming of good butter and green pastures. The Mathieu-Saint-Laurents would never know such deprivation. Their villa was festive. GIs came over with smiles as wide as jeeps filled with nylon stockings. Their arms were loaded with cases of whisky and cartons of Lucky Strikes.

Lucienne grew even more beautiful. Her lips were redder, and she wore sandals with a little wedge heel. She went out in a black crepe dress with square sleeves, like a Parisian woman in Hollywood. At night, she would attach a bouquet of daisies, cornflowers, and poppies to her plunging neckline. Instead of a necklace, she wore a plastic cross on a black velvet ribbon. Yves was sometimes a rascal. "We were near Oran, in the countryside. My father was away, and my mother kind of ran off: she went to a party at an American base. We children secretly followed her with the servants: we wanted to see Maman dance. The windows were high, so a servant lifted me up in her arms, and I saw my mother in the ballroom."[1] The sight of Lucienne in this black crepe dress was his first vision of fashion, and he always preserved it as a precious memory. Thirty years later he reproduced this design, which evoked the memory of those last happy moments in Oran.

Everything changed when Yves turned six and his grandfather died. According to Lucienne, Yves was "his sunshine." One day, forced to leave his mother's side for the first time, the child hung onto her skirts and shrieked. At age eight he started attending a religious school, the first stage of a different life. He remained at the Collège du Sacré Coeur until age sixteen. The only brother of two sisters, Yves Mathieu-Saint-Laurent grew up surrounded by doting female figures. The family's stories of him after he started school are nothing more than dates and places whose overall meaning seems to have been drawn in invisible ink. He slipped away to a place where the grown-ups couldn't go. Yves often went to play at the house of Fernand Baron, a neighbor on Rue de Chanzy who was four years older. What does Baron remember of these times? "We made up our own world and invented dramatic stories. For instance, we'd be a family of exiled aristocrats fleeing the revolution in a carriage. We also played hide-and-seek and 'stroke of midnight.' We played with his aunt Renée, a very mischievous and imaginative person." The game involved making the room dark and placing objects in the way. "The loser had only the disappointment of having lost. Yves had a way of thinking that matched my own. He was part of everything we invented. I wrote, and he drew on loose sheets of paper."

Yves's head was filled with dreams, ghosts, and serpents. He was one of those children who stand apart but pretend to be ordinary children to reassure the adults. Although he could be a little devil, he could also arrange lovely bouquets of flowers and spend his Thursday afternoons flipping through *L'Illustration*, a magazine popular with families in the provinces (his parents had every issue). Alone, he drew queens and princesses. His family wanted him to have nothing but the best. Albert Mulphin, head of Oran's École des Beaux-Arts, taught art to fifty students, all from the Saint-Michel neighborhood, and had them do drawings of plaster sculptures. In 1992, the eighty-six-year-old former teacher remembered, "Every year, we had a big show of their drawings in the hall of the school. Madame Berthouin-Maraval, a regular on Thursday afternoons, said, 'Do you know the Mathieu-Saint-Laurent boy? He invented an extraordinary white.' It was true, he had put silver powder in his gouache, something that indicated subtlety, meticulousness, and elegance. But I found it a little irritating that [his drawings] had a frame made of Venetian glass: the other students' drawings were just attached with four thumbtacks."

The people around Yves were intimate strangers. It was as if they doted on a ghostly form that sometimes became solid, tender, and affectionate. In Trouville, September storms encouraged indoor games such as I Doubt It, Old Maid, and canasta, and especially Monopoly. "I remember marvelous, unending games of Paris Monopoly," said Simone. "We'd play for the whole day. We scorned the blue cards, Rue de Vaugirard and Rue Lecourbe. We called them *raï*—common, mediocre. In Oran, a *raï* woman was a woman with no elegance, no style." A prankster, Yves threw potatoes at the windows of the neighbors across the street. He cut up dresses from his mother's closet to make dolls.

Those around him were ready with devoted affection. "We always left him alone," Simone said. "He had to call on us. It has stayed that way." He made up funny stories. Once he dressed up his younger sister Michèle, had her sit in the living room with her back to the door, and told his mother that a duchess had come to visit. He was sometimes ill-tempered, but he didn't get scolded. But Lucienne and Yves had a lot of fun together, brought closer by their inability to communicate: they talked about trivial little things, grazing the surface of each other's lives, as if they had both discovered secrets that were more delicate than Venetian glass and could suddenly be broken by any sincere, spontaneous revelation. Lucienne did share a taste for silliness with her son. They pretended to be afraid of the portrait of the Baron de Mauvière as he stared at them fixedly and pursued them into every room. One day, he turned up in the cellar! But then the inevitable happened: Yves threw a dart and hit the baron in the eye. Frantic, they called the framer Jacques Abécassis.

"Do something!" begged Lucienne.

"It's impossible, you should send it to the Louvre."

"No, my husband's coming back, you have to fix the painting. Look, he's the one who did this!" For the first time, Yves hid, blushing, behind the door.

Yves was twelve years old. The atmosphere of Paris materialized before him every Thursday in the newspapers and magazines at the Manès bookstore. In *Vogue*, he devoured all the reports of opening nights, the Paris social column, and the photo-journalism of André Ostier, who made the rounds of all the parties armed with his Hasselblad camera. "Fridays at the Opéra have brought back devoted music lovers and ruffled gowns," *Vogue* declared. "Men in tuxedos flock around the young pupils of the Opéra's ballet school." The pages came alive with watercolors and enchanting names: Éteignons Tout by François Villon, Divine by D'Orsay, Vous Seule by Pierre Dune. There were mysterious fragrances of Russian princes, serpents made of rose gold, and sheer stockings. Most enchanting of all were ball gowns embroidered with stars and secrets revealed by a chance calling card, a long black glove, or a kiss. And oh, how many styles of kisses there were! The *Capucine, Pervers, Troublant*...Paris had redis-covered the elegance of glamorous pumps and feathery flowers, in images such as those by Horst P. Horst or by Erwin Blumenfeld. The photos looked like paintings. Fashion was a stage featuring drama in mousseline and comedies of manners in black skirt suits.

By following the drawings of fashion illustrator René Gruau, Yves could keep up with the pace of Paris, where every hour of the day had its charms. Captions such as "Seen at the Ritz at noon" and "Glimpsed at the Théâtre des Champs-Elysées" evoked an alluring and stylish atmosphere. Women with seemingly endless last names smoked Chesterfield cigarettes. Decorators and migraines were *de rigueur*. American women put all their skill into coming up with improbable stories of their origins. Their husbands liked beautiful objects and young artists. In a bejeweled atmosphere, their youth and high spirits enlivened Louis XV sitting rooms with celestial blue wall hangings. Their charming eighteenth-century mansions exuded luxury, with royal silver engraved with old coats-of-arms that sparkled under the bright chandeliers.

Then came the world of the theater. It was pale and dark like Jean-Louis Barrault in *Hamlet*. Anger was red, happiness was blue, the windows didn't open, the birds were two-dimensional, and the palaces had only three columns, but they were enormous.

Yes, Paris was the refuge of the marvelous. It was like a golden cloud far above everyday life. Mysterious, splendid nights were starred with artifice. Dior's new tiered bun hairstyle created a scandal, enraging the critics. Of course, Yves noticed it: years later, he was able to remember and reproduce this haughtily elegant style that seemed to have been borrowed from some queen in a Hans Christian Andersen tale, or from Khmer dancers with gold in their hair. Under the Irving Penn photo of Dior's woman in black, the *Vogue* writer's amazed, ironic, excited, and trenchant prose was the stuff of Yves's dreams: "Extremes meet. The ridiculous can approach the sublime and even blend with it, and genius has always loved excess. An apparent exaggeration often reveals itself to be a fertile idea later on."[2] At age thirteen, Michèle Mathieu-Saint-Laurent recalled, Yves told his sisters, "One day, my name will be on lights on the Champs-Elysées."

Alas, Oran was not Paris. In the City of Light, the chestnut trees were in bloom, inviting leisurely strolls and a chance to fall in love. In Oran, there were no trees, just heat that crushed the town during the obligatory afternoon nap. Oran was made up of eight plateaus stacked one upon the other. The winds swooped in breathlessly. The highest point did not reach 2,000 feet. Mount Murdjadjo was draped around the bay of Mers-el-Kébir like a nonchalant arm. There was no Kasbah in Oran, just a *village nègre*. No winding streets, no domes, no snake charmers. Just low houses where women in white *haiks* (mantles wrapped around the body and head) walked close to the walls and vendors selling *calentica*—a kind of chickpea purée referred to as poor man's meat. Oran was not made "for the nuances of taste."[3] It was impossible to get lost there.

Albert Camus described the town in this way: "Oran is a great circular yellow wall covered over with a leaden sky. In the beginning, you wander in the labyrinth, seeking the sea like the sign of Ariadne. But you turn round and round in pale and oppressive streets, and eventually the Minotaur devours the people of Oran: the Minotaur is boredom. For some time the citizens of Oran have given up wandering. They have accepted being eaten. It is impossible to know what stone is without coming to Oran. In that dustiest of cities, the pebble is king."[4]

Everything was mapped out, organized, set in stone, as predictable as the "Sea Correspondence" column in *L'Echo d'Oran*, which published the names of the ships, the movements of the boats, and the lists of passengers leaving on the *Sidi-Bel-Abbès* on a daily basis. In the port, fishmongers wrapped red mullets and dogfish in newspaper. The conquering General Bugeaud's brave soldier-laborers, originally from Gascony and Roussillon, had taken the city back from Abdelkader's rebel *sharifs*. Their sons were rooted to the land like orange trees. When school let out, the grandsons would fight. They'd roll in the dust, as sturdy as the olive trees of the Tell Atlas mountains and steppes, with shouts of "Whore!" and "Fuck your mother!"

Girls and boys moved about in groups. They all saw adolescence simply as a stage before marriage. At this stage, they could "see each other" in certain places: Rue d'Arzew, the Stand Gasquet (a local spot for games and dancing), or the Carmen ice cream stand. The girls wore lightweight dresses; the boys strutted around like American actors. In Oran, you didn't go for a walk, you "did the boulevard." Woe to the isolated, the targets of all insults. The worst such insult was *mariquita* (fag). Before the war, young gay men didn't dare say hello to their mothers' male friends, for fear of ruining their reputations. Oran was a town where solitude stood out like a black spot. Silence was heavy as a stone. The two immense streets, Rue d'Arzew and Rue d'Alsace-Lorraine, ran parallel to each other endlessly.

*

However, at the Mathieu-Saint-Laurents', life was cheerful. Parties took place one after another. Hidden in a thicket in the Trouville garden with his friend Martine Ducrot, Yves watched the couples shimmy to the fiery mambo. After dreaming of white telephones and sighs in Macau, the mothers put away their veiled hats and curling irons. They acknowledged they were older now, but bought corsets that promised the bust of a twenty-year-old. Their dresses no longer glided, but their bosoms rose above shapely waists. How time flew by. But these married women did not sacrifice their charms to the dull routine of marriage. They mischievously flattered their husbands and made them proud as they appeared in new outfits at every event. "I had it all—fox, squirrel, skunk," acknowledged Lucienne, although the temperature never dropped below freezing. She couldn't resist the smooth sales pitch of Dina Fourrures. She had the seamstress, Madame Bonave, make her a "New Look" dress, completely pleated. "It was stiff as a brick." Other times, Yves marveled at his mother's beauty when she danced in her airy tulle dress spangled with white discs. One day he would bring this poetic vision back to life.

Lucienne took Yves to Promé Couture on Rue d'Alsace-Lorraine, a boutique on the second floor, where women from neighboring Rio Salado fought over the newest designs. Aware of Dior's success, Promé Couture bought the right to reproduce his designs, such as the Maxim's dresses, which were good for highlighting the figures of these self-styled gypsy women when they pretended to be Madame de Pompadour at the Canastel casino. Too rich, with too much make-up, they looked like women of loose morals who read novels about illicit affairs. They strutted about in their high heels when it was a hundred degrees in the shade. In fact, in 1950, the Colisée Cinema held a contest to crown the "Carmen of Oran." The character of Carmen, that wild, haughty creature, was a huge hit: after loving Rita Hayworth in *Gilda*, Oran thrilled to her performance in *The Loves of Carmen* with Glenn Ford.

Lucienne thought their husbands were a lot less fun. "When one buys a piano, the other one buys two." Did they even use them? When the colonists went to Paris, it was to hear cabaret singers. In Oran, the only culture was agriculture: wheat, wine, oranges. Oran didn't like intellectuals; Oran liked a good show. Especially the women. They might forget the name of the play they saw, but they always remembered what they wore to the theater.

On Sunday afternoons, Lucienne Mathieu-Saint-Laurent took her son to the opera, where the entire nineteenth-century lyric repertory was performed (*Aïda, Tosca, Carmen, Werther, Rigoletto*, etc.), along with Viennese waltzes and operettas (*A Waltz Dream, The Merry Widow, Das Dreimäderlhaus*, etc.). The city was an important stop for productions on tour in North Africa, along with Algiers, Bône, and Constantine. Duke Ellington played there in 1947. In December, women named Gaby or Monique, their skin as golden as biscuits, thrilled to Yves Montand. At the Colisée, he sang, "I like to kiss you because you have soft skin, because I like the spring. I like kissing you because I like stroking your twenty-year-old body." Virtuoso pianists, Spanish stars, singers with hit records, and "first-class" theater troupes (Jean Weber of the Comédie Française performed in *L'Aiglon*) all stayed at the Grand Hôtel. The Sunday issue of *L'Echo d'Oran* had a page titled "Theater Gossip" anonymously written by "the Prompter." During the week, the theater reviews were handled by "Grain of Salt." As usual, the actors were "amazing," their performances were "brilliant," and they drew the audience "into a whirlpool of excitement" or a "wonderful, romantic story that you will long remember."

Yves had an audience of children as director, actor, and costume designer of his own productions. His sisters, Brigitte and Michèle, were there, along with Aline, the maid's daughter, Paulin, the concierge's son, and his cousins Patrice and Catherine. Yves opened secret doors and, lighter than a shadow, transported the group into Cocteau's imaginary world filled with silent lightning bolts, angels of death, and talismans. Storms knocked down trees, and the children were bowled over, fascinated and terrified by this boy who, like the queen in Cocteau's *The Eagle with Two Heads*, dreaded nothing so much as tranquility. This play, which Edwige Feuillère and Jean Marais performed at Théâtre Hébertot, was made into a movie in 1948. Yves pasted photos from the film that his father brought back from Paris into an album. His sister Michèle recalled, "We were wrapped up in those stories for hours. We were sprawled out on the bed, falling over. We were shaken up. We found ourselves in a castle with arms coming out from the walls. We were terrified."

On May 6, 1950, Yves Mathieu-Saint-Laurent experienced enchantment in red and gold at the opening night of Molière's *The School for Wives*, with Louis Jouvet in the role of Arnolphe and Dominique Blanchar ("this very youthful pupil," as described by Grain of Salt in *L'Echo d'Oran*) as Agnès. The theater was packed. The production premiered in Paris in 1936 and traveled to Switzerland and then Latin America, where Jouvet fled during the war. The curtain rose on a set by Christian Bérard. A city in the background, with a square and a garden. Chandeliers like starbursts were painted onto a mauve ceiling. Where and when was this? There were no historical details indicating an exact time period. Everything was implied. Yet it was the seventeenth century, at the Jardins du Palais-Royal in Paris. For Yves, this play was a revelation. The simple techniques, the skillful interplay of the lights, and the costumes that were spots of yellow, purple, and green revealed a world to him—his world. "Becoming a director is like falling in love," Jouvet once said. Yves found his true family with Christian Bérard and Louis Jouvet, these two tireless explorers of shadows and artifice. He memorized whole scenes from the play. He had discovered the magic of illusion.

He was soon cutting out silhouettes from cardboard and dressing them in old sheets or scraps of fabric that the laundress gave him. His characters performed above a wooden crate with a marquee that read "L'Illustre Théâtre" in fancy script. It was a magic box. The stage was a painted set with candelabra and a trompe-l'oeil curtain. Yves recalled, "I had created an entire machinery to place the sets and the lights."

But one day, the candles set the sheets on fire during a performance of George Bernard Shaw's *Saint Joan*. The little room was now off-limits, given over to the laundress. But the show went on, in a more private manner. Brigitte remembered, "I must have been about five and it was so magical. I received invitations. My sister read them to me, I was too little. He asked me not to tell anyone. He waited for our parents to go to sleep to slide these little papers under our doors." He also sent invoices from "Yves Mathieu Saint Laurent, Haute Couture, Place Vendôme"[5] that were written in royal blue ink on big pages of grid-lined notebook paper and addressed to important Parisian ladies. One of them read:

> *First bill for Madame de Henlé's order*
> *1 morning ensemble from the shop: sweater, skirt, bag, 30,000 F*
> *1 Stanislas grand collection design, 70,000 F*
> *1 Shogun grand collection design, 60,000 F*
> *1 hat, Shogun grand collection, 10,000 F*
> *1 Yolanda grand collection design, 80,000 F*
> *1 Mata Hari grand collection design, 150,000 F*

The total, which was underlined, was 400,000 francs. The budding designer was very well-informed: the prices were quite accurate, and the order included a sweater and skirt ensemble. At that time, Elsa Schiaparelli, the former queen of shocking pink and eccentric designs from the period between World Wars I and II, had hired a young designer who made the first separates, blouses and skirts that were fresh and flexible, in marked contrast to the stiff, constricting suits of Dior. His name was Hubert de Givenchy, and he would start his own line in 1952. For the young dreamer in Oran, Hubert de Givenchy was a model, just like Christian Dior and Cristóbal Balenciaga—he closely followed the collections of all three designers.

However, Yves Saint Laurent's teenage years were traumatic. As he recalled, "Once I got to high school, I had to lead a double life. On the one hand, there was the cheerful life with my family, the world I had created with my drawings, costumes, and plays. On the other, the ordeal of Catholic school, where I was an outcast."[6] Another student at his school, François Catroux, who was originally from Mascara, remembered Yves well. "He lived off-campus. I had noticed him in the yard: students who boarded at the school wore black smocks, but he always wore a hound's-tooth jacket with a burgundy vest and flannel pants. He looked like a Britisher in Oran. He must have been in ninth grade. He spent his free periods alone, leaning against the windows of the chapel. He didn't hang out with anyone. He didn't seek out friendship. He was a loner."

Oran, where gossip cemented friendships and hatreds, held much suffering. A nonchalant attitude concealed strict, virtuous thinking. In this city, conformism was rock-solid. Wearing a chain bracelet made you a "snob," and a boy who came back from a trip to Paris with a pink shirt would be called a "fag." The sea views were beautiful, but obstacles were everywhere: the sun, the stupidity, the past. Good taste. A restrictive notion of what happiness could be. Each community was wary of the others, and scorn was passed down from parents to children. You had to let Oran break you to then be reborn far off, across the sea. At age fifteen, Yves Mathieu-Saint-Laurent started reading Marcel Proust's *Remembrance of Things Past*. In *Sodom and Gomorrah*, he would surely have read these words: "Supposing their vice to be more exceptional than it is, they have withdrawn into solitude from the day they discovered it, after having carried it within themselves for a long time without knowing it, for a longer time only than certain other men." From then on, any intimacy with one person or another was merely an isolated facet of his personality. It was impossible to piece them all together: they seemed to break apart on their own, in almost diabolical fashion. There was his nervous laughter, and the way he would suddenly conceal it by hiding his face behind his hand. And his long silences, as if he withdrew inside himself and became a different person. Like the heroes of romantic stories, he could instantly go from laughter to silence. Everything was "frightening" and "terrible"—or it was "marvelous."

At this time, his bedroom started to turn into the product of his fantasies. "Always seeking a kiss—that's who you will be. Oh, yes!" he wrote under a red and black drawing in the style of Cocteau, with two profiles touching with their eyes closed; the man's hair like lightning, and the woman's like clouds. Yves covered his Empire bed with panther print and put curtains around it. He was clearly different. How could he recognize himself in the future that the postwar bourgeoisie planned for its children? Or in these pronouncements in *Elle* in 1948? "A woman with a turned-up nose is very flirtatious." "Men with thick eyebrows are very virile." Or: "Heavyset men make good husbands. They're more affectionate, cheerful, sociable, and even-tempered. Tall, thin men, who are the darlings of the ladies and the pride of Hollywood, are usually nervous and tend to be melancholy."

He spent long hours in his room writing and painting intimate watercolor scenes of the Moulin Rouge. In one drawing, a man in a tuxedo with a waxed moustache poses among all his lovers: "the small blond woman with her round bosom," "the haughty brunette, pretty as a picture," "the sensual redhead, with a delicate body and beautiful legs!" No flirtatious gesture seemed to escape him. The women are half-naked, with jewelry, black stockings, mermaid busts, and legs like Hollywood starlets with red sandals. They hang onto the man, who is wearing nothing but pants. This Rhett Butler look-alike sticks out his chest, and tufts of dark hair burst from his pants, with his outspread legs forming an upside-down *Y*. Underneath the image, Yves wrote, "You will be a Don Juan." He wrote stories that were always about unfaithful wives, who chose "ugly, old, rich, and important" husbands and took lovers who were "handsome, young, but poor and working-class." In one picture, a woman appears in a red one-bedroom apartment. Opening the mauve curtain of the scene, she grazes the bald head of her husband, who is looking at her blond lover in shirtsleeves. "All women are vulgar except the one we love!" In another image, a woman is stretched out naked in a blood-red alcove with a black crucifix; it includes the following poem:

> *How well I know you*
> *You will seek out the smooth, white bodies of your mistresses*
> *But don't go so far*
> *As to become a sadist.*
> *For then no one*
> *Will want you for a lover.*

On large notebooks whose lines he traced with pencil, the student copied Alfred de Musset's *Les Caprices de Marianne* in black ink and Gustave Flaubert's *Madame Bovary* in red. This novel about an adulterous wife consumed by boredom in a provincial town and wanting "to die…[but also] to live in Paris" was key for Yves. Later in his life and career, everything seemed to harken back to it. In his drawing, Madame Bovary is alone, in a huge white dress whose skirts look like waves. She has her back turned to a man who appears as a blue illusion. Her clothing is draped over the gate of the garden like a veil. Yves also drew a love scene that takes place under the awning of "M. Lheureux, fabric dealer." The odious bespectacled merchant spies on the lovers. We see him pulling at Madame Bovary's dress in the scene where she cries, "You shamelessly take advantage of my distress, sir! I'm to be pitied—I'm not for sale!"

As with *Remembrance of Things Past*, Yves would identify and take inspiration from *Madame Bovary*. But first, he simply observed the costumes, the sets, the characters, and Mademoiselle Emma's little clogs, "her dreams that were too high, her house that was too narrow." He painted them in watercolor, capturing the details with the meticulous attention of a dreamer who closes his eyes in order to see better. "She had a pale saffron dress with three bouquets of pompom roses mixed with green." He used ink to draw the scenes that struck his imagination, such as the ball at the Château de la Vaubyessard, a starry whirlwind of dresses, white gloves, and extravagant hairstyles. Every page staged a scene, with lovers holding each other before stormy landscapes and husbands playing cards in rooms painted like stage sets, with wall hangings and chandeliers. We see a theater box, a pair of gloves lying across a top hat, and always the night sparkling with stars. Through his dresses, he would bring this dramatic aura to life. "Lucie stepped forward, half supported by her women, with a crown of orange blossoms in her hair, and paler than the white satin of her dress."[7]

Another remarkable encounter was with Scarlett O'Hara of *Gone with the Wind*. On sheets of Canson paper, folded like theater programs, he reproduced colors and sensations: a black dress in the middle of a ball, a virginal white dress with a green belt, the red and purple of Belle, the prostitute with the heart of gold, and so on.

Yves also wrote poetry. He began a series of poems titled "Why Speak of Love?" Each of the thirteen pages was illustrated with adorable creatures, country sweethearts who might extend an almond-colored glove above a trembling pink bodice. A redhead cast smoldering glances from under her pillbox hat with red downy feathers. The veils on the women's hats were more delicate than butterfly wings. These slender, small-chested bodies—especially "Annie" with her long black gloves—recall the drawings of Jean-Gabriel Domergue.

Yves Mathieu-Saint-Laurent also drew in the styles of Tsuguharu Foujita and Maurice Utrillo, and Oran's municipal art gallery mounted an exhibition of his work. But perhaps Jean-Gabriel Domergue influenced him more. The illustrator considered himself the inventor of the pin-up. After arriving in Paris in the early twentieth century, Domergue painted actresses and love scenes, characters from *commedia dell'arte*, and duchesses riding in gondolas. In the early 1940s, he created portraits with erotic ribbons and hats that revealed the mysteries of the ideal Parisian woman. "I don't like mass-produced women, however beautiful they may be," said Domergue. "Back home, when we marry a woman, we marry a whole harem. We go away for a few hours and find in her place an entirely different woman, a stranger. She is multiple, full of whimsy and unpredictability. She constantly changes her shifting moods, the expression of her eyes, her clothes, the funny little hats that she wears with such style, her make-up, her hairstyle, and her hair color. Today she's a little girl, tomorrow a great lady; she can be sentimental, or she can be a street urchin."[8]

Woman. For Yves, this magical word didn't stimulate carnal desire, struggle, or possession, but rather the ritual that proceeds them, a kind of pleasure that is superior to conquest. In "Why Speak of Love?," he wrote:

You'll have many a lover
Whose touch you'll discover
One day they'll leave you behind
But other loves you will find
Never be the lover of married women
Adultery is always vile
You'll find crimson lips that beguile
You need not look far and wide
For a blonde or brunette by your side.

As in the stories of anguished love that appeared in *Elle* every week, where the women were ravishing and distant, the teenager's heart began to smolder. He knew that the object of his desire would never be named Caroline or Antoinette.

> *Do you recall walking some place*
> *And seeing a lovely stranger's face—*
> *She smiled at you with desire,*
> *A smile as bright as fire.*
> *Your heart began to race*
> *When you saw that lovely face.*

The lovely vision was perhaps Lucienne, his mother, when she came in, wearing her ball gown, to kiss him before going out at night. Wasn't she the first one to pose for him? Her lips, her eyes, and her style made her look so much like the actress Danielle Darrieux. The public celebrated the star's return to the screen. This time, she was no longer the ingénue Mademoiselle Mozart or Marie Vetsera of *Mayerling*, but a 1950s version of Madame Bovary in the film *The Earrings of Madame de...* directed by Max Ophüls, in which she appeared with Charles Boyer. One woman containing multitudes. Behind her exclamations and her little lies, Yves perceived the smothered sobs of the bourgeoisie. In his sketches, we find the influence of the femmes fatales of French cinema: Michèle Morgan's slips in *Les Orgueilleux* (The Proud and the Beautiful), Micheline Presle's hats in *Le Diable au Corps* (Devil in the Flesh), and Simone Signoret's jet necklace in *Casque d'Or* (Golden Helmet). These characters were reminders that through all the pleasures of love, Parisian women never lost sight of their interests. They were no fools! As Yves wrote,

> *Women love men*
> *Not for their tenderness*
> *But for their wealth.*

Slim glasses interrupted his olive face, which stood apart in the sunshine. A fellow student described Yves this way: "He was taller than the rest of us. The way he presented himself was different. It seemed as if he was hiding his height. He was a little bent over and, above all, shy. But shyness can be a sign of pride!" At the beach, he often wore white, with espadrilles that he wore like mules, stepping down on the heels. He sunbathed, swam, and sometimes played tennis. He was so thin. Mothers adored him. They all wanted to have their portraits done in the style of Domergue. Wearing striped skirts and smocks, they arrived with their canvases. "So, will you do one for me?" He would paint dozens of female heads, which they hung in their living rooms. All his female childhood friends, now young ladies, seemed to be in love with him. His friend Simone recalled, "We had moved on from rompers to shorts." For Oran had all the styles. The town adopted the capri pants of Sicilian fishermen, tied under the knee, and light sweaters and cotton fabrics that breathed in the Mediterranean sun. The first plunging necklines revealed copious cleavage.

The first parties and the first flirtations began. Yves and Simone learned the samba, blew bubbles with pink Bazooka, and could stay out until midnight. The big attraction was still the Neptune movie theater in Bouisseville. It was an open-air cinema, with a shabby screen and a water fountain display at intermission. Simone described these outings like this: "We walked there with a flashlight. It was ten minutes away. It was just an issue of getting permission. He always got it. I had to beg my parents. The road went past a half-built casino whose construction had stalled when the money ran out. It looked like a huge abandoned meringue in the middle of the darkness. Arab families had moved in and had a simple life there, with their chickens. There were no doors. All you could see was darkness. It always gave us the shivers. Dogs were barking. We weren't really in danger, but the anxiety was a ritual that gave us a feeling of adventure." At the Neptune, they discovered the emotions of a slow dance, watching Alfred Hitchcock's *Notorious*, where Cary Grant and Ingrid Bergman had what was reported to be the longest kiss in the movies.

For his female friends, Yves embraced the Left Bank. He re-created Saint-Germain-des-Prés, where philosophical thin youths dressed in black and danced to bebop in smoky cellars. He reproduced this existentialist Paris in the garage of his house, which he named "La Licorne" (The Unicorn). It was summer 1951. On the white-washed walls, he drew bearded musicians and ballerinas straight out of Le Montana, the haunt of Juliette Gréco and Annabel. His lines were more assured, with an accurate observation of real details, from the shape of an ankle to the roofs of Paris. Musical notes floated on the walls. It was a mixture of enthusiasm and mockery, sentimentality and cynicism, dreams and a vivid slice of reality. Under a frenzied cow, between a child couple in love and a solitary muse, Yves recopied a poem from Jacques Prévert's *Paroles*:

> *Three matches struck one by one*
> *The first to see all your face*
> *The second to see your eyes*
> *The third to see your mouth*
> *And all of darkness*
> *To remind me of all this*
> *Holding you in my arms…*

Yves threw parties here. At the bar, orangeade was served in big glasses. The girls colored their lips with Rouge Baiser for boys whom they didn't dare kiss. And also for all the others, whose very existence they were unaware of: all the Habibs and Mohammeds who walked the sands of Bouisseville and Paradis Plage in the hope of dating these Catholic girls who symbolized France for them. The girls of Oran cut their hair short, like Dany Robin, the young, fresh, and flirtatious florist in *Deux Sous de Violettes*. *Elle* magazine had a page for girls seeking other girls to be their pen pals: "Age eighteen, looking for a pen pal in Paris, a student like me. Don't like Delly, Tino Rossi, discipline, or anything moralizing and boring. Like modern books, movies, theater, and music." The ads were signed Darn It, Blond Demon, Finette, or Rose Jasmine.

They wanted to look like the stars in the newspapers. At age fifteen, Yves had the thrill of appearing in the paper himself. In 1951, *L'Echo d'Oran* published his name for the first time in the "Talk" column. He had just created the costumes for Little Princess, the annual celebration organized by Mesdames Mailland and Medousa, directors of the city ballet. The scenes were titled "Ice Skaters," "Snow White," "Three Skiers," etc. Yves's sisters were part of the company. In a mousseline tunic with satin shirttails, Michèle danced in "Snowflakes and Dominos," while Brigitte played "The Gold Nugget" surrounded by Mexican couples loudly shouting the ritual cry of "Gold, gold!"

It was a bouncy parade of black chimney sweeps, slaves from the *Arabian Nights*, and parading little soldiers. The amateur journalist, an elderly lady from Oran who had sent in her article to the newspaper, called it "a performance whose splendor we cannot overstate." She praised the "original paintings of a young fifteen-year-old artist, Yves Mathieu-Saint-Laurent, who, with no guidance and no teacher, led by only his own imagination, created several sketches of costumes, the drawings for the 'Drawing Lesson,' and two large posters at the theater entrance." Lucienne cut out the article and saved it in a large notebook titled "Fashion" with a sky blue cover. The lady's name was cut off. In large letters, Lucienne wrote in pen on the first page these four letters: Yves.

In fall 1952, he started at Lycée Lamoricière to prepare his *baccalauréat* in philosophy. Unlike his previous school, which was a Catholic institution, this was a public school. It served the sons of well-off families and had a solid reputation for classical education. Located at the end of the Boulevard Gallieni, the school seemed to dominate the sea. Two thousand students underwent the ordinary routine of a large French high school, with roll call at eight o'clock and one-thirty for the day students, free periods, and cigarette smoking that was more or less tolerated by the teachers. Colonization was on the philosophy syllabus. The class had thirty-three students. One of them, Étienne Tiffou, still remembered forty years later, "The class was mostly day students. The boarders were obvious from their gray smocks and purposefully sloppy dress. The day students wore jackets and ties. Yves Mathieu-Saint-Laurent dressed with a certain affectation. I remember a white shirt with blue stripes and a collar whose tips had two little golden balls that pinned down his tie."

His impeccably styled hair seemed long at the time, even though it didn't cover his neck. He had the second desk in the first row. I don't think he was extremely interested in philosophy, at least not the philosophy they taught."

Yves's drawing portfolio didn't just contain sketches for his family and friends. In *Paris Match*, he had read about the first-ever fashion design contest organized by the International Wool Secretariat. The rules asked for a black and white drawing measuring thirty by twenty centimeters in three categories: dress, coat, and suit. Entrants also had to send a fabric sample—wool, of course—to create the design. In November, Yves learned that he had won third prize. This success nabbed him another article in *L'Echo d'Oran*, illustrated with a photo from his I.D. card. He told the journalist, "Up until now, I've always let my imagination lead me, for any type of drawing. I still intend to do decorating and especially to paint theater sets. I hope to study in Paris in order to improve my skills."

In this poem, the ambitious teenager already imagined himself back in Oran after conquering Paris:

Go rest
Far away, in the country!
And come back to Paris!
Here you are again!
Like the prodigal son
You'd had enough
Of that place!
Paris adopted you!
Paris, eternal Paris!
Now Paris welcomes you,
Good old Paris!
The women!
The little cabarets!
Many women!
Many little cabarets!

He felt a world of enchantment discovered in art and literature. He seemed to have gleaned the idea that only women were able to embody the limitless promise of life. As Domergue put it, "Paris—its light, its sky, its asphalt—is what gives women their unique look and inspires fashion designers. The Parisian woman, this exquisite and unbearable being, this chameleon, is the woman I prefer."[9] While other students were aiming to enter elite competitive schools in Paris or the Sorbonne, Yves was dreaming of exalted love affairs and balls. Individuals from the most established bourgeois families may in fact feel the keenest instinct to flee a reality whose limits they are aware of before others. This gives them a respite from mediocrity and boredom. "Carry me off, take me away, let's leave! All my passions and all my dreams are yours," said Emma Bovary. Yves took with him a hatred for quietness and virtue, and a hatred for bourgeois people who always think that mere accusation is proof of guilt.

2 / A PARISIAN EDUCATION

n December 1953, seventeen-year-old Yves Mathieu-Saint-Laurent arrived in Paris with his mother to receive the third prize in the International Wool Secretariat design contest. In a dark suit that lengthened his six-foot frame even more, the teenager strolled the streets of a city that he knew by heart: Paris, "this fortress that all young people in the provinces prepared themselves for," in the words of Balzac.[1]

In Oran, Yves had written this first-person poem about the sun, which also seems to be about himself:

> The Seine is my sister
> and, just as one day,
> my mother's womb gave me birth,
> She springs forth each day
> From the womb of the earth

The Seine shivered under its silver mantle. Yves had dreamed of dead leaves and vermilion autumns, of shadows and storms. Paris meant liberty, far from the cruel brightness of Oran. The sound of the coffee urns. The scent of hot chestnuts. The buses with passenger platforms on the back, where employees still wore ticket machines strapped to their waists to stamp riders' tickets.

This was his first great journey. He had never traveled anywhere but to the beach in Trouville, except for a few stays at his cousins' house in Mascara or with his great-grandmother in Saïda. Yves Mathieu-Saint-Laurent wanted to melt in the arms of the woman he had so desired, this inaccessible Paris described by Violette Leduc in *Vogue* as a city "of dresses and coats that were visible in my fashion bibles, but invisible in the street."[2]

Yves had built a world of castles where queens hid their pain under their veils, haunted by humiliating memories that made them more beautiful and mysterious. The woman who took shape in his drawings lived in a décor sketched with a curtain and a curved chandelier and an almond background that contrasted with the raspberry color of her dress.

Yves Mathieu-Saint-Laurent was the kind of traveler who went to the same café every day. Other young people from Oran got ready for Paris as if for a rendezvous with a woman of easy virtue. They rushed to Saint-Germain-des-Prés, ordered a *jambon-beurre*, and picked up female students riding motor scooters. Then they told their friends, "They're easy," in the same tone of voice as their parents said, "The Louvre is nice, but there are too many paintings!"

Yves had prepared this trip like a conquest that required calm determination and fine manners. Of course, he was frozen by shyness and couldn't go work up a sweat at the existentialist haunt Le Tabou like the others. But this cellar, where wild-haired existentialists did the boogie-woogie to the sounds of Boris Vian's trumpet, had already become part of a mythical past.

It was as if the curtains had risen on the fabulous Paris of *Vogue*, with red velvet at Place Vendôme and around the windows of Hôtel Lambert. Yves entered Paris with the same wide eyes he had when going to the beautiful movie theaters of Oran, where the children dreamed of inhabiting the images that the seventh art promised them. In the movies, it was merciless struggles and deadly kisses. Betty Grable played *That Lady in Ermine*, and two men fought over Joan Crawford in *Daisy Kenyon*. What memories!

He found similar passions expressed in the underground images of Saint-Germain-des-Prés cut out from *Samedi Soir*. *Vogue*'s table of contents: "It Rains on the City," "Invitation to the Château," with their heroines wearing esoteric black sun symbols. He had grown up with the idea that fashion was costume, and that a theater costume illustrated what Cocteau called "the heart of fashion."[3] Yves had discovered black-and-white photographs signed on the side by Horst or Irving Penn, masters who made the studio a theater box where the women looked like apparitions. He felt the excited buzzing at intermission, the crisp sounds of taffeta, and the crackling of tulle. He dreamed about the scent of the woman in black, angels, and bad boys.

Living meant finding a way to express the visions that would weave the web of his work. He kept his dreams, while others had theirs stolen as easily as wallets. He stroked them without breaking them. They were his angels.

He was as familiar with the posh neighborhoods of Paris as he was with the map of the Paris métro, where he already coasted along like a pro, distractedly handing his ticket to the ticket-taker before stepping into the red first-class car.

And pulled into a whirlwind of parties,
you'll have the time of your life!

It was as if he had already experienced life's disillusionment before beginning to live. In Oran, at age thirteen, he wrote these lines:

How happy you are!
you don't need anything
you have it all! Wealth,
beauty, youth
It's wonderful to be this way
But you're already weary

of this life,
your desire is gone!

He knew that high society still lived in the beautiful neighborhoods of the green cards in Paris Monopoly. Aristocrats still had a feel for adverbs (an artist was "monstrously gifted"), were charmed by villages (the Île Saint-Louis was "adorably picturesque"), and appreciated painting. In that sphere, ugly women were called "interesting," and the beautiful ones had a knack for making people forget that they hadn't grown up in the mansions where they entertained. But why didn't anyone ever say the aristocratic particle in last names? Why did they refer to "the Noailles" instead of "the de Noailles," and "the La Rochefoucaulds"? Right away, he realized that to be a Parisian you had to know what Parisians did. He knew the itinerary of the elegant Rive Droite: eleven o'clock in the Bois de Boulogne in a three-quarter-length beaver coat, five o'clock at the Ritz, six for an opening at Galerie Charpentier, eight at the Théâtre des Champs-Élysées.

His ambition had homed in on a destiny that he imagined like a novel. These words were written in fine, narrow handwriting above lines traced in black pencil:

Society life! Society life!
You'll have to get used to it.
It will play a big role
In your life;
For your great soul
Will certainly hold
More than women alone.
The first balls!
And the first conquest!
Shows!
Tomorrow, an evening at the opera!
Monday, exotic party at Porfirio Rubirosa's.
Tuesday, everyone will be at Maxim's.
Wednesday, cocktail party for "La Belle Que Voilà"
Thursday, gala for the Artists' Union
Friday, you'll be at Anne de Bourbon-Parme's
Saturday, costume ball, theme:
"The fables of La Fontaine." Masks
By Antonio. Sunday:
You sleep. That's enough for one week.

On the other side of the Seine, people were more unstable, always on the edge of wealth or poverty, always verging on love or suicide. They got their mail at the hotel, had dinner in town, and entertained at the cafés. The wealthy dressed as if they were poor, and the poor reigned like princes. Beauty was expressed in lines that were harder and darker. Writers for the *Nouvelle Revue Française*, theater people, students, old gentlemen from the Académie, and muses with strong features ruled the Rive Gauche.

Yves had already captured the artist's life in his sketches, where he wrote about the "the sun, an unattached drifter who likes sleeping by the banks of rivers or under bridges." The tone and style were no longer the same: "And he throws himself in the river and the paramedics turn up." Already in Oran, he had tasted Parisian melancholy:

And the Seine continues on its way
flowing under the Saint-Michel bridge,
and, far off in the gray,
the archangel and the demon and the fountain
are there, where pass by
an old back-alley midwife an unhappy boy scout
and a gentleman sad and stout
who has made a miserable fortune.

With his heart given to bohemian life by the time of his Paris sojourn, Yves already knew the attraction of old booksellers' stands and drew street lamps, the icy edges of the Seine, and street urchins with torn pants and striped undershirts. In these drawings, the street people's legs and hands are so beautiful that they look like dancers disguised as bums. One of them hides behind a mask. He dances near a beautiful woman with a moon-like face. Thus he is the "big lewd sun" who "plunges his big hot hand into the cleavage of the night."

Other visions influenced him, stacked one on top of the other like thin glass panes that together form an opaque block. He had read and thought a great deal. With simple manners, but sure enough of himself to know that he wasn't looking for flattery, he hid the pangs of devouring ambition under a Great Gatsby attitude. His delicate dreamer's silhouette hid true strength of character.

"I'll go alone," he told Lucienne, referring to the awards ceremony, with the hurtful selfishness of a son who asks his mother not to pick him up from school. They say love is blind. His had a demonic acuity: he saw everything, sensed everything, and lived constantly on the lookout. But he had a nervous temperament and didn't go in for long studies of people's characters. Seeing a heavily made-up woman, the grandmothers said, "She's quite done-up." Children were direct: "Wow, look at her lipstick!" With her Mediterranean generosity, Lucienne's wide smile exposed her teeth. It left little traces of red when she laughed.

Yves's relationship with her was ennobled by the distance that separated them. He showed her his drawings, but never spoke about his life. There was a silent pact between them. She avoided asking questions, instinctively knowing that despite their bond, he would never be fully open with her. She could be amused at little things, by turns capricious and serious, one of those women who are stronger than men and who, having learned to play all roles, have a knack for being what each person wants them to be. That included being coquettish for her son. In Oran, when she drove him into town in her "Petite Biluc," they looked like a couple of lovebirds. In Paris, Lucienne changed outfits like an actress: she slipped on a dress made at Madeleine Couture's—her son's first black dress. But when Jacqueline Delubac awarded the prizes on December 20 during a reception at the Théâtre des Ambassadeurs across from the Élysée Palace, Lucienne was waiting in her hotel on Rue Clément-Marot.

Yves Mathieu-Saint-Laurent didn't want bronze, but gold. Had one of the members of the jury, Christian Dior, already noticed this? Yves had never belonged to the world of haute couture, but he was familiar with it from the pages of *Vogue* and *Harper's Bazaar*, and he had already realized that it was becoming a thing of the past. Dior had accurately predicted its cracks: "1952 began in a serious mood. The iron curtain had fallen across the West. They talked about 'making' Europe. They were worried about the fires started in Indochina and Korea. The awakening of Arab nationalisms was declared. The euphoria of the 'New Look' was over, and so was the craziness. The new thing in fashion was now to be serious. That's why I offered the 'sinuous' line for spring and summer, indicating that fashion, being logical for once, was following the harshness of winter with summer suppleness. Jackets and sweaters became the main theme of the collection."[4]

Yves Mathieu-Saint-Laurent astutely assessed the distance between the splendor of the Bérard era—chandeliers, arabesques, frills and flounces, velvet, etc.—and the era that was moving forward under the standard of facts, progress, and mass production. A world was disappearing. The first one to close his ateliers was Lelong, in 1947, followed by an American working in Paris, "Captain" Molyneux. Robert Piguet closed up shop. In 1952, Marcel Rochas stopped designing clothes and kept only his perfume business. In 1953, Elsa Schiaparelli, the Surrealist sorceress, had to pack her bags, after having dressed her eccentrics—such as Maxime de la Falaise—in impossible dresses with straw sharks and angry poufs. Such boldness had been exiled by the ultra-feminine look. Wives of industrialists who built the postwar period and trim-waisted aristocratic women did not want to dress like exotic creatures of fantasy. So in her salon on the Rue de Berri, Elsa, the magician who had dressed high society outrageously with evening gowns printed with giant lobsters and hats shaped like shoes, cast her lot for a place of penitence: America.

America was incredibly new. It was as young as nylon, packaged soup mix, and blenders. America meant ladies wearing comfortable sweaters. The United States opened the way for *prêt-à-porter*. *Vogue* launched a budget collection and a selection of the month. Women started to prefer the ready-made to the tailor-made. Pleats were swapped out for flat skirts with straight lines, and fashion entered the world of television, which meant live, instant stimulation. In 1950, there were only 3,794 television sets in France. In June 1953, 60,000 TV sets were tuned to the first live broadcast: the crowning of the queen of England.[5] The same year, however, did not see Yves Mathieu-Saint-Laurent on a motor scooter. He preferred riding in taxis, his eyes drifting toward women's bejeweled upswept hairstyles. There was already nostalgia for a vanishing world. Visconti's *Senso* also came out in 1954. Beneath the black tulle of Alida Valli, Yves recognized the face of this beauty who seemed to say, "I am not a woman, I am a world."

Of course, he was also irresistibly attracted to this new era. At the theater, he recognized Hubert de Givenchy in the first row and said to his mother: "Maman, I'm jealous." Givenchy was gently loosening the constraints of design. At a height of six feet six inches, he was the "Giant Baby" of couture, handsome and distinguished. He knew countesses. His models had the names of flowers and candy, such as Capucine, Praline, and Gigi. He was part of a young set that frolicked about the Château de Corbeville, where Jacques Fath, the playboy of fashion, gave magical parties, with activities such as watering a dress made of ivy all night long and letting it die early the next morning. Givenchy was from an aristocratic family in northern France. After working as an assistant to Fath and Schiaparelli, he started his own company in 1952. A new wind was blowing over these organdy blouses, Doux Doux suits, boleros with rose petals, and swan coats for young watercolor artists. Dresses that remind you of "the first glass of champagne, which is the best!" They received the biggest ovation since Dior's "New Look." The Americans were crazy about this "April in Paris" look. On Seventh Avenue, copies of the famous Bettina blouses were for sale for under nine dollars at Reid & Reid. *Life* put Givenchy on the cover, and *Harper's Bazaar* sent Avedon to take his picture. His muse, the red-headed Bettina, became the most photographed model: she represented this new Parisian woman who smoked in a cotton shirting blouse at the Bar des Théâtres. With a supple waist, doe eyes, and lips wearing Rouge Baiser, she had a new kind of insolence that thrilled Penn: "Don't move, hold it!"

Where was Yves headed? Rive Gauche or Rive Droite? His severe suit emphasized his thinness. Young people knew that a delicate build inspired violence in their peers but earned protection from their elders. "They brought him before us as if to catechism," recalled Edmonde Charles-Roux years later. She would become editor-in-chief of *Vogue*. She described him arriving in Paris like "a tall beanpole, a teenager shaped like a giraffe, fighting with big glasses that always slipped down his face. A deceptively idle look, more reserved than shy."[6] A meeting with Michel de Brunhoff, editor-in-chief of *Vogue*, had been set up while Yves was still in Oran. Hélène Ducrot, a large landowner in Oran and the mother of Yves's friend Martine, had written a letter of introduction to her friend Michel. A rotund man with white sideburns, he had the look of a great bourgeois gentleman, smoked a pipe, collected Staffordshire porcelain, and was good at discovering new talent.

From a great publishing family, Michel de Brunhoff had taken over the monthly *Jardin des Modes* in 1921 with his brother-in-law Lucien Vogel, the founder of the *Gazette du Bon Ton*. He had edited *Vogue* since 1929, and his good taste and curious mind made him an important figure of Paris life.

Brunhoff had experienced the golden age when, as his friend Christian Dior wrote, "We had all the time in the world, instead of being busy all the time."[7] During the Jazz Age, Paris was cosmopolitan and scandalous, filled with sleepless nights and *bals nègres*, clubs with Caribbean musicians and dancers. Cubist paintings were still for sale on the street. Plays by Giraudoux, Claudel, and Chekhov were put on in warehouses. It was a wealthy time. Chanel made poverty into a kind of luxury. One day, the designer Paul Poiret ran into her wearing a black sweater and exclaimed, "You're in black! Whom are you mourning?" "You, my dear."[8] It was the time of the famed cabaret Le Boeuf sur le Toit. "We couldn't tear ourselves away from either this euphoria of pain or this whirlwind of pleasures that danced over the city like a tall straight flame, of which only the smoke would one day remain."[9]

Michel de Brunhoff had maintained a spirit of creative energy from intimate evenings of old spent with Christian Bérard, Sauguet (who worked on uncompleted operettas), Christian Dior (the dilettante of Granville had opened an art gallery), and Max Jacob (he danced in red socks, imitating an entire ballet company to Chopin preludes). During the Occupation, Brunhoff published what he called a "little advertising catalogue" for Renoir perfumes for the Duchesse d'Ayen, calling on his friends Derain, Matisse, Van Dongen, Bérard, Montherlant, and Colette to help.

Yet Michel de Brunhoff was a broken man. His son Pascal had been in the Resistance and had been executed a few days after the D-Day landing. In an abyss of despair, beauty can sometimes provide the only relief. Brunhoff started editing *Vogue* again, after interrupting publication in June 1940 under the German occupation. His two daughters, Marion and Ida, joined him to work on layout and fashion writing, respectively. In January 1945, he published a special issue called *Vogue Libération* that he said was "worthy of the past."[10] Its contents included "1945 Silhouettes" by Cecil Beaton and Christian Bérard and "The Lights of the City" by Alexandre Astruc. "Maillol is dead," André Ostier announced in these pages, while Germaine Beaumont conjugated the verb "respirer" (to breathe) in every person, celebrating the rediscovery of violets and sky in Paris. Christian Dior later told Michel de Brunhoff, "It's the photo of your daughters that brought us good luck." The designer made his first "New Look" dresses for them in January 1947. Brunhoff and Dior saw each other and spoke on the phone frequently. Their relationship showed how fashion, theater, and criticism—these "friends of the press," as Dior called them—could be a family, where shared connections sometimes meant that dresses, authors, and theaters could all share the same name, such as Edmond Rostand, Sarah Bernhardt, or Jean-Paul Sartre.

In the early 1950s, Michel de Brunhoff was seen at fancy-dress balls, big theater premieres, art openings, and backstage at the ballet, and of course he attended the haute couture shows to which the Paris elite flocked in early February and late July. After all, his magazine was "the constant reflection of everything that makes up the charm and spectacle of Paris."[11] *Vogue* was a who's who in pictures of a café society that glowed with luminaries such as Lady Diana Cooper, Rosita Winston, Carlos de Beisteigui, and Arturo López-Willshaw, a Chilean whose huge fortune came from guano (a powerful fertilizer made from the excrement of sea birds) and who was married to a very elegant woman who was not amused by Paris society. Able to sing verses by Mistinguett by heart, Arturo loved cabaret singers, bistros, and humorous young people. As the gossips said, "He's not like the Windsors, who only speak English and live in Paris because of the fashion designers and jewelers." Paris was no longer the capital of the art world, but café society meant it was still the capital of parties.

The city was international and brought together loads of odd birds of every color, who met at the Ritz or at Maxim's on Fridays and who might get a phone call from the eighth or sixteenth arrondissement or a telegram from Buenos Aires or New York. Crazily elegant foreign women, young aesthetes, ambassadors' wives, worldly decorators, and personal secretaries made the cocktail hour a time for exquisite dry rosé and turned bistros into "hilarious" places where women in evening gowns tossed their clutches onto the checkered tablecloths and stuffed themselves with boudin tarts. These ladies had a special way of being at home everywhere, calling all the concierges at the finest hotels by their first names and heading off to the Eden Roc on the French Riviera as casually as they had ordered a quick lunch at the Tour d'Argent the day before.

Michel de Brunhoff was a socialite by profession. It was just as important to him to be received by Marie-Laure de Noailles as to see *Waiting for Godot* at the Théâtre de Babylone. He was as comfortable giving an opinion on a puffy sleeve or a flat pocket as greeting Jean Genet as he argued endlessly at Café de Flore in white pants and a pink shirt.

Brunhoff was also seen at the Thursday gatherings of Marie-Louise Bousquet, who, along with Lise Dehanne, the Duchesse de La Rochefoucauld, and Marie-Laure de Noailles, was one of the last women to have a *salon*. Bousquet, who was a correspondent for *Harper's Bazaar* and the former mistress of Henri de Régnier, received members of the Académie and literary figures in her salon on Rue Boissière. As the years went by, she opened her doors to the more mixed strata of café society. Yet she remained one of the people who made Paris Paris. "Who would go see a woman who isn't young, beautiful, or rich? But everyone rushes to her house because she is clever," the unpleasant novelist Violet Trefusis once admitted, although she kept her distance from women after her thwarted love affair with Vita Sackville-West. Just steps away from *Vogue*, at the Place du Palais-Bourbon, Bousquet received guests in her charming eighteenth-century apartment, where you were guaranteed to meet someone important in one of the adjoining rooms: critics, decorators, theater people, and so on. It wasn't necessary to prove your credentials. Anyone could get in, and attendees included Cecil Beaton, Julien Green, Jean Cocteau, and Bernard Buffet, who came with Pierre Bergé, the mentor who guided his meteoric rise.

During Bousquet's Thursdays, this "mirror of Paris, famous all the way to deepest Texas," as Dior put it, the mixed glories of art and fashion were constructed.[12] Ugly as a post and overflowing with wit, this old lady leaning on her cane would have looked upon Hubert de Givenchy and said, "I salute you. You are the future of French haute couture."

"Retake your *baccalauréat* exam." That was Michel de Brunhoff's only advice for Yves Mathieu-Saint-Laurent. He had to prove that he was different by being the same as everyone else and going back to Oran to become a regular high school student again. "Only elite minds and people of Herculean strength can leave the protective shelter of their families to go struggle in the immense arena of Paris," Balzac wrote in *Lost Illusions*. Yves took a plane home with the humility of those who lust for glory but agree to disappear into the background in order to come back stronger. As he waited to take his exam, his passion for fashion only became more intense; he stayed locked away in his room, constantly drawing the idols that had grabbed hold of his imagination. As his former classmate Étienne Tiffou, who later became a Latin professor in the department of linguistics and philology at the University of Montreal, recalled, "One day, the assistant principal burst into the class and praised Yves Mathieu-Saint-Laurent, saying that he had an extraordinary gift for fashion design and drawing. We were a bit surprised: the future which he seemed to be destined for seemed imaginary to us and relatively enviable. That's the only time anyone ever talked about him, and, I do believe, he didn't enjoy it. I have a feeling that the time spent at Lamoricière must not have been the highlight of his existence."

Obviously, Yves Mathieu-Saint-Laurent was not seen at the Thursday athletic competitions at the Magenta stadium. Or Sunday at the Clichy, the café hangout of Lycée Lamoricière students, brought together by the virile camaraderie of soccer and the latest goals of the SBA, the Sidi-Bel-Abbès team, in a town that was a Foreign Legion stronghold. He never experienced playing the card game *belote* in the dorm, having pillow fights, or sneaking out when the monitor was asleep in his room. Since he lived at home, he left when the others rushed to the cafeteria, and went home in the evenings while they dragged their feet to evening study hall. One student remembered him as "a very straightforward and reserved guy, who didn't really get close to anyone." Yves Mathieu-Saint-Laurent wasn't in the habit of "dabbling" in his classes like his sisters. Nevertheless, he had to repeat the year. In June 1953, he was flunked by Yves Vié-Le Sage, a philosophy professor with whom his relationship seems to have been bad from the beginning. Vié-Le Sage was a card-carrying Cartesian, an alumnus of the Fontainebleau artillery school, and a lieutenant in the army reserve. The teacher was still angry as he recalled, "That boy cordially hated me! He never did better than four and a half out of twenty. He was an introvert. He didn't have any relationship with his classmates."

During the 1953–54 school year, Yves Mathieu-Saint-Laurent had Jean Cohen as a teacher. Behind his tortoiseshell glasses, this alumnus of the school (fired in 1942 after the Crémieux decree granting French citizenship to Algerian Jews was revoked by Vichy), taught less traditional material: "I talked to my students about Sartre." That got him a warning from the administration. With a few intellectuals such as Paul Bénichou, he founded a little group to resist the city, which he considered to be "a scornful place." His tolerance didn't prevent him from reprimanding Yves in class: "I didn't allow students to look away. He wasn't taking any notes. I approached him. He was drawing women's dresses! I said, 'How can you do such pointless activities during a philosophy course!' He blushed. I never saw him again. Except once, ten years later....He was still blushing."

In 1953 and 1954, Yves seemed to exist between Oran and Paris. With Michèle and Brigitte, he would go to Michel, the fabric department store, and leave with a roll of fabric under his arm, with a spoiled child's attitude: "Send the bill to my father." "The big city sucks up the elite," the colonists philosophized, indifferent to those who looked at the sea with envy.

Yves Mathieu-Saint-Laurent was alone with his dreams of glory. His best friends were people who were absent: his memories of them, cut out and collected, would fit into a small black suitcase. Christian Bérard had passed away in 1949, and Jouvet died on stage on August 16, 1951. From these theater people, he had learned rules that were written down nowhere, because they were not part of theory, nor part of reason. Observing. Learning to see accurately. Transposing poses and situations. Summarizing in a gesture or a brushstroke the elegance of a time period or the character of a person. Margot yellow. Roxane red. Agnès white. Knowing these thousand little facts that make the false more true and the real more striking.

Michel de Brunhoff put the student on this path. The *Vogue* editor wrote to him on February 21, 1954: "Dear Sir, I was very interested in your drawings and I can only repeat to you what I said during your trip to Paris. You are undoubtedly gifted for fashion. I marked the drawings that I thought were the best with a cross. If I were you, I'd take advantage of this year when you are still at the mercy of your *bac* to work as much as possible from nature, not only in drawing fashion figures but also landscapes, still-lifes, and portraits. Indeed, I'm a bit afraid that the gifts that you have may keep you from working hard enough on your drawing skills. I see that you are still influenced by Bérard. That's wonderful: he was one of my old friends and you couldn't choose a better master. I should add that he worked a great deal on his drawings, and the few wonderful portraits that we still have by him were remarkable. It was unfortunate that at the end of his life he was focused only on theater sets, costumes, and fashion."

Less than a month later, Yves sent him more sketches with this reply: "Dear Sir, thank you for the advice that you gave me in your last letter. Rest assured that I will put it to good use. As far as paintings are concerned, I have made many of them, especially portraits, for landscapes don't interest me. It is too bad that you can't see them, but I'll try to have photos of them taken that I can send to you." He seemed to miss nothing of the current fashion scene. Like René Gruau, who noticed an elegant woman at the Ritz, he spotted designs in the new collections and copied them. Fashion changed so quickly. It was a thrilling serial drama. At the time, new styles replaced old ones as rapidly as prime ministers came and went (eleven governments since Liberation). The press often published witty formulas along the lines of, "Hello, this is Paris, the tailor is dead, long live the tailor!"

Yves's brush carefully followed the development of a suppler and more natural silhouette. Goodbye, wing sleeve pleats and nervous zigzagging energy. Seeking a "breathing" ease, Dior enhanced the body in lines named after flowers, such as Tulip (summer 1953) or Lily of the Valley (summer 1954). Cardin started his own company, and Chanel was back in business. But, that icy February of 1954, abundance was still too new for a shepherdess from Auvergne to indulge in reinventing poor luxury. Society never really forgave this daughter of gypsies to have dressed a generation as maids. An ordinary little black dress could be worn during the good years. But in these difficult times, when servants were more and more costly, the ladies of the Faubourg Saint-Germain hung on to their last privileges: tapestries, solitaire, and charity. They didn't want to have their day of receiving anymore, but they went into the street and served soup to the people, having gone nuts for Abbé Pierre, the founder of the charity Emmaus, when they discovered that the poor were also dying like dogs.

The new Coco was therefore met with an outcry. She declared, "When I showed it in Paris, I had many critics. They said that I was old-fashioned, that I was no longer of the age. Always I was smiling inside my head and I thought, I will show them. In America, there was great enthusiasm. In France I had to fight. But I did not mind. I love very much to battle."[13] It was too soon. Having barely made it out of the deprivations of war, fashion first had to astonish, as Dior's theatrical creations did. They were applauded season after season because they restored Paris's reputation for excellence and its status as a reference point. Dior, the master of artifice, understood this. He was the first one to remodel the female body to emphasize its advantages: plunging necklines, exaggerated hips, frills and flounces and inventiveness. "Women don't wear what they love, they love what they wear."[14]

Cristóbal Balenciaga ruled as master of the cut. The invisible construction of shapes around the body gave his models an aloof presence, making them untouchable in a unique way. He was the most expensive and most mysterious designer in

Paris. He would disappear before the bravos and would only allow his designs to be published a month later than the others. Dior strangled the waists of his darlings, but Balenciaga liked rounder shapes. They said he wanted his models to be a little bit ugly, so that their looks wouldn't distract from the clothes. He refused to sell his toiles (test garments in inexpensive fabric) to buyers and scorned the press. Yet he was the one the press talked about the most. Balenciaga was about distinction, Dior made women beautiful, and Givenchy came up with the charming audacity of flower-cloaks and grasshopper-dresses. With her pixie haircut and black flats, the ingénue Audrey Hepburn became Givenchy's good-luck charm with *Sabrina* in 1954. Yves observed and took it all in, comparing what was beautiful, what was pretty, and what was just right. He resolved any contradictions by designing each time "in the style of" Balenciaga, Givenchy, or Dior. Chanel didn't draw, she cut. But Dior was passionate about sketching. He liked to say that he scribbled everywhere, in bed, while walking, in his car, during the day, at night. These were veritable fashion engravings that distilled his ideas for dresses: "The drawings could sometimes be vague, sometimes specific. They came through the movement of my hand and the chance position I found myself in physically or emotionally. What mattered above all was that they were expressive. The big mistake of fashion design schools is to teach students to make drafts and abstract diagrams. To ignite the enthusiasm of the *première* who will make it, as well as my own, a sketch must suggest a movement, a look, a gesture. It must evoke a silhouette in action. It must already be alive."[15]

This kind of thinking reflected Yves's own attitude, which was influenced by his dual love for fashion and theater. His two obsessions were interwoven. He was haunted by emotional heroines, like Lucile in the play *Duel of Angels* by Giraudoux. The production starred Madeleine Renaud, Jean Desailly, Simone Valère, and Edwige Feuillère, and Christian Dior did the costumes. In this drama, the heroine kills herself so that she won't survive the collapse of her ideal. It is a drama of purity under the sun of Satan: "Your restraint and modesty are merely your inability to become accustomed to your sex."[16] In the photos, Yves could identify the elements that were part of the theater's magic: velvet wall hangings, long pale hands protruding from a white dress on which Lucile had thrown a black veil. The teenager was excited. He copied the play and illustrated it as if he also wanted to conquer the audience and splash it with red. "You have put the taste of Hell into unconsciousness and innocence....Like sainthood, purity is an excess of the imagination."

He was directed and devoured by his visions, peopled with nuns with bags under their eyes who whipped little match girls, such as a fifteen-year-old "with chilblains on her feet and cracked hands." "And the sister's wimple was as white as the girl's underwear." He saw "the truth of poverty, completely naked and bloody" and wrote about the "rape of the night." Even his dreams and nightmares were draped with fabric:

And in black, bloody shreds of satin
the early morning appears
the stillborn early morning, feverish and pale
that desperately moves
its ghostly little body
entangled in its gray shroud.

In his room in Oran, Yves continued to draw and write. The rotund *Vogue* editor and the thin teenager were involved in an epistolary duel pitting the wisdom of a mature man against the passion of an inspired youth who sketched virgins and devils. Michel de Brunhoff wrote on May 6, 1954, "My dear Yves, I think we have been writing to each other long enough now that I can call you by your first name? I continue to give you my sincere compliments. I was extremely interested in the photos of your paintings in your last letter. Naturally, it's difficult to make a serious judgment based on these photos without color, but they show that you are passionate and hard-working. If I have any advice to give you, it's to paint as much as possible from nature, whether it be portraits, still-lifes, landscapes, nudes, etc. It is absolutely necessary to underpin your drawings with knowledge that, once you have acquired it, will allow you all kinds of creativity." He went on, "I was very interested in your Lucretia, although your illustrations are a bit too extreme in my opinion. I hope you will pass your exam and be able to concentrate on your art."

Yves would not reply until late June, when he announced that his "exam results were fully satisfactory" (he received his degree, but without honors) and that he would move to Paris in the fall. "Perhaps my plans are too vast. Like Bérard, I'm interested in several things which in reality are all one: theater sets and costumes, decoration, and illustrations. On the other hand, I feel very attracted to fashion. My career choice will certainly come about from some opportunity in one or the other of my possibilities."

In September 1954, he moved to Paris and took courses at the school of the Chambre Syndicale de la Couture. The trip didn't have the excitement of the first time. He was alone, without Lucienne, whom he liked to surprise and charm. He moved into a room he rented from the widow of a general, Madame Buisson, at 209 Boulevard Pereire, in the seventeenth arrondissement. Lucienne had skillfully arranged this through her seamstress, Madeleine Couture. Yves's childhood friend Simone had also graduated. She was also leaving Oran to study for the entrance exams for France's elite schools. Simone recalled, "He saw us and laughed. He made fun of the way we were over-dressed." Before leaving Oran, he took her to Mathilde Montier, his sisters' favorite seamstress, to have a red skirt, a gray jacket, and some other clothes made in preparation for her studies in Versailles. In France, they would sometimes get together and go to the movies. But after some good laughs—over Madame Buisson's broken porcelain vase, whose pieces they tossed into the gutter—

they no longer saw each other much, even though the friendship continued. It was like the theater, where the same backdrop can look totally different in different lighting. At this point, two years had passed since the existentialist party at Aïn el-Turck and the parties at Ginou Noss, listening to Sidney Bechet and Claude Luter records on the Teppaz record player. People from the provinces tended to flee each other once they got to Paris. And people from Oran didn't have a great reputation. People said that they exploited the Algerians and that they still had camels and slaves. Like young men who practiced eating a tart with a fork in front of the mirror in their rooms, Yves put on airs even in his writing: "I happened to run into Madame Ducrot, who holidays at the beach in a villa near ours, and she sends you her very best regards."

Charles Mathieu-Saint-Laurent, Yves's father, traveled to Paris to sign his son up for the school of the Chambre Syndicale de la Couture. It was located at 45 Rue Saint-Roch, near the Tuileries. Founded in 1927, it had about thirty students in 1954; most of them were girls. Spinster women with gray hair in buns taught them about cuts, pattern-making and grading, drawing, and clothing history and gave them a feel for lines and shapes. Yves was deeply bored there. Yet he was in Paris. So why did these women seem so uninteresting? Their dull stares seemed to reveal a lucid hostility: they knew that these boys who weren't real boys but liked trinkets and flowers would be the first ones hired by the designers (although the girls were more "deserving"). The hours were strict, and the students learned how to complete a piece that was neat and impeccable. The room was lit by ugly spotlights and peopled with mannequins with horsehair wigs. They still used a gas iron.

He left no mark on the school and none of his drawings remain there. But at his desk, he met Fernando Sanchez, another very slim boy who also wore dark suits. He also liked Cocteau, Bérard, and Maurice Sachs, and he lived alone in Paris, in a studio on Rue Dauphine. This would be Yves's first Parisian friendship, and one of his lasting ones, continuing for decades over the Paris-New York-Marrakesh circuit. "I'm either very indifferent or very loyal. We found ourselves sitting next to each other. The skill of his hands was magical. We became close," Fernando recalled.

Born in Spain and raised in Antwerp, Fernando had grown up in another world. His mother dressed in Balenciaga and he remembered teas where the women of the Spanish aristocracy looked like great crows. He also dreamed of colors and freedom and was hired by Jacques Fath and brought to Paris. He recalled that Yves commanded attention like a star. With their intense way of staring and their ill-timed bursts of laughter, the two young men sometimes had the arrogance of young unknowns who resent their lowly position: "They hated us at school. They said, 'You both think you're geniuses.'"

It was an eventful time. On November 25, 1954, Yves won the victory he had been waiting for: he was awarded both first and second place in the dress category of the international wool industry competition. He had become the youngest-ever winner of this prestigious contest. From the six thousand sketches that had been anonymously submitted, seven had been selected. Three were by Yves Mathieu-Saint-Laurent. First prize in the coat category went to Karl Lagerfeld, a twenty-one-year-old native of Hamburg who had moved to France in 1952. Yves had the honor of being mentioned by the patriotic narrator of the Gaumont Theater newsreel: "At age eighteen, his talent has been crowned with double success. With Yves Mathieu-Saint-Laurent, North Africa has scored a point against Paris."

Along with members of the press, the awards committee included Jacqueline Delubac, Pierre Balmain, and Hubert de Givenchy, whose workshops produced the design. "I'm thrilled," Yves said in an interview with Janie Samet, a neophyte journalist writing her first article for *L'Echo d'Oran*:

> He's 18 years old, with the look of a serious and reserved student at Sciences-Po and revolutionary ideas about fashion: "Elegance is a dress that's so stunning you won't dare wear it twice. I love things that are eccentric, funny, unexpected." With one shoulder exposed, this sinuous black dress is worn with long gloves, in the style of Yvette Guilbert, with a sparkling rhinestone cuff...."My dream would be to be a designer for a great maison de couture. Oh, to create joyful, lively dresses that make people turn and look, to imagine bold accessories, and couture jewels that are so much cleverer than real ones."[17]

Yves, who could be found backstage at the Théâtre Français more often than in his fabric cutting class, also had another ambition: theater. "To design sets and costumes, to always be in contact with the public that raves or criticizes." His father wanted him to be a lawyer. "He just didn't believe in my calling," said Yves, with a slightly mocking I-told-you-so tone. "Now he is resigned and accepts that I am 'the artist of the family.'"[18] The award money that Yves received was in fact worth much more than a 300,000-franc check. It justified a secret struggle, a challenge, an absolute "no" to the kind of life that his nature would not accept. Yves knew he would never be one of those earnest, hard-working fiancés, the proper kind of boy whom chic girls dream about and who are respectful to their in-laws. What happened between Yves and his father? Yves looked at Charles the way Emma Bovary looked at her husband: with irritation that provoked suffering instead of turning away from it. "She wished Charles would beat her so that she could have more right to hate him and avenge herself on him." Yves sometimes seemed exasperated by this father who talked loudly and was always overdressed when he went out, strapped into his tuxedo, with a shirt with a stiff white collar that strangled his neck. At some point, Charles Mathieu-Saint-Laurent had realized that his son would never continue his lineage. This man, who believed in inherited values and the ideal of Napoleonic glory, was chilled by this revelation, which wracked him with guilt. As if to compensate for all his absences, Yves's father, who could be rather strict but who was, according to his daughters, "a big softie," would watch over Yves and protect him, without his son's knowledge, even though it was too late. Yves would continue to seek out this protection later, despite the disgust that he felt for this security and these well-meaning intentions that smothered him.

Yves didn't bother to get his degree. Circumstances made it difficult. He was drowning, in his words, in "the deep and dark abyss, the hallways full of shadow" of his solitude. After the euphoria of the first months in Paris, he fell into a horrible depression, as inescapable as the smell of veal cutlets in the staircases of the seventeenth arrondissement. It was a sad, "suitable" neighborhood. There were little trees, as bare as combs with missing teeth, and women who always looked guilty for sins they hadn't committed. The trains that went under the Boulevard Pereire marked the interminable hours. In his typical student's room—a tiny place hung with neutral wallpaper, with the sink and bidet hidden behind a screen—the boy king discovered the boredom of Sundays.

Charles Mathieu-Saint-Laurent knew that he didn't get his son. But his ignorance made him humble, and he did not withdraw. This respected and often betrayed man was the only one in the family who was brave enough to consider that his son was suffering through something darker than just the doldrums of a sensitive artist. In any case, he had no respect for artists—since it was well-known that they lived undisciplined, bohemian lives. He cautiously referred to Yves's "shyness," in the same way as people in the nineteenth century said "It's nerves."

Yves didn't know that his worried father had decided to write to Michel de Brunhoff. The letter is dated January 14, 1955.

Dear Sir, Please forgive me for writing to you without yet having had the pleasure of meeting you, but all the kindness that you have shown to my wife and the interest that you have shown in my grown son Yves encouraged me to do so. We have just received our first two letters from Yves after he returned to Paris following Christmas vacation in Oran. They reveal a bitterness we did not expect after the euphoria of the first semester and especially after the excitement of his success in the wool competition. Indeed, during his vacation, his excitement continued and he was full of projects. Of course, I realize that the transition from home to his student room as well as the memories of two weeks of vacation spent with his old friends must have given him a bit of the blues. But it seems—and in fact he says so himself—that the classes he is taking are no longer enough to fill his time. He is seeking out several activities to prevent gaps in his day so that there will not be chances for the "blues" to increase. You must have noticed his great shyness and his fear of imposing on anyone, and this is why, given the immense trust that we know he has in you, I am taking the liberty of asking you if you will advise him and prod him a bit, if necessary, when you see him. I think that at his young age he needs work obligations and you alone can show them to him in the profession that he has chosen. I apologize for the length of this letter and ask that you not mention it to him, and I thank you very much for all that you have done and may do for him…With my kindest regards….[19]

Michel de Brunhoff replied a month later, on February 16, 1955. "You must have heard from your son that I have been quite unwell following a very serious operation." Yet he announced that he had introduced Yves into the Comédie Française by way of Suzanne Lalique, "a very talented woman" who had just designed the sets and costumes for *Le Bourgeois Gentilhomme*. "Suzanne Lalique told me that it would be very difficult to find a job for your son there, since the Comédie Française has a great deal of regulations, but she promised me that she would invite him to the theater for rehearsals and set installations, which could be very interesting for Yves and put him in touch with people who could be helpful to him later on….While I'm writing to you, I'd like to add that I like your son very much and think he is very talented. I will do all I can to help him find his way and make his time in Paris a true success."

Yves kept on working and observing. The offensive took place. He went to see Michel de Brunhoff again and gave him fifty sketches he had done in Oran. Elongated silhouettes with the narrow line of the bust flaring below the waist. Struck by the resemblance to Dior's A-line, Brunhoff immediately called the designer. This is the letter that Edmonde Charles-Roux received a few days later in Italy: "Young Saint-Laurent came by yesterday. To my astonishment, out of the fifty sketches he showed me, at least twenty of them could have been by Dior. I've never met anyone more gifted in my life. I got him an appointment with Dior right away, explaining that I was insisting on it in order to prove to him that his designs couldn't have been leaked, since the boy just turned up yesterday and Christian's collection is only two days old….I'm taking him there personally in a little while….If only you were here! If this boy becomes great one day, think of me." A destiny was unfolding before his eyes.

On June 20, 1955, a young man as thin as a dark line headed for 30 Avenue Montaigne. Two days later, Yves's father would write to Michel de Brunhoff to thank him. "Dear Sir, Yves has realized his dream. He joined Christian Dior day before yesterday and I'd like to thank you with all my heart. You have obtained one of his greatest joys for him and for us it is great happiness to know that our son is happy and on his way along the path he loves….You know how shy he is, not only because of his youth but also because of his character, and since in his letter he complains himself of this shyness, which he said somewhat paralyzed him on his first day, I'd be grateful if you could apologize on his behalf the next time you see Christian Dior."

He would be an assistant, like all the young men, such as Guy Douvier or Marc Bohan, aspiring decorators and designers who would spend a month or two, sometimes more, in the holy of holies, the Studio. They told him where to sit. Noiselessly, he slipped behind a little wooden desk. The studio was a separate world. Everyone who didn't belong rang before entering. The staff wore lab coats. Monsieur Dior did not at all fit the image of a fashionable designer. He called his dresses Love, Happiness, and Tenderness, but he looked like someone's dad. He liked to eat, was quite plump, and was always dressed in a gray suit. He had certain good luck charms, such as his cane, which was made of wicker with a gold knob, and which he called his "magic wand."

Here, from sketches to toiles and from toiles to fittings, these collections of 200 designs were created and made the magical name of Dior shine all over the world. Owned by Marcel Boussac, the richest man in France, the Maison Dior was a fortress in front of which tourists posed for pictures. Inaugurated on February 12, 1947, by the "New Look" show that made Paris the capital of elegance once more, it had twenty-seven different ateliers. After starting out with sixty employees, by 1955 the company had one thousand. In 1954, Maison Christian Dior was responsible for 49 percent of all haute couture exports to America, including Dior Perfume, Dior Stockings, Dior Furs, and Roger Vivier Shoes for Dior. In 1953 the couturier had opened a shoe department with Vivier, the only designer with whom he ever agreed to unite his brand. After two successful years, they started a *prêt-à-porter* department that created the biggest French sales network ever offered to a shoe designer. The licensing agreements multiplied. The small Dior shop of the early years grew to occupy eight floors of the building on the corner of Avenue Montaigne and Rue Francois I and soon received 25,000 people per season.

A maison de couture was a theater, and at Dior, invisible tickets allowed some people to sit on the gilded chairs in the pale gray salon. While the side door of a theater is the performers' entrance, in fashion, it's for the employees and tradespeople. At 8:58 AM, freshly perfumed women workers in white gloves clocked in. In a frock coat with a stiff collar, Ferdinand the porter sometimes let the salesgirls in through the Avenue Montaigne door, but they were always scared of getting caught by Suzanne Luling, the sales director. Roger Vivier's shoe salon was on the right. Vivier the magician continually sharpened the toe of his designs, making it as pointed as a bird's beak and shaping the slender leg of the 1950s with designs called Virgule, Cancan, or Guignol heels. His shoes were worn by socialites and stars, from Elizabeth Taylor to Marlene Dietrich—his neighbor, who inspired him to create a pump with a heel that was a rhinestone ball.

Everyone who was anyone came to Dior, including the Duchess of Windsor, Ava Gardner, Lana Turner, Lady Fellowes, and Countess Volpi. Elizabeth Taylor, too, even if, as a salesperson is recalled to have said, "Monsieur Dior never came down for her. He only loved the greatest talents." There was no better example than the incredibly stylish Gloria Guinness, for whom he once designed a black dress. She commented, "Yes, Monsieur Dior, you are completely right. This white dress is exactly what I needed." The designer was impressed and inspired by women who knew what looked good on them and didn't hesitate to try something new. This encouraged him to be unafraid to challenge conventional wisdom. Every day, at three o'clock on the dot, forty-five saleswomen in black took their positions on the grand staircase. They were called "the crows." The collection was shown on twelve models. Some clients, such as Lady Marriott, came every day. Her name appeared in the appointment book, arriving at two o'clock and departing at seven. She was a fashion mystery: at the Ritz, where she dined alone, or at the Lido in Venice, she always seemed to be wearing the same suit. She was a woman who was seen, but not noticed. The American women were often identified by their gloves and their practicality: when they went to Roger Vivier's shop, they didn't buy one pair of shoes— they stocked up on ten. Some of them ordered three of the same outfit, like a certain Mrs. Beedle—one for Paris, another for the country, and a third for New York. There are those who showed up devastated: "My husband is ruined this season! I can only buy ten dresses!" And there are those who, like Patricia Lopez-Willshaw, dressed "very simply" during the day, and went out at night with their jewels.

It was a time when women still chose dresses to match their diamonds. The saleswomen knew their clients' maids by their first names and the hotel concierges were their most valuable informers. Strange little envelopes were passed back and forth. The relationship between female clients and their luxury designers were subtly depicted by Max Ophüls in *The Earrings of Madame de....* "Our male clients are there for our female clients. Secrecy is our specialty."

A maison de couture was a school. Everyone who entered for the first time was nothing without a specific role, or without being called "my dear." Everyone had a place and a sphere, established by the rigid laws of the hierarchy and relationships. Only some hangers-on and the telephone operators had undefined identities. The others were called "Monsieur" or "Madame," followed by their first name, which gave these middle-class workers, many of whom came from Christian Dior's hometown of Granville, the feeling of a big family, with its titles, its ideal of silk perfection (being considered a "good tailor" was the highest compliment), and its rules: never wear boots in the winter, and always wear stockings, even in summer. The saleswomen were hired through personal connections, after a trial period that could last up to a year.

Women played the biggest roles around "the boss." Raymonde Zehnacker was the first person hired by Dior, in 1947. His confidante and advisor, she was constantly at his side, whether behind the scenes or out in society. "She complements me perfectly," he said, adding that she "brings reason to creativity, order to imagination, and rigor to freedom."[20] Marguerite Carré headed the ateliers as technical director. Eighteen years working for Jean Patou had given this fresh, plump-faced woman the absolute authority of a technician who carefully watched over the "fairy-fingered" execution that gave the house of Dior its prestige. "She has pins that speak," said the workers, many of whom came with her when she left Patou.[21] At Dior, skillful tailoring was paramount. "It must stay stiff." The dresses were so stiffly constructed, controlled, and pinned that they could stand up on their own. The wooden tables were riddled with traces of needles.

And then there was Mitza Bricard, the muse. Her fourteen rows of pearls revealed that she was a woman of expensive tastes. An insider told me she had the habit of telling her crowd of eager admirers, "My florist is Cartier." She usually turned up in the late morning wearing a bodice sparkling with rubies and other jewels under her lab coat and always wore a mysterious band of mousseline wrapped around her wrist. Some said she had been shot by a lover; others that she had tried to kill herself. Stories followed her like her perfume: they said she had been the mistress of the son of the German emperor Wilhelm II and married a Russian prince before appearing naked in a London theater and marrying "a little guy" named Bricard. She had one of the most beautiful jewelry collections in Paris and wore fur like no one else. As Monsieur Dior said, her point of view "is that of the Ritz."[22] She gave her opinion on every design, and her experience with Balenciaga had sharpened her innate sense of elegance. She wouldn't hesitate to tell the boss, "This has one too many buttons!"

Shh! Get to work, *mesdemoiselles*! In a maison de couture as in a theater, everything happened according to the rules. But fashion was more about how to be quiet than how to speak. Discretion camouflaged millions of disputes under its golden curtain. Your professionalism was judged by how well you could hide what you knew: a client's hunchback, a horsehair half-slip under a Trafalgar dress, wealth and its origins, the name of the gentleman who pays the bills, the line of a shoulder, or financial distress. Fashion was a thousand secrets whispered over a shifting background of little dramas writ large, which ended in tears, but the dresses got made. The girls would "die" over two centimeters, they'd make a dress and then have to make it over again. When sewing wedding dresses, the apprentices would wipe away a tear thinking of the husband they might find, if the little strand of hair they had slipped inside the hem brought them good luck. Fashion was a profession: one entered the atelier as an *arpette*, a low-level apprentice who picked up pins and stuffed mannequins, warmed the irons, cleaned the floors, and served the *première*. The next levels of sewing apprentices were: *petite main, petite main débutante,* and *petite main qualifiée*. To get ahead, you had to rise through the ranks. At Dior, the workers were tested. They were given a length, a pattern, and a mannequin. Grades were given for elegance, finishing, and execution. The *première* instructed and graded. Her *seconde* outlined the toile in pencil. She alone cut the fabric and transformed the sketch into cloth. The *première* arrived at ten o'clock in the morning and "went down" for the client's fitting. It would have taken the *première* fifteen to twenty years to acquire this title, a qualification which was a great honor. Before the war, at Patou, a *première* did not deign to speak to her *seconde*. Everything loosened up at Dior, although Madame Germaine and Madame Monique "kept their distance," as the workers said. The workers ironed the *première*'s dress, shined her shoes, and took her coat. In a natural manner, without affectation, the *première* exerted her authority over everyone. First of all, over the clients, who always gave her little gifts—a brooch, a gold bracelet. At the top was Madame Marguerite, who as technical director was the *première* of the *premières*. She was the one who would go to the Plaza for Madame Parke Firestone's fitting. She could fly into a rage over the way a sleeve or a collar was put together and make the apprentices start over three or four times. But, as Monette, the *seconde main* who had known Madame Marguerite at Patou, pointed out, "No getting around it. Taking a sleeve apart because of two millimeters—that's what haute couture is all about."

Such were the ramparts that defended this kingdom, where Italian buyers were taken to task for having taken measurements with packs of Lucky Strike cigarettes. Dior was wary of knock-offs. The designs were marked with permanent ink that was invisible to the naked eye. It could only be seen by subjecting the fabric to ultraviolet light. "No dress leaves my maison without this identifying sign."[23]

Yves wrote to his parents about his first day at Dior. The way the apprentices flitted about as gracefully as ballet dancers, the expert movements of the fitters, who placed a special black ribbon to measure lines and called out instructions to the *secondes*, the difficult decision between two shades of white fabric, the *paruriers* (accessory and finery makers) unwrapping their treasures—feathers, jewels, embroidery. He had suddenly entered another world, one which was as complex as the inside of a dress—blue thread was for the pleats, white thread for the gathers, and green thread was never used because it brought bad luck. Claude Licard, who had started working at Dior in 1947, when the company had only 120 employees, recalled Yves's arrival at Dior. "He was like everyone in the studio: frozen with respect, excited to learn....He learned very quickly that you had to be demanding, that you could always do better....For example, I only saw Monsieur Dior sit down in his chair once. His head had to be elsewhere. That season, everything was for Fath...." Hired on a one-month basis to handle merchandise, Licard ended up staying for thirteen years. His role was to check orders, to stamp the studio's sketches and to note them down in a special register. Every collection had 270 styles, with an average of 500 garments. "Monsieur Dior let us suggest people to help him," he recalled. "He asked for drawings. Generally, the person was sent back after a month and a half, but Yves's sketches got through. I could tell that he had respect for Yves. Under the assured manner of a gentleman sitting calmly in his chair, perhaps he had already sensed that he had a rival."

On his first day, Christian Dior showed Yves the ateliers. Madame Esther, who had worked in fashion since 1937, recalled Yves as "a rather gangly young man, a bit shy. He didn't seem like a fashionable young man." This folksy, kind-hearted woman was the *seconde* of Mademoiselle Christiane, who had been a *seconde* at Patou before being promoted to *première* at Dior. Yves's first sketch for Dior was stamped at the studio with the number 335 and the date July 5, 1955. The following description was written in ink on the sketch: "Sheath dress in black velvet. Very tight sleeves and plunging neckline. Wide draped satin belt, placed above the natural waist." Yves Mathieu-Saint-Laurent had written this description in his own way for the *première*, the person to convince in order to be taken seriously. He didn't know anything about technique. But this inky silhouette tied with white whose two arms form a Y has remained incredibly modern. Yves's first dress for Dior is shown in "Dovima with Elephants," a photo by Richard Avedon taken on August 30, 1955, for *Harper's Bazaar*.[24]

Yves's other sketches are still in the Dior archives, and through them we can follow his development. He was consistent in his use of faux jewels and other embellishments, including clips with baroque pearls and mink bracelets, but he played around more with the woman's poses, her sapphire stole, her blue-gray satin gloves, and her slim shoes. With a coral teardrop earring and narrow, motionless eyes, she looked as if she could sigh in your arms or fiercely assert herself. She seemed to have been caught in motion on the paper by a keen observer. While her expression was more restrained, more stylized, you could feel something coming to life around her: the life of a maison de couture. "I arrived in the morning and spent the day alongside Christian Dior, without talking very much. I have to say that I learned a great deal. Christian Dior over stimulated the imagination, and he trusted me totally with his work. One of his ideas would give me ideas and one of my ideas might give him ideas. This was something that became stronger over time and happened much more at the end than at the beginning. There was no discussion between us. I had an idea. I drew it. I showed him the sketch. The big demonstration between us was the proof. Since I'm not talkative, I prefer that, it's a *tour de force*."

So who was this young man who kept such a low profile? His very slim silhouette and dark blue suit, his large black shoes, those arms that he unfolded like antennas, everything about him was intriguing. "I live at an old lady's house in Pereire. On Sundays, I eat apples and cry," he told Jean-Pierre Frère, another studio assistant, a bundle of nerves jovially perched on two little legs. The little group sometimes dragged him off to dinner: Karl Lagerfeld, Jean-François Daigre (who started off in the furs department and the gentleman's boutique), and Fernando Sanchez, whose hope was shattered with the death of the man with whom he wanted to earn his stripes, Jacques Fath. There was Victoire, a model whose looks many women at Dior didn't like. They said she was too short, her hair was too dark, and she didn't know how to walk. But Monsieur hired her and defended her against all the furies in black. Victoire brought him "a little Saint-Germain-des-Prés look" that he liked.[25] The other models included Lucky, a pretty girl from Brittany with prominent cheekbones and the shoulders of a longshoreman, Renée, the image of a chic lady (according to a one-time Dior employee, the men said she was "a bit boring"), and Alla, who represented the mysteries of the Orient ("She's a stereotype, but what class!" said the saleswomen). Victoire seemed very different and wore her first name cheekily. She knew she was the star. "I drag all these young unknown people behind me," she said. When she walked into a restaurant, married men's mouths went agape, and it was often said that if their wives had had guns in their bags, Victoire wouldn't have gotten out of there alive. In the group, there was also Anne-Marie Poupart, the niece of the composer Henri Sauguet, a loyal friend of Christian Dior. Born in Arcachon, she moved to Paris at age nineteen. First she answered the phones at *Vogue*. Then she spent two years in Madame Simone's atelier, learning to thread needles fast, block fabric, and loosen dress waists with an iron. After four months, they had her make a bodice. It was Lucrèce's bodice, and she cried over it all Saturday. She went to work for Christian Dior in 1953. On her first day, Madame Raymonde said to her, "Anne-Marie, dear, we organize the fabrics by colors." Anne-Marie and Yves became friends. What more is there to say, except the essential: "I did this profession because of him."

Yves's Parisian education had begun. It included uproarious evenings at the Bar des Théâtres on Avenue Montaigne, a strategic observation place across from the Théâtre des Champs-Élysées. He had his first lunches at the Ritz, where the price of an omelet reflected the prestigious environment around it, and his first outings to the Fiacre, a gay bar. As Jean-Pierre Frère recalled, "We went out almost every night. Karl had the most money. He had a Volkswagen convertible with a Grundig radio. We went all the way to the Place de l'Étoile (he said he only knew the way from L'Étoile!) and we'd go out to dinner." The nucleus of the group attracted other friends, usually models, such as Vania, Brown Puck, or the Serbian model Ivanka Boyevitch.

Le Fiacre was on the Rue du Cherche-Midi and had a small restaurant seating under thirty people on the second floor. You could bump into the international elite on the staircase. On a dance floor the size of a postage stamp, people danced the cha-cha. All of fashionable Paris came through, such as Zizi Jeanmaire, Jean Marais, and Michèle Morgan. And fashionable designers like Pierre Balmain came to dine with the women who managed sales for them. Sometimes they even ran into the boss, accompanied by his chauffeur, Pierre, and his troops: Suzanne Luling, Raymonde Zehnacker, Yvonne Minassian, and Gaston Berthelot. But Mitza Bricard always turned in early to keep her skin looking fresh. With wide eyes Yves discovered the seedy Paris of the Bal de la Montagne Sainte-Geneviève, a strange club run by a former actress who was like a happy, rowdy fishwife. On Mardi Gras, the butchers' apprentices dressed up as women. They were quite the sight with their shaved chests, shaking their hoop skirts to the accordion music—irresistible! Yves fell in with a group of flirts who partied every night. One Christmas, the girls dressed in costume. With a velvet crescent and rhinestones on her head, Anne-Marie looked like a Spanish countess. Yves had fun. Perhaps this was the Christmas when he forgot his date with Simone. For her, the memory remained "cruel."

Yves laughed at all the gossip and all the incredible stories told about the clients. There was the hearing-impaired client, whose hearing aid wire Madame Marthe, a *première*, accidentally cut with the scissors while trying to remove the collar of her dress. "She was cutting and pinking, and the woman couldn't hear anything anymore!" There were many superstitions about pins. If the scissors fell onto the point of the pin, it meant death. There were also the mean and catty remarks of the fashion trade. The horsehair busts of the clients that were made to their measurements were called "the cemetery." At seven o'clock in the evening, the studio emptied out. "Vania's alcove" was a storage area for scraps of fabric and skirts. One night, Jean-Pierre took a red piece of fabric that had come from a black taffeta gown with a heart-shaped neckline. With a red skirt and a gondolier's hair, he became Vilaine Lulu (Naughty Lulu), a character Yves invented (he would publish a comic book about her much later, in 1967). The next day, Yves came in with sketches: Lulu in love with a firefighter who sets her building on fire, Lulu who was fat and mean, always with two favorite expressions: "schmuck" and "pluck." She tore up schoolchildren's books and notebooks and picked flowers from the flower beds in the park. As a nurse, Lulu got kids drunk on cheap red wine and raised white rats. She was a real troublemaker. Amused, Monsieur Dior noticed the drawings: "I have never seen this person. I thought I knew everyone here."

Having gained Monsieur Dior's trust, Yves now attended all the fittings and shared his ideas. The master selected more and more of Yves's sketches for his collections and praised him warmly. The young designer even created sets for "Musique de Foire" for the Ballets de Monte-Carlo. At Dior, Yves made his first dress for star ballet dancer Zizi Jeanmaire. When she and choreographer Roland Petit had gotten married in December 1955, their photo appeared on the cover of *Paris Match*. They had known Christian Dior since the Liberation. He had designed costumes for them several times, particularly for *Treize Danses* in 1947, even if he did not have fond memories of the experience. "We were finishing the sewing on the backs of the dancers while they were already on the stage, facing the audience."[26]

In fact, the first clothes that Christian Dior designed under his own name were costumes for Sheridan's *The School for Scandal* at the Théâtre des Mathurins, when he was still working for Piguet in 1939. Dior didn't have a special passion for the theater world, though he created dresses for ballets and movies, such as Roland Tual's film *Le Lit à Colonnes* and René Clair's film *Le Silence Est d'Or* (Man About Town), but he never sought to develop this activity after he started his own maison de couture. Only his passion for the Second Empire made him agree to make costumes for *La Valse de Paris* (The Paris Waltz) at the request of Odette Joyeux. Most often, as of the early 1950s, Dior preferred to give dresses from his collections to his actress friends to wear in their movies, as Marlene Dietrich did in Alfred Hitchcock's *Stage Fright*. In 1956, he dressed Ava Gardner for Mark Robson's *The Little Hut* and Olivia de Havilland and Myrna Loy in *The Ambassador's Daughter*. "The disorder of backstage demands improvisation, a 'good enough' mentality, and a sacrifice for dramatic effect that are not in my temperament," admitted the designer from Normandy, who defined himself as "taciturn" and preferred the quiet of the countryside to the artificial lights of the city.[27]

Of course, Yves still felt what Cocteau termed a "red and gold" passion. Unbeknownst to them, Roland Petit and Zizi Jeanmaire, the two defectors from the Paris Opera Ballet, were his idols. In Oran, Yves had kept up with the adventure of Petit's Ballets des Champs-Élysées in the newspapers. When the future designer was eleven, Roland Petit was practicing his tap-dancing, Jean Babilée was angrily ripping the petals from his costume in *Le Spectre de la Rose*, and Boris Kochno was walking Christian Bérard's little dog Jacinthe along Avenue Montaigne. And then there was *Carmen* in 1949, a sacred moment when, on the stage of the Théâtre Marigny, Renée Marcelle, with her hair cut short, became Zizi Jeanmaire. Like Roland Petit, Yves played Pygmalion: he cut his little sister Michèle's hair "like Carmen's." Six years had gone by. While the gold and velvet Opera Ballet faded away, Roland and Zizi had become the new stars of the music hall. Zizi was to do a magic show with Fernandel at the gala of the Union des Artistes. She and her husband set up an appointment with Christian Dior. "I'll give you my young assistant," said the designer, who was busy that day. "We saw a very thin young man arrive....The ritual took place as usual, in an atmosphere mixed with a bit of anxiety. Sketches, test costumes, fittings...and the big day came." Roland Petit remembered: "It was a white dress. Its tapered shape lengthened her figure. He had put fake pearl and diamond necklaces at the shoulders. It was made of rather thick duchesse satin, with a slit along the leg....He had removed all the awkward hoops. He found the perfect, true shape for her." That night, Zizi wore the dress at the Cirque Médrano. A wonderful relationship had begun.

Christian Dior understood Yves's dual fascination with theater and fashion quite well, since he himself dressed a woman the way a director directs an actor and invited the public every season to his "opening night." Wasn't his dream "to dress a woman in Christian Dior from head to toe?"[28] But the times were changing. Haute couture still supported a female workforce of twenty thousand, but the prices increased by 20 to 30 percent between 1955 and 1956. People started calling it a crisis: the fashion houses feared being copied and raised the entrance fees for buyers. Christian Dior had opened a luxury prêt-à-porter boutique in New York, and he understood the Americans' love of everything that was new. He wasn't fooled by this country "where air conditioning prevents not just bodies from gradually heating up, but also minds."[29] America had made French luxury affordable to all. Empires had been built on what some deemed "*haute* mass production." In magazines, advertising photos had replaced illustrations. The opinions of Russel D. Carpenter (I. Magnin), Lawrence Marcus (Neiman Marcus), Russeks, and B. Altman now counted more than those of the elegant ladies who set the styles during the time of the Comte de

Beaumont's balls. These department store owners were now the ones being interviewed: "What do you think of the new hemline?" Elegance became more conventional, and the beautiful, broke foreigners left Paris. Buyers' influence was increasing. Didn't Grace Kelly say that she now bought all her clothes at Macy's, the most popular store in Manhattan?

Coincidence: the same year that Yves arrived on Avenue Montaigne, Dior opened the *grande boutique*, an enlarged version of the little nook selling fancy goods that he had launched in February 1947. Christian Bérard had suggested the décor: cream and sepia *toile de Jouy* along with wicker mannequins—a little gem of a place fabulously filled with baubles, jewels, and scarves. Starting in 1948, a boutique collection was shown. Soon gloves, stockings, and perfumes made their appearance, and then objects, ties, gifts, and so on. "The boutique risked bursting open like magicians' eggs that hide heaps of multicolored scarves."[30] After negotiations with a bar, two stores, and several tax collectors, the renovations started. The *grande boutique* opened in June 1955 at 15 Rue François Ier. In the neo–Marie Antoinette/1900 spirit that Dior loved, his decorator, Victor Grandpierre, arranged medallions of white stucco, small lampshades, and kentia palms that went with the pearl-gray salons. "I wanted a woman to be able to leave the boutique with a complete outfit, even with a gift in her hand."[31] Every saleswoman had her domain: stockings, perfumes, belts, purses, jewelry, girdles, gifts, porcelain, etc. Women spent fortunes here and always left empty-handed: "The chauffeur will come by." They all knew each other, but usually ignored each other. The saleswomen could tell when the formidable Comtesse Volpi arrived from the clicking of her fan, and they knew the Comtesse de Chavagnac was there when they caught a whiff of her rose perfume and powder. Business reached a fever pitch in January and July, late November (for Saint Catherine's Day, which celebrated seamstresses and single women over twenty-five), and December. They decorated the windows. At Christmastime, the boutique was filled with the scent of pine. Yet the true madness started at night, after closing. Even then, the new designs continued to flood in.

Yves designed holiday cards and "special" designs that in Dior language are called "zinzins": fussy dressing gowns and "sensational little tops." He actively participated in decorating the shop with Jean-Pierre Frère. That is how he first met the sculptor couple François-Xavier and Claude Lalanne. They remembered these creative all-nighters with emotion: "We made decorations with wire frameworks, birds made of beads, little fauns of moss, and dragons made of stovepipes," recalled François-Xavier.

Yves sometimes wore a little leather jacket and tight pants. He was twenty: how could he remain indifferent to the strong wind of youth that was shaking up the wary world of couture, closed off with its own certainties and privileges? While the Americans envied the French their courtyards and monuments, they themselves inspired dreams of comfort and better, faster ways of dressing. Young women who just yesterday had to resort to dresses from the "girls" department now posed in dresses by Jacques Fath Université and tight sweaters by Korrigan. They bought their first coats for shopping, for the car, for the weekend. Their idol was Françoise Sagan, the lauded young author of *Bonjour Tristesse*. "No powder, a little lipstick, disheveled bangs over the forehead."[32] They also admired Audrey Hepburn, Givenchy's good-luck charm: with her slender figure, ballerina flats, and her pixie haircut, she drove a scooter in *Roman Holiday* or, as a bookseller in pants and a sweater, played the star model in *Funny Face*. All this youth suddenly brought out the conservative side of fashion—the papal shot silk of Paquin, the tulle mouche of Lanvin, the double rows of pearls and Ming blue velvet pillbox hats. This unchanging attire of women who weren't yet the stuff of nostalgia, but no longer corresponded to reality.

But Chanel was different. Ever since her comeback, she had never stopped working with jersey, making it more and more pliable on the bodies of her scrawny models. Without rejecting her past, she adapted. She took the Chanel suit, which was the essence of the Parisian woman, and made it into a uniform that American women dreamed of. She was the only one who dared to say (probably because she knew no one could copy her): "Copying is healthy. Dressing fifty women is not at all interesting. But finding your own designs at moderate prices in department stores all over the world and seeing women in the street adopt your style should be the goal and the glory of a couturière."[33] She was the only one who let photographers and illustrators reproduce her designs before the September 1 store date. Chanel enshrined the word "practical," and her vision inspired Dior's little group to venerate the 1920s. Her spare, simple lines made her more than a designer: she represented the spirit of this century and its struggles. "A man at least is free; he may travel through the world of passions and foreign lands, overcome obstacles, grasp the most distant blisses. But a woman is continually hindered. Inert and flexible at the same time, she has against her both her physical feebleness and her legal dependence. Her will, like the veil of her hat, held by a string, flies about with every wind; there is always some desire that draws, some conventional propriety that restrains."[34]

The temple of this attraction for the 1920s was the Boeuf sur le Toit. Jean Hugo had found it "full of Americans" in 1945.[35] Those were its final years; it was visited by tourists on pilgrimage. It stimulated dreams. How wonderful to still be able to say, "Let's go to the Boeuf," thirty years after the time when Henri Sauguet, Anne-Marie's uncle, went there with the same elegant walking stick as Léautaud. One might even run into the ghost of Princess Bibesco, shrouded in veils of black crepe starred with diamonds.

Yves's Parisian education included contact with high society. The key roles were played by Carmen Rodriguez and Lillia Ralli—women who had close contact with the clients—and especially Suzanne Luling, the sales director. It was a wonder that this feisty woman bursting with energy could work in an office that was only big enough for two stools! From her nook off the staircase, she could observe everything that went on through a bull's-eye window. Her domain went much beyond that. She was also in charge of public relations for the fashion house. A Granville native, she had worked in advertising for Marcel Bleustein-Blanchet before the war and turned out to be a sales whiz. She made an art out of seating people when the collections were shown. This wasn't always simple, since often the same gentleman purchased Dior clothes for two different women (and they might also have other gentlemen waiting in the wings).

Always wearing beige in the summer and gray or black in the winter, she made it a point of honor never to dress like the clients. Luling had lunch at Le Relais Plaza; she was invited to all the cocktail parties and went out at night in a long dress to the Epi Club or the Eléphant Blanc on Rue Vavin. Nothing seemed to affect her, not even white wine. Very popular in Paris, she hated petty gossip. She was a friend of the Duchess of Kent and a woman you could trust. According to Christian Dior, "She revives the saleswomen, stimulates the clients, and the excitement and health that show in her eyes are contagious."[36] She quickly took a liking to Yves. "He should meet people like you, it will make him Parisian," she told André Ostier.

André Ostier was a photographer and columnist who was on top of all society goings-on. He could tell the difference between the jewels given to Mitza Bricard by the Kronprinz and those that she borrowed from Cartier. He knew the "incredible" number of Balenciaga negligees bought by Nicole de Montesquiou. Henri Cartier-Bresson told him, "We don't see you with a camera very much, but many of your photos appear." André Ostier had no competitors. The paparazzi didn't exist yet. He was the only photographer invited to private parties. He was known as the French Cecil Beaton. Women adored him because he wasn't mean. On the contrary, he was always careful to show his elegant subjects in the best possible light. His natural manner could easily be taken for aristocratic ease but was in fact achieved through the kind of struggle that society people knew nothing of. He had no ancestors at the Crusades. He belonged to a tribe that lives only for beauty. And when he agreed to take Yves around Paris, it was surely because, despite the difference in their ages and origins, he recognized the same passion in him. Creative outsiders like Yves and Ostier had always been fascinated by the titled Parisian upper crust to which they didn't belong. They were then able to make this storied history live again through their work, while the aristocrats merely embalmed it to display it in their family chapels. This is a great tribe. It could be called the Tell-Me-a-Story tribe. André Ostier was twenty when he first went to see Lady Mendl, who, on her white sofa, always repeated to him, "It has to be beige." She only had one regret: not having known the dukes and Russia under the czars.

Unfailingly polite and always putting others first, André Ostier photographed Yves at the Hôtel Lambert. During the summer of 1956, the apprentice designer designed headdresses and hats for a *bal des têtes* (a ball where guests decorated their heads with elaborate creations) given by the Baron de Redé. These flowers, crests, and puffs of organza recalled the Domergue-style sketches that he had made for his mother's friends in Oran. But it wasn't exactly the same. He had to avoid conflict between the clients by never repeating the same design. He had to deal with little complaints and caprices. Basically, he had to find, as Molière put it in *The School for Wives*, "these thousand ingredients that embellish the complexion": "A skillful woman is quite another matter / Our fate depends merely on her whims." As in the watercolors, the faces were crowned with impressive crests that burst out whimsically. From their heads sprouted gardens with sprigs of lily of the valley, ostrich feathers, pyramids of flowers, and black lilies. These tulle headdresses sparkling with stars sometimes recalled a fabulous swan worn by the dancer Jean Babilée or Alida Valli's bun in *Senso*.

Ostier snapped a picture of Yves with his Rolleiflex camera during the party. His hands were long and slender. His eyes were elsewhere, observing everything with an apparently absent look.

With its chestnut trees and its buses with platforms in back, Avenue Montaigne was like a little village. The women workers would leave the ateliers singing. Their fiancés, factory workers at Kodak, were waiting for them. Models disappeared into big cars. And yet, the dream was ending. International events were having a disastrous effect on the haute couture business: during the Korean War, the Americans stopped buying. The news was about the new woman. The "evil fairy" of journalism, as Cocteau called it, had to be conquered. In fashion, there were several people who controlled these reservoirs of praise or venom that, with a headline, could make or break a collection. In the United States, there was even a daily paper focused solely on fashion: *Women's Wear Daily*. It was the bible. At Dior, the Marquis de Maussabré handled media relations. Among the editors who sat in the first row were Carmel Snow, who came up with the phrase "New Look" (*Harper's Bazaar*), Sally Kirkland (*Life*), and Diana Vreeland (American *Vogue*), who were all depicted by Stanley Donen in *Funny Face,* released in 1957.

Dresses had become more flat, as if they were being held back by the Cold War. Some people saw the flat bust of Agnès Sorel in Dior's "H" collection. From straight shoulders to waistless tunics, the silhouette only continued to become more drawn out. The A-line (summer 1955), the Y-line (winter 1956), the Aimant line (summer 1957), the Fuseau line (winter 1957): at Dior as elsewhere, the line was lengthened as the late 1950s harked back to the 1920s. The father of the "New Look" was not the founder of this trend: it was Coco, "this unsexed genius," as visionary Maurice Sachs called her thirty years earlier in *Au Temps du Boeuf sur le Toit*, one of Yves's favorite books: "Nothing did more to encourage the taste for homosexuality than this boy look that women adopted. And Chanel, because she took simplicity as far as possible, opened the doors to all eccentricities; it was like communism leading the way to dictatorships on a smaller scale."[37]

While Chanel gave luxury its simplicity, Dior associated it with skill and accomplishment, the air "of finished perfection" that was breathed in Paris.[38] In 1957, Christian Dior celebrated his fashion house's ten-year anniversary. He made the cover of *Time*. A kind of mutual respect united twenty-one-year-old Yves and fifty-two-year-old Dior, despite their contrasting appearances. While Yves was as slim as a spider, Dior was as solid as a country priest and always feared that people thought he was too fat. He had *paterfamilias* bearings and could smooth over conflicts between the women around him better than anyone. But Christian Dior only seemed calm on the surface. He was obsessed with his weight problems, binge-eating and then taking trips to weight-loss clinics. Nothing in his twelve-room mansion on Boulevard Jules Sandeau in the sixteenth arrondissement hinted at his doubts and suffering: Regency furniture, velvet wall-hangings, fringed sofas, and his portrait by Bernard Buffet above the mantel. But he always took a psychic wherever he went. The night before a fashion show, she would tell him where he should sit during the show. Though he seemed a *bon vivant*, Dior was eaten away by this secret insecurity and, although he was surrounded by others, often felt completely alone. Even if he couldn't discuss the technical differences between straight grain and bias, the *premières* respected him and loved him like a father. He was the most courteous man they had ever known. They made all these dresses for him, and he always had something nice to say: "How pretty this is."

Monsieur Dior taught young Yves a lesson he would never forget. "Something other than fashion and fashion design. The fundamental nobility of the *couturier*'s vocation." Yves regularly went back to Oran, where he designed dresses for his sisters and even supervised the fittings at Madame Montier's, which flattered her greatly.

In July 1957, Lucienne Mathieu-Saint-Laurent went to visit her son. Her daughters said she had changed since Yves left; she wasn't as cheerful. Yves had moved to Square Pétrarque, near the Trocadéro, in a big, light-filled studio. He had a new friend, Philippine de Rothschild, with whom he went out dancing. To celebrate the arrival of his mother, who was staying at the Plaza, he reserved a table at the Relais. Their lunch was disturbed by the whirlwind arrival of Suzanne Luling: "Well, aren't you secretive? You didn't tell us your mother was so pretty." And she went to tell Monsieur Dior. Charmed, he invited Lucienne to the studio next day. Yves was all worked up: "Wear this dress. You'll stand over here."

Lucienne went to 30 Avenue Montaigne with her son. "Leave us, young man," said Dior in a paternal tone. What did they talk about? Yves spent the summer he turned twenty-one in Oran. On October 24, 1957, Christian Dior died suddenly of a heart attack in Montecatini, in Italy, a small spa city where he had been going for years to try to lose those stubborn pounds. He was fifty-two. He had been terrified of death. He believed in dreams and cards, knocked on wood, and made the sign of the cross. To the very end, he had defended the mystery of fashion. The couture house mourned and, ravaged with sadness, the faithful quibbled again. "Madame

Delahaye had told him not to go to Montecatini!" lamented a former Dior worker. The former director of a little art gallery, the "dilettante" of Granville, had become the symbol of an empire in just ten years' time. He left behind a brand whose estimated worldwide value was seven billion francs.

His remains were brought back to Paris. On Tuesday, October 29, 1957, his funeral was held at Saint-Honoré d'Eylau church. Wreaths of flowers and bouquets of roses, orchids, and lilies of the valley, Dior's favorite flower, arrived from all over France, as well as Caracas, New York, Tokyo, and Rome. His body lay there the whole night, alone between two silver candelabra. At nine o'clock, a crowd gathered in front of the church. The apprentices wore sprigs of lily of the valley in their buttonholes. At ten o'clock, they closed the great doors of the church. Three thousand people remained outside. Inside, in the pews, there were many celebrities. The Duchess of Windsor and her lady-in-waiting Pamela Churchill, Carmel Snow, Pierre Balmain, Cristóbal Balenciaga, Hubert de Givenchy, Marcel Boussac and his staff, Jean Cocteau, Louise de Vilmorin, and Francis Poulenc. Henri Sauguet selected very moving music, old chants of overwhelming purity with few instruments. After the mass, the funeral procession went on its way. In accordance with his wishes, Christian Dior was buried at Caillan, in the department of Var, near the old eighteenth-century residence of bishops of Grasse that had been his refuge. Among all these women with black veils, their eyes red from crying, two men, unknown to one another, accompanied Monsieur Dior's walnut coffin: Pierre Bergé and Yves Mathieu-Saint-Laurent.

3 / A YOUNG KING AT DIOR

he Sun King was gone. Letters were still coming from as far away as Australia, Florida, and Japan. These stacks of condolences were like the final star crowning the heaps of accolades, invectives, or grateful thanks that had accompanied Monsieur Dior's last ten glorious years. He had been called a madman, a vizier, a fashion dictator. He had been compared to God. A ruined widow had even begged him to dress her so that she could "experience heaven."

There was an unhinged atmosphere after his death. Rumors. Costumes for Saint Catherine's Day that were packed away with heavy hearts. And, especially, the entrance of a character who made all these women act like little girls again: Jacques Rouet.

Dior's financial and administrative director, who was away six months a year on business, returned to the hive on Avenue Montaigne in full crisis mode. With a wide forehead and a build like a Grand Chamberlain, Jacques Rouet was Dior's right-hand man and a key player in the successful running of the Boussac organization. A traditionalist, he and the billionaire industrialist shared the same image of France: moderation and good form, plus a concrete sense of power. Mistakes were not tolerated. Rouet oversaw the company's expansion and its licensing agreements, balancing the dual goals of prestige and global presence. "We're businessmen," said the Master, who, although he was the first to put his name on stockings, always refused to sacrifice the prestige of his brand: "It was important to me to remain independent, which seemed to be the only situation that was compatible with the dignity, the reputation, and the supremacy of Paris couture."[1]

Rouet was in charge of an empire of fourteen hundred people. Dior contained eight companies and sixteen firms present on five continents.[2] From Gruau's illustrations in the magazines to the store windows "dressed" by the house decorators, Jacques Rouet made the name of Dior visible everywhere. The house was present at gala events in all the world's capitals, from the reopening of La Scala in Milan to the April in Paris ball at the Waldorf Astoria in New York City. Perfumes such as Miss Dior, Diorama, and Diorissimo allowed women from Paris to Tokyo and from Berlin to Caracas to partake of the mystique of Avenue Montaigne.

On November 15, 1957, three weeks after the tragedy at Montecatini, Jacques Rouet held a press conference. It was staged on the mezzanine, a strategic place that was like the couture house's antechamber. It connected all the sales rooms of the building. One door opened onto the fitting rooms, and another onto a lobby that was connected to the hat salon and the fur salon. The room was dominated by a rectangular table, as if for the Last Supper, in the midst of luxury goods for sale. On the left was Marguerite Carré, on the right, Raymonde Zehnacker. Along the table sat Mitza Bricard and Yves Mathieu-Saint-Laurent, looking pale in his black suit. Their backs were to the window onto the avenue. The center seat was empty. Jacques Rouet entered through a hidden door, sat down, and then rose with a piece of paper in his hand. He began to read in a solemn tone: "The couture house's future will be assured by those whom Christian Dior himself hired: the studio will be directed by Madame Zehnacker, technical management of the designs will still be carried out by the great Marguerite Carré, and the great Mitza Bricard will contribute her taste. All the drawings will be carried out under the responsibility of Yves Mathieu-Saint-Laurent, the favorite disciple of Christi—." Before he could finish his sentence, all the photographers rushed over to the young assistant designer and began snapping pictures furiously.

It was a historic moment. What had happened? Why didn't Jacques Rouet move when the photographers aimed their flashbulbs like spotlights at the twenty-one-year-old? Forty-five years later, Rouet reflected, "Marcel Boussac had wanted collective leadership. But Yves Mathieu-Saint-Laurent was instantly crowned by the press." But deep inside, a voice that was stronger than reason called and guided Rouet: his loyalty to his playmate on the beaches of Granville. To the friend that he met again by chance in Paris in 1946. Would the house of Dior have been born without the gold star that Dior picked up that day on Rue Saint-Florentin and that Rouet kept like a good luck charm? He remembered Christian Dior's last words to him in July, before leaving for Montecatini: "Yves Saint Laurent is young, but he is immensely talented. In my latest collection, I estimate that he was the father of 34 out of 180 designs. I think the time has come to reveal him to the press. My prestige will not suffer from it."

Yves had the sad and serious look of a young prince floored by the responsibilities of power. But he didn't look surprised. After Dior's funeral, he had written to his mother: "He was such an anxious man all his life that knowing that he is now in the full plenitude of his being, 'in the midst of the angels he has dressed,' said the priest in his favorite village…" Yves did not finish his sentence. "As for me, now I need to dress the 'demons,' and this will not be an easy task."

The day of his coronation, twenty-one-year-old Yves wrote another letter to his mother: "I can't tell you everything I feel, it would be too long: sadness, anxiety, joy at the same time, pride, the fear of not succeeding." But he promised "to fulfill his duty completely."

Yves Saint Laurent had been unknown on November 15; now, on November 16, he was famous. Two billion francs of revenue weighed on his shoulders.

All the newspapers announced the news in huge headlines. There was no more "Mathieu" between Yves and Saint Laurent. Along with the mysterious disappearance of "Mathieu," Yves himself also tried to disappear as much as possible. "The Invisible Yves Saint Laurent Was Tonight Crowned Christian Dior's Successor" was the headline in *Paris-Presse-l'Intransigeant*, where Simone Baron wrote, "For Yves Saint Laurent, yesterday marked the end of an ordeal. For two weeks, he had lived a semi-clandestine existence inside the couture house, leaving an hour after the others by a hidden door, not picking up the telephone, and fleeing the photographers. However, he didn't stop working. First, as he did every season, he needed to design the store's decorations and the holiday dresses, which will be shown next Monday. The decor isn't yet finished, but he will complete it overnight on Sunday.... He also had to choose which designs to send for a show in Australia, to see the collections of fabrics and accessories, and to think about the spring 1958 collection, which will give us a chance to decide whether Christian Dior really has a successor who is worthy of him."

Yves flew to Oran a few days later. He was in the habit of leaving about two weeks before each collection to make the sketches that he would then show to Monsieur Dior. *L'Echo Dimanche* of November 17 had an article about him: "Oran residents are happy and proud of the success of Yves Mathieu-Saint-Laurent, who has been chosen by destiny for his immense talent...." A bevy of journalists was waiting at the airport. "I have nothing to say." He could already answer questions like a homegrown star who was flooded with secret joy at the creamy compliments, but who was also nauseated when they were too sugary. On Rue d'Arzew, there were many excited whispers. At Promé, all people talked about was the "god of couture." "Oh, I knew him when he was only so high." In Oran, they still called him Yves Mathieu-Saint-Laurent. *L'Echo d'Oran* called him the "Antaeus of couture." What could the son of Poseidon and the son of an Oran insurance executive have in common? What connection was there between a giant and this young man who was thin as a wire? Antaeus was invincible, as long as he was touching the ground. The journalist believed that Yves Saint Laurent had come to his native land to restore his strength. The allegory was more complex, because Gaia, the earth, was the mother of Antaeus. Dior's successor was returning to his own mother.

"Fix your hair, Yves is here!" The women ran around hurriedly: Lucienne, who hadn't finished putting all the newspaper clippings into her big blue notebook; fifteen-year-old Michèle, still baby-faced but with a serious look; twelve-year-old Brigitte, the youngest, a prankster who was as nimble as a cat and whom Yves called his "model little girl," a nod to the Comtesse de Ségur. On the day of her confirmation, he painted her in her dress, crowned with flowers, with her hands clasped in prayer like a saint in a village chapel. This framed portrait was placed on an easel in a place of honor in the middle of the large parlor, in the familiar décor of the Chinese knickknacks and the grand piano. This was a slap in the face to the Baron de Mauvière, who remained stone-faced in his wounded dignity.

Nothing had changed. Yves returned to his Empire-style bedroom, *Vol de Nuit* perfume, and bouquets of zinnias. Angèle still made her wonderful Swiss chard tart. Lucienne dallied in her Hollywood-style bathroom. The Illustre Théâtre was brought up from the basement at the request of a *Paris Match* journalist. The little room where plays were once performed had become a laundry room.

"Only in the calm of my true home can I work," he told *L'Echo d'Oran* when he finally agreed to an interview. "People have talked a lot about the influence that an event or travels can have on a couturier. I don't believe that. On the contrary, I think we carry inspiration inside. For me, design isn't actually based on something that's physical or concrete. I don't think of a specific woman when designing a piece of clothing. I simply live intensely during these few days of retreat, but without having any fixed schedule. I may not pick up a pencil all morning long, and then do forty drawings of an idea that suddenly springs forth. I have to walk during this incubation period. That's why I like this large parlor." Seated on a velvet sofa, he spoke, volubly, while fiddling with his long pale hands. He looked like El Greco's Saint John the Evangelist, holding in his hand a gold chalice from which a snake emerges. What unsettling grace! He loved Bach and dogs. But not just any dogs. Mutts, the kind that are "ugly but very nice, stray dogs. I bring them in off the street. But they're so old that we don't have much time to enjoy them." He painted somber portraits. His favorite books? Plays by Gide (*Saul*), Anouilh, Green, and the works of Proust. "I'm especially interested in Madame Verdurin's parties, because I love Proust's descriptive little details, the complete re-creation we get of a lost atmosphere. Fashion, the way people put their elbows on the table, the way they hold their cup…The climate, more than the psychological value of the characters." He liked the late eighteenth century. He always hated sports but liked to swim. What he didn't like: the idea that one day he'd have to learn to drive. One last thing: he liked being alone while working. That was the only time he smoked (and then it was American cigarettes).

The lively way he answered the questions made the journalist remark on "this southern temperament that seeps through his nonchalant manners." Like a detective who has unmasked a criminal, the journalist wrote, "Paris doesn't see him like this, but I do. He finally gets excited. And his passionate tone is that of a true Rastignac."

He no longer had to go to the Manès bookstore to get the newspapers he liked. Now they came to him. According to *L'Echo d'Oran*, "Yves Saint Laurent looks like a shy professor." He had "the thoughtful look of a weary poet." The first thing they noticed about Yves, nicknamed the "Little Prince" by all of Paris and photographed on a bench in the Jardin des Tuileries, were his blue eyes encircled by tortoiseshell. Some thought he looked like King Baudouin of Belgium, while others compared him to "Byron with an attorney's glasses." He read countless such descriptions. They were so convincing that he was smart enough to fit them, like an actor who understands his public and continues to faithfully play the role that won him great plaudits.

In the writings of these journalists (the most influential ones were women of a certain age who took notes with mechanical pencils from under their little veils), Yves Saint Laurent's "shyness" became legendary. Along with his sketchbook, pencil, glasses, and suits, it became something of a good luck charm that made him "a tall, sad young man who is getting ready for a date with women all over the world." He flattered the protective instinct of men, who easily fell into his traps. At times he was serious like a child, or surprised like an old gentleman, and playful like both of them: "Deception is a large part of the craft of a couturier: I have permanently adopted this principle."

A twenty-one-year-old writer from Bordeaux, the same age as Yves, described the amoral youth of the time in thirty-five pages. *Le Défi* (The Challenge) was Philippe Sollers's first novel. The hero, Philippe, was born in 1936, like Yves Saint Laurent. He has a "nervous, absurd, absolute passion for independence, that had become a reflex." He is unmoved by death: "Looking at their faces, I realize that they take my silence for an abyss of sadness. This seems very touching to me." *L'Echo d'Oran* reported that when Yves Saint Laurent was asked, "Are you affected by the sorrow of others?" he replied, "I find there is enough to handle with oneself....What I'm saying is awful!" Was he interested in world events? "Not exactly. For me, these are matters that don't concern me personally." Hadn't he suffered enough?

In this way Yves Saint Laurent became what his imagination had turned him into: a legend. This young man with the face of a serious student, who had been known only to a few, now symbolized the romantic figure of a sacrificed generation. Born at the dawn of World War II, they turned twenty as the Algerian War erupted, with no promise of happiness other than progress. *L'Express* published a historic issue on this generation. Françoise Giroud invented the phrase "Nouvelle Vague," or New Wave. "All possible futures seem blocked to them. Already, their professional future is difficult....But this is even more true of the political future. It seems to have no solution. Algeria is the concrete materialization of this absurdity, the wall without a crack that blocks the horizon," wrote Father Jean Daniélou. "Now no one believes in the possibility of a national future anymore. The politicians' statements are all hot air. There is general disgust with political ideologies, communism, socialism, the new left....It's a wave sweeping everything away. The previous generation believed in too many things one after the other. None of them proved viable. This generation doesn't believe in anything."[3]

In the midst of a youth that lacked ideals, Yves Saint Laurent's passion set him apart. Others believed in happiness. He only obeyed the line that had led him here, that imposed itself as a necessity. By giving himself completely to this ideal, he escaped from himself. He did not know which way the wind was blowing him. But it was taking him away from the terrible *ennui* he felt. The die was cast.

His shyness did not restrain his ambition. He knew he wasn't intended to do fashion, but to create. When Yves Saint Laurent agreed to open up, it was only to hide the essentials. The Marquis de Maussabré, who handled public relations, tore his hair out. "I felt as if I were torturing my son," a Danish journalist told him after an interview. With him, an interview was a duel.

Yves Saint Laurent explained himself. He was made up "only of contradictions." His favorite artists were Henri Matisse and Bernard Buffet. How could one love both the artist who painted *Le Bonheur de Vivre*, the free, sensual lines of these nudes curled up into arabesques, and the hatched, lethal lines of the shivering bodies of Bernard Buffet?

In his portraits of sad little dancers, the solitary young man from Oran seemed somewhat influenced by this artist whom critics considered the best postwar painter. For François Mauriac, whose "Notepad" column appeared weekly in *L'Express*, "Bernard Buffet is simply 'the son of God.' His world is ours. A world he contemplated as a child under the Occupation, and as an adolescent at Liberation. Twelve years of French politics have not let him escape from this."[4] His success was phenomenal. From a middle-class Paris family, he studied at the École des Beaux-Arts and became an overnight success when he won the Prix de la Critique in 1948. Represented by prominent art dealers Emmanuel David and Maurice Garnier, he saw his prices soar. In January 1958, Bernard Buffet, who lived at Château d'Arc in Provence, a seventeenth-century estate looking out on the Montagne Sainte-Victoire, returned to Paris for the opening of his show at the Galerie Charpentier. On January 16, in a crush of mink, duffel coats, and crumpled ties, all of Paris crammed its way into the gallery to admire these angular figures, fish bones, flowers without petals, girls without joy, greenish crucifixion scenes, human spiders, funerals, and other "horrors of war" signed by Buffet in letters like large black sticks. From his early bleak self-portraits to his washed-out landscapes (the most recent ones were painted in Dallas that fall), one hundred paintings by this thirty-year-old painter covered the walls of a gallery that was known for only paying homage to "consecrated" works. "You look like a Buffet, go ahead. You'll enjoy yourself," Arletty would say on her way out to the critic Jean Fayard, who was tall and thin.

People were also talking about the man who had orchestrated his rise from an attic room to a château: Pierre Bergé. That year, he published a book on Bernard Buffet with Cailler in Geneva that featured images of almost two hundred paintings. Buffet's paintings inspired humanistic reflections in Bergé, as if he were defending artists in general, with a sensibility attuned to the psychological needs of the creative spirit. "The artist, despite a false exhibitionism, does not reveal himself easily. This young man who paints a canvas of two hundred seventy feet in record time, is the most reserved, shy, modest being imaginable. His sensitivity is pathological: he can't stand noise or imagination and can only work in quiet. He often reminds me of cats, even though he avoids them, because they are fearful and solitary like him. He inherited this sensibility from a chaotic childhood and an anguished adolescence.... He threw himself into painting the way others turn to drugs: this explains the large quantity of paintings he has made."[5]

Who was Pierre Bergé? At twenty-eight years old, he dressed like a gentleman and dashed about like a young man. He seemed eager to fight, in the turmoil of cannon fire in a Parisian war where he manned the ramparts. That's where he watched all that was said and done and planned. Christian Dior had had a house in Draguignan, not far from Bernard Buffet's château. Pierre Bergé remembered meeting him there: "We talked about art, literature, everything. Everything except fashion." He boasted of being one of the last people to see the couturier alive, in September 1957. The very day he returned to Paris, October 24, 1957, a friend told him the news: "Dior is dead." In the new year, Pierre Bergé received an invitation from Maison Dior to the show on January 29, but, for now, he only had eyes for his protégé.

The Trapeze collection was born in 1957 at the Mathieu-Saint-Laurents. According to *L'Echo d'Oran*, over two weeks, "more than six hundred drawings" burst forth. Anne-Marie, Yves's friend, remembered his return to Paris fondly. "He came back in early December. Everything was there in his suitcase. Rigor. The line. Transparency. All in one burst." Yet his welcome at the couture house remained professional. There was no kowtowing. "We could tell he was very determined. There were forty-five saleswomen. There were fourteen hundred of us working there. There were two hundred designs to make," recalled Sophie Gins, one of the "crows." Brigitte Tortet, Suzanne Luling's niece who worked in the public relations department, described the attitude toward Yves this way: "He wasn't loved or hated. He was accepted. Dior had chosen him. He was part of the studio. The *premières* said, if Monsieur Dior accepts him, then he's good." Lily-of-the-valley Radio worked well.

One man worked with three women: Madame Raymonde, still with dark circles under her eyes due to the absence of her kindred spirit—she'd never scrawl little notes saying, "Faster, boss" again; Madame Marguerite, who never again would say, "Did I express you correctly?"; and the last member of the trio, Mitza Bricard. A personality with great vision. The meanest said that she didn't have nice legs, that she had one of the first nose jobs. People commented on her caprices, such as the mousseline blouses that she would only wear in iridescent pink-blue. Yves Saint Laurent felt closest to her. This magnificent woman reminded him of the fictional heroines he adored. She was really a woman. A Parisian courtesan. She sold her favors in a way that honest women scorned. He admired her because deep down she was like him: she only depended on herself.

The countdown started. In the large studio that occupied the whole floor, the Little Prince showed his sketches to the Regent, Madame Marguerite—of whom Dior said, "Life exists only in her dresses, an unrepentant Penelope, she undoes, redoes, cuts, cuts again, wearing me out but remaining tireless herself."[6] Once again, Madame Marguerite handed the sketches out to the *premières*, being careful to let them choose according to their preferences, since one seamstress had the right touch for the fine tailoring of a sand-colored suit in woolen fabric, while another had a feel for the flowing design of the Promenade ensemble in Shetland wool. The couture house was buzzing with the back-and-forth of deliveries from the warehouse and the apprentices carrying the mysterious white packages. Once again, the telephone operators were overwhelmed with calls asking for invitations. Or by brief, enigmatic orders—"Find me a cyclist, dear"—which made them cry for an hour in the bathroom until they finally realized the request was not for a courier but for a snap fastener.

The "young ladies," the models, Alla, Arlette, Catherine, Christine, Denise, France, Lia, Nicole, and Odile, waited in the models' room to be called to try on test garments. Once completed, they would become "simple dresses," "cocktail dresses," or "visiting dresses." Victoire, the newest model there, would wear thirteen designs at the show. She had just married Roger Thérond, and Yves was her witness.

What would he do? This was the question on everyone's mind. It echoed in the lobbies of the luxury hotels where the foreign buyers were waiting. The answer would determine the couture house's future. The last collection designed by Christian Dior himself, shown in July 1957, didn't win over the press. On January 28, Hélène de Turckheim and Viviane Greymour asked in Le Figaro: "Has fashion reached a dangerous and perhaps unique turning point in its history?" The shirt dress, the hot thing that winter, made them worry that couture might be impoverished by fashion that was too "practical" and "comfortable." The highlight of the time was the irresistible rise of ready-to-wear. The couturiers had to give in and choose hip, attractive names for these new lines: Jacques Heim Vedette, Nina Ricci Boutique, Jean Dessès Bazaar, Maggy Rouff Extension, Jacques Griffe Evolution, Madeleine de Rauch Boutique, etc. The young hot shots of couture were also eyeing America. Pierre Cardin, an ambitious thirty-four-year-old from Venice who was a former fabric cutter at Dior, had a fashion house with one hundred seventy workers. That year, he was showing his third large collection. Thirty-four-year-old Guy Laroche had fifty workers and was also on his third collection. A former assistant designer at Dessès, this energetic, friendly designer from La Rochelle had won the Americans over with simple, fun designs that were easily adapted to mass production.

Christian Dior's death couldn't have happened at a worse time. The world of luxury and haute couture, shaken by international tensions, was clearly weakened and divided. Balenciaga had retreated to his ivory tower. Chanel was playing the maverick. Dior's death raised almost political questions. On January 30, 1958, Madame Express asked anxiously, "After Christian Dior's death, what designer could impose a revolutionary line on his own? Will he find a successor inside his fashion house? Or outside? After the dictatorship that he exerted over fashion in France and abroad, can each designer now seize a bit of his glory? Or, on the contrary, will the profession as whole suffer from the loss of its leader?"

Thursday, January 30, 1958. 9:55 AM. In the Trianon gray salons that had witnessed Dior's triumph for ten years, the elders of the international press waited emotionally for the debut of couture's youngest face. Two women had the most enviable positions. The first was Hélène Lazareff, the editor of the weekly magazine Elle. The second was Edmonde Charles-Roux. She had taken over Vogue Paris in

1957 after Michel de Brunhoff retired. Now she reigned over this luxurious monthly magazine, whose title she stretched out, pronouncing it "Voh-oh-gue." Matthieu Galey described her this way: "Looking a bit like a schoolmarm, with her glasses and her hair pulled back in a bun, but wearing a suit by Chanel or Cardin, she reigns like a mother superior over this convent of chic. When Maurice picks her up from Place du Palais-Bourbon to go to a reception, she becomes miraculously feminine. He is splendid, radiant. She is dark, trembling, seductive. Such a romantic couple."[7] Yves Saint Laurent's history is intimately connected to *Vogue*, of course. The magazine had given him, as a youth, a glimpse of the superior existence of high society women. And thanks to Michel de Brunhoff, he met Christian Dior.

On the sofa of honor, Carmel Snow of *Harper's Bazaar*, wearing a blue Dior suit, talked with CBS reporter David Schoenbrun, the author of *As France Goes*, which was translated as *Ainsi Va la France*. Marie-Louise Bousquet, who still had her *salon* every Thursday at Place du Palais-Bourbon, waited impatiently. Across from them were all the women who were anyone in Paris, the battalion of private clients whom sales director Suzanne Luling called "my darlings" and whose curiosity was skillfully cultivated at Le Relais. The day before leaving for Montecatini, Dior had told Suzanne, "I'm not worried. I'm leaving you Yves."

Yes, they were all there. It was just like the "Paris Lives Again" photo spreads by André Ostier that had once made teenaged Yves so dissatisfied with his province. Not that these women were more beautiful. But he had dreamed about them with all his heart, as if dreaming of a different life. He was no longer a child, but these dreams had only become more vivid, revealed in all their splendor by Dior. He could see them at the first Panache ball thrown by Christian Bérard for his female friends: all Paris's crests, blossoms, and ostrich feathers crowned "the prettiest heads in the world." The masked ball, where the beautiful Hélène Rochas came dressed as a bat in black tulle designed by Léonor Fini. Recalling the splendor of the past, Comte de Beaumont had reopened the doors of his music room for the Ball of Kings: Christian Bérard was Henry VIII and Patricia Lopez-Willshaw was the Queen of the Roses. Cosmopolitan Paris was bubbling with champagne and illusion. Its young women knew how to live in pretty apartments and enter the lives of older men like a breath of fresh air, to embody everything they had been missing until then. Regal women always lived up to their reputation: each dress could only be worn once, and every day required a new brooch. "Money was easier," Hélène Rochas remembered in the cream-colored sitting room of her mansion. For her, this splendor was a memory. For Yves Saint Laurent, who dreamed of moonlit sighs, grand haunted châteaux, and courtesans, that time was only starting. He would have his secret revenge against those upstanding women back in Oran who were obsessed with order, frugality, and planning.

For now, the house was haunted by one of the master's lucky charms: lily of the valley. It was sprayed into the air, and thousands of little white bell flowers hung around the mirrors of the salon. The sound of chairs scraping announced the last arrivals. Bernard Buffet came in with Pierre Bergé, the "terrible dominating cobra."[8] Bergé had never been to a fashion show in his life. Now he had been invited "to a show by a young man he didn't know."[9]

Aéroport, Air France, Alma, suits, shirts. The first styles came out. Hidden behind the door, Yves Saint Laurent had pinned a sprig of lily of the valley to his black suit. Several bravos were heard, at first intermittently, then regularly. At 10:30, it became a storm. At 12:30, people were crying. Yves Saint Laurent did better than win. He had gone to Oran to bring back a line, and he came back with two. The first line, the suits and dresses, was straight. So thin that it crushed the models' chests and spread out into skirts that were slightly bell-shaped. The hat, placed straight on the head, marked the summit of a geometrical shape: it was the Trapeze line. The program announced that it owed "its elegance above all to the sparseness and purity of its construction." The day designs had names like Café de Flore, Ciel de Paris, Passy, Plaza, Parc Monceau, Montmartre, Grands Boulevards. Paris was a smock-dress, number 116, right in the middle of the show—the time when the ladies would take out their compacts, as Monsieur Dior would have said. All eyes converged on this new silhouette: the smock and its sleeves weren't connected at the neck, but started at the shoulders. The shoulders gave these dresses their balance. They structured these smocks with wide, open necks—repeating, in expanded and shortened form, the proportions of the H-lines (Christian Dior's famous Haricot Vert, or Green Bean) and especially the A-lines (summer 1955)—a letter that had brought luck to Yves Saint Laurent because it announced the movement and the simplification of the cut. No bows, but darts. Basically, a trapeze. Very inspired by the geometrical lines of the 1920s. It was a "machine silhouette" that would have been lambasted by Christian Dior, the man who declared, "I am a couturier."

But, of course, the spirit of the house of Dior was there. Inflated like bubbles or domes, delightful dresses multiplied under the artificial light of the evening. This was the second line. The dresses had names like Scarlett and Arabian Nights. It was as if Yves were inviting the audience to the theater for the first time. The newest model, Victoire, with her sixteen-and-a-half inch waist, spun around, sparkling. Audrey Hepburn, accompanied by her husband, Mel Ferrer, smiled. The most acclaimed dress was called Muguet, French for lily of the valley. Another favorite was Nuit, because it was entirely black. The night before, at midnight, it didn't even exist; Yves was still sketching it. Raymonde Zehnacker helped translate it into fabric, and Marguerite Carré put together the test garment at three o'clock in the morning. The last dress appeared; it was the wedding dress. Then an exhausted Yves came out.

"Saint Laurent on the balcony!" Three hundred people and a few television cameras rushed to the corner balcony where Yves had just appeared. "We thought that as soon as he was celebrated, the young man might be smothered to death."[10] For the first time, the guests saw the Little Prince smile. In Dior's grand salon, covered with lipsticked kisses, he was followed by hordes of admirers crying with emotion and swarms of photographers shouting among the knocked-over chairs. "Adorable!" "Marvelous!" "Oh, it's one of a kind!" Carmel Snow of *Harper's Bazaar*, who invented the name "New Look" in 1947, murmured: "It's a good collection, a very good collection." "I'm tired, I'm going home to bed," Yves declared. It was midnight at Christian Dior when the biggest buyer in Canada asked to see one hundred forty dresses.

At the end of the day, Lucienne received a telegram. "Incredible success stop Marvelous stop With love Yves." He had asked his parents not to come. Madame Mathieu-Saint-Laurent would proudly glue the articles into her blue notebook. There were too many to count! "Yves Saint Laurent on the Balcony" was the headline in *L'Echo d'Oran*, with an article by the mysterious Velvet Glove, who wrote: "When our grandchildren and our great-grandchildren and our great-great-grandchildren talk about the scene on the balcony, they won't be thinking of Cyrano de Bergerac. I'm here on Avenue Montaigne. The crowd is standing about in front of a house with an awning."

The Parisian press felt Yves's collection was a triumph. "The little king of haute couture passed his *bac* of glory with flying colors," crowed the *Paris-Presse-l'Intransigeant*. On January 31, *L'Aurore* had an eight-column story headlined "France Applauds, Foreigners, too. Long Live the Trapeze Woman." "It's a success! Marcel Boussac won't regret having faith in Yves Saint Laurent, just as he had faith in Christian Dior."

The foreign press was exuberant. The *Manchester Guardian* had two columns headlined: "Emotional and Triumphant Atmosphere at Dior" and "Yves, Paris's Idol." As in a Hollywood movie, all the ladies with pearl necklaces sent cables: "Dior Without Dior, a Triumph for Yves Saint Laurent!" The austere *New York Times* reported, "A miracle rarely happens when you want it to. A miracle happened." Searching for powerful enough superlatives, the *New York World-Telegram* printed in capital letters and in French: "QUELLE MERVEILLE!" "I've never seen a better Dior collection," raved Eugenia Sheppard in the *Herald Tribune*.

It took just three hours for Yves to thrill his contemporaries. His first collection was a manifesto. It immediately revealed Yves Saint Laurent as the only intermediary between two different eras: 1947 and 1958. Dior had made clothes for a "time of rebeginnings": the return to the attractive and the pretty. The birth of his fashion house benefitted from a wave of optimism.

On the other hand, 1958 marked the beginning of an era of disillusion and progress. This collection functioned as a mirror with two sides. On one side, the day, the rigor, simplicity, sparseness of a Passe-Partout coat, which announced a "now look" following in the footsteps of Chanel. On the other side, the night, the theater, the whims of seduction: they revealed more clearly Yves's connection with Christian Dior, who, according to *Le Figaro Littéraire* of June 8, 1957, saw haute couture as "a treasure of conscientious craftsmanship."

Yves had to resolve all these contradictions. On the one hand, he felt obliged to remain faithful to the principles of his spiritual father who passed on to him his love of the craft. On the other, he was determined to become what he was: the couturier of a time that no longer meant gilded furniture and Couture with a capital *C*, but ready-to-wear and Formica. The Milan Triennial showed the first pass-through furniture, movable Formica bookcases, and living rooms with room dividers, which meant that a whole generation would stop eating and sleeping as their parents did, in an old-style sitting room with an ugly crystal fruit bowl on the waxed wood table. Yves had decided that he had to become the couturier who would dress this generation. He knew that you couldn't revolutionize fashion with hemlines anymore, but needed something more lasting than fashion itself: modernity. He was connected to his own time.

Caught between nostalgia and the need for new expression, Yves Saint Laurent had already begun by taking inspiration from a time that liberated the body: the 1920s. At Christian Dior's last collection in July 1957, which had many contributions by Yves, there were skirt suits with jackets, skirts tied around the waist African-style, and rather full safari jackets (the Fuseau line, winter 1957–58). Six months later, the dress that his enemies called "the sack dress" was a huge success. So much so that *Vogue Paris* celebrated it as "a ready-to-wear victory," for "nothing is more elegant than the movement of the body under supple fabric that moves with the slightest gesture. This is definitely *the* dress to have this season!"[11]

The seeds of the Rive Gauche style were sown in 1958; it would be launched exactly eight years later.

Yves Saint Laurent was neither a psychic nor a sociologist. But he had a tough intelligence that made him invincible. When there was a break, a transition between two decades, he gave the best of himself. He lived apart, skirted the limits, flirted with debauchery. He exposed himself. And he dangerously sampled life drop by drop and then distilled it onto the turbulent canvas of passing time, paying attention to be the first to spot decadence, "this great minute when a civilization becomes exquisite," as Cocteau put it. While he didn't paint landscapes, or real portraits, or still-lifes, his main "subject" contained them all and was vast enough to be offhandedly categorized as the spirit of the times. He sensed this spirit simply by waking up each morning: "I never felt that I had important moments in my life. I was simply engaging in situations that were more or less important but in which my inner self remained withdrawn."

Yves Saint Laurent seemed to have put into his dresses this worldly sophistication that others use to their advantage as they move through life: the art of listening, talking, introducing oneself, answering, hiding, and seducing in way that was still inexperienced, but not totally innocent. And, starting in 1958, this is surely why observers had a great deal of difficulty categorizing him. He wasn't a partisan of order and good taste. Much later, he said, "Dior is a magnificent painting to be hung on the wall." Although he was the son of the postwar bourgeoisie of pretty ladies and good tailors, the man-child perceived its limits. Even if it restored Paris as the apex of elegance and gave "made in Paris" a halo of perfection (from Cartier to Hermès), it never stimulated new shapes but always strived to live "like before." After erasing four years of deprivation, it wanted simply to put the spotlight back on flirtatious ladies, corseted by received ideas and fearful of change. Yves Saint Laurent knew this world was coming to an end. Another world was beginning and was open to all kinds of possibilities, dangers, and seductions—a world where one could live and breathe without restrictions.

His muse was neither a blond charmer, like the newcomer Brigitte Bardot, nor a severe postwar intellectual in a suit like Simone de Beauvoir. There was another type of woman whom his eyes scanned, a free woman, a wild girl of 1958 who was just as much of a chameleon, perhaps, as Cécile, the heroine of *Bonjour Tristesse*, who could be by turns a capricious child, a woman, an ingénue, cruel, in love, or indifferent. Or Amber, from Kathleen Winsor's racy historical romance *Forever Amber*, which was published in the United States in 1944 and translated into French in 1946. Yves's female friends in Oran read it in secret. "The Devil take it, my dear! You're the prettiest creature that hell ever did hold."[12] Is it just by chance that, in addition to Victoire, he chose another beautiful model with Eastern charm? Twenty-two-year-old Svetlana had well-defined black eyebrows, and her hair, when not done up in a bun for the fashion shows, fell naturally onto her shoulders in sensuous waves. Reds and rose pinks brought out something of Amber in her, "something luxurious and hot" that could stimulate "enticing suggestions" in men, something she was not responsible for, but of which she was acutely aware. "Young women were jealous of that more than of her beauty."

Yves told the press that he had no desire to meet Brigitte Bardot, in a slightly annoyed tone that members of a circle have regarding newcomers, especially when they themselves are quite recent arrivals. Bardot's success irritated more than one celebrity. From *Look* (five million issues) to *L'Express*, all the magazines fought to put her on the cover. B. B. had the world at her feet. *And God Created Woman* showed in New York for nine weeks! It was the first time since the war that a French film had been so successful. But it didn't matter: "the twentieth-century Eve" was not at all the couturier's type. How could she be, when his dresses made the chest disappear and were off limits to anyone measuring over thirty-five inches! For a long time, he had a certain scorn for what Proust called women who were "all ready." He only liked those who laid traps. Those who were called to dominate after a long initiation. Free, lively, bold, in love, lascivious, shameless, unbridled, vile, dishonorable, dangerous, unfaithful, fickle, flighty, breaking vows, devious, famous, pretty, witty, irritating, provocative. After all, when he wrote "Why Speak of Love?" in Oran, he rhymed *femme*, or woman, with *infâme*, or dishonorable.

"By being natural and sincere," Dior said, "real revolutions happen without anyone looking for them."[13] Yves Saint Laurent was like Dior, and he created the same kind of revolution. With him, there was no message. You couldn't be a "Saint-Laurentist" the way you could declare yourself Sarrautard, Butorian, or Robbe-Grilletist. Later, fashion designers Courrèges and Paco Rabanne would seek inspiration from conceptual artists and futurists. In 1958, at the Philips Pavilion, Le Corbusier—whose Radiant City, first considered "the nut house," had become a model—composed an electronic poem that summarized human development in eight minutes. During the same period, Paris was discussing the concrete and spatial music of Edgard Varèse. Artist Yves Klein showed the "void" at Galerie Iris Clert.

Yves Saint Laurent was definitely not avant-garde. Always in classic dark blue or dark gray suits, he looked "dressed" and his ties were perfect because no one noticed them, exclaimed journalists. He made no noise, no gestures. But if he stood in line in front of a movie theater on the Champs-Élysées, fans approached him with notebooks and ballpoint pens. In restaurants, people started whispering when he came in. Like a Hollywood star, he received letters: nice letters, crazy letters, letters offering advice.

He renewed fashion, but in a classical language he had learned from books—perhaps from the preface to *Bérénice* by Jean Racine, a little beige and purple Classiques Larousse edition from his teenage years, which he put away with his mementos. "The secret is first of all to please and to move the audience."

It was the first time since Chanel that a couturier was not judged as such, but as a privileged observer of contemporary life. "Paris had two sad children, Françoise Sagan and Bernard Buffet. Now they have a little brother, Yves Mathieu-Saint-Laurent," read the February 6 issue of *L'Express*. In early 1958, these three people dominated Paris news. Françoise Sagan's play *Rendez-vous Manqués* was first performed at the Opéra de Monte-Carlo with sets by Bernard Buffet. The Paris premiere took place on January 20 at the Théâtre des Champs-Élysées. Between two fittings, Yves made a point of seeing it. "It's not so bad," he said. It was as if these Parisian celebrities were on the verge of an expected meeting. Among the weekly news outlets that put him on the cover, *L'Express* had a drawing on the front page of the February 6 issue that was specially made for the magazine by Bernard Buffet: a trapeze dress threaded with black needles and captioned by a quotation from Edgar Degas: "Drawing is not form, it's the way of seeing form." Pierre Bergé trumpeted to anyone who would listen, "I'm the one who asked him to do that drawing!"

Two days after the show, the Little Prince appeared at Maxim's to celebrate, surrounded by the women Jean Fayard called "the fairies": Raymonde Zehnacker, the fairy of fabrics, Suzanne Luling, the fairy of sales, and Marguerite Carré, the fairy of technique. The pillars of the kingdom framed them: Jacques Rouet and Jean-Claude Donati, head of advertising. On February 3, *Le Figaro* described Yves as follows: "He barely looks his twenty-one years. As tall as a morning glory vine and very thin in his proper suit jacket, shy-eyed and nearsighted behind his glasses, he looks like a junior high school student being rewarded by his family, or like a little crown prince out for the first time in public."

There was already something powerful in the eyes of these women with whom he had just worked. As if they had just discovered the child they never had. These women, as well as female journalists and clients, immediately had an almost maternal feeling for him.

Since with this couturier they could talk about something other than hemlines—which was the single topic in fashion at the time—the critics felt protectively affectionate toward him. Plus, Yves Saint Laurent didn't put on airs.

His Parisian education had begun. While other people his age were going wild in the dance halls, Yves Saint Laurent looked like a model young man living a proper life. His salary had been multiplied tenfold. So what? Of course he decorated his one-bedroom apartment himself. It looked out over a dead-end street near the Trocadéro. He covered one of the walls with blue velvet, and he loved very large sofas. He had bronze Louis XIV sconces. He asked the phone company for an unlisted number. He ate all his meals in restaurants. He went out with friends to the movies or the theater. "Now he has to agree to serious lunches and grown-up dinners!" wrote Jean Lohain, whose "Le Paris des Parisiennes" (Paris of Parisian Women) column appeared in *Marie Claire*. Everyone believed him.

With his legendary courtesy, Jean-Claude Donati, head of advertising, told people all day long, "It's not possible to see Monsieur Saint Laurent." They discovered his powerful work ethic. As Alice Chavanne wrote in *Elle*, "He gets up every morning at seven and gets to the studio at nine-thirty. Around eight or nine at night, when he has completed the dresses, he goes down to the boutique, which he arranges and decorates himself. He has a light lunch in the studio: grilled meat or fish, salad, and fruit. He doesn't drink or smoke. He eats a sandwich for dinner, standing up, in the boutique. He doesn't go out."

The elegant women who experienced the enchantment of the postwar years were grateful to him for restoring their lost youth. Geneviève Fath, widow of the couturier Jacques Fath, responded emotionally to Yves's collection: "It's a success, it brings back so many memories." Four years had passed since Jacques Fath's death, and this Parisian woman who traveled with twelve large trunks, seventeen hats, and sixteen pairs of shoes felt that Yves Saint Laurent's creations resuscitated the image of a woman who was a bit frivolous and mischievous, who walked around during the day like a young girl but at night became a princess in embroidered tulle who was lighthearted and covered with flowers, always with some whimsical creation on her head: a fencer's mask with a veil on it, a cloud of feathers, or ribbons—a sassy detail that seemed to say "Who cares?" Older women who admired Yves described him in spiritual language: "Genius has no age, it's sublime," said Marie-Louise Bousquet.

And it was at Marie-Louise Bousquet's house that Yves Saint Laurent and Pierre Bergé met again. Like a journalist, Pierre Bergé had his sources: he had a knack for surrounding himself with the right people at the right time, when he knew they were useful. This man of action, who zipped around town in his Jaguar, had his eye on everything that was said and done in Paris. This was the source of the energy for his battles. He was attracted by different cliques, but he understood them strategically and was able to avoid getting trapped by them. It was a risky game. He was comfortable with intellectuals, cultural arbiters, important women, and young men with Proustian physiques. He was welcome at 11 Place des États-Unis in the mansion of Marie-Laure de Noailles, who, along with Louise de Vilmorin, was one of his dear friends. He also stopped by 4 Place des États-Unis, the home of Francine Weisweiller, a patron of Jean Cocteau (her black Bentley driven by a uniformed chauffeur made an appearance in Cocteau's film *Orpheus*).

Pierre Bergé appeared and disappeared at society receptions "in a charming and elusive breeze."[14] He might be seen at Françoise Sagan's or Marie-Louise Bousquet's; at an out-of-town ball given by the Baronne de Cabrol on a rainy day in Normandy (which no one wanted to attend, according to André Ostier) or at the Bar du Pont-Royal, a hangout for the publishing house Gallimard. Or even at Boncourt. Carmen Teissier had a farm there called La Bergerie. It produced honey that she was going to sell at gourmet purveyor Fauchon, with the label "le miel de la Commère," as announced by *Vogue*. Pierre Bergé even thought about having the label designed by Bernard Buffet. Moving effortlessly between the Right Bank and the Left, Bergé was all eyes and ears, his finger on the pulse of the city, his lively personality always pushing ahead to what was most essential.

His ideals of justice and liberty and his position against French Algeria revealed similarities with Louis Aragon, the editor of the very serious publication *Les Lettres Françaises*, and he already shared with him masculine affinities that leftist intellectuals were too virtuous or too sectarian to acknowledge. Unlike Yves Saint Laurent, whose first travels were only in his dreams, Pierre Bergé's life was a series of developments shaped by changes in history. He was born November 14, 1930, on the Île d'Oléron, under the sign of Scorpio. Pierre Bergé was not part of the New Wave generation. He grew up in a time when art and writing were politically engaged. Everything was black and white. War was war, and liberty was a duty. Life exempted this pragmatic mind from dreaming of masters because he met them at age eighteen. He moved to Paris in 1948, and there he met Jean Cocteau and became very close to Jean Giono. In December 1948, Bergé founded *La Patrie Mondiale*, which published writers such as Camus, Raymond Queneau, André Breton, and Jean-Paul Sartre. The newspaper's address was Bergé's own: 12 Cité Dupetit-Thouars, near the Carreau du Temple. He recalled those early days: "I was lodging with a lady behind the Place de la République. I didn't have a cent. I started earning a living by buying books from the booksellers along the Seine and reselling them to bookstores. I ate at the City Club. I was broke, but I spent every Wednesday at the Rostands'. Mauriac and Arletty were there. It was interesting. It all went fast, too fast." Just a month after its launch, his subscriber-only newspaper moved to the Avenue d'Iéna in the Passy neighborhood. Now it cost fifteen francs instead of ten. This short-lived publication—there would only be two issues—supported the American Gary Davis, the "Citizen of the World," with the manifesto, "Pour un Rassemblement Contre la Guerre" (Gathering Against War). Those who signed it included André Breton, Albert Camus, and Maurice Rostand, who dedicated his poem "Les Vrais Pacifistes" to Pierre Bergé. Most of the articles were written by Bergé himself. He handled the literary and theater criticism under the pseudonym J. B. Sicard. In fiery prose, he didn't hold back: "After having murdered Proust, M. Malaparte has now slaughtered Karl Marx." He raged against "hollow" writing, texts that "dragged on," or "the ridiculousness of a masked ball that adds nothing." Bergé was always raring to go.

His cultural appetite had no boundaries: "I read everything very young." An old local poet, a pal of Jules Laforgue's, played jazz 78s for him, along with "all of Beethoven, all of Wagner, Brahms, and Schumann." To him, nothing was as important as culture. Even his childhood—about which he was quite reticent—was rife with references. His German teacher was also Sartre's. But although Pierre Bergé could stroll through the world of quotations as comfortably as through an elegant living room, he felt all his knowledge melting like wax armor when faced with true artists. His only defense was the physical power and dominating energy that others devoted to their creative work. "Creators are monsters before whom all yield and all must yield." This struggle drove him on, stimulated him, and channeled his ambition.

Since 1950, he had managed Bernard Buffet's rise. In fact, he belonged to no party but his own, admitting that he didn't "see himself in anyone else." He shared with other wanderers the privilege of feeling at home everywhere. Very young, he "rubbed elbows" with high society (his words)—and this education developed his verbal skills, including the art of making cutting and very clever remarks. Like Yves Saint Laurent, he had several reasons for hating the sanctimonious bourgeoisie. The first and main reason was that he made his way on his own, and that he was never afraid. With this weapon, he could stand up to anything. Well, almost anything.

There was just one thing whose solitary battles and agitated bursts fascinated him. One thing he would fight for, ready to give whatever he could: talent. He had experienced loneliness and distress, and he had a sharp, cynical understanding of human nature. For this reason, he admired those who were different. "Submerged by his painting," he wrote, "the artist doesn't direct it, but lets himself be guided by it." He had a weakness that few men were humble enough to share but which he defended with honor: "Nothing amazes me more than talent." He was soft-hearted and sentimental, with a habit of being wary of people in general but not enough in particular. Effusive, funny, and rebellious, he often got angry when he realized he was wrong. Fashion seemed secondary to him in comparison to music and the theater. Pierre Bergé claimed not to understand anything about it. He had dinner one night at Francine Weisweiller's with Balenciaga, a rather secretive person who usually avoided high society life. Balenciaga disappeared at the end of every fashion show, without waiting to hear the applause. On January 30, 1958, Pierre Bergé came to congratulate the young Yves Saint Laurent: "Bravo, that was magnificent!"

The official meeting of Yves Saint Laurent and Pierre Bergé took place in the first week of February at La Cloche d'Or, a restaurant on Rue Mansart that was popular with actors after their performances. Five people were there: Marie-Louise Bousquet, Raymonde Zehnacker, Yves Saint Laurent, Pierre Bergé, and Bernard Buffet.

The painter was charmed by the Trapeze collection. A friend of Christian Dior's, he published a panegyric to Yves Saint Laurent in *L'Express* titled "Yves Mathieu-Saint-Laurent, a Shy Young Man with a Great Destiny"—with another drawing, this one a portrait that Pierre Bergé had requested. Buffet wrote, "Yves Saint Laurent doesn't talk about his craft, but we can tell that we haven't heard the last of him and that he has an admirable understanding of what he wants. We're not dealing with a child prodigy but a man whose qualities seem unquestionable to me.... People said that Christian Dior was a magician. But his final accomplishment was surely, at the most essential moment, to make the right young man appear—not to replace him, but to continue his legacy."[15]

However, Bernard Buffet would be shunted aside from the adventure that was starting. Some observers placed the break during a summer weekend at the Château d'Arc, which someone who was there described as follows: "Pierre left with Yves, Buffet with Annabelle, and Sagan stayed with her bottle." The eventful breakup would be heavily covered in the tabloid newspapers. Bernard Buffet even published an open letter in *Les Lettres Françaises* in which he criticized this invasion of his privacy.

Yves Saint Laurent and Pierre Bergé would form the most famous gay couple in the history of fashion, their private life mirroring their respective talents: the designer and his artistic director. They were two men shaped by the art and culture of nineteenth-century France who were thrust into a rapidly changing world they felt compelled to master. For different reasons, they both grasped the world that was coming into being: money and America. They would have a role in a sublime and decadent play that would make them say for a long time to come, "We arrived ten years too late."

They understood their surroundings the same way, and they complemented each other, pushed by the same instinctive hatred of boredom and the "idiotic petits-bourgeois" who ruined Madame Bovary's life. These two men of the provinces both had dreams of grandeur that they expressed differently. Pierre Bergé's admiration for beauty, whether it was Iznik pottery or a black Senufo bird sculpture—the first piece Yves acquired from the antiques dealer Raton—seemed to have convinced him, like Dorante in *The School for Wives*, "that money is the key of all great undertakings; and this sweet metal that strikes so many heads, in love as in war, makes conquests move forward." He never bought anything inexpensive. "I don't hang around flea markets," he said. On the contrary, Yves Saint Laurent was not a collector. But he acquired lots of good luck charms. The only value he attached to objects, rare or not, was their connection to his imaginary world. He hated museums "because they're dead." Another difference: like Dior, Yves Saint Laurent hated to travel. It frightened him. He didn't like feeling like a foreigner in a city. But such unpredictable mobility was a special weapon in the hands of Pierre Bergé.

"I knew nothing. I had seen two women wearing the same Dior dress. I thought that every couturier came down with his yardstick in his mouth and his pins," declared Pierre Bergé. Starting in March 1958, he somewhat nervously discovered the theater of couture, the salons of 30 Avenue Montaigne, the entrances, the role playing, the aesthetic dramas that were silenced by the sales curve. "I admired Jacques Rouet right away." The couple was seen out on the town. Lunches at Francis on Place de l'Alma or at the Ritz, evening get-togethers with chic friends.

In 1958, Yves Saint Laurent gave his new definition of elegance, as if he realized that the dresses he had thought were chic were exactly the kind of thing that chic people wouldn't wear. For him, elegance wasn't "a beautiful bodice" or a pretty dress, but a way of living, "of translating oneself." Yves found this quality in Marie-Louise Bousquet. He sometimes went to Bousquet's Thursday salon and had compared her "to a Goya painting," without specifying which one. Pierre Bergé called her "someone who was both a socialite and an intellectual—which is rare!" Francine Weisweiller remembered her in this way: "She entertained a lot.…She brought in much freshness at her age. We'd have tea or whisky. We talked about anything and everything. She would tell me about the era she lived through. She loved to surround herself with young people."

Yves Saint Laurent also met the Comtesse San Just, one of Dior's first clients, who remembered Yves as "very sweet, very modest. He didn't put on airs. He was someone truly great." She was one of the couture clients who would disappear over time: her clothing wasn't noticed by those who didn't have the right taste. At that time, she ordered about four dresses per season from Dior, including one to go to the races, where she sat in a box belonging to her mother, Madame Jean Stern. She often wore a blouse with a knit tie. "Oh, how pretty," said Yves Saint Laurent, using Monsieur Dior's little phrase. In the summer, she entertained in her beautiful house in Cap Martin "with a garden beautiful enough to die for" and where Cocteau would stop by. In her mansion in Neuilly, she described never organizing balls or "things like that." "We got together among friends," like women who saw their peers ostentatiously made-up and whose response was "the Baron de Redé was never her type."

At age twenty-one, Yves discovered "the trap of his life": "the fortress of celebrity." Dior left him a throne of gold in a palace of mirages. In his room in Oran, this highly sensitive teenager sometimes built up the golden existence of these women into a fantasy that would rescue him from boredom and shame: beauty. He had dreamed of beauty, but arrived to love her too late: she had fled. In Oran, he dreamed of Paris, and in Paris, he dreamed of Oran.

At age twenty-one, the couturier gave his designs a "little girl look"—coats with round collars and storybook dresses—and gave them names like Récompense, Sophie, and Jeudi, or Thursday. He charmed women with paradise—a lost paradise, but also one that he invented as if then to lose it better. Did the society lady who ordered this pretty gray suit know that it got its name, Zouzou, from a little dog? And did the bride-to-be have any idea that her wedding dress was the one that Yves had designed for Simone Tronc, his childhood friend? Other dresses, in tulle embroidered with gold or silver or sparkling water droplets, and dresses made of mousseline or printed with transparent flakes, completed his album of real and imaginary memories. Of course, there were Scarlett, Séduction, Roman, Senso, and Fiesta, a sheath dress for evening wear. They were seen at Promé Couture in Oran, where his sister Brigitte modeled them, and at the shop of Madame Dufihol, who maintained "the prestige of haute couture" in Algiers.

Yves continued to have flowers thrown at his feet. "Fashion: The Curtain Rises" was the headline of *Paris Match* on March 1, 1958. But the threat was there: there was the drama of the Algerian War that had been building for nearly two years now, the khaki uniforms on the mountain slopes, the green berets of the French Foreign Legion, the photos of the *fellagha*, armed Algerian nationalists, being led behind barbed wire that were published in the same issue. But who was worried? *L'Express* adopted a playful tone: "At his age, theoretically he should be doing his military service. But he was not deemed fit to serve and was granted a deferment. Even if he gains weight, any minister who cares about France's interests may hesitate to put a uniform on a young man who can put women around the world into a French uniform...and into a little girl's uniform at that."[16]

He had a title. Glory. Nicknames. "Christian II." "The little prince traveling on the clouds." "The young stranger with the periwinkle eyes." But a danger was present, periodically stalking him and yet attracting him. In an interview on April 9, 1958, with *Le Journal du Dimanche*, something imperceptible and serious emanated from him. It was his way of talking about death, Christian Dior's death in particular, as if, in the midst of the immensity around him, it became part of himself, as if he were transformed into a dramatic hero.

"I felt a void, the same void I experienced after my first collection. It wasn't the void of fear, but the void of nothing. I had so much faith in him, faith in everything he said and did, and I felt a kind of apprehension thinking that no one was there anymore to say: this is good, this is bad. It was the first time that I discovered the moral meaning of aesthetics, so to speak." When he was asked, "Are you afraid of death?" he answered, "I'm afraid of old age especially, and experiencing so early what others experienced so late brings me a certain anxiety. People forget what they loved so quickly." In *L'Echo d'Oran*, the mysterious Velvet Glove gushed, using the Algerian slang word *zaoui* for a celebrity in France: he was "the one who has become the most *zaoui* of all the *zaouis* in France in just a few hours." The Velvet Glove prompted him, "This must be going to your head!" He replied, "No, it's just nice to think that I've succeeded, that I've reached my goal. A goal that is always receding, because ambition is all-consuming, and it constantly pushes back the limits of egotism."

He had to learn to dream anew in order to keep on living. He had to forget that he was born in Oran. But no matter, he lived only to dream.

> *You must be rich*
> *And a socialite, so that the women*
> *Whom you'll choose as victims*
> *Are covered with jewels.*
> *Money is necessary for love*
> *Your mistresses will only be wealthy,*
> *Poor women will give you no pleasure*

He had written this poem eight years earlier in Oran. In 1958, he could dress his dreams. They would need "dresses with character, evoking Renaissance Venice and its splendor, eighteenth-century Orientalist art, and Goya": his "dogaressa dresses," his "evening dominos," his "theater cloaks."[17] Often, he left through a concealed door, saying nothing. Walled up in his loneliness, despite the tumult in his head, he perceived, like Flaubert's Saint Antoine, "an enormous silence that separated him from the world."

4 / THE DRAFT, THE PRINCESSES, AND THE ALGERIAN WAR

year had passed since Dior's death—an eternity. His aesthetic had become part of history. It was his sense of pomp. A certain formality. A way of imagining dresses as if all women rode in black coupés with uniformed chauffeurs. Yves Saint Laurent had gotten rid of the "bracelet" waist, freeing the body from the rigid architecture that held it prisoner—the famous Dior stranglehold. Once, an important politician had told the father of the New Look the following story: "I'm always late to the Presidential Palace and to diplomatic receptions. People think I'm delayed by matters of state. In fact, I'm helping my wife get into your dresses. They're veritable tarlatan armor, with secret corsets to lace up, three or four zippers that are impossible to find, connecting underwires, and rows of snaps. And you have the nerve to call these very simple dresses!" The couturier's secret could be discovered by turning the dresses inside out: Christian Dior was selling women a new youth, filling out what was too flat, squeezing the waist, lifting the bosom, and emphasizing the curves.

Yet it was still the school of Dior: every season, the new collection gave women the illusion that everything else was out of style now, and convinced men that their wives had changed. Dior said: "Agreeing to yield to the difficult laws of elegance is a way to acquire self-discipline, and also a way to find harmony with everything that isn't you: the world of other people and the world of things. However, let's not forget this personal, emotional aspect of fashion, which is the desire to please, to change one's appearance in order to keep someone in love with you."[1] This didn't stop Saint Laurent from moving away from the house repertory. With him, fashion was not just a silhouette—it was a look. Stiff construction gave way to movement.

He already had a special way of moving around the body, accentuating the paleness of the arms and face, lengthening the silhouette and making it dangerous. He defined various shades of black: Mystery black of an elegant cocktail hour, Lady's Battle black, Detective black, Diamond black, Lily black. If his designs could have talked, they would have sounded like Louis Malle discussing his movie *The Lovers*, which scandalized Venice in September 1958, "In fact, you see, I was interested in making a movie about a woman, to say what I wanted to say about a worn-out theme that was still new: love." He created a sense of capturing his era, of walking around with a camera-pen and watching those to whom he dedicated dresses called "Quatre Cents Coups" (Four Hundred Blows) and "Season." Would he become the New Wave couturier? One of his salespeople recalled the changes at this time: "In 1958, a little breeze of youth and modernism arrived. With Monsieur Dior, the dresses could stand up by themselves. Now, it was different: they were suppler, more relaxed. The Americans liked it."

In fact, Marcel Boussac was thrilled. The triumph of the Trapeze collection, whose rehearsals he attended, reminded him of the wonderful time of February 1947. Pictured on the cover of *Vogue* in March 1958, Bonne Conduite (Good Behavior) was the best-selling design of the season with eighty-five sold. The number two and three best sellers were 1958 and Aurore (Dawn). The collection increased revenue by 35 percent. "I was right to have faith in him," said the entrepreneur, always faithful to his motto: "Clothes don't speak—only numbers."[2] The pressure from American buyers was intense. At that time, French fashion was a more lucrative export than French automobiles. American department store magnates were now keeping the French couture houses alive.

Yves Saint Laurent's position was made official. A press release on August 12, 1958 announced, "All designs, whether for the Paris, London, or New York collections, will be designed exclusively by Yves Mathieu-Saint-Laurent. Marc Bohan will assist Monsieur Mathieu-Saint-Laurent only in executing designs for London and New York in September and March."

Yves Saint Laurent was couturier at Dior from January 1958 to July 1960 and created six collections: Trapeze (spring/summer 1958), Arc (fall/winter 1958–59), Longue (spring/summer 1959), 1960 (fall/winter 1959), Silhouette de Demain (spring/summer 1960), and Souplesse, Légèreté, Vie (winter 1960). He showed the Souplesse, Légèreté, Vie collection in July 1960. It would be his last for Dior.

Dior was like a father, a head of household, a husband to the women he dressed. Yves was like their lover. He would be their Léon, their Rodolphe. Like Emma Bovary, they would say to him, "Take me away! Carry me off! Oh, I beg you!" Along with Pierre Cardin and Guy Laroche, he was one of three young people who had rejuvenated fashion. But he had a secret. He was neither a pioneer nor an innovator. Through some mysterious alchemy, he was the only one who could captivate girls by making clothes for women.

Dior had renewed the language of seduction. Yves Saint Laurent dramatized it, with a formidable sense of humor that always flirted with parody. With him at the helm, Dior press materials read like theater programs, along with a summary that set the scene and kept the viewers on the edge of their seats as if they were about to witness a new battle of *Hernani*. "This line breaks completely with the last collection....Although the waist is short, this line rejects all Napoleonic inspiration...." He described the accessories as if he were meticulously preparing for the stage entrance of the Parisian woman: "Stockings: the trend for winter revolves around black: marcasite, which is a smoky gray, and charcoal, which is a false black." Paris gray-blue, cashmere- and fog-color tweeds, and English flannels already made an appearance in these collections. Dresses for outings to the theater or cinema had names full of promises: Lever de Rideau (Curtain Rises), Suspense, Entracte (Intermission), Enigma. A bridal gown was called Haute Fidélité, or High Fidelity. Claude Licard, who assisted with the fittings under Yves Saint Laurent as before him under Christian Dior, summed it up: "It was kind of like the theater. We explored. Actors try to find the right tone, lighting directors try to find the right lighting. We tried to find the right cut and the right model to highlight the dress."

People found Yves eccentric. He was soon categorized. In August 1958, *L'Express* printed two photos. On the left, a Chanel suit: "Dressing up." On the right, a Saint Laurent dancing dress: "Or having fun?" As tensions in the world ramped up, fashion became more subdued.

Yves Saint Laurent shattered the image of the young French *bourgeoise*. At the time, designs for women were split into two opposing camps. On one side, the mothers, with their suits and pearl necklaces and crimped hair. On the other, the younger women. The new generation was starting to become an all-powerful entity. Some praised it to the skies ("It's the country's lifeblood!"), but others were terrified and condemned it: "They're all bad seeds. Just look how the girls are made up as if it's Carnival! They need to be reined in."

Yves Saint Laurent rejected rhinestone sheaves of wheat and strings of pearls. Instead, he used semiprecious stones, such as two big round agates or pieces of turquoise. Plus large fake jewels as buttons. With Saint Laurent, the pearl necklace hung between the shoulder blades. Yves depicted daughters of Eve who dominated men with their magic, courtesans who precede the Wise Men in the kingdom of heaven, as stated in the Gospel of Matthew. Journalist Hélène Cingria described his flair as follows: "Formal dresses revealing the cleavage and plunging all the way to the waist in back hide nothing. This is especially where Yves Mathieu-Saint-Laurent triumphs, with his designs with proffered busts and short bodices belted in satin that recall the Venetian painter Carpaccio and take us back to a time when the courtesans of the Serenissima Repubblica of Venice awaited the return of ships loaded with gold from Byzantium."[3] These brunette women with powerfully lined lips, their profiles accentuated by Callas-style buns, had a look that took journalists by surprise.

His dresses, after all, were called Circé, Souricière (Mousetrap), or Siren. For passionate Victoire, he created dresses with stories, such as Salade (in garden green taffeta), Bowling Pin (shaped like its namesake), and Main Chaude, or Hot Hand (in mousseline). Along with Fidélia (a Eurasian) and Déborah (a Russian), there was a new model from Australia. Her name was Gay, and she was very tall. Her black hair contrasted with her freckles. Between Bleu de Paris and Bobby, Gay appeared in Blouson Noir, an afternoon outfit in black leather. The leather helmet (very much inspired by the one that Cardin showed the year before) matched the blouse. "I was just as shocked as everyone else," remembered Hélène Rochas, "but I ordered a black suit. Balenciaga was chic. But Saint Laurent was chic and modern." Yves Saint

Laurent was indefinable and his silhouettes were delicate and flexible. They were Parisian, Asian, and androgynous, all at the same time.

Unaware of the troubling times looming thanks to the Algerian War draft, Yves expressed his life with his own colors. Christian Dior was fond of colors from fields and gardens: mauve violets, green lawns, yellow buttercups, blue cornflowers, forget-me-nots, and larkspur—shades of beautiful nature and opaline. Color made his dresses pretty. With Yves Saint Laurent, color erupted into a supernatural setting. He used its texture to create more intimate connections. Dior dreamed of the blond hair of the queen. But Saint Laurent imagined silk organdy the color of clouds. He fell in love with color like a child with his first box of colored pencils, which he knocks over in his excitement. He drew feverishly, playing with names more than with materials, which he hadn't yet mastered. For the first time, Yves Saint Laurent showed how color was a vision for him. Like a great bazaar of everything that amazed, charmed, and overwhelmed him—all the heroines, films, and stories. Colors weren't there to "brighten up" the design. They weren't a distraction from it—they were inseparable from it. The influence of Christian Bérard, the Ballets Russes, and the decorator Léon Bakst, the Delacroix of costume, were clearly visible. Oriane was red. Clélia, the ingénue of *The Charterhouse of Parma*, was pale blue. Acid green made Philaminte in *Les Femmes Savantes* even more domineering.

Then came the peasant dresses, wrapped in shawls but bedecked with diamonds. Genoa velvet was specially woven "in colors dear to Bronzino"—deep purples embellished with gold and copper embroidery. Color was a drama, a game. A way of seeing that turned more toward the Renaissance and the Romantic era than to Dior's eighteenth century and 1900. No preciousness, no little bedroom ribbons, no love poems. But monologues, blood-red camellias. Velvet masks, austere woolen fabric, and gorgeous faille celebrated a woman who was closer to the courtesans of Carpaccio than the marquises of Boucher, whom Dior courted with ribbons and pastels.

Yves Saint Laurent's colors were not those that fashion usually used for its fabrics: the traditional soft blue, magenta, pale salmon, stem green, beet red, smoky gray, light candy pink, sea green....He illuminated them by giving them a different intensity. His blues dropped Dior's references (Fontainebleau, Marie-Antoinette) and were less about defining a quality than creating a hot or cold sensation: delightful blue, Mediterranean blue, swordfish blue, Turkish blue, university blue.

For night, his palette was a gallery of characters and emotions: Siena red, Venetian red, hussar red, vivid red, purple, flame red. Fire red, lacquer red, flash red. Hot jazz red, dahlia red, Bergamo pink red. Saadi red, bishop red, Roxane red, Cinecittà red. And there were still Gauguin pink, fuchsia pink, begonia pink, Etruscan pink. Sulfur yellow....Everything was there, stimulating the imagination.

He walked around with a sketchbook that he filled with eighteenth-century orientalist images and village scenes taken from the art history books he devoured, hoarding their pearls, sultana necklaces, crystal teardrops, and silk tassels in the same way he used to cut out images to transform them into figurines for his Illustre Théâtre. He stole a straw hat from Manet, a fur cap from Piero della Francesca, and Antonia Zárate's black dress from Goya, leaving her on her yellow sofa. He selected, combined, cut and pasted. At that time, Yves Saint Laurent was still a viewer: his dresses looked more like the work of these painters than his own.

Journalist Hélène Cingria described his creations like this: "Thanks to him there appeared a long supple creature, light and bouncy, who seemed to be born from the same breath as Botticelli's nymphs, and who, like the flower-girls of Umbria, with their bodies comfortable in flowing rainbow-colored clothing, their foreheads crowned with jasmine, their arms bare and their legs barely covered, will serve as the most perfect symbol of spring in the coming months."[4]

Yet a strange force seemed to possess him. Dresses with character, dresses with panache, dresses as full as Persian lanterns, bullfighters' culottes—all these visions were layered and ended up, with a thousand gathered details, forming a universe in the world of the artist who mastered them. He seemed to use his visions to fight a reality that oppressed him. As time went on, the world of the fantastic seemed more and more like his only refuge. At age twenty-two, Yves had discovered the loneliness of accolades. In April 1958, he was asked to inaugurate the World's Fair in Brussels. As *Le Figaro*'s correspondent observed, "For the first time ever, Brussels welcomed a silent Parisian." Duck à l'orange at Chez Joseph, a tour of the French pavilion, and an evening in the neighborhood of the dance halls of what was promoted as "joyful Belgium." The couturier signed autographs for groups of students. Nevertheless, Yves Saint Laurent continued to return home to Oran regularly, always laden with perfumes and scarves for his mother and sisters. But soon this would no longer be possible. In November 1958, he showed the Dior collection at Blenheim Palace, about sixty miles from London, to Princess Margaret and two thousand of the richest women in England. He was asked to design a wedding dress for Farah Diba, the future empress of Iran. What glory! On December 19, 1958, he was at the Opéra, where Maria Callas sang the great "Miserere" scene of *Il Trovatore* and the second act of *Tosca*, which would one day become his favorite opera.

Yves had become an important personage. A new era had started. Boutique stylist Jean-Pierre Frère described how things changed: "I still went to Le Fiacre. He didn't go there anymore. You'd see him at Le Relais or Chez Francis. That's when he started taking tranquilizers and drinking. Like a Hollywood star taking all kinds of stuff just to get through it all. I didn't see him anymore. I just ran into him sometimes. I had to request an audience." His mother confirmed the difficulty of this period for Yves: "When he went to Dior, I think it was a marvelous time for him. He was cheerful. He had fun with his little group, Victoire, Anne-Marie. He would tell us about weekends in Honfleur, and the Bar des Théâtres. And then there was work, and the burden of the journalists and photographers. His youth stopped abruptly in

1958." By realizing his long-held dreams, he closed the door on his life. Yves became a supplier of illusions.

There was personal loss to endure as well. Suffering from cancer of the liver, Michel de Brunhoff died on May 14, 1958. Who would replace him? What new father figure?

Yves was able to find female allies at Dior. One of them was Yvonne de Peyerimhoff, head saleswoman at Dior, an extremely important person. A client of Balenciaga and Patou back when she was Madame Charles de Breteuil, this proud soul had won her independence with an energy that dazzled the men around her, whether gay or straight. "You know the United States, you are well-liked there and I need you," Dior told her in 1947. She became fond of Yves Saint Laurent as soon as he entered the couture house as assistant designer in 1955: "I never had time to eat lunch, and neither did he. And he was shy, so he didn't want to eat with everyone. So he would sit down with the apprentices to have a sandwich. Or he would wait for me. We'd have fried eggs and tea in the cafeteria. That's how we became very close. He was so charming. He had female friends. He palled around with young women his age. I was older, and I was his friend." She added, "When you work with Yves, you can only love him. He was an extraordinary boss. He always had a nice word, even though deep down he was quite blunt. If something wasn't the way he wanted it, he had a very gentle manner of making you understand, even though he could have said, 'You didn't get it at all, leave and come back tomorrow with what I asked for!' He tried to arrange things on the spot. I really saw him. I saw all his rehearsals. I was fascinated. It was wonderful to see him construct something."

Constructing? Around 1959, a smell of anger, of provocation, of dangerous beauty invaded Yves Saint Laurent's fashion shows. These six collections, extraordinarily rich in their contradictions, are nevertheless the least well-known. And for good reason: the box with the press articles is missing from the Dior archives and those of Yves Saint Laurent. It has been lost. So those two years have been left aside. Dior did preserve the "charts," the large cardboard-backed sheets with the drawings, the names of the designs, fabric samples, programs, and photos. But in Dior's retrospectives, only the 1958 Trapeze line is frequently mentioned. In fact, everyone prefers to pass over those years quickly.

Late in 1959, the news hit like a bomb: "Next year, Yves Saint Laurent will be wearing a new couture ensemble: Government Issued," Hélène de Turckheim wrote in *Le Figaro* on November 28. The young couturier had benefited from a military service deferment, but would be enlisted on September 1, 1960. A notice had been published in the *Journal Officiel* on November 27: "The deferment was granted to him on March 22, 1957 and was thereafter automatically renewed on an annual basis. Exerting the powers granted by the ruling of July 12, 1958, on the oversight of the renewal of deferments, the minister of the army has decided that this deferment will not be renewed."

Military service was for a period of twenty-seven months and fifteen days. Yves ignored it all. He boldly announced that he would go to Algeria, but to design his collections.

By this time the threat that had been building was becoming clear and forceful. In retrospect its presence could already be felt in his designs, such as amphora-shaped skirts that were so tight at the knees that they impeded walking. They were like trap dresses. Did he, in turn, want to immobilize women where they stood? Keep them at attention? Perhaps the Little Prince (or "choir boy," as the English called him) was actually a little devil? His reputation floundered. In July 1959, his caressing taffeta dresses, and especially his famous sheath dresses that were tight all the way to the knees and displayed "a deliberate desire for spectacle"[5] were received coolly by the critics: "It's not a question of whether these paper lanterns in which Yves Saint Laurent enjoyed enclosing women's bodies are beautiful or ugly, or even whether French women will want to wear them or not. At another time, we might have feared an incredible fiasco, while still recognizing this young man's indisputable sense of a certain 'present': he is surely the contemporary of Zazie and Lolita. He has an admirable ability to dress up little girls and all those who want to adopt their juvenile impudence," wrote Christiane Collage in *L'Express*. In fact, buyers did buy the paper lantern dresses. But the journalist continued, "Since in any case there is a basic fashion this year whose various interpretations are generally very successful and quite diverse, no buyers can limit themselves to Dior—as some of them could when Christian Dior was designing."[6] The American press described Yves's new line as "a tube of Vaseline," and the French called it a "drop of oil." Hollywood would even declare war on the Dior collection in the person of Kim Novak: "I prefer to be true to nature instead of Dior. I like simple dresses that follow natural lines, the curves that nature gave us." Janet Leigh also expressed a negative opinion. Corinne Le Ralle, who was a saleswoman at Dior, described a delicate situation: "We had a problem, because we had to explain to the clients that they had to take off the dress to go to the bathroom."

In March 1960 *L'Express* reiterated a certain "carelessness regarding the proportions of the female body, which has played tricks on him in the past." With an international crisis going on, extravagance seemed out of place. Paris was no longer the capital of the world. On May 13, 1958, the takeover of Algiers revealed the fragility of French institutions. The government was in crisis and anti-parliament sentiment reared its ugly head. In October, Charles de Gaulle deplored the death of 7,200 French soldiers and 77,000 rebels killed in the fighting in Algeria. The French were glued to the news. Fashion journalists were the messengers of a guilty conscience.

Hell was starting for Yves Saint Laurent, too. Every day, *L'Aurore*, the newspaper owned by his boss, Marcel Boussac, ran big headlines supporting French Algeria. The noose was tightening. A Dior employee recalled giving a ride to soldiers home on leave in summer 1959 who asked mockingly, "So, will Saint Laurent sew up our pants for us after we get creamed?" There was even an association of mothers against draft dodgers. Anger was mounting. People talked about "the Saint Laurent affair." Ordinary people felt outrage at the simple unfairness of it all. Why wouldn't some-one from Oran go and fight when boys from Brittany were getting blown to smith-ereens by the *fellagha*!

But Yves did not lie low. On the cover of *L'Aurore*, he posed surrounded by his young female workers. They were wearing white haiks, like the Arab women in the *village nègre*.

It was an explosive atmosphere. At the same time, the Charrier affair broke. Just two weeks after being drafted, Jacques Charrier, the most famous enlisted man in France, and Brigitte Bardot's husband, was admitted to Val-de-Grâce military hospital. "Clinical signs of illness" was the terse statement of the military authori-ties. Was he getting special treatment? Would he be dismissed from the army? Did his "nervous depression" have a specific cause? Did Charrier try to kill himself? Was he even sick? Marcel Boussac's *L'Aurore* led the most aggressive campaign against the star of *Young Sinners*, the Marcel Carné movie that came out in 1958: "It is very hard to understand why a famous actor should get special treatment."

There was no solution for Yves. Everything seemed closed off before him, as in a prison. Return to Algeria, where seizures of land, arrests, and attacks were only increas-ing? In January 1960 the so-called "week of the barricades" had ended in blood. In Algiers, a sixteen-year-old boy was buried. A hastily scrawled sign hung on a plane tree announced that he had fallen "for French Algeria." On February 26, 1960, Oran held a general strike as a sign of mourning. At noon, five thousand demonstrators gathered at Place des Victoires. Many of the men carried weapons. Tramways stopped, angled across the streets to block traffic. The landowners marched down Avenue Loubet and laid flowers at the monument to fallen soldiers. The rest of the city was deserted. The curtains were lowered. "The OAS was our only chance," said Brigitte Mathieu-Saint-Laurent, who thoroughly defended French Algeria, referring to the secret right-wing paramilitary organization that carried out terrorist attacks against Algerian national-ists trying to overthrow French colonial rule. Yves's little sister, who was fifteen in 1960, remembers hitting her classmates when they said, "Your brother's just a fag!"

Goodbye to happiness in Algeria. Goodbye to distant Paris. Yves only had one way out: imaginary travels.

"Dresses that evoke exotic gardens, folk songs and dances, vows of love, dreams, and all the extravagance that the hours of darkness produce, dresses whose marvel-ous colors are as beautiful as a work of art whose brief life we bitterly regret," Hélène Cingria wrote in *Les Lettres Françaises* on February 4, 1960. The only other time Yves Saint Laurent would use color so intensely was in 1976, a tragic year for him.

This is how he fought his battle: with all the weapons of his profession. On Wednesday, January 27, 1960, the salons at 30 Avenue Montaigne were decorated with pineapples and exotic flowers. Murmurs of surprise came from guests on gilded chairs. But the colors shone forth. Garden green, lacquer red, fuchsia, Turkish blue. The names of the dresses referred to the most famous restaurants and clubs in Paris: Petit Bedon, Benoît, Eléphant Blanc, Epi Club. Then more dresses came out: Nuit aux Antilles, Nuit de Bagdad, and more nights, these in India, Miami, Isfahan, Singapore, Tehran.

"Marvelous!" exclaimed the Duchess of Windsor.

"At night China comes into view, with gossamer coats and long tight sheaths. Egypt is present with pharaoh tunics that are made stiff as armor by their gold embroidery."[7] Of all the journalists, Lucien François of *Combat* best described these travelogues. Printed on the front page, his review was especially moving: "What affects me the most about Yves Saint Laurent is the ease with which he is always able to combine elegance and poetry. There is nothing more delicate. An artist's style is dangerous when it comes to fashion. Here, art is present without trying to draw attention to itself. Its gentle vibration animates a world of artifice that sums up a thousand obsessions and childhood dreams. Art is finally expressed without restraint in sparkling and fragile materials. Peau d'Ane, Sleeping Beauty, Tania, the girl-flowers, and Armide are dressed in Dior. Like armor, they put on satin Milky Ways and muslin fogs, golden fleeces and the invisible cloak, without forgetting a little dress for a woman-child, which is so bare, so simple, so foolish, that only clair-voyants, lovers, poets, and princes can recognize it."[8]

His line was evolving. It was thicker and firmer. And, at the same time, more subtle. He no longer designed gloves, but a gesture, an attitude, like putting one's hands in one's pockets. The coats were split open, the bust was elongated, the line become more supple. It was less rectilinear, less polished, more expressive. "Yves Saint Laurent Smiles on the Woman of Tomorrow," read the headline of an eight-column article in *L'Aurore*. The newspaper had never printed such a long article about him, with an entire page describing "this tropical flower vision of a girl, with Persian hairdo and shoes, shaped like a Chinese woman, with Parisian jewels and gloves.... As of yesterday, the tropics are passing over Paris.... In one hundred twenty minutes and one hundred eighty-nine designs, a new woman was born, delicate, mysterious, exotic, and precious." At the end of the show, the women rushed to smother their Lollobrigida-sized chests, to flatten their big hairstyles, and to alter the lines of their too-round eyes.

During this time, Yves made two important connections: one was Mitza Bricard, the Jewish-Romanian woman who jealous women said would kiss a man for a ruby. With wit and whimsy, she gave shape to Yves's ideas: headwear for a masked ball, doge caps, feathered fez, domes to attach to a bun, Tower of Babel, minarets, ostrich feathers, crests, point d'esprit embroidered tulle cages enclosing the faces of the first *Goyescas*: Española, Marquesa, Duquesa…

*

The other encounter was with Roger Vivier, who created shoes that looked like jewels. Vivier was born in Paris, in the eighth arrondissement, and grew up on his own: he was orphaned at age nine and entered the École des Beaux-Arts at seventeen. In order to become a sculptor, he sketched his first designs for a factory with a telling name: Paiva. In 1937, he opened his own studio at 22 Rue Royale and sold shoes to Pinet, Salamander, Rayne, and then Delman, in New York. His first shoe was a Chinese-style platform shoe made of cork. Rejected by buyers, the design was adopted by Schiaparelli and worn by Marlene Dietrich. During the war, he designed in New York under the label Roger and Suzanne. He met Christian Dior in 1947.

Vivier and Yves Saint Laurent respected each other right away. The couturier would later say, "Monsieur Roger Vivier is a great craftsman. He modernizes the sketch and gives it the inevitability of something pure and refined. His great sensitivity makes him an artist. He can heat up the sometimes cold, cutting perfection of an arch and an admirable heel with the warm softness of lace, a darling ribbon, a garland of guipure lace flowers, a moss rose, the flight of a variegated feathers or tulle with jet sequins." Roger Vivier described their meeting as follows: "The first time I saw him, it was in Dior's studio. Christian had invited me to show him the collection I was working on. I spotted a thin young man with glasses on his nose who looked very serious. He looked more like a student in the exact sciences—mathematics or physics. There was something very strict, very diligent about him, which clashed with the traditional image of a fashion designer. He seemed incredibly diligent and meticulous. When I got to know him better, this strong impression of rigor and determination never diminished. He knew very exactly what he wanted, and it was simple for him to get it. I was also struck by the fact that, despite his great youth, he spoke to me so accurately about what my own work inspired in him. It was as if he were able to suss out very easily, under the finishing details, all the little secrets that led me to a particular design." He went on: "Dior and Saint Laurent were very different in the way they displayed the designs that they had imagined. Dior, who was not very skillful at drawing, preferred to make corrections to the test garment, which was based on his words alone, by pointing with his stick on the model herself. This didn't prevent him from specifying very swiftly what he was looking for. But Saint Laurent, who was remarkably good at drawing, expressed the ideas that came to him very succinctly in his rapid sketches. With a few spirited pencil strokes, and very few words, everything was clear. The efficiency of his sketches reduced his shyness, which would have been exacerbated by verbal explanations. It was a chance for him to out-maneuver his shyness through the accuracy of his sketches."

Just as he had done for Christian Dior's collections, Roger Vivier designed a line of shoes for each Yves Saint Laurent collection—for the morning, afternoon, and evening—and created multiple variations of the upper, the arch, and the materials: the Pied de Biche (Doe's Foot) line in lavender crocodile leather or gold faille, and heels called Polichinelle (Punchinello), Crête de Coq (Rooster's Crest), and Choc (1959), which resulted in angry letters because it tore up rugs from the floor. In these designs, Vivier pushed his imagination to the limits: Persian sandals, heels in a harlequin pattern, Rhodes blue satin, or minaret green, all of them splendidly decorated in the spirit of eighteenth-century gardens of paradise with beads, lace, and even kingfisher feathers. All these shoes flirted with an Eldorado strewn with gold nuggets, coral, and beaded and crystal fringes, which were a perfect match for *Arabian Nights*–style dresses like Nuit de Bagdad, Nuit d'Ispahan, Nuit de Téhéran, Nuit de Grenade, and Nuit de Venise.

However, some critics were concerned. By its very charm, all this exoticism seemed troubling. One critic griped that "ultra-sophisticated headwear, heavy jewelry, violent makeup. On defeminized bodies, these hyper-decorated heads look like a parody of femininity.... Saint Laurent has even put evening skirts over tight, embroidered toreador pants.... It's extremely imaginative, but it expresses a strange male-female combination that adds humor to the spring atmosphere...."[9]

After the parties of indebted café society came the glamorous balls. Debutantes strutted around in Versailles-style white dresses with crowns of pearls on their perfect buns. The "cheaters" had aged. The outcast youth of Saint-Germain-des-Prés had become bourgeois. They vied for success, the Goncourt literary prize, or the Légion d'Honneur. They had opinions, apartments, social security cards, and bank accounts. "Have you read the books people are talking about?" "Do you like Brahms?" asked a young woman in a little black dress imitating her mother. The pirate pants, ballerina flats, and windblown hair were discarded. The young women were serious students. "My mother doesn't want me to go out too much at night, she's afraid I'll get pregnant." They traded their whisky for fruit juice, wore pearl necklaces over their twin sets, and read Albert Vidalie's *La Belle Française*, a love story in the Fontainebleau Forest. They went to the movies to see Doniol-Valcroze's *L'Eau à la Bouche* and got excited about filmmakers. They no longer said something was "fab," but called it "divine." What else did this woman need to be happy? A boyfriend. They took advice from *Elle*: Laughter makes you pretty; take care of your hands if you want to get a ring. In the early 1960s, young women didn't idolize Sagan's heroines anymore. They had grown up wanting to be wild and free, but now they struggled to find happiness after their marriages dissolved.

As for Yves, he was no longer the daring young man with the flying trapeze. His statements were ambiguous: "No, I'm not in love. No, I'm not thinking about getting married."[10] And the press stalked stars: during the summer of 1959, the break-up of Bernard Buffet and Pierre Bergé was ripe for tabloid gossip. Artists were no longer judged for what they did, but for who they were. Yves Saint Laurent no longer fit the image that people now expected of a couturier.

The press celebrated Givenchy's dresses as easy to live in and praised Balenciaga's black suits. And Chanel was at the top of inspirational couturiers. La

Grande Mademoiselle made all the magazine covers. "Delicate, smart, rigorous, well-mannered, charming, warm: these are the words that come to mind when Mademoiselle's collection files past you. These words could also describe a woman who is admired, the woman we'd all like to be," wrote Hélène Lazareff.[11]

Chanel was first and foremost "this great elegance with mischievous details." Women went to Rue Cambon as to a temple, to admire suits that grazed the body, soft tweeds, and white wool trimmed with navy silk braid —details that were all perfected more meticulously than stone carvings. Choosing young society women as her models was her ultimate revenge on the Faubourg Saint-Germain. Chanel also made Christian Dior models' runway poses outdated. Kouka and Alla walked down the runway with their hands on their hips, arms outstretched—basically a "goddess" pose. But Chanel favored a more natural, casual style. Hélène Lazareff got model Paule de Mérindol a job at Chanel, and she recalled her modeling work in this way: "I played with a certain naturalness in my femininity. No artifice was allowed. I walked as if in someone's living room. There were no conventional ways of presenting the clothes." During the fashion show, there was absolute silence. As in a Cocteau film, the models appeared from mirrors as if by magic. Some observers thought they looked as if they had just broken up with their boyfriends over lunch, pushing their indifference to the point of walking down the runway like it was no big deal. On the staircase, the queen who believed herself invisible betrayed her presence by casting reflections in the mirrors.

Others tossed off new collections like darts. Ideas came and went, but Chanel's style triumphed. Dior's woman had a small waist, somewhat rounded hips, and a nice chest. Chanel's woman was boundless. She charmed "these women who don't ask their clothes to wear them, but who know how to wear their clothes....No one designing clothes today can neglect the Chanel priorities: ease, suppleness, comfort," wrote L'Express on February 11, 1960.

After observing and reflecting, Yves Saint Laurent concluded, "I don't think that women dress for other women. They dress for themselves and for men. A man always notices a well-dressed woman. If he doesn't see what she's wearing, that means she's dressed badly."[12] He would become Chanel's spiritual son.

Chanel's influence on him became clearer. He announced in January 1959, "The figure takes a backseat to style."[13] In his couture collections, he soon started using jersey, a fabric that was specifically associated with Chanel. This was a risky idea when couture, made more and more vulnerable by mass production, had started to look like an old authoritarian lady. Feeling their power declining, the couturiers were on edge. They hunkered down in the bastion of fashion bordered by Rue du Faubourg Saint-Honoré, Avenue Matignon, and Avenue Georges V. The instructions were for heightened secrecy. The drawings were locked away in trunks and the collections were planned in black and white, with the fabrics selected at the last minute. The length of the dresses was decided only the day before the show.

The hunt for "copiers" became more intense: up to fifty plagiarists were foiled every season. The authorities inflicted punishments on those who didn't play by the rules. For instance, Pierre Cardin, who opened a men's boutique in 1957 and showed a collection of ready-to-wear for spring 1959, was expelled by the Chambre Syndicale de la Couture for five years.

As for Yves Saint Laurent, he was convinced that this evolution was inevitable. Along with others, such as Jules-François Crahay at Nina Ricci, he tried to adapt this contemporary spirit to haute couture. He sought to achieve ease and movement: his jackets softened into sweaters, his coats were no longer of stiff canvas, his polo shirts moved with the body. His line became even more simple, seeking a silhouette that fit the era of the independent woman. His pencil lines were more precise; he cut straight dresses traced with a saber, striped sweaters with leather buttons, jackets with cut-out pockets in the shape of mathematical symbols, the stitching indicated to the *première* like a staff on a musical score. Balenciaga's influence could also be seen.

But Yves wasn't a technician, unlike Balenciaga. Also unlike Crahay or Cardin. Yves Saint Laurent was closer to the line than the fabric. These tall collars and spindly coats still had a Dior fragility that made Chanel say, "Dior? Flights of fancy built on cardboard."[14] Despite these cutting remarks, Yves Saint Laurent succumbed to fascination with the old empress who managed to make people talk about her every season while always redoing the same suit.

Chanel didn't draw—she cut. She draped onto the model. She made suits for women she knew like the back of her hand, because she was her own first model. For his part, Yves Saint Laurent was a voyeur. He still sketched for the ideal image of woman. "The models? They're just models. I don't think of them as women. If something about them draws my attention, it's just to make a particular shape stand out." These visions of heroines drew him into a world that was rejected by a fearful era. It thought that the height of refinement was Marie-Chantal, who was humorously sketched by Yves's friend society journalist Jacques Chazot. "She threw away her car because the ashtray was full."

The collection shown in July 1960 had a strange emphasis on dark purple hues. It evinced a preference for shades of purple. All shades, from plum to black tulip. The first number was called À Bout de Souffle, or Breathless, and the last "Zurbaran." Too complicated. Uncopiable. Yves Saint Laurent appeared whimsical and eccentric. *Paris-Presse-l'Intransigeant* saw him as the man who seduced "stars and starlets." A quite gratuitous assertion. In fact, the new Hollywood was eager for respectability. Actors had become businessmen. On Sunset Boulevard, air-conditioned Cadillacs had replaced the Duesenbergs in flamboyant colors. And the divine leading ladies sank into the hell of lonely nights fueled by drugs. The producers found replacements for them: Italian stars like Sophia Loren and Gina Lollobrigida, with full lips, doe eyes, high heels, and heaving chests. Even as Jayne Mansfield posed naked with turquoise fingernails in her pink heart-shaped bathtub for *Paris Match*, the golden age was still ending. It took with it the mystery of these leading ladies whom Yves Saint Laurent would continue to celebrate devotedly.

Thin, supple, and feline, his models wore dresses that set them off perfectly and had names of forbidden nights. They were Folie Douce, Whisky, Iris Noir, Fumeuse, and Dolce Vita, after Fellini's film, which had just been condemned by the Vatican. These dresses seemed to be intended for women haunted by mysterious disappearances, like Jeanne Moreau in *La Notte*. With the sensuality of the sheaths, which emphasized their shape without seeming to touch them, Yves Saint Laurent directed his models as Antonioni directed his actors: "I try to encourage them to lose control of themselves without them realizing it."

He had doubts. But he knew he wouldn't give up this danger. Even if *Le Figaro* stigmatized his "sophisticated and unhealthy airs that are the opposite of refinement" in a list of "outrages that are harmful to the reputation of Paris,"[15] he realized that his power lay in this so-called flaw. He struggled, he experimented, he pared down, carefully reflecting the changing world and finding an unrestrained technique to dress new gestures and allow modern women—and not just well-mannered women—to get in touch with the wonderful wildness inside them.

On the one hand, he simplified. He embraced movement. He championed these women who didn't ride around in the backseat with a chauffeur holding their packages. His car coat was airy, with wide sleeves, two slits on the sides, and a half-belt. On the other hand, he invented a past, with the same beginner's enthusiasm that made Delacroix say, "They want to put in everything and sacrifice nothing." Yves glorified his Infantes. For them, nothing was too heavy or too precious: chains, pearls, pendants, point d'esprit embroidered helmets, puffed tulles, jet embroidery, silk tassels, drop beads, embroidered camisoles, satin plumes. These decorations grew more and more ostentatious and created a sublime distance from reality. For current events were more and more troubling. The papers reported that the elite French paratrooper units had only one mission: to scour everything and tear it apart, to leave nothing to the rebels, not the mountain or the night. They were led by General Marcel Bigeard, a warrior whose toughness was legendary, and whose khaki torso was displayed on the nightly news.

It was too late for Yves Saint Laurent. "Saint Laurent needs to have a thick skin," Lucien François severely noted in a review of the July 1960 collection that criticized "women-relics." "Yves Saint Laurent is a decorator."[16] He had especially designed these thirty black dresses to go with the jewelry. The Americans referred to these slim black dresses as "tunnels." The shadow of Dior became more distant, leaving the heir apparent alone once again. He received his draft letter. He would be called to serve on September 1, 1960.

5 / A MAN DISAPPEARS

n April 1960, future soldier Yves Saint Laurent traveled with Pierre Bergé to the southeastern French town of Le Cannet to visit Alice Chavanne, who edited the beauty column at *Elle*. Another fashion editor, Susan Train, American *Vogue*'s Paris bureau chief, remembered how unhappy he was when she saw him there. "He rarely went to the beach. Pierre supported him, and we tried to take his mind off it."

His personal misfortune coincided with a turbulent turn of events. The month of September 1960 began in Paris in the explosive atmosphere of the Jeanson trial, when a group led by philosopher and activist Francis Jeanson was accused of assisting the Algerian National Liberation Front. The open letter known as the "Manifesto of the 121" made a forceful statement in favor of the rights of conscientious objectors. Academics, intellectuals, writers, and journalists stood together to support the young defendants. Jean-Paul Sartre, who had signed the manifesto, advocated for the cause in a letter to the military court, while Jean-Jacques Servan-Schreiber published an aggressive editorial in *L'Express* on September 21 in support of ending colonial rule: "This is truly gangrene. The authorities can tie it off and cut and slice away, but the ill is too strong.…The struggle between citizens and mercenaries has begun. We can all take action in the most honest and unquestionable way, by supporting the best of our young men…This crusade can achieve the victory of stopping an absurd war and giving birth to a new France."

Petitions against censorship. Seizures. Fear. Arrests. The older generation, represented by the owner and management of Dior, thought it was of utmost importance to save France's honor and maintain its colonial possessions. Dior's management remained fixated on military service, although, as Jacques Rouet acknowledged thirty years later, "We knew he was meant to hold a pencil, not a gun." The daring young man with the flying trapeze fell into a deep abyss. "Suppleness, Lightness, Life," the program of his latest collection had announced. Then he became a number, one of 500,000 young men drafted into a black hole in 1960, with his always-elegant way of seizing the momentum of his era.

Indeed, 1960 was a tumultuous year. With fear of rebellious teenagers and fear of attacks, everyone's nerves were on edge. Five earthquakes, sixty-two days of riots, 366 days of war in Algeria, seventeen countries obtaining their independence, a Nobel Prize (Saint-John Perse). There's the summary. The young people cast blame. The families were quiet. "You don't talk about rats at the table." The age of suspicion described by Nathalie Sarraute had started. Heroes ended up in cemeteries: Albert Camus, Boris Pasternak, Jules Supervielle, and Jacques Becker.

Sleepless nights, coffee, tears…many young people from good families discovered a hidden talent for acting so they could land the role of "unfit for service." Those wounded by life easily found ways to expand their flaws. The environment only helped them.

The Bégin military hospital at Saint-Mandé in the eastern suburbs of Paris. Room 39. Then Val-de-Grâce military hospital, which Molière celebrated three centuries earlier as an "August building, majestic temple, / Whose splendid dome rises into the clouds. / Decorate this magnificent street of great Paris." Yves Saint Laurent was admitted on September 20, 1960.

A brief news item appeared in *Le Monde* two days later: "M. Yves Mathieu-Saint-Laurent, who has in recent years been the designer of the Maison Dior, was recently drafted and is currently under observation in a military hospital. Although the Ministry of the Army has declined to provide any information concerning one drafted soldier among many, it has confirmed that the health of M. Saint Laurent, who had already been suffering from nervous depression for several months, made this measure necessary."

He was discharged in November, since "his health has not improved." In the news stories, Saint Laurent's situation was associated with that of Jacques Charrier, who had been temporarily discharged as of December 10 of the previous year. An army doctor had sent the young actor back home. But Yves Saint Laurent stayed in an isolation ward for six weeks.

Only one person was allowed to see him every day: Pierre Bergé. He said, "I pleaded the cause of Yves's mother with Professor Juillet, a doctor at the military hospital, so she could see him at least once." Lucienne recalled:

> When I got there, he was in a fog from all they had put him through. He was half dead from the drugs. But I had gone to see a general, I don't remember if his name was Durand or Dupont. But he didn't want to hear about it. It was awful. He was always so elegant, so concerned about his appearance, and so private. They had taken everything away, even the doors of the bathroom. He didn't eat. He was lying on the floor. There were photographers waiting outside. They beat him down, to make an example out of him.

"This will take a permanent toll on you," Yves later said the doctor told him.

Although he was floored by suffering that he would not reveal until thirty years later, he displayed a new fierceness. He asked his mother to go back to Oran. He was now the son of someone else. Pierre Bergé—the fighter who had written ten years earlier, "Whatever it takes, we'll open the window that they want to keep shut; and if it's impossible, then we'll break the glass"—put the energy he devoted to his earlier political battles into his new mission.

At that time, Bergé was living in an apartment he owned on Rue Saint-Louis-en-l'Île, which still resembled a little village. "This apartment is a veritable Buffet museum," Matthieu Galey observed in his *Journal*. "Most of the paintings—the most beautiful ones, the first ones, which were hard, angry, and accusing looks at the sordid side of life—are dedicated to him. His name appears on the back in the painter's handwriting. There are paintings everywhere—against the walls, in the closets, hallways, the entryway. Their omnipresence doesn't seem to bother the master of the house at all. He loves these paintings for their own sake, and also because he considers them partly his work. It's as if they remind him of nothing except what they depict: a smoked herring or a skinny girl astride a bidet. Brutish insensitivity, or magnanimity that rises above any break-up? Hard to say. Pierre is a force, a torrent, a bull, nothing can stand up to him!"[1]

On September 30, the Maison Dior issued the following press release: "As Yves Saint Laurent has been obliged, due to his conscription, to interrupt his activities with the Dior company, the fulfillment of his contract is suspended during his military service. The creative management of the studio is entrusted to Marc Bohan, who designs Christian Dior's London collections."

On November 14, Pierre Bergé celebrated his thirtieth birthday. "Yves didn't come, he was too sick." Afterward, Pierre took him to spend several weeks in the Canary Islands. The hotel was called the Santa Catalina. Pierre Bergé describes this trip like a honeymoon. He took multiple photos of Yves to preserve these happy times: Yves, suntanned in his white polo shirt and canvas pants, is smiling. "1960 was only fifteen years after the war. The tourists hadn't yet invaded the island. There were more paellas, not so many hamburgers. And the beaches were still deserted." But during this time the war machine was being established. "It was the time of Marc Bohan's success," Pierre Bergé adds dispassionately. "It was snowing in Paris. And we were in the sunshine."

From his first collection, Marc Bohan, who started as an illustrator at Piguet and had solid experience at Molyneux and Patou, established himself as a couturier of the straight and narrow. No waves, no excess, the waist in its place, slim shoulders, a harmonious look of distinction. Jean-Pierre Frère remembered his first days replacing Yves: "He arrived in conquered territory. And to think that during Monsieur Dior's time he wasn't even received in the studio!" His flowery dresses, his ruffed collars, his tiny pleats, and his great wide-brimmed hats revealed an inspiration drawn from the garden parties of Buckingham Palace in tame, natural colors, closer to the lily of the valley than the lily: fresh garden green, jade, daffodil, pink quartz, frosted mandarin orange, Provence apricot, or curry yellow. The eternal second fiddle of couture, he would remain creative director at Dior until 1987.

Back in the city, Yves Saint Laurent was free to discover a different Paris. The Paris of little plots, of stillborn love affairs, or smiles that said nothing and polite nods that made you want to flee. Fashion fearfully draped itself in nostalgia. It took refuge in the attic, as if to see nothing, not the old ladies dying or the young hooligans who terrorized them. In a definitive farewell to the pin-up, Parisian couturiers brought back the style of 1925 for winter. A few journalists talked about the lasting influence of the Trapeze collection. The dance halls made the charleston fashionable again. But memory was fading, like the shadows of the old muses of Montparnasse, who had become distressing alcoholics in turbans. *Les Lettres Françaises* wrote that the English eccentric Nancy Cunard, the "woman with the hundred bracelets" (who had won the heart of Louis Aragon, its publisher, among others), was sinking into decline.

Yves Saint Laurent discovered this special brand of Parisian indifference, where "I love it" can quickly lead to a neglectful "I don't like it anymore." "Yves Saint Laurent, the successor of Christian Dior, has proved his mettle!" "Yves Saint Laurent, a French national hero!" His memories were like empty pockets. Two years earlier, he was spoken of in the same breath as Dior, the man who had saved French couture. At age twenty-four, Yves Saint Laurent was already mourning his own past glory. He had already lived too much to be young, to dance like the others to the rock and roll of Elvis Presley or Bill Haley. The British invasion was starting. He didn't see it coming. In 1959, Mary Quant opened a shop on King's Road. Young female baby boomers would soon fill the street. Yves Saint Laurent seemed to belong to a different generation.

Victoire said, "He came out of the hospital worried, in a stupor, and alone. Yves, a soldier? You might as well try to turn a swan into a crocodile!"[2] People were already considering him a sick man. The exile in the desert had begun. "But Pierre and I helped him," Victoire continued in a motherly tone. "We supported him, believed in him enough to lie to him by making up names of investors who would make this beautiful boat seaworthy, with the name 'Yves Saint Laurent' shining in gold letters on its prow."[3] Yvonne de Peyerimhoff stated, "Yves never recovered his equilibrium. He would never have become what he is without Pierre Bergé."

It's easy to understand the disgusted melancholy into which a proud spirit surrounded with meaningless attention can fall. "The Return of Yves Saint Laurent: The Shawl Dress," *Paris-Presse l'Intransigeant* nevertheless announced on April 18, 1961. For his star model, who remained his closest female friend, "the former Monsieur Dior, torn away from fashion by the army," picked up his designer's pencil once again. The pink mousseline dress edged with wispy ostrich feathers was made at a dressmaker's workshop on Rue Saint-Louis-en-l'Île. "The first one he designed since his conscription, discharge, and nervous depression."[4] Victoire posed for front and back views of the dress, which she wore to the wedding of her friend Philippine de Rothschild. Yves also designed twenty-five costumes for Henri Sauguet's ballet *Les Forains*, choreographed by Roland Petit and shown on French television.

His line had changed once again. Supple and playful, it expressed the excitement of middle-class youth who went slumming: bad boys at the dance halls on Rue de Lappe, lithe male cancan dancers, little match girls, circus acrobats, chimney sweeps in red caps, handsome young bathroom lurkers—a seedy city of poets and bad boys celebrated by Jean Genet. There, on the dark streets of Paris, he could find the forbidden pleasures that novelists reserve for dandies and princes dreaming of a sailor who would take them far away in a tiny windowless cabin.

The sudden loneliness of anonymity allowed Yves to see Paris in a different way. Its hidden corners. The dark little streets where, finally, he could lose himself. Now he could breathe in the immense "night with the soft moon's face," as when, in a long poem, "Once Again on the River," he described in Oran "the tremendous hobo with the triumphant awakening," "this lewd, easygoing sun":

and his heart beats as in the past
and he finds himself as in the past
so young with a clean shirt
that he took off to make love
and he looks at the Seine
and thinks of her
of life and death
and love
and he shouts
oh, Seine
don't be angry if I throw myself
into your bed
these things shouldn't happen

But events rushed ahead. The break-up with Dior would soon be complete. He had a meeting with Marcel Boussac.

The meeting was disastrous. "Right away, I found the man and his environment likable," Christian Dior had written in 1946, after Jacques Rouet took him into the office to meet his future investor.[5] But this man, whom Dior described as having "a stubborn forehead, a willful jaw, [with] dry and direct words and gestures," would become Yves Saint Laurent's and Pierre Bergé's bête noire. Dior was forty years old when he met Boussac, and liked parsonage gardens, slowly simmered stews, and country churches.

Yves Saint Laurent was twenty-five. His thin face, sharpened by sadness, had a silent look of rebellion. How could he get along with this old-style paternalist who gave toys to his employees' children at Christmastime and for whom managing meant "controlling everything"?[6] The owner of fifty-two factories, where he often made surprise visits, Marcel Boussac, "the Impassive Frenchman," as the Americans called him, ruled over the biggest French textile empire (21,000 people).[7] Proud of his 288 looms, Boussac gave authoritarian orders: "I want the Boussac name only on flawless merchandise." With the famous checked gingham—which Brigitte Bardot had used to make her wedding dress—Marcel Boussac had struck gold. He had the most powerful horse-racing stable in the world—orange jerseys and gray jockey caps —cars, planes, and estates with Louis XIV furniture that was energetically polished. His entire life obeyed this will to power that was commanded by an unshakable sense of order and duty. He backed the Dior company in order, as he put it, to "get my hands on this indefinable thing called good taste."[8] Two visions of the world were clashing. Yves Saint Laurent imagined a hero's destiny. How could he bend to Boussac's ideal? "Dressing fashionably basically means making women prettier, making children more charming, and making men more proper."[9]

Pretty, charming, and proper: this was everything Yves despised. His heroines were unclassifiable rebels and bedroom empresses. They drew their strength from their impurity, their skill at devouring, spending, bankrupting, breaking themselves for love and then dying from having loved. They were named Rosa, Marguerite, Divine, Elisa, Bijou, Olympia. Streetwalking marquises and women of questionable morals, they all had sins in their pasts. They only recognized themselves in forgetfulness, their ability to reinvent pleasure every day, a pleasure that was never big enough to hide their scars.

Pretty, charming, and proper. How could Yves agree to the common sense of Marcel Boussac when he had fled a city that was smothered by exactly the same clichéd views? His disillusionment helped him to join the steadfast heroines whose doubts and secrets he shared, the women about whom other women asked, "What have they got that we don't?" What did they have? Everything. The art of giving themselves to everyone without belonging to anyone. This fascination with money, and also this scorn, since no wealth could make them faithful. Having absorbed so many romantic stories, Yves Saint Laurent kept boredom at bay by dreaming of these women who constantly flirted with extremes, in both pleasure and danger in order to survive. How could he fail to recognize himself in these women, who knew that at any moment they could fall, become once again ladies of the evening, be sold like pieces of fabric, or end up in these sinister shops "where one hears a consumptive wheeze under a shawl, just as the agony of poverty hides under a gold-lamé dress"?[10] But reality was as heavy as a bag of old fabric scraps. Despite all his clairvoyance, Marcel Boussac was a man of the past: he considered couturiers tradespeople. Boussac rejected the solution suggested by Jacques Rouet: opening a small couture house for Yves Saint Laurent. The numbers from his time at Dior weren't bad, far from it: in 1960, the couture house had revenue of 41.5 million francs (with a profit of 3.3 million), while in 1955 the number was only 21 million francs (with a profit of 1.2 million). Boussac offered the ambitious young man a consolation prize: to be the designer for the New York subsidiary. The philosophy of Boussac, who was one of the six richest people in the world, could be summed up as follows: "Men can be controlled through fear and through money."[11]

In May, Yves Saint Laurent engaged a young lawyer, Jean-Denis Bredin, and took Maison Dior to court. He sought to be restored to his previous position. He also demanded 430,000 francs in severance benefits and 250,000 francs in damages for breach of contract. The court gave the parties a two-month period to try to come to a settlement. On October 16, the court ruled that Dior had to pay damages.

Pierre Bergé had thrown himself into the battle, and later said he was "convinced that Marc Bohan was no threat. And Balenciaga and Chanel wouldn't stop a twenty-five-year-old man's career from taking off." In July, he rented a one-bedroom apartment on Rue La Boétie and bought a desk and some chairs at the flea market. They asked the typeface designer Cassandre for a logo. Yves Saint Laurent sketched his first designs on a wooden board, surrounded by bundles of silk remnants. Behind him, three photos were inserted into a mirror on the wall: they were of Christian Dior and Yves's deceased dogs, Zouzou and Eglantine. There was also a calendar. All day long, suppliers arrived, along with the apprentices who would work in the four ateliers they expected to set up.

The idea was to start a small company, with a great name. As Victoire told it, "I thought of Yves, who wasn't yet 'Saint Laurent.' And I wondered if Pierre, despite all his energy and all his faith, would manage to pull off this gamble, which was, if not the gamble of his life, at least a gamble on a crazy dream. Meanwhile, in the one-bedroom apartment he had rented, we played along. Because if we stopped believing in it, all would be lost. The time came when Yves had to choose the fabrics for his first collection under his own name, which would be shown to the press on January 29, 1962. But the phone still wasn't ringing, and my melancholy thoughts began to wander."[12]

Around Yves Saint Laurent and Pierre Bergé, the staff ate on the run. They used trunks as tables. On the menu, *jambon-beurre* sandwiches and champagne. On the walls, framed drawings by Yves told the story of his collections for Dior. He had brought talented people on board. Claude Licard, the studio manager, left Marc Bohan after one season: "The collections were put together with lists. There were no eureka moments anymore. Now I rediscovered Yves's ability to get what he wanted from us." Twenty-three-year-old Gabrielle Buchaert had been a public relations assistant at Dior and became the head of Yves's advertising department. Promoted to sales director, Victoire didn't hesitate to inflict on other women the humiliations of a boss for the servant she might have become—if luck, beauty, and instinct hadn't decided otherwise. Women hated her. Men preferred not to notice it. "A little jewel, a rosebud," hairstylist Alexandre, who knew her at Dior, remembered. "She came in almost every day. I gave her mountains of hair that made her taller." But four years had passed, and Victoire had taken the advice of Mademoiselle Chanel, whom she met in 1960: "Cut off that bun!"

On Avenue Montaigne, at the salon run by Alexandre, whom the society ladies nicknamed "Butterfly," Yves Saint Laurent's name took flight once more. Whispers about the tremendously famous pouf skirt, telephone calls. Victoire began her charm offensive: "Saint Laurent is opening his own couture house." The women got ready: "Do you have a fitter yet?" Victoire was married to Roger Thérond, and through her influence an enigmatic article appeared in *Paris Match* on August 5, 1961: "Two Parisian women seem to be wearing Saint Laurent. Yves Saint Laurent, who has just recovered from a serious illness, has granted the requests of his two best friends, Zizi Jeanmaire and Victoire. He designed four dresses for them that have been spotted on the streets." It looked as if the photos had been taken without their knowledge. The mystery was skillfully orchestrated. Pierre gave a little party to celebrate this first press article.

As of 1961, Pierre and Yves were living together on Place Vauban, near Les Invalides, in an apartment that they rented from the Duc de Sabran-Ponteves. "The beginning of our life together," Pierre Bergé remembered. Barcelona chairs by Mies van der Rohe, a Roman marble placed on a Knoll table, a pyramid lamp by Noguchi, bookshelves made of boards, a Lorjou, and many paintings by the omnipresent Buffet—everything reflected a style inspired by Roger Vivier that combined modern furniture with African statues. Victoire and Roger Thérond were there, along with Françoise Sagan and her sister Suzanne. Yves, leaning over his copper globe, was smiling, but his mind was elsewhere. The evening ended with whisky at Régine's.

In the ateliers of 30 Avenue Montaigne, the news made the rounds in secret. At Dior, two allies would play a decisive role. First, Yvonne de Peyerimhoff, who would go to work for Yves in October 1962. Then, Suzanne Luling, who put Yves in touch with many people, starting with her own secretary, Maryse Agussol, a young woman from a good family who lived with her parents on Boulevard Flandrin in the sixteenth arrondissement. "It was really nice. You left one company, and you came to another one that was already familiar to you: we all knew each other," Agussol recalled. Having learned the right way to do things, she would be in charge of the saleswomen and the purchase orders in the style defined by Dior: "Deference and subservience, but with class." Large spiral notebooks, a chart with numbers, descriptions of each suit with extra copies for the atelier. It was pure Dior: orderly and rigorous.

Suzanne Luling, who didn't join the Saint Laurent team (the gossips said she was too expensive), also helped Yves hire Denise Barry de Longchamp, who worked in accessories at Dior. "Goodbye, hats! Now I'm head saleswoman," she said. "It followed very naturally. There was only one winter vacation between the two jobs! I don't remember feeling scared. However, in retrospect..."

When Christian Dior started his fashion house in 1947, he hired many women away from Patou, with the help of Marguerite Carré. The same thing now happened fourteen years later. The Maison Dior reacted: six months later, Jacques Rouet sued

Yves Saint Laurent for corrupt business practices in the form of raiding its employees. Yvonne de Peyerimhoff, former head saleswoman at Dior and the future sales director of Yves Saint Laurent (she replaced Victoire), was the principal target. "Monsieur Rouet even had the criminal investigation department call me in!" This woman was able to build a veritable state within the Dior empire. Pierre Bergé admired her. After all, wasn't she a bit like him? She made her own way in life. Some months spent as a volunteer nurse at the Vaugirard hospital and then in a surgical setting had given her a supreme scorn for men and their weakness. This Parisian woman in light-colored stockings and a black dress with her hair in a bun used all her skill to hide her murky past, and stated succinctly, "I've chosen the people I spend my time with."

She traveled to New York, gave cocktail parties at the Hotel Pierre and lunches at Le Pavillon, and went to visit clients on Seventh Avenue. During buyers' season, she worked eighteen hours a day. Her friends included Patricia Lopez-Willshaw, whom she saw every Sunday in Paris and over the summer at Saint-Tropez, where they both had houses. Marie-Louise Bousquet used to say to her often, "We're related!" Peyerimhoff explained, playing with her pearl necklace: "She was already old when I met her! She had been the mistress of my father-in-law, the Comte de Breteuil. She had a very eventful life." Madame de Peyerimhoff was smart enough not to ask questions, because she figured everything out on her own. Her life had given her what she called a "woman's strength." Her secret was never discussing the past, even though she sometimes mechanically repeated, like all the old hands at Dior, "He never should have gone to Montecatini!" That phrase was more than a memory. It was a code, the sign of belonging to an elite group with the highest standards.

Half of the eighty workers hired by Yves Saint Laurent came from Dior: the *secondes* became *premières*. This was the case of Esther Jadot, who had gone to work at Patou in 1937 and who learned the craft from Marguerite Carré: at Dior, she earned 680 francs per month (equivalent to about 1,250 euros in 2018). At Yves Saint Laurent, her wages rose to 1,500 francs per month. She was responsible for sewing the first design, ordered by Patricia Lopez-Willshaw. A black and white dress with the lucky label "Yves Saint Laurent 00001."

Catherine Devoulon was a third-level seamstress and became a *seconde*. "When Monsieur Dior died, I had already started taking clients at home, to develop my skills." She was thirty-four. Catherine, who later became Madame Catherine, the *première* of the *atelier flou* (where the loosely cut designs were made, in contrast to the *atelier tailleur* for tailored designs), celebrated thirty years at Yves Saint Laurent in 1992 and described these early days: "I only knew him by sight. The day of his first collection, we were out on the sidewalk to applaud him. And we saw him on Saint Catherine's Day [November 25]. We knew he was talented. We had to prove to him that we had guts. He intimidated us. We were just starting out and the clients were waiting for us on the street corner. We didn't want to disappoint him." This was an unspoken tribal law. It wasn't based on order and constraint, but on a mysterious energy that combined sacrifice and pleasure. You didn't just work for Saint Laurent. You dedicated yourself to him. Either you quit, or you loved him. Moreover, establishing a couture house depends most of all on the memory and instinct of the saleswomen's connections, their sing-song welcoming, "Bonjour, Maadaaaame," and the notes of the *premières*, where they jotted down secrets that husbands and lovers were often unaware of. Basically, this mysterious network of couture that the concierges at the Ritz and the Plaza knew so well. They even pulled Ferdinand the doorman out of early retirement in Saint-Lô. Pierre Bergé hired the staff. There were about ninety of them. "We did everything big," he said, sounding ready to celebrate with champagne.

Pierre crisscrossed Paris in his Jaguar. The countdown had started: he had until December 1 to find the money they needed. He had contacted Paul-Louis Weiller. Elie de Rothschild declined to invest: "We're probably making a mistake."

Pierre had sold his apartment on Rue Saint-Louis-en-l'Île as well as some of his Buffet paintings. In a stroke of luck, Buffet's sordid period was exactly what collectors were seeking.

Then, a financial savior arrived—from America, of all places. Philippe Caron, Suzanne Luling's nephew, introduced Pierre and Yves to J. Mack Robinson. This discreet businessman ran the Delta Life Insurance Company of Atlanta and was a partial owner of ten other companies. He had heard of Yves Saint Laurent from a 1958 article in *Life*. It was his first investment in France. Yves Saint Laurent, who always made it a point of honor to forget the names of his investors, quickly found him a sobriquet: the American from Atlanta. The contract was signed on November 14, 1961, Pierre Bergé's birthday: "Yves had 15 to 20 percent of the shares, and I owned a percentage as director. Robinson put in the rest." It was the first time an American had owned a French couture house. He would invest 700,000 dollars over three years. But his name remained a secret until 1963, when *Newsweek* revealed his identity. The news was quickly picked up by Carmen Teissier, whose gossip column ran in *France-Soir*, and, of course, by *Women's Wear Daily*, the fashion bible edited by John Fairchild, which would soon have a special relationship with the Maison Saint Laurent. *WWD* got information first, well before the French newspapers.

From the beginning, the Maison Yves Saint Laurent's relations with the press were shrouded in mystery. With very little information in hand, journalists maintained an aura of suspense: "Yves Mathieu-Saint-Laurent is getting his collection ready in great secrecy. Some of his competitors are losing sleep over this secrecy. Not because they want to copy him, but because they fear some exciting new trend that will eclipse their own designs. The latest word is that this exciting new trend is the complete absence of low-cut necklines."[13] But the network was starting to get established. Short news items appeared here and there, in the *Evening Chronicle* of Newcastle, the *Birmingham Mail*, the Frankfurt *Abendpost*. Gabrielle Buchaert began conscientiously inserting the press articles into big black leatherette binders that bore the brand name and, not by coincidence, the phrase "Cover-Girl."

Yves Saint Laurent stayed out of the spotlight again. He did appear in a tuxedo at a premiere at the Lido. Victoire was with him and drew attention with the soft look of her satin top and skirt and her new hairstyle. Other sparkling personalities were there that evening, including Francine Weisweiller in Dior, Patricia Lopez-Willshaw in Balenciaga, the Duchess of Windsor, Hélène Rochas, Melina Mercouri, and Annabel Buffet.

The excitement was cleverly maintained: Pierre Bergé charged the biggest buyers an entrance fee of 1,000 dollars. Those who came only to see the collection would pay only 400. "It will be dog-eat-dog!" Bergé warned in accented English. "There won't be enough for everyone. We want to help the buyers. We want to recreate an atmosphere in which couture cooperates with the buyers, and not with cheap stores and bad copies." With his amazing business acumen, he turned the tables and transformed the company's weakness into its main asset: "We are only a small couture house. We cannot produce more than 120 pieces between January 29 and February 22. If you commit to buy a specific number of dresses from us at 550,000 francs, I guarantee that you will have them on time." It was such strokes of genius on the part of Pierre Bergé that made Yves Saint Laurent say, "If Pierre Bergé didn't exist, we'd have to invent him. He handles business like an artist. In this way he is unique."

But there was panic behind the scenes. "Madeleine de Rauch let me down," recalled Pierre Bergé. "We had a verbal agreement to use her mansion." She withdrew her agreement at the last minute. So they found "a 'house without a roof' at 30 bis Rue Spontini, a classy street, located on the edge of the Bois de Boulogne." It had once been the studio of the painter Forain, who was famous in the late nineteenth century for his caricatures of Parisian life. Rue Spontini was not at all a central location. It took faith to believe that it would work. "Yves said, 'No one will come!'" Pierre Bergé recalled. But Yves discovered a drawing by Forain in the basement titled *La Bohème*. He also stumbled on a good luck charm: "I saw a playing card on the floor, face-down. I picked it up: it was the ten of clubs."[14] Dior had also found a lucky charm as he prepared to open his maison de couture, a gold star on Rue Saint-Florentin. Work on the building would take two months. So where would they work on the collection in the meantime? On Rue François Ier, in the former ateliers of Lucile Manguin. As bad luck would have it, the mover they hired called in sick on the appointed day. So Pierre Bergé rolled up his sleeves and did the job himself. He was also the night watchman. "He can do everything—except sew!" said Gabrielle Buchaert.

The adventure had started! They put an ad in the paper looking for models. All the streetwalkers from the notorious Rue Godot-de-Mauroy showed up to apply. And Zouzou, who used to dance the twist in Saint-Germain-des-Prés and whom

Yves Saint Laurent was crazy about, was sleeping in a corner. She was a strange character! The seamstresses forgot their pride. They put their whole hearts into their work. Monette, who had been promoted to *première* when she was hired by Saint Laurent, recalled the atmosphere, telling the story in her Parisian street kid accent: "It was dirty. We cleaned it up. We did everything. We went to get the old mannequins and stuffed them with hay. We flattened out the chests and broke the hips. Monsieur Saint Laurent passed out the sketches, and we made the toiles."

Along with his collection, Yves Saint Laurent designed some two hundred fifty costumes for Zizi Jeanmaire's show. "It got me back in the saddle," he said. They were sewn by the famous Russian costumer Karinska, on the second story of an atelier on the Rue Washington, near the Champs-Élysées. For Zizi, there was a gold jacket, a sunburst made of swan feathers, a corset of black diamonds, and a man's sweater. She was given a wedding dress that showed her legs. "Don't weigh her down, impede her, or restrict her with the constraints and tricks of yesterday, but let her go wild in all her supernatural ability," Yves wrote.[15] In December, on the stage of the Alhambra, Zizi triumphed night after night in front of an audience of 2,400.

With her legs sheathed in black silk, wearing pumps with rhinestone heels, she sang "Eh l'Amour," "Mon Bonhomme," and "Toto l'Aristo." Eighteen chorus boys waved ostrich-feather fans, her "feather thing" that would become world famous. These pretty boys wore black tank tops and Parisian street urchin pants that moved with them as they glided around the stage. Right in the middle, a surprise appearance provoked laughter: a woman with orange hair in an impractical bubble dress.

Alexandre, the hairdresser, has great memories of the show. "Zizi? Great peepers, great gams. A phenomenon on the stage. Jet-black eyes, dramatically short hair, and this low-cut, short peacoat with those two long legs in stretch pants. Zizi as designed by Yves was magical. It was as if a fairy, with a magic wand, had opened the doors to the music-hall for her. And it was nothing at all. It was a shirt with sequins. It was modern."

The press loved it: "Yves Saint Laurent's costumes, often black, smoky black, with black backgrounds and bright, matte colors, are in perfect taste. It's hard to believe that this young man who used so much fabric at Dior to dress women in monumental dresses that were so hard to wear was able to limit himself to the tiny amount of fabric that dressing these impeccable ballerinas requires. We have to get used to this: he can dress you with nothing," wrote Jean Freustié.[16]

The show was a success. "If this keeps up, I'm going to be working as regularly as a postal employee," the great Zizi joked with Matthieu Galey. Galey recorded the event in his diary: "Zizi Jeanmaire. A show that was part variety show, part ballet, with wonderful costumes by Saint Laurent. Everything was focused on her, this dark bird of paradise, flashy and feathered. In her dressing room, she's another person: there's nothing left of her inside this white terrycloth dressing gown that she tightens over a flat chest and boyish hips."[17]

The maison de couture officially opened on December 4, 1961. Yves was the miracle worker. Once again, he reshaped the reality of a world that he didn't want to see, in order to re-create it as something more true and more real in costumes. His work revealed someone who was true to the best of himself. He was an old young man who liked Proust and Marlon Brando (who was said to be horribly out of fashion). The real young people read Sartre, Malraux, and, especially, Camus. Camus's death in a car accident on January 4, 1960 struck everyone "like a blow that the gods of Greece reserved for men who were too proud," as André Rousseaux put it. Albert Camus was the hero of all rebellious men. He soothed their despair at life by telling them of a new humanism where it was less important "to be happy than to be conscious…on ground level."[18] This was exactly the world that Yves Saint Laurent was fleeing. He was incapable of choosing a course of action. Or this course would be broken, shattered, whipped. Under duress, he resisted, finding the strength to fight until he became unhinged from the mediocrity of existence and headed for the limits of death, danger, madness, and institutionalization. As if he always wanted to tell himself, "I have escaped." Fashion prepared him for this. Yet everyone looked back to his 1958 success and asked, "Will he be able to surpass his Trapeze line?"

The stay at Val-de-Grâce hospital left a scar. It revealed the hardness of a shy person who, suddenly, preferred to vanish, to disappear into himself as in a submarine. And then there was the void. A black hole. Other people ceased to exist. He had no age anymore. This terrible experience revealed to him what his world would be: going so far as to lose himself, to be destroyed, and, in his fall, regenerating himself through his desire for beauty, the only antidote to "this fatal boredom" that Serge Gainsbourg was singing about at the same time.

This total experience would not stop Yves from experiencing more suffering. But it was the only way to escape the memories that haunted him and made him fixate on the bars that he enjoyed sawing: "There is a strength inside me, a fierce will that pushes me toward the light," he said. "I'm a fighter, and a winner." He was exceedingly vulnerable, but he had never had more doubts about his strength, or his gift for sadness. Suffering had emptied him out. He didn't play love games with his mother anymore. This new challenge would put back together a life that had shattered into pieces when he tumbled, when he fell on his face and everything evaporated. Fashion had already killed him once by robbing him of his youth—but did he ever want to be young? Now fashion would give him back his name and his life in golden letters.

Seated at a table, Yves Saint Laurent plunged his outspread fingers into a necklace of imitation diamonds. As if the body of a woman slipped through his hands. Pierre Boulat, the "Frenchie" of *Life*, documented his work on the collection for seven weeks with his Leica camera: "Looking at Saint Laurent, I see only Orson Welles. The same deep sincerity in the true or the false. Nothing fake." More than five hundred photos detailed this adventure that was made up of waiting, doubt, and concentration. No other photographer caught with such truth "that terrible year of his debut," as Victoire called it.[19] Pierre smoked and bit his nails, Claude sharpened pencils, Yves sketched. He counted the days on a Belleville Reneaux cardboard calendar. Boulat, invisible, caught his silent fits of anger. His showoff side. The way he simpered to Pierre Bergé. His joys. A white hat on Victoire, like the flash of a smile. Her eyes were still heavily made-up, but her hair was short. A puddle of silk lay at her feet. Victoire, a magical name. What happened between her and Yves? Something fatal and ephemeral. The meeting with this demon named Woman whom he made his black Virgin: "From one collection to the next, the same image is present in my mind. That of Victoire, a sublime model and a marvelous muse. I remember a black dress embroidered with giant chrysanthemums, and, especially, the veil she was wearing. Since then, the veil has become a tradition in my collections. If I had gotten married, Victoire is the woman I would have chosen!" After all, this petite, dark brunette woman had the same slim, graceful silhouette as Lucienne, his mother.

A terrible tension was in the air. Fear was mixed into the employees' diligent focus on their work. The improvised studio was in creative disorder. Bundles of samples were attached to the walls, which were hung in white canvas. Ribbons were draped from curtain rods. The fittings were totally silent. In a sweater and dark skirt, Madame Esther, who had been hired as the *première* of the *atelier flou*, pinned the first version of a skirt on Victoire. All eyes were glued to the mirrors. In the greatest of secrecy, the collection would be transported by truck, in the dark, wee hours of January 29, to 30 bis Rue Spontini. Workers in coats climbed the steps with white garment bags. "Ghosts," Monsieur Dior would have said.

6 / THE CHILD WITH NERVES OF STEEL

January 29, 1962, arrived.

The décor of the show was carefully put together in order not to over-shadow the dresses. Curtains of ecru canvas, white walls, a Havana brown rug, a chandelier by César, Swedish chairs covered in black leatherette. The style of Pierre Bergé and Yves Saint Laurent was expressed through simplicity that modernized tradition. There was a clear break with Dior's neo–Louis XVI spirit and extremely feminine style. Yves Saint Laurent knew just what he wanted: "I want very understated fashion, carefully selected clients, a setting without pomp. A boutique—certainly not. At the very most, perfume and scarves. Bouquets are out of the question. A few green plants, but nothing more." The guests of honor didn't sit on eighteenth-century-style divans, but on two comfortable sofas covered in dark brown canvas from Mobilier International. The only thing left of the Dior spirit were the salons: one for the press, and another for clients and celebrities. Among the men, there were many artists as well as the photographers Norman Parkinson, Hiro, and André Ostier, the choreographer Roland Petit, and the decorator Victor Grandpierre. In the first row were seated Geneviève Fath, Madame Stux-Rybar, Zizi, Patricia Lopez-Willshaw, Mrs. Randolph, Doris Duke, Hélène de Turckheim, and Françoise Sagan. Roger Thérond was seated next to the Vicomtesse de Ribes, who commented, "Yves Saint Laurent and Pierre Bergé were very excited. They felt that day as if the world would soon be theirs." Yves had stayed up all night. At two in the morning, he added another design. Next to the Comte and Comtesse de Contades, at the end of the row, were Lucienne Mathieu-Saint-Laurent, who made a special trip from Oran in a Caravelle aircraft, with seventeen-year-old Brigitte and twenty-year-old Michèle. They were spending four days at Hôtel Frontenac. "Some people recognized us," recalled Brigitte, with some excitement in her voice. "Yves left when I was nine years old. He always dazzled me. In fact, in terms of gifts, he was so much more talented, we were nothing in comparison."

With her bedroom eyes and milky complexion, her dark hair hidden under a huge musketeer hat, Victoire opened the show in a suit with large green and pink checks. No tassels, no frills. The dresses no longer had names, but numbers. The 104 designs were briefly described in white folders: Ensemble. Dress in gray wool. Coat in gray and white checked tweed. Suit in natural shantung. Casino dress in black and white printed twill.

Lines: the blouse, the peacoat, the striped sailor shirt, the suit. Skirts. Natural tones, supple shapes, a rather nonchalant elegance. Slim shoulders, a supple bust, a waist casually cinched with a leather tie over floaty blouses. Yves Saint Laurent's women could be the models for those who listened dreamily that year to the Beatles' first single: "Love, love me do / You know I love you." They embodied Good, wrapped in a white shawl, just as adroitly as they played Bad in long velvet gloves. Morva, Heather the Brit, Fidélia the Eurasian, Paule de Mérindol—who quit Chanel in November 1961—and Victoire walked in a casual and sophisticated way. He seemed to have written a love letter to each one of them, and they pretended to believe it marvelously. Suits, tunics, sailor shirts: the first impression was the simplicity of this spring line, which crossed out everything that stood in its way with a black line and in a few flashes of red and green. "The fashion world flutters with 100,000 frills and 100,000 lace edges, but he chose simplicity."[1]

Edmonde Charles-Roux, editor of *Vogue Paris* at the time, remembered a "frightening suspense. Everyone was watching him. We were aware that Dior's time was past and that the crown prince had become king. There was even a double suspense: was he as talented as we thought? Could this talent be expressed given that he had lost the previous context for his work? It was a double triumph, the triumph of talent and technique."[2] They realized that Yves Saint Laurent worked the way Monsieur Dior did: in a lab coat, but without protective oversleeves. This was agreed on, but from there opinions differed. "Very Balenciaga," "Not young enough," "What class!," "Modern," "Gorgeous." There was no agreement. Replacing the traditional references for long and short, Yves Saint Laurent brought a breath of fresh air to his light frock coats and his mousseline sheath dresses. With the subtle skill of his time, he made a new statement: his own. *Elle* summed it up: "We were expecting a collection by a young man of tomorrow, but we saw the collection of a master of today."[3]

Yves Saint Laurent was the youngest of the five "New Wave" couturiers. Gérard Pipart of Nina Ricci was twenty-eight. Philippe Venet was thirty-two. The Roman designer Roberto Capucci and Jacqueline de Sthen were twenty-nine. They all opened their own fashion houses at the same time. But a special atmosphere emanated from Yves Saint Laurent. A few days before the show, he was interviewed by the novelist Dino Buzzati, who was a special correspondent for *Corriere della Sera*. "I was curious to see this phenomenon up close, since he already had a legendary aura." Afterwards, he departed "with the painful certainty of having looked like a total idiot….Maybe I'm an idiot, but famous people, even if they're barely twenty-five years old and still act natural, always intimidate me. Plus, I was in a world that was entirely new to me. I'm shy, and he was, too, so you can imagine the results. He was turning a paperweight shaped like a hand over and over in his fragile and extremely elegant hands."[4]

Yves's return to fashion, which had been the stuff of so many rumors (that the money had run out, or he was unable to do it by himself, among others) did not receive only bravos and cheers. They sized him up, analyzed him, criticized him. Yves Saint Laurent was the little prince no more. Those who had once found him too eccentric now thought he was too cautious, not young enough for his age (*Le Figaro*, *La Dépêche d'Alger*). "We were waiting for him like the Messiah, and he declined to establish rules. We expected extravagance, and he refrained from making bold statements. His colors were mild. His line of blouses with loose-cut backs is comfortable, made for taming sparrows in town squares. His designs are neither street Parisian nor high-class Parisian," Lucien François wrote.[5]

Those who wanted to see what this young designer had to prove got only one result, without any fuss and bother: Yves Saint Laurent was a classic.

"Yves Saint Laurent's nerves were shattered when the crown prince of the perfumed salons experienced the atmosphere of the barracks," Lucien François wrote. "How could it be otherwise? Fortunately he is at an age when you can recover your health as quickly as you lost it. He's learning to spread his wings."[6]

With his first collection for his own company, Yves suddenly became a great couturier at the age of twenty-five, alongside Chanel and Balenciaga. When *Women's Wear Daily* came out the next day, it gave him a cumbersome title: "Yves: Fashion's Third Force." But was he really the same man? His face had changed. His shoulders, his attitude, his mouth harboring a faint smile, his eyes shielded behind thick tortoiseshell glasses—everything revealed a different person. In January 1958, the Trapeze collection had burst forth from a drawing. This collection summed up a man who had matured over two years of absence: "I don't intend to be revolutionary. The dresses will develop according to the events and inspirations that guide them. I am an artisan," he told the *New York Herald Tribune* one week earlier on January 21. It was no longer about the exquisite vibration of feelings. It was the ambitious and precise movement of an intelligence that managed, selected, simplified, and tackled the essential, i.e., the paradox of couture: show something new, but at the same time clients were always looking for a design that, judging by the rigor of its shape and the solidity of its fabric, seemed built to last. Although Yves seemed fragile, he had found the line that would keep him from getting lost. He came back and staked his place. He set his standard of clarity and lines. A new mastery led him to reject excessive lyricism and color. He made this plan the base for his art: he would sustain and direct it and submit it to laws that life refused him. "I want to create style more than fashion."

From the beginning, the American press was the most enthusiastic. Especially *Women's Wear Daily*, the only newspaper to have had a special preview. A few days before the show, Yves Saint Laurent showed John Fairchild his designs. Twenty years later, Fairchild summed up the situation in a fatherly manner: "Balenciaga was in decline, Dior was becoming boring, Givenchy had adopted the repetitive style of Balenciaga, Chanel was a veritable dictator of fashion, and Saint Laurent, who observed everything from behind his big glasses, knew this better than anyone."[7] *Life* celebrated Yves as the best suit-maker since Chanel,[8] and American *Vogue* was in love with a collection that was so "calm, gentle, marvelously wearable."[9] *Vogue* even had a six-page spread on the day dresses and cocktail dresses, photographed by William Klein on black backgrounds with neon stripes that emphasized the colors that couldn't intimidate New York.

Yvonne de Peyerimhoff's arrival in October 1962 as sales director reassured everyone and attracted new buyers. She made it a point of honor to welcome them as VIPs: "I wanted everyone to have a better experience at Saint Laurent than anywhere else," she said. "We did everything to make them happy and comfortable. Some of them came to buy before lunch and stayed until one-thirty in the morning."

The kings of the textile industry were there: Sidney Gittler (Ohrbach's), Russel Carpenter (I. Magnin), Alvin Walker (Holt Renfrew), Andrew Goodman. Madame de Peyerimhoff didn't hesitate to take financial risks: "When a manufacturer was afraid of a sleeve, I told him, if you don't hit it big with this, I'll pay you back for it next season!" Her assistant, Corinne Le Ralle, said, "The scariest accents were from Chicago and Dallas! But I knew the drill: we had to be fast, and avoid selling the same thing to everyone. And we had to get on the good side of André, the concierge at the Ritz. He would get them tickets to a show."

The French liked being excited rather than reassured. Strict elegance would be quite dry if it weren't jazzed up by the pleasures of love: that was the theater lesson of Monsieur Dior. At Yves Saint Laurent, the jacket buttons were gold jewels, and the espadrilles became strange mules of braided leather. At night, a mysterious black mousseline often veiled his princesses, and turbans decorated his rajas with brocade. The decorative spirit of his latest collections expressed itself in accessories. Amid a flood of jewels worthy of Topkapi—black jet, rubies, garnets, black emeralds, giant flowers of mother-of-pearl or coral—as well as in his stormy purples, one could already pick out a slightly subversive beauty that disrupted traditional standards of chic: "No pastels, no monochromes, few colors, never any flowers, but violent combinations of tones."

Zizi Jeanmaire would be the first to kiss Yves Saint Laurent that day. This insatiable woman dressed all in black lit up a cigar while sitting on the sofa with the other guests of honor. The Duchess of Windsor, who was seated next to her, must have been awfully shocked.

The Duchess of Windsor's reserved manner didn't stop her from applauding. She ordered two suits, three dresses, and a coat from that first spring collection—one of the biggest orders for the brand-new company. The *premières* often gave her fittings at home: by 1962, the duchess didn't go out very often. Clients included Patricia Lopez-Willshaw, Suzy Delbée, Baronne Guy (de Rothschild), Francine Weisweiller, Liliane Bettencourt, the Comtesse Chandon de Briailles, and the Vicomtesse de Ribes. "Madame, I put the dress in your suitcase": on stationery embossed with Passy 43-79, Danièle Portheault—a former Dior saleswoman—wrote those words to her customer, Baronne Geoffroy de Courcel, who lived in London, where her husband was the French ambassador to England. In April 1962, on the day when her husband officially accepted the ambassadorship, she was seen in a sheath dress in emerald and blue silk with a matching coat and turban. "It's extremely attractive! What an experience! It gives you confidence in yourself. It's like armor even if it's made of tulle." She remembered, "There were two fittings, and three for the evening gowns. I followed Yves Saint Laurent enthusiastically. On Rue Spontini, I found the atmosphere of a prewar maison de couture. It was like the atmosphere at Schiaparelli's. It was classic, but with the wildest inventive spirit. It was like a club: you knew who was having a fitting next to you. We were among friends. We were experiencing the heroic time of a young man who was suddenly setting up his own couture house."

The women nicknamed the company "the candy dish" and "the hive." At Dior, the saleswomen wore black. At Saint Laurent, they had a beige period before going back to black. "Wearing bright colors would be a faux pas," explained Denise Barry de Longchamp, the senior saleswoman at Saint Laurent in 1992. She was, she said, a "dissident" because she wore suits with some muted color. Her motto: Stay below what you are offering to the clientele. She acknowledged that "at Dior, the saleswomen formed a group. At Yves Saint Laurent, they asked us to be in uniform. But it was more intimate: a little army in black!" The prices weren't as high as for Balenciaga or Givenchy, but were far above Carven (which was one of the least expensive). In 1962, a Saint Laurent suit cost 755 dollars (versus a price of 900 dollars at Dior). The coats were proudly bumped up a little bit (807 dollars at Saint Laurent, 800 at Dior). A discount might be offered to certain clients, but mum's the word!

Yet this was an unusual couture house. It didn't fit in at all in a neighborhood filled with families of doctors and bureaucrats. The streets were gray like the hallways of these big bourgeois apartments where children dressed in navy blue played hide-and-seek. Without the Café Spontini and the Boulangerie Veinachter, where the apprentices bought their croissants, the area would have seemed gloomy, haunted by subjects that aren't discussed at the dinner table and wives who all looked as if they were kissed on the forehead. For clients arriving with their chauffeurs, 30 bis Rue Spontini was like a remote magical island. Some ordered in meals from the Ritz. Others showed up with shoeboxes full of jewels. The Comtesse de Casteja brought caviar sandwiches and a bottle of vodka. The decorator Jeanne Laurent came by bicycle. The telephone crackled. Saleswomen with dresses draped over their arms passed back and forth. "Clients in skimpy clothing wearing lots of perfume and with their hair in snoods entered noisily and gave kisses all around," as Hélène Cingria described it.[10]

The collection was shown every day at 3:30 PM. Marie-Thérèse Herzog traced copies of Yves's sketches for the foreign clients. Yves gave it his all: "I would go downstairs with earrings, gloves, and hats, and sometimes he would do more sketches during that time."

*

Everyone did everything. Pierre Bergé peddled the collection skillfully. He recalled, "Yves and I divided up the roles very quickly. We were in agreement on our attention to detail. We had no time to lose." He learned to set prices and negotiate contracts. "No one was going to tell me that you had to graduate from an elite academy to run a couture house!" Yet he wasn't a man of numbers and tedious calculations: after taking a year to fill out the first paystubs, he hired Madeleine de Rauch's accountant, Monsieur Edouard. What animated Bergé was the amazing intelligence of power: knowing how to surround yourself with the best people. Investors who would bet on the house's future. Journalists he could count on. Staff that he sometimes hired too quickly, but usually selected with keen understanding. His office was next to the studio. Louis Aragon would sometimes stop by. And with the same fiery energy that burst from his pen in his writing for *La Patrie Mondiale*, Pierre Bergé rushed forward, got angry at a buyer. Everyone was aware of Monsieur Bergé's temper and was familiar with the way he made up with people by sending bouquets of white roses. The Americans really felt as if they were in a Parisian comedy. James W. Brady, a journalist for *Women's Wear Daily*, remembered, "Bergé also had a subtle sense of humor, ironically calling himself 'the money-changer in the Temple' or adding a few zeros on the labels of a series of dresses the day before the show because John Fairchild, after getting a glimpse of the collection, had said that it would be a sensation." When an American buyer asked if he spoke English, Pierre Bergé answered, "I know how to count in English!"[11]

The novelist Dino Buzzati described a scene that would repeat itself many times over. "He was wearing a blue lab coat, and he seemed very busy. I explained who I was, and he apologized and temporarily put me into the hands of Pierre Bergé, the maison's business manager, who was also very young, but short, with a rather hard and willful face. People say that Pierre Bergé is a marketing genius: the stunning success of the painter Buffet is to a great extent due to Bergé's friendship and protection. Now he champions Saint Laurent."[12]

On the other floors, the strictest professionalism was expected. The workers punched in at nine o'clock. If they were three minutes late, their pay was docked a quarter of an hour. But there was no risk of that: they put their heart and soul into these dresses. "We didn't have great working quarters," remembered Madame Catherine, "but we worked wonders. We met with the suppliers in the stairwell in front of the door to the studio. We couldn't put a mannequin on top of the table because the ceilings were too low. To make the hem of an evening gown, I'd go next door."

Sometimes the close quarters exacerbated tensions. Quarrels became everyone's business. They would only bring the family closer together, with its network of secrets, disagreements, and jealousies. There were rivalries between the former Dior employees and the "intruders" or between the *premières* and the saleswomen. The clients were often quite considerate and so generous. So if one wanted to change the shape of the neckline of her dress, the saleswoman didn't always have the heart to say no. This made the *première* furious: "It's not the same design anymore! If the client doesn't like it, she can just take it to the seamstress down the street!"

Victoire's mother, Madame Devis, a freelance seamstress, lent a hand. "She saved the first suit collection," admitted Pierre Bergé, who arbitrated the catfights with rare humor. But the former Dior workers put up a united front: "We respected her age, but she wasn't a professional. We couldn't replace Madame Marguerite. The seamstresses didn't know how to cut along the grain properly. They thought it was okay just to fold the fabric in half and cut it. But we had squares. You put a thread into the weave of the fabric to find the direction. [Instead,] the seamstress marked it with chalk every twenty centimeters. I can't accept that!" said Monette, who treated herself to her first silver thimble while at Yves Saint Laurent.

And Yves Saint Laurent? According to John Fairchild, "He was the true boss of the company. I always thought that he was in charge of everything. He wasn't this poor shy animal, this Bambi of fashion. He was a real lion. The lion of the fashion jungle!"

This would come out clearly in July 1962. In salons blooming with Indian rosewood, magnolias, and flowering cherries planted in every corner, Yves Saint Laurent garnered another ovation like the one he had received at Dior four years earlier. Heroines were in fashion then. The movie industry had rediscovered giant films. In Rome and in Hollywood, they built cardboard empires and played with dynasties, Technicolor exoticism, and billions of dollars. This became Yves Saint Laurent's opportunity to return to his feats of magic. Four years after the Trapeze collection, *Vogue Paris* put him on the cover for the second time, in September 1962. The photo was by Irving Penn. The salon was full of shoving, shouting, and applause. Marie-Louise Bousquet lost her hat when she threw herself into the arms of Suzanne Luling, who had finally left Dior in 1961. Two great tears rolled down Pierre Bergé's face as he consoled all the women who were, he would later recall, "dying of happiness."

America, "which isn't the country of great luxury but of great spending,"[13] in Christian Dior's words, was back. In the first row sat Lee Radziwill—Jackie Kennedy's sister—who had split with Givenchy after wearing his clothes for six years. Great publicity for Saint Laurent. In 1962 New York had become the capital of elegant parties. People went to the opera on Mondays or the April in Paris ball at the Waldorf. At night, women always went out in long white gloves. Jackie Kennedy invited Shakespearean actors and forty-nine Nobel Prize winners to the White House. It was the Camelot era. And the billionaires wore Yves Saint Laurent.

The first collection established a radical line. The second revealed the project more overtly: it was a look. A way of throwing a black oilskin battledress over an evening gown. A way of being theatrical: velvet butterflies on hats, giant ties in Ranch mink. Whimsical accessories, like an ostrich feather cocoon combined with organdy petals. The inspiration was very Givenchy, but the Saint Laurent touch was clear. He already had this way of making each woman the rival of another. Of fanning the secret flames of a special connection that seemed sometimes as if it didn't need men at all. These women were too beautiful to be loved. They shone for an audience.

In addition to the type of American woman who drove toward Sutton Place settled in the back of a Rolls-Royce Silver Cloud that matched her jewels, other presences were noticed. The powerful image of faithless priestesses resonated with women wearing elaborate jet stone necklaces, their loose buns speared with diamond hairpins. Was it Maria Callas? In December 1961, she performed *Medea* at La Scala, addressing this introductory phrase to her frustrated public: "Ho dato tutto a te." This voice bursting from the shadows, this luxurious bird, was perhaps the "Black Magic" of winter 1962–63.

"The silhouette is elongated as it is everywhere, but in a certain way that can't be seen anywhere else, and which has as much to do with the way the head is carried as with the waist suspended under the breasts. A certain dark light emanates as much from the lacquered silks and jet stones as from the eye make-up," Lucien François raved in *Combat* in a July 31, 1962 article titled "Yves Saint Laurent, the Poet of Fashion."

That season felt like a contest between the youngest couturier, Yves Saint Laurent, and the oldest, Gabrielle Chanel. As if, in what she called a "farewell collection," Mademoiselle would see her successor burst forth in the storm.

Yves Saint Laurent said that he never met Gabrielle Chanel. "I never wanted to have lunch with her, I would have been too afraid that she would eat me up." But La Grande Mademoiselle told Robert Goossens, who created jewelry for her starting in 1953, "I had lunch with a young man who will go very far. Yves Saint Laurent." One of them was lying, but which one? Well, what does it matter? Starting that year, they engaged in the only battle that meant anything to them: the craft of the couturier. For Yves Saint Laurent, Chanel was truly an obsession. "I wanted to know everything about technique," he said. Yet how could he have held his own against this *grande dame* with a way of looking at you that was as unforgiving as his own? Didn't he feel closer to her like this, with his eyes on images, his hands in fabrics, sharpened by the instinct of what luxury itself is? There is a line in *The Eagle with Two Heads*: "Would a queen allow someone to come into her room and faint?"

These two stars shared the awareness of their greatness. They both considered their profession a sacrament. They persisted, they absorbed the blows. Because they were looking for something other than recognition. They turned their solitude into a temple and elevated couture into something greater than just an issue of cuts and hemlines: a judgment of the world. With her short hair and black sweaters, Chanel obstinately opposed the ruffles and frills of the Belle Époque with the modern look. "Her elegance, even for a layperson, was stunning. With a sweater and ten rows of pearls, she revolutionized fashion," said Monsieur Dior. Saint Laurent's style also avoided anything that flattered vanity in too sugary a way, or emphasized the look of the 1950s: charming, adorable, excessively feminine. "We never made taffeta dresses with big shirred puffs and roses," observed Madame Esther, the *première* of the *atelier flou* at Yves Saint Laurent. He shared Chanel's aversion for styles that were small, precious, flowery, or cutesy—woman as trinket.

Yves Saint Laurent was alone. He was searching. He plunged his hands into fabrics and turned them over and over. At some point he'd understand it and be able to explain it, but he didn't yet have the words. And the apprentices who had been trained at Dior, who could handle and stitch fabric like no one else, would have to tame these fabrics, which they found too soft. But the fabrics got their revenge. They fought, furrowed, or frayed. They resisted the hand that sought to control them without managing to find the right movement. For Madame Esther, Yves was definitely "a master of drawing, with demands that were sometimes difficult to produce. He didn't want any darts or zippers in the back. No one could get into the dresses." Yves Saint Laurent saw a Chanel suit up close in 1961: it was pink and green, weighed down by the famous gold chain. Mademoiselle Chanel had given it to Victoire. At the time, Yves Saint Laurent had officially disappeared. Three years later, he was filled with questions. How did she give so much suppleness to this sequined jersey that, instead of being stiff and brittle, rippled like a silvery fish? How did she come up with this bold cut that let you move your arm without the jacket moving an inch? How did she manage this simple little skirt that made the whole outfit? She had the secret for giving women this silent, devoted, present, sweet, bitter, anxious, and passionate look that belonged to them. This casual way they moved—whether mothers, mistresses, or wives—without getting lost, without weighing themselves down with anything except a simple suit, a cigarette, an item of jewelry, and a little perfume. The suit was always the same, and made them stand out from their clothing: Anouk Aimée, the star of Fellini's *8 1/2*, posed for *Vogue*, reclining like an odalisque: yet a man's strength was visible in her eyes. Even Brigitte Bardot, the champion of the busty look, gave in: she started dressing in Chanel. She came to see Chanel one day, after admiring the designer's ethereal dresses on Delphine Seyrig in *Last Year at Marienbad*. She wanted a long, black silk mousseline dress. "My dear," Chanel told her, "your best feature is your legs." So the mousseline let the legs show through. But Brigitte also wanted a black camellia in her hair. "No," said Chanel, "maybe you can get away with playing Ophelia, but not Lady Macbeth." Brigitte didn't get her camellia, but she was transformed.[14]

Male designers, whom Chanel called "these gentlemen," were all fascinated by her suits. Robert Goossens recalled, "Balenciaga admitted to me that he bought a Chanel suit and took it completely apart. There were strips inside. Everything was close-fitting, and he didn't understand it. That's why he admired her so much."

Yves Saint Laurent increasingly revealed the influence of Chanel: suits without padding, slim coats, light, porous wool pieces, and so on. Black, which dominated the winter 1962 collection, revealed its nuances even better. It was no longer the Cinecittà black of his golden youth, but the more languid and voluptuous black of the Woman, which was very much inspired by Delphine Seyrig in *Last Year at Marienbad*, the black of a fluid silk sheath dress. The delicately pleated crepe flowed over the body. It would be the jersey of the "Easy Look" collection. Then the white blouses. Then the suits, which became two-piece outfits in Shetland tweed. The line became lighter and almost disappeared. The face had disappeared. The wide-brimmed hats floated, the ties were loosely tied, and the blouses seemed airy.

Yet fundamental differences remained. A collection by Chanel was appreciated between the thumb and forefinger; a collection by Yves Saint Laurent was judged by the eyes. "Chanel manipulated fabric constantly. She worked on the material, but he worked on the design. We made toiles. Chanel picked up a fabric, cut it, felt it, until it was as worn as an old English tweed," recalled Paule de Mérindol, whom Mademoiselle used as the model when she made her own suits. "A Chanel suit might take three and half months to make. I would pose for a month and a half. It was a struggle to transform it, to subdue it, to make it something very personal. Yves Saint Laurent was the heir of Dior, a very structured kind of couture. He produced an image that they tried to reproduce and fulfill."

Another difference: Chanel, the peasant girl, had a concrete way of working: she touched the body and draped the fabric over her models. But Yves Saint Laurent limited himself to observing them. From this distance, he invested them with all the love he could not give them: they were women. For Chanel, they were just physiques: "If it looks good on one, it'll look good on another," she used to say, with feigned aloofness. Yves Saint Laurent, on the other hand, was inspired by their differences. He translated these differences, from the most obvious to the most imperceptible, into dresses that were inspired by an attitude. Paule de Mérindol recalled the fittings: "Everything happened without the least little gesture. When Chanel wasn't happy with a design, her mouth became square. Sometimes she cut a dress to humiliate the *première* who had done too good a job making it. Monsieur Saint Laurent concentrated, or went to the other side of the room. With Chanel, the silences were heavy. With Saint Laurent, they were muted." But Robert Goossens noted, "Coco put a lot of pressure on herself, something that Saint Laurent couldn't do. Maybe because he wasn't in the habit of fighting with himself. People were afraid of Mademoiselle Chanel, they weren't afraid of Saint Laurent. Chanel was Saint Laurent and Bergé all in one."

Indeed, Chanel had that formidable energy that Yves delegated to Pierre Bergé. As John Fairchild said, "Yves, you're missing the pleasure in life." Fairchild described Yves: "Ever since I've known him, he [Yves] has had no contact with reality. If there's a problem with a toilet that won't flush, Pierre has to deal with it." Determined to discover every arcane detail of technique, Yves Saint Laurent sometimes stayed alone in the studio until the wee hours of the morning.

Thus he became the couturier of women like Marie-Laure de Noailles, who didn't resemble the ones he loved. She was "strange, with an extreme look and elegance," according to Pierre Bergé. She found herself invited to city celebrations; the city of Hyères offered her her weight in artichokes. "May 16, 1963. An additional dress with organdy collar for Marlene Dietrich. 18, Avenue Montaigne." What is a name when it slips from a magical screen down to the little lined notebook of a couturier? Wasn't Yves Saint Laurent closer to the one on screen, the femme fatale who wore her "Miss Dietrich Gowns, by Adrian" and whispered on a silk sofa, "I did exist, but I didn't leave"? Would he be able to adapt to the commercial shift of the 1960s? How could he stay true to his dreams while still keeping up with the times? Private clients were not enough to keep the ateliers running full-speed. Dior's magnificently rich clients had quietly entered a legendary golden age. In 1928, three dresses cost as much as a car. In 1963, one dress did. Yvonne de Peyerimhoff said, "I calculated my salary at Dior myself. Saint Laurent didn't bring in a tenth what Dior did. I wanted it to work. We worked extremely hard." Thirty years later she added, "Pierre is very aware of what I did for the company. But Yves never thanked me."

Sylviane Hodgkinson, a head saleswoman who retired in 1988, recalled, "The women who received an invitation weren't always the ones who bought." And those who bought weren't always the easiest to dress. There was the elderly American woman who only wore pink. The Texas billionaire who wanted to add chinchilla to all her dresses. The wife of a filmmaker who was covered in psoriasis. One woman had to press down her breasts with a washcloth to get them into her bra. Another always traveled with her own silk sheets. "Once she forgot them here and we had to deliver them to the Hôtel de Crillon for her!" recalled a saleswoman. Another client was a fortune hunter but was very stingy. "When she ordered dresses, she practically counted the flowers on the print. One day, she came with a plumb line." Tall and thin, like a schoolteacher who eats candy, Sylviane Hodgkinson summed it up: "Women who don't know anything are often the biggest pains in the ass."

Times had changed. Now that designers had become stars, the combined world of couture and commerce gently submerged the old high society of Paris. The idle rich disappeared and were replaced by those who worked. A newspaper in the Rhineland even offered an editor's job to Soraya Esfandiari Bakhtiari, second wife and Queen Consort of Mohammad Reza Pahlavi, the last Shah of Iran. But the old ladies still wore hats. And in the front row the influential journalists stubbed out their last unfiltered Gitanes of the evening with the weary, professional look of judges.

Now America projected its dreams in Technicolor. The new glamour girls had marble bathrooms with gold fountains, golf and bridge instructors who spoke nine languages, and servants from the Bahamas. They divorced on Park Avenue and tanned at Gstaad, and sometimes admitted to their masseuses after a morning whisky, "Darling, I don't think my figure is good enough for ready-to-wear clothes."

Champagne flowed in palaces for the jet set. "It was unclear where these rich women who traveled were from—they had chalets in Switzerland and houses in Barbados," said Pierre Bergé.

The manager of Yves Saint Laurent also felt nostalgia for postwar social mores. It was described in this way by Parisian Bernard Minoret: "There were random acts of creativity. Louise de Vilmorin, Marie-Laure, and Léonor Fini knew that they were theater shows unto themselves. People loved paradoxes. They liked turning a monologue into a work of art. Being provocative was a game, and no one was offended. Jouhandeau and Sauguet did their shows. Pierre Bergé may be the last representative of this world." The death of Jean Cocteau on October 11, 1963, marked a break between the golden age of theater and the era that was beginning: the growth of the Maison Saint Laurent.

But there again Bergé and Saint Laurent arrived a little late in terms of the economic development of haute couture. Pierre Cardin had already launched his Paris-Tokyo line in 1957. Pierre Bergé moved fast: just eight months after the company started, he made his first trip to Japan to sell the Yves Saint Laurent brand. In London, Fortnum bought the collections. His first trip to New York would take place in 1963.

In terms of culture, Yves Saint Laurent was able to stay "with it." When Algerian independence was ratified by referendum on October 28, 1962, de Gaulle's Republic seemed to recover its calm. But then new "troublemakers" made their appearance: teenagers. These young people gathered under the banner of Daniel Filipacchi, who edited the magazine *Salut les Copains* (circulation: one million) and had a radio show with the same name on Europe 1. Johnny Hallyday sold seventeen thousand 45s per day, the same number as Elvis Presley at the height of his fame. His hits made the girls swoon. Kids danced the Mashed Potato and the Madison Twist. It was the time of doo-wop and Dalida's hit song "Vingt-quatre Mille Baisers." Yves Saint Laurent was crazy about Johnny along with the rest; perhaps since the famous singer had deferred his military service in Algeria, Yves could understand his anxieties better than most.

He listened to "Retiens la Nuit," which Johnny sang for Catherine Deneuve, and "Poupée Brisée" while sketching in the bathroom that he turned into an office. His room became an isolation chamber. Pierre Bergé remembered, "How many times did I see him in our Place Vauban apartment, lying prone on his bed for hours? We said, 'Yves is behind his screen.'" In 1960, the press nicknamed Yves "the Johnny Hallyday of couture" because of his leather jackets, but he didn't have the attitude of a rocker. He was more like a child playing diva—or a diva playing at being a child. He became a fictionalized character, to the point where the famous Japanese writer Mishima wrote about him in his novel *The School of Flesh*, which was published in 1963, the same year Yves Saint Laurent had a show in Tokyo and signed his first manufacturing agreements for exclusive designs with Seibu. Mishima wrote, "There was going to be a charity gala on the evening of April 10 where Yves Saint Laurent, a designer whose glory was beginning to rise in the firmament of Parisian fashion, would show his collection. Taeko had decided to go and be seen in public for the first time with Senkitchi." The suspense was there: "It was all a mess! Saint Laurent has finally come to, but now he's crying like a child! One third of the collection hasn't made it through customs yet and Haneda is not nearby." Because of "Monsieur Saint Laurent's great fatigue and many worries," the show is put off. Finally it begins, and Mishima describes it as follows: "The first model appeared nonchalantly before the golden screens—it was Ara, a famous *Vogue* model, a woman of average age and Asian origins, whose false eyelashes were glued exaggeratedly far from her eyes and who wore under a navy blue suit a white quilted blouse—it was already past nine....The diaphanous Ara seemed to be walking on clouds. Leaning imperceptibly forward, swaying her hips, with a look full of meanness, she moved proudly through the audience." Mishima seemed fascinated by the attitude of the Saint Laurent women: "They all had large bowl-shaped hats and the attitude of goldfish enclosed in a bowl, and they walked emotionlessly, flashing sudden smiles."[15] But the beauty of mauve pink coats and dresses embedded with gold seemed far from the concerns of the young generation.

"Now there rises a huge, well-fed, historically ignorant, realistic, apolitical and apathetic horde of French people under age twenty," François Nourissier wrote in *Les Nouvelles Littéraires*.[16] France's rock and roll generation was a gold mine: there were seven million of them. A group of four "in" boys sang "She Loves You," and Beatlemania swept over Europe. Twenty-year-old Françoise Hardy had twenty songs, sold 250,000 records, and, with her sad little girl eyes, invented what *Vogue* deemed "graceful boredom." As Ophélie in the Roger Vadim film *Nutty, Naughty Chateau* (based on a Françoise Sagan play), she posed in a black sweater and a vinyl playsuit by Dior Sport. She made the cover of *Vogue*, photographed by Helmut Newton. She smiled, she moved, her daydreaming eyes lightly made-up in Make-Believe Pink. "Not since Brigitte Bardot has any figure or youthful attitude attracted as much attention as Françoise Hardy's figure, style, and youth."[17]

Yves Saint Laurent was torn between the need to uphold the staid couture tradition and his desire to experience the youth he never knew. "I had had enough of making dresses for blasé billionaire women," he would say two years later.[18] The clients' custom-made mannequin busts were lined up on shelves in the ateliers. The nickname in the couture industry for this area was "the cemetery." The skill of a *première* came through in her talent for making humps and fleshy flaws disappear. "Salons see women as they should be. Couture salons see them as they are."[19]

When designing for dance and theater, however, Yves did not have to improve the human form but could clothe it in dark or whimsical ways. The costumes and decorative elements that he designed for *Maldoror*, a show directed by Roland Petit at the Théâtre National Populaire in January 1963, were full of demons and distress.

Shivering old ladies, skulls covered in red pastel, a procession of witches, skeletons in cruciform black oilskins, with eleven scenes set to music by Maurice Jarre ("The Lice," "The Funeral Procession," "The Spider") expressed all the horrors of nature under the gaunt features of Maldoror (the hero of Comte de Lautréamont's book, a cult novel of ill-fated youth).

Yves's designs were clearly inspired by Francisco Goya's *Caprices*, a series of engravings including the famous image of the artist asleep at his desk, attacked by evil birds, titled *The Sleep of Reason Produces Monsters*. In the shadows of witches' Sabbaths, Yves designed grotesque figures and bestial contortions like those the painter raised to the level of the sublime. The kind of "monstrous realism" described by Baudelaire gave Yves Saint Laurent's drawings their diabolical evocative power, somewhere between nightmare and reality. Nothing could better express the couturier's tragic fascination with the enchantment of theater than this photo of him working, staring strangely at this black-and-white silhouette, which could be an actor, a real skeleton with make-up, or the Angel of Death. "He loves this photo," his press officers said laconically.

That angel could be André Courrèges. Anticipating the year 2000, he launched his first cosmonauts in July 1963. It was as if a gigantic explosion had suddenly cut the world in two. From this breach there burst a universe that was incredibly new, futuristic, sterile, and stripped of everything that weighed it down: beehive hairdos, elaborate buns. Fake hair, cake mascara, high heels, and girdles. Courrèges's style was like an explosion. Everything was new, space-age, futuristic. There were now two very different kinds of white. The white of yesterday: a bit of white, a scrap of organdy, a mother-of-pearl necklace, the white of white gloves by Chanel. The white of tomorrow: sparkling, slippery, lacquered, plastic white, which was unruffled by wind, waves, or, it seemed, even cosmic disruptions. It was the "All White" established by the designer, who was already being called "Doktor Courrèges" in America. Optical, dynamic. Yves Saint Laurent had shown his first pants for women in his inaugural collection of 1962. Courrèges made them his image. Hyper-constructed. Structured. With little white boots. Ready to fly off to the moon.

After Courrèges, the "lady look" seemed ten years out of date. Couture would never get over this affront that suddenly made it look like an old mistress, much too staid with its beautiful waved hair and pleated elegance to burst into the world of business, contracts, and the race for licenses. In the 1950s, names had become symbols. In the 1960s, these symbols became brands. Couturiers found themselves with limited choices. Become businessmen (Cardin), or lock themselves up in an ivory tower that isolated them from a world whose memory they were nevertheless preserving (Chanel, Balenciaga). Postwar ready-to-wear clothes were anonymous, but now the lines had names: Mary Quant, Biba, Sonia Rykiel—the queen of knitwear—Michèle Rosier—the queen of plastic—and so on. In London, the first happening boutiques opened on King's Road. Girls tried on clothes to the sounds of the Beatles' "Help!" and "Yesterday" or the Rolling Stones' "(I Can't Get No) Satisfaction." Victoire had left Saint Laurent to launch her own line, Victoire. She designed vinyl suits and denim-colored jersey pants. She posed for *Vogue* with her mother working as her fitter at her feet. It was a brief career.

What direction would Yves Saint Laurent take? He had put lily of the valley in the pockets of his first collection to bid farewell to Dior. He would attach camellias to his giant bows of black gauze. But Chanel was slippery: rejecting her symbolic camellia, she quilted gardenias on the backs of her jackets and hats. It was only later that Yves truly would be able to dialogue with Chanel, once he had mastered the knowledge that allows style to express itself and distinguishes true homage from imitation. Would he forget to be himself? For now, overly fascinated, he seemed to doubt his own strength, even though it was emphasized by Lucien François in *Combat*: "Chanel chic is always the same. The only changes are the materials, the fringed edges, the secrets of the weave and finishings....Yves Saint Laurent, on the other hand, constantly invents new clothing, new behaviors, to golf, to do the morning shopping, to go to the movies or the cabaret, to eat at a bistro or in an embassy, to wander, to make love, to be happy."[20]

Despite his success, Yves found himself out of favor again in 1963. He would later explain the winter 1963–64 collection by saying, "That season, I had bad models," putting into this admission all the humility of his pride. "It was the only time that I was wrong." The *New York Herald Tribune*'s Eugenia Sheppard called it "the quiet look." To her, Courrèges was "the power influence." Classicism had fallen into conventionality. "Yves Goes Back to Grey and Grandma" was the *Daily Mirror* headline. Sales to professional buyers continued to decline, with winter 1964 numbers dipping below those for winter 1962. Only the private clients were satisfied.

In 1964, Mademoiselle Chanel invited Pierre Bergé to dinner at her home on Rue Cambon. She asked him to manage her couture house. Pierre Bergé recalled it thusly: "Mademoiselle Chanel told me, 'I'm offering you an empire. Yves Saint Laurent is only a couture house. Come here tomorrow—your contract will be ready.'" Bergé said that she told him he could name his price. The next day, he sent her white roses in apology for his refusal.

For Yves Saint Laurent, an era was ending. J. Mack Robinson was looking to get out of the fashion business. Yvonne de Peyerimhoff said she found a purchaser for his shares: Richard Salomon, the manager of Charles of the Ritz, who held the American license for Y perfume, which was launched in 1964—considered a good French perfume, light and classic. At that time, Charles of the Ritz was a powerful empire with 1,800 employees. Its revenue placed it behind Elizabeth Arden and ahead of Estée Lauder.

A new world was beginning, full of promises and concepts. The children of the Baby Boom wanted life to be fast and practical. Straight from American colleges, campus style replaced the twin set and pearls. In Paris, *Elle* style meant Sylvie Vartan, the young twister who posed in t-shirts and Levi's with her hair in the wind. A junior version of *Vogue* came out in January 1965. Everything was brand new. The Instamatic: "Fantastic photos, a unique camera, click, clack, thanks, Kodak." Toasters, electric orange juice presses. Mentholated Kleenex and instant soup. A Teppaz record player was manufactured every thirty seconds. Everything was mini. Dining rooms were replaced by breakfast nooks, couches became sleek armless seats, radios turned into cubes, novels shrank into cheap paperbacks. Women were always busy, managers got promotions, and couturiers were now visionaries. Scientific discourse eliminated imagination. Literary figures were no longer novelists, but academics named Michel Foucault, Claude Lévi-Strauss, Fernand Braudel, and Roland Barthes, who even wrote an article for *Marie Claire* on the "Chanel-Courrèges showdown." "The unchanging chic of Chanel tells us that women have already lived (and known how to live). The obstinate newness of Courrèges tells us that they are going to live," wrote the champion of the New Criticism. Fashion entered an experimental era. The new women would be helmeted, zipped, booted, metallic, patented.

Sucked in by this impressive desire for freedom, Yves Saint Laurent turned back to the luxury of the past and saw only a fearful world, huddled up inside its old principles. The keeper of a memory that was being lost—one which the producers of new ideas wanted to wipe out—he anticipated all the limits of an era that would make newness its only raison d'être. He found an outlet for unbridled creativity in the theater: he designed sets and costumes for Zizi's show at the Théâtre National Populaire. The Renaud-Barrault company commissioned him to make costumes for *Il Faut Passer par les Nuages* and *The Marriage of Figaro*. All the characters written by Pierre-Augustin Beaumarchais were sketched gracefully, as if they paraded before you. It was the Saint Laurent version of the eighteenth century, with young boys in black morning coats and Hogarth-style peasant women wrapped in orange shawls, with dancers' busts. Yves designed everything—the wigs, the furniture, the shoes—revealing once again his obsessive attention to detail and his vision of the whole. There were at least five or six different shades of white. His careful observation came through in the image of the countess, even if everything was part of the moment, the free line, strokes of felt-tip pen that turned into a stole made of spotted tulle. His sense of humor also came through: he cut out the classified ads from *Le Figaro* to make a skirt for the character of Marceline with the big black hat.

His muses were definitely not Bond girls, or robots, or old perfumed ladies. Where would he find them this year? Surely in the sheltered woman Gloria Guinness discussed in *Harper's Bazaar*. A way of matching something to her sweater, of smoking a cigar, of wearing fake jewelry with courage, of slipping a man's raincoat over an evening gown, of traveling in white linen, and of putting a black bikini on in the summer. Chic is a dry martini, *Time* magazine, American clothes.

At a time when everything was being simplified—skirts, apartments, style ("Are you old-fashioned or modern?")—he found a third way: his own. Obeying his intuition and guided by the only ones who never betrayed him: women. "I was stuck in traditional elegance. Courrèges got me out of it. I thought: I can do better." He had to make Courrèges go out of fashion, as he had done with Dior. He launched his first peasant skirts, motivated by a romantic sensibility that made him distance himself from the city in order to see it better from afar. A necklace of gold branches intertwined with pearls, a beautiful Italian woman posed in *Vogue Paris*: Benedetta Barzini. Yves Saint Laurent had designed a wedding dress for her in white piqué. Her braided hair was decorated with white jasmine and orange blossoms. This lover of beauty extracted grace and the candid purity of childhood from his own era in order to invent a different time, making this supernatural journey seem like the most natural thing in the world.

n a suit and tie, Yves Saint Laurent is dining alone in his apartment on Place Vauban. The table is set in the living room. A carafe of wine and a crystal goblet are in the foreground. Behind him stands Bernard, the valet, in his white uniform. Yves Saint Laurent isn't eating—he's drawing. This photo was taken by Pierre Boulat in December 1961. Four years later, another image by an unknown photographer shows him transformed. He's at New Jimmy's with Rudolf Nureyev and Pierre Bergé. Yves has long hair and looks almost British: his tie is more colorful, and he has traded his dark suit for a corduroy jacket. This new Yves Saint Laurent thought the beatnik style was "incredibly chic." He defined elegance as "being yourself" and added, "There are two kinds of couturiers I can't stand—the alchemist couturier who, wearing a lab coat, locks himself up in his laboratory and prays to Saint Le Corbusier before designing the least little trinket, and the mystery couturier, whom you never see and who never sees anything because he lives outside his time."

Three years after starting his company, Yves Saint Laurent, having assimilated the lessons of Chanel, Balenciaga, and Givenchy, freed himself from imitation and stylistic exercises. He would take inspiration from the new era that was starting. The 1964 World's Fair in New York ("the Olympics of Progress") promised paradise for all—underwater hotels, laser tree-felling machines, and car dashboards that looked like airplane controls. But Yves rejected the overly formal French idea of progress: a way of moving abruptly from embroidered pleats to a spacesuit helmet, from Duchesse satin to mica—basically, to turn the couturier into an architect. Saint Laurent was a time bomb.

Between the Chanel tradition and the Courrèges moment, Yves Saint Laurent offered an alternative to women who didn't feel young enough to pretend to be ladies, or old enough to dress up like little girls. Starting with his 1965 collection, Yves Saint Laurent would be known as the couturier of the "Now Look": he created a synthesis between futuristic shock and timeless chic. As *Combat* put it on August 7, 1965, "Yves Saint Laurent has successfully created a new line from old principles." The kick-off was the Mondrian collection of winter 1965, which was shown in July. Ten shift dresses crisscrossed with black lines and rectangles and squares in the primary colors of yellow, red, and blue marked a new stage in Yves Saint Laurent's rise. As he described the dress, "It's like a block, a colored prism."

The couturier gave a long interview to his friend, the journalist Patrick Thévenon, in *Candide*: "I understood that we had to stop thinking of clothing as sculpture. Quite the opposite—we should think of it as mobile. I understood that fashion had been stiff and that now it had to move."[1]

After having made Dior's 1950s look outdated, he now did the same to Courrèges's futuristic style. Yves Saint Laurent didn't deny the demiurge of plastic; he shifted haute couture entirely. "I was imagining more and more elegant dresses. It was disturbing." But rejecting the fashion of yesterday didn't mean jumping on board Sputnik into the world of tomorrow. While Courrèges's ideal, as Violette Leduc wrote in *Vogue*, was "a girl who traveled to ancient Sparta," Yves Saint Laurent's ideal was first and foremost a woman. This woman didn't dance the moon kiss in a mini-mini-skirt, nor did she experiment with dresses made of paper or plastic. She liked to drink, and smoked light cigarettes. "Oh, to kiss the hand of a society woman. And scratch my lips on her diamonds. And then in her Jaguar, to burn her leopard skin with an English cigarette": these Gainsbourg lyrics could have been written about her.

For her, no celluloid glasses or white nylon wigs. But long eyelashes that were fluffy with cake mascara and a bun that just barely displayed the nape of her neck. Yves Saint Laurent didn't offer her get-ups, but dresses. "Between [Watteau's] *The Embarkation for Cythera* and the moon launch, there is room for an era that no one seems to care about: our own. In the past, luxury meant being mummified in mink. Little girls dreamed only of Rolls-Royces and diamonds. Today, luxury means living. And a woman isn't living when she's a prisoner of such constraints. However, we shouldn't make the opposite mistake and work for the year 2000. Certainly we should get rid of high heels, but we shouldn't replace them with unsightly boots that hide the prettiest part of a woman's leg: her ankle."[2]

After a difficult beginning, the company began to soar. The Mondrian collection gave wings to the sales figures. In one season, sales to buyers went from 790,000 francs to 1.4 million francs.

Sales to private clients went from 1.6 million to 2.3 million francs. It was a total success. This change had a big impact on Madame Esther, the *première* of the *atelier flou*: "Monsieur Saint Laurent had me make a completely straight toile. He put on the bands. We pinned it. That's when it all started. Mondrian was the big takeoff. After that, we never stopped working."

It was the first time that Saint Laurent was copied heavily. Although these dresses will always be associated with the 1960s, they're powerful enough to have escaped it: today, they haven't aged a bit. The Mondrian dress would become the first haute couture dress that was shown, exhibited, and cited as a consumer item. One sign: in three years, Roger Vivier sold 120,000 pairs of black buckle patent leather per season. The shoes were intended to go with the Mondrian dresses, both real and fake. In 1965, the dress was photographed by Irving Penn, David Bailey, and Richard Avedon. It made the cover of *Harper's Bazaar* and *Vogue Paris*. In 1969, it was on the cover of *L'Express*, and in 1990 the cover of *Connoisseur*. Despite the weight of retrospectives and honors, the years that pass only made it more timeless. In 1982, Helmut Newton photographed the Mondrian dress worn by Catherine Deneuve.

While it's true that 1960s haute couture was frequently based on experimenta-tions—Pierre Cardin paid homage to Op Art, Courrèges to BMPT (Buren, Mosset, Parmentier, Toroni) and the futurists, and Paco Rabanne to the realists—the Mondrian dress was an accurate illustration of the era. The couturier didn't just stick a painting onto the body; he made it move. That's the whole difference. It wasn't an adaptation or an enlargement. Yves Saint Laurent didn't reference Mondrian in order to show off his knowledge, but to re-create the artist's spirit in his own couture context. In the same way, and in the same year, Godard filmed the painter's primary colors in *Contempt*: the red Ferrari, Bardot's black wig, her yellow robe, and the smooth blue of the Mediterranean.

As if he were sketching with charcoal, Yves Saint Laurent divided his dresses with black bands, enjoying constructing balanced blocks. He had very personal knowledge of what the leader of the constructivist movement De Stijl expressed in his manifesto: "Relationships of pure lines and colors that lead to pure beauty."[3] But by adapting the Op Art graphics of the time to the rules for designing clothing, with their requirements for cut, production, and details, he simplified appearances with-out breaking with tradition. And above all while staying true to himself, consider-ing the true avant-garde to be classical. Starting with the 1958 Trapeze collection, he had already anticipated the need to make form fit the functions of modern life. His world was always about proportions and lines. Seven years of reflection later, Yves Saint Laurent started from the same foundations as Courrèges and Cardin—flat and fleshy fabrics, straight collars, close-fitting felt hats—to create a look instead of a concept. He softened these geometrical shapes in crepe and jersey, with a sense of moderation that proved to visionaries that newness is neither seeking to be original nor stylizing the shapes of yesterday, but something obvious: "You can cheat with pleats, but with simple dresses, there's no way," said Madame Esther.

The young man on the balcony had become the Parisian wonder boy. According to a 1965 *Women's Wear Daily* headline, "Chanel Is the Greatest. Castillo Is Better. Madame Grès Is Couture. Yves Is Today." "Saint Laurent's Star Is Rising Again," observed *The Herald Tribune* the same year. France had always responded to Yves Saint Laurent with enthusiasm tempered by patriotic hesitation, due to the presence of American capital, and bad memories of the Algerian War. But now his success was complete. As *Marie Claire* wrote, "America made him a star. In France, we didn't know if Saint Laurent owed this special place to his personality or to his talent as a couturier. Today, we applaud America's choice: Saint Laurent's latest collection is a marvel of youth and style." He was witty: along with homages to Mondrian and Poliakoff, he showed a white mink tied with black imitation leather (the sausage fur) and a babushka-bride, made out of 150 balls of wool and six meters of ribbon.

Now, according to Patrick Thévenon,[4] he had "Ringo's hair, John's mischievous-ness, George's style, and Paul's success: he's the Beatle on Rue Spontini." Although he had once perfected Balenciaga-style mystery, he now appeared around the city without giving up his seductive charm. He showed up incognito at the *My Fair Lady* Ball Hélène Rochas gave in September 1965 at the Grande Cascade Waterfall in the Bois de Boulogne. Henri Sauguet had composed music for the queen of perfume. The film, with costumes and sets by Cecil Beaton, was one of the year's hits. In boas, straw boaters, striped suits, and ostrich feathers, all the youth of Castel arrived in a greengrocer's truck decorated with damask roses. In a pavilion set up like a Covent Garden pub, the tables were covered with pink satin. The Vicomtesse de Ravenel was spotted under a ribboned straw hat, Pierre Cardin was seen in a white tuxedo, and Dany Robin wore mousseline frills. Excited girls with feathers in their hair danced the polka and the jerk.

Yves Saint Laurent had conquered this village of the seventh arrondissement, which scorned cocktail party chatter and small talk. Times had changed: they got together at nine for drinks with friends and had dinner on Spanish time in Parisian bistros: Allard and Benoît, where the checkered tablecloths, the *tête de veau* with *sauce ravigote,* and the spirited waiters were "way more fun" than the great temples of gastronomy with fine silver and maître d's.

Socializing was now based on simplicity: they gave up boring elegant soirées for enchanting parties where all the young people had fun. Yves Saint Laurent designed a point d'esprit dress for young Sybille de Vandeuvre, whose grandmother threw her a ball for her eighteenth birthday. The room was decorated with a riot of flowers: hortensia bushes, beds of azaleas, and an arbor covered with bouquets of daisies. At another enchanted evening, the Château de Ferrières was draped in tulle and chairs gilded the old English garden: shining in the white dress that Yves Saint Laurent made for her, Baronne Guy de Rothschild welcomed her 1,500 guests, including Maria Callas. The crystal chandeliers were ablaze with candles, and the stone urns were overflowing with white flowers. A ghost ship passed over the lake.

"The world has become young—I want to do the same," said Hélène Rochas, one of Yves Saint Laurent's friends and admirers. She added, "Chanel had the idea of modernity, Yves had the idea of the street." When Yves was at Dior, she had been one of the few clients who ordered the black leather suit that "ennobled leather." Now she naturally adopted "simple skirts that weren't at all dry or artificial" that were seen in *Vogue,* and she continued to follow Yves, just as she followed the Beatles, Sagan, modern painting, and all those people who taught her that boredom was no longer tolerable. "I realized that I had to sign on to these developments and listen to the world instead of resisting it," said this woman who came up with a new language for her enduring style. She had blond hair, lips delicately pearled with pink, and a face that matched her supple and regular body. She resembled the beautiful ladies of François I's court, whose limpid enchantment was celebrated by the Fontainebleau School, or Diane de Poitiers.

On the night of Rochas's *My Fair Lady* Ball, a man in a tuxedo smoked a pipe near Baronne de Vandeuvre. He sported a gigantic moustache made from a straw broom and a black bow tie that was almost a foot wide. The newspaper *Détective* recognized him as "the most elegant man in Paris": Yves Saint Laurent.

Later, when Yves created a series of comics for adults, he would have the heroine, Vilaine Lulu, or Naughty Lulu, say, "I love me, I love me not." For now, he had dinner at Maxim's, danced at Régine's, and took exercise classes from Hélène Rochas's private instructor. To sum up, he was temporarily disconnected from his Oran past.

He seemed to distance himself from his mother, even as he began to resemble her by becoming just as fashionable. The gardener in Oran had died. In July 1962, the Mathieu-Saint-Laurents had definitively left Oran, obliged to travel separately in the chaos following the Algerian population's strong vote for independence. Lucienne recalled that difficult time: "I had to leave by way of Mostaganem. They stuck me on a boat filled with sheep. Fortunately, the captain gave me his room. When I got to Marseille, they brought out my car. It was terrible." Yves usually was hard only on himself, in relation to his work, but he could be insensitive to his family. "Come on, don't play repatriate!" Yet he still felt an indestructible link to his mother, and he saw how this relationship enhanced his artistic image. Yves Saint Laurent had assigned the roles. In interviews, he gave his mother a glamorous significance (she was the one who gave him a book on Mondrian "one night"), perversely irritating Pierre Bergé, who was relegated to the role of the surly son-in-law who didn't understand anything about women's intimate secrets.

Pierre said, "Yves's language is not that of speech." Yves communicated in a different way. "Knowing Yves Saint Laurent was knowing a great French artist," declared Philippe Collin, who was then Louis Malle's assistant. "I think his relations with women are more classically simple. Women were his craft."

The young couturier, who straddled the Right and Left Banks, moved through Paris with a grace that astonished society women and actresses. He was what the Americans called a "crazy fashion success." And they were all there at Rue Spontini to applaud his success: Jane Fonda, Leslie Caron, Catherine Deneuve—who was no longer the young girl from Auteuil or the single mother from *The Umbrellas of Cherbourg*, but a dazzling blond who took flight in the photos of David Bailey, her husband. Elsa Martinelli, who lived in Paris, Rome, and Saint-Tropez, would pose in *Vogue* with her false eyelashes and a stunning dress in crepe with gold embroidered sleeves by YSL.

His apartment was also changing with the times. In the dining room, white-lacquered Regency chairs surrounded a Saarinen Formica tulip table. A seventeenth-century Chinese checkers set was placed next to a kinetic sculpture by Jean Chall. This minimalist décor contrasted sharply with fellow couturier Castillo's museum-like rooms, where the bedroom was covered with gouaches by Modigliani, Matisse, Cocteau, and Bérard, and the dining room was filled with Neoclassical vermilion. Pierre Balmain had one of the most famous collections of Greek Tanagra figurines in Europe. In his bourgeois-style, wood-paneled rooms, hundreds of Gallé vases and Chinese porcelain figures were displayed in glass cases. Yves Saint Laurent was more bohemian.

In Yves's place, amethysts, rock crystals, jasper, agate, and onyx were spread throughout the rooms, on low Knoll tables, bookshelves, and even on the floor. "I only like surrounding myself with objects that attract me by their size or their feel. I hate the collector's mentality: it's the death of the object."[5] Pierre Bergé, on the other hand, was concerned about giving a more Parisian touch to the apartment, combining objects with a sense of dramatic placement that put a Mesopotamian urn next to a watercolor by Sonia Delaunay on top of a Boulle Regency chest of drawers. Who inspired him in the art of decoration? "The Noailles. And also Christian Dior, a man of taste whom I respect a lot." One could tell that Bergé had methodically observed Roger Vivier's apartment. Vivier, on the other hand, collected, he said, "while having fun. The way I conceive of interior design may seem sophisticated, but in fact it's utterly simple: seek out beauty and the elegance of form that is justified by its very universal nature."

It was clear that Yves Saint Laurent's apartment was very connected to the couture house. Pierre Bergé, who admired Chanel, wanted to make it a salon—a place for high society guests, professional connections, and friends that would artistically make people forget that forty years before, couturiers were viewed only as tradespeople: "When Yves gave a cocktail party, I welcomed the guests," said Yvonne de Peyerimhoff. "Once everyone got there, I left: you should never get too close to the people you work for."

On a more personal level, the Saint Laurent clique was already getting established. A new woman joined who would play a key role: Clara Saint. This redheaded heiress who was born in Santiago, Chile, and was rich enough not to show it was a serious ballet lover. Her name appeared in the newspapers on June 16, 1961: she helped Nureyev stay in France. Questioned by two officials from the Soviet embassy who asked him to return to the USSR—when he was about to leave for London with the Kirov Ballet—the young dancer shouted in Le Bourget airport, "I want freedom," thereby renouncing, at age twenty-two, the possibility of ever returning to his country. Clara introduced this "winged dancer" into the Parisian milieu that was like her family—at a time when everyone, from Giacometti to Jean-Pierre Léaud, met up at La Coupole. She still wore Chanel when she met Pierre and Yves, with whom she immediately became close. She was able to handle them effortlessly, listening to one without bothering the other. She always saw them together. Wearing one of the "astonishingly modern" navy dresses tailor-made for her on Rue Spontini, she would introduce them to people, including Margot Fonteyn, Philippe Collin, and Jean-Paul Rappeneau. She drew Yves and Pierre into this Left Bank world whose regulars, such as Charlotte Aillaud (the sister of Juliette Gréco and the wife of the architect Émile Aillaud), collected "crazy," "funny," "quirky" things, like a desk shaped like a submarine or sheep with cast-iron feet who had escaped from the Lalannes' surrealist bestiary. They all hung around with "amazing" people, united by the same lack of passion that they nonchalantly displayed, annoyed by whatever was too noisy or new, and which made the people across from them say: "Why did he put up a Zao Wou-Ki in his hallway? No one gets it!"

Clara's dog was named Joke and her fiancé Thadée. He was a writer who didn't publish, but filled up black notebooks, played pinball in cafés, and spoke "only to children and dogs." (Clara, who had never worked, would become the publicist for Saint Laurent Rive Gauche in 1966, doing the job as others welcome friends or host parties: with the natural distinction of the wife she would never be.)

Yves Saint Laurent had rejoined his era. In 1965, he designed clothes for Sophia Loren in *Arabesque*, the extraordinary film by Stanley Donen in which the heroine, a collector of thigh-high boots, takes off with her Eastern lover on an incredible chase. Who can forget the moment when she climbs up on her mare and her brown dress pulls up to reveal her perfect thigh? Science-fiction comics took over the movies: Joseph Losey filmed *Modesty Blaise* and Vadim made *Barbarella*. Movies were pop.

Roland Petit commissioned Yves to make costumes for *Adage et Variations* as well as *Notre-Dame de Paris*, two ballets performed at the Opéra in December 1965. Dressed as a student, he attended the rehearsals, and soon tore up his romantic costumes, then stayed up all night to design more. In colors recalling stained-glass windows, they matched the sparse choreography, which avoided any bohemian or gothic elements. Thus, in *Notre-Dame de Paris*, the slender Claire Motte (Esmeralda) with gold rings wore a white tunic whose plunging neckline laced up with black suggested the eroticism of a young man's bust. The muscles of Jean-Pierre Bonnefous (Phoebus) appeared in transparent tulle crisscrossed with vinyl like a wrestler's uniform. Helmeted, with arching backs, their hips strung with straps with leather shells attached, the king's knights wore red, white, and black bodysuits in a bold move that was generally praised by critics. For *Le Figaro Littéraire*, this world of color was reminiscent of "Christian Bérard's costumes," while for *Le Monde* it was more like "the uniforms of motocross riders."

It was as if Yves were giving up his internal visions to project images collected from television, magazines, drugstores, and elsewhere directly onto his era. And yet, "He had never been in a supermarket!" Richard Salomon, who bought Saint Laurent from J. Mack Robinson, remembered with astonishment. Salomon, a distinguished businessman and Brown University graduate, loved Paris, where he had once lived in the mansion of his uncle, the owner of Coty, while taking classes at the Sorbonne. In the fall of 1965, Yves Saint Laurent traveled to the United States to launch his perfume Y. For ten days, Richard Salomon was Yves's official tour guide. At the supermarket, he saw women in Mondrian dresses pushing their shopping carts. Amazingly, Yves's response was, "That's the mark of success!" This almost agoraphobic couturier went on a whirlwind tour of San Francisco, Los Angeles, Dallas, Houston, and Atlanta, the hometown of J. Mack Robinson, where, defiantly, he made a scene. He left in a huff when he discovered that the store windows that Rich's department store gave to his line looked, with their medallions and pastels, like those of Dior.

In *Les Choses*, which won the Prix Renaudot in 1965, Georges Perec depicted a generation that was born to buy. Yves Saint Laurent spoke to this generation by name: "We're starting with dresses, then we'll tackle fabrics, men's fashion, and furniture. I'm convinced that we're on the threshold of an art of living that will be as important as the 1925 International Exhibition of Modern Decorative and Industrial Arts in Paris [which launched the Art Deco style to the public]. Down with the Ritz, down with the Moon, long live the street!"[6]

He already idealized the street: it was his escape. He remembered exquisite moments like the inconsolable Naughty Lulu dreaming of "Jojo Savora, a naughty boy, an exquisite toy" and going off with a vigorous firefighter with a moustache whose love she won by setting her own house on fire. The street was an anonymous world where he could lose himself within the boundaries of his celebrity, a role he already knew by heart: "I'm sick of being young, rich, and famous," he complained one day to a female friend who ran into him sunbathing at the Deligny swimming pool. Yves was also like Naughty Lulu when, like Narcissus, she looked at her reflection in the river and commented, "What a beautiful child!" Or when she looked in the mirror and exclaimed, "I'm as good as gold!" A few pages later she appeared in the guise of a red demon riding a little cloud: "I've finally found myself." He seemed to enjoy being adored by women just as much as being hounded by men. Unlike Lulu, he never really did anything stupid. As a teenager, he wrote impassioned texts in his journals, denouncing "the terrifying gray-uniformed cops," a justice system "that judges and condemns poverty." He defined that system at the time as "the ludicrous and unpleasant parody where sworn lies order poverty to tell the truth, the whole truth, and nothing but the truth." There were times when his love of the street made him cut loose a bit too much. A fan of James Dean, he sometimes had a tendency to see the road as a giant track. On May 4, 1966, Yves Saint Laurent was summoned to traffic court after his black Volkswagen Beetle hit another car, slightly injuring the driver. The judge was easygoing: the fine was only 400 francs.

He was close friends with Nureyev, who became the best-paid dancer in the world in 1965. Nureyev made the cover of *Time*, an honor he shared that year with Jeanne Moreau, Ho Chi Minh, the Vietnam War, Martin Luther King Jr., and the computer. Four years earlier, who could have guessed that Nureyev would partner with the most famous star in Europe, Margot Fonteyn, the wife of the ambassador Roberto Arias and the recipient of countless distinctions and honors? Yves Saint Laurent venerated her. Nureyev and Fonteyn were the most prestigious couple in ballet: at Covent Garden, Londoners lined up for hours to see them in *Swan Lake*, *La Bayadère*, *Le Corsaire*, and *Raymonda*—all the ballets that the Royal Ballet proudly took to New York and then as far away as Baalbek, Lebanon. When they performed in Paris in November 1965, the entrance of the Théâtre des Champs-Élysées looked like a casino. Scalpers were selling tickets for 5,000 francs apiece. That night, white mink trailed from the most beautiful shoulders in the world. The Bégum, Callas, Ludmilla Tchérina, Ira von Fürstenberg, Yvette Chauviré—they all paid for the best seats. Rudolf Nureyev and Margot Fonteyn danced for over an hour, to the applause of an ecstatic crowd. Yves Saint Laurent met up with the dancers afterward at Maxim's, and they ended the night at New Jimmy's.

Yves Saint Laurent and Nureyev had many things in common. They both found fulfillment through their professions, with the same iron will that makes hypersensitive people invulnerable: "You'll see, little sister, one day, I'll be a great dancer, the greatest dancer in the world," Rudi vowed as a child. Like Yves Saint Laurent, he devoted himself to his passion despite his father's disapproval. "Dance elevates the soul and means you are able to create movement forever," Nureyev said.[7] His mischievous eyes peeked out from beneath a wide-brimmed hat and he wore his hair like the Rolling Stones. "He looked like the kind of British gentleman you see nowadays in Lord Snowdon's circle," Le Figaro commented. Though they were always eager to move as fast as possible, they both had a rigorous approach to their professions that brought them back to the sources of their art and made them observe the rules taught by the greats: Chanel and Serge Lifar. Additionally, each had a kind of artistic sensibility that attracted the protection and respect of mature women—with Margot Fonteyn, through her grace and generosity, as the most noble example. "When you dance with Nureyev, you simply have to submit," she said. Yves Saint Laurent and Rudolf Nureyev also complemented each other with their differences. While Yves suffered from shyness that was sometimes paralyzing, Nureyev made his body into a work of art. "I'd like people watching me dance to feel the same thing they would before a great painting," said Nureyev, sounding like Yves Saint Laurent talking about his dresses.[8] Yves tested himself only with a pencil; physical strength was what he never had and what he admired in Nureyev.

One year later, in July 1966, Yves Saint Laurent celebrated his tenth collection by flying the colors of Pop Art: a bubble-gum pink heart, a two-tone jersey suit, Campbell's red and gray, and a bright green dress with a purple collar. Once again, America stimulated all consumer dreams. And in America, Op Art triumphed. At the Museum of Modern Art, the exhibition The Responsive Eye was the hit of 1965: lines, shimmering, sparkling surfaces, juxtapositions of planes and primary colors in the work of Stella and Kelly, and checkerboards, static black and white waves from Bridget Riley. Paintings by Vasarely would soon be reproduced on dresses sold at the supermarket.

From then on, Yves Saint Laurent would prove to the world that couture wasn't just about technique, but also reflective of the times. In this case, the chaotic 1960s as highlighted by Warhol: counterculture, subculture, superstars, drugs, lights, and discos. Invisible elegance gave way to the electric light of flashbulbs, and theatrical artifice was replaced by the neon of advertising. Superlatives were a substitute for criticism in a fast-moving time that consumed everything it saw. Yves Saint Laurent made fashion into a medium: he reproduced paintings on his fabrics the way Warhol depicted everyday life on his canvases, starting with press photos that were enlarged and silkscreened. The couturier became a star. For the third time since 1958, Yves made the cover of *Life*.

Inspired by Wesselmann's *Great American Nude* series, a pink trompe-l'oeil body stood out on a column of black jersey. "Wear everything that looks like you: haute couture, like Art, expresses the whole meaning of an era, everything you are feeling. Express your pop opinions on a face dress," *Le Jardin des Modes* excitedly advised its readers in September 1966. For these new times, Yves changed models. He chose a twenty-year-old Danish woman who looked fourteen, with hair as straight as straw: Birgit Frostholm. Next there was a Swedish model, Ulla. Nordic girls with soft skin and long legs replaced the divas. His models' eyes were always shaded in black, but their mouths were pink and their skin light. It was the "Little Ritz Girl" look.[9] From the Factory to Carnaby Street, blonds were in fashion: Anita Pallenberg, Pattie Boyd, George Harrison's wife, Edie Sedgwick, the heroine of the Andy Warhol movies *Vinyl, Vacuum*, and *Poor Little Rich Girl*. Yves Saint Laurent tacked up a photo of Sylvie Vartan on the big bulletin board in the studio. The divine brunettes of the 1950s were gone: their statuesque beauty no longer fit the movement of the time. Time had given the *premières* their revenge on the models of the previous decade, who were a little too sure of themselves. The *premières* would say, "We knew her, she drank whisky, and she ended up drinking cheap red wine in Montmartre." The men of the couture world would wrap their disgust in silk paper: "She's gained a little weight."

Yves was thirty. His preference for an androgynous look was emerging. The models appeared as ingénues or little lords. In 1966, Yves Saint Laurent's navy style would embody the male-female body. Once again, we see the influence of Chanel, who strung her pearls on top of big sailor pants in the 1920s. Like her, Yves Saint Laurent repurposed men's clothing. But his sea was more hectic, more urban: the Saint Laurent peacoat, traditionally worn by northern fishermen, was also the coat worn by Nico, the singer of the Velvet Underground, who danced at the Dom in New York in 1966 dressed like a boy in a beige cashmere sweater. Functional and sophisticated, the navy look would never leave the Saint Laurent cruise ship: from one season to the next, he created variations: the peacoat dress (1967), the Lurex sweater for music hall sailors (1974), the jersey sailor shirt with disco sparkles (1979), the officer's suit (1988). These infinite variations on the same theme followed the inspirations of the day. Yves Saint Laurent loved spending weekends with Pierre Bergé in the midst of the menhirs in Carnac or among the rocks of Concarneau, a city surrounded by fifteenth-century granite walls. He brought back with him a burst of inspiration from the sea air. And elegant women turned into old sea dogs. In 1966, the year when Claude Lelouch's *A Man and a Woman* won the Palme d'Or at Cannes, Yves buttoned up his pea jackets with golden anchors and launched his eveningwear sweaters. "Yves Fires a Naval Salute" was the *Women's Wear Daily* headline. "Yves Saint Laurent Hits the Jackpot," read the headline in *Candide*. Catherine Deneuve went out in a long sheath sweater with navy blue and white stripes. The sequined fabric sparkled like mother-of-pearl shells.

"Elegance has changed. Allure has taken its place. A look that's mannered, starched, or too perfect irritates us. Today, a well-dressed woman is someone who can construct a certain harmony between her clothes and her personality," he said as he saw these women who loved to wear their hair down and rejected both the science-fiction look and the push-up bra necklines of the past in order to slip into dresses with neat little armholes and simple collars, which one slid into with a quick zip. "Where are we going?" *Vogue* asked in March 1966. "Toward a faster, livelier, bolder woman. We see a lot of her legs, it's true, but also her arms, and often her back....We're moving toward a kind of fashion that has never been so much based on the body. For a few years, we have seen fashion become simplified, freeing itself from details and building itself very rigorously around the body. Not the modified female body, with the cinched waist, the lifted breasts, the swelled hips, but the real female body as it is naked. We don't ask fashion to amaze us or couturiers to shape us anymore. We ask them to obey us, to help us, to give us our freedom." This new way of being had no sleeves and no restraints, and it became even more liberated with flat heels and sheer pantyhose that Dim sold 3.5 million pairs of in 1965. Yves Saint Laurent added a touch of mystery and ambiguity to this new arsenal of seduction. His designs had that certain *je ne sais quoi* with which Paris titillated puritanical America, by adding charm to comfort. Perhaps because in Paris there were roving hearts who put on dresses so that men could take them off. Jeanne Moreau sang, "No ring on my finger, just a silk thread."

Yves Saint Laurent designed sweetly extravagant looks, airy creatures in baggy cigaline pants and gold mules, with moonlit faces and Pearly Silver eyelids. In January 1966, his models wore crystal slippers by Roger Vivier—translucent shoes with rhinestone heels. That year, twenty clients would be his Cinderellas, among them Marlene Dietrich, Farah Diba, the Duchess of Windsor, Michèle Morgan, and Sophia Loren. "Yves Designs for Eve," the American press observed. His mousseline dresses with a little something underneath and embroidery in all the right places made people exclaim, "Oh!" Increasingly, Yves Saint Laurent's designs yearned for sun, heat, and liberty, such as the series of short evening dresses from summer 1966 (numbers 99, 100, 101) in silk organdy that was navy or flesh colored, embroidered with gold sequins whose zigzags covered the breasts and the upper legs. The Americans called it the "nude dress." The wedding dress that season was a huge organdy scarf tied around the hips. Sewn inside, mousseline flowers bloomed into a bouquet around the body.

"We gossiped, we laughed, we said silly things. We were united by good cheer. We were curious about everything. We saw the same ridiculousness in the same things," recalled Charlotte Aillaud, the wife of the famous architect. She concluded, "Yves liked to see his dresses." A close-knit group would get together at his apartment on Place Vauban on Sundays, with Philippe Collin, the photographer Jeanloup Sieff, Mireille Darc, Fernando Sanchez (who lived on Place Furstemberg), and Clara Saint, whose apartment was also a meeting place. "These were the Place Vauban tea parties," said Philippe Collin. It was a family atmosphere: sunk back into the cushions, the clan discussed opera performances in between remarks on people in the fashion world, such as Cardin or Givenchy, who was called "Givenchère."[10] Late at night, they'd go to eat at the Chinese restaurant on Rue du Mont-Thabor, unless Pierre decided to whip up some spaghetti. Often, the night would end at Régine's. "Those were the Naughty Lulu years. Yves would play us the latest 45s he'd gotten at the record store. He would show us the clothing sketches he had made during the week. He was an impressive observer. We had gone to a medieval restaurant on Rue Jacob, with parchment menus and rustic décor. In five minutes, he had noticed all the details. He had a great ear and a perfect eye," said Philippe Collin. In fact, in "La Bonne Histoire de Poulaines," Lulu appears as a Cathar innkeeper. She serves suggestive dishes in period helmets: monk in a jacket, Charlemagne cotton candy, the pilgrim's dream, and so on. Lulu punishes a customer who has knocked over a glass, spilling cider on the new tablecloth: "Wicked imp, you will be punished, to the dungeon, to the dungeon!" Lulu is a little devil, and her author took care to specify that "any resemblance to persons living or dead is completely intentional. All these adventures are based on real events." The tone is very caustic, almost cruel.

Yves Saint Laurent started writing the Naughty Lulu comics in 1955. The tone never changed. The events and names can be used to date the stories. Like her author, Naughty Lulu experienced her era to its fullest. As soon as one story is over, Naughty Lulu starts her life over elsewhere, in a different way. By turns she is black jacket Naughty Lulu, a hip singer, Lulu XIV, Lulupoleon, Lulu Carmen, Lady Lulu, Patriot Lulu, Lulu with a thousand and one facets who also needs something to battle against so she can put herself back together. By looking outside herself she is able to forget herself and can make her cutting remarks. Naughty Lulu plays on the beach in a metal dress: "I'm a sausage, but a sausage by Rabanne." Her big target is Courrèges. One day, Naughty Lulu decides to go to a debutante ball and goes to see a new couturier. A woman garbed in white welcomes her. Even her boxing gloves are white. "Here everything is constructed," says the saleswoman. "We are architects. Our god is Le Corbusier—it's modern." Naughty Lulu is annoyed by the racket of tom-toms and an oompah band. "Enough, enough," she shouts. "I only like black." Grabbing two white inkwells, she pours the ink all over the white carpet of the beautiful white salon. "Oh! You want to play? Here you go, vile vestal virgins!" She dips her hands in black ink, then proceeds to smear it all over the saleswomen's faces. Her governess takes her hand: "Come, little Lulu, we should just go see Laurent Saint Yves." A big red heart appears above Naughty Lulu's head: "Yes, yes, yes, I'm sure he'll understand me."

8 / THE RIVE GAUCHE SPIRIT, FROM *BELLE DE JOUR* TO ANDROGYNY

A woman in tears because the last coat was sold. Tags torn off in the turmoil. An outstretched arm struggling to fit into a knockout dress in studded jersey. The other arm won't go in. Too fat. Breasts and hips, too big. Not Saint Laurent enough. Furies in pantyhose who grab men's silk ties, shirt dresses, big gypsy-style chain belts, short two-tone kilts, skirts in suede calfskin. "Do what Mireille Darc does, come at lunchtime," *Vogue* advised. Saint Laurent Rive Gauche. The first name had disappeared. But his full-length portrait by Arroyo presided over the Plexiglas stands. With his arms crossed over his black suit, he seemed to watch his double: one thrives on the Right Bank, and the other on the Left, at 21 Rue de Tournon. All these women wanted a little something by Saint Laurent.

Pierre Cardin was the pioneer of ready-to-wear in France. But it's not all that significant that he came first. With Cardin, it was just an experiment. But by personally overseeing the design, production, and distribution of the ready-to-wear line he launched, Yves Saint Laurent gave ready-to-wear a good reputation. "With him, everything changed," Pierre Bergé said proudly. Until then, ready-to-wear was simply an economic necessity; Saint Laurent added a new pleasure to it, that of designing for his era and astonishing it. "Ready-to-wear," he said, "isn't just a last resort for couture. It's the future. We know we're dressing women who are younger and more receptive. With them, we can easily be bolder." Yves Saint Laurent sowed envy completely innocently. He had a way of telling a story exactly right, of offering women a thousand charming Parisian items whose attractiveness he knew since he had designed and arranged similar things in the Dior boutique nearly ten years earlier. "Rive Gauche? We were already dreaming about it at Le Fiacre," recalls Anne-Marie Muñoz, the director of the haute couture studio. In 1957, the whole group saw Billy Wilder's *Love in the Afternoon* in a dingy little movie theater in Saint-Germain-des-Prés. How could he have forgotten that scene where Gary Cooper, playing an aging playboy, finds himself under a table in the Ritz holding the little shoe of a girl in pants, Audrey Hepburn, who pretends to be a sophisticate: "There is something *rive gauche* about you."

It was the first time that a couturier opened a store that was completely independent from his couture salons. It quickly became a Parisian club by day. With nylon carpeting and Barcelona chairs by Mies van der Rohe, the interior design was by Isabelle Hebey, a functionalist with shock power, the designer for all well-known Parisians who took pride in not having any "Louis" furniture in their homes, such as Hector de Galard, publisher Christian Bourgois, and advertising executive Pierre Grimblat. Hebey had short hair and was sure of herself in a suit cut by a tailor from Valence. She likely considered steel and laminate the modern answer to wood paneling, and her motto might have been, "If I die, the drawings are clear." She had been contacted by *Vogue* the previous year to write a story on the apartment that Yves Saint Laurent and Pierre Bergé shared. After the article, Yves called her up: "I'd like a warm boutique, not cold, but contemporary. A store that makes people want to come in and touch."

Out of a long, narrow space that had been a bakery, she created a sparse boutique with red and black lacquer. The clothes were hung in the open and there were wall racks for scarves and belts, along with pedestals with clear jewelry boxes on top. "I didn't imagine Biba for Saint Laurent. I couldn't help but think that he was a couturier. At that time, other designers' dresses were hidden in armoires."

Women entered, they touched, they loved it. He was the only one of the great designers to combine the mystery of the golden genius with prices designed for the general public. Parisian women embraced ready-to-wear: they had their star boutiques, such as Laura (Sonia Rykiel) and Dorothée Bis, and they even started using brand names to describe the staples of their wardrobes. In 1966, they began saying "a Cacharel" for a blouse, "a Harry Lans" for a jacket, "a Korrigan" for a sweater, just as the French still today call a trench coat "a Burberry" or a polo shirt "a Lacoste." To this comfortable familiarity, Rive Gauche added something attractive and exciting: a belt was no longer a restraint, but a jewel, Le Smoking became "the rage of Paris," as the Americans put it, and a dress became known as *une petite Saint-Laurent*—something simple enough to be worn on ordinary occasions, but special enough that even a widower would notice it: "I think you're very elegant. Do you like money?"[1] These chaste dresses and these skimming skirts protected the body while they also excited a desire to possess it, not because it offered itself, but precisely because it refused to.

From the beginning, the Rive Gauche style had just a little scent of the forbidden: far from the curves that were properly emphasized by a straight skirt and a twin set, you could already see the silhouette of a woman who didn't follow the rules, a lover with a childlike body. The store opened on September 26, 1966, with Catherine Deneuve as its patron. The actress was living in London, but returned to Paris to act in Luis Buñuel's *Belle de Jour*, in which she played the role of a well-off bourgeois housewife who, every afternoon, becomes the most in-demand worker at a house of ill repute. Author Joseph Kessel had previously refused to sell the rights to the novel from which the film was adapted, but eventually he gave in.

Catherine Deneuve appeared for the first time in her Saint Laurent suits, showcased at the height of her power by this surrealist comedy. From that moment, the cold, blond beauty definitively abandoned her role as a *demoiselle de Rochefort* for her own role, which she would no longer leave: "Catherine Deneuve is one of the women who move me the most, because she has a radiant beauty and she is the greatest French star today....I think we have liked each other very much ever since the first film for which I designed clothes for her. It was *Belle de Jour* by Luis Buñuel." It took Romy Schneider a long time to leave behind the image of the ball gowns she wore in *Sissi*. And Brigitte Bardot was still associated with her dark sunglasses and the invasion of her private life by photographers. In 1966, Deneuve, the young girl from Auteuil, affirmed the sense of artifice that made her seem both close and elusive. Neither her red suit nor her black vinyl raincoat seemed to weigh on her shoulders: they grazed her, revealed her for who she was. Not one woman, but an infinity of women, with a natural abundance to which she lent all the charm of artifice, a false innocence that made her as desirable as forbidden fruit. "With strangers—it must be horrible!" Without corset or ruffles, Belle de Jour is a blond who earns a good living and whose little vinyl coat the redheads envy. "Carducci?" one asks jealously, looking at the brand. "You have expensive tastes." But another sneers, "Don't sweat it, it's a knock-off."

At the store's grand opening, Catherine Deneuve looked as if she were on set. She arrived in sheer stockings, patent-leather loafers, and a peacoat with gold buttons. Her outfit shed subtle light on the character to whom Geneviève Page, the madam hiding behind the sign reading "Madame Anaïs, Seamstress," seemed to say, "You are nice and fresh, that's the kind that does well here. I bet it's the first time you've worked."

This goody-two-shoes side was a facet of her style. It was expressed in the spot-on, unexaggerated perversity of a black dress decorated with white quilted details that doesn't press against her body, but manages to look both proper and sultry at the same time. Michel Piccoli, the Valmont of *Belle de Jour*, takes it off: "Pretty dress. You look like a precocious schoolgirl." Clothing played a special role, and Buñuel enjoyed filming it. He seemed to suggest that under the polished appearance of Deneuve's character, fetishes overwhelm her. It's the hand searching for the zipper under the prostitute's collar. "You're starting to excite me and you won't let me kiss you."

Yves Saint Laurent designed clothes for Catherine Deneuve in this role with an intimate understanding of the story, the "voluntary servitude" about which Proust wrote, calling it "the beginning of liberty."[2] By entering Buñuel's vision, Yves Saint Laurent restored his own with greater sincerity, as if he could become more himself by admiring a master who was a genius of perversity. In an early scene in which Belle de Jour is thrown out of the carriage by her fiancé, tied up to a tree, and whipped by the coachmen, Catherine Deneuve recalled, "He had designed a jersey dress for me, but inside he had put a strip of Velcro. It was as if he was preparing me for the role, by suggesting a particular way of acting it....When the dress is torn away, the noise of the Velcro immediately creates the atmosphere of a rape."

Rive Gauche didn't express a luxury of wealth, but one of attitude: clear shapes, free colors, a refusal of gossip and simpering airs. Yves Saint Laurent got rid of suit blouses, little scarves, little chains, and hair clips. He replaced blouses with t-shirts. He rejected the innocent look, giving the Parisian woman an authenticity that was totally separate from the popular traditional lace or the 1967 version of Madame Bovary filmed by Chabrol in *The Unfaithful Wife*. Yves's new woman was neither the spoiled woman of loose morals of the 1950s, nor the heroine in fake Chanel who discreetly yawns before her *canard à l'orange*. Nothing pastel or quaint. Just this Rive Gauche look, which made a woman seem to free herself from her clothing, like a chameleon—a caterpillar during the day, and a butterfly at night, Chanel would have said.

Although he started with dresses and pantsuits, he gradually (with the pantsuit and the black color palette of 1967) drew women toward the smoking rooms where only tomboys and dandies ventured. Saint Laurent wasn't about stealing the shirt from men, but giving the shirt back to men. He dressed women like his male heroes: he offered them Brummel's vests, Dorian Gray's golden curls, the scarves, make-up, jabots, and ruffs of Watteau's Gilles, and the stacked heels and jewelry of flamboyant men.

Yves Saint Laurent's Now Look responded to women's situation and their struggles, but it spoke more to women as individuals than as an organized group. While Valerie Solanas proposed "cutting up men" in her SCUM Manifesto, a radical feminist tract, Yves offered them a much more powerful weapon: ambiguity that electrifies mystery. In an approach that was the polar opposite of that of Courrèges and Cardin, who considered a woman's body to be a vase and imagined clothing as shapes and geometry, Yves Saint Laurent saw the body as a vine, a serpent, ready to move seductively, as a changeable being like Virginia Woolf's *Orlando*. "His form combined in one the strength of a man and a woman's grace." Hence Yves Saint Laurent employed a touch of melancholy in creating this portrait of the feminine charms that he appreciated in men, and the masculine virtues that gay men love so much in their female friends. With a sharp, extremely expressive line, he led fashion into the terrain of adventurous sexuality, from the perverted paths of Violette Leduc's lesbians with the look of junior-high school students to the soft-skinned young men of Saint-Germain-des-Prés. "Beauty? Not interested. What counts is seduction, shock. What you feel. It's purely subjective. Personally, I'm more sensitive to movement than to glances, shapes, or anything else." Yet he still had models who were his abiding "knockouts," with deep physical beauty that he would later enhance in his orientalist travels. His first Rive Gauche collection took a clear and uncompromising view of the female shape. If women with full figures couldn't fit into his clothing, it was because his lines expressed this sentiment of Proust's: "If loose women attract us so little, it's not because they are less beautiful than others, it's because they're too easy."[3]

For his Rive Gauche collections, he worked on only one model, Danielle Varenne, a redhead, and said that when he imagined a dress on her, he didn't think of the audience at a fashion show but instead "of life." Varenne recalled, "I had a very casual way of walking. Putting on a jacket with your hands in your pockets—no one did that at couture shows. With Yves Saint Laurent, design is osmosis, an understanding between the fabric and the way you move. He draped the fabric until inspiration came. The way you stood helped him to express himself." He got rid of darts on the bust, preferring to add panel lines that were more supple. He chose fabrics that had previously only been used in menswear: canvas for safari jackets, woolen military cloth for coats. Like Chanel, he was always careful to make sure that the buttons buttoned and the pockets were useful: "Pockets are very important. Take two women, both wearing a slim jersey dress. The one who has pockets will immediately have a feeling of superiority over the other. It's an awkward handicap to have to let your arms hang or have to cross them or turn your wedding ring round and round on your finger."

His style encouraged women to play with artifice, with jewelry, with make-up— basically, with the art of appearances. "A woman is only seductive in pants if she wears them with all her femininity. Not like George Sand. Pants are flirtatious, they add charm—they're not a sign of equality or liberation. Liberty and equality aren't bought with a pair of pants, they're a state of mind." The 1968 pantsuit, tennis-striped jacket and pants worn with a mousseline blouse, were the height of the IL style, which was masculine and feminine at the same time: Yves wanted to find an equivalent of the men's pantsuit for women. With Rive Gauche, women could all be the same while each remained different: "Now there is women's fashion that comes directly from men's fashion, and [expresses] a need to be comfortable, to use their clothing and their taste, without trying to impersonate them, or copy them, or emasculate them. Simply to join them."[4] In his sketches, the silhouettes were now face to face, about to meet each other, to clash. Before, they judged each other, asking, "Who is more beautiful?" With Rive Gauche, they understood each other, were attracted to each other, and observed each other in a couture salon that had become a kind of club where the members recognized one another without needing to be introduced. Paradoxically, this intimacy was justified by the severe elegance of the Saint Laurent name, combined with a strict line, a passion for black, and an economy of detail. You didn't buy Saint Laurent, you *were* Saint Laurent. Françoise Darmon, one of the faithful of "Saint-Lolo," as those in the know had begun to call him, remembered:

> Rive Gauche was an extension of one's attitude. I was submissive enough to get married and later wanted freedom. Everything split open. Saint Laurent marked this break. He was the perfect eye for that time when we wanted to invent the future without destroying all the past; to stay the same and be new. We were dressed in men's suits during the day. And at night, like Oriental women. I loved the huge bows, the necklaces, the woven belts. We weren't butch women or tarts. He made references to so many things. We were both liberated and very feminine. I started on Rue de Tournon. Then I

went to Avenue Victor-Hugo. The saleswoman would call me on the phone. We'd run over. I had blind trust in him. I wore Saint Laurent top to bottom and didn't shop anywhere else. People noticed me for my elegance, but they didn't know why. At a dinner one night, there were three of us wearing the same Saint Laurent dress. But we hadn't accessorized it the same way.

While in life Yves often played the victim, in fashion he took a leader's role and was sure enough of himself to refrain from turning his power into tyranny. He was the only one to tell women, "Wear what looks good on you," with that unforgiving look that they understood.

With Rive Gauche, he became truly interested in the movement of his time, rejecting the too-formal look of high society to express the achievements of a new generation in his clothing: the liberty of the body and the sexual revolution. "Before him, there was something orthopedic about haute couture. At age twenty-five, you didn't see yourself in Balenciaga or Dior. It was for ladies," recalled Claude Berthod, who wrote a classic article for *Elle* at the time under the title "Saint Laurent Coupez pour Nous" (Saint Laurent, Cut for Us).[5] She also met him on *Dim Dam Dom*, a television variety hour that captured the spirit of the years 1965 to 1970 with a quirky patchwork of reporting, songs, and clever references to theater, literature, and fashion. The hosts changed with every episode and included Marie Laforêt, Bernadette Lafont, France Gall, Romy Schneider, Françoise Fabian, and Mireille Darc. Produced by Daisy de Galard, *Dim Dam Dom* (tag line: the meeting place for clever and curious viewers), offered "an hour of attitude and elegance." Its reporting made it, along with *Cinq Colonnes à la Une*, one of the cult shows of the time, despite its very small audience. In January 1968, Saint Laurent appeared on the show and spoke for fifteen minutes about his profession and his era in an unguarded tone. His way of thinking came through in various ways in this interview, as well as through his fashion and his caricatures (such as Naughty Lulu).

"I hate bourgeois women. Their rigidity, their spirit. They always have a brooch pinned somewhere and carefully combed hair," he said in this televised interview, which remained the longest and best-known interview he would do until 1993. "He was wonderfully young," Claude Berthod recalled. "A lot of humor and cheerfulness. We felt that he was unbreakable, but at the same time consumed by disillusionment, a temptation to leave, to escape."

There were now two kinds of fashion sprung from the same dream: inventing an equivalent of the male wardrobe for women. Helping women to be what they were as much as what they were not. A Venus with two faces whose elongated silhouette, the willowy neck and legs, announced the Saint Laurent body, the polar opposite of the "womanly woman" body promoted by Dior. According to Claude Berthod, "Saint Laurent is the first couturier who stimulated women's desire, beyond the regular tailor-made clients. He de-bourgeoisified couture by creating couture clothing for everyday life. He took basic clothes that everyone wore without thinking about them and made them sublime." No luscious busts or blossoming décolletés: "For a woman to be easy to dress, she must have a neck, shoulders, and legs. I'll take care of the rest."[6]

One of Yves's closest friends was Betty Catroux, whom he met in 1967. "It sounds like a joke, but he picked me up at Régine's through a mutual friend," she recalled. Catroux had worked as a model at Chanel for two years, but got into modeling originally just "to make a little cash." Hidden behind her blond bangs, she would pose, but she hated "everything about creating appearances." She was six feet tall, with endless legs that she would stretch out while drinking an Old Fashioned. "I think elegance means finding your style. I found mine, just as my hair found its part, just by following nature....I always wear my hair in a single slim braid on the side. It's like my signature." Her number one accessory: her belts. Number two: her cigarette holder. Her colors were black and brown. Day and night, she lived in a t-shirt and black pants. When she went out, she wore a tuxedo jacket, with nothing underneath. "The more people disguise me artificially, the uglier I am. I hate all those photographers who stick fake jewelry on you everywhere. My kind of attractiveness is totally backward. I'm almost happy to have dirty hair. I almost think it's chic." People often thought she was a young man, which she enjoyed, especially when they thought she was David Bowie.

Out of all the women Yves met who inspired him, Betty had a special place. She was his pal, his close friend, his double. He liked seeing something of himself in her. "His hair was platinum blond. Thin as a rail, with tight jeans. A sublime person," she said. "We looked alike." With him, she would travel everywhere. "I had the best and the funniest part of him....With Yves, you're either very up or very down. We didn't talk about work or fashion. We talked about our moods. Pierre and my husband were the big questioners. But Yves and I never did things deviously. We were pure." With Betty, Yves finally showed his wild side. "Everything important in my life happened at night. Even in dives." She was the first one to wear the couture Le Smoking in high society, with a transparent blouse. At the opera, she was booed.

La Coupole was their cafeteria, the starting point for endless nights. The famous brasserie of the Roaring Twenties became the place to be for young people in Montparnasse in 1968. People who would later say, "May 1968? I missed it all," with a touch of snobbery, nevertheless have deep-seated memories of exceptional nights there. "La Coupole? It was a dream. Now it's just a brasserie."

Rive Gauche was like a gigantic sketchbook of things seen: tall dreamlike creatures in laced-up shirts and black satin pants, handsome boys scribbling their numbers on scraps of paper napkin, cover girls focused on their hot fudge, irritable Lady Janes wearing black felt wide-brimmed hats, mysteries of Paris, stars, ordinary people gasping, "Did you see who's here?," part-time hippies walking across the room with the pretext of a phone call or the need to comb their hair. "Let's talk soon!" La Coupole had its rules and its games. The regulars entered on the right, pushing the swinging doors nonchalantly. There was also the La Coupole attitude: extending your hand while looking over to the side. La Coupole games. Pretending to look for someone, and pretending not to notice anyone, while kissing everyone. César, Sean Flynn (Errol Flynn's son, who devoured a steak tartare every day), Maurice Béjart, Belmondo, Ursula, Giacometti, and Mick Jagger, with whom Yves and Betty had dinner several times. "We were friends, it wasn't serious."

In fact, it would have been a huge mistake to think that Yves would attract the daughters of his clients. They never came. He thought of them when putting two pop art squares on his logo, one red, the other pink. And also when hiring his friends' daughters as saleswomen. They smelled like Y perfume and wore Shetland sweaters and kilts. They looked more like Claude Jade in Truffaut's films than like British model Twiggy, the star of swinging London whose sunset eye make-up was copied all the way to Minneapolis. Why didn't he realize that his clients' daughters weren't looking to SoHo, the New York galleries, Lichtenstein's comics, and Tom Wesselmann's *Bathtub Collage* series as he was? Instead, they were focused on King's Road, Carnaby, mauve pants from Biba, and Mary Quant's lamé vests and mini-mini-skirts. The year Rive Gauche opened, Lady Plunket, aka Mary Quant, was decorated with the Order of the British Empire by Queen Elizabeth II. Her mini-skirts were selling like hotcakes: in 1966, she exported four million pounds' worth of mini-skirts. Girls who had the "knack" wore Mary Quant: "They're prettier than their older sisters, and we're designing for them. They weren't raised eating bread and potatoes like we were."[7]

He wanted to offer them short transparent raincoats made of a synthetic with the sweet name of cigaline. Artists' wives came to buy them for their servants, because the prices were "extraordinarily low."

The designer, whom Americans already found "intellectual," soon understood his mistake. Instinctively, he pulled back, and avoided being taken in by a time period whose excesses he caricatured like Gainsbourg, whose hit at the time was "Qui Est In, Qui Est Out?" His audience was not made up of the adventurous, trendsetting girls, the intrepid co-eds and young women whose smiles were so beautiful that they didn't need to dress up. "A twenty-year-old only needs a t-shirt and jeans. At age thirty she starts to become interesting."

But, once again, youth was a hot topic for fashion journalism. Yves Saint Laurent was totally absent from the raging controversy of the 1960s, the new hemline wars that turned into an international political issue. The Polish Communist party said yes to the mini-skirt, the Dutch Parliament said no, and in Great Britain traffic experts observed unusual traffic slowdowns. It was a fashion success: in 1966, French women were said to have bought 200,000 mini-skirts. The controversy became more radical: "I think it's dirty and shameless. To whom is it supposed to appeal? It's pretentious.... A woman looks old when she shows her knees," said Chanel. French education minister Alain Peyrefitte thought it was "inappropriate in high schools." The conservative press called it a "provocative get-up." Readers also complained: "an affront to modesty," "the mini-skirt is breaking up households." Yves Saint Laurent remained uninvolved and continued to draw fleeting apparitions, little trifles, a profile, a situation, a hat, or Naughty Lulu.

He was not at all a rock-and-roller, either. On the contrary, he started to cultivate the charm of a dandy. He was loyal to his tortoiseshell glasses from Gualdini, but now dared shades of pink and purple, wore Moroccan jewelry on his velvet suits from Renoma, and sported Hilditch & Key socks with elegant Tilbury shoes. "The love that dare not speak its name" had emerged from the shameful shadow that the postwar bourgeoisie had cast over it. The gay man even became a fashionable character, at a time when fashion was no longer about clothes, but about attitude.

Yves Saint Laurent, "the young couture star," agreed to answer the Proust Questionnaire. His greatest flaw? "Shyness." His greatest quality? "My will." The height of misfortune? "Solitude." The height of happiness? "Going to sleep with the people I love." The talent he would have liked to have? "Physical strength." How would he like to die? "Quickly." His favorite person in history? "Chanel." Who would he have liked to be? "A beatnik."[8] On *Dim Dam Dom* he said, "I love my era, I love nightclubs, even though I don't go out very often, I love what she [Chanel] calls the rock-and-roll generation, I love the stores. Basically, I love everything about this era, and all this has a huge influence on what I do, but I think it doesn't have any influence on what Chanel herself does. I think that Chanel has completed the cycle—she has become a legend. A Chanel suit is like a Louis XV or a Louis XVI ensemble. She's part of the history of fashion. It's a wonderful document." He added, "The word 'allure' has replaced the word 'elegance.' It's more a way of living than a way of dressing."

The impulse of a new passion animated this lover of beauty who also loved the women he made beautiful. Chanel only believed in their weakness. Yves believed in their strength. He found them "astounding." He shared their aversion to punctuality, routine, common sense, and the art of cooking with leftovers, along with their hatred of "honest" women who keeled over after one drink.

If woman was a demon, he was her best accomplice. Selfishly, he didn't judge her. He shared her desire to wow men, perhaps expressing the fascination and fear that men inspired in him. He had no sympathy for young men in suits and ties who were on the cover of *Time*: ambitious young executives who ate frozen food from an orange plastic tray, read *Le Défi Américain* by Jean-Jacques Servan-Schreiber, and went to the office reeking of Balafre. He was still the child who loved Bach and dogs, but also Picasso, Céline, and Aragon. He "hated the snobbery of money."[9] He campaigned with a pencil and sheets of white paper. Committees for peace in Vietnam were forming in Paris. Dutronc sang, "Sept cents millions de chinois. Et moi, et moi, et moi." And him? He wasn't the son of Mao or of Che Guevara. And certainly not a defender of the old bourgeoisie in Passy whose teeth chattered in fear in their big labyrinthine apartments. Where was he? While some were engaged in cultural guerilla warfare, and while families from the sleepy provinces came to see Tutankhamun's treasures in the Grand Palais, he remained an observer, carefully following something everyone seemed unaware of, in the name of the final struggle or of prudish morality: the danger of the physical encounter.

The costumes he designed for *Le Paradis Perdu*, a ballet by Roland Petit staged in Covent Garden (with Margot Fonteyn and Rudolf Nureyev and a Pop Art–inspired set by Martial Raysse), revealed this discovery of sensuality. Fashion wasn't just about lines, but about bodies in movement. Adam's chest was bare, with an open, low-waisted leotard held up by two thin straps. He flew across the stage like a cat, radiant, bound by his desire for woman, an Eve who was given a mink. In December 1967, happening Parisians in black silk Mao suits and hippie wigs gave it a mixed reception. But the audience put on a show, too: Lee Radziwill was sitting next to Ava Gardner with white camellias in her hair. Leslie Caron had on a sequined mini-skirt, and Mick Jagger was there with Marianne Faithfull. Maria Callas made the trip to see the ballet. The young king was there, surrounded by his club of adoring women: Baronne van Zuylen, Hélène Rochas in Le Smoking, Kim d'Estainville, and Zizi Jeanmaire in a pink dress with a feathered hat.

In the midst of the commotion of his era, Yves had a calm attitude that revealed his strength. He didn't make any paper dresses, go-go boots, or even the "shower curtain" tunics sold in New York at Paraphernalia that would end up in video art installations. There was never a couturier who claimed to be less revolutionary. Starting in 1966, Paco Rabanne announced that he wanted to "blow up" fashion and showed his metal dresses at Galerie Iris Clert. But for Yves, there was no iron, no sharp points, nothing that shaped the body too arrogantly. He would challenge the body without damaging or hurting it. He verged on limits, he suggested, he invited in a rather supernatural and exclusive way. His clothes were neither a murmur nor a slogan. They were a necessity. "Just as an artist finds his style, a woman must find hers. And when she is aware of it, whatever the fashion of the moment may be, she is sure to have seduction value."

Sonia Rykiel, who was nicknamed "the queen of knitwear" in the United States, revolutionized her medium and material. Yves Saint Laurent described her as "an important figure" in 1993. He didn't invent any new clothing; he chose the best, and made ready-to-wear into a style. Relying on the trust that his era had in him and the special relationship that he had with androgynous bodies, he would quietly turn fashion upside down. Couture had been buried alive in its châteaux, but he saved it and made it fresh, removing its old accouterments, its ribbons, its scent of old garment bags, and breathed new energy into it that saved it from death. But, like elderly ladies whose children move them into modern apartments, couture knew it could never be happy in its new place.

"Couture is not an art, but a craft. This means that its starting point and its goal are concrete: a woman's body, and not abstract ideas that might have some interest in and of themselves. A dress isn't architecture, it's not a house: it's not made to be contemplated, but to be lived in, and the woman who lives in it must feel beautiful and good inside it. Everything else is just hare-brained ideas."[10] While he borrowed expressions from Chanel, he added something desperate to this vision. He had a rather dark way of defining his profession in terms of linking and enclosing, adding something fateful to the obstinacy that this implies, and speaking of himself like a thousand-year-old object that people would dig up, clean, and evaluate, before displaying him in their windows: "I'm a fossil, I'm in my cage. It's not so easy to get out of haute couture. I make dresses and I sleep." Why did he speak so naturally of himself as a prisoner? We see here the obsessive visions of the teenage Yves in Oran, this way of observing himself and feeling compassion for his own fate, like the sun that must wake up "the lioness in the zoo" every morning. Back then, he copied poems by Jacques Prévert:

What a dirty job
and how desperate and beautiful
and harrowing
and unforgettable it is
the look she has when discovering
as she does every morning
when she awakes
the dreadful bars of dreadful
human stupidity
the bars of her cage she had forgotten when asleep

Well before the historic date of May 1968, Yves instinctively anticipated the social collapse to come. Yet—and this is the Saint Laurent mystery—he kept a certain distance between himself and those events—a distance that he expressed in his clothing. You don't throw your arms around the neck of a Saint Laurent woman, you look at her. His dresses didn't illustrate a point of view—they were their own point of view. Yves Saint Laurent designed feelings. In this way he would cross over eras without belonging to any one in particular, but while letting each one believe he belonged to it.

What was he doing on the night of the barricades, from May 10 to 11? Was he in Paris, struggling with a fil-à-fil coat, in Marrakesh in an apricot grove, or elsewhere? In his clothes, we find no traces of cars on fire. During the events of May 1968, the maison de couture stayed open. Sales for fall/winter 1968 remained stable in terms of the number of buyers, but sales to private clients increased from 2 million to 2.8 million francs. But this peak was the beginning of a lasting crisis. "We made a lot of Rive Gauche clothes on Rue Spontini," Madame Esther points out. "For three weeks I didn't go to work," a worker recalls. "There was no métro service to go back home." Yves belonged to a bohemian Left Bank that, in a shut-down Paris, dined at Brasserie Lipp, where Madame Berthe, the bathroom attendant, kept the regulars stocked up with Marigny and Montecristo cigarettes, which had become impossible to find.

Time flowed by harmoniously. Yves Saint Laurent and Pierre Bergé had four months of vacation per year: in the summer, they did music (Bayreuth and Salzburg) and spent a bit of September in Venice, at Cipriani. They did their Christmas shopping at Maison Jansen on Rue Royale. That was where Yves noticed Hélène de Ludinghausen. He called her two days later. "Are you hoarse, or is this your regular voice?" Indeed, Hélène de Ludinghausen had a voice that you couldn't forget. Born in Paris and raised in Brazil, she went to college in Switzerland and said that she spoke six languages. This White Russian, the daughter of the Countess Stroganoff, Princess Scherbatoff, seemed to have the whole world in her address book. She was twenty-five. Pierre Bergé would be in charge of hiring her: "Yves Saint Laurent would like to create a new job for you: to represent him all over the world."

Yves Saint Laurent and Pierre Bergé were always seen together. They had dinner at the home of Charlotte Aillaud, who threw "very pretty little balls" in her mansion on Rue du Dragon, with performances by "a little orchestra," the Zingos. What exactly did go on around Yves? Even Matthieu Galey, in his diary, would not spoil the mystery: "In life, one must know how to keep quiet, that's our *modus vivendi*. Saint Laurent, a smiling spider, surrounded by his long-haired court. Quite likeable, behind his glasses."[11]

Alongside his society engagements, Yves was also intrigued by the seedier side of life. In 1967, he met Serge Gainsbourg, who was more of a fellow traveler than any couturier. Gainsbourg was a seducer. He was also a street performer, who declared his love to his "bella donna" and sang a ballad to phenobarbital. He loved Deneuve, to whom he dedicated "Manon." He sang about prostitutes and dreaded only boredom. In his smoky apartment, he drew women's bodies on his Pleyel piano. Like Yves, he combined a sense of graceful aesthetics with a dark and moody sensibility.

Chanel had banned pants from a woman's city wardrobe. They were still considered leisure clothing, like Courrèges's astronaut outfits. But Yves made pants classic. In 1966, pants were at all the big social events: black pants in silver lamé for the premiere of Truffaut's latest film, *Fahrenheit 451*; a sporty version at Brassens's rehearsal; a Sunday version before Vermeer paintings at the Orangerie museum, and even at mass in Passy. But while pants were allowed into the street for shopping and dinners, they remained completely prohibited in the business world. "Pants still don't have the right to work," Franka de Mailly wrote in *L'Express*. But two years later the same magazine announced: "Pants have entered the city." Female board members wore pants to meetings and, under lawyers' robes or doctors' lab coats, you could see two black pant legs. Saint Laurent's collections issued the female body "a permit to live without keeping your knees together," as the designer himself put it. In one month, the store on Rue de Tournon sold four hundred pairs of pants.

Yves Saint Laurent had become someone who engaged in battles and won them, with no other adversary but himself. For the haute couture collection of summer 1967, he showed designs that evoked Bonnie and Clyde, a double-breasted jersey suit with tennis stripes, a blouse in lawn cloth, and a wide tie. Starting in 1968, he made the suit appropriate for evening wear. "A jersey jacket, masterfully tailored over a blouse with a tie. You drop the jacket and you're ready to go out. The idea will make a fortune," wrote Hélène Lazareff, a close friend of Chanel. In a historic editorial,[12] she announced: "The spirit of fashion has changed, with Saint Laurent in the lead. The youngest of couturiers has set the tone, the excitement, and the 'shape' of the new style. We think that these city and evening pantsuits can be worn by the great majority of women regardless of their ages or their figures. We think this change is just as important as Balenciaga's sack dress or Dior's 'new look' in 1947."

On Sunday, February 11, 1968, at 9:45 PM, Chanel designated Yves Saint Laurent as her spiritual successor on the France 2 television channel, "since one day or another it will be necessary for someone to carry on what I do." Yves was the first couturier since Chanel to speak of seduction when asked about fashion: "It's an issue of intelligence. You also need a little bit of narcissism, or at least self-awareness: loving yourself a little bit in order to be very attractive to others." He brought back big costume jewelry: "No stones, no colors, nothing flashy. Just gold, or, actually, imitation gold, because I only like fake jewelry." In 1967, at the time of the first bohemian skirts, he made black his color. And of course black meant Le Smoking. The design was shown in the July 1966 haute couture collection, but only one example was made, and it was ordered by a woman known as Madame Kenmore. "We didn't see her much after that! She disappeared," remarked Maryse Agussol, who has managed Yves Saint Laurent's haute couture orders since 1962. Three months later, the Smoking was on sale at Rive Gauche for one hundred dollars.

The declared enemy "of women who are den mothers, pleasantly plump, or athletic," Yves Saint Laurent became the leading designer for women who weren't afraid of black. They never carried a purse. They went out with nothing more than a pack of Gitanes and their keys. They rarely danced, but talked and smoked, first tapping their cigarettes on the table to tamp down the tobacco. Among these early fans were Maïmé Arnodin and Denise Fayolle, who launched the Prisunic chain and endorsed its particular style: white dishes by Andrée Putman, lithographs by Bram van Velde or Matta—they made three hundred copies of each and sold them for one hundred francs apiece.

His black wasn't the black of a habit or a uniform, which absorbs light under the stiff jacket of a notary's suit or a religious zealot's dress. It was a powerful and simplified black that surrounded the figure without confining it, a black that condensed and elongated it. "I like black because it affirms, it designs, it stylizes. A woman in a black dress is a line drawn with pencil. But, careful, not the 'little black dress' that is worn with pearls and a mink stole. Modern black. I always light it up with gold, on buttons, belts, and chains. I illuminate it with very long, floaty scarves, which are usually white…. Black is just as beautiful in the light as in the sun, where I hate bright colors: yellow, orange, pink, turquoise—too easy."[13] In the shadow of a grain de poudre overcoat, a hero of the high life was sketched in black wearing high heels; the softness of a silk velvet doublet with an embroidered collar imitated the radiant portrait of Philippe le Roy by Van Dyck in the Wallace Collection in London. Jean Shrimpton, the most photographed model in the world, posed for Guy Bourdin in this lordly ensemble. "Black? It's good for funerals," André Courrèges would have said. He considered a woman beautiful when she was naked.

Ten years after having been crowned prince of Dior, Yves was named the successor to Chanel. He couldn't resist exhibiting the vanity that consists in looking older than one is. He posed in a lab coat with Monsieur Dior's cane. He borrowed expressions from Chanel and pronounced authoritarian judgments. This honor made him realize that he was no longer the little prince. He was a man, in spite of himself. He said so: "Before every collection, I have a pathological fear, one that is ultimately reasonable. Since the age of twenty, I feel myself loaded with a responsibility that crushes me: my failure would put many people out of work. Often I rebel. I feel frustrated. I've never had the time to be young, to be carefree." But what would he have done with this freedom from care? He would have had to forget his dresses, which he spoke about even more warmly than he spoke about women—his dresses were always alive. "There are dresses that the model rejects. It's like someone who doesn't love you."

Yves Saint Laurent liked being admired and loved, and he turned his sensitivity into a strength. Bloomingdale's suggested that he open a pocket boutique in a corner of the New York department store. "You're lucky to be with us. If things don't sell well, we get rid of them right away," said Mrs. Fitzgerald, the store's fashion coordinator. "Let's call it off," said Yves Saint Laurent, cutting short their lunch meeting at the Ritz. The child king wanted his own store. He would get it, on Madison Avenue, no less. When it opened on September 26, 1968, women lined up to get in. At three o'clock, sales totaled 25,000 dollars. The bestselling item was the "city pants," an exact copy of the haute couture design, but at a tenth of the price, between 145 and 175 dollars. The store sold out its entire stock in three weeks. "Yves's name is magic," *Time* magazine raved. Why such a victory? For the first time, a couturier offered women modern clothing that, as the magazine pointed out, "isn't exclusively for those under age twenty-five, like the minidress or culottes."

After the Courrèges bombshell, after the mini-skirt scandal, which led Yvonne de Gaulle to shorten her skirts by two centimeters, the fashion world was shaken by the hippie movement. A healthy exoticism unfolded in couture salons: safari suits, loose African tunics, and Andalusian outfits. Evening looks were African, Cuban, Creole, Tahitian. Society women wanted to become invisible. Girls were more interested in cars than debutante dresses. Cardin, who had seen the writing on the wall a long time ago, positioned himself by distributing his designs everywhere. He seemed more like a businessman than a couturier.

Quite the opposite, Yves Saint Laurent staked everything on women's sense of difference, sophistication, rarity, emotion, and desire. In 1966, thanks to Pierre Bergé's vigorous pursuit of the deal, an agreement was signed between the Maison Saint Laurent and Mendès, a clothing manufacturer that had been established in the early twentieth century and was directed by Didier Grumbach, the nephew of Pierre Mendès France (prime minister of France for eight months during 1954–55). At first, Didier Grumbach rejected the offer, arguing that it was unthinkable for an industrialist to produce a collection for a boutique. But it was too late: Pierre Bergé had already announced the news in *France-Soir*! The first order (500 pieces) was placed in 1966. Those numbers quickly rose to 6,000 pieces per season in 1968, to 20,000 in 1972, and to 135,000 in 1980.

Mendès had a reputation for quality. The company even had production studios headed by *premières d'atelier* who had been let go by haute couture. Disappointed by Madame Germaine's pear-shaped shoulders, Yves didn't want to do anything similar. "He had his vision of what his ready-to-wear should be. Others considered it a necessary evil, and they settled for adapting designs from the previous haute couture season. Saint Laurent went much further. He had a real passion for Rive Gauche. He didn't bring couture 'down' into the streets," said Didier Grumbach. All the prototypes were made on Rue Spontini, in Monsieur Georges's atelier. Anne-Marie Muñoz, who was hired in 1963 as director of the Haute Couture studio, worked closely with Yves Saint Laurent. She became his Madame Raymonde. With a severe eye, Muñoz selected the suppliers and checked the measurements of all the designs before they went into production. After a few failures—clients complained of clothes "cutting them under their arms" because of armholes that were too tight—the maison hired a quality manager in April 1968. His job was to go to the factory every week and oversee production. He was called "the biker." "Our patterns were sacred," recalled Jean-Claude Rossignol. Cutting, treating the fabric, stitching, ironing, finishing: he watched over all the stages and pointed out "the basic rules of the Saint Laurent technique to all these people used to making Jupiter polyester raincoats. A round back dates a woman. Our thing is very straight shoulders....We like well-placed backs. A seam in the back holds a piece of clothing together and slims the silhouette." Creating the line of the shoulders and putting together the sleeves and neck required painstaking work. Ten hours for a jacket. The darts couldn't be slack, and the shoulders had to be nice and straight. His fabrics had secret code names. Series 8: velvet from Giron. Series 32: cotton gabardine. 701: voile fabric. And the great classic, jersey from Racine. "You understand, we were aiming high. Yves Saint Laurent wanted to be in the street, but in an acceptable way. We weren't concerned about the profit," said Rossignol. In these standards, Yves Saint Laurent's contradictions are revealed.

"Culture is dead. Achieve orgasm," proclaimed graffiti scrawled on the walls of the Sorbonne. Yves Saint Laurent didn't identify with either destroying the past or venerating it. He hated "gloves, hats, diamonds, the fashion of 1947 to 1964." But he also hated "sectarianism, the avant-garde, young executives, the idea of going to the moon and the idea of making it, not to the moon, but in life." Starting in 1969, science fiction was again all the rage. The only "optimistic" alternative to the muddy mess of Woodstock, futurism came back even stronger in the late 1960s, on the ruins of the de Gaulle years. An orderly society was collapsing, dying like a mean old lady who throws her gold into the Seine to punish her heirs. "The Plaza was empty. Paris was empty. Everything had collapsed. We used to sell fifty pairs of shoes. We turned out the lights. We were scared. It had become unfashionable to dress well," recalled Michel Brodsky, Roger Vivier's business partner.

Yves Saint Laurent didn't question this development in fashion. He went with it, and even accelerated its pace, seeing an opportunity: "The future is in ready-to-wear, of course. It is perfectly immoral, whatever one's income may be, to pay 4,000 francs for a jersey dress. Today, my ready-to-wear dresses cost 400 francs. That's still too much. I hope to be able to bring out dresses in jersey one day. By the thousands, naturally. I don't need ateliers and atelier methods to express myself," he told *Elle* on March 7, 1969. He wore ready-to-wear himself, claiming that he didn't have the "patience" to have suits made by a tailor. Why wait for six hours? That's how long it took to fly from Paris to New York! Fashion seemed to have replaced the old conventions of style very quickly with the permanent coup d'état of the "totally new." The new style was like an ultramodern skyscraper with enforced playfulness and no imagination. Shirt collars soon looked like flippers, armchairs resembled sacks full of marbles, beds were like boxing rings, rooms became gyms, and kitchens turned into labs where everything was built in. Adults played at being big kids in the comics. Hélène Rochas reigned as a female CEO. Her office on Rue François Ier was a white cocoon with snow-white carpeting on the walls and ceiling and mushroom chairs, luminous moon-shaped mirrors, and a James Bond–style instrument panel. Paris was dancing on a volcano of polyurethane. Art had become egalitarian. It was no longer consumed, it was up to the viewer to produce it, to settle into it as in a television stage set (Vasarely) or an erotic-technological game (Soto's plastic *Penetrables*).

Everything was back again, but more massive. Bras weren't made of lace anymore but metal. Like Raymond Moretti, fashion dreamed of accomplishing a gigantic total work of art. Emanuel Ungaro introduced the woman of the future in tempered steel. "Ungaro is the era of rockets and inspiring women with skeptical minds," *Vogue* wrote in October 1969. Fashion was keeping up with Stanley Kubrick's *2001: A Space Odyssey*. A "Moon Shoot" cocktail was invented at Harry's Bar, and a Miss Moon was elected at Le Bilboquet in Saint-Germain-des-Prés. At Au Nain Bleu, mini Apollo rockets and lunar modules sold like hotcakes.

Paris was talking about the giant 11,000-pound breast sculpted by César for the Rochas perfume factory and the metal pantyhose of the astronaut Jane Fonda in *Barbarella*. Style was stuck in the conventional fashion-show-as-happening era. "Women are no longer present, they either serve as material or as bulletin boards. And these holes through which you observe female 'holes' have already been made by Henry Moore for forty years now," an angry Romain Gary wrote in *Elle* on March 10, 1969. "Stop having one foot in fashion and the other in the Museum of Modern Art, because the female body loses out in the process." Yves Saint Laurent's Mondrian dress was on the cover of *L'Express*, in the studio of the sculptor Nicolas Schöffer, but curiously, in the midst of these colored lights, it looked quite alone, torn from its context, and as if a stranger to its creator.

Yves Saint Laurent denounced futurism: "The most attractive woman I know is Barbara—the opposite of the abominable Barbarella. Barbara is a moving Avedon photo: the way her body occupies space is miraculous. Plus, Barbara is a miracle: a popular singer who is the height of sophistication and refinement. I'd really like to design clothes for her."[14] As for upper-middle-class women, they got a taste of dangerous heroics when they put on their patent leather shoes and wore pants for New Year's Eve at Hélène Rochas's house, the same way they'd cross the Seine to go to Les Halles and eat an "amazing" andouillette. Yves Saint Laurent made the mature woman seductive: "Elegance means being noticed in a black dress. It's poise. It's an attitude. A woman doesn't look old because of wrinkles or gray hair—it's her gestures. That's where my accessories play a big role. A scarf you can play with, a shoulder bag that frees up your hands—there's nothing uglier than a bag dangling on your arm. A flexible belt—always a chain—that gives an attractive sway to your hips, and pockets. My accessories are gestures."

In the United States, Saint Laurent's "city pants" became a sign of style. Hélène de Ludinghausen recalled, "I spent my life in airplanes. I'd help to do the windows in the department stores. They'd put up a sign: 'Meet Baroness Ludinghausen. Third Floor.' We had specific codes. We had to teach them a new way of dressing—how to wear a flowered skirt with a safari jacket, how to have few clothes and lots of accessories, how to dress in a way that was both interesting and comfortable. It was anti-bourgeois training. The noon-to-midnight pants remained a symbol of this."

One story, in particular, has become a legend. In 1968 in New York, a woman went to a restaurant wearing a tunic and Yves Saint Laurent pants. She was not allowed in. She went to the ladies' room and came out five minutes later in a mini-dress. "Welcome." Sao Schlumberger claimed to have been the heroine of this adventure at La Côte Basque. But other clients claim the story as well, citing other restaurants, such as the 21 Club or Lafayette. "It's like a piece of clothing—they're all fighting over it," Betty Catroux said of the story, laughing.

Rive Gauche style would have been nothing without the excitement of these women. Nothing seemed thought out. Everything happened very spontaneously, and it all depended on craftsmanship. At Mendès, there were only thirteen women handling restocking and inventory for the boutiques. Monsieur Bernard went out on expeditions. The hangers got caught in the elevator's sliding gate. Small series were made here: a woman was paid by the item to produce them. There were no fashion shows, but a few looks displayed on two mannequins on the fifth floor of a building on the corner of Rue d'Aboukir and Rue Léopold-Bellan. They were like family. Journalists made appointments. Clara Saint, the publicist, showed them the designs: they touched and tried them on, imagining the story or the photographer—Penn, Avedon, Bourdin, Newton, Sieff, Klein, Bailey, or others—who would highlight them. The great Diana Vreeland, editor of American *Vogue*, stepped over the garbage cans on Rue du Sentier to come see the handful of designs that would be the next big thing next season. Yet Yves still continued to launch haute couture "bombshells," such as the safari look and evening mini-dresses made of wooden beads (African collection, summer 1967) or alpaca wool tuxedo shorts with a transparent cigaline blouse (summer 1968), photographed on model Penelope Tree by Richard Avedon. In 1968 he also introduced a safari jacket with a bronze ring belt that would become a classic.

Haute couture and Rive Gauche complemented each other perfectly. The history of ready-to-wear would never experience anything comparable to the early years of Rive Gauche: low costs, quality production, and extremely competitive prices for a style that was the rage of Paris. After the first Paris store, two more Rive Gauche boutiques opened in Paris and Marseille. They were a smashing success. In three weeks, the stores were sold out. The factory that Mendès had operated in Chalonnes (in the west of France) since 1967, which employed a hundred people, was now entirely devoted to Saint Laurent. By 1969, there were eighteen boutiques in Europe and ten in the United States, each of which sold twenty jersey pants per day. In Bordeaux on Cours Clemenceau. In Nice on Rue Paradis. In Madrid on Calle Serrano. In Rome on Via Borgognona. In Munich on Burkleinstrasse. In Toulouse on Place Wilson. In Geneva on Rue du Rhône. In Venice at the Cipriani. In Milan on Via Santo Spirito. And the list went on. Pierre Bergé was a firm believer in good locations. He was careful not only to examine the place, but also to make sure that the store manager's style matched that of Saint Laurent. No perfumed *grandes dames*. A large lady from Hamburg was politely shown the door. But how could they resist sincere enthusiasm? In London, the editor-in-chief of *Harpers & Queen* quit her job to open boutiques. Didier Grumbach related the story: "Lady Rendlesham was waiting for us in her Rolls with a uniformed chauffeur. During lunch, she gave a little speech about Saint Laurent—about its future, about what it represents. I looked at Pierre Bergé, and he had a tear in his eye." Lady Rendlesham went on to open five Saint Laurent stores: the first, on Bond Street, was inaugurated by Princess Margaret. That day, Yves arrived surrounded by his muses, all wearing pants. The TV station sent its star reporter, who asked, "Are these really women?" "Yes!" shouted Pierre Bergé, grabbing him and throwing him out. Very soon, a veritable army of Rive Gauche stores was established, unified by their décor: store windows edged with metal, orange-red carpeting, and purple seating by Olivier Mourgue. Isabelle Hebey recalled designing some 530 boutiques between 1966 and 1990.

Each store had a giant poster of Yves Saint Laurent on the wall. The king had become an idol. In Milan, he sued a chain of Bologna department stores for unfair competition. One night in 1969, the store on Avenue Victor Hugo was plundered by robbers. The crooks were connoisseurs: they stole only the new collection, leaving the older clothes hanging on their displays. In the street, in the studios, everyone would pose for him. Princess Theresa von Fürstenberg in her black raincoat. Princess Antoinette de Mérode in her checkered kilt-dress. And in this era when they didn't need anyone and rejected the tyranny of yesterday, he hooked them with clothes that made them more beautiful, thinner, more alive, and more free. It was as if, following in the footsteps of Van Dongen, he said, "My essential rule is to lengthen women and especially to make them thinner. After that, all I have to do is make their jewelry bigger. And they're thrilled!"

Wide-eyed, with fake eyelashes, Marisa Berenson moved in a jersey ensemble with her hands on her hips for photographer David Bailey's camera. It was a slim, supple look that lengthened even more the era's low-waisted silhouette, the "tough" look that Yves Saint Laurent dramatized in its simplicity. Flexible, aloof, wearing precious jewelry shaped like serpents, the women wore pants, even the bride. A silk scarf nonchalantly tied around Nicole de Lamargé's neck lengthened her silhouette so she seemed to dissolve in the black of a long cardigan and jersey pants. Paradoxically, although his designs seemed unobtrusive, emphasizing the women who wore them, they also required careful staging. Newton highlighted the mystery of the models of the era by photographing them as if they were unknowns, sitting on the edge of a bed in a hotel room where, near a Cinzano ashtray, one saw hundreds of crumpled bills. "I only like luxury when it's thin. A girl in a black tuxedo. A long dress in black jersey in the midst of embroidery and sequins. People are always overdressed."[15]

In September *Vogue*, Betty Catroux posed for Penn in a huge cape that brushed her ankles. This "Davy Crockett" coat created the illusion that the mirror was too small to reflect her. She was also seen seductively stretched out in an ultramodern apartment on Quai de Béthune that had been decorated by her husband, the designer François Catroux, with a platform bed, acrylic glass cubes, and a built-in television across from the bed. "I endure his taste nicely," she said, with that *enfant terrible* look that endeared her to Yves. Night and day, she lived in pants and t-shirts. When she wore Yves Saint Laurent, she chose jersey pants and roll-neck tops, and she wore a dressy version of the same thing at night, with transparent shirts that veiled her boyish chest.

Like Terence Stamp, the actor whose biblical beauty Pasolini celebrated in his 1968 film *Theorem*, Yves Saint Laurent was soon able to charm not only women, but men. With a six-meter façade, red lacquered walls, and cylindrical spotlights, the new store on Rue de Tournon, which opened on May 12, 1969, was the mirror image of previous Rive Gauche boutiques. But there was one important difference: it was for men. "I'm not embarking on men's fashion," said Yves, the boy with the long hair. "I'm getting into it naturally. I'm motivated by selfish reasons, because I want to dress in a certain way that I haven't ever found in stores." Was this forgetfulness, or just the sin of pride? Yves Saint Laurent was a loyal customer of Renoma, on Rue de la Pompe—the store where men like him shopped, since they didn't cotton to sloppy student clothes or fussy suits with stiff jackets and narrow pants.

At Renoma, corduroy suits with pointed collars, safari suits, and shot silk blazers thrilled hip, elegant dressers and showbiz greats. You could run into Brigitte Bardot, Catherine Deneuve, Eddy Mitchell, Sylvie Vartan, Johnny Hallyday, and Antoine who sang, "Sell the pill in Monoprix." "What I'd like," said Yves Saint Laurent, "is for men to free themselves from their constraints the way women now have—women are so much more open, more modern than men. I'd like French men to stop believing in the pleat of their pants, the dull, serious-looking tie, the 'business suit' (and, why not, in the business lunch) and in their famous good French taste. In France, there's a way that people meet others in the street and judge them from atop their tradition, and it's the most unpleasant thing in the world. The English don't all have the natural elegance of Terence Stamp or David Hemmings, but at least they know how to look at people without staring at them." In low-waisted pants, a canvas tunic, and a big belt, he posed for Helmut Newton hugging his younger sister, Brigitte. In one photo, they are both wearing the laced gabardine safari jacket, the liberating must-have item of 1969.[16] Completely innocently, Yves Saint Laurent denounced conformity, a form of boredom to which he was especially sensitive. "I'll let others make boring suits for boring people and boring circumstances," he said. "I'm speaking to free men."

But this ideal of simplicity couldn't sustain him. What he loved above all was exposing himself to danger. For this *bel indifférent* was constructing his destiny, a self through which he could finally live, a god to which he would sacrifice his life: Saint Laurent. He dreaded nothing as much as tranquility: in tranquility, he collapsed.

That was the other part of himself. He needed stimulants, excitement, theatricality, near misses. He only lived when shaken by forgetfulness, shock, surprise, excess. "Fifteen aspirins when he had a headache. He sometimes felt suffocated. I understand him," said his sister Brigitte. He just wanted to experience everything. As if he had mixed the blood from a secret wound into the lifeblood of a generation. An artist looks at the world and says, without needing to speak, "The important thing isn't what you think of me, but what I think of you."

9 / YVES, LOULOU, AND THE SERPENTS

New York had crowned Yves Saint Laurent the king of fashion. But he wanted to prove to the world that he could exist without Americans. "They have a false opinion of fashion, because they like exclusive things. And exclusive things are out of style," he said in a slightly defiant short film.

Woman Is Sweeter is a whimsical walk through New York directed by Yves's childhood friend Martine Barrat, with trippy music by Galt MacDermot, the composer of *Hair*. It featured Red Riding Hoods dancing in Central Park, Puerto Ricans in turquoise shirts, and Berber princes on horseback. As the sun sets in the background, a naked young man comes out of the water: it's Yves Saint Laurent's double. "When Mack Robinson saw the film, he almost had a heart attack!" said Martine Barrat. The film was never publicly distributed but is preserved in the Saint Laurent archives.

At Dior, Yves had dropped a bombshell by showing a collection that was entirely black. Ten years later, he was even more disturbing, with an almost angelic insolence. The more he became himself, the more distant he became from Americans' image of him. They expected from a couturier something they would never have tolerated from a politician: that he be a dictator.

In January 1968, headlines screamed that Yves was joining the topless move-ment. That month, controversy swirled around Rudi Gernreich, an American designer who scandalized the country by designing a one-piece bathing suit whose straps left the breasts outrageously exposed. Yves Saint Laurent's version of this trend was to showcase breasts by covering them up. America saw this as a much more subversive attitude than feminist protests where women shouted, "Ban the bra!" And Yves would go even further. Once when he was asked to design a bathing suit, he "forgot" the top. "Oh, I didn't realize women still wore those," he is supposed to have said.

He had no liberating message. Instead, he expressed the liberation of an era. The problem was that he belonged to the marijuana generation and worked for the dry martini generation. Bare-chested under his lab coat, he nonchalantly said, "It's very hard to have two different mind-sets, when you do Rive Gauche and when you make dresses for billionaire clients." He continued to offer the jet-set its extrava-gant embroideries and finery. For Marie-Hélène de Rothschild's Bal Oriental in 1969, Yves Saint Laurent created elaborate and exotic costumes: jewel-encrusted tunics, long, baggy shirts of Isfahan rose silk, rope belts with silk tassels, large Persian coats, Russian tunics seen in *Vogue* in photo shoots in Ahmedabad or Delhi, where models with kohl-rimmed eyes posed barefoot in front of mosques. In his haute couture collection, he showed tapestry coats reminiscent of kilims. *Elle* celebrated "Yves Saint Laurent's splendid gypsies: the exoticism is Oriental. Silky, mysterious, enchanting."

But this opulence was not the essential thing. Yves Saint Laurent's true concern was the nude. The body came out of its confinement. The couturier fell in love with movement, secret waves, and caresses. He wrapped his figures in mousselines that recalled the "woven look" dear to Orientalism. This inspiration affected the costumes he designed in December 1970 for Le H, a show at the Paris Casino. They revealed the dual influences of Delacroix (shirtless *femmes d'Alger*, wearing only embroidered velvet boleros) and Bakst. These bodies lightly touched by beaded harem pants and veils evoked Ballets Russes productions—particularly *Salome, Cleopatra*, and especially *Scheherazade*—for which Bakst designed costumes and sets. Bakst once said, "I have often noticed that, in every color of the prism, there are gradations that sometimes express honesty and chastity, sometimes sensuality and even bestiality, sometimes pride, sometimes despair. This can be suggested by making use of different shades. This is what I tried to do in *Scheherazade*. Against a gloomy green, I placed a blue full of despair, as paradoxical as this may seem.... There is the blue of Mary Magdalene and the blue of Messalina!"[1]

Yves Saint Laurent was oriented in the same direction. The pants were a rain of delicate stones. The positions of the arms, legs, and torsos revealed a mastery of movement that emphasized the design of the dance and of anatomy. Around his bust, Jorge Lago wore a rattlesnake that wound around his muscular body, curling around his groin with scales raised. Slave shackles gripped his wrists and ankles. Chains were sensuously twisted around bodies, following the curves of the buttocks and breasts like dotted lines. This time, Yves Saint Laurent didn't attach a jewel between the shoulder blades, but a black ponytail. A dancer from Cuba's National Ballet, Lago arrived in Paris in 1967. He fascinated the designer and the public—which called him "the new Nureyev," as if trying to forget that Nureyev was irreplaceable. Jeanloup Sieff photographed him in this provocative, half-nude costume for *Vogue*. The dancer lived with Pierre Bergé and Yves Saint Laurent for some time. This encounter was a sensual revelation. Through these new paths, Yves Saint Laurent's style would become more languid, more secretive, and more hedonistic. As Yves put it, "Manliness is no more linked to gray flannel or full shoulders than femininity is with a swelling bust. I think that the time of doll-women and dominating men is over. Men don't need to stick out their shoulders and curl their moustaches to make people think they're men."[2]

Yves was thirty-three years old. The age of Jesus Christ Superstar. He had changed once again. His hair was longer. He wrapped himself in big Indian scarves and didn't wear glasses anymore. He spent three months a year in Marrakesh. Marrakesh, "the daughter of the desert," which Churchill called "my beloved," had initiated him. It was his capital of light and desire. Loulou de la Falaise shared these times with him: "It was truly a vacation. We lived at night. We swam a bit, but life started around tea-time. Yves could dance on a table for four hours, doing his one-man show. When we gave him a Camel cigarette, it was like a hash pipe for him." She concluded, "With him, everything happened in his head. He needed to invent stories for himself." In Marrakesh, he could finally experience what he had only had hints of in Oran.

The combination of dust and colors, the noise of the souks, the pyramids of purple and dark red fruits stacked up in the markets came back to him like familiar memories. The steer was still bleeding on the turquoise blue tiles, and the lemons were so yellow that they looked fake. Yet everything was alive. Men in robes sat and smoked. The women had hard lives. Their baskets were overflowing with pink onions, black soaps, and packets of rassoul (a natural mineral clay used for cleansing skin and hair). The spice merchants' shelves were a riot of color, with glass jars of red pepper, cinnamon, and cardamom. Mysterious little vials promised love. Unlike Oran, Marrakesh was a place where you could lose yourself, swallowed up by the noise, the powerful colors, and the darkness of these little shops that sold everything. Time couldn't penetrate the souks. The men worked, unperturbed, letting foreigners think they were the only ones watching. A barber shaved a young boy's head. Everything was offered and everything was secret. In Oran, the Europeans felt they were in France. In Marrakesh, Yves felt he was home. All in white, he strolled through the souks, invisible, happy to lose himself in this labyrinth of colors. He could have written, as Théophile Gautier did when defining "supreme happiness" in *Mademoiselle de Maupin*, "I would be there, motionless and silent, beneath a magnificent canopy, surrounded with piles of cushions, having a huge tame lion supporting my elbow and the nude breast of a young slave like a stool beneath my foot, and smoking opium in a large jade pipe."[3] In Marrakesh, he could endlessly extend the moments of pleasure that were furtively seized in Oran. He moved like a young prince among all these men with soft, olive skin.

In 1967, Yves Saint Laurent and Pierre Bergé bought their house from Maurice Doan, Prince Champaçak, Barbara Hutton's brother-in-law. "We were going to Libya. A famine drove us out. We went through Tunisia to Morocco and fell madly in love with Marrakesh," recalled Pierre Bergé, expressing his passion for a place by feminizing it. "Three days later, we bought the house." Located in the heart of the medina, just a few minutes' walk from Djemaa El Fna, the house was called Dar El Hanch, "the house of the serpent." Yves painted a coiled red and blue cobra on one of the walls. The rooms were like little boxes, linked together by steps. You'd walk down three steps to enter a room, and then walk up four steps to go into a different one. Mustapha Lahbali, who began working for Pierre Bergé and Yves Saint Laurent in 1967, recalled, "The house was small, but it seemed to never end!" Mashrabiyas (traditional Arab latticework) made of cedar carved the light into intricate designs. The house had a charming simplicity: wooden niches for books, mats on the floor, and a fireplace made of a plain block of chiseled plaster. The furnishings were basic: the main room, the living room, had a big white sofa, copper candlesticks, and many Moroccan objects found in the souks. In the kitchen, tagines were piled up on bamboo shelves and pots hung from hooks. "It was small, but always bursting at the seams," recalled Betty Catroux. Friends usually came to stay at Easter: Clara Saint and Thadée Klossowski, Hélène Rochas and Kim d'Estainville, Charlotte Aillaud, Fernando Sanchez, and Loulou de la Falaise. Betty, who was the kind of woman who wore the pants and left the skirt to her husband, remembered wonderful times there. "Everything was funny. We went there on our honeymoon. The four-poster bed collapsed!"

The house had two terraces, which kept it private while opening it onto the world. One terrace looked out on the wide clay path that became lively at twilight. In the evening, the sound of shouts would rise in the dust. The air was warm. The mimosas gently dropped their yellow seeds. In the sky, pink turned mauve and shimmered like mousseline. The sun burst like a big orange threaded with red. That was where Yves liked to draw. He later recalled, "Before, I only used dark shades. Then Morocco came with its colors…colors of earth and sand. But also the colors of the street: the women in turquoise or mauve caftans…And the sky."

Inside the house, the atmosphere was calm, touched with shadow and coolness. Pots of ivy, a few mandarin trees, and jasmine flowers framed a fountain and pool. That was where Yves, the most sensual of designers, decided to have his photo taken for *Vogue*. With his long hair lifted by the breeze, he posed with his hand on his hip. A tobacco-colored leather safari jacket lovingly shaped his body with its folds. His chest could be glimpsed through the untied laces. But he had a good sense of humor about playing his role: "I'm an artistic fag," he said one day while turning over the cushions on his couch. What a strange character!

Loulou de la Falaise recalled, "At these parties in Paris with Jeanloup Sieff, Philippe Collin, Pierre, and other very cultured people, everyone did the Proust Questionnaire. Yves would vanish, showing just one hairy leg from behind the door. He lifted up his pant legs like a tutu. Yves always had a very childish side. And also a sense of humor that everyone understood, even the best-behaved people. He was a born star!" In any case, he had the androgynous beauty of the time, as seen in figures such as Helmut Berger (who wore Rive Gauche safari jackets), Jim Morrison, and Mick Jagger, who started the fashion of transparent tunics on stage and who also mocked hypocrisy in songs like "19th Nervous Breakdown" and "Mother's Little Helper."

At that time, the haute bohemia of the 1960s was having a last golden age through its memories of past extravagance: the Roaring Twenties of La Mamounia, the Marrakesh hotel whose regulars included Josephine Baker and Maurice Chevalier. American billionaires had fallen in love with the city. For instance, an extremely wealthy heiress named Mrs. Taylor came from the United States by yacht and then by mule to monitor the work on her house on a ten-acre spread. Marrakesh's golden era went back to the 1950s: Pierre Balmain gave a memorable party at La Mamounia, Aly Khan and Rita Hayworth strolled amorously in the souks, Erich von Stroheim acted in *Alarm In Morocco*, and Hitchcock made *The Man Who Knew Too Much*. Some even say that La Mamounia's gardens inspired him to make *The Birds*. Fernando Sanchez, whom Yves and Pierre met in 1954 in Paris, recalled, "I went to Tangier. That's where my Moroccan life began. Pierre and Yves came a different way. We all met up in Marrakesh. It was even more intense: another step. We had dreamed of these Arabian nights with Moorish kings kidnaping princesses."

In 1969, Marrakesh was enjoying its last boisterous period. American architect Bill Willis later told me that "tourism hadn't yet invaded the city. It had a fascinating purity." He followed Paul and Talitha Getty there from Rome in 1966 for a two-month vacation, and he ended up never leaving the pink city and decorating billionaires' houses there with local craftspeople.

Marrakesh was a garden of paradise and an adventure. Today, no one dares touch this past, whose absence hurts. Even years later, Pierre Bergé became emotional when remembering it: "It was a golden age. The Orient. Wonderful dinners. People wearing caftans. Servants, orchestras in the gardens. The atmosphere was like the Arabian Nights. We were crazy about Wagner. We'd head off into the apricot fields, we had faraway picnics." His memories seemed to have been shaped by cultural references: "We were in a landscape by Alma-Tadema or Benjamin Constant. Of course, it was completely decadent. People were high a lot." Bergé, who couldn't resist the pleasure of loving a place for its "amazing" characters, listed them in a spirit of erudite friendship: "We met Paul and Talitha Getty, Ira Beline, Stravinsky's niece, a Russian woman who had designed costumes for Louis Jouvet, Bill Willis…"

Yves Saint Laurent's memories were focused on himself. "I always had problems with fear and isolation during the collections. But I had fun. We were a little group. The Rolling Stones were there. Very beautiful women were there. We rode bicycles. I've never been as happy as during those years. That was when I met Talitha Getty. Afterwards, it turned into drama, because of opium." Bergé sentimentally added, "I've always admired Yves for this honesty. Talitha Getty looked like a Burne-Jones or Dante Gabriel Rossetti painting. An impressive woman." This is a surprising statement considering that for Pierre Bergé, only well-dressed people were worthy of being noticed, especially by a designer. As Loulou de la Falaise saw it, for Yves, Talitha embodied the sexual freedom of which he had been deprived for so long: "There's something very conventional and very provincial about Yves. Talitha had the charm of ephemeral people, like a wilder version of Romy Schneider. She was very sensual, very sexy. She had a very pretty accent. Yves would've liked to jump on top of her, but all of a sudden he got a headache. He had finally found someone crazier than he was."

Talitha Getty, the wife of Paul Getty Jr., was born in Bali to Dutch parents. She lived in Rome and spent her vacations in Marrakesh, in a palace where dinner was never served in the same place and always included no fewer than fifteen people, with dancers, acrobats, and magicians. "I would have rugs in Turkey and cushions for my dreams on each of my divans," this beautiful, freewheeling stranger said. Jeanloup Sieff photographed her for *Vogue* from behind, naked under her thick mane of hair. She embodied the modern romanticism that had taken hold of the magazine. From that point on, girls began to seem weightless. They looked as if they would float up from the photos. They lived in the midst of open suitcases, on an eternal psychedelic trip. The journalist concluded, "They travel the world with a certain way of loving life while also remembering that life is horrible; that there are wonders on earth, but also so many horrors that no one has the right to believe they hold innate truth, or to want to impose outdated conventions."[4]

Yves was fascinated by this beauty who looked like an artist's fantasy. Wearing red boots on a hot day, Talitha Getty was beautiful and serious like a Venus Verticordia by Dante Gabriel Rossetti. A witness to the era told me, "Not a drop of her blood was human. But she was made like a soft sweet woman." Under her flowery, floppy hats and behind her kaleidoscope eyes, she had the secret wounds of a spoiled child. In this strange part of the world, a kind of chemistry gilded the trees with sparkling sequins, changed the mountains into elephants, and made the grass catch fire and turn pure red, like certain times that are associated with a particular color. At night, the beautiful women danced with their heads in the stars, making little noises like Tom Wolfe's heroines in *The Electric Kool-Aid Acid Test*, as if to say, "Oooh, it sparkles!" In this luminous fog, many people passed through, including Andy Warhol, Mick Jagger, Brian Jones, and, as Mustapha Lahbali recalled, "other strange people, who slept all day."

Some days, Yves hid behind smoky lenses. He was an enigmatic and secretive person whose decisions were unpredictable and just as sudden as his transformations and his troubling promises. Loulou de la Falaise concluded, "Yves was much more fragile than all these people who didn't work. Back then, he was able to take advantage of this euphoria to produce his collections." He managed this despite his frequent, brutal crashes, due to what Jeanloup Sieff called "this trouble with existence that paralyzed him." Loulou described Yves thusly: "At a basic level, Yves is a scoundrel who has been very damaged. An ambitious man with outrageous agility." According to her, at this time Yves cast Pierre in the role of Père Fouettard, the companion of Saint Nicholas who would flog naughty children. "'Oh là là,' he'd say, 'he's going to beat me.' This excited him, actually. Pierre was like Captain Haddock. They were a true couple. I've never seen such a close and passionate couple."

Once again, Pierre Bergé and Yves Saint Laurent were slightly out of step with their time. Yves hadn't been swept up in the movement, and now the movement was ending. Beat mania was fading away. Kerouac died in 1968, and now his road was about economic development, not dreams. Yet dreams continued to stir. On the stage of New York's Biltmore Theater on West 47th Street, black and white naked bodies came together in the rock opera *Hair*, with its hit "Let the Sunshine In"—the biggest hit musical since *West Side Story*. Fashion was focused on afros and patched jeans. In all-night bookstores in the Village, the last beatniks reread Hermann Hesse's *Siddhartha*, the bible of an Age of Aquarius that now had its back against the wall. For Yves Saint Laurent, the Age of Aquarius was only now beginning. The Beatles with "Lucy in the Sky with Diamonds" and the Rolling Stones with "Brown Sugar" and "Sister Morphine" explored the forbidden world of drugs; like them, Yves also felt sympathy for the devil.

Plus, America had found other idols. Halston, the ex-milliner who dreamed of becoming "America's Balenciaga," had opened his couture house in New York in November 1968. Dubbed the "Orchid Palace" by *Women's Wear Daily*, it was a colorful place where crazy parties were held, where Babe Paley, Lauren Bacall, Liza Minnelli, and Puerto Rican transvestites all mingled. The other idol of the time was Giorgio Sant'Angelo. He offered the WASP elite a return ticket to the land of the American Indian.

The New World was looking for its roots. The age of disillusionment was beginning. Weakened by the Vietnam War, America counted its dead, suddenly discovering what the noise of B-52s dropping bombs on Hanoi had covered up: the fury of a generation. It was a revolt against the values of the American way of life. In January 1967, Jim Morrison, the Rimbaud of rock, said, "I've always been attracted by the idea of rebelling against authority. I'm interested in everything that has to do with chaos, rebellion, disorder, all activity that seems to have no meaning."[5] Ambulances parked outside concert venues. Drugs had become a national scourge.

Yves's journey of initiation to Marrakesh revealed his eternal demons: women-serpents, accursed queens, shadowy bodies with thin hips and made-up lips that called painfully for love. The symbols of pre-Raphaelite painting and the Decadent literary movement, stars, serpents, white lilies, and redheads entered into his world. His idols were Maria Callas (who played Medea for Pasolini) and Silvana Mangano (the star of *Bitter Rice* and *Theorem*, who went on to star in *Death in Venice*, one of Yves's favorite films). Still others were there, leading him to paint this vanishing world with fabrics.

Far from the social approach that reduced art to happenings and cinema to a slice of life (André Cayatte's *The Pleasure Pit* in 1969, or Barbet Schroeder's *More* in 1969), he struck out into a world of precise physicality: that of the beauty of the devil. His vision of "the Orient" remained very pictorial. He chose two very young women to present his collections. Elsa, from Chile, and Amanda, from Germany, would put on long-sleeved black dresses and printed silk scarves that were exclusively designed by Abraham from a drawing by Yves. With their eyes lined in black and their necks encircled by delicate chokers, they posed for *Vogue* as *The Two Sisters*, an 1843 painting by Chassériau, a former pupil of Ingres—an attentive pupil, judging by his classically severe line and his sense of contours. Yves Saint Laurent hewed closely to this way of seeing: he recomposed reality according to an ideal of perfect beauty, emphasizing the oval shape of the face and the lower neck according to rules of balance and harmony. His sensuality seemed almost severe, compared to the kaleidoscopes of colors used at the time. "We weren't dirty hippies," said Bill Willis, with perceptible scorn for such "sloppy" people.

Discovered by the Beatles, hippies, and tourist agencies (ten thousand French people were soon spending their vacation in India), the all-purpose "Orient" was the new Saint-Tropez. From Périgueux to Miami, the "gypsy look" was a huge hit. Fashion was all about upscale second-hand clothes dealers. Mohanjeet in Paris and Malabazar on Brompton Road sold Indian tunics and Afghan vests to all those who were trying to find their "inner selves" in the verses of Lao-Tze. Yves Saint Laurent let others with less style dig through and appropriate this bazaar of amber necklaces and mauve skirts. He bided his time with a slight distance that allowed him to sense that something was ridiculous before others could. Unconscious of the danger, women went out in the most garish colors: "To open the eyes, I pluck the eyebrows Oriental-style and draw an Inca triangle on the forehead," said Gil, Max Factor's make-up artist. He emphasized the collarbone with yellow, drew on the larynx with Nile green, and lit up the earlobes with a little touch of turquoise. Everything was crazy: the mouth lacquered with vinyl red, the fake eyelashes made of the wings of a real fly, the silver thigh boots photographed by Henry Clarke in the sunshine of Persepolis, the purple baby-doll dresses and ponytails, the baggy pants and the golden gladiator sandals.

In December 1969, in an orgy of sequins and shawls, mauve and paprika, members of Paris high society—led by Brigitte Bardot—with Indian scarves tied around their heads, staged a new Woodstock at the Lido for a gala premiere, with the same enthusiasm as Jane Fonda and Roger Vadim arriving in a Rolls-Royce to be one with the pop tribes on the Isle of Wight, or the jeweler Bulgari displaying his giant emerald hearts on a Buddha in *Vogue*. Yves Saint Laurent was certainly too individualistic to take part in this rush to India. It's as if he sensed the signs of a return to moral order underneath the mauve-painted eyes. "Kids are sliding down a slope that always leads to mental and moral destruction, to madness, or to death." Those are the words of Jean Cau, the author of the libretto for Roland Petit's ballet *Paradise Lost*, who, in *Elle*, slammed shut the doors of perception: "There must not be any understanding, or excuses, or resignation. Drugs are the plague."

Yves Saint Laurent was the first to dress women in nudity. But he hated nudists. Aware that great art can only inscribe itself in its time by escaping it, he returned to the sources of the ideal: the ideal of the Decadent movement of the late nineteenth century. "Evoke, don't paint." As of 1969, escaping labels that imposed their own requirements, he distanced himself from an era that had suddenly decided that the body wasn't taboo but had to be shown everywhere. It was a heady era that rushed with its fly open into everything that could be consumed: movies, books, theater, travel.

In 1969, sex guides written in the style of household manuals came out. The pleasures of reproduction entered into the confessional of scholars and sociologists. That year, no fewer than eight sex dictionaries and encyclopedias were published in France. *Emmanuelle* was adapted for the cinema. Sade was taken out of the forbidden books section of the French National Library. A decree from the interior ministry authorized the publication of Henry Miller's *Sexus*, and in eight months, it sold more copies than that year's Goncourt Prize winner.

But Yves Saint Laurent would make sin fashionable again: body-hugging vests with golden chains for men; skirts fringed with leather, like the whip of Sacher-Masoch's Venuses; savvy transparencies, long mousseline dresses covering the hair but revealing the bust. In January 1968, the portrait of a lady in black with an open frock coat revealing her bust enveloped in organza troubled the public. The next year, she dominated Paris nightlife. Wrapped up and wearing a turban, she moved her arms like silk wings, with a sad, tender grace.

While women militated for equal pleasure and unisex fashion, Yves was focused on something quite different: the caress of a feather and light, transparent fabrics. "Femininity is in woman, not in what she wears." He dressed Catherine Deneuve once again, this time for François Truffaut's film *Mississippi Mermaid*. The actress had conquered the United States in 1968 with *La Chamade* (released in the United States as *Heartbeat*), a film by Alain Cavalier based on the book by Françoise Sagan and featuring costumes by Yves Saint Laurent. The British called Deneuve "the most beautiful woman in the world." But she had a beauty that superlatives couldn't touch, as if, by turns light-hearted and serious, vulnerable and indifferent, she pushed away the unchaste assaults of the mob with a smile barely tinted with mango lipstick. A blond with beautiful manners, Deneuve was not one of Yves's close friends. "What ties me to him is admiration and unspoken agreement," said the actress, who never missed one of his shows. "He's a man who really loves the women he loves. He gives you signs." In *Mississippi Mermaid*, her body, radiant under the white latticework of guipure lace, was covered with a black cloud at her bust. Everything was revealed, but without showing anything, chastely. Under her legendary coldness, Yves fanned the flames of seduction. "We get dressed in order to get undressed," as Françoise Sagan summed it up in an opinion piece in *Vogue*. "A dress has meaning only if a man wants to take it off....A man doesn't love you for a dress, he loves you for a missed rendezvous, a word, a glance."

Instead of the trivial imitation of reality or the "erotic" bodies of the late 1960s, Yves created the dream of a temptation veiled in shadow, a woman who appeared in black mousseline, her waist encircled by a golden serpent. For Yves Saint Laurent, the body needed an atmosphere of myth, like the smoke that made the tormented sky in Visconti's *The Damned*. Around these women there was the delight of danger, of a shadow stalking its prey while gently swaying. It wasn't the body itself but the sculpted body that he emphasized: he would shape his mousseline dresses around golden waists, necks, and stomachs sculpted by Claude Lalanne from molds of actual women's bodies.

Yves Saint Laurent met the artist couple Claude and François-Xavier Lalanne at Dior. They worked in Ury, near Fontainebleau. Their house was a surreal animal preserve. Their hands created flying horses, monkeys sitting at the table, and all kinds of unreal animals that seemed full of life. They replaced raw reality with a strange yet familiar world with items such as an egg bed and a hippopotamus bookshelf. Yves remained their friend and client. He had a bar they'd made, as well as some of their famous sheep, and mirrors framed with bronze branches that seemed to have been torn from the knotty trees of a fantastic forest. The sculpted dresses did not find any buyers. But in 1969, Claude Lalanne created accessories for the collection: hats made of bamboo leaves, butterfly bracelets with golden wings, and lip necklaces molded from Yves's own mouth. François-Xavier Lalanne described Yves in this way: "He's a relaxed god. Yves doesn't make people crawl. He tyrannizes them in his own way." His wife, Claude, who shared Yves's shyness, had a more intuitive understanding of the designer: "We don't talk much, but I think we understand each other. He is sunk into a deep darkness that he has a hard time getting out of. It was always there. Of course, back then, it was less visible. But he has a sickness inside him. He was born like that, with this deep anxiety that paralyzes him."

During these eventful years Yves Saint Laurent's fashion expressed games of attraction-repulsion to death: the time period offered him a new version of this game that he had known for so long. It was all downhill from there. Two years had passed since the Age of Aquarius in Marrakesh. Soon enough, the miracles of LSD had become "spiders on my tuxedo shirtfront," as Gainsbourg sang in "Intoxicated Man." A wonderful journey was ending with hard drugs and overdoses. The Rolling Stones sang, "Please, Sister Morphine, turn my nightmares into dreams....Sweet Cousin Cocaine, lay your cool cool hand on my head." The time of the prophets was ending, and that of the martyrs began. The Beatles broke up. On July 3, 1969, Brian Jones died. The Rolling Stones celebrated his memory with a concert in Hyde Park attended by 250,000 people. The Doors paid Jones homage by passing out a poem by Jim Morrison dedicated to the "angel man" that included the following stanza:

Hot buttered pool
Where's Marrakesh
Under the falls
the wild storm
where savages fell out
in late afternoon
monsters of rhythm

Loulou de la Falaise went to work for Yves in 1972 and never left. She would become his muse, the Salome of the 1970s, the daughter of Babylon. Sparkling with jewels and magic, she was one of those women who caused people either to flee or to fall in love. In 1969, she was twenty-one years old and Yves was thirty-three. Loulou lived in New York, where she posed for *Vogue*. Diana Vreeland loved her. She designed fabric patterns for Halston. She lived with Joe Eula, "the guru of chic," an American-style Bérard whose apartment on West 54th Street was a white cave filled with portraits of his muses. He went on a road trip with Loulou to show her America, from the Rockies to Santa Fe, in his Plymouth convertible. He found her to be full of surprises: "A delightful mess. Something like a pre-Raphaelite dream!" Loulou plucked her eyebrows to look like Marlene's and dyed her hair red. Loulou didn't dance, she fluttered. Her suitcases were tied with string. She was the kind of person who might have nothing in her bag but a safety pin, or a diamond bracelet from the queen mother. She could make four different outfits out of a scarf. "I'm not an obsessive collector. I've always left things behind." She started getting dressed for the evening at three in the afternoon, appearing in a whirlwind of bracelets, long necklaces, and silver belts from King's Road, depending on whether she felt like a man or a woman, a pixie or a dandy, a blue angel or a red demon.

Fernando Sanchez, who, in his words, was designing "fur lingerie for movie stars" for Reveillon at the time, recalls meeting Loulou at a party thrown by fashion illustrator Antonio Lopez. "I had just arrived from Marrakesh. I knew her mother, who was already a legend to me. Purple velvet pants and a crown of flowers—that was Loulou. She looked like a fairy from an Irish folk tale. She represented everything amazing about that time. There was an aura around her. Her excesses thrilled me. Our friendship grew deeper in Paris, at Place Furstemberg. Lots of amazing things happened in that apartment. Loulou belonged to the mythology of exoticism."

Her life was like a novel. She was born in a country house in Sussex, England, at tea-time according to her grandmother, or cocktail hour according to her mother, Maxime de la Falaise. She came from one of those families where beautiful, broke women married men—and not the contrary—with a romantic attachment to duty that didn't exclude their gift for loneliness, dreaming, and forbidden games. Elegant and silent, the husbands found satisfaction in tending their English gardens. Loulou's maternal grandfather was Lord Oswald Birley, the official court painter and favorite of Queen Mary. Loulou's father was Count Alain de la Falaise, a pillar of the Jockey Club who, according to his wife, Maxime, was "very handsome—short with sublime legs, a puny torso, and a delightful mouth." At age seventeen, Maxime signed up as a volunteer medical aide in the air force and read books to soldiers for five dollars a book in New York. She met Alain de la Falaise at a publishing party. "For him, work was something you do before lunch. I was a furious gust of youth. Alain was perfect for having children. By marrying him, I married my idea of France. It wasn't sexual, it was just recognizing destiny." Maxime recalled Loulou's birth as follows: "She was born in the bathroom, while I was doing a translation for a fashion magazine. Alain was putting little wads of ether under my nose and it burned." Loulou admitted that "the English are not physical." When she tried to kiss her grandmother, the older lady would pull back and make the sign of the cross. Loulou grew up with tamed monsters who scared her at night but then ended up becoming her pals.

She learned to imagine the way other children learned to read: by teaching herself. Sent to live with a religious couple in Seine-et-Marne, she had an upbringing like something out of *The Night of the Hunter*. This is how she describes the couple who served as her foster parents: "She was from Brittany, he was from Lille. She had almost become a nun. One day, the church fell on top of her. She was paralyzed. She had to go to Lourdes to walk again. To thank God, she married him. He had been a Scout. During the war, they had captured him for pissing on a Nazi." Loulou's voice was somewhat haunted. Her bony body wouldn't stay still, moved by memories that spit fire like the dragons on her Ossie Clarke pants. "I was the big sister. Alexis was little and Catholic. I was a pagan. I wrote prayers to the wind. His belief in the Holy Virgin was rock-solid. I didn't have that baggage."

The independence that she was forced to acquire gave her an unusual strength. "When you're a child, you get along well with madness. It makes you resourceful," she explained, instead of saying, as Flaubert would, that it "masculinized" you. Loulou moved through all kinds of worlds while creating characters for herself. Loulou had the beauty of a late bloomer. When she talked, the words shifted into a world that wasn't about lies or dreams, but was beyond good and evil. As a teenager, her imagination ran wild as she explored the Marquis de Sade's château. Expelled from the Lycée Français in New York for unruly behavior, she went to work at the Iolas Gallery, owned by "a Greek man with forty thousand gold necklaces and diamonds," and then was sent to London by her mother and married an Irishman, Desmond FitzGerald, in great splendor. Lady Birley threw a ball for seven hundred guests. "There was a very big estate without a cent. Some Americans came just for the day. My husband gave speeches, but we acted crazy."

She never lost her pull, even as she left destruction in her wake: homosexual jealousies, unlikely couplings, women she seduced—like Ira von Fürstenberg—or pinned down so fast their heads would spin. "I never needed to be sexually liberated. I've always frequented ambiguous circles. We ambiguous people are all brothers." She and Yves got along right away: "He liked to do silly things. Betty [Catroux] was the same type."

With her pointy face and androgynous body, Loulou had, as Fernando Sanchez gallantly put it, "her head in images and her feet on the ground. She's kind of like a tall tree with deep roots whose top is in the stars." Her attitudes and her body moved as nimbly as a chameleon. She didn't need to burn her bra, because she didn't ever wear one. "For a long time, I thought I was a boy. I refused to put a skirt on until I was forced to. I was ashamed to wear high heels." She fascinated Yves. When she visited Yves and Pierre on Place Vauban, she became the "pal of the two girlfriends." For a long time, she was a child with dirty fingernails filling people's boots with slugs in the Fontainebleau forest. Then she went to a boarding school in Sussex, thin as a rail in her green and gray uniform. It was surely because of Loulou that Yves Saint Laurent could confidently say about a woman and her wardrobe: "She must have intelligence and imagination. You can always transform everything." Such as putting a strip of fabric on the bottom of your skirts? "Oh, no, how awful! I don't know. Cutting something to make a tunic. Changing your accessories. Adding tights in a similar shade. Today's fashion is above all a state of mind, an attitude."[6]

Loulou expressed her mystical sense in the moment; Yves gave it shape. He would create dresses for tomboys who ran out of velvet, "lamés brocaded with purple and copper feathers" for a costume ball thrown by Étienne de Beaumont. They attended with Tristan Tzara in jersey polos and big rolled-up pants. They announced a theatrical passion for the 1920s, a powerful time when Paris nightlife was world famous.

Loulou could improvise accessories just as easily as she used to put salt into containers of yogurt as a child. She turned a napkin ring stolen from Petit Saint Benoit into a bracelet. Her neck was sometimes covered with bruises—from her chokers, she said. So she added more. She was a kaleidoscope of jewels, colors, Taroudant coral, Victorian chains, blue stones, and an azure, green, and orange turban she took off a dragon she found at the flea market. She inherited this sense for combinations and color from her maternal grandmother. Mad about the Ballets Russes and a close friend of Diaghilev, Lady Birley was the only woman allowed to take part in the fox hunt in Ireland. She rode her horse in a buckskin jacket with a Hindu turban, and went to the opera with a shopping basket. She wore her veiled hats as naturally as her garden gloves, which she used to maintain one of the most famous rose gardens in England. She put together outfits in an economic and luxurious fashion, cutting up saris that she bought during her diplomatic travels to Nepal. Loulou, who was also a keen user of pinking shears, called her "the first hippie."

Metaphorically sprayed with Shocking perfume at birth, Loulou had always been charmed by Maxime's style. Her mother was a high society saleswoman at Schiaparelli. Maxime reigned in the postwar Paris imagination, the society that Yves Saint Laurent dreamed about back when he was flipping through copies of *Vogue* in Oran. A society "ambassador" for Schiaparelli who was invited to the Noailles and Polignac families' homes, Maxime was especially amazing at premieres and balls, when she appeared on the arm of Hubert de Givenchy in a diamond dress "that stuck out like a sore thumb." Maxime lived in New York. She reigned over the artistic and literary scene like Oscar Wilde's Herodias. Her dinners were happenings: around a medieval dish, she would regularly receive Warhol, Bianca Jagger, and Gloria Swanson (her sister-in-law). Still drunk on those endless nights when the muses burned their sables, Loulou moved to brown and gray Paris, which she found "provincial." She recalled, "Dressed in gigantic bell-bottoms, I was suspect. A Zulu. The women wore kilts."

The ingénue Loulou, who spoke French like a child, added a poisonous candor to her lack of understanding: "No one spoke English. When Fernando talked about Yves and Pierre, I thought it was Pierre Cardin." She stimulated Yves's imagination. His lines for Rive Gauche sometimes had a very tough, almost ascetic quality. Loulou posed in Fernando's apartment on Place Furstemberg. Behind her, in the bedroom, one can see a photo of Pierre Boulat, Zizi, and Yves and another of the kiss on January 29, 1962, the day of Yves's first collection.

Eight years had passed since that debut. By trying to become young, the city had aged. Balenciaga had closed up shop in a chivalrous farewell to a time period that didn't suit him. "It sends chills up my spine to think that we are dressing women with locks and covering them with metal, nails, and chainmail," said Gabrielle Chanel.[7]

Paris became bitter. While Paris pouted, resting on its laurels, its competitors refined the industrial know-how that would make Italian fashion so famous in the 1970s. Ready-to-wear now had its star designers, including Karl Lagerfeld (Chloé), Emmanuelle Khanh, Cerruti, and Sonia Rykiel. Licenses (sweaters, ties, raincoats, lingerie, etc.) provided a royal income for Cardin, Féraud, Torrente, Scherrer, and Esterel (eleven thousand points of sale on five continents). Pierre Cardin had become a businessman, eager to diversify: menswear made up two-thirds of his revenue, and he was getting ready to open Espace Cardin.

"When I arrived," recalled Kenzo Takada, "all the women wore beige and brown." The new models were Francine Gomez and Gilberte Beaux. It was the beginning of the Pompidou years. The future was the practical woman of Rexona deodorant. "My nose tells me it's five o'clock." It was the Formula 1 woman, who wore madras pants, long shirts, and tank bras, bought low acrylic tables, dreamed of a casual home with a huge kitchen and transparent pots, and went shopping in air-conditioned malls wearing capris and zipped boots.

This atmosphere did not suit Yves Saint Laurent at all. He counter-attacked: "For my latest collection, I chose this suit, which is a real man's suit, to represent the woman of the future. I think that in twenty years, it will be just as relevant: the body of the woman of tomorrow is evolving toward a lengthened, slim, androgynous silhouette, like the body of an adolescent, and this ambiguity creates her charm and seductiveness. The truly modern piece of clothing in a woman's wardrobe today is pants. Why shouldn't it be a suit tomorrow? It's an elegant, ironic, and very humorous way of asserting her liberation."

Yves Saint Laurent tried to keep his distance from the controversy that roiled the fashion industry: for or against long skirts? "Making us ten years older in one week is really a hard blow," sighed those who were against. "For us, Saint Laurent is a bellwether," the manufacturers answered, without really understanding. *Paris Match* followed suit: "Designers are divided into three clans: the 'shorts' (Ungaro,

Courrèges), the 'half-ways,' (Cardin, Dior), and the long (Saint Laurent)."[8] The break between the street and the couturiers was final. It was the boutiques, now, that started fashion trends. Kenzo opened his store, Jungle Jap, in January 1970 in the Passage Choiseul, shaking up the sleepy capital. A fan of the Saint-Pierre market, Kenzo had a bride in espadrilles walking through a gallery painted with water lilies. ·He received wild applause in this ambiance of country folklore. Kenzo was about color, cheerfulness, and combinations in a time whose mottoes were "everything goes with everything," "you make your clogs yourself," and "let's be creative together." All the girls were named Pom and Mary. Indian ponchos, Fruit of the Loom t-shirts, Afghan bags, and denim overalls that were bought at the Saint-Tropez market for ten francs were the uniform for a power grab: "the Estates General of Women," organized by *Elle* magazine.

On August 1, 1970, protesters walked through Paris chanting "Long dresses, short ideas! Long dresses, frustrated men! Long skirts, betrayal!" Yves had thought all those debates were over. Now he had to justify himself: "It's true that a certain kind of long dress makes a woman look old. If you simply lengthen your skirt, it's absolutely dreadful. It looks like we're back in 1950 again. But long dresses are something different. You have to change everything. The fabrics are softer, they have to move with the body, so you can feel the legs, the thighs."[9]

The Kenzo woman was fresh and cheerful: she was full of life. The Courrèges woman was still in space: at his shows, they laughed, they danced, they jostled each other on the white runway. But the anarchist sisters had every reason to resent a designer who was a little too rich, a little too handsome, a little too famous, and a little too bourgeois: "We see that Saint Laurent works with a capitalist's money," his enemies might have said. "He must have had a heartbreak this winter and to help himself think better, he went to meditate in the attic. He opened up his trunks and found his old designs."

In Marrakesh, at least, he could feel good and forget about everything: time, society, and women who talked to him about his dresses. As when he was a child in Oran, distance was what made Parisian life more desirable and more exciting.

Once again, theater translated his visions through pure expression. He was once again the child who designed costumes for a vanished world. Paris was bringing the 1920s back with variety shows featuring dancers on staircases with feathers in their hair. In May 1970, Yves designed costumes for the Casino de Paris. It was a variety show war: the Alcazar, owned by Jean-Marie Rivière and Marc Doelnitz, bought the Casino de Paris's costumes, including Mistinguett's stage dress. The 100-year-old Casino had been owned by Henri Varna, but after his death in June 1969, his estate put it up for sale. It was almost bought by the owner of the London Palladium. Finally, Roland Petit and Zizi Jeanmaire acquired the right to run it for a two-year trial period. Many artists volunteered their talents: César gave them two giant plastic breasts, Vasarely designed the stage curtain, Guy Peellaert did the posters, Erté made the scenery, and Yves handled the costumes. He showed up at the Casino in brown corduroys and a Liberty shirt, with a scarf tied at his neck and his chihuahua in a canvas bag. He was fully committed to the production and went to all the rehearsals. Zizi's silhouette no longer had the dark boniness of the Alhambra, where the influence of Bernard Buffet could still be felt. This time, everything sparkled and shone, and the design was studded with stars made of jet and diamonds.

The show was to be called *Champagne Rosé*. In the sketches, the bodies were in circus poses, their faces lit up in pastel pink. Big red circles dotted the *i*'s in Zizi. Naughty Zizi, with her long eyelashes and husky voice, admired Yves: "My feather headpiece is like Maurice Chevalier's straw hat. Yves made me with that. I have two men in my life, Roland and Yves. We're high-class acrobats." In 1968, Yves designed the costumes for her show at the Olympia. Now, two years later, she was singing "J'ai fait ça en douce" with her cocky duchess of the streets attitude. She had a striking black bouquet and a burst of feathers on her head. André Lemarié, a designer of accessories who had worked with Yves since 1958, described the effect of ostrich feathers in this way: "They're flattering, they're supple, they're impressive, they're truly nightlife. You can curl them, shave them, cut them to give them a cleaner look, or wrap them like a boa. Zizi is very thin, so nothing should weigh on her. The osmosis worked perfectly. We work together effortlessly."

Yves rediscovered his excitement from the 1961 show, when Zizi's feathered headpiece and the thrill of the costumes soothed his personal purgatory a bit: "Mademoiselle Jeanmaire shines—as soon as she steps onto the stage everything comes alive and lights up. That's the privilege of showgirl queens: just the outline of their silhouette sets the audience on fire—it's a mirage, a dream," he wrote.[10] Some time before, he had designed costumes for Johnny Hallyday's performance at the Palais des Sports: the rock star appeared in an ensemble embellished with red and gold flames, with a big black belt with a bejeweled sun and rhinestone wrist cuffs.

With Rive Gauche, his company had grown even bigger. How would he manage to get through to the other side of the decade? Once again, his eyes led him to women who were more chameleons than even actresses are. There was Betty, with her tall, boyish frame; Paloma Picasso, the femme fatale; and Loulou de la Falaise, the dandy. Loulou, the dissatisfied foreigner, slipped from one place to another, from the finest neighborhoods to Pigalle, from Montparnasse to the Rue Sainte-Anne, guided by her love of wine and unknown places. The adventurous Loulou was first in line at places where women dressed as boys and, at night, looked like cross-dressers.

Yves was also influenced by meeting Paloma Picasso. The first time he saw her, he exclaimed, "It's Dora Maar!" Like Proust's Swann, he had a mania for finding connections with paintings, selecting the aspects of reality that allowed him to flee it. "That day, she was wearing a dress and hat of her mother's from the 1940s. She had very red lips, and that was also a very great shock." The daughter of Pablo

Picasso and Françoise Gilot, she played with colors the way others played with dolls. For Paloma, it was not about "beauty in and of itself, but about things that can make us laugh, dream, travel. And things that do nothing. I like fashion because it's a game." In Paloma Picasso, Yves Saint Laurent had found the inspiration for his retro style. After the joys of pop style, she discovered the delights of kitsch, turning into a babushka in a multicolored skirt she brought back from England or a mystery woman in flea market furs.

"I wore extravagant clothes. It was a way of hiding myself, of twisting people's attention to me so that they wouldn't see me only as Picasso's daughter." Paloma often wore turquoise, red, and bright yellow, along with large hats. "I was very silent. The way I dressed was a way of communicating. Yves and I clicked because we're both very shy." She described meeting Yves through Clara Saint, "the great organizer of all the dinners." Paloma was mad about the Gloria Swanson–style dresses she found on Portobello Road, and she made up her lips with an old stick of rouge that stung her lips: "But it was no worse than that. I suffered but I got through it." At that time, Paloma lived with her grandmother in Neuilly, just outside Paris. She discovered Yves through Penn's photos of Betty Catroux in *Vogue*. "I recognized myself in his style!" she said, while still pointing out the difference, like a woman from the South examining the androgyne: "You can't see Betty's lips."

The Saint Laurent attitude, as it can be reconstructed from his designs, resides in transforming reality. It's a way of leaving yourself behind to play all kinds of different roles. The uncompromising dreamer, Yves could not handle reality when it became mundane. "He couldn't stand the tiniest physical failing, someone who limps, someone who doesn't have elegant gestures," said Paule de Mérindol. "He had this diabolical desire for purity tinted with black humor which places the mind above the body. His need for perfection made him exaggerate things. But he managed to create a symbol of life that a whole generation identifies with." Yves Saint Laurent, a cannibal of memory. Only women sat on his jury. But in 1971, the public was on stage: no one wanted just to be in the audience anymore. They created together. The stars wore clogs. That vision was still intolerable, especially when you yourself looked like a fashion plate. "There are women who don't deserve the gentle name of woman," he said one day to Jeanloup Sieff.

As a true esthete, Yves Saint Laurent loved beauty for its aura of desperation. He venerated women as saints and whores. What he loved about women was himself. As Proust observed, "Homosexuals would be excellent lovers if they didn't pretend to love women."[11]

But for the first time, Yves wasn't alone. He shared his aesthetic tastes with Argentines and Cubans in Paris, a whole generation of exiles who were forgotten in their countries and still little-known elsewhere. Javier Arroyuello, a native of Buenos Aires and one of the wave of Argentines who moved to Paris in the late 1960s, once described to me the feeling of the times: "Once again, the past existed. We believed in the incredible power of the imaginary. We had to reinvent our belonging." This family of artists brought Paris the new creative spirit it needed to be reborn. Jorge Lavelli put on his first play, *La Journée d'une Rêveuse*, at the Théâtre de Lutèce in 1968; Alfredo Rodriguez Arias directed *Eva Peron* at the Théâtre de l'Epée de Bois, the place to be for pure camp: dance-hall lighting and sparkly costumes by Juan Stoppani, kitsch sets by Roberto Plate, and tangos made the character of the holy whore of Argentina gleam. The title character was played by a cross-dressing mime, Facundo Bo. "Eva Peron is a monster. What's more monstrous than a man-woman?" said Copi, the playwright.

The adventure of Arias's theater group, the TSE, had started in front of empty benches at the Musée d'Art Moderne de la Ville de Paris with *Aventuras, Dracula,* and *Futura*. It grew strong with a faithful audience. Unlike politically engaged theater, it promoted the necessity of artifice and myth. Like Saint Laurent, TSE actors loved opera, Visconti, Rouge Baiser lipstick, and Hollywood stars. The Cinémathèque Française became the meeting place for elegant men: transvestites dressed to the nines, hairless and beautiful, trotting around in their velvet overalls from Biba and gold pumps. How many films dubbed into Greek with Danish subtitles did they see while fanning themselves with their fans? Marcial Berro, originally from La Plata, moved in high social circles in New York and met his first clients at the home of Dalí. The painter ordered a jewel from him that would kill whoever touched it. In Paris, his first client was Yves. He bought a silver pill box shaped like a globe, which opened at the equator.

"We said we had to be beautiful and not bored," said Javier Arroyuello of the TSE company. Arroyuello was then staying with Rafaël Lopez Sanchez in a little hotel on Rue Malebranche where they wrote TSE's first plays. Le Sept, a club opened by Fabrice Emaer on Rue Sainte-Anne, had replaced the defunct Fiacre. Those who couldn't get in called it "Maxim's for queens." Its regulars included Roland Barthes, Michel Guy, Andy Warhol, Pierre Cardin, Karl Lagerfeld, Kenzo, and, of course, Pierre Bergé and Yves Saint Laurent, one crossing the Seine in his Jaguar, the other in his black Volkswagen Beetle.

In this new Parisian hotspot, the codes were specific but invisible. When Fabrice, six foot four with wavy platinum hair, greeted you by saying, "Hi, dream child," you knew you were in. "Everyone slept with everyone else. But we respected people's choices," recalled *Le Monde* journalist Frédéric Edelmann. Yves often didn't get home until sunrise. A breeding ground for the Palace, which would open eight years later, Le Sept was a fiefdom. Seduction and witty gossip flourished. Guy Cuevas was at the turntables. Sometimes a glass of champagne was spilled onto an enemy's shirt or spaghetti with caviar dripped from the ceiling. "It's a Klee!" shouted Warhol. In its narrow space, Le Sept combined the privacy of a club and the underground movement of an American-style disco, where everything became fun at 2:00 AM, when the gentlemen talking about Cocteau and Jouhandeau disappeared after their last vodkas. "Then the back room initiation began, to the sweet scent of poppers," a witness once told me. All around the Rue Sainte-Anne, where many young men fraternized, was a string of bars and clubs where young elegant men in satin suits with perfectly blow-dried hair were invited to dance by Spanish hustlers with loose hips and high-heeled boots, who accompanied them to their seats and then left for one-night or one-hour stands in the arms of rugby players. What aficionado—if there are any left—doesn't remember the time spent in Le Sept as the best years of his life?

Women were not excluded—on the contrary. They were expected and venerated. This was not the lot of the typical "fag hags," whose make-up sometimes stimulated these gentlemen's mean-spiritedness.

The whole Saint Laurent clique was there: Clara Saint, Pierre Bergé, Patrick Thévenon, Anne-Marie Muñoz, Betty Catroux, Jeanloup Sieff. However, Sieff was less at home there: "I wasn't part of the inner circle. Guys cheek to cheek just isn't my specialty." Loulou danced on the tables. She was disorientingly energetic—sparkling and bubbling like champagne, said her admirers.

"Le Sept saved me," she said. She felt chilled by this city where different worlds didn't mingle. Loulou preferred New York. Life there was more fun. "First Avenue has become a kind of Rue Saint-Benoît to the 1,000th power," Philippe Labro wrote in *Elle*. "People pass joints at picnics in Central Park." Patti Smith lived with Robert Mapplethorpe in a loft with no kitchen. Warhol wasn't yet a household name; billionaires weren't hung up on surefire investments, and artists weren't concerned about their careers. A group of "girls" gravitated around designers Giorgio Sant'Angelo, Halston, and the illustrator Joe Eula. They were Naomi Sims, the black iris, Betty and Marisa Berenson—the granddaughters of Elsa Schiaparelli—and other unconventional beauties, such as Heidi Gold, Karen Bjornson, Jane Forthe with her Cruella mannerisms, and a brunette from Florence named Elsa Peretti. Plus Loulou de la Falaise and Pat Cleveland. "I love New York," Yves Saint Laurent said, adding that he found the city "wonderful, generous, and full of inspiration."

Yves Saint Laurent observed these women dressed as men and these men dressed as women. He stole their image to create an idealized version of it.

Loulou, the high-class hippie, the woman of a hundred faces, the supreme vice, had entered his life. Loulou, as secretive as all her transformations, a woman of the past in her eccentricity, showed him the paths where serpents become young again by shedding their skin, while everything condemns man to death. In December 1970, Yves Saint Laurent sent a curious New Year's card: the first of his "Love" cards. He would continue to produce different versions until 1992. On a white background, four capital letters, with four reptiles wrapped around them. What poison had love put into his veins?

L ove me forever or never," read the multicolor letters embroidered on the bride's black coat at the end of Yves's fall 1970 show. But the public was fickle. On January 29, 1971, for the first time, Yves Saint Laurent did not come out to greet journalists after the show. It was clear that the collection had fallen flat. During the show, Nathalie Mont-Servan of *Le Monde* wrote her review of Carven, while a journalist from *Le Figaro* read the newspaper and Christiane Collange told Pierre-Yves Guillen of *Combat*, "We should start booing." Some people even left the salon on Rue Spontini before the show was over.

What had happened? With a flowery, almost outlandish style, Yves Saint Laurent had sent out vamps before a public in maxi coats and peasant skirts: this was the Liberation collection. It made Yves Saint Laurent the first couturier of this new decade to adopt a retro style. But it caused a huge scandal. Eighty-four designs were shown without music. A flaming redhead and a black goddess strode along the two large salons without a trace of a smile. They had painted nails and crimson lips. Proclaiming their frivolity in opposition to the neutral unisex style, they were found disturbing. The crepe de Chine had the strident sheen of synthetic fabrics and early Technicolor films. Shockingly, an absinthe-colored fox coat revealed the model's legs. With permed hair under turbans, slender shoulders, and sharp hips, models strolled by in mousseline blouses printed with Man Ray's famous lips. They wore kid leather sandals with double straps, with poppies on their ankles, as if to say, "Come on, boys." It wasn't the clothes that shocked people so much as the styling, the make-up, the hairstyles, the attitude—the very spirit of the collection. Yves Saint Laurent had depicted a complete woman who was almost a parody: she no longer sought to be man's equal, but his opponent. She displayed her power. Under blazers, the dresses looked like silk stockings under a man's robe. A certain version of Paris was back—Paris as imagined by those who hadn't grown up there. A certain way of walking, smoking, and sitting down. "Ruffles annoy me. We need a clean break." And Dior was back. The "Saint Laurent shoulder," built up with padding, and the narrow, braided, reinforced jackets were just as constructed as Dior's dresses when he lined them with percale or taffeta, reconnecting with a forgotten tradition. It's as if Yves Saint Laurent had his arms full of presents—"some gorgeous merchandise," as Marlene Dietrich's character in *A Foreign Affair* might have said. He knew women couldn't resist red silk flowers, polka-dots galore, low-cut Hollywood necklines, and topaz boas and turbans.

Yves Saint Laurent directed women as if they were actresses. The character he created in 1971 was a cabaret singer. Her life was the cabaret, pimps, and bars. But she had a weakness for nice fabric. It was Arletty, and also Marlene in *A Foreign Affair* singing "Take all I've got....Take my lovely illusions." Her sandals looked as if they'd been traded for a typewriter; her American cigarette was purchased with a smile. This retro provocation looked like a defense of the angels of sin. He shared their scorn for men. And also their scorn for women of establishment elegance who were weak enough to think they could imitate them. In these mascara-heavy eyes, there was an echo of Viviane Romance in *Naples au Baiser de Feu*: "If I had been a proper lady, I wouldn't have been your mistress, darling."

It was a critique of the conventionality of haute couture, which he called an "old lady."[1] Ten days after this collection was shown, a press release appeared in *Le Monde* to announce that Yves wanted to focus exclusively on ready-to-wear. Yet in this family dispute, he had the role of heir. He was the heir to Dior because he established a shape. He was the heir to Chanel because that shape remained characteristic: the famous Saint Laurent shoulders. This time, he went on the offensive. The retro bombshell established the ground rules of contemporary style: collage, mixing the old and the new, and demystifying haute couture by using the flea market, as if to say, "It's a love story between me and the street." There was also the arrival of street girls among the ladies, through nostalgia for a time when Paris was still, as Balzac called it, "this great prostitute."[2]

That year, the fashion journalists sat calmly at Yves's show as if witnessing a public execution. *France-Soir* sounded like a broadside from the French Revolution: "Why this slavery, this anachronistic discomfort?...Couturiers no longer have absolute power, the crown has slipped. They grow more infuriating every year." A wave of anger against such "bad taste" overtook reviewers. The ethical stance that was thought to have been done away with in 1968 came back with a vengeance. Except for *Elle* and *Vogue Paris*, the entire French media was irritated at this pot-stirrer who, not satisfied to have escaped the deprivations of war and the postwar period, indulged in the unheard-of idea of making a style out of it. Pierre-Yves Guillen's article in *Combat* was the perfect example: "Why these too-square shoulders, these heavily draped hips, these violent colors, and these shoes with wedges that are the finishing touch to an ugly look? It's hideous and shameful. All we can do is cry. Because it's in very, very bad taste: these turbans, the hemlines above the knee, this is what we saw in Sacha Guitry plays in 1942....What a scandal for someone with as much talent as Yves Saint Laurent! Or what arrogance to think that, like sheep being led to the slaughter, we would applaud this carnage of good taste, this mass grave of elegance, this crematorium of prestige! Evening dresses are decorated with prints depicting men with their members in their hands. A souvenir of Nazi virility, no doubt! I rejected all that in 1944. You did, too, I hope. But I'm afraid there will still be at least one crazy woman in every neighborhood or town who will wear this. You know, one of these crazy women you see sometimes: seventy years old and dressed like teenagers. That's it! Yes, these clothes are made for crazy women who don't want to get old. They're made for people who miss the Krauts—for idiots. Maybe *they'll* like them! Saint Laurent, it's over."[3] In *Le Monde*, Nathalie Mont-Servan also struck a blow, like a schoolteacher who had been assaulted by a rich boy: "Yves Saint Laurent has lost all sense of moderation and good taste, and if ready-to-wear follows his style as it has done for years, women will be forever disgusted by a style that doesn't give a damn about them."[4]

Yet the retro style that Yves Saint Laurent dramatized was already in the air. The day of the show, his muses were guests of honor. Paloma Picasso wore a flowered crepe dress she had gotten at the flea market and a bolero jacket made of monkey fur. "He knew with the previews that the reviews would be bad. I was still a young baby. I didn't know I was his inspiration. He only revealed that to the press in the early 1980s. But that day, he put me in the first row." Loulou de la Falaise, who was living with roommates in New York and was just passing through Paris, wore an electric pink satin jacket and black pantyhose. Yvonne de Peyerimhoff remembered exclaiming, "Those two are a carnival act!" She never forgot the scene that followed. "Yves turned toward me incredibly fiercely and said, 'How dare you talk that way about my friends!' He was usually so sweet and tender, and now he looked like a rattlesnake ready to bite. I went back into my shell and I never opened it again."

In America, retro was also the rage. "Old is in," said *Life* magazine, which even published a special issue on the phenomenon with a pink cover showing movie stars: photos of Rita, Ruby, Paulette, Myrna, Joan, and Betty were depicted inside a heart-shaped anniversary cake. "All the movie stars buy my dresses, even Lana Turner," Halston claimed.[5] But the retro trend didn't stop Americans from trashing Saint Laurent's collection. What right did a European have to appropriate a legend? Wasn't Hollywood glamour the only thing that Americans—who had a complex about their lack of history—insured more heavily than their limousines? Their chastisement was harsh indeed, with headlines such as "The Ugliest Show in Paris" (*New York Herald Tribune*), "Yves Saint Laurent Debacle" (*Time*). The *New York Herald Tribune*'s Eugenia Sheppard declared the show to be "frankly, definitely, and completely hideous." She praised Givenchy, Lanvin, Patou, and Ungaro: "the right clothes for the right people." One buyer told me, "There's no more leader. Paris has been over for three years."

This fiasco exacerbated tensions between Paris and New York. American ready-to-wear didn't think it needed couture. Style, not fashion was the watchword of the day. The rise of Ralph Lauren, the boy from the Bronx, had begun. After a decade filled with all kinds of experimentations, America was rediscovering its classics. Halston, who was defended by the press and Seventh Avenue buyers, was the heir to this supple and functional easy line. In 1969, he won a Coty Award, the equivalent of an Oscar in the fashion world. The next year, Ralph Lauren won it for his men's collection. In the United States, everything had to look new—even things that were old.

The Americans thought they'd already had their share of decadence. Their hypersensitive puritanism was stimulated by the moral and political crisis sweeping the country: the ravages of illegal drugs, the painful readjustment of Vietnam veterans to civilian life, and political crises including the Pentagon Papers (published by *The New York Times* in the summer of 1971) and Watergate (Nixon would resign on August 9, 1974).

It was neither the first nor the last time that Yves Saint Laurent would encounter American criticism. He was fascinated by the look of American women, who always had pockets, even in their evening gowns, and slipped on turtlenecks and hot pants under their mink coats. But he never thought they had the boldness that made European women so charming and fragile. "In France, fashion is part of social life. You play with it. American women like fashion, but it worries them. They need to be reassured by the newspapers, which are kind of their bible," explained Susan Train in the March 1971 *Vogue*. For this reason, the Americans eagerly protected themselves, anticipating solutions to future problems and automatically rejecting anything that resisted this logical system. "American women thought the New Look was a conspiracy," Train concluded.

Although she was shocked by this bordello collection, Susan Train thought Yves Saint Laurent had many good qualities: "He's disciplined. He's smart. He's rigorous. His strength is to lead the way." Nevertheless, for the first time, Yves was oblivious to the questions that Americans were asking of couturiers. In fact, he pushed them to liberate themselves from such things: "I want to free women from the tyranny of hemlines."[6]

When he scattered American stars across his crepe de Chine coats, it was an innocent nod to the GI's. But this was disturbing and troubling. In 1947, the New Look had also caused a wave of anger. When he went to Chicago, Dior was met by "ladies who were half suffragettes, half cleaning ladies," "Bacchae in a fury," who held signs reading "Burn Monsieur Dior" because of their hatred of emphasized hips and long skirts.[7] This was still the era when a couturier wanted to be judged only on his dresses. Since Yves Saint Laurent had burst through the plush walls of the salons and was more exposed, he himself provided the weapons that were turned against him. But he remained an amazing acrobat who always landed on his feet to deafening applause with a smile on his face. He loved the dizziness of the void.

When he turned thirty-five, he revealed a new side to his personality, one which hadn't come out in the 1960s. First of all, his appearance: long hair and a beard, a velvet Rive Gauche safari jacket, a rust-colored satin shirt with a rhinestone star, black boots and discreet jewelry from Cartier, one of his favorite jewelers. The shy, handsome young man faded into the background. His sketches revealed strong lines and he revealed a stubbornness that would earn him insults. Yet Paule de Mérindol, who temporarily left the company at this time, remembered his strength of character:

"Yves is theatrical. The others have to hold him back. He is so powerful that he has to tie himself up to be protected from himself. He's provocative. He just wants to blow up whatever annoys him. Order. Established people." His demands and his whims were the price of his ambition. He knew that he was his own harshest critic. He told *Elle* in February 1971, "I'd rather shock people than bore them by repeating myself."

The fashion critics slammed the door and trashed the collection, and the clients disappeared. Yet Yves Saint Laurent had done nothing but obstinately follow his line. He hadn't given up the "beautiful skinny women" who were so sophisticated: they illustrated more decadently the feminine-masculine style that he had sketched out long ago, when he first starting working for Dior, with the Trapeze dress for flat hips and an adolescent bust. But this was the first time that he had exposed himself with such fierce sincerity. It was his way of protesting propriety, puritanism, and the censorship of his time. Yet, as of 1971, the greatest provocation by a couturier was to make dresses, pants, and jackets that were neither aggressively new nor half-heartedly boring but that simply put themselves out there on the strength of their style. His fans judged him more astutely: "Very contemporary," they said. The collection even made an impression at Cardin, where it stunned a nineteen-year-old design assistant named Jean-Paul Gaultier.

With this collection-as-manifesto, Yves Saint Laurent went back to his childhood demons: the women of Oran with their dyed hair and plucked eyebrows, whom the women of Algiers found "rowdy." He hinted at this to *Vogue,* as was reported in the March 1971 issue: "What I want to do is shock people and make them think.... Young people don't have any memories." His silk poppy pinned to a black dress was his first tribute to Lucienne. Would anyone believe that through these women he was sketching out an almost autobiographical portrait of himself?

In this portrait he was both aggressive and charming, tragic and frivolous—a man who wanted to reign over all hearts since he couldn't be a ruler over one alone. His retro collection was not an "easy" style. It didn't evoke the health, youth, and realism that journalists wanted. It was a reverse New Look. Saint Laurent redefined himself by rushing ahead to meet that era—the retro style that already existed on the streets. He didn't simply reconstruct the past; he stylized it. He did this in a powerful way, through a puzzle of references that he made his own. He recycled documents and things he observed, holding life close. This kind of style could be seen in New York in Betsey Johnson or in Stephen Burrows' World. In *Elle*, Yves Saint Laurent acknowledged, "If I had any influences, it was American pop artists: I discovered the black legs and the very high heels on Andy Warhol's pin-ups and loved them. So what if it's not distinguished? I think it's seductive. Aggressive, but seductive."[8]

Yves Saint Laurent got the message that "people weren't so much visually shocked as morally shocked."[9] The next season, he coldly banned his critics from his show. Outraged, the press took a stand. The Association Française des Journalistes

Professionnels de l'Elégance issued a press release in "most vigorous protest against the deliberate ostracism" of some of its members: *Le Monde*'s Nathalie Mont-Servan, Europe 1's Christiane Collange, *Combat*'s Pierre-Yves Guillen, and Eugenia Sheppard, whose column appeared in some eighty American newspapers. Pierre Bergé was a bundle of nerves.

But Yves Saint Laurent was ready for his great solo. With Rive Gauche, he had adapted the rigor of couture to the movement of a generation: in less than five years, black, navy blue, jersey, the safari jacket, the trench coat, the tuxedo suit, and the women's pantsuit had become classics of the contemporary wardrobe. In 1971 he declared, "It's hard to offer people only the option of work clothes for a life of work. Of course, we have to take that into consideration. I also paid my dues to reality: everything I've done up until now was about serious, responsible, 'appropriate' clothes. But that's no longer enough. We need fun, humor, freedom. Revenge. Fashion should also be festive, it should help people to play. To change. To compensate a bit for a world they're doomed to live in that is so terrible, so gray, and so hard. We also have to design for their dreams, their escapes, their craziness." Modern women no longer wanted couturiers to be fashion dictators. But Yves still had a vision that he wanted to impose.

Paris was burning. Police buses were everywhere. Leftist students and far-right activists clashed with iron bars. The real shock of 1971 was the manifesto for the right to abortion, which Catherine Deneuve had signed. So all this meant that Yves Saint Laurent's nostalgic dream came at the right moment, restoring the aura of a world where couturiers, and Yves at the head of the pack, sold bath towels and bed sheets. Yves Saint Laurent was defending something quite different than his professional status—even if he knew quite well that the greatest threat to couture wasn't being copied, but *not* being copied. He was the only one who was building his fortune on the suicide of the profession.

The trend of the time made women servilely dependent on a natural style that—like Marie Antoinette playing shepherdess—they thought they'd use to banish all their ills. "*Le monde entier fait l'amour,*" Esther Galil sang that year. People drank thyme herbal tea and rode bicycles, after reading that cars pollute. Medicine was alternative and cuisine was vegetarian. They threw crepe parties in the white-plastered studio. And here came Yves Saint Laurent declaring war on the great sect of love, on modern sanctimoniousness, which was concealed like a sewing kit in a hidden Formica cabinet. In 1971, the fake young ambitious style triumphed in a clumsy hodgepodge of dried flowers and orange ottomans. Everything was smooth and practical, like a pair of Karting pants that looked the same in the back as in the front. Everything was built-in: the dining room was now a breakfast nook and the living room was a lounge. In their rustic cottages with psychedelic flowered wallpaper, mothers now had only one idea: to look like their daughters. And the body! It started floating in grandpa-style shirts, house painter's overalls, bulky sweaters, or huge flowered skirts. This natural style drove Yves mad. He was a luxury hippie who had never cooked a meal.

Yet, as Paule de Mérindol explained, "This young man had an amazing aura. He took himself for the Chosen One." The sheaf of wheat that a model held in her hand during the famous fashion show on January 29 symbolized this power. In a Hellenic style, Yves Saint Laurent drew figures of Achilles and helmeted gladiators drinking, fighting, and dancing among fantastical animals, and these were printed on silk crepe dresses. It was a way of inviting women to regain the individual strength that they applied to collective struggles. He would prove that women's liberation doesn't start with burning your bra or not shaving your underarms. Everything was emphasized, molded, low-cut. That year, Yves Saint Laurent made the girlfriend go out of style and celebrated the woman who could bring about misfortune. The couturier embodied the role that existence had refused him: being the male who decides, the pimp who flexes his muscles for a tease, the handsome officer of the French Foreign Legion who fascinates gays.

More than ever, the Saint Laurent woman was an apparition. Other women said, "She's not natural. She's very Saint Laurent." With make-up in shades like purple smoke, for the lips, and misty champagne, she exhibited a special kind of beauty that wasn't about perfect features but the truth she expressed. She wore her fox stole like Lucienne Mathieu-Saint-Laurent, pinned over one shoulder. It was as if he were inspired by the Marcel Carné film *Children of Paradise*: "Traditions are disappearing, the public constantly asks for something new. Something new, something new—what would that look like? Newness is as old as the world itself!" Followed by her perfume, the Saint Laurent woman was as skillful at hiding her past as upper-class women were at hiding how they spent their time and American women were at hiding their relatives. Her dog had to be named Nobody. She needed rivals and admirers. Lipstick and make-up. Love letters and a solid gold cigarette holder, on which an unknown hand had engraved, "Mad about boys." At age twenty, she liked to act like a seductive thirty-five-year-old, giving herself over to love without being fooled by it, but believing in it enough to indulge in it at least twice a day. This was completely out of sync with couturiers whose only reality was a commercial one: "Chanel was from the Rolls era, I'm from the Matra era. She worked for rich leisured ladies who got pearls by the millions, and I work for modern women who just have average budgets," said Courrèges, who had started showing his ready-to-wear Prototype line at the same time as his couture collection. While couturiers were apologizing for their title, Yves Saint Laurent only strengthened his connection to his profession. Then a sudden event would open up new possibilities for him.

"Chanel is dead!" The news fell like a bombshell. The "Grande Mademoiselle" passed away on January 10, 1971, in her apartment in the Ritz. For Yves Saint Laurent, the real struggle was starting. He would have to fight the myth. Become his favorite historical character, the shade who enlightened him: Chanel. He had borrowed her camellias. Then her suits. He had freed himself from imitation, renewing Chanel's spirit in its eternal truth: French classicism, decadent British elegance, Russian exuberance. She had once suggested a collaboration: "I will give you an extraordinary gift. You'll take the Chanel collection and the Saint Laurent collection to America. We'll give them a big surprise at the end. For the brides, Saint Laurent will make a dress. And I'll make pants," she told Pierre Bergé. It never came to pass, as the circumstances were never right. Too early. Too late. And then she was gone.

"I make my men's collection the way Chanel made her suits," he told *Le Figaro* in 1971. But he quickly added, with the seriousness of an anatomical expert: "A man's body in jersey is soft, rumpled, old." Making men look good was personally satisfying, but he needed a more spectacular success, one that would be more scandalous. True kings seek out war. Coco had dressed worldly women as maids. Yves Saint Laurent never had to avenge himself on poverty, but on a morality that named wise men and fools. So he dressed worldly women as tarts. Thus he reminded them of what they preferred to forget, under their prudishly-tied scarves. The Yves Saint Laurent suit would become what the Chanel suit was. With this difference: he didn't dress proper wives, but amazons. Those who played on the ambiguity of double sexuality. I was told ten years later he would say, "Chanel is a marvel. She understood her time. She created the women of her time. When she died, my success increased tenfold."

The Saint Laurent suit widened the shoulders and lengthened the legs. This role play was disturbing enough that people asked in 1971 whether he was dressing women as men or men as women. Either way, it was clear he had the same thing in mind as Helmut Berger when he parodied Marlene in the first scene of *The Damned* by Visconti, Yves Saint Laurent's favorite filmmaker: "I'm sick of gigolos. I want a real man, with a heart of fire." The 1970s were starting up against a background of disillusionment. An aggressive, troubling, suicidal time.

Around the world, the hippie dream was burning up in the darkness of a lost generation that had traded its pop standards—sunsets and strumming guitars—for the closed fists of rock and roll in leather jackets, motorbikes, and black jeans. Love is sex. An album cover created a scandal that year: *Sticky Fingers*, with its close-up on a man's crotch in jeans. The newly released Rolling Stones album was an invitation to hell. In a February 1971 issue of *Rolling Stone* magazine, John Lennon described Britain in the darkest terms: "We've grown up a little, all of us, there has been a change and we're all a bit freer and all that, but it's the same game. Shit, they're doing exactly the same thing, selling arms to South Africa, killing blacks on the street, people are living in fucking poverty, with rats crawling over them. It just makes you puke, and I woke up to *that*, too. The dream is over. It's just the same, only I'm thirty, and a lot of people have got long hair." The same year, Milos Forman's *Taking Off* mocked American conformity: a meeting of parents of runaway children turns into a marijuana party. At the edges of these little distractions, death was lurking. It carried off the beautiful Talitha Getty when she overdosed in her fabulous bathroom.

Yves Saint Laurent had found his way. The extreme. The edge. The excess of appearances. The cross-dressing of the world. He expressed his own style—just as Dior had found his in postwar optimism: "We were coming out of a time of war, uniforms, women-soldiers. I designed women as flowers with soft shoulders," Dior wrote. In 1947, he wanted to forget the "detestable" fashion under the Occupation: "Skirts that were too short, jackets that were too long, soles that were too thick, and, worst of all, the horrible way Parisian women's hair was piled over their foreheads like fontanges and spread out over their backs like manes. Basically, the zazou style, which surely came about as a challenge to the arrogance of the occupier and the Vichy authorities."[10]

In 1946, after all, women obtained the right to vote in France. That was exactly what Yves Saint Laurent put back in the spotlight in 1971, in the tragic and laughable mystery of a woman in a man's jacket who stuck a feather in her hair and lifted up her skirt to walk through the mud like a queen.

In 1971, Yves Saint Laurent invited women to reinvent their past. On this journey, he played the roles of couturier, of friend and guide, and of the lover whom they dreamed of belonging to—as if, in a void left by men, there were hearts to reconquer: "At that time, women had a special kind of seduction, perhaps because of the anxiety in this climate of men, dreams, and heroes," he would tell *Elle* in 1986. His conclusions on the Liberation collection were positive: "Women—in films, in photos—were never so attractive. Because they looked free, decisive, and happy. Perhaps because they expected wonderful tomorrows from the future, and that lit up their eyes. That made their high heels click cheerfully, and with delight they rediscovered silk, colors, the pleasure of getting dressed, the pleasure of being attractive. They didn't care about fashion with a capital F. Just like me."

Now he was committed. He had completed a break with the public that brutally surprised him as much as it affected him. "I even think the word 'scandal' is not too strong, and I'm sad and flattered."[11] Yet he continued to believe in his instinct: "Manet's *Olympia* caused the same kind of reaction."[12] Somewhat awkwardly, he sometimes felt the need to surround himself with references, even though an artist usually doesn't need them. Manet himself said, "It's the effect of sincerity to make artworks resemble a protest, even though the painter thought only of rendering his impression. He tried to be himself and not someone else."[13] None of the criticisms of Yves Saint Laurent were about the stiffness of his suits or the pleats of his pants that sometimes made the stomach stick out a bit too much. They attacked the spirit of the collection. Under those assaults, everything would explode, as if in a big family fight. People had always loved Saint Laurent for what he wasn't. But in 1971, they still had trouble loving him for what he was. In fact that was what excited him and encouraged him to struggle and not to betray himself or adopt the bourgeois desire for petty honors. During the same time, the press praised "the brave pleats" of Jacques Griffe, "the easy fashion" of Ted Lapidus, and the "reassuring" white and navy wool suits of Dior.

"This collection established the basis of fashion for the next twenty years," said Paloma Picasso. Sharper than the angle of the blazers, redder than the braid that emphasized these jackets like eyeliner, it offered a chance to discover a man's vision. "I think that after trying to blend into the crowd for a while, seeking refuge in the anonymity of a uniform, today people prefer to stand out, to stage themselves, with everyone as a star. And to exhibit their 'type': the boys wanted to let their beards grow and the girls want to express their profound femininity." He would stimulate this idea in a terrible demand for perfection. This hypersensitive designer would always fight the quaint, the average, and the unbearable tranquility which, if it dominated completely, would sign his death warrant. As Yves put it to Claude Berthod in *Elle*: "I'm not the one who changed, it's the world. And it will never stop changing. And we're forever condemned to adjust our ways of seeing, feeling, and judging. Certitude, tranquility, a clear conscience—that's over. Elegance is part and parcel of that. Why should a bunch of graybeards claim the right to decree in the name of elegance that one thing is good and another bad?"

The passage of time—Saint Laurent time, "ciné-réalité" as Loulou de la Falaise called it—would only make this decried collection more lively. He said, "It's one of the youngest collections I've done. It's the result of a memory....I still have this vision of my mother in that dress." Yves Saint Laurent imagined the women of Oran atop the ruins of a collapsing world. They'd been the first to lead him into a world where red is the color of nail polish and reality is permanent cinema. Ever since then, he had never stopped trying to revive that enchantment in a sort of communion with the women he guided without knowing them. Virna Lisi borrowed the green fox coat to act in a remake of *The Well-Digger's Daughter*. To show the collection, actress Maria Kimberly posed in a black evening tuxedo suit with a rose in her hair and what *Paris Match* called "all the accessories that we thought had disappeared." The couturier added, "You have to see her with a sense of humor and without preconceived ideas. This time, the men will be happy."[14]

While Yves Saint Laurent wasn't addressing everyone, his preaching touched all those who shared his solitary struggles. After being long repressed in shameful secrecy, they came out from the shadows that year with their lipsticks, dresses, and wigs. Having attended religious school, they had dressed up to play Joan of Arc or Bélise in Molière's *The Learned Ladies*. Teachers by day and seductresses by night, they loved Saint Laurent because he was the first couturier who openly came out as the impresario of the homosexual set. Like them, this man had been formed by women. He knew these capricious, fickle, horrible, troubling creatures better than anyone. And what he preferred in them was himself—and his desire to be the fiancée of a heartthrob through his dresses. An aesthete fascinated by dives, Kasbahs, and prisons, Yves Saint Laurent had conquered his public. At this time there was a sort of Saint Laurent club whose members put little YSL rhinestone stars on their satin jackets. It was the symbol of a real group that didn't identify with any party, even the outrageously subversive. They were closer to the effete artistic circle of Rive Gauche high culture—Barthes, Foucault, etc.—than to the bearded guys wearing bras who protested under the banners of the Front Homosexuel d'Action Révolutionnaire. Each one of them was a movement all on his own.

The enlightened bourgeoisie of Paris liked to go slumming—in a proper way, of course. On January 26, 1971, three days before the Liberation collection was shown, the cabaret La Grande Eugène launched its new show, which would run for 700 performances. Many personalities of the Saint Laurent clan would be seen there: Philippe and Marie Collin, Clara Saint, the Muñoz couple, Zizi Jeanmaire, and Loulou, the first woman in Paris to wear jeans with her YSL tuxedo jacket. "She was ravishingly elegant. Incredibly nice and funny. No airs," remembered Jérôme Nicollin, alias Belle de May. Jérôme "had a beard and shaved it off to enter La Grande Eugène the way others shaved to enter a monastery." He used Lechner eyebrow pencils and Caron powder. His gold kid leather sandals with red soles were by Saint Laurent. "My good luck charms," he called them. "Originally they were made for the model Veruschka." Every night, "the approximately celestial angel," as Le Monde's Frédéric Edelmann called him, embodied his idols: Yvonne Printemps, Mistinguett, Lillian Gish, Marlene Dietrich, Sara Montiel, and even Zizi Jeanmaire in her feather outfit. Belle de May recorded her voice and then lip-synched her songs in order to emphasize her physical poses, which were close to the theater of attitude and gesture where the Saint Laurent women excelled. "Cross-dressing was the only way to get on stage when you were unknown," Jérôme Nicollin said. "I was very handsome…and very beautiful." In the first Grande Eugène show, Belle de May did a Soeurs Étienne song wearing a tight-waisted suit and platform shoes.

The circuit was launched: La Grande Eugène, Le Sept, Les Puces, Casino de Paris, La Cinémathèque, and the Théâtre de l'Epée de Bois (which was always under threat of eviction). A whole court surrounded Yves Saint Laurent: the actors of worldly theater in the camp mode.

In 1964, Susan Sontag defined camp in "Notes on 'Camp,'" which became a user's guide in Europe for all those who weren't part of the camp world. "The essence of Camp is its love of the unnatural."[15] "Camp is the answer to the problem: how to be a dandy in the age of mass culture."[16] It offered a way to love Aubrey Beardsley's drawings, old Flash Gordon comics, boas, transvestites, operas by Bellini, and Visconti. A way to reinvent myths through memories—Joan Crawford's jungle red, Jean Harlow's negligees, or Marlene's eyebrows—that had established the image of absolute and parodic femininity. "I'm fascinated by luxury magazines, fashion stereotypes, the uniform, mechanized movements of cabaret girls, and advertising posters. These are daily references that belong to everyone, and as soon as I make them theater and put them into the context of the stage, into the machinery of acting, I draw the audience into this game, into this universe, at least I hope so," Alfredo Arias was quoted as saying to Colette Godard in *Le Monde*. In *Dracula* and *Aventuras*, Maria Félix in a dominatrix role with heavy make-up, held up by female dwarf servants, ruled over operetta peasants. At the time, Arias staged L'Histoire du Théâtre: the actors moved while deconstructing their gestures, demonstrating their characters like models. As for Helmut Newton, he photographed models like movie characters. He considered himself to be a Pygmalion and said he "trained" the girls he photographed: "I had a crew of two or three women. We always worked together. They were fascinated, and thrilled to become famous. It's true that they were crazier, and that the magazines didn't require 'selling' images." He added, "For a fashion photo to be successful, first of all it has to not look like a fashion photo." This master of the lens would be one of the only photographers of his time, along with Guy Bourdin, to refuse to photograph certain clothes. "Preparation is often more important than the photo. I work very fast. I use very little film. I always have a very specific idea, even if everything can change at the last minute. The second rule is that you must always have your antennae up."

Born in Berlin in 1920 and naturalized as an Australian citizen, Helmut Newton had an encyclopedic memory. *"Femmes fatales* always interest me more than virgins. Because that's my entire youth in Berlin. I started taking photos at age twelve." In the same way, Yves Saint Laurent rediscovered his youthful enchantment with fashion. Draped, low-cut dresses that emphasized the hips and waists, pleated crepe shorts, Naked Van Dongen–style backs under alpaca wool suits would be published in the same place where they were born: the pages of *Vogue Paris*. The magazine defended him, much as it chose to publish the glossy pin-ups by Helmut Newton. "Farewell folklore and costumes, farewell neurotic fabrics. No, Yves Saint Laurent isn't hideous, as they claimed. No, Paris hasn't killed fashion," read *Vogue's* "Point of View" column in March 1971. "I want clothes that give women a new range of ways to seduce," he told the magazine. In *Vogue*, Yves Saint Laurent posed for Jeanloup Sieff with his models—Annie, Elsa, and Jacqueline—and the dancing girls of the Casino de Paris. It was then clear that the retro collection was more than an issue of fashion. It drew its necessity from something deeper than a couturier's inspiration: a need to create theater. To express one's fantasies on stage, in a world where everything is fake, in order to be more real.

For Zizi Jeanmaire's new show at the Casino de Paris, Yves Saint Laurent, liberated from his company and his clients, made his true declaration of love to Paris. "Yes, you, Mademoiselle, step forward, please," said the young couturier who, backstage on the Rue de Clichy, looked like a living version of Duduche—the young and naïve cartoon character—lost amidst the sparkles. In one of the sketches for the show, a lady of the night comes forward almost naked, a redhead wearing black stockings. One rhinestoned hand is perched on her hip and the other twirls a little evening bag. Red and white swan feathers burst forth from one corner of the stage. It was Paris singing "On m'suit" in blue mink with sleeves delicately wrapped with pink ribbons. The figures wore black fox stoles and diamond necklaces. Yves had already drawn such redheads in his book *Pourquoi Parler d'Amour*. Twenty years later, he brought them to life. "You will be fiery, fierce, and insistent to them, so that carnal pleasure will take hold of their entire bodies." It was as if he had erased their pillbox hats, their little veils, their Domergue-style faces. They were hussies with hearts of gold. Girls who weren't born with silver spoons in their mouths. A past on the streets. A future in a mansion. These women whose lives create a stir, and whose deaths often pass unnoticed. These women idolized by gay men for being bewitching, dramatic, tragic, and glorious. They were monsters. Adorable, indifferent. Egocentric, calculating. They put on an act so that they wouldn't fall, so they could defy what brought them a bit closer each day to terror. Women whose elegance was always noticed but who, at the serious times in their lives, had no handkerchiefs to wipe their mascara tears. Unable to seek happiness, they just avoided boredom. Betrayals, murders, whims, and hopeless love affairs distracted their ill-fated existence.

This show, *Zizi Je T'aime*, was the height of extravagance, as Roland Petit later recalled he wanted "to rehabilitate bad taste in good taste." With no geisha cha-cha or noche flamenco. Thirty-six scenes, thirty-two female dancers. Four hundred seats, crimson velvet and gilded stucco. Circus lighting, rhinestones, sweat, and feathers. Serge Gainsbourg wrote all of Zizi's songs. "*Du champ, du brut, des vamps, des putes, des stars, des tsars, d'l'amour, des filles d'amour à boire ou à plumes.*" Michel Legrand and Michel Colombier wrote the music.

There were six hundred costumes in all by Erté, Pace, Léonor Fini—who handled the witches' Sabbath—and Yves Saint Laurent, who was totally committed to the project. Nothing was beautiful or luxurious enough for Saint Laurent the magnificent.

"We need white fox," Yves said in a gentle voice. "That'll cost a million!" exclaimed Hector Pascual, who worked with Yves. He was calculating the cost of these dreams: "I'll try to see if I can get it for a little less." "Oh, of course," said Roland. "But, ultimately, darlings, we have to have what we need!" "Of course," Saint Laurent murmured, "especially since each time we tried to save money…" The show cost five hundred million francs. At least, at first. On stage, the streetlamps were arranged. A gondola descended from the sky. "It's an undertaker's gondola for a burial in Bécon-les-Bruyères! Go stick it in a suburban yard with geraniums in it!" shouted Roland Petit. "And make me another one!" The new one would slip into the Venetian night, matching the dominos in red velvet and black vinyl.

Madame Fougerolles, who was devoted to Roland Petit's dance company, made the costumes. She was a professional who was first in her class at the École du

Spectacle and was head costumer for the Théâtre de la SNCF in the 1950s. She owed her understanding of the profession to Karinska: "White Russia, the aristocracy of taste. A great atelier!" That was where she made the costumes that Yves designed for *Cyrano de Bergerac* (1959) and for *Notre-Dame de Paris* (1965). "He knows exactly what he wants. But he's able to listen. He's not a tyrant. He likes to learn." Yves Saint Laurent understood the battle between the world of costume and the world of fashion, where the worst insult was to make something that looked like Scheherazade, while in the theater it was to do haute couture. He was torn between two opposing universes. What *première* would agree to work with those barbarians? In haute couture, they scorned entertainers, who treated fabrics disrespectfully, gluing them or dyeing them to create the desired effect, "what they call their fullness." On the contrary, in the theater, they mocked careful needlework. "A true couture dress, on stage, is just nothing," said Madame Fougerolles. "It has to be adjusted according to the viewpoint of the audience." She handled pink taffeta capes, fountains ringed with iridescent acetate, crinoline skirts with garlands of three thousand beads. "In couture, they're used to looking at things closely. Theater is an added crazy dimension. You have to go," she said, as if looking ladies who only talk about clean lines and millimeters up and down. But even in theater, you can't overdo it. "If we put twelve meters of flounces, the dancer can't turn around!"

At the Casino, they rehearsed. There were sixty technicians. "Clear out in front, barbarians!" an electrician grumbled at two British intruders who came in to take photos. There was an incredible amount of coming and going. Clowns and jugglers. Powdered noblemen. Sets that rose up and came down. A Bridge of Sighs. A seven-meter gorilla. Snug inside a big marmot coat, Zizi curled up like a cat in her corner, her eyes on the lookout, ready to leap, her claws extended on her white tights. Zizi as a brunette Venus. Blond Zizi. Zizi as Elisa, Zizi melancholy in bruises: "Bruises are jewels, hit me again, you thug." That was her job. All performers knew discipline was mandatory. "You have to know your technique before you forget it. Without technique, you'll break your face."

Two dancing singers wrapped arms: "I'm mixed up with a mixed-race guy." Gainsbourg could be seen in a cloud of smoke. His appearance offered a strange contrast to that of Erté, as dashing as a young man with chain bracelets and a polka-dotted porcelain blue ascot. Around him, everyone seemed too young or too old, and just plain vulgar. "I only had trouble with Lillian Gish," this Russian aristocrat would sometimes say. He had gone to work for Paul Poiret in early 1913. That was where he made his first dress: a costume for Mata Hari in *Le Minaret* by Jean Richepin. "I started with a revolution in the body. Before, the bust was leaning over." He was eighty years old and "hated monotony," someone familiar with him told me.

A transvestite came out of the wings, as if bursting from one of Yves's drawings, waving a headdress of pink feathers: just a gigolo with plump arms, in a 1920s-style red silk dress with a long necklace of pearls as big as candy. Yves was having fun. But his passion was an Orientalist scene, "The Awakening of the Sultan," whose costumes and sets he designed. "A new career has started here, one which can make us forget about Bakst," Louis Aragon wrote in *Les Lettres Françaises* in February 1972 about the costume and set designer for the Ballets Russes, with the same excited tone that Apollinaire had for such "soirées de Paris" sixty years earlier.

Filled with wonder, Yves Saint Laurent plunged into the colors of the Blue God, Thamar, and the sultana Zobidé. After the discovery of Christian Bérard, he had found a new master. Léon Bakst invited him into the magic box that was theater to perfect what he had always been seeking: to free the body from the costume, to enhance its expression and decorate it with pure fantasy that did not hinder movement, but which needed to "go boom," as Zizi would say. Yves Saint Laurent was in fact much closer to Bakst, who died in 1924, than to Erté, the eternal young man. With feminine, mannered lines, Erté slid bodies under nymph tunics, with the same meticulousness that was seen on stage in his sphinxes and his crystal columns, and in his own house full of rare shells and flowers with mother-of-pearl petals. Erté's blue was fluid as water and fragile as Wedgwood china. He was more interested in details and the harmony of contours. Bakst focused on groupings of colors and unpredictable sensations. "There are reds that are triumphant and reds that are murderous. There is the blue of Mary Magdalene and the blue of Messalina!"[17] "Astonish me," he seemed to say to Saint Laurent.

Just as Bakst broke with the vanished convention of periwinkle and violet sets, so Yves Saint Laurent rejected the typical eroticism of "Gay Paree" or of colonial love with a backdrop of the Kasbah. No chiaroscuro, but masses of color and arabesques. As a disciple, he copied. It was as if he wanted to assimilate a technique before forgetting it in order to express his sensations more intensely and create his own rhythm.

In his drawings, color was still sequestered: the watercolors had clear lines. They didn't blend. He was heating up. But you could tell that this creative ferment had taken him over, that he would reveal himself and find in this adventure the Saint Laurent who made colors explode, as in his Turquin marble blues, his Mediterranean blues, his Garance reds, and his Coq Hardi greens. The romantic excess of his 1960 designs for Dior had already foreshadowed this. "Splendidly decadent," wrote François Nourissier about the show in *L'Express*.

In this green and red garden of delights, odalisques in beaded harem pants waved fans, languidly stretched out on orange and blue silk cushions. The sultan then appeared, naked with silky skin, a god of love with a thousand beads rolling over his delicate muscles like kisses. There was no phony exoticism, but a body superbly wrapped in a silk loincloth that was admired like a magician's turban: Jorge Lago, the *maravillosamente sexy* dancer "for whom dance is clothing," as Pierre Marcabru, wrote in *France-Soir*. Yves was very much in love.

All of fashionable Paris was there for the opening night of *Zizi Je T'aime* on February 14, 1972. Ursula Andress wore a Cossack outfit. Marie Bell had pink feathers and Françoise Dorin sported a silver spacesuit. At the end, Zizi came down the great staircase. The curtain fell, and the audience burst into deafening applause. On stage, everyone took a bow: Roland Petit, Serge Gainsbourg, Erté, and Yves, in a black tuxedo with a giant bow tie. *Elle*'s headline was: "A Glorious Paradise for Yves Saint Laurent!" "Zizi's Got Legs and Smarts," raved *France-Soir*. There would be 170 performances. "We made our billion in ten months," announced Roland Petit, who considered that "Giscard d'Estaing saved my life." The minister of finance kindly forgave the Casino's back taxes. The Zizi girls and the black pearl, Lisette Malidor, tossed their furs over their shoulders.

Yves Saint Laurent gave women their high heels back. Roland Petit, the new owner of Casino de Paris, gave the star performer her staircase—these forty steps that Mistinguett and Cécile Sorel once descended.

The biggest surprise was the Parisian and slightly snobbish excitement that the show inspired. That same week, two great friends of the maison Saint Laurent, Edmonde Charles-Roux and Louis Aragon, each wrote an article about Yves in *Les Lettres Françaises*. Edmonde Charles-Roux wrote, "Le Casino de Paris is presenting an authentic cabaret with no mothball scent," and celebrated the "many little details of this profession that no one notices. It's the dress on ball bearings that seems to walk by itself, the crinoline skirt shaped like a gondola that folds up like an umbrella, it's the masterpiece of the Marinette and Aumont ateliers, and it took three months of labor to make this confounded dress go on and off the stage." Yves Saint Laurent had described his difficulties with this dress to the woman who still called him "the Parisian from Algeria": "You must have both a sense of excess and a postcard way of looking at things. Even more than theater, cabaret is life inside-out. Poor materials look luxurious and vice-versa." Cabaret taught him "speed. At the cabaret, everything is there. Three accessories can create a whole world. So, with a big bunch of black feathers, you can make a great hat. Perch it on the head of a tall nude black girl and when she goes on stage, it's simply a marvelous effect."[18]

"I'm not ashamed of what I love. Shame on those who are ashamed to love," wrote Louis Aragon. It was two years after the death of his wife and communist muse, Elsa Triolet, who had never been a model of frivolity, and it was as if Aragon had now rediscovered the excitement he had once known when he introduced his Surrealist friends to Montparnasse nightlife and experienced a mad passion for Nancy Cunard, "this creature of flesh and smoke."[19] Under the headline "From Zizi Jeanmaire to Alfred de Musset," Aragon described the "quivering of pleasure that is still totally new."[20] He was the first to set foot on the red carpet that Saint Laurent unrolled at the feet of intellectuals—whom he called rather ironically "cultured people." "This show is like a great gift that's been given to us. Lower your eyes, hypocrites!" he wrote, going so far as to say that Yves Saint Laurent's costumes "bring back to life" those of Ingres and Delacroix. "People will say…I certainly know what people will say: feudal art, the bourgeoisie, decadence, Western corruption, etc. But let me have my own idea of the future, and, hence, of socialism: imagine that its victory, in France at least, will not make men and women less beautiful. And pleasure is their main occupation."

However, some critics had a more mixed assessment. "It's both garish and distinguished," wrote *Le Monde*'s Claude Sarraute, who was charmed but also annoyed by "this confusion of a show that rushes off in every direction, comes and goes, starts up again, hesitantly waltzes between *Vogue* style and hara-kiri style, and is like a runway show with models who look like glossy photos, plus a show of monsters, cross-dressers, and fat ladies who are mocked in the style of Averty."

But the little prince hadn't finished challenging people. Having acquired a police record early on for liking Arabs and smoking hashish, he had always found ways to criticize order and narrow-minded people through his work. Occasionally resentful, he had found his target: *Le Figaro*, the newspaper that Pierre Bergé and Clara Saint sometimes bought the morning after a fashion show, eager to read a review of a Saint Laurent collection. But in 1971, *Le Figaro* got angry and called the collection "a sad occupation." Yves Saint Laurent was a charming rascal; he could be as irritating as he could be appealing. In 1971, he made fun of *Le Figaro* in his ad for Rive Gauche. The ad depicted a slightly prudish woman with a pearl necklace who sat next to a man, both of them in complete silence, and read *Le Figaro*. The scene took place in a café. Then a red-headed woman wearing lots of make-up meets a group of friends—one of Yves's friends, Philippe Collin, played one of them—and devours a big messy slice of cream cake. Her poppy mouth was as red as the VW bug that she drove, almost running over a policeman. "There was once a time when women were docile, submissive….They were so good at staying in their place! Rive Gauche isn't a perfume for unassuming women." Proper people could be quite offended by these bold slogans.

The launch of his first men's cologne was more spectacular. "What if we called it 'Eau de Zizi?'" he asked, laughing at this childish word for "penis." He ended up calling it simply "Rive Gauche." He decided to use his own image to promote it. At a time when the female nude had already lost its commercial attraction, Yves Saint Laurent posed in his birthday suit, becoming the first male advertising object of the new decade.

"I want to shock. I want to pose nude." Yves posed in his friend Jeanloup Sieff's plant-filled studio on Rue Ampère. He even brought along a fake perfume bottle that he wanted to put between his legs. "I wish I had taken those photos," said Jeanloup Sieff, who remembered "a mix of provocativeness and a certain unease…I hesitated. I took photos that were more close-up." The shoot lasted an hour, with Sieff using his Hasselblad with an eighty-millimeter lens and an electronic flash. And Yves's image appeared, enveloped in shadow, showing him without revealing anything. The photo was published in the November 1971 issue of *Vogue*. "For three years, this cologne has been mine. Today it can be yours." It was the first time that a fashion designer advertised a cologne himself, posing thoughtfully behind his glasses, surrounded by a halo that gave him a vaguely biblical look.

The image created a scandal, reawakening all kinds of hatred. *Le Figaro* was one of the first to react: "It must be because of nostalgia for appearing before the medical board—although he never did his military service—that Yves Saint Laurent appears as naked as the day he was born," Philippe Bouvard wrote in November 1971.[21] He was called "Christ with glasses" (Carmen Teissier, *France-Soir*) and "a cherub" (Hélène de Turckheim, *Le Figaro*). But soon a storm of insults, comments, and caricatures followed what became known as "the naked CEO affair." It created a precedent. *Cosmopolitan* published a centerfold with a reclining pose of the first "pin-up boy:" Burt Reynolds. It had record sales. But Yves Saint Laurent was neither married nor a father. What seemed normal for dancers like Baryshnikov, Nureyev, and Jorge Lago, who made a gift of their beauty to the public, was a scandal when it was a man whose name was connected to the idea of fashion and was more serious. Several newspapers, including *Jours de France,* refused to run the ad. Others printed it for free. The ad was even criticized in the ateliers, where apprentices said they were shocked to see their boss in the buff.

Yet, what a success! No other cologne had created such a stir. More than one hundred articles and other references appeared in the press, in publications ranging from *Témoignage Chrétien* ("living to sell") to the *Sunday Mirror* ("Yves Bares It All"), along with *La Revue du Liban* ("Saint Laurent Under the Gun"). One of the most memorable reactions was a caricature by the artist Tim in *L'Express*. It was a political parody called "Eau de Chirac, UDR." "For three years, power has been mine. Today, it can be yours." Everyone had an opinion on the scandal. The gimmick was turned back against him: Yves Saint Laurent belonged to everyone. The critics became more familiar and touched on his private life. That was the most direct way to target the man, whereas the artist always found a way out. The prince had "uncovered" himself, and was no longer "respected": "He's actually not bad. Saint Laurent. He's certainly not the hottest item in Paris. Some say quite the opposite. But he's pretty muscular, with no trace of fat and his glasses give him a certain dignity," André Halimi wrote in *Pariscope*.

He was the talk of the town, to the point where Bernard Pivot wrote two articles about him in *Le Figaro*: "Isn't the irritation primarily with Yves Saint Laurent's boldness? If an unknown exhibits himself to earn a living, it's more pitiful than revolting. If a celebrity doesn't hesitate to do a strip tease to sell a product, then there's a type of cynical provocation."[22]

But was it cynical provocation? Yves was making a gift of his beauty to the public, just as he gave himself over body and soul to his art. He exposed himself in this image, just as he would expose himself to the dangers of perfectionism, overwork, and addiction in the name of his sublime visions.

"My style? A slow-moving Rolls-Royce
playing an old dance-hall tune."
—Yves Saint Laurent

Dear Yves, divine Yves. That's what the women called him now, as they kissed him, imprinting their red lips on his cheeks—the same red lips that he had just embroidered on the black velvet of the collection that was received so harshly. He was thirty-seven years old. The Liberation collection was a financial disaster: the company's haute couture revenue dropped from eight to five million francs, its level in 1963. But two years had gone by, and no one remembered that this retro collection had launched a fashion-world scandal. By 1973, it had been copied all over. In his ready-to-wear collections that year, Yves Saint Laurent had gone back to his classics, giving them a new, campy twist: the first dressy shorts with black pantyhose (stolen from Marlene), and shocking pink or electric green satin leather safari jackets. Loulou de la Falaise looked especially spectacular in those, and she was photographed for *Elle* playing pinball in a bar while wearing one.

In 1971, *Herald Tribune* journalist Eugenia Sheppard publicly apologized to the couturier, with a professional humility that the French didn't bother with: during the swinging sixties, she went to check the length of mini-mini-mini-skirts at the Cheetah Club in New York. She acknowledged, long after the fact, that the retro style was indeed on the streets. The flea market style was being sold in stores. Unflappable, Yves Saint Laurent was already distancing himself from it like a seducer who fell asleep in the arms of a young woman and wakes up next to an old mistress: "The street is monstrously ugly."

He had weathered the storm, coming out not only unscathed, but even more powerful from a crisis situation in which he seemed to have been the victim—but which he wiped out as if he were cutting a scene out of a movie. The Liberation collection that scandalized the American press contained everything the couturier would now play with in a softer way, such as flannel pants and a gold cardigan, masculine/feminine mixtures adapted to interest in the 1930s. From what scene, from what film did he borrow the imperceptibly colonial white suit worn by Catherine Deneuve photographed by Helmut Newton for the cover of *Vogue*? Or his Twentieth Century Fox negligees? Loretta Young in *Café Metropole*? Jean Harlow in *Dinner at Eight*? Worthy of a maison de couture filmed by Cukor or Lubitsch (the Cinémathèque Française featured tributes to them), luxury had once again found intimacy. Clingy, slinky, satiny—the look in black velvet chenille idealized a new homespun glamour: the extravagant style and acrylic blond colors of Wesselmann were over; the complexion was pale, more fragile, more tender. The Cukorian image of 1972 beauty as pushed by the magazines: blue masks, sea-extract creams, and lily-white necklines coming out of a milk bath, with a glass of whisky mixed into the shampoo, and magical little containers that emerged from a toiletries kit for a trip from London to Istanbul on the Orient Express.

The "naked CEO" had put his clothes back on. It wasn't the time for scandals anymore. And for good reason. In 1972 Yves and Pierre Bergé bought back the couture house and the licenses from Squibb, which had merged with Charles of the Ritz: the payment was spread out over fifteen years at two percent interest. Squibb CEO Richard Furlaud kept the perfumes. For the publicity photo, Yves posed in a white suit, with the easy manner of a 1930s seducer with just a few touches from the early 1970s: bell-bottom pants, his hair swept back and blow-dried, white socks, and shoes with white laces. He tried wearing contact lenses, but in vain. The advertising pages appeared in *Connaissance des Arts*, which was found in doctors' waiting rooms in posh neighborhoods. He was no longer the big unshaven Duduche in jeans and a crocheted tank top. But his charm was there. He played with it, crossing and uncrossing his long legs like a Metro-Goldwyn-Mayer star. "All of his gestures seemed calculated, and he moved with an extraordinary aura," remembered an observer. He smoked menthol cigarettes and watched his figure, never using sugar, but saccharine. He had himself photographed in Marrakesh's main square, the Djemaa El Fna, in white pants, a white short-sleeved shirt, and supple white leather moccasins. He recommended the restaurant La Maison Arabe to the *Vogue* journalists, "even though it has become touristy." In New York, he was stopped by autograph seekers. In March 1972, *Harper's Bazaar* described his spring collection in these terms: "Today this man is purely and simply the greatest designer in the world." His ambition was limitless. Didn't he say he was speaking to twenty million Frenchwomen? Wasn't he the first couturier to put his photo in his stores?

But an era was ending. "I didn't go back to Marrakesh after 1972," Philippe Collin said. Jeanloup Sieff remembered, "We didn't keep up with each other. The 1960s must have ended then. We had lived through a relaxed era. I started traveling. The Saint Laurent fashion house, where there were always thirty chairs for the family, became a big commercial machine. Things came apart at the seams. I didn't see the others either—Charlotte Aillaud, Philippe Collin, or Hélène Rochas. I saw Pierre Bergé again in 1982. Ten years later, Yves called me. He wanted me to do a portrait of his mother. He sounded terrible. He was clearly drunk. I'm still convinced that he has passions. But success is terrible. You have to have incredible character to resist it, or you can't accept the least criticism. He has this mixture of arrogance and great dissatisfaction. He's really tormented."

Yves Saint Laurent became the French star of couture, with his demands, his whims, his ups and downs, his thing for Roederer Cristal, his male desires that made him suffer so much, his narrow escapes in his black VW Beetle, and his Indian summers in Venice, where he stayed at the Cipriani in late August to see the Regata Storica gondola race with historical masks and costumes, as celebrations took place all along the Grand Canal on the first Sunday in September. He belonged to a divinely decadent Paris. Champagne, feathers, joints, and Vaseline. At Le Sept, Cuban Guy Cuevas, with the physique of a big baby, became deejay without realizing it. The phrase "dance hall" had disappeared, but no one said "disco" yet.

Yves, who was never a big fan of nightclubs, remained a regular. He gave his car keys to the valet and got back behind the wheel at dawn along the Avenue de l'Opéra. "I once saw him so drunk that he was talking to the taxi stand!" one source remembered hearing another say.

At Le Sept, Fabrice Emaer honored his guests as if he were a grand duke in a Visconti film. Sophisticated, warm, and haughty, the former hairdresser knew how to make each customer feel that he was the most important. Everyone was there: Karl Lagerfeld's clique, Saint Laurent's clique, and Warhol's clique, ready to report all the gossip in Andy's monthly magazine, *Interview*. Françoise Sagan played cards with Peggy Roche, Claudia Cardinale lost a pair of diamond earrings, and Helmut Berger arrived in a mink coat. Only one thing mattered: looking good. Everything was an excuse to dance. The French singer Barbara's hit *L'Homme en Habit Rouge*, Stevie Wonder, bird songs, or *Swan Lake*. The queens didn't yet have moustaches and would go with women as long as they were "beautiful." They went out with "divine" girls who put on quite a show. Donna Jordan was Marilyn, Jane Forthe was Cruella, and Pat Cleveland danced naked on the bar. "I don't get why she didn't become Josephine Baker," some people from that era still say. Loulou was the most unpredictable of all.

Loulou de la Falaise went to work for Yves Saint Laurent in 1972. "In New York, I stayed with various people. It was practically a gypsy life. When you remain a gypsy too long you annoy everyone. They're rich girls." She lived with Berry Berenson, who left for the West Coast and later married Anthony Perkins. Loulou had crossed the Atlantic with her trunks, her tricks, and her odds and ends. She stayed in an attic room that had been "renovated in a very chic style" before finding an apartment on Rue des Grands-Augustins, where she had a troubled love affair with the Catalonian architect Ricardo Bofill.

"When you create personalities for yourself, you can go anywhere," Loulou said. She was as thin as a Giacometti sculpture with the uninhibitedness of an odalisque. Morning and night, Loulou had real presence. She turned up on Rue Spontini with her little striped sailor sweaters, her big jewelry, and her strange friends. "People would stop by. They knew we were a company with more freedom than the others." She spoke all the time. Right away, Yves and Loulou completed one another. "He has an intellectual vision. But I'm more influenced by nature, the organic side of things." Imitate Loulou? Impossible. With a bit of chiffon, she could create something amazing. As for rare items—a Russian cross or an Order of Malta set with "gray, barely cut" diamonds—she could wear them with a regal nonchalance. Only she would dare to wear extravagant fake jewelry, brightly-colored velvet, with that boldness that irritated the women in black. "I hate things I can't lose," she said bafflingly. "I don't like little real gems. I'm not crazy about pastels."

Her way of being and dressing was unique. She acknowledged, "The more you tend to look bad, the more you tend to dress up." And the more she dressed up, the more she highlighted her pale skin, dousing it with powder to bring out her very red lipstick. Like a moth, she fluttered, a bit unreal, through Paris. She was Naughty Loulou dancing with Kenzo on the tables at Le Sept, where little vials of poppers swung from the necks of handsome young men. "We went out to have fun. Yves was more mental, more perverse. With him, everything happened in his head." An ex-hippie in Wales, the ex-wife of Desmond FitzGerald, Knight of Glin, Loulou didn't delude herself. She lived in her own fairy tale, playing the role of the poor princess. "Her beauty was dazzling," Serge Bramly remembered. "And she was very funny. At six AM, she was still dancing. In her frail frame, there was an incredible will to have fun, to make her head spin. She was always up for anything."

Between Yves Saint Laurent and Loulou de la Falaise, design and life stimulated each other. "Think of one woman to dress all the others," said Yves. In his sketches, he captured attitudes, lively movement, a chameleon look. And Naughty Loulou went wild: "I love to put on costumes. I was never the marquise. I always try to be the boy in the story." An androgynous Venus, both incredible and marvelous. One day a femme fatale, and the next a gypsy, she reinvented herself every day in front of the mirror. She embodied the Rive Gauche spirit.

With haute couture, Yves gave Paris the "perfect, polished look"[1] that the whole world came to take in. Now he was the new hero of a black-and-white Paris, the capital of a gigantic Hollywood play, where yesterday's flappers indulged in sensual tea gowns in crepe de Chine and wealthy gentlemen enjoyed a Brandy Alexander or a Porto flip such as F. Scott Fitzgerald's characters might have sipped at the Ritz. Selfish and frivolous, pearl-colored Paris lost its head at bals blancs, where eligible young men and women went looking for love. It was a flashback to the days when Zelda danced the charleston on the tables at the Waldorf, the tragic entertainment of a society that was jaded from too much amusement and too many holidays.

Nostalgia was in fashion. As if to mark its distance with wild urbanism and the era of new cities, the La Coupole generation constructed an homage to old-fashioned décor: a new version of the restaurant Régine—Les Années 30—opened on Rue de Ponthieu, with a bar that was an exact replica of the one on the cruise ship Île de France. One kind of snobbery replaced another, in a gentle revolution that was subtly illuminated by the artificial light of the spotlights. After storage cubes, the sharkskin armoire; after white laminate and stainless steel, black lacquer and skins of wild animals, loaded with memories. Like wallets, interiors filled up. Everything became oversized: TV screens, ties, watches, coats, and platform shoes. The cult of the gadget and of science fiction in pop colors was ending. It made room for tawny leather, carpeting with giant prints designed from tapestry cartoons, all these curiosities, magic lanterns and Hindu hands, vases that were a bit too black filled with arum lilies that were a bit too white, interiors of 1970s nabobs where, between the feet of an Art Deco table, one could recognize a lithograph by Messagier printed by Prisunic. The living room, an undefined zone with rows of down-filled armchairs, was once again a smoking room where plots and political conquests were hatched, giving a whole new elite of producers, decorators, promoters, and designers the illusion of re-creating the golden age of leisure.

In 1972, in keeping with an effective tactic tried out by Pierre Bergé, Yves Saint Laurent made his brand exclusive. He didn't show his haute couture collections to the press for two seasons, offering the coveted title of VIP to those he invited to his shows. He counted more and more American women among his clients, and they were quite flattered to wear dresses for which no line-for-line copies were available. While he still had department store buyers, there were only three American department stores at this point that had acquired the right to reproduce his haute couture designs, minus the label: Ohrbach's, Alexander's, and I. Magnin.

Dior once said of American women: "Their essence is to be impeccable. They have all the shine of a new penny."[2] But American women had proven that they cared not only about fashion, but also about its history—a history that Parisians thought they knew so well that they neglected it. And weren't the Americans the only ones who still dressed like Parisian women? Who still had perfect legs sheathed in black stockings, who still took care of their hair and polished their nails? Who said yes or no. They expected a couturier to do his job. That year, America did him the honor of continuing to call him the "king of fashion." He knew how to offer billionaires clothing for the Ritz and Rolls existence that Florence Gould had used sixty years earlier to make people forget that she was the daughter of a farmer from the Gers. With dresses that were made for singing, "But my heaven will be in your arms," he charmed America with the only thing that money can't buy: memory. New York was becoming a giant conservatory of fashion. The Metropolitan Museum of Art opened its Costume Institute, whose collection dated back to 1937. Here, in America, fashion was studied: professionals came to consult the thousands of garments, fabric samples, and illustrations that were sold off for a pittance by the Drouot auction house in Paris. It was at the Metropolitan Museum, and not in Paris, where the first Balenciaga retrospective took place the year he died, attracting 300,000 visitors. The curator was none other than the great Diana Vreeland, who had moved from editing *Vogue* to highlighting this heritage that gave a new meaning to luxury and to the necessity of elegance. Yves Saint Laurent was once again the son of America. The circumstances were right: with the triumph of *The Great Gatsby* and *The Sting*, Hollywood once again became a dream factory.

Marisa Berenson, recently named the most elegant woman in Paris, tried on ivory shantung suits and mousseline blouses, an evening gown in crepe de Chine and a swan down bolero jacket. "The trouble with your collection is that you have to choose. I'd like to take everything," this stylish woman, the granddaughter of designer Elsa Schiaparelli, would have told Yves. She had given up modeling for acting and had a role in the lagoon miasmas of Visconti's film *Death in Venice*. Always jetting off somewhere, the actress, who had to attend the premiere of *Cabaret* in New York, posed for *Paris Match* in 1972, like a Hollywood starlet, in clothes by Yves Saint Laurent. The staging was perfect: Yves, who had refused to let photographers into his show, appears in one photo like a star in black saying no: "No flash, please!" Bianca Jagger posed for the *Daily Mirror* in full Saint Laurent garb. "I want to look like Rita Hayworth." Lauren Bacall ordered a sweater with black and silver embroidery under a short evening ensemble in satin bordered with marten. "He always thought she was very chic," said a saleswoman.

Yves Saint Laurent reinvented the mystery and aura of a thirty-year-old woman with flowing Neoclassical dresses. The Americans praised these sporty deluxe separates. *Women's Wear Daily* ran the headline, "Saint Laurent Leads New Paris Harmony." They saw Yves Saint Laurent as "the Chanel of the 1970s." "Yves Saint Laurent's collection is a definite triumph. It's elegant and supple, and extremely refined," wrote *Women's Wear Daily* in July 1973. His winter collection was one of the company's biggest hits since the triumph of the Mondrian dress in 1965. *Le Figaro* sharpened its claws, but was kind enough to pay him some backhanded compliments: "Since Yves Saint Laurent always tends to repeat himself, we also have a tendency to repeat our comments. Why is it, in fact, that in discussing Saint Laurent, everyone forgets to ask the question: Does he have ideas or not?" asked journalist Hélène de Turckheim. "It's because, starting with the same basic clothes, which he deems essential, the long knit cardigan, the eternal shirt dress, the long flowing 'ambassador's wife' dress, as my neighbor Françoise Giroud called it— items that can be found in the collections of almost all designers this season—Saint Laurent manages to create superb combinations of refinement, which are often very removed from the conventional wisdom." After all, for Yves, an ambassador's wife dress was never safe and proper. It still hid in its folds the secrets of a femininity that only transvestites inspired in him, a way of crossing one's legs or smoking king-sized cigarettes under a white fedora.

Balenciaga and Schiaparelli both died in 1973. Yves Saint Laurent understood that he was now the guardian of a priceless treasure. "In the world, there are only three thousand women who dress in haute couture, not one more. I have two or three hundred clients. They wear my designs because they love them. How would the opinion of a journalist influence them? Haute couture is an artistic process."[3] His vision of the world would form itself from the crumbling of the past. What was he planning?

The more the years faded into the distance, the more this invisible thread connecting his collections stretched and became finer, always ready to break the man who invented them. "I tried to understand Chanel's success: she didn't try to create, she perfected."[4] In the artistic and powdered blurriness of Sarah Moon's photos, Yves Saint Laurent's white suit stood out, with an ivory safari jacket made of a heavy silk blend with gold buttons. Every season, he got closer to the beautiful, which Chanel compared to a jealous god. "Dior taught me my profession. Thanks to Chanel, I found my style."[5]

The Saint Laurent woman didn't drink rose tea while reading romance novels. She didn't make good home-cooked meals, nor did she knit Christmas sweaters— she smoked. When a lover said to her, "I love you just as you are," she detected the beginning of indifference. But did she even have time for a husband? She wasn't an organized "sportswear" woman who read the advice column in *Cosmopolitan* and thought, depression is an illness and can be treated. Yves Saint Laurent offered liberated women additional sophistication, and he gave the others the certainty that they were modern. Saint Laurent was a man's suit with a little something extra. Pearls, a crepe de Chine blouse, a way of moving, a way of smoking, an indefinable allure. The art of living became a business.

Elsa Peretti knew Yves as a client and a model. "I like his voice and his kindness. And I always felt stunning in his clothes." She lived in New York, in Halston's former penthouse, where the Knoll style was combined with Japanese furniture. Her life was very eventful. One day she burned a fur coat that Halston had given her. Above the mantel, she hung Japanese paper with a haiku in calligraphy: "I return alone when the moon is exactly at its zenith."

But Betty Catroux, along with Loulou de la Falaise, perfectly fulfilled Yves Saint Laurent's androgynous ideal. He experienced their friendship as an extension of himself. He found the dandy in Loulou and the tomboy in Betty. As in Oran, when he directed his sisters, women played a role for him and were put on a pedestal. Stretched out at home on one of his two white sofas, Betty posed with her cigarette holder and her YSL Bakelite bracelets starred with rhinestones and wearing a gold cardigan over a crepe de Chine blouse with flannel pants. A "perfectly happy nonchalance" as American *Vogue* observed. Helmut Newton would later take her photo in exactly the same position, but naked.

At this time, Yves Saint Laurent's line liberated itself. His silhouette, which was always very long, become softer in contact with swanlike necks and satin crepe sheath dresses worthy of Marlene Dietrich in *Desire* drinking her tea in a crystal cup with bouquets of pale yellow roses. The fluid lines slid over bodies that were barely of flesh, everything tied, untied. Long pearl necklaces skimmed crepe de Chine blouses. His dresses were intimate friends. They followed him, let themselves be handled, tempted by these little escapades, these exercises in style that renewed romantic feelings, with a flower in the buttonhole. He also had a special relationship with the past. He wasn't new, he wasn't old, but present at the instant when he gave himself over, without make-up, without dust, with this very Paris simplicity. His white was never fragile, sappy, or eggshell. Neither was he a futurist or sporty. His style just made people wonder how others could still make ruffled flounces, embroider bodices, or wear themselves out with trivial details. "Fashions change, style remains. My dream is to give women the bases of a classical wardrobe that, escaping the fashion of the moment, lets them have greater confidence in themselves. I hope to make them happier."[6]

Seeking a doomed love, Fitzgerald's Gatsby threw parties that were so glamorous and extravagant they made him realize that he would never force open the door of a world whose manners he was imitating. Yves Saint Laurent, the Gatsby of fashion, became a billionaire, and, like the last witness of a world that was distant from his origins—the world of the Polignacs, the La Rochefoucaulds, and the Noailleses (setting aside the fact that Marie-Laure de Noailles often went around with a basket and that she was, according to a Saint Laurent saleswoman, "undressable"). Yves was building his castle, taking back the influence that the Faubourg Saint-Germain had lost in the early 1970s as it yielded power to the business bourgeoisie. He was the subject of envy, controversy, and amazement. "A designer that no one wants to copy isn't a couturier but a dressmaker," he would have said in 1971. Like those places that lovers of Paris history were eager to see landmarked so as to protect them from developers, Yves Saint Laurent had already entered into history. To Pierre Bergé, he was already "the last living king." That was how he gained a title that birth had refused him: this world where one exists before being born. With Yves Saint Laurent, haute couture would be like the aristocracy that was collapsing before his eyes.

With the power he used to improve upon reality, this lover of the last age of classicism gave himself over totally to his role, to the point of constructing a set where he could play it marvelously. In 1972, Yves and Pierre left the apartment on Place Vauban and moved to Rue de Babylone. The apartment had belonged to Marie Cuttoli, who had commissioned tapestry cartoons from Picasso, Braque, and Miró that were made into tapestries in Aubusson. She even bequeathed paintings to the Musée d'Art Moderne before moving to the south of France. The first time he visited the apartment, Yves thought the courtyard was "gloomy," but then the door opened, "and right before me was a window opening onto a garden, and that was it."[7] He never moved again.

Yves Saint Laurent didn't start fashion trends. He salvaged them. He did the same thing with interior design. He was one of the first wealthy art lovers in Paris to collect furniture from the 1920s and 1930s. "It was Karl, Hélène Rochas, and us," said Pierre Bergé, who remembered buying two Dunand vases in the middle of the 1960s from Galerie Jeanne Fillon, along with a Ruhlmann chaise longue and a big lacquer painting by Dunand from Jacques Denoël. In 1972, the 1930s style saw a big rise in popularity: it was the year when Eileen Gray was named a "Pioneer of Design" in London and the Doucet auction took place. At the auction, Yves purchased two Miklos stools, a Legrain stool, and an Eileen Gray table. At the Biennale des Antiquaires, some exceptional Art Deco pieces sold for higher prices than eighteenth-century ones. The 1930s style would be to 1970s café society what Louis XVI style was to the 1950s: the gold standard of social status. The luxury of that prewar decade was a nostalgic echo to the economic situation of the 1970s, a way for the wealthy to take a provocative stance in the midst of financial crisis. Recession? What recession? The crisis of 1972–74 was also a refuge: the future was over. And while the word "pollution" entered the French dictionary, France discovered the retro style, with even popular newspapers covering the phenomenon: "Everywhere, movies, records, dresses, posters, bric-à-brac, the past is all the rage.… An overwhelming wave of collective regret sweeps away the splendor of yesterday, lived or dreamed, real or imaginary. Images of 'the good old days' reduced to symbols? The shock of the future has become the craze for the past."[8]

But Yves Saint Laurent knew how to tap into the spirit of things. He seemed to make it a point of honor to pick out objects for their symbolic value, something related to his fears and fascinations: "I have a passion for objects depicting birds and snakes, but in real life, these animals scare me," he said twenty years later. He was just as sensitive to the design of an object as Pierre Bergé was to its value. Things like Eileen Gray's "cobra" chair, Dunand's tray shaped like a coiled snake, or the boa constrictor holding up a console by Cheuret. The apartment on Rue de Babylone was said to look as if it had been decorated by Jean-Michel Frank for a rich American. Original wood paneling, glass wall lamps, and the chrome banisters were the last traces. Jean-Michel Frank applied his pared-down style to the décor of the years from 1925 to 1930 the same way Chanel designed for her era: rigorous shapes allied with materials that were either raw or sophisticated, such as cowhide or ray skin, travertine or straw, applied piece by piece to furniture. He worked with Alberto and Diego Giacometti, who designed iron furniture in gnarled shapes for him, as well as Christian Bérard and Emilio Terry. They were all Yves Saint Laurent's idols. Attentive to custom, this designer knew how to emphasize timeless shapes that were almost manly and sometimes massive, such as large oak chests. He reduced furniture to shapes (a cube-chair made of sycamore wood, a low U-shaped table), just as Yves Saint Laurent reduced clothing to lines, with a similar sense of luxury. In the same way, the couturier simplified, paying attention to the accurate relationships between material and function, space and shape. Yves Saint Laurent, "the Parisian from Algeria," and Jean-Michel Frank, from a German Jewish family—"the prune in gray flannel," as his critics called him—were not born into high society. Yet they were both among the last heirs to French aristocratic taste, forty years apart. They struggled with these high standards that were sharpened by their flawed origins: "We don't work with centimeters, but with millimeters," said Jean-Michel Frank, whose tragic destiny—he killed himself in 1941—was part of Yves Saint Laurent's worship of him.

Yves identified with many figures in addition to Frank. The more time passed, the more the subjects of his identification multiplied. Yves and Pierre's large drawing room seemed to be a replica of Jacques Doucet's studio, which was praised by *Fémina* in 1925 as a "temple of modern art" and had since become an almost mythic reference. But there was a difference. Doucet had asked Legrain to frame his Picasso paintings and asked Iribe to handle a Manet. He knew how to surround himself with contemporary artists, with demands that some people found vulgar. Hadn't he asked Masson to add a bird to one of his paintings? But he had stimulated the birth of decorative art and fancied himself a discoverer of talent. Pierre Bergé and Yves Saint Laurent weren't interested in being patrons in this area, and although they collected Eileen Gray, they didn't care for her message: "The past casts only shadows." From this moment, they no longer bought any paintings by contemporary artists: the last was the portrait that Yves commissioned from Andy Warhol, just like so many other beautiful people and businessmen's wives of the period, ready to pay 70,000 dollars to see four colored images of themselves on canvas.

Their souvenirs from Place Vauban were absorbed into this décor. What was left of the Mondrian period? The Senufo bird was still there, as well as the Eero Saarinen table. But Yves had already begun his search for lost time. He seemed to want to re-create it through souvenirs that he collected. Moreover, Yves's favorite piece wasn't the museum piece, but the large white drawing room that opened onto the garden, like an expanded replica of his room on Place Vauban. In the drawing room on Rue de Babylone, the walls were covered with bookshelves, and Yves had a special way of arranging books in relation to photos and objects that were emotionally connected to them. This is where all his chosen idols appeared: Maria Callas, Andy Warhol, Christian Dior, Françoise Sagan, Pat Cleveland, Princess Mathilde, Le Clézio, Colette, René Crevel, Violette Leduc, Lilya Brik (Elsa Triolet's sister), Louis Jouvet, Mitza Bricard, Louis II of Bavaria. For instance, behind a photo of Marie-Laure de Noailles with Natalie Barney, he placed books about his friends, including Christian Bérard. Watercolors by Bérard and Bakst (including a study for a costume for *Salome*) were next to books by Giraudoux, Proust, and Cocteau, who was represented by an opium pipe. A photo of Callas was placed next to the cover of his high school Classiques Larousse copy of *Bérénice*. Books on Morocco were behind a portrait of Maréchal Lyautey. Behind the large sofa, he set up his bar, as well as two sheep by the Lalannes. On low tables, he arranged boxes, an ivory letter opener, framed photos, bronze sculptures, Berber jewels, and Arab daggers. "Every nook is decorated," Yves would later explain.

Here he had his Paris parties. At that time, Yves was still very close to Karl Lagerfeld, with whom he had discovered Paris, starting in 1955, during the Fiacre years. Karl lived on Place Saint-Sulpice in an apartment that he had redecorated four times in ten years. Lagerfeld, who claimed to be the heir to the Gloria Milk fortune, lived like a grand duke. At age twenty-three he had his first Rolls-Royce. This exuberant man shared many affinities with Yves. Like him, he had studied many issues of *Vogue* before the war, he loved Brassaï and Arletty, and he hung out in the movie theater of Saint-Germain-des-Prés. They spent weekends together on the coast of Normandy.

Karl Lagerfeld seemed more like Pierre Bergé in terms of his personality: the same drive to experience the present moment, the same will for order and power, and the same regret at not having been born an artist. Karl Lagerfeld was a brilliant designer. He could sketch clothes in a flash. But this mercenary of couture, who had outstanding success at Chloé, never attained the glory of Yves Saint Laurent. Could that be why he decided to move as soon as the Rive Gauche boutique opened on Place Saint-Sulpice? Karl Lagerfeld was condemned to leave behind what he had created: he had to prove his existence as he remained professionally anonymous. He had no maison de couture. At that time, his name was known only to people in the profession who were amused or offended by his extravagance. Paloma Picasso shared this memory of him: "Karl can be exceedingly ridiculous. I saw him at Saint-Tropez in a 1900-style bathing suit with black patent leather high-heeled mules. He was never an Adonis! I remember one day in Milan when he wore red thigh boots. People wanted to lynch us. The Italians are so macho! Yves never had to do all that. He experienced all the pitfalls of celebrity: being famous—too famous. He wanted this celebrity as a revenge on the petty humiliations of his childhood. Yves reigns supreme." Yves constantly doubted and challenged himself, but then stuck to his guns with regal serenity: "My style? It's still the same. I don't change! More pared down, more truthful. I like women to evolve, but not to change continuously at the risk of losing themselves." His white, supple, belted, roomy sailor sweater was already there in 1962 and also in 1969, when it became all black, with a low-cut neckline for the androgynous denizens of Montparnasse. "I made these a long time ago. It's classic to fashion in general, but especially classic for Yves Saint Laurent. I felt like doing something with them again," he said, like these women who "discover" an "old" Rive Gauche tunic in their closet that they wear perpetually—knowing that dressing too young is the best way to look old.

Both Yves and Karl acutely felt the advantages and disadvantages of their mutual situations. Pierre Bergé described them diplomatically: "This profession is made of two essential things: on the one hand, style, and on the other, fashion. Style was Chanel, Balenciaga, Yves. You can't say that Yves designs for every season. He refines his designs. On the other hand, Karl Lagerfeld does fashion. It's thanks to these fashion-makers that this job exists," he concludes, acting as if the main difference between them was not important. "Yves is very withdrawn, and Karl is an extrovert," explained Helmut Newton. Karl Lagerfeld worked with music, but Yves Saint Laurent worked in silence. He was so courteous. "When Yves turns off the radio, I imagine him apologizing to the speakers," Isabelle Hebey, who designed the interiors of Rive Gauche boutiques starting in 1966, joked affectionately. "In exchange, he demands that we leave him alone." One of Yves's jet-set acquaintances, Rafael Lopez Sanchez, said, "At dinner, he asks for the salt the same way he would ask an assistant for a pin, in a whisper."

"Yves reminds me of someone who pinches his nose on the phone to pretend he has a cold and avoid going out to dinner. The problem is that he got caught in his own trap," said Maxime de la Falaise. He kept himself isolated from business, living the way he had always dreamed of: above other people, above the risks and vagaries of everyday life. At this time, Pierre Bergé got into his producer role, nervous and smiling in his gray suits, establishing himself in fashion as what Irving Thalberg, the master of Universal, was in the movie industry, employing a savvy strategy of showing money in order to attract it. "Yves Saint Laurent, a 50-Million Dollar Label," ran a headline in *Women's Wear Daily* in 1973. That was when he revealed the blank check that Chanel had offered him. "Leave? Oh, no. Chanel offered a fortune to leave, but I was never even slightly tempted. No, you see, I am a winner. I would go with no one else. I don't want to be a loser. But Yves would have been YSL without me."

"Yves couldn't live on his own. Pierre was like a father. Yves needed that. When he said, 'I'm exhausted,' or 'I'm not hungry,' Pierre would say, 'Work,' or 'Eat.' He was really like a nanny, a trainer with a horse that doesn't run very well. He dominated him and pushed him. He could have used someone more affectionate to give him a little gentleness." Thus spoke Boul de Breteuil, a great lady whom the couple spent time with in Marrakesh. She met Yves in the late 1960s. "With me, he was relaxed. We didn't talk about his career. We talked about pretty things, pretty houses." Boul and Yves used the familiar "tu" form with each other like overgrown kids: they complemented each other. One found the son she had lost to an overdose, and the other found the mother whose strength he admired: "She hates women," he said amusedly.

She lived in the splendid Villa Taylor that the Breteuil family offered her. "A gift from my mother-in-law, the countess." Alongside her guest books, the social registry looked like a common phone book. All kinds of celebrated people stayed with Boul: from Yvonne Printemps to the Duchess of Windsor, along with Roosevelt and Churchill, who had a secret meeting in the dining room. Churchill even painted a view of Marrakesh from one of the towers of the house. "Whether it's John Doe or Churchill, for me it's the same thing. I don't go overboard." The countess spoke with a Paris street urchin accent, as if she understood that the best way to make people forget this flaw was to emphasize it.

Every day, followed by Miss Love, her little Scottie, she walked over the property. Then she swam for an hour in her blue swimming pool with a pergola, in the shade of a seven-acre garden where the plants grew in an artistic jumble. She had always avoided whatever was shiny and new, with an energy that unsettled the nouveaux riches, whose tics she noticed immediately: "I'm suspicious of people who come here and stare at the ceiling," which was a way of pointing out to the ignorant that it was authentically Moorish. The house was a huge Art Deco palace. You didn't visit the Villa Taylor; you strolled through it along the two riads where the tortoises bumped their old shells. Everything here—the silver, the bound books, and even the collections of marble eggs that she arranged near the sofa, as well as the photos placed on the tables like invitations, seemed to have been polished by time. Nothing demanded your attention. As if being chic meant making people not notice. "My staff is deaf and dumb. If you tell them, 'Paris is underwater,' they'll be upset for two weeks. But I don't care." Women in flowing robes passed by with bouquets of roses. The countess received her guests in the green drawing room. Coca-Cola and dry cookies were served. She lived, she said, in "old pants" and always wore sweaters and caftans in the evening. "Coco told me: 'Take whatever you want.' I wasn't going to take something just to take it. In a Chanel suit, I looked like a retired hausfrau. Chanel suits look too old lady, there are too many buttons." When asked about style, she laughed, "Oh, chic, with several c's, like chewing gum!" Then she answered briefly, "Luxury is comfort. I'm not into jewels—they don't look good on me. Great hair, a good lipstick, a ring and there you go." About her pants, she said pragmatically, "If it's wide at the bottom, you don't look at the top so much."

Boul always lived outside herself, for men. Yves always lived inside himself, for women. United by their difference, they didn't dread loneliness. And neither one could be fooled by the other. Like Betty Catroux, like Loulou, Boul didn't fall into traps, and that's why he admired her: "Listen, you're not going to be shy with me! Give me a break." They saw everything; nothing escaped them. "I recognize who's real and who's not," said Boul. "Too many compliments. Too much flattery. People are like jewelry. If someone gives me something fake, I can tell right away." She sincerely admired Yves. "Saint Laurent and Chanel brought simplicity to fashion. It was clear. And then he dared to create color combinations that others didn't. Givenchy is a great gentleman. Yves is a great guy. It's like the goose that laid the golden egg. He couldn't get over what he had done. He didn't realize he had that talent."

"You're good with simplicity," Boul told him. But the most elegant women weren't the ones who bought his dresses. On the contrary, his clients bought them because they wanted to be elegant. In 1974, there were eighty Rive Gauche stores in the world. YSL was worth as much as Dior, almost a third less than Cardin. Yves was still a man of contradictions. On the one hand, he embodied the movement of this era, whose development he felt before others did. He made it unfashionable to dictate fashion rights and wrongs and to create an entire couture line that would change every season. Jackie O., photographed on Fifth Avenue in a fox-collar cardigan by YSL and a Valentino blouse, was a one-woman illustration of women's independence vis-à-vis their couturiers. Yves initiated that liberation by showing that fashion was no longer about hemlines or colors but a way of living.

On the other hand, he knew that this profession was doomed. In France at the time, the "tailor-made" represented only 18 percent of haute couture revenue. But by excessively cashing in on their names, some companies were selling off their prestige. From Jean-Louis Scherrer to Ungaro, Avenue Montaigne polished its black lacquer and its smoky mirrors. Everything could be sold with a prestigious name. Pierre Cardin bicycles in the streets of Tokyo, YSL bath towels in Fifth Avenue department stores, rugs in Kyoto, Féraud stockings in Prisunic in the Benelux countries, Balmain velvet in interior design stores in Milan. All these royalties, fees, and licensing contracts gave haute couture the illusion of experiencing endless prosperity, despite the oil crisis. The maison Yves Saint Laurent—strengthened by the alliance of two personalities, one who handled fashion and the other who conducted business like an impresario—would resist. "Putting one's name on an item that is just one product among many designed by other people is not design, but prostitution!" Pierre Bergé said indignantly. Coming out of the shadows, the passionate CEO put the couturier on a pedestal where he would reign as if on a throne.

Yves became king at a time when haute couture faced the danger of not being copied anymore. From Gstaad to Marbella, luxury was becoming standardized. Women were liberated: they had traded their wedding rings for three Cartier rings. In December 1974, Pierre Cardin was featured on the cover of *Time* magazine, just like the shah of Iran or Faisal of Saudi Arabia: "The image of the designer as a shrinking violet covered in scarves and surrounded by fashion victims is completely outdated," he would have said, clearly targeting Saint Laurent.

Yves Saint Laurent's beauty and charm stimulated desire and jealousy. This was reflected in the special relationship he had with his models. Each one wanted to be his favorite. Then, once she was his favorite, she feared being replaced. Who would wear the heart this season?[9] Yves Saint Laurent had found new models: he hired Nicole Dorier, who was nicknamed "Nicou Crawford," and Vesna Laufer, the Garbo of Rue Spontini: "At Chanel, they dyed my hair dark. They said: no blonds this year. I showed up at Saint Laurent....Gradually, my hair turned light again. I was blond after two weeks," said this Slavic beauty with porcelain eyes. When she smoked, with plum nail polish and very white hands, it always looked like she was just pretending. Yves reconstructed a personal world through gestures and attitudes that these women inspired in him: they curled their hair with electric rollers, plucked their eyebrows, and went to dance at Castel in wide-brimmed hats and golden sandals. In his designs, they explored their acting talent and developed their desire to be, for him, even more redheaded or ash blond, to have even glossier lips, and, like the Neoclassical beauties of the big five movie studios, to wear fur as easily as a dressing gown: "We always had to have our hair done and wear make-up. We were always beautiful for him. He had a very discreet touch. With the fabric, he would touch a little more, and then wrap you." After coming from Ljubljana to spend a year at the Sorbonne studying French, Vesna ended up staying at Yves Saint Laurent until 1981. "It's as if we were taking religious orders. With him, communication happened right away or not at all. It was without words. Something happened. Afterwards, it's kind of for life," said Nicole Dorier, who modeled for Yves Saint Laurent for eleven years before becoming the modeling director: "He asked you to walk. He watched you very carefully. He would say, 'Thank you, Mademoiselle.' There was fascination, mystery, and the anxiety of disappointing him. It was like having a fiancé whom you wanted to charm all the time. Nothing was ever taken for granted."

This idealized image of the *femme fatale* protected him from himself. It was as if beauty purified him. Perhaps it was because he feared the dreadful side of life—the humiliation, suffering, and destruction—that he wanted at all costs to escape it. Meanwhile others, who hadn't experienced it, tried to reveal its awfulness. He took no part in the trend of exploiting the darker impulses in human nature, as seen in images of whips, chains, transvestites, Marlenes in X-rated movies, leather boots, black masses, games with broken glass. How many uniforms with swastikas on posh stages in cabarets or operas, and how many torturers and victims had there been since Visconti's *The Damned*? How many crime novels were about virgins tormented by the SS? With *The Night Porter*, Liliana Cavani created a scandal. "All cheap eroticism was now associated with Nazism," Michel Foucault explained.[10]

Yves Saint Laurent was able to spare his retro style from loaded and nauseating pretentiousness. Of course, his entire style was part of the resurrection of the vanished mythology of the star, the Hollywood vamp whose every facet—from the most glamorous to the most androgynous—he would celebrate. But Yves Saint Laurent preserved the enchantment of his idol.

He evoked the ambiguity and exceeding perfection of the kind of woman Peter Handke would describe as "so beautiful that you're scared."[11]

He thought of Marlene Dietrich when designing the tuxedo suit, for the actress who kissed women on the mouth and gave gardenias to men. Black grain de poudre was for Yves Saint Laurent what tweed was for Chanel: the material for variations on a theme, his walk on the wild side. "I've always admired Yves Saint Laurent's work," said Helmut Newton. "The woman in a tuxedo suit became this androgynous figure. It wasn't a woman, it was a being who could be a very handsome boy or a very beautiful woman. I'm attracted by this ambiguity."

Yves Saint Laurent expanded on this mystery. With him, thinness became the height of elegance. The enemy of gaudy color schemes, couture details, and curves, he obstinately followed his line: "Lots of pants. Pants. Pants. Wide. Roomy. Easy. There's nothing inside. Ungaro's models were slim, Féraud's were skinny. Saint Laurent's models skirt the edge of death from malnutrition," René Barjavel wrote in *Le Journal du Dimanche*. "When they turn, there's a moment when they're in profile. You can't see them anymore. They only have a tiny bit of flesh at the top of their legs." Boul de Breteuil identified the problem right away: "Yves makes dresses for ideas, for women who are too thin. But if we don't eat, we look bad and don't get thin. Women have derrières, there's no getting around it."

The figure and presence of Loulou de la Falaise clearly influenced Yves's style. In March 1973, with red hair and a tie, Loulou, channeling Marlene Dietrich, posed for Scavullo on the cover of *Interview*, Andy Warhol's magazine, in a tuxedo suit by Yves Saint Laurent. "I looked kind of like Régine, didn't I?" Yves dedicated his tuxedo to Marlene Dietrich, the transforming angel, the goddess of the cabaret, the victim of men's desire and their stupidity, the embodiment of the idealized adventuress who fought wearing a little hat with a veil. It calls to mind a Dietrich line from *The Devil Is a Woman:* "All men are the same. I throw myself at men's necks to tell them, 'Don't touch me.'"

In June 1973, Marlene Dietrich performed in Paris at Espace Pierre Cardin. Yves Saint Laurent saw her at the Empire and the Olympia for her first return to France. That night, cheered by her fans, Marlene ended her set with "Falling In Love Again" and "Naughty Lola," shaking hands as usual with her fans in front of the stage, hiding behind a voice that protected her to the point of becoming a parody. In December, *Vogue Paris* put her on the cover of its Christmas issue: "I love sweaters, short shorts, leather, big hats, light-colored shoes with light-colored stockings, men's suits." The name Saint Laurent appeared nowhere. As her daughter, Maria Riva, wrote, Chanel was the only one who impressed Marlene: "She really did a number on everyone. She invented a single outfit that she reproduced a thousand times and she passed for a great designer."[12]

Yves Saint Laurent seemed to be possessed by Dietrich's spirit, at the very time when Dietrich gently withdrew into silence and alcohol. Yet they both seemed linked by a similar awareness of their profession, which ruled their lives to an unforgivable point. Marlene spent her life "spotting the bubble, the false pleat, the imperfect line." Yves Saint Laurent was never closer to her than when he was demanding. "What I hate? Lack of inventiveness, badly made shoulders, ugly shoes, imitation." Saint Laurent's daytime and evening wear resembled the different clothes in which Marlene appeared on tour: cross-dressing in tails and a top hat, and then in a white dress. "The first part for the men, the second for the women," said the star.[13]

Yves Saint Laurent had totally expressed the spirit of this character, her attitude, her legs, her nails, her gaze, her way of being, acting, and smoking. "Only men have managed to imitate me," she said. In the Saint Laurent universe, they were all there: the trench coat from *A Foreign Affair*, the furs from *The Scarlet Empress*, the real fake diamonds from *Desire*, the white skirt suit from *Morocco*, the black dress from *Angel*, and the feathers from *Blonde Venus*. But seeking them means nothing, for though they cannot be separated from these characters, they are not what makes the character. Sternberg said of Marlene, "No, I didn't give her any personality other than her own. Everyone sees what he wants to see. I didn't give her anything that she didn't have already."[14] In a similar way, Yves expressed the essence of Marlene without emphasizing her features. He resisted the spirit of caricature that would culminate in Fassbinder's outrageous *Lili Marleen*, the absolute and vampiric treatment of the myth. There were no invasive quotations. He preserved her sovereign spirit, possessing its meaning without trying to appropriate it for himself. Marlene Dietrich surely embodied this ideal woman: "A woman is more moving, and therefore more seductive, when artifice starts to come into play."[15]

With his hands behind his back, Yves Saint Laurent came out to greet his public. A 1973 snapshot by Pierre Boulat froze the couturier's smile. He was the man in the white suit. He spun around, waved, and disappeared. What could be more chic than these Prince of Wales suits, this feminine style that was barely masculine that the models wore with a crepe de Chine blouse, flowing hair, and lots of pearls?

That year saw him more fortunate in fashion than in the theater costumes he made for *La Chevauchée sur le Lac de Constance*, a play by Peter Handke that was staged by Claude Régy at Espace Pierre Cardin. Michel Cournot's reaction to Jeanne Moreau was as follows: "a hideous hairstyle, the body deformed by a dress without a heart."[16] Yves Saint Laurent also designed a dress with silver sequins for Delphine Seyrig. The expressionist influence of the time could be seen, and everything, even the red rag that polished the silver, evoked the memory of *The Damned*: white make-up, painted eyebrows, and actors who slowly sank into the frozen shadows of existence. "Transvestites would have done a better job expressing and betraying Handke's intentions," Matthieu Galey wrote in *Combat* in 1974.

But Yves Saint Laurent had enough resources to remain indifferent to the critics. In September 1973, he saw the TSE's new show at the Palace, *Luxe*, ten times. It was a new love letter to Paris, and Arias, the Argentine director, displayed his girls with golden lacquered hair, his boys with made-up lips, and his Miss Marucha Bo naked under her raincoat: Miss Eliott, who dreamed of being a star, stretched out under a gaslight and imagined a handsome Prince Charming, studded with diamonds.

A charmer of Parisian high society, with his mischievous laugh, Yves was at the Prix de l'Arc de Triomphe horse race in September with high society people dressed to the nines, including the Begum and the Aga Khan, Jacques Grange in tails and a white bowler hat, Marie-Hélène de Rothschild in a fox hat, and François-Marie Banier smoking a cigar in his flannel tennis outfit. Marisa Berenson and Hélène Rochas wore little veils with an art that made it look as if Paris was a film set, or even the capital of the new seduction. The future president of France, Valéry Giscard d'Estaing, walked down the Champs-Elysées, posed in a bathing suit, and soon invited sanitation workers to the Élysée Palace. One generation was disappearing, nobly defending, in a slightly outdated and obsolete way, ideas that were henceforth for sale.

Yves lived his career and his life like a movie. At the famous Battle of Versailles Fashion Show on November 28, 1973, Saint Laurent models appeared on the runway getting out of a white Hispano-Suiza. "Yves Goes to the Movies," was the headline of *Women's Wear Daily*. That year, he designed fifteen dresses for Anny Duperey in the 1974 film *Stavisky* by Alain Resnais. The dresses were all black and white and decorated with diamonds and pearls, "cut and almost sewn on to me, I slide in as if into the character's skin."[17] For *Elle*, the Stavisky affair was also the Saint Laurent affair: "Fluid, swaying, sensual, a whole nostalgic elegance for the period which is the mark of 1974 fashion."

Handled by Resnais as an intimate drama, the story of the biggest financial scandal of the 1930s brought back the charm of a period when luxury was the primary character: costumes in ermine and white satin crepe, and wasn't Arlette Stavisky the most fabulously elegant woman in Paris? Like Yves Saint Laurent, she liked lilies, as well as money, as long as she was spending it: "I'm not virtuous, I don't respect the sacrament of marriage. But I belong to a man. Only he can deliver me from this servitude. I fear only one thing: that he will give me back to myself."

12 / THE MOVE TO FABULOUS AVENUE MARCEAU

On July 14, 1974, a French national holiday, Yves Saint Laurent left Rue Spontini and moved into a Napoleon III–era mansion on Avenue Marceau. To Yves, "Couture is a mistress who costs a lot of money, and she has only seven years to live." He described his vocation like La Traviata, who gives herself over to pleasure to escape from her sorrows. "It's his way of giving Couture a beautiful place to die," *Women's Wear Daily* suggested after a visit to the construction site on June 10, 1974. That day, it was raining. "Rain means money," said Pierre Bergé, dressed in a gray suit. At that time, there were eighty Rive Gauche stores around the world, and they brought in revenue of more than eight million dollars.

Yet it was just when their company was becoming international that Yves Saint Laurent and Pierre Bergé decided to give the store the look of a Second Empire salon, almost as if to compensate for another decline: the revenue from couture was less than that of the two Rive Gauche stores in Paris. Even the billionaires were buying ready-to-wear.

It was not a time for extravagance. Chile under Pinochet, Watergate, the Yom Kippur War, and the oil crisis had all marked the history of the period. The entire planet would soon discover that it was addicted to "black gold," as people discussed at dinners in Paris. Europe was already the special operating ground of international terrorists. The image of the American model was crumbling: Nixon announced his resignation in tears. His successor tripped on airplane ramps. Was there still a place for luxury? Halfway between the Place de l'Étoile and the Eiffel Tower, the determined duo took a new gamble: "We only have one goal: maintaining quality and prestige," said Pierre Bergé.

Worth was the first couturier. Yves Saint Laurent would be the last. "The 1960s continued until 1975," said Pierre Bergé. "With a desire to be anarchist and carefree, we didn't draw any conclusions about this profession. Everything was cool, no problem. We didn't realize that couture was going to melt in the sun. One collection after another went by. It was an assumption. This craft became a profession. An artistic profession. The values on which this profession was based were being lost."

Starting at this time, the rivalry between Pierre Bergé and Pierre Cardin became sharper. Did it originate in homosexual jealousy? In the early 1970s, the war between the two clans was expressed as a struggle for influence. Each had its stronghold: as in the great nineteenth-century novels, the Saint Laurent-Bergé clan still saw Paris as the capital of the world. For Cardin, who bought apartment buildings in many great cities, Paris was just once province in the universe. Living like a monk, Cardin refused to enjoy the spectacle of luxury: "I don't need to be visible, I just am." He called himself a "traveling salesman" for his own products. A manager with a golden touch, he built his empire by selling loads of licenses abroad. "Selling bras and bidets by the ton is fine, but it's not based on anything. I've never seen a woman wearing Cardin. It's bogus," said Pierre Bergé. Cardin was eight years older than Bergé. Were they too similar to be able to stand each other? Cardin, whose clothes had been worn by the Duchess of Windsor, was also very close to high society during the café society era. But that world was dead. Once again, the aesthetic refuges were opposite: Cardin devoted himself to the religion of the twenty-first century. Bergé and Saint Laurent found their ideal in the nineteenth. The Venetian Cardin swore only by concrete, sleeves shaped like missiles, and science fiction. He lived for the race for success and futurism: "I love life too much to love the pauses."

In contrast, Yves Saint Laurent and Pierre Bergé were based in nostalgia. They always needed models, anti-models, and references, and expressed this through loyalty to tradition and craftsmanship. One example: Pierre Cardin purchased sewing machines that could do zigzag stitching for his ateliers. At Dior, they had started making lace embroidery loops or picots by machine. But Yves Saint Laurent made it a point of honor to have everything sewn by hand and to have the grain of the fabric identified using the traditional technique of thread marking. These little details revealed a mentality that expressed itself in loyalty to people: "Yves Saint Laurent was the first couturier who didn't make me use the service entrance," recalled embroiderer François Lesage. This respect for the men and women of the profession went along with an old-fashioned power system that was anti-technocratic. A nineteenth-century spirit of imitation and eclecticism gave Pierre and Yves's passions a theatrical setting. "Every walk in life has interest, and it can be just as fascinating for an artist to show the ways of a queen as the habits of a seamstress."[1]

In 1974, Yves Saint Laurent was applying his desire for splendor to fashion. His imaginary journey was beginning. In 1968, he destroyed the accouterments of the "vile" postwar period: "Feathers, stoles, faille fabric, diamonds, long crinkled gloves didn't glorify triumphant femininity, but the triumph of cash and ostentation." Six months later, he spoke of couture like a woman to whom he gave everything, as if forgiving himself for not belonging totally to her: "My profession? You can't choose it, it's like family."

Like Empress Eugénie collecting all the objects that had belonged to Marie-Antoinette—to whom she was almost superstitiously devoted—Yves was seeking a vanished world, that of Dior, "our dear nineteenth century," said Pierre Bergé. Yves had an obsessive fascination with the past. Monsieur Dior's cane came into the Avenue Marceau store. Pierre and Yves spoke to Victor Grandpierre, whom Christian Dior had design his couture house on Avenue Montaigne. They even bought furniture that had belonged to Dior.

On Avenue Marceau they founded not only a historical monument to couture, but also an altar dedicated to the only god the bourgeoisie venerated, after money:

art. Yves Saint Laurent was one of those romantics who found refuge in aestheticism, whose ultimate references were Maria Callas, Luchino Visconti (*Death in Venice* came out in 1971), and Marcel Proust. Starting in 1971, Saint Laurent was the designer in chief of this nostalgia. He designed the most elegant dresses for the Proust Ball given for the writer's centenary by the Baron and Baronne de Rothschild at Ferrières. The glamour and pleasure of this party still hid the true motives for this attraction for death, which he sublimated through his work. For now, the past was trendy. Opera was popular again, with an audience that included Pierre and Yves. In Paris, New York, and London, the opera houses were consistently almost full. To get tickets to *Faust* at Paris's Palais Garnier, *bel canto* fans waited in line starting at four in the morning. However, the life of great opera had never seemed so precarious. The financial directors routinely called for help, often enough for *Le Figaro* to reference their "chorus of lamentations" in 1975.

Pierre Bergé polished the throne where the "last living king" of couture would reign. Yves Saint Laurent glorified the desperate imaginings of the main character in *La Dame aux Camélias*: "I hate plans, I make my decisions every morning when I get up." Yves got into the habit of canceling plans at the last minute, let Louis Roederer Cristal champagne go to his head, and adopted the glamorous manners of the demimonde. Pierre was a businessman who went out to dinner after the theater, in love with a demanding mistress who was ruining him and for whom he built a mansion: "600,000 dollars cash," he told *Women's Wear Daily*, revealing the construction costs in a rather unsophisticated move. Pierre came to work every morning in a chauffeured Rolls-Royce. Yves Saint Laurent drove himself in his Volkswagen Beetle. But what they had in common was their sense of staging and theatrical role-playing that was managed down to the least little detail. After all, why decide to move on July 14, a French national holiday? Why say, "Couture has only seven years to live" in the same year when the candidate from the right, Giscard d'Estaing, was elected president?

The inspiration for the salon de couture was Princess Mathilde, a "masculine woman" admired by Edmond and Jules de Goncourt, who nicknamed her "Our Lady of the Arts" and "Queen of the Gay Science" in their journals. "Her house was a kind of ministry of grace," Sainte-Beuve wrote. For Marcel Proust, the most striking thing about Princess Mathilde was her simplicity: "'The French Revolution?' I once heard her say to a lady from the Faubourg Saint-Germain. 'If it hadn't happened I'd be selling oranges in the streets of Ajaccio!'"

They called it "5 Avenue Marceau" the same way people said "Princess" when etiquette required "Madame." The entrance was not actually on Avenue Marceau, which rolled like fabric from the Place de l'Étoile to the Pont de l'Alma, but around the corner on Rue Léonce-Reynaud. The wrought-iron gate, the purple velvet curtains, and the chandelier held up by thick red shot silk ribbon all invited even the most hurried visitor to slow down and be welcomed by a forest of kentia palms on each side of the eleven steps leading to the reception desk. There, behind a glass desk, a blond woman in a black skirt and a pearl-colored blouse seemed to have sat serenely forever. Some would have fallen over a long time ago, but her education prepared her for the art of thinking of nothing, for hours, as clients came and went in a parade of little indiscretions and secrets—occasionally interrupted by a door slamming upstairs. One of Monsieur Bergé's whims! "I'm not intimidated by people who lose control," said an unflappable long-time employee. In the large salon, the sofas with red silk cushions were reflected in the mirrors. Orchids stretched out proudly above porcelain Chinese vases. And just as plaster once replaced wood paneling to save money and create an aesthetic effect, here panels were painted to look exactly like marble. It was Second Empire style via the 1970s: thick rugs with a pattern like bound books, false Greek columns lit up by spotlights, and large black lacquer screens. Across from the entrance rose a large staircase with a gilded wood railing, which turned sharply enough to the left that visitors down below didn't notice they were sometimes being observed in the reflection of a mirror. There were many doors, but they were invisible, as in a brothel. "That was great," remembered Helmut Newton. "One of my favorite photos was taken in the Avenue Marceau store as if in a luxury bordello. All the girls are there, dressed and waiting. You feel like telling them, 'To the salon, ladies!'"

Pierre Bergé's office looked out on Avenue Marceau. It was almost bigger than the studio where Yves Saint Laurent worked, surrounded by Anne-Marie Muñoz, Loulou de la Falaise, and the rest of his team. Every day, this entirely white room seemed to shrink, invaded by blue camellias, purple crosses, fabrics, books, and a whole jumble of colors and trifles. Here, dresses where born like flawless jewels. It was a bazaar, nicknamed "the château" by the inner circle. "There's a gypsy and family atmosphere here," said Loulou, the only person, except Pierre Bergé, with whom Yves used the familiar "tu" form.

The first fashion show was held on July 23, 1974. Garlands, batting, tassels, gilded decorations. People said hello, exchanged kisses. Everyone was waiting for the great event to begin: in the front row, Hélène Rochas and Kim d'Estainville, Françoise Sagan, Zizi Jeanmaire, Olympia (the beautiful wife of David de Rothschild), Nan Kempner, Betty Catroux, Françoise and Oscar de la Renta, and Earl Blackwell. Catherine Deneuve appeared in a Prince of Wales skirt suit and a bronze silk blouse. At 11:00 AM, the models came out, pushed by Pierre Bergé; Régine's gypsies played the violin when the guests arrived and left.

Yves seemed to have been inspired by a painter's countryside landscape, where women celebrated the harvest among bouquets of wheat and gold-colored cakes. "My new décor brings back past times whose nostalgia I love. But my naïve and peasant fashion has nothing retro about it." In white blouses with gathered collars and muslin skirts sprinkled with country bouquets, there was all the freshness of a folk tale, where the shadow of an impossible love lurked among the flowers. Something beautiful and sad slowly moved forward. Strangely, a new model, Anna Pawlowski, who was one quarter Mongolian and three quarters Polish with prominent cheekbones and eyes like two long dark lines, walked down the runway without ever smiling. Next to her, the others looked very "womanly." "I have an unattractive physique," she said. Another break. She had arrived by chance, in an old suit, encouraged by her best friend, who happened to be Jean-Paul Gaultier, with whom she went dancing in nightclubs in Montreuil. With very white make-up and very red lips, she smoked little cigars. She dressed in long skirts and big sandals she bought at the flea market. At home, she always walked around in her underwear. She was told, "Make an effort." She answered, "Okay, I'll put shoes on." She wasn't pretty, but Yves saw her as beautiful. And she became beautiful, and royal, in caftans and embroidered coats. "I remember him draping me with fabric. It was hot. He liked touching the fabric and wrapping my body. He looked in the mirror. He knew. You have to have a wonderful imagination to know that it will turn into this, and not something else. I admired this sincerity, all this kindness that he gave with his hands, this fabric that he made into something that moved." Following in Dior's footsteps, Yves became once again the "master magician," the one who launched a line every season. This collection seemed to be for redheads, with wool muslin dresses in autumnal shades such as deep purple, bronze, and copper, and cashmere coats that the press described as moving jewelry boxes, in a color range of browns and burgundies. "Yes, I remember, we called it 'Clara's collection,'" Pierre Bergé recalled with emotion.

Nothing was like before. The colors had code names. They didn't copy drawings by hand anymore; they were photocopied. In the move to Avenue Marceau, something was lost. It was even more precious than the box with all the archives of two years at Dior. On Rue Spontini, they were like a family. The celebrations of the Feast of Saint Catherine. Monsieur Edouard, who answered questions before you finished asking them. Yvonne de Peyerimhoff leaving Pierre Bergé's office, wiping away her tears with the back of her hand. "It's nothing, tomorrow I'll get a bouquet of white roses." In 1971, the retro collection had marked a break. Madame Esther, who had left Dior to follow Yves when he started his own company, understood in 1971 that "a world had ended."

"We were cut off." Madame Esther, the *première* of the *atelier flou*, described the company like a piece of fabric. "On Rue Spontini, we were all together. Now, everything was structured. We only ran into each other by chance. It had gotten so much bigger!" Two hundred fifty people worked at 5 Avenue Marceau in a space that was over 20,000 square feet. There were three ways to reach the ateliers: by the service entrance (that the seamstresses used); by the door at the end of the hallway along the studio; and by another door that opened into the press office, which was next to Pierre Bergé's office.

There, a spiral staircase led up to the ateliers. "The Bridge of Sighs," Monsieur Dior would have called it. The company had changed: it was an empire worth 50 million dollars. The number of YSL licenses had increased to 80 by 1974, although this was a smaller number than Dior (120) or Cardin (440). Manhattan Industries and the Bidermann Group launched a collection of suits and shirts under the YSL name that would bring in 15 million dollars in the first year. Yvonne de Peyerimhoff, aged 73, was replaced by the 28-year-old Hélène de Ludinghausen, a White Russian with a Rolodex that was bronzed in the sunshine of the jet-set. "She has a voice like a party animal," said the long-time employees. There were new clients, including Texans and Brazilians. Including women about whom people whispered that they were named John before being named Mary. Including those who, after being forty years old for ten years, suddenly disappeared. Including those who still came at three-thirty in the afternoon and fell asleep in the front row, startled awake when Jacqueline Miller, a black model who loved to play pranks, burst in. One afternoon, in the grand salon, in the middle of a private show of the collection for clients, she came in wearing a housecoat with a broom in her hand, speaking pidgin French to Countess Volpi, who had fallen asleep in the front row.

Times had changed. Now when someone wondered where a model had gone, the answer was usually, "She must have gone to have a little something in the bathroom." Loulou de la Falaise had become Yves's muse. Of course he hadn't informed anyone. We can imagine how nervous the staff from the Dior era were: they had learned the profession with tears, and now this foreigner was admitted into the holy of holies without ever having to struggle to get there. Loulou acknowledged, "My drawings were terrible. I had looks and ideas." When she got there, she simply said, "I hate navy blue and I love shocking pink." Her best professional experience was her life.

With Loulou, the studio became open to unusual "suppliers," Argentines who showed mock-ups made of crazy fabric. It was also opened to Paloma Picasso, who designed her first jewels, in the shapes of suns, clouds, and glass ladybugs. "Yves Saint Laurent is the only Frenchman who hired me," she said. It was a new era. With Maxime, Loulou never had to fear what people would say. She made fun of bourgeois people who were "weighed down with conventions." Paradoxically, she had an extreme sense of order and respected institutions such as tea, marriage, and the queen. But she had no self-control. She spoke about herself as a field experiment. In Andy Warhol's magazine *Interview*, Loulou and Maxime aired their dirty laundry and talked about anything and everything, including the incest fantasies that Maxime's husband, John McKendry, harbored about his stepson, the two months Loulou was hospitalized, and how she liked to spend her time at the doctor's or the hairdresser's instead of cleaning the house. "You're kind of a domestic," she said to her mother, who was about to publish a book on medieval cooking. Maxime said that when she was pregnant, she looked like "a snake that had swallowed a chicken." As usual, Andy had his tape recorder on.

A very raw and unkind conversation then took place. "I was offered a lot of money to start a maison de couture. I never wanted that kind of life. Being responsible for a maison de couture means agreeing to see only fashion people. Nothing, not money, not glory, would make me accept that kind of prison," Maxime de la Falaise said confidently. She was the "best-dressed lady" who was always noticed at parties, between Truman Capote, Babe Paley, and Princess von Fürstenberg. "Yes, that's like Yves," Loulou replied. "I would hate to be Yves, because he can never stop working. There's always more and more, and sometimes he goes crazy, because he knows there is always something else to make and wonders how we will do it."

For his part, Yves always kept the good manners of couture. He knew that some were made to design dresses and others to wear them. In this way, wasn't he the son of Dior? His politeness toward the ateliers was legendary. He always said, "Bonjour, Mademoiselle," to the young women, as loyal to this etiquette as he was to the finest fabrics. Dior had passed on to him an obsession with construction and finely done work, which all the long-time employees who came to Saint Laurent from Avenue Montaigne practiced. Like Madame Catherine, they had a way of saying, "No, my jacket isn't ready. I still have to clean it up a bit." He had that sense of the profession and its secrets that are written down nowhere and are transmitted through craftsmanship, the eye, and the hand. "If you're wearing navy blue and you do good, careful work, it bleeds," Monette explained. "I'm old-fashioned, a lab coat is much cleaner."

There was a special sensibility that flowed through the company like a wave. The way that Madame Hélène, who was in charge of wrapping the clothes, talked about the fabrics: "Mousseline is long, it flies away. It's like hair. You have to use tissue paper, fold it, and fold it again, so there are many layers." These women maintained an inalienable sense of pride. Waiting for a late client who had an appointment for a fitting, Madame Catherine was a bundle of nerves. She would fiddle with her yellow ruler, then jump up suddenly, her blond braid swinging in the air. "Punctuality is the politeness of kings. And this lady isn't even a baroness."

But everything changed. In her interview with Warhol, Loulou described the differences that came about: "The profession became weighed down. The Rive Gauche collections were limited to a few outfits, but everyone remembered them. Who can forget the laced boots and the safari jackets? But the job started to get more burdensome for Yves. He became anxious and sometimes infuriating to those around him, suffering more and more from the burden of the business and this emotional relationship with Pierre." She added, "He can be very mean. But he has this wonderful sense of humor that gives him some distance. He doesn't apologize, he makes fun of himself. When he falls in love, it makes him mischievous. Afterwards there's a fit of hatred." Spanish blood flowed in his veins. Andy Warhol did a portrait of Valentino and Halston. Furious, Yves told *Women's Wear Daily* that he would hold a "private ceremony" to burn the portrait that Warhol had previously done of him. Of course, he did no such thing.

The more successful he was, the more doubts he had. What was expected of a king? Glory and conquests. Yves played for a demanding and crucial public: America. Every season, he had to offer a private preview for John Fairchild and his team from *Women's Wear Daily*. Pierre Bergé was seated at his side—the salon was empty—filled with doubt and fear. "Usually I took the photos," Vesna Laufer remembers. "He said he wasn't ready. He was in an incredible state, so anxious. Almost more than for the main fashion show." He had phobias and superstitions. For him, the suit of spades, especially the ace of spades, were bad luck. He was afraid of fire, mice, and cats (especially black cats), peacocks and birds in general, and "everything that's in horror movies," according to Loulou. "But the main creepy-crawly is himself. He likes being scared of big mean wolves. He lives in an invented world. He quickly goes from euphoric fantasies to fits of rage and discouragement." At night, he escaped himself, losing and then finding himself in the Paris he had dreamed of in Oran. The man in the white suit liked to dress in costume, with black leather and diamonds. "He loves slumming. But like everything about him, it's fake. He pretends. He puts on a costume. At that time, he was too good-looking. I always thought he looked like Roger Moore," Loulou remembered in a slightly mocking tone. More than anyone else, she was able to give new things the look of having already been worn, in a sloppy chic style. But Yves amazed her. She let herself be led like a little girl by this crazy driver: "It was incredible! He drove so fast. He'd stop all of a sudden because he saw something in a store window. He could run over the feet of an old lady who would say, 'What an honor, Monsieur Saint Laurent!' When he heard a siren blaring behind him, he'd dart down a one-way street. His old fear of the army and uniforms. It was a crazy ride through Paris." But sometimes he got caught and ended up in the police wagon. He was once arrested for drunk driving, taken to the police station, and even, according to Loulou, "beaten." "They stopped when he said his name was Yves Saint Laurent. That's what shocked him the most." The policemen let loose a barrage of jokes: "You must've seen a lot of beautiful babes naked."

In Marrakesh, he could have a simple life again. He enjoyed it even more since he knew it was only temporary. Mustapha, the butler, wearing loads of Rive Gauche cologne, described what Yves was like in Morocco: "He's a Leo. Occasionally, he explodes. But it's rare. He's a guy who doesn't bother you. He comes here to forget. He's a family type." On August 28, 1974, Pierre and Yves moved into an Art Deco villa in Marrakesh that was designed as a smaller-scale replica of the Villa Taylor. "Yves said, 'I'd like it to be the color of the skin of a pretty woman.' He had torn out a page from *Vogue*," Bill Willis, the architect, recalled. The ironwork looked like lightweight netting along the bay windows. In this house, there were no restraints or hindrances, no trinkets that you could only look at, but objects that were bought by chance on afternoon strolls through the bazaars. Baskets, pottery, painted tables, copper trays. "He likes simple things. Something real keeps its value, but sometimes it's not useful for anything," said Mustapha.

The approach to the house was, as at the Comtesse de Breteuil's estate, through a living, chaotic garden where trees grew like children in a big family. It was an open house, looking out on a garden with banana trees, hibiscus, and bougainvillea whose pink hair tickled the second-story balcony. Nine calm, white rooms, barely troubled by a designer's Orientalism, with Syrian furniture inlaid with mother-of-pearl and drawings and watercolors depicting sharifs and Kasbahs seen from the Arab quarter in Constantine, or a very beautiful ceiling from a palace in Fez. But Yves's favorite room was the "sitting room for all seasons," which was slightly out of the way, and dominated by a pink mantel with a black bust of a woman, on which he put a red coral necklace. The screens of sculpted cedar, the armchair nonchalantly draped with a cashmere shawl, a tiger skin rug at the foot of a bench tucked away into an alcove, little openwork wood tables like pavilions: everything created an exquisite sensation of winter in summertime. Pierre Bergé preferred the large salon, which seemed more lively, even when it was quiet. This must have been because of all the books it held. It was the library of a vacationing book lover that contained bound sets of the complete works of Jules Verne and Anatole France as well as Giono's *Solitude de la Pitié*, rhyming dictionaries, and *Les Bêtises* by Jacques Laurent, which were displayed on shelves of dark wood, surrounded by Yves's drawings, including one that was full of snakes. The house was called Dar es Saada, the house of happiness. The napkins were made of mauve linen. Yves wrote in his room, which was as blue as the swimming pool. He strolled about in a white cotton caftan and pants and smoked Kool cigarettes. He drew Loulou in a turban and Pierre with a beard and even caricatured himself, with an absent look and a cigarette. In the garden, Pierre immortalized him with his Olympus camera. Pierre was sometimes grouchy, and when he abruptly shouted, "Yves!" everyone grew silent. A sign of his presence and his great affection. "They were still happy," photographer Pierre Boulat said. Boulat recalled being surprised at the couple's touchiness when he wouldn't reschedule his flight home to stay and have dinner with them. Yves posed like an odalisque, with his instinctive ability to merge into a place or situation, to be one with it the way women became one with his dresses: "The silence of clothing, i.e., the moment when the body and the clothing are one and you completely forget what you are wearing, when the clothing doesn't speak to you, i.e., doesn't grab you, when you feel as comfortable in your clothes as you are naked."

The years from 1974 to 1976 were a gestation period. Always attracted by contradictory worlds, Yves felt the noose was tightening around him and preventing him from exploring all of them. He experienced his passions totally and extremely. Everything was in conflict within him. The hip young 1940s-era Frenchman and *The Earrings of Madame de…*, the hermit and the Queen of Sheba. Two worlds that were inseparable, that completed each other, rejected each other, and were passionately attracted to each other. They found expression in his designs. On the one hand, the androgynous woman, and on the other, the femme fatale, a goddess of vengeance, who appeared in summer 1974 in a canary yellow crepe dress tamed by Guy Bourdin.

Once again, in Yves's mind, reality and dreams were confused. As he became a hero, the "last couturier" started seeing women as queens: "His women are not only well-dressed, they're heroines," *Vogue* wrote.[2] After designing for their ambiguities, he began depicting them as mistresses, powerful women, women for whom one would burn down a castle for love. With characteristic lyricism, he would offer them everything that they sacrificed in their struggle: the fantasy of expense and the pleasure of seeing men bankrupt themselves for them, nostalgic echoes of the passionate, powerful women of the Belle Époque. "Without fashion—and pleasure—life is silly," they sang at the turn of the century in the show *Paris s'amuse*. He would give himself over to couture in a frenetic, expensive, decadent way. But what did money mean to a man who was in love with a doomed idol, whom he would make his impossible love in order to justify his unhappiness?

This awareness of following in the footsteps of his master and of being the last Napoleon of fashion placed Yves definitively above his doubts, above men, above chance. But he risked cutting himself off from the world and life.

His nostalgia for Dior and his attraction to theater and artifice made contact with reality more difficult every day. "They're a mess!" he said in New York when models showed up without their hair done and with no make-up for a show at the Pierre. There was the side of him that wanted to shine, that launched his impressive designs and waited for applause. But he was also a misfit who saw everything, and chronicled his time—its brilliance and its transgressions. From Jackie Onassis to Cher to Pat Buckley, he was the darling of showbiz and the jet-set. Yves and Andy Warhol came up with a musical titled *To the Fog* featuring billionaires at the fashionable restaurant La Grenouille. Yves, who wasn't able to take a plane by himself, instinctively chose on his own those who would represent him abroad, women built like young men who looked like him: "Before Yves, I always had a complex about my big shoulders. Afterwards, it was divine." In the span of ten minutes, the former model Marina Schiano, a brunette Betty Catroux with jungle-red lips, would become executive vice president of Saint Laurent in the United States, managing media relations, advertising, twenty-three licensing agreements, and fifty-five Rive Gauche stores. On the phone, people often called her "Sir" because of her unusually deep voice. Up until then, she had been in charge of the men's boutique on Madison Avenue. "Everyone came by: Andy, Tony Perkins, very chic black men, and lots of women who dressed in silk Mao shirts and black pants. The best tea-time in New York!" Invited by Fernando Sanchez, Marina first met Yves at a cocktail party at his Rue de Babylone apartment. "It was a July evening. He was dressed all in white. I remember his kindness and politeness most of all," she recalls. "This strange night among the flowers was like the calmest part of *Suddenly Last Summer*. Except that it wasn't the last summer." In New York, Yves felt a special kind of freedom. "He was like a child who never had any money on him!" says Marina. They had dinner with Mick and Bianca Jagger and Silvana Mangano at Pearls or Le Jardin. Marina sums it up as "Yves's very healthy period."

The summer 1975 collection was surely one of Yves's most modern collections. Was it just by chance that it came out when the West was celebrating International Women's Year for the first time? In France, Françoise Giroud was named Secretary of State for the Condition of Women. And several laws ensured the lasting liberation of the so-called weaker sex: starting in 1975, adultery and abortion (the Veil Law) were decriminalized. Yves Saint Laurent's clothes fit this contemporary spirit of freedom. The spirit of the early days of Rive Gauche was there, along with new maturity. "In this profession, fashion comes second. We try to express an art of living. Of course you may overlap with fashion, but there comes a time when fashion doesn't interest you anymore, when you seek instead collaboration and friendship with women."

There was almost no color. It was all black, white, and navy blue lines. "I think we went too far, myself included, into folklore and retro. It was time to update all that, to create fashion that was simpler and more current." The tuxedo became a jumpsuit, and the long flowing dress turned into a scarab green crepe sarong with black flecks. "Here come the sirens," wrote *Women's Wear Daily*. "Forget Nostalgia," read the headline of the *Daily Express*. "Forget the naïve chemise, the big skirt." All at once, Yves made his most faithful clients look out of style, in a seductive game that consisted of saying temporary farewells now and then in order to come back looking even better. As they left the show, all the women in flowered shift dresses were completely depressed: "We look like dead leaves!" said Hélène Rochas. They all decided to go on diets. "He did a t-shirt, but what a t-shirt!" It was the lean look of summer 1975, a season that was nicknamed "the Pitanguy summer" after the most famous plastic surgeon of the era. Some critics thought the cult of thinness went too far. René Barjavel issued this critique: "They don't show us the breasts from the side anymore, because there are no breasts. Every year, when I go back to Saint Laurent, I wonder if the devoted girls who model for him will have managed to get even thinner. Well, yes. A year will come when there will be nothing left of them. The crepe dresses will float weightlessly over their ghosts. This year they let their master construct completely masculine skirt suits around them, with no trace of obstacles from their chests, hips, or buttocks....We'd like to see some curves. Alas, it's all flat or even hollow. Where can our poor hands go?" Barjavel described seeing a "monk in black velvet followed by a cloud of melancholy." The body was lengthened, slipped into a long silk jersey cardigan. It was a sweater that could be rolled up in a suitcase and be dressed up for evening with coral jewelry and an anthurium flower.

"That collection was me," said Marina Schiano, with the confidence that Saint Laurent women had of seeing themselves in a time period that seemed to exclude all others, and especially all other women. The Americans called it the "pure look." This "contemporary silhouette will have a great influence on the clothing of the future," Yves Saint Laurent promised. Thirty-five out of seventy-four designs were black. With the others, he revealed an extraordinary mastery of tones, in subtle mixtures of muted mauves, blue grays, and olive greens. "The jewels are poor." In 1975, Helmut Newton shot one of Yves's favorite photos. It was taken on Rue Oudinot in the seventh arrondissement and you can see the influence of Brassaï—"my master," Newton said. A silhouette with slicked-back hair stood out against the damp twilight. The androgynous woman looked very sophisticated in a gray wool man's suit with tennis stripes and a pearl gray Moroccan crepe blouse.

This was all very far from the curves and decorations of the nineteenth century. "It's difficult to give a new look to the same design every season. I am evolving toward more precision. Every year I improve the proportions, because, seeing my clothing live on women, I correct my mistakes. My goal is to reach prototypes that will no longer go out of style. Like jeans, which have reached perfection." Was this a challenge from Yves Saint Laurent the man to Saint Laurent the couturier? "I have only one regret: that I didn't invent jeans," he would later say. Jeans had no sex, they were wearable by all men and all women in any season, day or night, in any climate, at any age, and by any social class. In jeans, you could go anywhere. Their sales skyrocketed. Factories were set up. Five hundred million pairs were sold worldwide in 1973, including ten million in France. In 1975, the number one brand worldwide, Levi Strauss, surpassed one billion dollars in sales. *Playboy* called jeans "the backdrop of the twentieth century" while others considered them the fabric of decadence and the havoc of May 1968. Yves was the first designer to have shown them not as an outfit with something to prove, but as a classic.

It was this Saint Laurent who, season after season, reworked the things he borrowed from the male wardrobe: trench coats, sweaters, pantsuits, raincoats, shorts, safari jackets, and t-shirts. The sparse, clean lines created intimacy with the body's movement, adapted to suit women while respecting classical rules. That Saint Laurent was the one who changed life. He simplified it, because he lived it. His dresses started with a t-shirt. His pants became the basics of the contemporary wardrobe. By 1974, after their fragile victories, women had bought twenty-five million pairs of them. There was also the man's jacket, of which he was the best observer. It's as if his nighttime escapades only gave him one desire: to transform life immediately into a fabric of memories. He chose to make pants out of the fabric from café waiters' jackets and to create skirts from Saint-Étienne velvet—the velvet of riding helmets. Photographed by Guy Bourdin, the tuxedo suit of winter 1974 was inspired by bellboys' uniforms. Yves Saint Laurent was the first one to use a type of satin that was only used for bartenders' imitation leather. "That fabric smelled like fish glue! It was terrible to prepare," recalled Josiane Dacquet, director of materials, who started at YSL in 1968. "We asked the suppliers to improve it." It was first used for the inside of the tuxedo suits, and then expanded to jeans, safari jackets, and shorts of all colors. It was the "Saint Laurent leather satin."

Other classics of the maison were dry, masculine fabrics. "My golf flannel, my grain de poudre," Yves would say, speaking of them as if they were people. They were tough guys with hearts of gold, who seemed to say, "Come on, you fool, kiss me!" They stood up very straight, with clear lines. They were imperturbable, and able to endure any test. "He loved rustic silk remnants," recalled Josiane Dacquet. "At first, the seamstress didn't want to cut it. She thought it had too many flaws!"

Yves also liked "English flannel," which had this name even though it was made in France. These were all the raw materials for a transformation: "A woman in a pantsuit is not at all masculine. Through the rigorous cut, her femininity, her seduction, and her ambiguity come through even better. This androgynous woman, who is man's equal by her clothes, deploys all the secret weapons that belong to her alone, especially make-up and hairstyle, to triumph over what might seem a handicap. If one day we must depict the woman of the 1970s, the choice must be a woman in pants."

Finding the permanence, the silence of lines. Going toward the essential, that which cannot be undone. This Saint Laurent wants to be done with fashion. He was no longer in the wings pinning illusions. He designed for daily life in the footsteps of Chanel. His clothes were seen on the men and women who came to his fashion shows. "The Other Yves Shows," ran the headline of an English newspaper. Elsa Peretti, all in white. François and Betty Catroux. "It's my jeans or him," she said of Yves. François-Marie Banier. That Saint Laurent dreamed of becoming a haute couture garment whose greatest luxury was to be forgotten. In Oran, he dreamed of seeing his name in bright shining lights. In Paris, he sometimes dreamed of disappearing, of becoming the anonymous person he never was.

But something stood in his way and kept him frozen. The fear of not succeeding, which had haunted him since 1958. "I never felt that I had important moments in my life. I was simply engaging in situations that were more or less important but in which my inner self remained withdrawn," he had said as the head of Dior, the greatest maison de couture in the world. "Success doesn't happen overnight—all you can do is deserve it or disappoint your fans." The more time passed, the more fear settled in. The only way to escape it was to belong to it.

At age twenty-one, Yves entered the kingdom of the doomed, swallowing the poison that had made Dior king, offering him his greatest joys and his greatest suffering. "Yves is naughty, he's mischievous, just like Monsieur Dior," said one of the long-time employees on Avenue Montaigne, Micheline Ziegler, who was there when Yves's career was first starting and he decorated the store windows. But there was a difference between them. "Monsieur Dior was a reserved man. But he accepted himself as he was: fat, homosexual, and superstitious. His only anxiety was the shows." Micheline was hired by Yves Saint Laurent in 1962 and left the company in the early 1970s after a dispute with Pierre Bergé. She acknowledged, "Monsieur Dior was affected by war and poverty. He liked bourgeois comfort. Yves is rootless. He is alone. He's rebellious and very intransigent about his creative process. And at the same time, he's more vulnerable. When Monsieur Dior had appointments with the suppliers, he went." Yves's only anxiety was himself. The saleswomen saw a doctor come to administer Monsieur Saint Laurent's "shots." He might have an interminable sleep that lasted a second. He liked books that cultured people thought were stupid. "It's just a novel!" they would say. Specialists bored him. A trifle could transport him. A trifle could break him.

For how much longer would he be the son? The deadline was approaching. Yesterday, he was called "shy" the way people used to say "artsy" instead of "homosexual." Changing times? Starting in the early 1960s, people began to say "neurotic": psychoanalysis on glossy paper had started. "I'm in the middle of my life. Accepting the change from adolescence to maturity isn't easy." Who was he? Old enough to become young, and young enough not to have to be afraid of being old someday. He hardly had time. Living. Disappearing into the shadows of an unbearable freedom that doomed him to create every moment. Or roaring like a wild beast in a gilded cage, whose bars protected him against the cold, the sun, and himself. He always had to keep inventing: other refuges, other Illustres Théâtres. For the people, he became a brand. For his court, he was simply Yves. But what did he fear the most? Others? Or his loneliness? Surrounded, he felt smothered. "He hates people to think he's normal," said Loulou. Alone, he was drowning. He ended up wishing for an obstacle to arrive by chance, as if he needed to do battle with an enemy.

13 / BLACK IS A COLOR

On July 28, 1976, Yves Saint Laurent showed his haute couture collection in the Imperial Salon of the Hotel Intercontinental in Paris. Before then, the shows had been held in the Avenue Marceau headquarters. This was the first time that fashion was staged like a spectacle. The event would have lasting influence. His favorite model wore the fake ruby heart that had been around since his very first show on Rue Spontini. From its place hanging in Yves's room near a crucifix, it was put in a shoebox and specially delivered by the chauffeur in a twilight-hued Rolls-Royce. The Ballets Russes collection had 110 designs. Yves would later say of this collection: "Perhaps it wasn't the best, but it was certainly the most beautiful."

At age forty, he had rediscovered his kingdom of shadows. Something inside compelled him to explore everything, to burn everything, to feel everything, to see those truths "that dominate death, preventing us from fearing it and almost making us love it."[1] Like a ghost, a mysterious lady in black appeared that year, illuminated with gold spangles: Yves posed for Lord Snowdon in his garden on Rue Babylone with his arm around actress Dayle Haddon. They looked like two lovers turned to stone among the trees.

That season, crescent moons with blue stones and big earrings with golden threads interlaced in a dusting of green and red beads had no goal other than decorating and beautifying the woman-idol. Yet this idol shone with a strange intensity. Everything rumbled. Everything stunned. Red satin with orange and gold lamé. Burgundy faille against emerald crepe de Chine. Everything was electric. This woman was not coldly ideal. But too beautiful. Too alone. Too divine. She seemed to say to her servant, "No, I won't be going out tonight," and to walk forward, on this elongated stage, turn, and disappear, sucked into the void, while another woman arrived and walked right over her shadow.

That day, Yves Saint Laurent revealed visions that brought together Paris, the devil, and woman. "I wanted to have fun, to get out of the constraints that had enclosed me. I wanted to give women the possibility of creating a universal wardrobe. When I dressed them like men in blazers and pants, that fit practical everyday life. But all of a sudden I wanted something imaginative. I was weary of fashion being stuck in the humdrum and the serious, which was paralyzing it."

Now he was enchanted by color. He expressed its restlessness in his sketches. Living like black flowers on mauve mousseline. The yellows were like bits of broken sun. The astonishment of a solitary Indian pink. The flow of reds. The slow elevation of colors of earth and spice, saffron, cinnamon, chili powder, among the brightness of sapphire and emerald. Everything was transformed: the salon became a harem, and the diva was a daughter of the desert, aristocratically revealed by instinct as happens to rulers of the world. They appeared with their gold turbans pinned with black butterflies, their necklaces, their magic. Beauties of the devil. The portrait of Woman, like Balzac's girl with the golden eyes who was "an abyss of pleasure where one tumbles endlessly."

That season there were only two pairs of pants. Betty Catroux rushed to order them. Everything changed, everything would change. Exalted by the use of impressive fabrics such as shot silk, taffeta, and faille, Yves's lines were at the same time more flexible and more energetic. It was as if he were led along by the expansiveness of his gestures, such as coats with expanded, rounded shoulders. The capes touched big, gathered skirts. The waist was emphasized by velvet camisoles or bodices. "After so many years, I understood that the most important thing about a dress was the woman who wore it."

Yves's new favorite model was an Indian woman named Kirat, whose skin sensuously lit up a dress of Indian pink lamé. "She walks like a goddess, rests like a sultana,"[2] in the words of Baudelaire. Purple velvet bolero jackets, open at the hips, permitted glimpses of her proud and regal body, where there rose shoulders as straight as those of Egyptian goddesses, with very long necks and legs.

Photographs of these designs by Duane Michals appeared in the October 1976 issue of American *Vogue*. Three women in red and pink turbans and long taffeta skirts were leading themselves to the seraglio. Guy Bourdin had them pose like the Delacroix painting *Women of Algiers in Their Apartment*. Yet they had mink ushankas and gold leather boots. Color made the peacock.

The fabrics convulsed. They swelled, filled with threats and distant hopes that exploded passionately in these hot, brilliant blacks that looked as if they had come from red: the black ink with which he wrote this Ballets Russes collection. It was no longer the black of a black silk jumpsuit, thin as a line. It was black as dense as fever, lining the belly of the world. His colors and the intensity he gave them reserved him a separate place. He would launch a taste for exotic styles in fashion. On that day, he sent out his first great invitation to a journey. The critics were floored. René Barjavel wrote in *Le Journal du Dimanche* on August 1, 1976 (Yves's fortieth birthday): "This man who had attained the heights—or the depths—of sobriety and starkness six months ago with his striped gray skirt suits has suddenly transformed into a sumptuous volcano where lava of magnificent fabric flows in compositions of amazing colors and shapes. It's more than a change—it's a revolution." Barjavel waxed even more poetic when describing the dresses: "And then the voice of Maria Callas resounded and the splendid evening gowns appeared. I can't describe them, I'm not a seamstress....Each one was breathtakingly beautiful, and the next one always turned out to be even more beautiful. This is more than a couture collection. It's an event. Paris hasn't seen anything like it since Paul Poiret and the Ballets Russes."

Was it a new way of sensing his era? Of defying it? With an opera background, he celebrated the decadence of the 1970s, the irresistible rise of narcissism and the nostalgia industry.

The mood for exotic travels was shared by other designers that year. Jean-Louis Scherrer with his Turkish-inspired looks. Ungaro, who someone told me said he was "tired of real coats. They're out of fashion. I like envelopes." Or Jules-François Crahay of Lanvin, who was the first to bring back traditional cuts, such as capes and peasant dresses. He posed for *Vogue* eating Petrossian caviar. It was the return of full shapes, with women wrapped in fabric instead of buttoned-up. But Yves added his own special vision to this trend. There was nothing small, sweet, or charming about his designs. No fanciful Pierrots or child-women who "protected" themselves in their Pulcinella outfits, just as they "liberated" themselves yesterday in their space-suits. Yves Saint Laurent preferred to magnify the head and the gaze. He didn't lose himself in little ribbons, princess ringlets, lace, or flattering pink. Nothing senti-mental or precious. Nothing that sought verisimilitude or historical exactness. His dresses were the opposite of period costumes. Starting with the material, he depicted a personality, the truth of a character, and he made it visible. As if he distanced himself from the theme and from literal history in order to return to the source of the work. To restore the truth of a character that predated the work and was revealed by it. "I'm not focused on the past. But when the past is perfect, it is totally present." When he was inspired by Vermeer's *Girl with a Pearl Earring*, he gave the impression that she posed in a blue and yellow Saint Laurent dress. Looking at the painting once more, it's astonishing to discover that the girl had no dress—or, rather, that it wasn't visible. Vermeer painted only her face. "I tried to imagine the dress she was wearing," Yves Saint Laurent said calmly.

Why in 1976 did this man reach the point of neglecting himself? And of forc-ing others to see his physical degradation? While his dresses enveloped women in magnificence, Yves, of all people, was abandoned by beauty. Through this transfor-mation that the viewer internalized, thousands of sensations came and broke the lines. Everything exploded, everything resonated. The fabrics quivered like voices, and the colors rose into a song dedicated to passion, suffering, and death.

That year, the evolution of Yves Saint Laurent the artist imposed great strain on Yves Saint Laurent the man, who drank up to two bottles of whisky a day. His own life was drowning in the flow of the lives he imagined. "I selfishly expressed all my dreams, my paintings, the opera, the ballet. Women also need to dream," he said. He celebrated his heroines, the prima donnas of passion, to tell them, "Accept me among you." The most important one was still Maria Callas: "Diva among divas, empress, queen, goddess, sorceress, magician, poverty-stricken, divine," Yves would write. Another heroine, Tosca, who listened powerlessly to the cries of her lover being tortured. Or Visconti's Countess Serpieri, who shouted the name of the lover for whom she had betrayed her people, humiliated by a man who loved to look at himself in the mirror. Scarlett O'Hara mourning a love that had never existed, and that left her emotionless and alone. Finally, Emma Bovary, invited to her first ball, whose memory would leave a kind of hole in her life.

Four months earlier, in March 1976, the Rive Gauche collection set the tone for this imaginary adventure. "Yves Says Big Shapes" was the headline of *Women's Wear Daily*, which published forty sketches by the couturier, like a manifesto for change. The street followed his lead, as seen in the new way women were wearing their shawls, over just one shoulder. Yves didn't only design clothes, he designed attitudes. The fabric gave itself over to him, revealed in a mysterious whirlwind of pinks, purples, and reds. With the haute couture collection in July, everything asserted itself. The fabric shivered, lifted by the storm that was arriving. A world of unknown harmonies finally entered him, possessed him, attracted him.

Perched on their gold heels, the uproarious 1970s were in full swing—eye-catching, seductive, individualist. Intoxicated with parties, alcohol, and drugs. They set the stage for all kinds of travels: disaster movies, the rediscovery of history, fascination with the opera. Yves Saint Laurent extracted his truth from this energy of death. Beyond the splendor, an irresistible force pulled him along.

Yves once again became the boy king who flipped endlessly through *Vogue*, at a time when perfumes were called Attente by Verlayne, Vous Seule by Pierre Dune, and Espoir by Paquin. "You must learn to love women, you will give them all your soul," he had written in "Parlez-Moi d'Amour." He restored fashion's power of expression, as if he had injected sensations and emotions into the fabric that gave it new color, gave it a brand-new yet familiar strength. Never, since 1959, had he given such intensity to color, to these visions that he made almost tactile. The material was serving this expression: he tamed it, glorified it, and extracted all its possibilities. His velvets in the colors of precious gems were distilled like liqueurs. But his wool muslins, his matte, rough woolen fabrics, grew dry in the terrible cold of the desert night, where olive trees struggled against the dust and sun. Colors of earth and spices revealed the route from Marrakesh to the Ourika Valley, bordered with eucalyptus, across from red mountains. The stones had a blue-gray sheen. The plants, like a curled mane of hair, stretched their tips, burned by the sun, toward the sky. Men in sandals waited for centuries. Women in gold dresses carried bundles of sticks. At little makeshift markets, the heat burst open brown paper bags filled with hot peppers and garlands of rough-skinned figs. A street barber tossed a pink cloth over a child's shoulders.

He caught these beings and these worlds in a single vision—as when he tied a scarf with magnetic fingers to reveal a face. "How many times I saw him arrange the fabric. With him, a turban became a hat. The milliner went crazy. It was as if his hands were magic," recalled Felisa Salvagnac, who went to work for Yves Saint Laurent as the *première* of the *atelier flou* in March 1976, after thirty years at Balenciaga and eight at Givenchy. When journalists asked him about his taste for exoticism that year, Yves answered, "I met Madame Felisa."

The imposing bespectacled blonde who smelled like roses became his fairy godmother, his queen, that year. "Crepe is my weakness. It falls attractively. It drapes. It feels you. You don't need to overdo it." It seemed that she was closer to Saint Laurent than to all the "old" designers. She had already noticed it: "Balenciaga was scandalized by his transparent blouses. I thought, 'This is someone daring.'" She describes her initial encounter with Saint Laurent: "Our first meeting was at his apartment on Rue Babylone. Ecstasy. An arrow in the heart. Love at first sight. The second time was at the couture house. I felt as if I were entering a mansion. I arrived with my *Seconde*, Madame Jeanine. She is like an extension of my fingers. The first thing came for me: a buckskin jacket. I thought: 'It's a test. He wants to see.' I put my whole heart into it. I looked at the sketch. I prepared the test garment. He was so happy. Then I felt liberated. From then on, he gave me the spectacular things, the eveningwear."

How did he manage to travel through so many countries and centuries without getting lost? Crossing Czarist Russia, surprising Catherine the Great in Saint Petersburg, and finding Delacroix in Morocco, where a slave served tea in a blue caftan? Dyeing faille fabrics the pinks and yellows of a Bombay market? How did he manage to enter a place without deforming it, to enter a century without reconstructing it, with that strength that took him in the right direction when he seemed to describe everything at once—Degas's dancers with their black bodices, Marlene Dietrich, the red empress in her pearls and mink, the silky rustling of the dresses in *Senso*? How could he channel all of it while also forgetting it all—the books, operas, paintings, the historical and documentary truth? "Few men have received—in full—this divine grace of cosmopolitanism," Baudelaire wrote. "But all men may acquire it to a greater or lesser degree. The most richly endowed in this respect are the lone travelers."[3]

No trace of struggles or possession. He gave exactly because he didn't try to take. The journey began when the curtains closed. In his studio devoured by color, a man pinned a piece of white paper onto a bulletin board: "There is nothing. One can only breathe in immensity." He knew from then on that he could go anywhere, no matter whether his feet would carry him. Any period—the American Civil War or the Risorgimento—and any place—the Paris of *La Dame aux Camélias* or the Morocco of the Orientalists—belonged to him as soon as he seized it.

We can see the influence of Schiaparelli, whose memory he made sublime. This is what he wrote about her in December 1976: "She slaps Paris. She hits it. She tortures it. She enchants it. It falls madly in love with her! She comes to Paris, enigmatic and spectral, trying to blend into the crowd with her trunks filled with episcopal silks, cardinal purple, and toreador jackets. Rolls of drop beads, candy bags filled with gold nuggets and silver sequins, papal shot silk, faille, and silks as sharp as scimitars, Oriental dressing gowns, officers' Brandenburgs and braided trim, accessories from the Commedia Dell'Arte, a harlequin costume, sprays of bad, stiff vulture feathers, smart little crests from circus horses. A whole world of strange, disturbing, and exciting things."[4]

Coco Chanel, a poor girl from the Auvergne region, was the first designer received by high society. Elsa Schiaparelli, a transplant from Rome, was able to amaze high society with her tragic frivolity. "Schiap" whipped them to a froth and sprinkled in sparkling streams of pink and gold. Yves Saint Laurent, who was high society's last couturier, was clearly the heir to Schiaparelli from 1976 onward. Maxime de la Falaise, who was Schiaparelli's former ambassador to the aristocratic, described her accomplishments: "She taught me everything. With her, I understood a certain style. She immediately showed me how to avoid anything overly sweet or charming. Schiap raised fashion to the level of art. People wore art even if it was ugly. It was better than wearing a pretty dress. Yves has this same hardness in his style." Yves Saint Laurent was the only one who could be the spiritual heir to both Chanel and Schiaparelli, two great enemies in the couture world. Chanel once scornfully called Schiaparelli, "the Italian artist who makes dresses." But Yves, a child of the South, found in her a new star he could identify with.

Elsa had themes, and would tell her *première*, "Do Egypt for me." But with Yves, it was a more spectacular voyage, with no other destination than himself. He created impossible meetings, between Scarlett and Anna Karenina, or La Traviata and a woman of Algiers. It happened where the warm, cracked gold of Byzantine mosaics met thick green palm trees. Where the full, yellowish blue of Moroccan pottery held in outstretched hands met the astral blue of the frozen waters of Antarctica. And the observers were there, traversing these golden steppes with boyards who would soon be lost in the steam of a Turkish bath. It was as if portraits had stepped out of their frames, queens had fled from their tombs, for the supreme rendezvous of beauty and damnation. Pierre Bergé recalls Tatiana Liberman saying to him that day in July 1976, as she left the fashion show, "This is the work of a madman."

No plan, no designer poetry came between these designs as they appeared one by one. "*Numéro dix-neuf.* Number nineteen. Long evening ensemble. Emerald velvet and sable bolero jacket. Orange and gold lamé mousseline blouse. Red satin skirt." It was like a travel diary. Words that had slipped out. Notes for a painting that would never exist, even if he acknowledged, "It's a painter's collection." Colors burst into view, following no rules except those of Yves's spontaneous visions. He would later describe being inspired by the random arrangements of colors in Morocco: "On every street corner in Marrakesh, you encounter groups that impress you with their intensity and relief, men and women mixed with pink, blue, green, and purple caftans. These groups that look as if they were drawn and painted, evoking sketches by Delacroix, and it's amazing to realize that they're just made of the improvisation of life."[5]

From that day, the dresses remain, along with something else: the vision of the world that lit them up from the inside. They were the only traces of its artistic expression. And like the great artists described by Proust who, although they are bad, "use their flaws to conceptualize an ethical rule for all" (*Remembrance of Things Past*), he spoke of love with the strength of those who have suffered from not loving and one day, when it's too late, feel the sadness of abandonment.

That year revenue from the collection was 5.61 million francs, the best year for Saint Laurent since 1962. Madame Khashoggi alone ordered four dresses. Almost 40,000 yards of taffeta entered the ateliers. They were overwhelmed, and had to outsource the underskirts. The clients had to be served. They were all there: Mrs. Hyatt, Princesses Aïfa and Sarah Fayçal, Hélène Rochas, Madame Englehart, Baroness van Zuylen, Baronesses Alain and Guy de Rothschild. Viscountess de Ribes, Princess Firyal of Jordan, Bianca Jagger, Madame Pierre David-Weill, Madame Francis Lopez, Empress Farah Pahlavi, Baroness Thyssen, and Madame von Bulow, who placed her last order that season.

Yves was forty, and once again became that tall, old, sad young man who had a love affair with women the world over, as in 1958 with his first collection for Dior—the day when the crowd yelled, "Saint Laurent on the balcony!" His Russian collection earned him his first front-page story in the *New York Times*, by Bernadine Morris. "A Revolutionary Saint Laurent Showing," read the headline. Writing for *Women's Wear Daily*, Sidney Gittler compared the collection to Dior's "New Look." "Paris Opens Today: Couture Extravagance." Between July 26 and August 9, 1976, *Women's Wear Daily* devoted six front-page stories to the collection: "The Russians are Coming."

He seemed to relive an experience that, while erasing time, made the memory of what preceded it and followed it even more painful. The wonder boy who hoped to "make jersey dresses for forty francs" had become a couturier whose last collection had cost over half a million dollars. "I don't need atelier creations to express myself." The journalists' applause made him understand that he was no longer the son of Dior, but Dior himself, reincarnated in Saint Laurent. *Time* called it "The New New Look."[6]

Yet Yves had always fought and dreaded the idea of revolution in fashion: "My dresses will evolve in keeping with the spirit of the time and the inspirations that guide them," he warned when opening his couture house in 1962. The trap had closed. Fashion reporters saw Yves Saint Laurent as presenting the fall couture collection that would change the course of fashion around the world. His collection's impact was compared to Christian Dior's New Look in 1947, the one that transformed how women dressed everywhere.

He discovered once again the brilliant mourning of glory. The glory that isolated him and condemned him to experience even greater loneliness when he was surrounded than when he was alone, because, to compensate for this ludicrous world of sycophants, he had an even stronger feeling that from now on, the only critic who could destroy him, and therefore spur him to progress, would be himself. On the one hand, he was praised to the skies in articles that read almost like parodies of a bygone world—the world of Dior and of postwar exhilaration. On the other hand, many designers were dismissive of the collection. It was all too easy to imagine how they would have lashed out: Halston would have deviously called it, "a costume party for America." Sant'Angelo would have commented, "Beautiful, but it looks like a very old revolution." "I don't think going back to costumes of the past is a revolution," Calvin Klein might have uttered, indicating that he disagreed with the *New York Times* review and judged it "irresponsible." One of the only designers who wasn't critical was Oscar de la Renta: "*Time* is late! All this was in the ready-to-wear collection in March. There, it was more luxurious. I must say that I think that Yves Saint Laurent deserves this recognition, because he has a great deal of talent."

In the United States, less than ten days after the haute couture show, the "Saint-Laurentians," as *Women's Wear Daily* called them, had already appeared. Full shot silk skirts by Anne Klein, Afghan vests from Liz Claiborne, operetta sultanas from Oscar de la Renta. Yves was the one setting the styles: "You just have to see the peasant dresses in all the big Fifth Avenue stores—they're all inspired by Saint Laurent, who is at the height of his influence here," said John Fairchild in *Women's Wear Daily*.

But a fashion show is a spectacle that isn't repeated—it takes place only once, before an audience of professionals who ask themselves, as they do every season, "Where are hemlines this season? What colors are in?"

This profession with no other escape route other than nostalgia aggravated Yves's heartbreak. "Doing fashion at precise times isn't fun for me. All these dresses that die after one year, and at the same time all those I have to make. It's an ossuary and a womb. I feel torn between life and death, between the past and the future."

But as a couturier Yves knew, like Dior, that he would put his whole life into his dresses. He was an "innovator of illuminations chosen by the master of fireworks."[7] He would reply to "women's joy," excite their tumultuous existence. Fuchsia and red lit up the night. The velvet flowed. The lamés flashed. It was as if he had spilled an elixir of love and originality onto fashion. *Vogue* journalist Susan Train described it like this: "We were wearing pants. We found ourselves in long skirts with boots. While remaining invisible, he had his finger on the pulse of the time. He seemed to know what we wanted before we realized it. He put everything into place." A man was there for them. A way of feeling and seeing, of attaining this beauty that was more infinite than evil, for which it was the poison and the antidote.

14 / THE OPIUM YEARS

n September 1976, the 112th Rive Gauche store opened on the Champs-Élysées. Yves Saint Laurent was at the height of his glory. But the heads of the boutiques were aware of the negative side of this fame: "They watched him carefully at the beginning of every fashion season, because he set the style. They imitated him so much that it became bothersome," recalled an observer. Yves's victory looked very much like a tightrope walker balancing on a wire over the void. The crowd looking up at him from below gave him wings. But if he became even the least bit distracted, they could easily make him fall.

"I can't do it anymore." The article appeared in the December 1976 issue of *Le Point*, written by Barbara Schwarm. "There is a Saint Laurent mystery. The who's who of the fashion world has been buzzing with the strangest whispered rumors for weeks, even for months. At age forty, while he celebrates both his birthday and the tenth anniversary of his ready-to-wear collection, Rive Gauche, the man is more intriguing and fascinating than ever. Yet no one sees him or hears from him anymore."

There was a revelation. "I am sick, very sick. I was already sick before the haute couture show in July—but no one noticed. Yet I was having intravenous treatments: I was seriously depressed." It was true, his physique had changed. His pupils were darker, his hands trembled, his face was growing heavier. He no longer smoked the same way. The cigarette was perched on the edge of his lips, about to fall. It seemed to hang there all by itself and burn on its own. He had another characteristic gesture: his immobile hand, which was as still as his behavior was volatile. His moods were dark, suspicious, irritable. A vicious cycle was underway: alcohol, cocaine, depression, I.V., a new collection.

However, this man who staggered and rolled on the ground revealed extraordinary strength. It was as if a metal carapace protected his burning body. "There was energy in him that came up from the inside," said Bénédicte de Ginestous, the modeling director. Her nickname was "the Voice," because she announced the designs at every fashion show (*"Numéro un*, Number one"). "I saw something come about like that, during the test garments. He would arrive completely despondent. All of a sudden, looking at a fabric, something would light up in him. It was a sacred flame of talent that dominated his own physical state."

In fact, after he announced his depression, his collections became even more lyrical and sumptuous, with the Spanish and Romantic looks of summer 1977 and the Chinese styles of the Opium show (winter 1977). The Rive Gauche collections had the same flights of inspiration. The most impressive one was shown in

October 1976: 280 designs, peasant women and odalisques, long-necked idols decorated with "endless gold sequins" and flowers, with shawls edged with feathers and tassels. According to Loulou de la Falaise, it was "the most beautiful collection of all." She still speaks of it with shining eyes: "There were Irish women dressed up to be Spanish."

Although he desired glory and honors, he didn't completely recognize himself in them. In order to escape their attraction, he had to find the truth of beauty somewhere else: in his memory. His sketches for the Rive Gauche collection expressed the same jubilation as those that he made in Oran or during his early years at Dior: there was a sense of decoration, a stylishly tied scarf, a clearly suggested earring, the tilt of a broad-brimmed hat, and the sketch of a laced-up espadrille (indicated by two black crosses over the ankle). They all expressed once again the sensibility of a man of the theater. As if he had to go back to the source each time, giving back the mauve scarf to Manet's Mademoiselle Victorine and returning the pink and black jewel to the artist's *Lola de Valence*. "To dress a woman, you must think of all the others," he said.

Did these references become, through his eyes and hands, a crepe de Chine dress? The worldly woman who was suddenly adorned with a girl's grace, beautiful and desirable in this flame lamé taffeta dress that set her body afire when she walked, was certainly unaware of the dark alleys that might have inspired these dresses. She instinctively let herself be enveloped by the fabric as by a stranger whose caresses seemed familiar to her right away. Yves Saint Laurent loved women. By loving them, he also loved his own love, "love discovered outside town, pure, simple, eternal love."[1]

Though Cocteau's influence came through in these bodies that resembled those of young men, these high foreheads and profiles that recalled ancient coins, Yves was done with imitations, habits, and other stylistic exercises. His pencil danced on the page.

Two hundred eighty designs. A show that lasted two and a half hours. At the end of the spectacle, they kissed and hugged him, intoxicated with light, dazed by the lemon yellows, the oranges burst by a hand furiously squeezing out all their pulp, the same hand that made the reds bleed, slit the throats of the purples, and brewed exciting greens. Saint Laurent slapped Paris just as Schiaparelli had. Until then he had been influenced by American ready-to-wear, but this time he freely devised magical spells: "I was irritated at being constantly copied. I wanted to play a trick on my colleagues....The American designers are furious."

There were forty-six Rive Gauche stores in the United States. Every season, the Americans waited for Saint Laurent's colors the way they had once waited for Dior's lines—one day A, and the next Y. But Yves Saint Laurent's creative energy took its toll on his nerves. He "exploded" with ideas: "I'm assailed by them," he said, like the Horla. His mystique of color surprised women with its brilliance, but he suffered from the demands of creating a collection. He now knew that the worst part wasn't the trials that his fashion put him through, but the very risk of such a high position: that having reached the summit, he might come back down one day. The Americans were starting to have international influence in ready-to-wear. They were the kings of the casual look as represented by rising star Ralph Lauren, who dressed Diane Keaton that year in supple jackets and men's shirts for Woody Allen's 1977 movie *Annie Hall*. On the other hand, Yves Saint Laurent belonged to the eternal world of couture and champagne—the sublime Paris that was idolized by American women. As Andy Warhol noted in his diary, after having lunch at La Grenouille with Maxime and Loulou de la Falaise: "All the chic girls were in YSL fur hats."

In January 1977, the front row rustled with birds of all colors. Catherine Deneuve in green, Marisa Berenson in blue, Sao Schlumberger in mauve. Muslin blouses, cashmere shawls, braid-trimmed bolero jackets, Russian boots. Nan Kempner, one of Yves's loyal clients (she met him at Dior in 1958), recalled it in her Park Avenue living room, barefoot on her flowered sofa: "That was a time when my husband, Tommy, asked me every day, 'Nan, who are you today?' I love to dress up while still keeping it simple. All those collections were marvelous."

As in Oran, when he dyed chiffon in secret to make costumes for his marionettes, he returned to the infinite world of artifice that his masters Jouvet and Bérard had opened for him. He did it with even greater ease than before, since this time he was no longer an audience member, but the director. Women were his stars, and he managed them with absolute authority. "She must look imaginative," he said, speaking of a woman. "I want her to be amusing and cheerful. She must learn again to become sexy, to dress up as someone else. I offer her a huge selection." Like Jouvet, he preferred "the spells and enchantment of the stage" to "the insidious seriousness of life."

His close childhood friends were primarily the characters he met in books, such as Madame Bovary or the queen in *The Eagle with Two Heads*. Like him, they were all heroes who had dreamed of becoming heroes. By living together, they ended up being similar. The queen from *The Eagle with Two Heads* said, "I dream of becoming a tragedy. Which isn't convenient. One cannot compose anything good in chaos. So I lock myself up in my châteaux." Balenciaga disappeared after his runway shows. He was the untouchable couturier. Chanel suffered from loneliness that she couldn't prevent, and managed to resist it by her intransigence: "Never admit your disasters." Chanel had wanted glory so she could liberate herself from it. Yves Saint Laurent wanted it so he could lose himself in it.

The name Saint Laurent was now linked with depression. Rumors spread: "Apparently Pierre Bergé is going to lock him up." Everything that soothed the ambition of the couturier consumed the man a little more each day. His isolation became public and his invisibility became a hindrance. Gustav Zumsteg, the CEO of the fabric manufacturer Abraham in Zurich, which made exclusive fabrics for Yves Saint Laurent according to his sketches, acknowledged, as a witness reported, "When you have that much creativity, you pay the price." The noose was tightening around a man who, according to Loulou de la Falaise, "realized he had a kind of madness. He even used it. But he was a person who couldn't manage to live in today's world: this world is too flat, too ordinary for him."

In a sense, he was in a familiar role. A slightly yellowed photo shows him at age thirteen dressed up as the Beast for a costume party: he was already hiding behind a mask surrounded with beauties. In 1977, Saint Laurent rebuilt his Illustre Théâtre in real life. Pulling the strings of his marionettes, which he ended up dyeing in his own colors, he stole superstition from Dior, the love of beautiful things from Chanel, mystery from Balenciaga, enchantment from Schiaparelli, maternal feelings from Proust, and imagination from Yves Mathieu-Saint-Laurent. The whole world was at the premiere. The bell rang. The audience waited quietly. He recited like an actor, "The worse I feel, the more I need to create cheerful things."

Esther or Salome, odalisques or Upper West Side gypsies, the models walked Saint Laurent–style. Strode down the runway Saint Laurent–style. Spread sensuality around them. It gleamed, it shone. It took flight and put on a show. Here, they wore their hearts on their sleeves, and mirrors as necklaces. "Their hair was too curly and their legs were too thin. But they were divine," recalled Loulou. "People said we were reverse racists because there were almost no white women." Yves's female ideal was at odds with classic notions of femininity. He always wanted very flat busts, very square shoulders, and endless legs. Even when corseted, belted at the waist, or with low-cut necklines, the bodies never seemed to be held in by the clothes, never seemed to need to spill over or come loose when the clothes were unzipped. Because these women clearly had nothing in common with Mediterranean mammas. Without hips or breasts, they would never be real Carmens or real women of the East, whose archetypal femininity created an instant carnal connection for the male gaze. A man looked at them to make them his. "In the fashion house, the models tried to assimilate the movements. To know how to be withdrawn. To be in a waiting position in order to give even more of themselves, always ready, always beautiful, but not exuberant. He had an ideal figure in mind: not too much chest, legs, a stride," explained Bénédicte de Ginestous. "Each one had a special relationship with him, but it didn't always continue—which is very hard to go through," added modeling director Nicole Dorier. Yves Saint Laurent always gave special importance to his models: "To design and construct my dresses, I have to work with a living model. A body in movement. I couldn't just work on a wooden mannequin. For me, clothes must live, and to stage them in real life, I need the presence of a woman's body."

But the Casanova couturier found other muses. Starting in 1977, the women in tuxedo suits found rivals in women with amber skin on whom the reds, pinks, and hard blues glowed in puddles of light. Yves Saint Laurent became the man they fought over: "This design was made for me. He loves me in this." Time had changed, and the models no longer scratched one another's faces, but traded insults. ("The black models have corns on their feet.") These bursts of passion sometimes compensated for declining love. For they were now unfaithful. As of 1977, they started taking other jobs, showing up late, and being replaced. But isn't that what gave them the look of mistresses, always about to leave the man who got under their skin? He divided them in order to rule over them even better: "I don't reject what I've done. Women in pants aren't out of style next to a Spanish look. But I wanted to show that there is not just one way to look good and above all I felt that the masculine style that represented the avant-garde, liberation, and freedom was going to enter a bourgeois cycle. I had to get out of it." Now there was competition between the women from the provinces, the Yugoslavian models, who arrived in 1973 as if straight out of Yves's favorite black-and-white films, and the new arrivals from 1977 to 1979, whether Indian (Kirat), Argentine (Mercedes), or African (Mounia, Amalia). "Obviously, shocking pink looks better on black skin!" said Nicole Dorier, who one year earlier had dominated the stage, blond with red nails and wearing masculine-looking flannel skirt suits. "Of course, this wave of girls of color brought in something exotic. But beige isn't really Parisian, right?" she said, with a slight Nice accent. For her, 1976 was a break: "The notion of a runway show had changed. All of a sudden, it became a spectacle. The star system started." Fifteen years later, Vesna, interviewed at the Mayfair Regent bar in New York, added in her cool voice, "In 1976, six months after giving birth, I wore the black bodices of the Spanish collection. We already didn't have any eyelashes. But with the Oriental collection, I could tell I was no longer his muse."

The reign of retro beauty was ending: farewell, mauve-shadowed eyelids, wavy hairstyles, and lily-white complexions. Black that was soft as mohair and fluffy as mousseline now spat fire. Farewell to androgynous women, farewell to the feminine scent of Madame Peau Fine perfume. Paris put away its tough guys and its bistros. "I loved to hear the names of the couture colors like absinthe. He spoke gently to us. He made us dream. He lit cigarettes for us. We felt as if we were in a movie," remembered Mercedes Rubirosa, a model who came to Paris from Argentina in the early 1970s with her high heels and her dreams. During a fashion show, she forgot her flaws: her chin, her huge mouth, emphasized in an unnatural and excessive way. "Yes, she was one of those he found 'interesting,'" said one of Yves's long-time employees from Rue Spontini, a bit scornfully.

But there had to be spectacle. He could turn a cloud of black mousseline into Eva Perón. She had three minutes to say it all: her extremely thin body rippled and performed. The more the bodies took shape, became round with hips swaying, became Eastern, the more the face became made up and artificial: "We knew how to make ourselves beautiful, we didn't need anyone," said Nicole Dorier. "Later, the make-up artists came." One of these make-up artists, José Luis, preferred a different title: "I'm a beautifier, a cheater. My role is to follow the magic of the clothes, respect the gaze, the movement, the cat eyes of a gypsy who struts about in a red skirt." The day of the show, every model wanted to be the most beautiful. There was a tacit understanding. "At this couture house, no one liked what was cute or pretty. The ideals were Ava Gardner and Rita Hayworth. Masterfully lined eyebrows and lips. Sometimes, Yves Saint Laurent made a drawing for me. Sometimes Loulou told me, 'Look at that girl, make her Marlene, make that one Gilda.'"

This so-called immobile hand skipped over the paper. "Darlings, I'm in my bed making up stories for you," he seemed to tell women. The drawing looked written. It immediately evoked the memory of an encounter. Here, a Spanish woman waved her fan. There, a dreamer in a white turban nonchalantly stuck her hands into the pockets of her harem pants. This one, more flirtatious, jangled all her bracelets and seemed to study everyone's eyes on her. Yves Saint Laurent might have been the most easily copied of all the couturiers, but his expression was inimitable.

For there were all these notes, on both sides of the sketch, like a painting to come whose composition he had planned in his beautiful black script: "Odalisque. Swirling cotton turban. Bright pink mousseline blouse. Bright green satin belt. White glazed cotton skirt with multicolored arabesques. Blue taffeta underskirt. Cashmere shawl."[2] These notes didn't explain the drawing, any more than the drawing illustrated the notes. The lines and the movement were one. Everything was unified—the bracelets, the braided necklaces, the stole with the Persian designs, the shoes in straw with gold braid, the odalisque turban, draped Loulou-style.

Yes, he captured what was fleeting and transitory in these lifelike sketches. It was truth in motion: "In photos, you could see that I wasn't beautiful. It was the movement that made my flaws disappear," said Anna Pavlowski. He was the first couturier to let imperfect models shine brilliantly, in a whole palette of artifices. "Cheating is part of seduction," he said.

He was flooded with applause. Between 1976 and 1982, haute couture sales for Yves Saint Laurent increased almost threefold, from 11.4 to 31.6 million francs. This boost in business came from sales to private clients. The figure for the buyers remained stable. Ready-to-wear had developed so much that they turned their attention from "exclusive" haute couture designs. "Respond to women's joy," said Yves Saint Laurent. Some seasons, the maison de couture could not accept all the orders.

Fashion needed to be destroyed in order to be reborn, and it flowed in his veins like a drug that made the user swing from depression and anxiety to euphoria. "I suddenly felt as if I myself were out of fashion, not my designs. In the past, I only enjoyed myself when making theater costumes. But for three seasons now, I've enjoyed myself like crazy in my profession itself."

He had become Saint Laurent. He had come a long way. His knowledge of the body was remarkable. The body no longer rejected the fabric. It let itself be carried along by it, as if tamed by invisible hands. Madame Felisa showed me a Polaroid: "Take a look, do you think this is a dress? No, it's just a piece of fabric draped on the model and held with pins into its shape and its exact folds. That's what Monsieur Saint Laurent is all about."

At Dior, the dresses had cute names. But at Yves Saint Laurent they were Attente, Rencontre, and Rendez-vous—references to the moments that preceded the dresses, moments of torment, madness, and love that passionately united a couturier to his maison. His fashion vibrated with him, loved him madly, gave itself to him. He drew all these women into the giddiness of a barbarian tribe, where mothers gave birth to daughters in order to sacrifice them on an altar of glory. "The discovery of my profession fascinates me. I know of no greater exaltation. How many times I thought myself powerless, desperate before the black curtain of habit, and how many times was the curtain torn away, revealing to me unlimited horizons that gave me my greatest joys, and, I'll admit, true pride."

Starting in 1976, everything rushed, everything flew, everything grew lighter. The designs that only yesterday seemed to be contained in geometrical shapes were suddenly animated by what journalists called "peasant style." That meant bias-cut, a technique that was utterly foreign to the Dior school, which was used to rules and structure.

Shown in January 1977, the summer haute couture collection (the Spanish and the Romantics) was significant in this respect. The rectangles became luminous flowering shapes, the t-shirts puffed out into airy blouses, and the stole flowed around the body like a fan of feathers. The stripes faded away, the gold evaporated from the mousselines, the tulles crackled, the black organza underskirts were puffed out from the inside, and the volatile influence of Loulou could be seen. The fabric no longer seemed cut at bony angles, there were no straight lines, the body sparkled, playing with the fluttering light of embroidered crystal and porcelain beads, sunrise and sea green ribbons, and the night shone with jet spangles, which lit up their movements.

The year 1977 marked his true communion with Madame Felisa. All the *premières* for tailored clothing were a bit jealous of her. "No one knows how to make flounces like she does," said Yves Saint Laurent. He cut loose and got as excited as a child when he learned a technique. These women found happiness in suffering for him, for why else would they stay at work sewing dresses late into the night? "Sometimes we slept there," Loulou remembered. How to explain this madness called couture? Its pleasure may seem trivial to those who have never seen the faces with bags under their eyes suddenly light up at the satisfaction of having given it their best. "I feel almost drunk," said Felisa. "This man has an orgy of ideas in his head. He explodes." Loulou also recalled, "He wanted to learn to make things that could fly. Everyone thought that the others knew everything. Nothing was worse for [Felisa] than the closures: the dress had to evaporate, so that it didn't even seem that it was held together. Some women hated her. You were held inside the dresses by an elastic, and you felt naked in them. With no tricks, she gave you a fabulous body." This lightness sometimes had disadvantages: "I remember a ball given by

Marie-Hélène de Rothschild. One of the women got up. Poof, her bustle fell down. It was a handkerchief. It was just a little bit of wind, held up by a dot." On the fourth floor, in her studio the size of an attic room, Madame Felisa—who played solitaire like a gypsy—cut everything in a chic way, with no measurements. "Balenciaga was the funeral of Count of Orgaz in the church in Toledo. Doña Sol, Felipe II and his bastards. You looked. You could contemplate this painting for hours. It was magnificent. Saint Laurent was a tragic ballet. The corrida. A festival. It shone. He transformed a torero costume into an evening dress. He captured beauty and put it into women. He was simplicity itself. Why try to be complicated with someone who goes to your core?" There was madness, there was an elixir of love, there was endless excitement: "Balenciaga cut the skirt suits when they came out of the atelier. He was thoughtful and structured. Saint Laurent was, too, but he caressed."

In July 1977, the same madness began again: "This time, I made too many things again, but for two years now I've been in a state of grace." Yves pinned the six hundred sketches he brought back from Marrakesh to the wall of his studio. In France, he became the "king of fashion." He was photographed with Kirat, his favorite model, for the cover of the weekly news magazine *Le Point*, which recognized his influence: "Now, from New York to Hamburg and from Rome to Tokyo, he reigns as Chanel and Dior did before him, meaning that he changes the shapes and colors of the landscape of cities."[3] In stores in Berlin, Hamburg, Stuttgart, Hanover, and Munich, the professionals acknowledged it: "He is the couturier of the moment. Every season, all of German ready-to-wear asks itself only one question: what is Yves Saint Laurent doing this time?"[4] Buyers turned up from New York, Munich, and Milan: "We only came for Saint Laurent. Of course, some of the others are good, very good, even excellent.…But Paris, you understand, is Saint Laurent. It seems that the French are the only ones who don't know this."[5]

And yet, the child who drew by imitating the style of others knew that by attaining glory, he had lost his illusions. He could no longer thrust himself into the future with the excitement that had always saved him from boredom. His first dress, which won the International Wool Secretariat competition, had been produced by Givenchy in 1954. Now he had this to say about Givenchy: "I don't usually look at magazines, but a while ago, in one of them, I discovered a photo of a white pantsuit with a tie-neck blouse from my last couture collection. 'Superb!' I thought. I looked at the caption. It was a suit by Givenchy. He had even used the same Abraham fabric for the blouse." The king was suffering. He didn't have the nonchalance of Chanel, who knew she could not truly be copied, and said, "For me, being copied equals success. There can be no success without copies and without imitation."[6] The pressure was intense. Although the company had only 245 employees, 10,000 jobs worldwide depended on it. Pierre Bergé described its success to *Le Point*: "We're number one in haute couture. We're the top couturier in ready-to-wear. And as for licenses, we're in the top three, with Dior and Cardin."[7]

The licenses were increasing, but Bergé was careful not to tarnish the Saint Laurent name and image. "A name is like a cigarette: the more you draw on it, the more it gets used up, and then there's only a butt left. So we have to be able to say no to licenses. We won't make Yves Saint Laurent tires, even though the Americans asked me to."[8] Yves would need to outdo himself continually. His designs would be daughters of fire, crowned captives confronting the demon, queens that fate doomed to criminal celebrations. He said that he saw a procession of Persian prints "as if behind a veil." Could Saint Laurent outperform Saint Laurent?

An American doctor who, Loulou said, "cured me of hepatitis in five days," prescribed "vitamins" to the couturier. His first injections of speed. "Do you want it to be hard-core?" asked the "injection lady," nicknamed "The Bee" by Loulou and Yves. What wouldn't he do to "navigate in the sea of illusions"? He posed for photographers, holding still beside a porcelain vase by Dunand and a bouquet of lilies, but he didn't look that way at the couture house. There, he was always in movement, arranging a pleat, fixing the way the fabric draped, his eye studying the mirror, in his studio-cum-bazaar where, as soon as he brought in his designs, an extraordinary wind stirred the fabrics and blew into the hallways, amidst the coming and going of the models and the *premières d'ateliers*. As Madame Felisa explained it, "He made his sketches. He spread them out on the floor. He called all of the *premières* over to see them. The next day, he told us to choose. But he knew perfectly well which ones we were leaning toward." He would sometimes lose his head, revealing a demanding, authoritarian nature. It unfurled over the fabrics. He exploded, liberating all this force, escaping the prison that he built for himself, against which he could only struggle by strengthening that same prison every day. Weren't the first hearts that he drew, at age thirteen, covered with black bars? Once, before the runway show, Yves put a crucifix surrounded by candles in the models' room, Loulou recalled. "He took himself for a toreador. I said, 'Watch out! You're going to set my hats on fire!'" Later, Yves would describe designing in this way: "It's a bit like the arena. The model is the bull and the couturier is the matador. The emotions are very intense."[9]

He used his physical destruction to accelerate his sensations. By late 1976, a piece of his life seemed to have come unhooked like a dress. Nothing was okay anymore. But where was he? Yves seemed to have disappeared from this world of shadows and transformations where everything was fake and everything was true, leaving behind only his fabrics.

It all began with rumors that spread like wildfire between October 1976 and March 1977, when the foreign press besieged the couturier's studio, in the expectation, as one of his friends said, to see "the corpse move." German journalists were sent by their editors. Pierre Bergé took them to the studio, opening the door to yell to Saint Laurent, "Yves, move your arm to show them you're not dead." But the rumors spread in Paris and on March 31, 1977, the day of an art opening at the Pompidou Centre, the gossip had it that "it's all over." In fact, that was the year Yves gave the most interviews: *Le Point*, CBS, *Women's Wear Daily*, *Elle*, and *The Observer*, which ran the headline "Yves Lives!" In the *New York Times Magazine*, Anthony Burgess wrote a nine-page article about the couturier, titled "All About Yves."[10]

So, where was the subject of the gossip hiding amid the shadows that lurked about 5 Avenue Marceau? Where was the Phemius of couture, who sang of the end of Odysseus? The night of his "death," Yves ran into Paloma Picasso at Le Sept: "If I had been your father, I would have been able to leave it all. But, you understand, I have a company."

The contradictory statements reveal all the facets of the person. As if his truth were not unified, but multiple. Every observer had a vision of him that was presented as the only one. Yves Saint Laurent only liked himself when he was unhappy. As his close friend Betty Catroux said, "Yves is an actor. Deep down he's very tormented and hypersensitive. But he wouldn't change places for all the gold in the world. He's enchanted to be what he is, instead of being Mr. Smith with a normal life. He does what he wants." At this time, he had several stays at the American Hospital in Neuilly. His sister Brigitte, who lived nearby, visited him twice: "They gave him a lot of sedatives. He wasn't able to speak." But she acknowledged, "Yves has always been depressed. In 1976, things hadn't really changed. I still saw him, when he felt like it. But from the beginning they separated us from Yves. And I think a lot of things were hidden from us." These words clearly targeted Pierre Bergé.

Wasn't Yves himself extremely secretive, the child who never really played in the schoolyard? "I'm going to play hooky," he warned early in 1976. He liked to "get in trouble," like his character Naughty Lulu, and he did it with his friend Betty Catroux. They spent two weeks in the hospital together: "We were there for the same reasons. Cocaine or alcohol overdose. It was a dream stay! We were little spoiled children. Imagine what a laugh it was: we had a doctor who was very impressed by Yves and whose mouth hung open with admiration at everything he said. It was hilarious! It was a carefree era for us. We could say anything, do anything. Yves sent me little notes via the nurses. We said, 'Quick! Let's get out so we can start up again!'"

That year, Pierre Bergé moved out of the home he shared with Yves on Rue de Babylone. "One day was the straw that broke the camel's back." Bergé cited the fatal date of March 3, 1976. "There was the alcohol, then the cocaine, then the tranquilizers. Since then, Yves has never really come back to life." As Loulou saw it, "Yves took himself for Callas abandoned by Onassis. He avenged himself through the brilliance of his talent, with collections that were more and more beautiful. He had recourse to artificial energy. Time passed very quickly, and he put himself into a position where it was physically impossible to live. Instead of aging, he let himself give in to his vice. Yves has the mythology of the drunkard, the aristocracy, pop stars, and betrayed women. He has a fascination for physical decay. He likes to play vagrant. He wrecked himself. He always said he would end up like an old lady sitting on her case of wine."

"I didn't leave Yves for someone else. I did it for me, to save myself," said Pierre Bergé. "Yves had started to live a self-destructive life that I didn't want to witness. This was the time when he loved Le Sept and other nightclubs. That was his life." On March 3, Pierre left, taking with him the pain of humiliation and sadness. "Yves was unfair to Pierre," whispered a female friend while serving asparagus with mousseline sauce.

What wouldn't Yves Saint Laurent do to tear away this "black curtain of habit"? He walked more slowly and sometimes everything seemed out of his control, his twisting mouth, his legs numb from alcohol, his collapsing body. "The bad years," as one of his fake friends said, refusing, like others, to reveal more, in keeping with the rules of the clan.

But the mystery could be entirely different. For him, suffering was part of a vicious circle, a necessary evil for his success, so that he could hear people say, "Yves, you've done it again!" He needed to struggle and now only found struggles within himself. So, like stars who write their own fan mail or divas whose driver and ex-lover reserves entire restaurants for them so they can still imagine that the audience is there behind the walls waiting for them, he offered himself the spectacle of his own demise. An observer recalled, "I remember the Rive Gauche show in April 1977. Everyone was saying he was dead. He was there, like someone being reborn from his ashes. All those rumors had made him very mad." But such stories had a terrible attraction for Yves. "Finally, I was apathetic about my death," Yves said with a smile. "What was unpleasant was all those people, even my friends, opening the door of the studio to see if I was alive."

These rumors only increased the drama around the couturier. He had challenged the Grim Reaper only to tame him. As of this date, Yves used all his weapons. Running off ("Yves fled with a kitchen knife!"), chases in Paris, suicide threats, statements to the press, for whom he became the victim, the "martirio San Lorenzo" as Titian painted him in the church of Santa Maria dei Gesuiti, naked over a fire with red and gold flames.

That year, he began identifying with Ludwig in Visconti's film of the same name, the betrayed ruler who locked himself up in his empty castles in order to live free to seek happiness in impossible love, and whose rather eccentric life was finally accepted by his ministers. Supposedly the Bavarian king took his servants as his lovers. In his madness, Yves wrote a love letter, then sent it with a plane ticket for a secret passionate rendezvous in Bavaria—which never took place. Loulou warned the recipient, who had a strange physical resemblance to Pierre Bergé: "Don't go. Pierre will make a scene!"

Now he was dreaming of white horses, frozen peaks, and endless soliloquies recited by an actor in the Visconti film, whom he envisioned as Romeo: "You will become my friend, you will be the only star in my theater." Finding it impossible to live in ordinary reality, Yves Saint Laurent found another self, another looking glass to go through and lose himself in. He was fooled by nothing, so he wanted to maintain the illusion of believing in everything, of becoming each time the character who could distract him from himself. And help him to become his own show, the only star in his theater. He needed the entire stage, or nothing. "Rehearsal is the actor's most difficult art. It's not the performance that's difficult, it's the rehearsal," Louis Jouvet told his students. "A text or a scene is an incantation, magic formulas that you are repeating. A soliloquy is like a prayer that you recite. When you have repeated 'Hail, Mary' a certain number of times, after a while, you are touched by a feeling, the feeling in the text. That's what we call grace."[11]

Like all depressives, Yves believed himself to be alone in the world. But he knew very well that there was only one Saint Laurent, the only couturier who could renew himself without ever destroying what he had loved. "I hate fashion," he told *The Observer*, even if he knew that only a temporary mental state could make him take such definitive positions: "Everything has to be re-evaluated every time. You can never be wrong about fashion. We don't have the luxury of being right in three or four years' time. I must always be connected to the outside world. People want the couturier to feel everything that is happening and everything that will happen and to translate it. I produced the rope to hang myself. I'd like to create fashion only when I want to, but I'm bound by my commercial empire."[12]

Yves bought a pied-à-terre in a new building on Avenue de Breteuil. It was a studio that looked over Paris, and he had it decorated by Jacques Grange. "He called me up and said, 'I want an Antonioni atmosphere.'" The studio was sparsely furnished with some Art Deco furniture and club chairs. Drug dealers stopped by. "I need it like a refuge. To be alone. I need more freedom. I can't stand being constantly assaulted and attacked. And I also come here to write. This has become a necessity for me, a kind of therapy. I'm writing a book that will be published in the spring, a book about me, my deep aspirations, and I will hardly discuss fashion at all. This is what is most important to me right now."

One year later, he told the society reporter Jean-Pierre de Lucovich, "In the evenings, I have dinner with close friends and then I write. I'm working on book that I started two years ago, when I starting going through this crisis. It made me want to write. I'm typing it up myself and editing it. The book doesn't tell a story: it's about me. I feel it may never be finished. Basically, in order to finish it, I'd have to get sick, like Proust. (*laughs*) Ever since I started it, I don't go out anymore. I feel as if I've broken up with society. Words hold true fascination for me. I study them. I do research. I haven't read the newspaper or watched television for a year. If no one tells me, I have no idea what's going on outside. My age? I don't know anymore. I think I'm almost forty-two."[13]

At Bobino music hall, for Zizi Jeanmaire's new show, "the dresses arrived, with pins," Roland Petit recalled. And instead of the enthusiastic young man who showed up with hundreds of sketches, his pens, and his whimsical ideas, they found a defeated man, swimming in his baggy pants. At a Rive Gauche show, he collapsed backstage. Model Anna Pavlowski tried to help him, but was pushed out onto the runway. The show must go on. People thought she was crying over a break-up. She was crying, besieged by a look of disaster: "The runway show is the only time he's happy. We all have a right to love. He doesn't have that right, because he's Saint Laurent. He has always lived surrounded and protected.... He knows that his life hangs only on his celebrity." That year, Anna's brother committed suicide. It was all too much, and she left.

Loulou, his companion in his downward spiral and his fancies, shared this sense of drama with him. In their bathrooms, they had the same baskets that they bought in Morocco. He put tranquilizers in his. She put jangly bracelets in hers. "The important thing is to invent yourself," she said, playing with words as she played with hearts, these charms that she pinned onto her extravagant outfits.

Yves threw a lavish wedding reception on an island in the Bois de Boulogne for Loulou when she married Thadée Klossowski. By what couture house magic did Clara Saint's fiancé become Loulou de la Falaise's husband? After having lunch at Angélina with Clara Saint and Paloma Picasso, Andy Warhol wrote in his diary that she was "suffering through the marriage of her boyfriend Thadée Klossowski to Loulou."[14] After all, she learned about it when reading the wedding announcements in *Le Figaro*. Warhol added wittily, "I said Clara and I should announce our marriage in *Le Figaro* to outdo them."[15] He was the only member of the Saint Laurent clan who didn't attend the wedding. That night, Loulou, draped in midnight blue lamé, seemed to embody all forms of passion, whimsy, and fancifulness, like a fairy with blue and silver half-moons on her head. "I've always put stars on my head, it works quite well on skinny people." In the heart of the Bois de Boulogne, the chalet was heaped with white hydrangeas and palms in the midst of Moorish heads draped with white turbans (designed by Yves Saint Laurent). "And the moon, a round and friendly thing, shone over this Brazilian vision," Hebe Dorsey wrote in *Vogue*. Pierre Bergé looked very much like the father of the bride in his tuxedo with its starched shirtfront, watching over everything. The funniest thing was how the guests arrived on boats bedecked with flowers. Loulou wanted this celebration to be true to the English tradition: "The parents and the children mix together, with no disdain. That's what lets you take flight!" This party would go down in the history of Parisian nightlife. It was the first great "mixing" of baronesses and punks, old society and gatecrashers. The Stinky Toys gave a surprise performance, and then, as Loulou recalled in a coarse voice, "vomited in the bathroom all night." Marina Schiano, a thin odalisque in laced-up boots, recalled all the "beautiful people" who were there: Marie-Hélène de Rothschild, Bettina Rheims, Paloma Picasso, Eric de Rothschild barefoot in tie and tails, Bianca Jagger, Princess Minnie de Beauvau-Craon, Kenzo and his alter ego, Gilles Raysse, Fury and Aphrodisia, Isabel Goldsmith, Karl Lagerfeld, Alexandre Iolas, a New York art dealer who looked like a devil all in red with silver studs and shouted to anyone who gave him a surprised look, "Los Angeles!" Many long taffeta skirts and blouses that everyone wore according to her natural elegance, one looking like a gypsy and another like Countess Serpieri and another like herself, a natural actress. Sao Schlumberger seemed to shiver in a corner, "a little thing draped in a white shawl," said the gossips.

That night, Yves played the enfant terrible. "I'm sick of tuxedos," he told Hebe Dorsey, with the look of someone who was dying to get into trouble. He was wearing a loose black suit with his shoulders draped in a huge black chintz shawl: "Dior 1958," he explained. Around his waist, he had tied a beige wool fabric that he found in Marrakesh. It was held on by a string: "Dior 1960," he said mockingly. Another attendee told me that, sipping her scotch, Hebe Dorsey exclaimed with astonishment, "What a life for him, you know! He's had to deal with so much since the age of nineteen! People hassle him with pompous titles. Golden boy, heir of couture, and now great pontiff of fashion. As he once said to me sadly, 'I had no youth.'"

His most beautiful creation, "the end of a dream," he offered to Maria Callas, who died of a heart attack in her Paris apartment on September 16, 1977. It was an essay that appeared in *Le Monde* on September 18. He knew that the only reason to write is to write yourself. In this portrait, the words sparkle and play-act like thousands of Saint Laurent women at the theater. Diana Vreeland described his writing style like this: "When he writes, he really gallops through the words."[16]

And suddenly, surging from the deep, a burning, deep, high, strident, supernatural, baroque voice, a voice unlike any other, tried to fight death. A miraculous voice, the voice of genius, with its bizarreness, flaws, syncopations, and amazing flights that took our breath away, its trills, its coloratura, its bursts of heat, its stridencies, and its irritations that burst into lightning bolts, into cataclysms, into orgasms. Valiant siren parting the oceanic masses whose magnetism made her listeners break on the reefs of her modulations and resonances.

Diva among divas, empress, queen, goddess, sorceress, magician, poverty-stricken, divine. Sublime, ravishing, explosive, nightingale, turtledove. She traversed this century like a great solitary eagle whose outspread wings have forever hidden those who will survive her.

Rainbow of light, Niagara Falls, underwater breeze, abyss of a bottomless well with chasms of an infernal forge, cascades of crystal, gauzy scarf unrolled under the breath of dawn, entrails of the earth, viscera of the Minotaur, torrents of honey, swamps, quicksand where one sinks in, where one forgets oneself to the point of being lost. You weave a long arachnoid web of threads, of braids, of ribbons, of straps in which we are entangled. Ghost of Duse and of Malibran, draped in Rachel's dress, you trip over Sarah Bernhardt and you arrive swiftly despite your fears, pure as a garnet.

Nereid, Morgana, Armide, Melpomene, monstrous performer. Outside of us, you have extended the magic circle of your arms and the crowd grew quiet. You sang and we did not know that this apotheosis covered the cataclysm. Everything melted away, everything shifted, everything died of love. Everything was going to die. Unreal, misty, fairy thread, stay, you wanted to make us believe in your weakness. And you drifted so you could take flight, a rocket, a firework, a brazier of the lofty furnaces. Your heavy coats of tragedy were lighter than a dragonfly's wings. You floated, you caracoled, you galloped, you reached unexplored elevations, virgin summits that you gently surpassed, as if it were easy, to flee even higher, even farther and enter the eternal system of planets and stars.

You sing no more, but you will always be there. Your voice broke on the reefs. You have left, eternal eclipse. You preferred to leave. You sensed death.

Yves Saint Laurent's depression would become as famous as his brand, with misfortune stamping the only beauty that the bourgeoisie respected: ill-fated talent. How could he not identify with Callas? "I went to hear her every night. People were waiting for her. Some wanted her to sing marvelously, and others were waiting for a false note."

As of 1977, Yves was promoted to the ranks of the dead while still alive. He was the first couturier who had retrospective articles in magazines—as if they wanted to preserve an era whose memory was fading. That year, Pierre Bergé and Yves Saint Laurent gave a splendid marketing lesson to a society that they directed as masters of illusion, a world they scorned but nevertheless couldn't do without. Like the Gena Rowlands character in *Opening Night*, which Cassavetes released that year, they knew all too well that theater, like sex, was about getting people excited. However, this theater required more sacrifices and struggles every day. They had to give things up and be ever more watchful, even if their commitment to couture required their mutual destruction. "It's an encounter between a killer and a suicidal person. But the killer defends the suicidal person," said an observer. Together, they built their empire.

The company on Avenue Marceau would be the scene of a double passion, where Yves Saint Laurent and Pierre Bergé would make gold from a destructive paradise. That gold was Opium, "the perfume of the wedding of the real and the unreal," and it would become one of the most fabulous commercial successes in all of perfume history. Until 1988, Opium represented over half the revenue of Yves Saint Laurent perfumes. In 1991, Opium was still the leading French fragrance for women (and sixth among all fragrances).

In July 1977 Yves Saint Laurent announced the launch of this perfume. He had created a very special atmosphere with the Chinese-inspired collection shown on July 27, 1977. That day, 800 guests watched this sparkling show at the Hotel Inter-

Continental, including Catherine Deneuve in a beige safari jacket, Paloma Picasso in chili-pepper red, Zizi Jeanmaire in a wrap printed with feathers, and François-Marie Banier "dressed like a gas station attendant," according to *Le Figaro*. There were 132 designs, the couturier's longest show since 1963. Paloma Picasso recalled, "At parties, women fell upon him like birds. They wanted to touch him and get his aura."

As with the Ballets Russes collection, Yves Saint Laurent brought a breath of enchantment to couture. That season, Guy Laroche chose dominoes and velvet breeches that recalled Casanova's Venice or the Spain of Velázquez. Lanvin ventured to Marrakesh and Saint Petersburg. All over, opulence radiated from the runway to the strains of Carl Orff, Stevie Wonder, Donna Summer, and Wagner.

In 1977, enchanted by new heroines, the couturier performed a great solo once again. Less than a year after Mao's death, he celebrated the splendor of imperial China. During his very public depression, it seemed that he was leaving fashion behind to write. But he wrote only his Opium collection: "The shadow of the Great Wall against which I shatter myself is more terrible than Genghis Khan's bronze shield. From the stupor of my shredded brain there surge forth all the dynasties, their fury, arrogance, and grandeur. I am finally able to penetrate the secret of the Imperial City from which I liberate you, my aesthetic ghosts, my queens, my divas, my whirlwind celebrations, my nights of ink and crepe de Chine, my Coromandel lakes, my artificial lakes, and my hanging gardens.... From the gates of the Celestial Peace hurtles down a mad flood of silk whose sensuous fluidity washes over the temples and tea houses.... From the terraces and pagodas of the Red Pavilion, I see my dreams dancing on the silver waters of the river of Love."

"Saint Laurent's Verdict: China Is In, Russia Out" was the headline of Eugenia Sheppard's article in the *Herald Tribune*. The girls were made up like Ona Munson playing the owner of a luxurious gambling den in Josef von Sternberg's *The Shanghai Gesture*. Once again, Yves Saint Laurent subverted traditional clothing to make court clothing, coats of black velvet embroidered with gold, jeans of red taffeta, shades of China blue soaked in a golden bath. Through hidden doors, he entered palaces, kidnapped women prisoners, wrapped them in organza dresses with gold spangles and mousseline kimonos that were lighter than scarves and draped his Madame Butterflys. The wedding dress was a butterfly of blistered silk, like those that he drew in black ink for Naughty Lulu.

Who would have suspected it? *Time* called him the "Sun King of fashion." This time, the items cost between 3,000 and 10,000 dollars. Some fabrics woven with gold thread cost as much as 1,000 francs per meter (the equivalent of about 815 dollars in 2018). It was an even more sumptuous collection than usual, where each piece seemed to have escaped from a private museum. Yves Saint Laurent used the colors of his *objets d'art*, the red and black of his lacquer boxes; his Chinese bronzes were reflected in the dresses of jade green satin, which moved like rivers. He borrowed porcelain patterns for damask jackets with gold thread and pagoda sleeves. There were also all the accessories: the fringed boots, the French cuff gloves in gold kid, the lamé hats and turbans trimmed with mink, fox pillbox hats, pagodas of shocking pink satin, tufts of feathers, golden Tonkinese cats. Yves Saint Laurent expanded the palette of blacks, making them more and more sensual, featuring soft black, shiny satiny black, and black as luscious as velvet.

It was as if he had already sprayed a few drops of perfume on the inside of the wrists from which burst taffeta beehives, or on a back whose fabric, tracing its curve, betrayed the warmth of the skin. "Opium. A gong resounds: in a jumble of splendor, the Idol abandoned herself to the audacity of my tribute....I chose Opium as the name of my perfume because I intensely hoped that it might, through all its incandescent powers, liberate the divine fluids, the magnetic waves, the curls and charms of seduction that give rise to mad love, love at first sight, fateful ecstasy, when a man and a woman look at each other for the first time," wrote Yves Saint Laurent, as if intoxicated. "Opium is the femme fatale, pagodas, lanterns! I am not able to disillusion you," he wrote in the introductory booklet.

On October 12, 1977, there was a party at the maison on Avenue Marceau for the Paris launch of the perfume. The red lacquer bottle, designed by Yves based on a samurai box, with a stopper seen as "a chiseled gold and silver billiard ball of the Klan Mughal,"[17] would become the scandalous object of the decade. The perfume was just as famous as its tagline: "For those who are addicted to Yves Saint Laurent." The ad campaign was orchestrated by Agence Mafia, headed by Maïmé Arnodin and Denise Fayolle, "his opium-addicted accomplices" who were affectionately nicknamed "the bad ladies." Jerry Hall, in a black embroidered Chinese vest and purple satin pants, was chosen as the face of the perfume and posed for Helmut Newton. Maïmé Arnodin recalled, "The photo was taken at Yves's apartment on Rue de Babylone. He did all the styling, even the rings, which he designed. When you are dealing with a designer like Yves Saint Laurent, the ad agency has to be modest and respect a personality like his—plus he is an exquisite being, full of humor underneath his shy exterior. The important thing is to have lifted Saint Laurent from seventeenth place in the fragrance market to first or second place."[18]

In Europe, sales reached thirty million dollars in one year. Opium was launched in the United States on September 25, 1978. On Wednesday, September 19, the couturier gave a memorable launch party in New York on board the tall ship *Peking*, which was docked at the South Street Seaport Museum. There were a thousand guests. Thirty-two television channels covered their arrival in a procession of gold and velvet. Squibb, the parent company of Lanvin-Charles of the Ritz, which distributed Saint Laurent's perfumes, spent 300,000 dollars on the party, according to *Women's Wear Daily*. But would YSL be there in person? Marina Schiano was pulling her hair out. The papers said he wouldn't come. For weeks, Schiano had been preparing this "waterside extravaganza." Until the last moment, Yves kept everyone in suspense, and then he appeared looking his best in a black tuxedo, commenting in his sumptuously provocative way, "Opium is a dignified drug." He spoke little, but his English was much better than Pierre Bergé's.

The boat was entirely decorated with bamboo, Chinese temples, and a giant Buddha. In this floating garden with a thousand orchids from Hawaii and a thousand lilies from Holland, chic young people, old society people, and other business and fashion royalty mingled in a vast crush on top of rose petals. "It's fabulous! It's fantastic! It's crazy! It's New York!" they shouted, while the sky above Manhattan, like a velvet dome, was lit up with "Yves" in sparkling letters in an amazing twenty-minute fireworks display. Among the guests were Cher, Halston, Diana Vreeland, Bill Blass, Oscar and Françoise de la Renta, Geraldine Stutz, Marion Javits, Calvin Klein, James Galanos, Doris Duke, Egon von Fürstenberg, and Truman Capote, who called it a "terrific" evening. Andy Warhol was in California and wrote in his diary about his regrets at missing the "big glamorous YSL opium party."[19] Yves was surrounded by his "opiettes": Loulou de la Falaise in a silk dress with large leaves and Marina Schiano in black. "He designed a spy's outfit for me!"

Yves stayed on board for three hours. The party continued at Studio 54. The writer John Richardson, then an expert at Christie's, described what Studio 54 was like: "Everyone was taking Quaaludes with their bourbon. What was exciting back then was the noise and the beauty of the people. People arrived alone or in groups. People from New Jersey were lining up outside. We got in easily, we had our own door." Yves saw New York and loved it, the same way he loved Paris when he got there from Oran. He felt a feeling of freedom. Wasn't this city, "where people get up in the middle of dinner and disappear," the true capital of the world? As John Richardson said, "When you're a foreigner in New York, you feel like a kid in a toy store. But people in this city are so puritanical that even when they lead sleazy lives, they all go to the same place, they all take the same drugs, and they all eat the same yogurt!" That year, the women would all douse themselves with the same perfume.

In the United States, the Opium ad campaign was voted best of the year by the Fragrance Foundation. In Opium's first four months on the market, sales in the United States totaled three million dollars. But the tagline was changed. "Opium, for those who are addicted to Yves Saint Laurent" became "Opium, for those who adore Yves Saint Laurent." Richard Furlaud, CEO of Squibb, was on the alert. The recently formed American Coalition Against Opium and Drug Abuse launched a campaign against the perfume. Furlaud defended Saint Laurent, saying he considered him a "genius" and evoking the name's connection to "the mystery of the Orient," Coleridge, and Cocteau. James Tso, chair of the Committee for Equal Opportunity of the Organization of Chinese-Americans, started putting pressure on Squibb to change the name of its perfume. Shelby Howatt, a member of the group, suggested replacing it with "Lotus Blossom" or "Mysteries of the East." He found allies in the Baptist churches and said he would swell his numbers with five other religious organizations.

The war began with petitions and buttons that read, "Kill Opium, Boycott Squibb." Some stores put up signs reading, "We sell Opium here." On May 4, 1979, protesters gathered in front of Squibb's headquarters. James Tso said he was disturbed to see an advertising campaign based on "a menace that destroyed many lives in China and other countries." Some newspaper headlines made fun of the outrage, joking about it being just a perfume. Despite or because of the scandal, the perfume was a commercial and media success. Not since Chanel No. 5 had a fragrance caused such a stir. The perfume of an unfaithful woman, with an animal eroticism, Opium was the pioneer of all the sensual perfumes that would follow—with Eastern notes of spice and ambergris—such as Calvin Klein's Obsession, Dior's Poison, and Guerlain's Samsara. It announced the coming decade of dangerous liaisons and fatal attractions.

Yves Saint Laurent had seen the women of Oran and the women of Dior. He knew their whims and their favorite movies. He had been to the movie theaters where they dressed up like princesses to see *Not Any Weekend for Our Love* or *Cass Timberlane* with Lana Turner and Spencer Tracy. The first idols he drew were nude, decorated with the "mortal drugs" that Agnès was forbidden to wear in Molière's *The School for Wives*:

> *These liquids, this fair make-up, these creams,*
> *And a thousand ingredients that make the complexion bloom.*

Who other than this lover of lipstick and black stockings could have launched gold lipstick tubes that let women do their lips without needing a mirror? Who else would have offered a range of beauty products in a line of colors—Indian pink, emerald green, intense blue, violet-red—that matched his fabrics? On March 30, 1978, the Saint Laurent beauty line was launched at Maxim's with thirty-eight products in eighty shades. Thick glass bottles, brushes made of pony hair, the perfect click of the compact, the choice of gold for the entire line, a double red and black square with the letters YSL. Every woman felt as if she got to take with her a little bit of this precious metal: in the last ten years, gold had become a safe investment. His product line was not described as shadows, mascara, lip gloss, or blush, but "make-up" for eyelids, eyelashes, lips, and cheeks. Starting in 1977, Saint Laurent make-up, symbolized by three universes—Carmen, La Mer, and L'Orientale—completed the couturier's vision. "The woman I design for was missing a face."[20] Once again, he was the first. Make-up in the 1970s had been dominated by transparent beiges and pinks, but he gave it back its Baudelairian qualities. Yet he wasn't fooled by these illusions. As a supplier of artificial beauty, he said, "The most beautiful make-up for a woman is passion."[21]

Yves Saint Laurent was caught in a vicious cycle. The more he proved he was alive by giving himself over to his profession, the more the doubts, suspicions, and rumors grew. The more he showed himself, the less he was forgiven for his absences. He thought he was protecting himself from Paris in Marrakesh, but Marrakesh became inseparable from Paris. He wanted to pull away from fashion, and fashion caught up with him. Painting? "I treat my fabrics like gouaches," he said. The hospital? There he sketched and called up his dealers. Some people even said that he enjoyed himself there. His room? It was photographed for the first time for the *New York Times Magazine* in 1977. His friends? He gave them sketches of his collections. And often he drew his women with a fiercer stroke, like a black knife mark on the page, on his personalized stationery. Everything was reversed: it was strangers who seemed to be concerned and very informed about his health.

Starting in 1977, an American journalist found Yves Saint Laurent in low spirits. People came to see him come out with his models at the end of the show: "Yves Saint Laurent is alive and well." Pierre Bergé gave health updates, including this one to Hélène de Turckheim in March 1977: "It's true that Saint Laurent has been suffering from nervous depression for two years, and he will need a year of treatment to come out of it completely. But I declare on my honor that he does not have cancer or any serious illness or anything that we need to hide. Plus, his stays at the American Hospital for treatment did not prevent him from creating even more brilliant collections that many healthy people are envious of." Bergé was guarding the temple. "In a way, Yves was born with nervous depression, but he didn't know it was called that. Yves is an artist with all his anxieties as he constantly seeks to perfect his perfection."

The book Yves was going to publish with Grasset in spring 1977 never came about. Yet he said that his model for writing was Marguerite Duras. "She is poetry itself. She uses two words and an image appears," he said about the author who described loneliness, inability to communicate, and absolute love in her novels. Her heroines lived "without knowing why" but waited "for something to come out of the world and come [to them]," according to her *Le Square*. But Yves Saint Laurent decided not to publish his writing. "It was like a cry, like *Les Chants de Maldoror*," he later said. "I wrote plays, essays, and then my opinion on women. I hid them so I wouldn't think about it anymore. Because it was horribly sad." Betty gave more details: "He wrote loads of things. Always stories of a man and a woman meeting, like in old movies. Some of his writing is lying around in old boxes. Some must have been lost, or burned. He's too lazy to go through it all. It must be a terrible mess." Yves Saint Laurent was once again like Gena Rowlands playing an aging actress in *Opening Night*: "As soon as I go to the bathroom, everyone thinks I've lost it." Watched. Spied on. A victim of the system that he established, one that also protected him and shielded him from the need for direct confrontation with reality.

In this respect, Paloma Picasso sees a vast difference between Yves's attitude toward glory and her father's. "I remember going out and having forty people around us after half an hour. But my father always ended up talking to the people who were watching him. He had a very open attitude. This access to people is very Andalusian.

Yves never wanted to go out without his buffer zone of friends. That's his nature: he always wanted to be protected. He's the one who wanted it, but then it became a disability. If I'm Yves's date, I know that I'm his guardian for two hours. True discoveries are made alone, when you expose yourself to everyday life. Pierre isn't responsible. He responded to Yves's request, the call of the void."

Energy shortages, terrorism, blunders of unfettered industry. There was no roadmap—it had been shredded into confetti. History morphed, once more, into the urgency of a decade that lived only for the moment. Countless trends were now in fashion: the first tanning pills, roller skates, disaster movies, and thrilling blockbusters (*Jaws*, *Star Wars*, *Close Encounters of the Third Kind*), jogging, and so on. The disco era had arrived, with feverish bodies struggling against all the demons of a world where children died asphyxiated by dioxin and where adults lacking an ideal invented new gods to survive—Filipino healers, cults, and fundamentalism. This world, like a living skin tattooed with the Sex Pistols credo "No Future," was like violent, visionary punk rock that flayed the beautiful face of European prosperity every day. There were 1.7 million unemployed people in France.

Haute couture glowed in its palace of marvels. Gold flowed over the fashion world: everything shone, everything sparkled like Ungaro's sequined hearts and Saint Laurent's lamé coats.

Women rediscovered fishnet stockings and stiletto heels. But no trend really stood out. There was no direction anymore. As if, in this kaleidoscope of events— the children of Mao discovering Coca-Cola and the children of affluence dying of overdoses—appearances also had to be shattered. The "freedom of styles" that *Elle* announced in May 1977 marked the dispersal of women's society into a thousand temporary personalities: "The After-Thermidorians meet the post-junkies, while the Novo-Modern mix in with the New Ecclesiastics and the After-Chics," wrote nightlife journalist Alain Pacadis in *Libération*.[22]

Yves was lost in the midst of this world that he had created but no longer recognized. Wasn't he the first one to have combined night and day, the outskirts of town and the salons, wood paneling and bazaars, the flea market and the finest neighborhoods? For his forty-first birthday, Pierre Bergé gave him a vermilion lion with ruby eyes. He wore a ring with the insignia of his astrological sign, Leo. "He had anger under his skin," said Loulou.

His predatory energy suffered from an abrupt stop of activity. It was as if, around 1978, he gave up the hunt in order to stop and contemplate how his accomplishments had been disastrously deformed by his imitators, how everything that he had given was now turned against him. Outrageous versions of cheap peasant style with colors that were too bright were now associated with the Saint Laurent style. "Starting at this time, he made things that were less daring, less sincere," said Anna Pavlowski.

He was just as lost inside his own empire, which grew on a daily basis (300 million dollars in products sold under his brand in 1978). He had planned for everything. Except one thing. That business didn't exist so that things could live, but so that they could sell. Now his brand was submitted to the women of the Gulf states. The day dress that sold for 2,900 francs in 1962 sold for four times that much in 1977. The quote for a dress special-ordered by a Middle Eastern princess could reach 55,000 francs. While mentioning the names of some new clients (the wife of the Sultan of Oman, women from Bahrain and Kuwait, Queen Noor of Jordan, the daughters of King Faisal of Saudi Arabia), Hélène de Ludinghausen expressed the maison's distance: "We didn't take the whole Arab market. We tried to limit the weddings. It wasn't like other lines that did nothing else."

But the transition was clear. The Saint Laurent style, which had once been associated with the liberation of the 1960s—women in pants—had taken on other connotations. Some women saw the jewel-like Opium bottle with a golden silk tassel tied around it as a break-up gift from the brand. "He could design for the whole world," said one of these women, a marketing director in Paris. "And all of a sudden, he puts women into slavery, with a rope around their necks. [Some women] were fooled. But women who…had a personality, who thought about who they were, who had found their style, didn't accept being led off to the harem like this.…He betrayed us over money. He betrayed himself." A very harsh judgment, but one that was shared by many professional women. They would still show up at Rive Gauche parties in their tuxedo suits, but they chose to buy their clothes elsewhere, finding that soft beiges made in Italy (Armani) or the Japanese unstructured look were invitations to peacefulness or action, while Yves Saint Laurent offered them a chance to shine, to create a certain appearance. Yet, among all those flashy designs, the shocking pink taffetas and the green mousselines embroidered with gold roses, there was a silent woman in a day ensemble that seemed much more elegant than all the dresses. "White flannel dolman. Pants of beige cotton gabardine, blouse of ivory crepe de Chine," read the description. Like a breath of freedom in the midst of the all the cloistered figures. But people came to Saint Laurent for the reds and the violets, and the audience would erupt in applause. They had to, just as there had to be sequins, lamé, and velvet for all these Middle Eastern princesses whose oil dollars flowed onto the luxury market.

It was Loulou who, starting at this time, gave new life to the Saint Laurent image, breaking the golden lid that sometimes smothered him. For who else would get married in wild pants with children's gloves and golden sandals? Who else could play with accessories like butterflies or turbans, and make her everyday appearance a continual surprise? Yves said, "Loulou de la Falaise's true talent, besides her professional qualities, is unquestionable. It's charm. Her special, moving charm. The strange power of a gift for lightness combined with the flawlessly sharp way she looks at the world. Intuitive and innate, Loulou's presence by my side is a dream."

Whatever he did, he spun like a ball of fire in his era, like Roland Barthes at Le Palace: "At each spot where I stand, I have the enjoyable feeling of being in a kind of imperial box where I command the games." The opening of this temple of the night coincided with the rising wave of disco. Fabrice Emaer, the owner of Le Palace, sent out an invitation for the opening night that read, "Tuxedo, evening gown, or as you like." In its first eighteen months, the venue made twenty-five million francs, beating all industry records. The Le Palace era had begun, with more than seventy concerts a year. Bette Midler, Madonna, the B-52's, Tom Waits, Klaus Nomi, the Talking Heads, Prince's first concert, Grace Jones, and more. A witness told me Emaer described Le Palace as "useless, free, purposely excessive, everyone defines their own place." One world was ending and another beginning. "Le Sept used to be a real club, a party at home," a regular recalled. At Le Palace, Yves entered an unbridled night of stars of a thousand colors, where couturiers found inspiration, society women sought their youth, the anonymous acquired some celebrity, calling themselves Paquita Paquin, Maud Molyneux, or Zaza Dior, and everyone entertained the illusion of being there together, like thousands of solitary people who sought and met each other in a melting pot of images.

Although Yves Saint Laurent was the first one to speak of decadence, he created the images of this great ball of confusion, where Warhol rubbed elbows with Jacqueline de Ribes, Régine dressed as Carmen Miranda, Marie Hélène de Rothschild as the fairy queen, and Olympia de Rothschild as Ophelia lost at the court of the Borgias.

On March 23, 1978, Loulou and Thadée gave a party at Le Palace with the theme Angels and Demons, Legends and Marvels. "I wanted a costume ball," Loulou remembered, "so that everyone had to make an effort. So they didn't all come dressed as punks and in black leather, or just in evening gowns and tuxedos. It was risky. But I could tell right away that it would be a hit. It was the only thing people talked about in between the collection shows (and often during them). People gave dinners to discuss their costumes. The night before, our friends raided the couture house. There wasn't a single jewel, feather, or piece of lamé left in the drawers." The splendid, excessive, phantasmagorical party brought together all of Paris, from fashion gurus to priests of the underground: "I want open parties like the ones I experienced in England," Loulou insisted. "Not rigid parties, I like mixing together different people. Old and young, rich and poor, bankers and students, intellectuals and athletes. It doesn't matter, as long as they're scintillating." Thadée, garbed in white, was an angel. Held up by golden lace, he wore feathered wings made by Maison Lemarié. Loulou, always dressed by Madame Felisa, was a demon in red and gold mousseline. "A hippie-fied outfit that was made at the last minute," she says. "I've always loved dressing up. As a fairy, a butterfly, or a tree. Once I was an acacia tree. It's very spiky. It was very extravagant, very pretty. I even gave some pruning shears to my tablemate at dinner." That night, Loulou sparkled in stars and moons. "I like having an outfit that I can dance on the tables in. A costume gives you extra freedom. If you dress as a demon, you're guaranteed to have a good night."

A Brazilian orchestra was on stage. There were flowers everywhere. Suddenly, the lights changed, and strobe lights plunged the crowd into darkness. Barbarella was flirting with Mephisto, and a fairy with a male voice was undressing a witch in a tuxedo with his eyes. Society women were costumed as cabaret stars. Men were seen dressed up as trees, birds of paradise, or Puss-in-Boots. Marc Bohan was Faust, Karl Lagerfeld was Merlin the Magician, strapped into a beaded jumpsuit that had belonged to Josephine Baker, and Edwige was Diana the Huntress. Jean-Charles de Castelbajac was Dracula, and Gonzague Saint-Bris was Rasputin, with Tarzan's Jane on his arm. François-Marie Banier was a white clown, and seemed to have borrowed his costume from one of the characters in his novels, where heroes played at loving and lying while dreaming of dying of love. Pierre Bergé was recognizable under a false leather nose from the Commedia Dell'Arte. Yves Saint Laurent had chosen an improvised kabuki mask, which he took off right away. He may have been the only one who was more elusive as himself than in costume.

There, Yves was armed with the ambiguous charm of a generation of nostalgic storytellers, hairdressers turned into duchesses, court jesters, evil fairies, catamites of a decadent magic city and other Trimalchios in garters, characters cobbled together from a night of cocaine, champagne, and disco. At this party, Pierre Bergé told Andy Warhol that he had started wearing a cock ring. Yves replied that he hoped everyone would start doing so, because that way "he could design new pants."[23] Would the era have the couturiers it deserved? Previously, Madeleine Vionnet had sent her design assistants to the Louvre to learn about the draped fabrics of antiquity. Yves Saint Laurent asked the fabric manufacturer Abraham to print gold moons and stars on his crepe evening coats and had Madame Brossin of Méré, who had supplied the maison de couture since its beginnings, to go see the disco lights at Le Palace to create similar light projections on velvet.

The lines of his sketches had become harder and more angular. The faces were rough-hewn, with accentuated cheekbones and pointy chins, and the shoulders were wider. Now gay men wanted muscles instead of dresses. Live from New York, the reign of gay power had started, with its networks, its sex bars, and its anonymous chained-up men posing for Robert Mapplethorpe.

According to Mapplethorpe, S&M stood for sex and magic. Everything would burn up in a great witches' Sabbath of sex, getting stoned, and every kind of experimentation. Showcasing a body girded for war, a generation exhibited its pleasures and its abuses: chains, whips, cigarette burns, and fascination with physical abnormalities. The pressured imagination became impoverished, overwhelmed by a more and more insistent reality that destroyed everything along its path. Styles were created by pushing back against each other, born of an individualism with no school or master. Writing in *Elle*, Robert Hossein described the fashion of the time like this: "Bubbles burst, something spurts forth. Sometimes it's terribly interesting, and sometimes it's terribly mediocre. The sporadic rules as master. It's the time of every man for himself. The defense doing things on an ad hoc basis. We're dwarves, sorcerer's apprentices, with confusion we feel something weighing on us. We're suffering from the lack of the whole, of connections, of coherence. The immediate triumphs. We're living day by day. It feels like we're in transit. The trends don't have time to be developed, to become a style, a school, a movement that makes society move forward."[24] It was a radical break, and one that Saint Laurent first glimpsed in 1976: "Society is divided into several fragments of society—and each has its style." He recognized this as a defeat: "I always thought that I'd find my way through designing. But I got lost."

There was no more future to be hoped for, or past to be buried. Just the immediate present. The shock of the images. Disco: "Boom boom on five floors," said Paquita Paquin, who worked as a bouncer at La Main Bleue at the time. The struggle was the other, who had to be aggressively seduced. "Getting noticed," said Loulou. Helmut Newton's photo of a naked woman in a Saint Laurent corset photographing her genitals with a long lens that is about to penetrate her is the best illustration of this mirrorless narcissism. The transvestites at Le Grand Eugène, with their legs finely sheathed in black stockings, smoking cigarettes like Marlene, were now shoved aside and knocked to the floor by others, who were built like longshoremen. "This was the time when men with moustaches started taking hormones," recalled Paquita.

The walls of shame fell down, the social barricades were broken—and replaced by others that were just as insurmountable, since they deprived one of even dreaming. The mystery disappeared. At a Thierry Mugler show, a pregnant model appeared on the runway dressed as the Virgin Mary. The transvestites in mousseline scarves vanished. Tested by bodybuilding, the body became a machine and sex was the product, with specialized rooms for practicing. It was exactly at this time that Yves Saint Laurent abandoned his beauty and chose to age prematurely.

In October 1976, Yves Saint Laurent appeared for the last time in a black Moroccan shirt and white pants with messy hair. By January 1978, the archangel had returned to the dark suits of his youth. He talked about "young women of the street" with a diplomatic elegance. Some people thought Yves's dresses weren't made for taking the subway. Yves replied with a certain cynicism, "My clients travel with forty trunks!" But he wasn't fooled by the image that they projected onto him. He emphasized it to challenge them. "Oh! Mercedes is very modern today," said the couturier, who could no longer recognize his model in a designer skirt suit with her hair in a topknot. At the Palace, Kirat was photographed with Claude Montana, who was wearing jeans and a leather jacket.

On the runway, the colors dazzled. Mercedes appeared in a leather overcoat with a red feathered hat and electric blue gloves. It was the era of slit skirts and pumps for afternoon tea. The models swayed their hips to Ravel's *Bolero*, and strutted to the strains of "L'Enterrement du Roi Arthur" sung by Klaus Nomi. In *Vogue Homme*, Jean Cau criticized the "frozen" exhibitionism of Le Palace, which opened one year after Studio 54 in New York, writing, "Petronius is the couturier and Messalina borrows dresses from him, Casanova is getting unemployment and working as a extra in between sessions with a tanning lamp. The Blue Angel is voiceless and her empty eyes watch the passing trains of a nostalgia without memory, without objects."[25]

"I knew the world of yesterday, I transformed it. I sensed the era that was arriving," said Yves Saint Laurent, who now spoke of himself in the past tense, as if better to promote his new role: the outsider. How could he be anything else? Even though he was still king, he knew that that world was definitively over. His strength was continuing to dream about women. Some of them wore a little of him and his past life in their dresses. "Being a couturier means observing, imagining women in all kinds of situations. I enjoy seeing my clothing move on a woman who doesn't need to be beautiful, because she is very elegant."

At the jet-set parties where all the other women were loaded with sparkling jewelry, Saint Laurent women moved about lightly and timelessly. They were noticeable at the ball given by Count Giovanni Volpi in Venice for his niece's eighteenth birthday. The terraces were carpeted with ivy and the rooms were hung with damask. Among the silver candelabra and the bouquets of roses, Betty Catroux was imperceptibly nude under a white crepe tea gown, as was Hélène Rochas in a mousseline sheath dress with a ruff of rooster feathers. Those dresses were friends; they hadn't betrayed him. "Thanks to Isabel Eberstadt for having been so beautiful in a dress that I made fifteen years ago," he said after the Opium party in New York.

He was ten years older than all these people of the night, who scribbled in their Le Palace datebooks with big purple felt-tip pens, "Go see drag show then Warhol film. Farida's party. Sleep 3-6 PM. PM—black with blond wig." In New York, groggy heads woke up with glasses of Perrier. Gossip became news, and private life became spectacle. Truman Capote told *Interview* about his implants and Andy Warhol discussed the beautiful kids he had spotted the night before. In her Saint Laurent suit, Bianca Jagger joined them at Quo Vadis after being interviewed by *Look* magazine.

Yes, his great strength was to blend in, without losing himself, with all these animals who read nothing and were surprised at nothing other than themselves. These people didn't get dressed but put on "threads" and thought everything was "swanky." For them, the name Victor Hugo referred to someone who worked with the New York designer Halston, and Casablanca was Donna Summer's record company (she sold three million records in 1977). But this strength also made him suffer and condemned him to be alone. As one of the initiators of the disorder of a society in which culture became a show, nightlife a business, marginality a market, he was also one of the first to grasp what was happening. Fashion was the mirror reflecting a society that no longer wanted to build anything except its own destruction. "I belong to a generation and a world dedicated to elegance. I grew up in an environment that was very attached to tradition. At the same time, however, I wanted to change all that, because I was torn between the attraction of the past and the future that pushed me forward. I feel divided between the two and I think I always will be. For I know one world and I feel the presence of the other."

Like everyone from nowhere, he could only return to one country: couture, where the roots were the rules that had been transmitted, from generation to generation, by other performers who had no land to cultivate other than memory. "My next haute couture collection will be an expression of my respect for the profession and my respect for the body of a woman with her seduction. My first collection was exactly twenty years ago," he said in January 1978. "I think that these long years have given me the right to pay tribute to the two most marvelous demands of my profession: craftsmanship and beauty. Whatever people say, couture is far from dying. The sincerity of its traditions is a force that is hard to bring down. Drawing on my own roots, in my own collections, what makes my style and what I come back to endlessly, delving into them and reworking them. The blazer, the safari jacket. The pantsuit, the crisp skirt suit with square shoulders, basically this classicism that is timeless and of our time."[26] And, like Scarlett O'Hara, he contemplated the landscape of his childhood with its torn-up trees and its houses in ruins, with the only certainty being the need to return. She plunged her hands into the red earth of Tara, where she drew her strength.

"Day ensemble, navy blue wool peacoat." "Day dress in havana gabardine." "Navy blue mousseline evening gown." He was alone with himself, with all the women he had loved, the hard-featured and the seductive, the androgynous and the fiery. "I want to be the reflection of our time. To give women back their appearance. The time when they had to change their wardrobe every six months has passed. Today, women are never out of style, and when I see them mixing my old clothes with those that I have just designed, I think it's great. Women are more and more liberated." It was as if he wanted to achieve Schiaparelli's great dream through his clothing: "Once I wished to be a man. The possibility of going anywhere at anytime has always excited me."[27]

The Saint Laurent suit finally reappeared. It was shown to the sounds of *Porgy and Bess*. *Women's Wear Daily* nicknamed it "Broadway." It was a straight jacket with patch pockets, ankle-length pants, and a blouse in crepe de Chine from Abraham. The Americans called it "straight line."

But this was also the time when everything became stuck, when the Saint Laurent line became something more clearly and permanently defined, whereas it had previously left invisible traces of a more aristocratic ease. It had been a way of life, a way of moving. Now he had to go over everything with a black felt-tip pen in order finally to be heard and understood. What he had done ten years earlier flowed naturally from his observation of women and their free, chameleon-like nature; in 1978, his clothing was the result of solitary re-creation. *Vogue* recognized its power: "Yves Saint Laurent showed a memorable collection. All by himself, he is able to reverse the trends and make the pantsuit appropriate for all hours of the day and the spencer jacket for all hours of the night."[28]

He came out of the shadows. But was it really Yves? His body seemed to dissolve in the dark. He tied a big red scarf around his neck. Where was the prince charming of yesterday? "I wanted to give it all up, but haute couture is a mistress I cannot do without. And also I feel responsible for the people who have made my success and that of the maison. Since I can hold up this abyss thanks to ready-to-wear, I must go on."

His face had changed. It looked like a mask pierced by two dark eyes with miniscule pupils. As in the early days on Rue Spontini, he had once again become the man who closed himself off in his studio, sometimes falling asleep there, and was awakened in the early morning by a cleaning lady. At that time he wanted to know everything about Chanel's technique. A different obsession tortured him in 1978: regaining this clarity from before the madness, this line from before the colors. It was an impossible dream that led him to caricature himself. His bold ideas tried too hard and lost their self-evident power. They were no longer surprising, astonishing, instinctive. René panned these tendencies in *Le Journal du Dimanche*: "Usually Saint Laurent is magically reliable in his discretion or boldness at matching colors, but this time his retinas seem to have revolted. His vague shapes try in vain to bring together acid greens, electric blues, yellows, and pinks the color of red currant ice cream, which set your teeth on edge and stink to your eyes like chemical odors.... When I tell you that his great new idea was to put flounces from an old lady's curtains everywhere, you will wonder, as I did, what mountain fell onto his head. Let's hope that this will be just one unsuccessful collection, and not the beginning of the end." Everything was more emphatic, thinner, and more shoulder-heavy. Saint Laurent was parodying Saint Laurent, seeking his other self: Monsieur Dior.

The skirts got shorter, acquired slits, and the fabrics sparkled with sequins. The act was more forced. Was it really him? The models caressed the chandelier with gloves the color of the sun. Kirat, dressed in green python, knelt down in golden sandals. Mounia, with her chocolate hands over the black velvet, supplicated the audience with her arms in the shape of a cross. They needed Jungle-red lips and black eyes, as shiny as leather. Backstage, the actresses got ready. That season, he did not come out at the end of the show.

Six months later, he reacted with a collection that was "very elegant, provocative and at the same time crazily modern, which may seem contradictory. I sought clean lines, but I introduced unexpected accessories: pointed collars, little hats, tasseled shoes." With these "nods," Yves wanted to "bring a bit of humor to haute couture" and "give it the same provocative and arrogant look as punk fashion."

*

From now on, he would continue on his path with his "aesthetic ghosts." Pierre Bergé encouraged him. Bergé had become director of the Théâtre de l'Athénée, located near the Opéra in Palais Garnier. Under the rafters of this Second Empire Parisian theater, he built a little experimental theater that he named the Christian Bérard Theater. He called the Italian Theater the Louis Jouvet Theater. Thus began the ascension of Pierre Bergé, who, for the first time, truly stepped out of the shadows and revealed his dual commitment to the theater—as both a lover of the stage and a man of action. He began organizing the very Parisian Lundis Musicaux du Théâtre de l'Athénée. One could say he was once again modeling himself on his longstanding nemesis, Pierre Cardin, whose Espace Pierre Cardin was a success in Paris.

Yves created the sets and costumes for Cocteau's *The Eagle with Two Heads* in the very place where, in 1936, the year he was born, Louis Jouvet directed *The School for Wives*, for which Bérard did the sets. Hadn't Yves secretly dreamed of becoming another Christian Bérard? Ten years later, Bérard would design the costumes for *The Eagle with Two Heads*, performed in Paris by Théâtre Hébertot, featuring Edwige Feuillère, Silvia Monfort, and Jean Marais.

Thirty-two years after that staging of the play, Yves seemed determined to revive Cocteau's ambitions: "I'm unapologetically bringing the audience back to the theater of actions. Actions that prevent boredom, which most audiences think means serious theater. They'd been sent to school, and it was time to take them out."[29]

This play, which was written as a tribute to Ludwig II of Bavaria, saw a widowed, virgin, dead queen, "who uses a fan to hide her face," confronting her assassin, Stanislas, who came to kill her and whom she awaited as her savior. "All of Cocteau is evoked in this set," Yves Saint Laurent told French television station TF1. His looks had changed once again: he was swollen from the effects of a recent stint in rehab. The segment revealed that he worked for six months making hundreds of sketches, including several different versions of the queen, such as a Wagnerian queen with golden wings and a pre-Raphaelite queen. In a very nasal voice, he talked about Geneviève Page's dresses: "A dress in a collection is made to be lived in. It moves. A dress in a staged space is fixed." Overall, critics were not fond of these sets and costumes. They thought they were too related to fashion. It was impossible not to realize that they were very linked to a Parisian fashion phenomenon. As the painter Garouste, who decorated Le Privilège, the restaurant at Le Palace, with frescoes and plaster casts, said, "Cocteau is very Le Palace."

The critics were pitiless: "Nightclub-style sets of staggering ugliness by Yves Saint Laurent," Michel Cournot wrote in *Le Monde*. The journalist nonchalantly squirted his last drops of vitriol: "The play was directed by Jean-Pierre Dusséaux. It's impossible to tell. The chief of police wears an elegant overcoat." Writing in *L'Express*, Robert Kanters was hardly more charitable: "Yves Saint Laurent's curtain is Wagnerian and kitsch, but the set in general is sparse, and as big as the gates of heaven." François Chalais of *France-Soir* was also unimpressed: "Is it because of Yves Saint Laurent's set, a muddle of styles, all at once Egyptian pyramid, Greek temple, Japanese shrine, and the Marly horses? Or the baffling appearance of a romantic drama that wants to be a tragedy? The same sparks are there, but not the same fire."

That year, more designers rose in the ranks, as everyone celebrated Thierry Mugler joining the Chambre Syndicale du Prêt-à-Porter, des Couturiers et des Créateurs de Mode established by Pierre Bergé. Two worlds and two eras clashed. Thierry Mugler was a former dancer in the Strasbourg ballet. He was born in 1948, like Loulou. He liked uniforms, Osaka, and comic books. Literary references bored him. What influenced him? Concepts such as air and ice. "Fashion for the Future" was the headline about him in a 1978 issue of Andy Warhol's monthly magazine, *Interview*. "No more Stendhal, no more Belle de Cadix or stuff like that," Mugler said, in implicit reference to Saint Laurent. "There's no more energy, and for now, I don't want that."

Jean-Paul Gaultier showed his first collection with his Japanese partner Kashiyama. Anna Pavlowski was the face of the collection. "I saw a bit of Yves Saint Laurent in him. Except that Jean-Paul loved to laugh and go out. Yves Saint Laurent cries through his dresses."

On December 18, 1978, there was a celebration for Le Sept's ten-year anniversary. Claude Aurensan, Fabrice Emaer's lieutenant, was there, along with Jacques Grange. Yves Saint Laurent was not there, although he had been spotted at Paloma Picasso's wedding seven months earlier.

As he distanced himself from life, he drew closer to himself, to Yves Mathieu-Saint-Laurent, the child who dreamed of making dresses for a world that didn't exist anymore. He was sewn to this suffering that condemned him to destroy what he loved and love what he destroyed. He borrowed what was fleeting, provisional, and individual in art, which was life, and condensed it in suicide-like fashion in dresses whose nature was to disappear. He kept himself alive, just as Madame Bovary kept herself awake by the window, while the ball at the Château de la Vaubyessard was ending, "in order to extend the illusion of this luxurious life that she would soon have to abandon."

While the double album soundtrack to *Saturday Night Fever* sold two million copies in France, Yves gently distanced himself from Le Palace, where all trends were born and died—Fassbinderesque sailors in Montana and fatal sirens in Alaïa. *L'Express* counted 3,500 discotheques in France. Twelve thousand people went to Le Palace every weekend.

Twenty years had passed since the little prince's rise. A generation. Now he spoke like the official couturier that Dior had been. "The frightening vision of this deformed and caricatured woman, this carnival puppet, this heap of old clothes from recent decades, this systematic commitment to ugliness and ridiculousness that the latest ready-to-wear collections have brought to the fore—this is completely foreign to me. I don't design dresses for vamps or women of ill repute. I want style to be seductive and not provocative."

But he was Saint Laurent, with all the contradictions that, in his hands, became beautiful. There were Spanish women with feathered fans. Gold toreros and laced sandals. Ballerinas in tutus. The mink pillbox hat of the red empress. Mounia, dressed as an aristocratic dandy, swept the first row with her black cloak. Alexandre the hairdresser recalled, "Mounia had to be born. He shaped his black pearl. She arched her back. It was a dance. She danced the pavane, she did glissades. She was jealous. She bowed with slow gestures, like a silent movie actress. He arrived. She awoke from a dream and stood up straight to greet him. Monsieur Saint Laurent is very sensitive to women's bodies. A beautiful body calls to him. He has always looked for something extra women had. Hair, or a divine shape. This poetry comes from that."

And then there was the dress, number 112, that appeared between *The Barber of Seville* and the Alan Parsons Project, while an endless blues number played. Two rhinestone bracelets. A slightly wavy hairstyle. A back with a lace cut-out, letting an oval of skin be glimpsed as if through a veil. With this mystery, he had announced the 1970s. Nine years later, it came back like a memory of love, and another story began. "One always surpasses oneself in this profession, which is inhumane and grueling. I'm the last great couturier. Haute couture stops with me."

15 / WORKING IN RED

n 1979, *Vogue* began celebrating the "great return" of haute couture to its original purpose: dressing a small number of very elegant women whose desires and needs were known. Loulou de la Falaise, on the arm of Cecil Beaton, set the tone: she posed in an Yves Saint Laurent ensemble: a black-and-white canvas spencer jacket, a black gabardine skirt, a black silk jersey t-shirt, and a pill-box hat. As *Vogue* put it that year, "the madcap years are over. There's a return to calm, to pure reason, to useful beauty, to comprehensible poetry, and to extremely refined simplicity."

In 1980, François Truffaut released *The Last Metro* with Catherine Deneuve, Gérard Depardieu, Heinz Bennent, and Andréa Ferréol. Who could forget the mink, the black stockings, the black skirts? Catherine Deneuve recalled, "The costumes were from the SFP [Société Française de Production]. But I had lots of Saint Laurent clothes: he had just launched a collection that was very inspired by the 1940s." For the first time the actress wore a hat with a little veil; it was made by Saint Laurent's milliner.

A whiff of nostalgia was noticeable in the air. Once again, fashion took a look at the past. The 1950s returned, along with high heels, as interpreted by Azzedine Alaïa and Thierry Mugler. Loulou the demon had transformed into an angel of the ritzy neighborhoods. She stopped drinking, as Andy Warhol noted in his diary on February 11, 1980. But Loulou said that having to be happy all the time sometimes made her sad. She added, according to Warhol, that Yves took "a millions pills." As for Pierre, he lived his own life, and had started what would be a long-term relationship with the young, slender American Madison Cox, who would become a landscape architect.

In July 1979, Yves Saint Laurent began a series of tributes—and the first one was to himself. He did another Mondrian design, this time as a suit. "I had to find a new equilibrium, a new stability," he said, as if, put in danger, he tensed up through the style of his clothes. The shoulders were straight and the legs formed a single line. "Mondrian is perfection and it is impossible to take perfection in painting any further. This perfection is like that of the Bauhaus. The masterpiece of the twentieth century is a Mondrian."

For the winter 1980 collection, Yves Saint Laurent also referenced Aragon (the embroidered eyes of Elsa) and Cocteau (the broken mirror). On a pink coat, he embroidered the words "Soleil je suis noir dedans," meaning, "Sun I am black inside." It seemed like a reply/tribute to Schiaparelli, who had illuminated the sun with golden rays, working from a sketch by Bérard. Through fashion, he kept his love of theater alive, while adding an extra dimension to haute couture: his ability to create the illusion that a woman putting on an evening gown was taking on a role. That same season, on a midnight blue coat, the words of Apollinaire were featured in gold: "Tout terriblement," or "Everything terribly." Yves Saint Laurent made another sketch, but didn't end up making the garment. It was to be embroidered with "Et je ne veux pas que tu aimes," or "And I do not want you to love." Next to the drawing, there was a handwritten note from Yves: "My coat was also becoming ideal."

In the early 1980s, he withdrew into his imaginary castles as if to gain a better viewpoint of the disaster movie of the world. The trip to the end of hell was beginning. It was nothing but towers on fire, bewitched little girls, black tides, and mass suicides (Jonestown happened in November 1978). Countless crowds proclaimed their hatred of America, kneeling at the feet of Ayatollah Khomeini. Faced with this rise of Islam, the West without god or master had nothing but entertainment to offer to its blasé citizens. "The end of an era," wrote Andy Warhol about the upcoming closure of Studio 54.

At Cannes, people said there were no more stars. Three years earlier, some people saw the special planes chartered for the likes of Gene Kelly, Fred Astaire, Cyd Charisse, or Johnny Weissmuller as a kind of swan song. Since then, the stars came to present their films only on an ad hoc basis.

The winter 1980 YSL haute couture collection was greatly inspired by Picasso, Diaghilev, and the Ballets Russes. The Bibliothèque Nationale de France in Paris had just staged an exhibition on the Ballets Russes, which triggered everything. Black velvet tutus, ballet flats with Pierrot ruffs, tulle skirts with gold spangles, dresses with satin fans or a lace shirtfront with an embroidered profile by Lesage, embroidered guitars, a torero jacket in pink lamé brocade—the list went on. Yves Saint Laurent referred to *Parade*, the one-act ballet that Diaghilev put on at the Théâtre du Châtelet in 1917 with costumes by Picasso. "I had started with toreador suits," the couturier explained. "But my idea hadn't crystallized. Then I saw models for Diaghilev's ballets at the Bibliothèque Nationale. After Bakst's Oriental inspiration, you felt the break of the war, and also a new impulse, a flame, with *Tricorne* and *Parade*. From then on, my collection was constructed like a ballet. I embroidered on Picasso, on a gentle kind of Cubism, on harlequins, the blue period, the pink period, and the *Tricorne* period. It's wonderful when inspiration arrives! I have no more doubts, I race ahead, I feel an immense joy!" he told *Vogue Paris* in 1980. "Some collections, like this one, seem special to me—I feel an artistic joy. And it's extraordinary to give this inspiration to a woman's body and not to close oneself off egotistically."

"Everything has changed," he continued. "The dresses are shorter, the necklines are more plunging, the shoulders are wide. Everything is deception—that's the only way to dress bodies that aren't perfect. I worked with planes of colors, like a painter.

There are many things inside me that I express in this collection. I project my admirations in painting or literature. I unwind with haute couture. It's a privilege to be able to make very special things. This kicks off my next collection. It's a very important step in my career. By going further inside myself, I go further in my profession, I advance." For *Vogue*, Horst photographed the black velvet and blue satin "guitar dress." Yves said, "Picasso is genius in its pure state. It's bursting with life and honesty. Picasso isn't orderly. He's baroque. He has several tracks, several arcs, several strings in his bow."

The distance between the two periods is very clear: an outraged Paris reacted to the ballet performed at the Châtelet on May 18, 1917, with shouts of "Opium smokers!" and "Draft dodgers!" What remained of the scandal? The cultural seasons had become events highly covered by the media. In the Marais neighborhood of Paris, the Hôtel Salé was being renovated as the home of the new Musée Picasso. In the Grand Palais, a gigantic exhibition was being prepared with eight hundred paintings, engravings, and sculptures from the Picasso donation. The muses had fallen into line. Paloma Picasso had married Rafael Lopez Sanchez, an Argentine writer who had experienced Parisian glory in the early years of the TSE theater troupe. He became Monsieur Paloma Picasso, the efficient artistic director of his businesswoman wife. Like Loulou de la Falaise, she posed for Sir Cecil Beaton. "Paloma Picasso is the very example of a certain kind of elegance made of both rigor and boldness, innovation and style. Over the years, her personality has developed more and more and she directly orients herself towards a sophisticated sparseness that is so personal to her," Yves Saint Laurent wrote.[1] But Yves hadn't lost his sense of humor. He had fun: that year, Mounia appeared in a wedding dress that was a black tuxedo. On her arm, an operetta toreador in neon pink. For the first time, he offered a dress to Paloma Picasso, who was now an heiress: "It's true that I was becoming visible."

The press praised Yves with grandiloquent accolades: "With harlequins for day and harlequins for night, Yves Saint Laurent makes color explode, expressing an optimistic vision of life and connecting to the most colorful periods of Picasso's work." "This was truly Saint Laurent," said *Le Figaro*. "The greatest night," opined *Vogue*. Paloma described her reaction to the show in this way: "He made me laugh, smile, and cry with emotion—not sadness—on various occasions. I must admit that I'm subjected to his charm, but how could I not be when some designs are dedicated to me? I become more Carmen, more 1940s, more toreador, better-behaved, more theatrical, ultimately more myself, with every collection." Yet she did observe later on: "He's becoming an institution. People read him like the truth."

With red—a color that he said in 1958 was his favorite "because red means stage lights"—he once again lit up the lights of his Illustre Théâtre. With black, he magnified the silence of matte and shiny lines, faithful to this search that had always haunted him: to be done with fashion, to be modern, to live.

"I don't yet know how, but I know, I can sense that this passion, this uniformity of young people all dressing the same, that there's an idea here, something that I'll end up finding, if it hasn't been done yet. Men dress more comfortably than women because they don't have to fulfill this role of object that has so often paralyzed women of previous generations. There's a concern for equality and not revenge in all these too-bulky sweaters, these blouses tied around the waist, all these things that are borrowed from men by women and that generally look so good on them. It will be stable. Comfort has now become a value that is as decisive as aesthetics. And it's not bad for a couturier to have to respond to it. It avoids errors or fantasies that are meaningless to people who live and work."

This is what he said to Françoise Sagan. On a rainy Sunday afternoon, he welcomed her to his apartment on Rue de Babylone, where, she noticed, "Every detail is a work of art." They hadn't talked for fifteen years. Everything separated them: she liked cats and lived in houses that were simply furnished. "Yves and I are connected by our professions. He designs his dresses the way I write my books: with feverishness and worry." Together they announced to their friends that they were "sick of working like dogs for twenty-five years." "He and I are forty-four and forty-five years old respectively," she wrote. "So, for years, we've carried terrifying burdens and responsibilities on our shoulders that are incompatible with our idea of life and our character. We're going to leave together next week and go sleep in cabins in the sunshine and never come back."[2]

With black, "the color of poise," the couturier stripped down his style. With red, the man of the theater would express woman in her most heroic manifestation. Andrée Putman, the Parisian decorator, was a fan of Yves's style: "I admire the abyss of his contrasts. This extremist finds the means for his classicism in strength and fragility. His boldness is a way of overcoming his shyness."

In Saint Laurent's designs, red would color dresses that seemed to have been designed in anger and in the memory of a past full of pain. The doomed image of his idol, Callas, was revealed: "Over your legend is lowered the heavy curtain of purple splattered with glory."[3] Everything that was intense and that sparked passion and ardor seemed to be concentrated in these fabrics, made to burn those who looked at them and cast spells on those who touched them: a blouse of copper satin, a dress of taffeta printed with red hibiscus flowers, a suit of ruby velvet.

"Red is a sign of existence," people in Marrakesh say. Yves Saint Laurent described the color like this: "Red is the base of make-up, it's lips and nails. Red is a noble color, the color of a precious stone—the ruby—and it's a dangerous color; sometimes we must play with danger. Red is religious and it's blood, it's royal. It's Phèdre, and a multitude of heroines. Fire red and battle red, red is a battle between life and death."[4]

His first collection in red was that of winter 1980–81, a tribute to Shakespeare inspired by a model, Violeta Sanchez, with dark fabrics that looked as if they had been stolen from a Renaissance palace. As if at the gates of hell, this being of violence and ambition had seen in these fabrics the revelation of his fate. Or how among the grays and blacks, the wave of burgundy velvet and emerald satin flowed like a poisoned liqueur, red like danger that one fears without understanding it, and which soon bloodies the public with despair and beauty. Number 105 was a long evening gown in Renaissance satin damask, Lady Macbeth red. A fleeting vision that had escaped from a drama, from one of the memories that are left on the other side of a door where the "do not disturb" sign is still dangling. A memory that had burst forth like a dagger, in the hands of a hunted man, who seemed to ask, like Macbeth, "Will all great Neptune's ocean wash this blood clean from my hand?"

Across from the maison de couture was the Saint Laurent museum directed by Hector Pascual, an Argentine who worked with Yves on his theater projects at the Casino de Paris and the Athénée. "Yves is the last visionary, the last nabob, the last artist." Like many people at the company, Hector Pascual seemed to hold a secret that others didn't have: "I'm lucky enough to know what influenced him." In his archives, there were 1,000 theater designs and 3,500 dresses, not counting the accessories. "In the beginning, we stored these things like old sweaters, in a bag of souvenirs. I didn't know that I could devote all my passion to it. I'm like a mother," said this perfumed gentleman, who "trained as a painter." For him, Yves Saint Laurent was primarily a man of the theater: "In his designs, there is the effort and despair of struggles," he said, showing the six versions of the queen's costume that Yves created for Cocteau's *The Eagle with Two Heads* And then Arletty's dresses for the 1966 revival of Cocteau's *The Sacred Monsters*, the entirely red Court of Miracles for *Notre-Dame de Paris*, the stilts for the Casino de Paris, along with the red and pink tuxedos, the clowns and their suits painted with flames. And then, through pages that came to life, a whole clan of acrobats, tightrope walkers, eagles, and ballerinas. Legionnaires and "women of easy virtue" in lipstick-pink bodices and sapphire blue fox coats. Yves Saint Laurent definitively belonged to "the same breed as Christian Bérard," Pascual said. "He draws on anything. It's very dangerous to leave him with paper. He draws all the time." Then Pascual grew quiet. "We're entering a banal world where directors will replace creators."

In 1980, Yves Saint Laurent created the costumes and sets for *Cher Menteur*, a play by Jérôme Kilty adapted by Jean Cocteau, with Edwige Feuillère and Jean Marais. But he knew, as someone who would have "loved to live on the stage with theater people," that a dream was ending:

"There was l'Athénée, Jouvet, Bérard. The first theater I fell in love with. There was the scintillation of this magic and unique swan couple that Cocteau made burst forth from the bottom of a Bavarian lake to transform them into royal eagles and reach the highest peaks. My first loves. There was all the trembling of my delayed adolescence before these unforgettable dreams. I had to be reborn.

Place myself once more in reality. Forget and destroy this sublime splendor. That's why I decided without a moment's hesitation to make the sets and costumes for *Cher Menteur*. I saw Edwige Feuillère. I saw Jean Marais. And she was a woman, and he was a man....

"My job was to serve them: to try to capture the emotion of their movements and hearts, released from the spells of this world of the past, however beautiful they may be. To make them what they are: an actress and an actor of today. I had to sweep away the shades and it was with much emotion that I did so. Surely the great names that led this theater and the spirit of this mischievous Academician will be there, somewhere, to express their affection. May I not disappoint them. For the love of theater."[5]

In his room, at age seventeen, he drew costumes for *La Reine Margot*. "Yves has always been possessed. He was already like that from the beginning," Alexandre, the hairdresser he met at Dior, recalled. "There was a light inside that was revealed bit by bit." For the second part of the play, when Queen Margot is forty years old, Yves imagined a black crown, a red dress, and embroidery like black spiders with two long wings of spotted tulle sprouting from her shoulders. The portrait of a bird of ill omen. Was it his own?

In any case, he gave up theater for fashion. "No, it's impossible for me to do both," he said in 1980. "I can't, I can't do it anymore: that would mean giving up everything I've done, and putting 500 people out on the street, people whom I respect and love a lot and who love me too."[6] But wasn't it because he wanted to be the only one once more? And for this insomniac to enjoy the only sleep possible? "I hardly have time to sleep between two collections."

In this struggle he found his strength. And this fierce energy spurted out like a flood of life in his dresses. Everything exploded in uncontrolled fury.

What inspired a dress? "A gesture," he answered. "All my dresses come from a gesture. A dress that doesn't reflect or recall a gesture is not good. Once you have found the gesture in question, then you can choose the color, the definitive shape, and the fabrics—not before. In reality, you never stop learning in this profession."

Before the collections, Yves felt like a "prisoner, empty," and then drew from his maison reserves of energy at the specific moment when he became the orchestra conductor once more: "One day, everything starts up, and then I'm the happiest of couturiers. I see in front of me a guy working, who has ideas and intuitions, who is only one aspect of me but whose exploits floor me. Alas, although I'm only one person when it doesn't work, there are always two of me when it works....Despite the incredible perfectionism of the ateliers, of the entier maison de couture, the anxiety remains, stronger with every collection, which I approach empty-handed, as if I knew nothing. There are two very painful weeks every time, when I wander from fabric to fabric, but afterwards, when it starts to come out, the ateliers are stimulated and work at colossal speed."[7]

At that point, Anne-Marie Muñoz, the head of the haute couture studio, would get involved. With black hair framing her very powdered face, she had the serious look of a *mater dolorosa* who had suffered heroically. There were two noticeable things about Anne-Marie Muñoz: first, her dark lipstick, and then her way of wearing wedge sandals with black net stockings in both winter and summer. She loved everything that was sharp, that held together. Sitting on a stool across from her, one always felt overwhelmed. Her bedtime reading is *Le Style Contre les Idées* by Céline. When she arrived at the studio, she didn't drop her coat on a chair; she hung it on a hanger, placed her suede gloves on top of it, and they didn't move an inch. She was the guardian of the temple. She seemed to be both Raymonde Zehnacker and Marguerite Carré from Dior all rolled into one. Dior said of his technical director, Marguerite Carré, "She, too, with the years, has become part of me, my 'couture' part."[8] She played her role so well that some said under their breath, "When Madame Muñoz isn't here, Yves knows how to make a phone call." She started at Dior, in this pitiless world of women. This only child, born in Arcachon, came to Paris with a will to learn. "She was short and fat, her name was Anne-Marie Poupart, she wasn't really part of our group," said Victoire, the muse of the time. Anne-Marie Muñoz said that she learned everything from Madame Simone, a long-time Dior employee who was Madame Esther's *première main*: "A good piece of clothing must be as cleanly made on the inside as on the outside." For Anne-Marie Muñoz, couture "is a blueprint, it's spelled out." She had a second sight. And a limitless admiration for Yves: "He's one of those people who make you go far. The path opens up. I had this career because of him. He never got taken in by money, conventions, or power. That's why he's always afraid, why he's so human, why he loves competition. Yves never designs the same way. Sometimes they're happy, sometimes they're aggressive." The 1980s would be his. "He's passionate about the cut. He has foundations, absolute structures. He loves straight shoulders and backs. The whole idea is to stretch you out toward the sky. It's ease and structure. You think a navy blue suit is going by. The whole thing is in the connection of the sleeve. The skirt is the hips. He wants to understand, he seeks, he takes the fabric in his hands." When there are many butterflies and it flies off, there's Loulou in the air. But the tailored look, that's Anne-Marie Muñoz. It's no wonder that the Libération collection was her favorite.

She was the only one with whom Yves Saint Laurent shared the intimate act of selecting fabrics. It was something to see them together engaged in mysterious evaluations. Everything happened intuitively. They hesitated among four wool crepes, found a duchesse satin too "hollow," one grain de poudre too "soft," and another one too "stiff." They could take ten minutes to choose the most perfect white. "The issue isn't finding a pretty fabric but the exact fabric," she said. For dress number 1043, she selected a very delicate black gabardine, with trim in white glazed piqué cotton. The *première* prepared it in a week, first using a wooden mannequin and then a live model, Kirat. Regarding the sketch, Yves said, "I gave it to Madame Catherine [the *première* of the *atelier flou*]. She didn't even make a test garment. It seemed simple to her. The design was eloquent." The alterations began. Then Catherine went to the studio, to show it to Monsieur Saint Laurent. Silence. He looked, without touching. He was able to dissipate the tension with a smile, and everyone was watching him— his silences were sometimes heavier than stones. "What a well put-together sleeve, Madame Catherine!" It was a success. There would be only two fittings. The dress was done.

Loulou played a different role. She was like Mitza Bricard, of whom Dior said, "Her love of nature is limited to loving the flowers with which she can decorate hats so well." Loulou arrived in the late morning, but unlike Mitza, with Loulou nothing was hinted at, everything shone forth. In this respect, her style was certainly more "cosmopolitan" than that of Mitza. Red and bright pink clashed on her body, which was always almost unbalanced. She never sat down on a chair. She made a face, laughed nervously, then grabbed a scarf in front of the mirror. She made up stories while watching Kirat, and wondered with Yves if this young woman were sad or happy, if she needed a mousseline handkerchief or a hat. "Not being a very happy person himself, he seems to live through these women who are excited for life." She corrected herself: "These aren't very specific women, not me, or his clients. Afterwards, when we start working, we say, 'This would look good on so-and-so.' Yves senses things, a bit like a fortune-teller."

Yves was a perfectionist. "It's a puzzle. We don't have the right to make a mistake, even on a little detail." Has anyone seen a billionaire who could have a breakdown over a row of buttons? Design 1043 was ready. The atelier record states that it required 2.25 meters of fine wool gabardine, 60 centimeters of white glazed piqué cotton for the Chinese collar, the tab, and the cuffs, plus six jeweled buttons of enamel and gold. Josiane Dacquet, the director of materials, specified, "Here, a client can reorder her black dress from ten years ago. The slightest detail is noted down. We always keep a button in a little envelope in case she loses one."

In the eyes of these women—often friendly, but still severe—he found a new reason to outdo himself: "I can't live anymore when it doesn't work, and I'm never really happy with anything until the day of the show, but in addition to me there are the seamstresses." He described the seamstresses as "women who work at the sewing machine day and night, and whom I sometimes make take everything apart. But I never insult them by making them work without believing in it myself: they would sense it, and would lose respect for me."

His sketching style changed once more. The outlines were clearer, revealing the essential details: the white trim, the collar, the placement of the pocket. The line became freer, barely troubled by a presence: that of a "thin young woman," he said, with that mania of associating, like many aesthetes of the 1970s, elegance with the absence of flesh. The memory of Carmen and the odalisques had faded. "He doesn't like big breasts. Right now, he thinks they're too big," wrote Mounia. "He makes them wear bands sometimes to suppress them. They look like women who've given birth who are trying to make their milk go away! He has a certain idea of female beauty, a little adolescent, never aggressive, closer to the romantic view of a work of art than to the real-life female."[9]

For *Le Journal du Dimanche*, Kirat posed exactly like the model in the sketch, with one hand in her pocket and one leg in front of the other. Just a few details were added to the model: a white-and-black pillbox hat, a blue grosgrain ribbon with a sparkling jewel that matched the earrings, black stockings, and "Deauville, white and black" pumps. And then a leather belt tied haphazardly around the waist.

However, under the sign of individualism and performance, a new generation would influence the 1980s. Traditional craftsmanship would be replaced by smooth talking. Feeling good about your life, feeling good about your body: the ego took center stage. Energy was the new god of a decade that was all about performance, where everyone held on tight, between unemployment and inflation, to survive among the wealthy of the world. Make way for living culture, many sided and connected to the present!

In France, François Mitterrand's election as president on May 10, 1981, consecrated the rise of government patronage of the arts. Between 1981 and 1982, the budget of the ministry of culture increased from three to six billion francs. Under culture minister Jack Lang, photography, design, graphic design, rock music, and comics were accepted as arts in their own right. Movements accelerated, along with the trend of producing trends. Lists of what was "in" and "out" proliferated, in a profusion of signs, codes, and video images, including ads and music videos, logos and fashion shows. Critics no longer analyzed; they took photos. The press raced after trends that appeared everywhere, in the euphoria of communication, pirate radio, and hip magazines. Fashion was no longer dictated by "the greats." After the future (the 1960s) and nature (the 1970s), the street became the main source of inspiration for couturiers and creative artists. From London to Tokyo, from Paris to New York, the moment justified all kinds of experiments, whether trashy (silk with holes in it from Comme des Garçons or the pirate fashion of Vivienne Westwood), avant-garde (Cruella by Thierry Mugler, Claude Montana's barbarians in studded leather), or transgressive (dresses with ice-cream-cone breasts by Jean-Paul Gaultier).

"Fashion has just recently become a complete spectacle," said Saint Laurent. "It happens on stages, with musicians, microphones, and artifice, which are mainly there to impress people, to create an effect more than anything else. It's not couture anymore, it's spectacle. The relations between couturiers, or between couturiers and their clients, are emotional and theatrical. But the result is often that the spectacle can be perfect, but the dress is unwearable. Another result is that names are released every year like hot-air balloons. The next year, the hot-air balloons have disappeared, replaced by others...."[10]

The 1980s had started. The children of Mao no longer protested—they communicated. East-West, North-South, everything was mixed together in world music. Fashion became media. A direct product of current events, it was consumed all over the world with urgency. Everything had to be new in order to exist: the new right, *nouvelle cuisine*, new philosophers, new life, new spirit.

Neighborhoods were transformed into store windows: in SoHo in New York, the artists left and were replaced by art galleries. In Paris, Les Halles got a shopping center, and Rue Bonaparte and Rue de Seine became a village of antique shops. The fashion world turned on the spotlights. "We made beautiful clothes that we showed to a few journalists. The real problem is the show," Pierre Bergé acknowledged ten years later. "Yves stuck to it. He did a real show. I'm not totally irresponsible." After all, thanks to his close relationship with Jack Lang, in 1982 Bergé arranged for the fashion industry finally to have a regular place to show its collections, the Cour Carrée du Louvre.

The Filofax generation had arrived. Relationships became public, and nightlife became professionalized. "The word 'party' no longer means anything," Loulou de la Falaise told Yvonne Baby. On January 1, 1981, *Le Monde* devoted an entire page to nightlife for the first time, in its art and theater section. "This word is now like a headline, a snappy look," Loulou said, while 3,000 people filled Le Palace every night.

"However, nightlife can be a party, joy, freedom. Everyone can bring out another self, break barriers, have a wild time or indulge in a crisis of poetic melancholy. I love giving parties. Hasty parties, at the last minute, that are improvised, without any lists or secretaries…It was 1977. Then, with the elections, when it seemed as if the left would win, all the rich people panicked. They said, 'You know, I can make a great chicken stew.' They said really shameful things. They stopped having parties to hide the fact that they had money."

In 1981, Loulou seemed already to miss a golden age: "What you wore was of no importance, there wasn't this aspect that annoys me: how to dress, how to look, how to borrow dresses from couturiers, how to be worthy of the party."

Yves Saint Laurent's name shone uptown, not in the streets with colorful graffiti on the walls where other designers found their inspiration in violence and euphoria. In particular, Jean-Paul Gaultier, whom the press called "the vandal of Couture conventions" and "fashion's enfant terrible," would be the symbol of this trend. "I try to destroy certain rules of so-called good taste," he said, with a silver ring in his ear, a shock of bleached-blond hair, and a little Popeye sweater. "I reinvent the ordinary. My tea ball becomes a pendant, a can of my cat's food becomes a high-tech bracelet." Wasn't his true teacher Cardin? "With him, I learned to make a hat out of a chair."

Yves, the leading designer of the salvage school of fashion, found himself dethroned by a son whom he had never acknowledged. The only one to say, walking in his footsteps: "Fabric has no sex." The only one to give a new twist to the classics, even if they weren't the same ones: the Levi's jacket instead of the peacoat, with which Yves Saint Laurent concluded his collection in January 1982, as he had started it twenty years earlier. A generation separated them: Yves Saint Laurent was imagination instead of image, novels instead of comic strips, women instead of girls, theater and cinema instead of television. "If he has a religion, its deity is without doubt woman," wrote Anthony Burgess.[11]

Yves Saint Laurent would lead all women to dream as he did of balls and parties, where "dolmans of gold lamé damask" shone.[12] They were there as mistresses of the night: Clio Goldsmith, Jerry Hall, sparkling in her "sardine" sheath dress with silver sequins. On the night of the César Awards (France's version of the Oscars), Romy Schneider looked splendid in her black taffeta dress, and Catherine Deneuve was on the arm of François Truffaut in a satin-lined coat. Yves Saint Laurent worked with "sturdy" fabrics (such as faille, satin, and gazar), as if to increase their effect. He worked to find Balenciaga's combination of starkness and power. In 1980, his haute couture wedding dress was all brocade. The bride was a divinity with countless necklaces of glass and black beads, and a diamond sparkled on her ebony forehead, held there by a gold turban. The next year, the bride was almost in black. Mounia appeared in a dress of iridescent dark purple faille with a bouquet of red roses in her hand. On her bust, hanging from a red cord, the fake rubies of the lucky heart dangled among the diamonds. "I love this great jewel against my chest, scraping and turning me into an icon," said Mounia.

Yves designed dresses made of bird-of-paradise feathers and coats strewn with a dusting of stars. People would wear them not because they were fashionable, but because they were by him. A sweater of diamonds. A cape of neon pink gazar. Or simply a black turtleneck and a black mink, with an attitude like that of Bette Davis in *All About Eve* saying, "It's going to be a bumpy night." During the same period, the body became the medium for all kinds of gadgets: coats with three sleeves, "anti-rape" pants and jacket, zipped jumpsuits ready to meet the little green men of the year 2000, and the female replicants of *Blade Runner*.

He stated, "A woman who hasn't found her style, who doesn't feel at ease in her clothes, who doesn't live in harmony with them, is a sick woman. She isn't happy, isn't sure of herself, and presents none of the characteristics that determine happiness." Yet he also talked about fashion as an "incurable disease."

When he was sheltered, he ended up more exposed: at the height of his power, the king was more and more vulnerable. Like people thrust into a foreign environment who had to expand their horizons to survive, now he had to define himself in these struggles that he was fond of: "Yves has always been torn between the Duchess of Windsor and the hepcat," said Loulou.

Hepcats? The gay ghetto was closing its doors. There, in those basements where women weren't allowed, Yves Saint Laurent had affirmed his homosexuality in a more individual way, in keeping with a solitude that was consoled by his aesthetics, his faith in beauty, and his absolute belief that it was the only reason to live. He could once again become the child who mentally addressed his schoolmates, saying, "I will avenge myself on you. You will be nothing, and I will be everything."

He may have been flirtatious, but his art was of incredible violence. It was because of Saint Laurent that there was no longer the obsessive fear of making a mistake, of daring, of dressing by undressing. He was the first one to strike a blow against haute couture while saving it every time from its predicted demise. At Dior in 1959, he was the first to design an haute couture leather jacket. The first to show black vinyl raincoats in 1962. To elevate ready-to-wear in 1966 and let women be as comfortable as men. To make, that same year, the pantsuit, the safari jacket, and the tuxedo into uniforms for an army of women. To bare breasts in 1968. To demystify traditional elegance with the flea market in 1971. At that show, some women left the room. "They didn't want to be around whores," he recalled ten years later, according to a witness. He was the one who imposed colors that the bourgeoisie thought exotic in 1976 and announced the rise of a woman "as mysterious as opium smoke." The more time passed, the more, in the early 1980s, he let the demon's face be glimpsed under the face of the protective angel: per Cocteau's *The Eagle with Two Heads*, "We carry our death with us and no one suspects it." By staging haute couture as a spectacle in 1976, he struck another blow. The year 1981 marked a new break, with video-taped fashion shows for clients. But the same year he returned to the source, with a "purely classic" collection, as the Americans called it.

Roland Petit explained, "Yves is a chameleon, you can't catch him." He reinvented himself each time, as if he had to begin the conquest of Paris yet again and reach higher. He had to imagine a new competition in which he would be both candidate and judge.

It was as if he smacked his own knuckles with a ruler. It was like Naughty Lulu talking to sinful women: "You must fast and deprive yourselves of these little joys that end up destroying the good moral health of your soul." He modified his clothing on the inside by submitting it to an act of advanced surgery. "I can't stand disorder. A garment must be perfect." He applied to fashion all the strength that life refused him. He made strictness into a dogma so that he wouldn't lose his way or get confused. A sign of style. A framework. An indestructible line, like the grosgrain ribbon that the workers on Avenue Marceau used to hold the waist in place, or the iron wires that supported a bustier. "Otherwise," they said, "the bustier is soft and the fabric collapses." He said, "No one can copy my suits. They involve maximum technique. It's a work of iron."

It was a reaction to punk fashion. For someone who caressed fabrics as if they were living matter, rags, loose threads, and holes in linings like shreds of skin were quite simply monstrous. The early 1980s coincided with the return to finished, controlled, decorated work. The fabric no longer flew; it held together, entirely shaped: a balloon of Persian satin or a pouf of aurora pink satin. Yves Saint Laurent had rediscovered a closeness with the princes of the tailored look, those who propped up the gathers, directed the pleats, using the same authority they wielded in life. Madame Catherine required cotton tulle for her bodices, or "otherwise, the women are irritated," she told the materials department in a gentle voice. Madame Catherine spoke little, but always to the point. Her body was knotted with muscles, and her blond hair was held back in a heavy braid that revealed the face of a Viking lady with prominent cheekbones.

And then there were gentlemen who came along to the maison de couture, like the cabinetmakers of the Ateliers La Ruche at the time of Jean-Michel Frank, and always wore suits. They referred to themselves as "academicians." Monsieur Jean-Pierre, the *premier* of the *atelier tailleur*, who went to work for Yves Saint Laurent in 1965 after spending seven years at Dior, explained aristocratically, "The seam-stresses put in the thread, I try to express the design." In 1979, Monsieur Jean-Marie was hired by the maison. He wore flannel pants with a shirt and tie, and always had a tape measure around his neck. "Crepe has no resilience. It melts on the body. Mousseline? It flutters away when you breathe. The *flou* crowd loves it!" He strug-gled with a jacket: "It has no shoulders, it's slumping!" In the atelier, they prepared the clothes, flattening the hems with steam, getting the shoulder pads ready. They were superstitious. A tape measure with a knot in it meant work to be done. If a box of pins got knocked over, it meant there would be an argument. Scissors falling, someone would leave. "Adeline, the neck goes too far down! Can't you close it up! Lucienne, ribbon!" Monsieur Jean-Marie would insist, "We must find the verticality of the shoulders."

Everyone felt entrusted with a special responsibility that conferred impor-tance. At the maison de couture, they didn't refer to Sao Schlumberger's or Marie-Hélène de Rothschild's suit, but to Madame Catherine's suit. Every seamstress followed her design. At the door of each atelier, an engraved brass plaque indicated the name of the *premier* or *première*. As in the theater. It felt as if you were backstage at the Comédie Française of couture. The *premiers* and *premières* were a bit like the members of an elite society. They didn't touch the needle. They met with the clients. "There is a lot of feeling in the work. Yves's secret is to have good people around him. We don't deal with cranky ladies."

The studio was its own world upstairs, where Saint Laurent's "goddesses" came when he called them, naked under their blouses. It was the cavern of all kinds of spells, pure head-spinning beauty. A roll of crepe that he unrolled at Mounia's feet. Hushed, the team attended this pagan ceremony in respectful silence. "How could it not be troubling, this man who makes me beautiful?" said Mounia. "Never will I have a lover as concerned with making me splendid. He speaks to me. He looks at me. He smiles at me. He touches me. He dresses and undresses me. I am a heroine." Meanwhile, in the make-up room which looked like a real star's dressing room—with lighted mirrors, little jars, half-eaten cookies, and crosswords—the others waited, redheads or brunettes, all in love, and all jealous. Who would get to wear the lucky heart this season?

He was joined to his ateliers by almost organic connections. He told *Le Monde*: "If I hesitate, my ateliers sense it, then they hesitate, and the current between us slows down. There's anxiety. An anxiety that can last three weeks, until the general lines become clear, and then everything circulates in the maison with incredible accuracy and speed. There's magic in the air, we're very united, and also happy." But in 1982, G. Y. Dryansky recalled, Yves said, "I get medical treatment at the beginning of each collection to relax me and stimulate me every time....I love my friends, but I see them rarely, because I'm required to follow certain medical rules. Celebrity means loneliness. Because you're locked away in one world and you don't leave. I had a more public image in the 1970s. For a while now, I've been withdrawn into myself."

Yves Saint Laurent would defend the catechism of the profession, like daughters of Spanish dancers who, having married English lords, raise their children according to religious principles. In fact, he would say, "I'm entering the collection" (around December 15, a month and a half before the runway show) the way novices say, "I'm entering the convent." Ironically, he appeared as the absolute memory of fashion, drawing on all the couturiers of the twentieth century, just as his own past disappeared, burned up by whiskey and cocaine. But reconstructing this memory of fashion's possibilities gave him the strength to support his failing body. Every collection was a process of building up and letting go; as Yves put it, "When the last pin is in place, you feel abandoned."

This is when people started calling a suit "a Saint Laurent." You could turn it inside out, go through the pockets, find dirt inside it, but the suit didn't collapse. It resisted, it held up. "It has a stiff inner lining, it has decorative borders, it requires perfect ironing. You have to have a good hand for tailoring. If you don't know how to iron, the result won't work," explained Madame Catherine. One didn't slump in a Saint Laurent jacket. It was as if the suit's natural authority forbade one to sit on the floor or let oneself go. "I think this coherence, this straight line like an arrow's flight define him the best," Catherine Deneuve said about Yves Saint Laurent.[13]

The suit was photographed by Helmut Newton in a staging worthy of the cinema: a man in a tuxedo kneels at a woman's feet and rolls a black stocking onto her leg. "He became her mistress instead of her being his," Flaubert would have said. People were watching from the top of the stairs. With square shoulders, severe lines, crisp fabrics, the swaying skirt opened up like a wrap dress. Black pumps. A fedora on a red mane. Gloves. A gray fox boa dragging on the ground. "With the Trocadéro photo, I became the chronicler of the bourgeoisie," Newton said with amusement. For Yves Saint Laurent, "The Parisian woman is a navy blue blazer, a black turtleneck, and a black suede skirt. Red nails. It's a very simple but very significant image. There's a very careful choice of accessories. You can transform a black suit with pale pink gloves and a fuchsia mousseline scarf." Men's fedoras and gloves reappeared. When he talked about Parisian women, he thought of the goddesses of the silver screen, a memory of the time when American movies and magazines increased the desire for Paris even more: Lauren Bacall, Bette Davis, or Joan Crawford, who set the audience at the Empire Theater in Oran aflame in *Flamingo Road.* "The role of her life," *L'Echo d'Oran* promised. Yves Saint Laurent seemed to say about the Parisian woman what Hollywood costume designer Gilbert Adrian—who accentuated the star's shoulder span—might have said of Joan Crawford: "Who would have thought that my career would rest on her shoulders!"

The Saint Laurent woman no longer appeared androgynous, serpentine, or dandyish, troubling men and women in her black jumpsuit or her beige safari jacket. Quite the opposite. She was subjected to the artifices of femininity that were the source of her power. Yves had her stroll down the runway while a man at her side walked her dog. Wasn't she a worldly woman, a real mistress finally? The Americans were won over. The Saint Laurent suit would become one of the best sellers of Paris haute couture (110 pieces per season). Between 1982 and 1983, sales to private clients rose from 28.2 to 41.6 million francs. They reached 45.1 million in 1984. The most popular suit colors were black and white. Each suit required between 80 and 100 hours of labor. The stages were very specific: sketch, test garments, paper patterns to correct the lines, interfacing, decorative borders, shaping of the jacket, and attaching the sleeves. Inside, the satin lining was attached by hand.

A veritable structure held up the jackets: bias-cut interfacing (for suppleness) and straight-cut interfacing (to prevent them from losing their shape). The seams were precise down to the millimeter: cut in half, a Saint Laurent jacket weights the same on each side. The shoulder pads required eight hours of labor. "We put in layers of cotton batting that we break down. Then we shape them," said Monsieur Jean-Pierre. Then there were the finishing touches: the buttonholes, with piping and embroidery done by hand, and then ironing, which could take an entire day. In the atelier, the big green Casoli irons were constantly on. Monsieur Jean-Pierre explained, "The jackets are very structured in the shoulders and supple at the waist. They're very constructed, but they follow the movement of the body." He added playfully, "As soon as there's a classic, poof! It's here."

The Saint Laurent suit, which was created in 1962 for the first collection, found its definitive structure twenty years later. It was strong enough to submit itself to all the variations of fashion: it would "move" on the inside, held up by shoulders with right angles. "A round back dates a woman. Our thing is very straight shoulders. Everything happens up there: the line of the shoulders, the attachment of the sleeve, the collar. If the garment is straight, it all holds together," said Jean-Claude Rossignol, the technical coordinator between the maison Saint Laurent and the Mendès factory. The Saint Laurent suit would become a Rive Gauche classic, a must for the 1980s. Like all the ready-to-wear designs, the prototypes were created at the maison de couture.

Colombe Pringle, who was a journalist for *Elle* at the time, summarized, "With the safari jacket, we were fashionable. Then, we were chic. We were thirty. We thought it was fun to look like our mothers. I had a Rive Gauche suit with tennis stripes that I wore with pumps and Brooks Brothers shirts. And at night, a divine gray velvet jacket with mousseline cuffs and fifty-two buttons. Everything else seemed incredibly vulgar to me."

The Saint Laurent suit had its inseparable component—the blouse whose first version was also created in January 1962: the gray satin "Norman blouse," a loose-fitting peasant tunic. It also went through all kinds of transformations: the transparent, rebellious see-through blouse of black silk cigaline (1968), the liberated dandy blouse (1969), the Romanian blouse (1976), and the blouse that was as silky as the wall hangings of a harem (1978). It soon seemed just as necessary for the suit as a powder compact in a lady's purse. "It's often made of crepe, satin, or mousseline," said Madame Jacqueline, the *première* of the *atelier flou*. "A shoulder seam, a seam under the arm, nothing is more difficult to do."

A Saint Laurent blouse required two weeks of labor. Its simplicity was also reflected in the trim: the collar was finished with a clean bias cut and hidden buttons ("Monsieur Saint Laurent doesn't like to see them") or twin buttons like those seen on men's shirts. The difference is that these were made of rock crystal or rhinestones. The cuffs were lined with organza to give firmness. The Saint Laurent blouse added brightness, comfort, and smoothness to a day ensemble (skirt or pants) or an evening ensemble (a tuxedo suit). The simple shape (the starting point remained the t-shirt) met an infinite range of colors: deep purple-red or chartreuse satin, which, Yves Saint Laurent said, "enlivened the suits." But only much later did he play with grazing the skin, meticulously structuring the fabric to create the illusion of a second skin. According to Monsieur Jean-Pierre, the telling characteristic of a Saint Laurent suit is "clean work. There is no heaviness. It's not cluttered. His motto is: The cleaner it is, the better I see."

The descriptions became as precise as scientific terms. "Burgundy grain de poudre suit. Pink and black satin damask crepe blouse." There was an impeccable faithfulness to the rules of haute couture: suits, day ensembles, formal dresses (including tuxedos), formal wear, long evening gowns, and wedding dresses. His obsession with elegance wasn't always the most elegant. But isn't that exactly why it touched the public and made it fall in love with his designs? His navy blue never looked as if it came from a boring Parisian suburb. His white was never calm. A whiff of danger always hovered above these women who were so rich, so beautiful, so Saint Laurent.

It was in July 1981 (the winter 1981–82 haute couture collection) that Yves Saint Laurent celebrated the great return of Le Smoking. The models strode down the runway with serious expressions, like Nicole Dorier, her hair in smooth waves and her red nails grazing her jet buttons. These women frightened men, because, across from them, the men could do nothing but subject them or break them, find the flaw behind this indestructible appearance, this very male and very female dream of being both the mistress and the lover: "Black satin and serge tuxedo-peacoat. Black grain de poudre skirt. Black silk jersey sweater." "Black velvet jacket and long skirt. Black satin blouse."

"If I had to choose a favorite design from all those I've shown, without a doubt it would be Le Smoking," said Yves Saint Laurent. Of all the clothes he made, it was perhaps the most famous and also the most mysterious. A beautiful woman could feel trapped in it. You couldn't see her legs or breasts. The pants? "Two pleats, a fly in front, a bias-cut pocket," summarized Monsieur Jean-Pierre. Each pair of pants required forty hours of labor. For Loulou de la Falaise, "The tuxedo makes everything gleam, makes you stand out, and exposes those whom I find unbearable. I think the tuxedo is very sexy."[14]

Since 1966, Le Smoking, "a sure thing that fits all times and seasons," as Yves described it, has been featured in every haute couture and Rive Gauche collection. Its black, like a pencil line on a white page, was "the silhouette at the apex of its perfection." Yves Saint Laurent gave it a material—grain de poudre, the fabric of amazons. This classic of the contemporary wardrobe has a rather shady past: the dinner jacket, whose origins go back to 1880, was banned in public until the death of Edward VII in 1910. With Saint Laurent, the tuxedo became feminine. It was a shadow lit up with rhinestones. A pair of legs in black stockings. Satiny hair. And a cigarette. Marlene Dietrich singing, "I am a free woman." The Saint Laurent Le Smoking was evening wear that let women cross their legs, serve wine, and not carry a purse. It was Betty Catroux, who always went out in a black jacket with nothing on underneath. Through it, he expressed the independence of a character, man and his double. For *Elle* magazine, he posed with Catherine Deneuve in a tuxedo, as he and his sister Brigitte posed in safari jackets in 1969. "When he saw that photo, my first husband asked me for a divorce," Brigitte maintained.

A chameleon outfit, Le Smoking has had versions as a coat, jumpsuit, bomber jacket, skirt suit, striped shirt, and peacoat. It could be haughty, as in the Seville tuxedo shot by Irving Penn (1968); it could be androgynous, as in the black tuxedo and its transparent smock that looked like a fairy crossed with a prince (1969); it could be scandalous, like the satin-lined tuxedo shorts inspired by Lola Lola in *The Blue Angel* (1971); it could celebrate the discreet charm of the bourgeoisie in the tuxedo skirt suit seen at the Ritz (1974); it could be extroverted, like the tuxedo with the black lace bustier under the disco spencer jacket (1978). It was liberated enough to expose itself, go to the front lines, and enter different worlds without losing itself. "Every client here has a tuxedo in her wardrobe," Monsieur Jean-Pierre revealed. "They put on their diamonds, and it's perfect." The most famous for it were Lauren Bacall, Liza Minnelli, and Catherine Deneuve. In 1982, Yves launched the tuxedo dress, which was photographed by Horst for *Vogue*, and which the magazine deemed "the most contemporary and sophisticated dress for cocktails and dinner."[15]

Of all Saint Laurent clothing, it's perhaps the design that is the most immediately recognizable—Le Smoking will forever be associated with his name—and also the one that most discreetly emphasizes the woman who is wearing it, as if by drawing her into the shadows it committed her to be daring and bold, to possess the night, to be both he and she, and to stand in a role that reveals men's vulnerability and women's true power: living not for procreating but for creating their personalities. As Elsa Peretti said in a hoarse voice, "The Saint Laurent tuxedo is the item of clothing that I've worn the most in my life. Normal things don't look good on me, alas."

"Dressed this way, a woman is at ease in her clothing, and her boldness is in her unexpected accessories and jewelry," Yves said, with his usual demanding vision. One had to have an attitude worthy of him, of the possibility he offered to play all the roles. To be a woman who saw another woman home. To walk in your high heels just as comfortably as if you were barefoot. To lead the conversation when other women, burdened by the need to be charming and cheerful, limited themselves to replying. Transforming the flaws of your irregular, imperfect body into a will to power. "It's by perfecting the essential items of clothing—a wonderful position—that I have created my style, that I have become what I am, and by doing this, I've gone beyond fashion."[16] Was he revealing his inner motivations? He seemed to have felt before others the danger of a decade: the breaking up of the world into a thousand little narcissistic individualities, into a thousand solitudes with no public. Fashions would blink and then die. He would resist them, being indifferent to what was momentary. But the break was there.

"My ambition is destructive," Yves Saint Laurent admitted. There were 160 Rive Gauche boutiques worldwide in 1981. Together with Indreco, Yves Saint Laurent had bought Mendès. Rive Gauche produced 70,000 pieces per year. Two hundred eight licensing agreements had been signed. "Thanks for the magnificent spectacle of your collection. The lines, the colors, the embroideries, the jewels. So much beauty 'cleanses the eye' of the sad sights of the everyday," actress Edwige Feuillère wrote to Yves.

In January 1982, Yves Saint Laurent celebrated the twentieth anniversary of his company at the Lido. As golden as an imperial eagle in her Saint Laurent jacket, Diana Vreeland gave the couturier the International Fashion Award from the Council of Fashion Designers of America. There were 1,000 guests at this "family party," a gala evening that cost 100,000 dollars. Catherine Deneuve wore Le Smoking. Jacqueline de Ribes looked like a black bird in her feathers. Horst talked about Greta Garbo with Cécile de Rothschild. Everyone who was anyone was there.

In his speech, Yves Saint Laurent, who looked very fit and was just a bit of a ham, couldn't stop himself from joking about the buyers, who weren't there. "We need their oil," he said, laughing. He resembled William Sheller singing *"Donnez-moi du ketchup pour mon hamburger... du gasoline pour mon chopper. Je serai votre pop star, je serai votre king. C'est une question... de feeling."*

Haute couture had started to disappear from the ritzy neighborhoods of Paris. In 1982, a haute couture garment cost between 16,000 and 65,000 francs (6,250 and 25,400 in 2017 dollars). But Yves remained a "restless and skittish child prodigy," the Little Prince who could rediscover "the little girls of his childhood": "With each of his designs, he seemed to try to revive, as if in a dream, light, acidic, and somnambulistic grace."[17]

In February 1982, *Le Jardin des Modes* published all of Yves's correspondence with Michel de Brunhoff. The maison de couture gave Yves a gift to commemorate its twenty-year anniversary: *Bravo Yves*, with the title in red letters, a splendid scrapbook with graphic design by Antoine Kieffer, the art director. On the cover was the famous picture of the "young man on the balcony" taken at Dior. Everyone in Yves's circle helped to create the book, which was full of anecdotes and accolades. "Don't put me next to Yves," Matthieu Galey is said to have requested of Pierre Bergé once. "I feel as if I'm next to his Royal Highness!"

But something shifted after that anniversary.

Now he was caught in his own trap. It was as if he had fallen in love with his character, in the same way he was in love with his body ten years earlier. He would be tested by his perpetual flight from reality into the "ciné réalité" that Loulou mentioned.

Like an actor, he played roles, and like so many other things in his life, those roles had been determined back in Oran: Queen Margot surrounded by her characters—the nursemaid, the confessor, the clown, the servant, the two lovers. She made the more recent one, the peasant Julien, more dignified by elevating him to Lord Saint-Julien. As Loulou put it, "As a child, Yves cut out a theater. He never gave it up. Whoever was able to follow him could do so." A passionate relationship with Jacques de Bascher, the Rasputin of Le Palace, lover of Karl Lagerfeld's, continued to haunt the history of Parisian nightlife. "He had the imagination of a knight. He liked to cultivate his country squire thing," said Paloma. "People projected their fantasies onto him." "I think he was a snobby idiot, but he had a nice decadence," said Loulou. "He was very obsessed with Yves. Then it became clear that his life was falling apart. He embraced fantasies, and caused them. We went out to have fun. It was less vicious. Yves is more mental. Everything's in his head. De Bascher went much too far. So it became very dangerous. With Karl and Pierre sitting in the middle, not really knowing what to do." On March 5, 1983, at the five-year anniversary celebration for Le Palace, Roxanne Lowit, "the girlfriend of the Divine" according to Karl Lagerfeld, photographed the two old friends, Yves and Karl, who still seemed to be very close. But they wouldn't be seen together again after Lagerfeld became artistic director at Chanel that year. From then on, they were linked by a professional rivalry: "It is important to have a style, but you have to recharge it like a battery," said Karl Lagerfeld. According to Paloma Picasso, "For a very long time, Yves was number one and Karl was number two; his aggressiveness came out at that time. The problem is that he never became number one—Yves was unquestionable."

Lagerfeld was tasked with giving a new look to Chanel. Around this time, Yves became the couturier shrouded in mystery: "These are the ghosts that protect me from the outside, that keep me company in this separate world that I invented for myself in my childhood. With age, imagination, like a river, sweeps along all the painting, literature, sculpture, and music that I carry inside myself and is expressed in the collections, these highlights of my work."

The maison de couture was his family. It was his refuge, even if he sometimes played with their expectations: "When he sees that everyone is worried about him, he does more so that they'll leave him alone. He has incredible resistance. But by playing this game he has destroyed himself. His body deserted him," said a source close to Yves.

Large glasses barricaded his face, whose flaws had been accentuated over time: the nose was wider, the mouth more horizontal, and his features grew heavier from alcohol use. He sought images and good luck charms: a duffle coat he had bought in Trouville in the 1970s, a scarf that made him look like a student who escaped from a boring party. "Why does he so rarely see himself young?" asked his friend François-Marie Banier in the catalogue *Bravo Yves*. "Does he forget that he's able, at any moment, to jump into his navy blue VW Bug and wipe out a police officer on the wet pavement?" Did he forget that he made the high society folks tremble by posing nude? That, like Naughty Lulu, to prevent boredom, his greatest enemy, he often thought about setting something on fire, about mooning three ministers having dinner at his friend's house? Banier "interviewed" the fictional character Naughty Lulu, who revealed a secret about Yves: "He often said that to relax the atmosphere there's nothing better than getting up on the table and showing your derrière."

Henceforth, his way of shocking would be to criticize the almost good enough, the deformed, the improvised, spontaneity—both real and false—and reality, when it was not idealized. In the early 1980s, this allergy to reality was expressed through a violent rejection of the street: "It's dirty, negative. I hardly go out anymore, but I just have to see one or two punks hanging around to understand." Warhol felt the same revulsion for these "dirty kids." He seemed less bothered by what the punks were than by what they awakened in him, as if they rubbed salt into his wounds. An era was ending, and skin was being peeled off. Yves seemed to live with many enemies he had confronted inside himself, and he had too many bleeding wounds to endure the spectacle that was exhibited before him: the cry of a dying world. He'd been the first to yell, "no future," the punk of a classical age: "And this sudden silence is so terrible, so desperately empty, so tragically disturbing that I can't help but think that the death of your voice was a fatal omen. It was the sign. It was the portent of the twilight into which we would sink. It was the end of the world of which you were the last festival, the last decoration, the ultimate flame."[18]

He would continue to play his role—like Ludwig, of whom people wondered every season, "Can the king still govern?" From his ivory tower, he observed the comings and goings of the court, "the paid friends," as one of Yves's servants said. Yves Saint Laurent became invisible.

The king suffered from an incurable mental illness. "Why this silence?" wondered François-Marie Banier in *Vogue* in March 1982. "Do you think Yves Saint Laurent is handsome? That's not so important to him now. Seducing, yes, perhaps. Do you want to protect him? Don't get too close. He fears embraces, these arms that put him into prison. While he speaks to you in his slightly muffled voice, with its childlike timbre, a subtle film is developing in him. He doesn't ask you to take precautions; he takes them with you. Extremely polite, nothing appears on his face, no emotions." The article was illustrated with a photo by Irving Penn taken in 1958, one of his favorite portraits. People waited for an audience with him. "Of course, every year, the month before, they start saying that it's not as good, that he's finished, that he's collapsing, that he's destroying his life and his pencils at the same time; every year they think he's dead to his friends and dead to couture, and every year they leave his first collection stunned and confused, and, if they're in good faith, delighted,"[19] Françoise Sagan had already written two years earlier.

Yves went to see his psychoanalyst five times a week. He now wore only black suits with dark ties. "The only thing to wear after age forty," he said. Yet hadn't he dressed that way when he was twenty years younger? He copied letters about suffering and framed them. Volume nine of Proust's correspondence became his bedside reading. And in these letters written by the novelist in 1909, in which he complained about his constant asthma attacks, Yves found the justification for renouncing life in society: "Anything, except going there, as I'm sick," Proust wrote to Max Daireaux around May 1909. So he sent flowers. Many flowers. Never enough. Armfuls of arum lilies. Orchids. Roses by the hundreds, in every shade. "They are always white. He chooses them one by one for me," said Francine Weisweiller, who still lived in the mansion on the Place des États-Unis. Smoking cigarettes that looked bigger than she was, she told stories about Venice with Cocteau, and the past that would never return: "Chanel was suits. Balenciaga was elegance. Then, there was Yves."

"I see life with the eyes of a child," said Yves. "That's why I don't age. My life is my profession, which continues youth, and where I project my dreams, memories, and thoughts into the future. One day, wisdom mixes into the rest, and you win freedom, you open yourself up more to others and to your era." Yet was it perhaps because he turned his back on his time that he escaped death? "He became sad in time. And I got married. If we're still alive, it's purely chance," said Loulou.

In gay circles, people were starting to talk about a strange illness that was mentioned for the first time in the *New York Times* in the summer of 1981. The death of Fabrice Emaer from cancer on June 11, 1983, truly marked the end of those years of opulence and madness. Farewell, dream baby. Farewell to Fabrice, who didn't hesitate to crack open 3,000 bottles of champagne for his friends for the opening party at the Palace in Cabourg. "It ended like the end of *La Dolce Vita*, with people sleeping on the beach," Guy Cuevas recalled. The prince was able to burst open Parisian castes and make the city feel like a true capital, attracting bohemians and punks, cross-dressers from the Bois de Boulogne on roller skates and the grandes dames of the jet set. "Bar owners have replaced the aesthetes," the survivors would say. For the new plague was devastating. In 1983 in Paris, Professor Luc Montagnier's team at the Institut Pasteur isolated HIV, the human immunodeficiency virus. The AIDS era had begun.

Yves Saint Laurent didn't go to Le Palace anymore, which caused rumors ("He's been grounded by Pierre Bergé!"), only adding to the legend of his reclusiveness. "I remember twenty years ago. I remember his laugh, his charm. Those around him have convinced him that he's this old gentleman now,"[20] said Karl Lagerfeld. Pierre Bergé acknowledged, "He's the cheapest staff member in terms of expenses!" The stage curtain would fall in 1983: at Paris's Théâtre du Rond-Point, he dressed Madeleine Renaud for *Savannah Bay*, a play written and directed by Marguerite Duras. After that, Yves did not design costumes for the stage again until 1993, when he designed a black dress for Zizi Jeanmaire.

While Karl Lagerfeld became a busy man, Yves Saint Laurent was recognized as the guardian of the memory of a past world. His universe was centered on the goal of designing dresses, which was his only consolation for all the tragedy—tragedy ironically born of those same dresses. Before their arrival he lived his most beautiful years. Finally, he could once again and for always become the child who dreamed of designing dresses for actresses, for women with countless lives: "Women are dual: he understood that during the day, we need to convince, and at night, to seduce," said Catherine Deneuve. For Deneuve, who opened the Cannes Film Festival in 1982, besides the smoking and the peacoat, two garments symbolize Yves Saint Laurent's world the best: "The almost sinful evening dress. Extremely elegant, but incredibly revealing. And then in the day, the suit, made to resist aggressiveness, men in the street, outside pressure. His clothing is very Doctor Jekyll and Mister Hyde. Very severe during the day, very debauched at night."

Debauched? His universe absorbed more and more references.

Starting at this time, he showed a black dress with red shoes in each collection, summer or winter. It was his way of punctuating the seasons, designed like the chapters of a story with divas in taffeta and the Tiepolo red evening coats of Oriane de Guermantes, whose clothing stunned with a triumphant air: "You had an all-red dress, with red shoes, you were unique, you looked like a great flower of blood, like a ruby in flames."[21]

In his long interview with Yvonne Baby,[22] he talked about his mother "going to the ball," of "the wait for the last kiss," as if he had to justify his own childhood and sometimes turn it into a Proustian pastiche. All these facets revealed the complexity of a character, the foreigner who had become ambassador of Paris, the story of a bourgeois man avid for honors, like Swann, the son of a Jewish foreign exchange broker who moved in aristocratic circles in the Faubourg Saint-Germain. Yves's consuming ambition, stimulated by the frustration of being a simple tradesperson, made him become in the 1980s everything that a couturier had never dared to hope to be: a painter, a man of the theater, a king, a patron of the arts, a man of taste who identified with the hero of Proust's *Remembrance of Things Past*: "Swann was one of those men who, having lived for a long time in the illusions of love, have seen the comfort that they have given to several women increase the women's happiness without creating any gratitude on their part, any tenderness toward them; but in their child, they believe they feel an affection that, embodied in their name itself, will make them live on after their death."[23]

In interviews, the rebel hid behind Proust quotations as he had previously hidden behind his shyness. He used them to parry, as a way of immobilizing his adversary, but especially so he could continue talking about himself, through another. "In what deep sadness did he find this unlimited ability to create?" he often said during interviews, quoting one of his favorite sentences.[24] "He was a being who was completely consumed by his work, a being who suffered deeply and who sacrificed his life so that this work could be the most perfect and the most astonishing," he said of his favorite writer.

He seemed to be working inside a gilded cage, where everything was organized to allow him to take a break from reality. Gabrielle Buchaert, the company's press officer, registered interview requests in black in her beautiful handwriting. "My job is to say no." They announced his hours. He got up at 7:30 AM and went to the office around 9:30. As of early 1979, he practically gave up any social life. He spent the month of August in a house he rented with Pierre Bergé near Trouville and watched over the renovations on his house, "an Agatha Christie–style castle," he announced.

He re-created worlds: that of Marcel Proust (Château Gabriel, in Bénerville-sur-Mer, near Deauville) and that of Jacques Majorelle, the son of the cabinetmaker from Nancy (Villa Oasis in Marrakesh). In Paris, he shut himself away in a world borrowed from Marie-Laure de Noailles and Chanel, where the scent of lilies and the sparkle of rock crystal suggested that he could only live when reflected in the image of these historical characters: "I cannot live in a room that has no mirrors. When there aren't any, the room is dead."

Just as Swann visited his former acquaintances—after belonging to "higher society"—Yves Saint Laurent chose in his house objects whose value had to do with the people to whom they had belonged: the Baron de Rédé, Chanel, the King of Belgium, the Archduke of Austria, whose coat of arms was engraved on a silver bowl. There, a candlestick from Maria de' Medici, here a large hexagonal crystal from Misia Sert: he liked the way the light moved inside, "as in a mirror."

The man who considered museums to be "dead places" lived surrounded by his treasures. And yet, according to Rafael Lopez Sanchez, "He doesn't have a landowner's attitude at his home. He's there, he goes into the kitchen, he steals a piece of bread."

Yves's apartment on Rue de Babylone became one of the most photographed "retreats" of the decade. The entrance door to the building was monitored by an electronic eye. "I don't collect, I accumulate," said the couturier. As one of Yves's acquaintances put it, "The house is for objects, not for people."

The objects seemed to wait for the visitors to leave so they could crawl, move, knock into each other, hold each other in a struggle that would set the bronze Hercules by Giambologna and the Senufo bird against all those snakes, cameos, bronzes, daggers in their velvet cases bursting from everywhere, in the midst of candelabra and lucky wheat sheaves. "There are people who change apartments every three years. But I move objects around, that gives them new life," he said.

As one entered, on the right was the mirrored room by Claude Lalanne, whose frames were twisted with pink water lilies. "I wanted something like Amalienborg, a dream room with little furniture and an aquatic atmosphere. Some nights, it can be a bit disturbing." The large parlor on the ground floor became a veritable modern art museum. What was their first purchase? Yves said a Mondrian, while Pierre thought it was a de Chirico. During the 1980s, the collection expanded still more: Fernand Léger (*Cubist Still-Life with Chess Board*, 1917), Picasso (*The Stool*, 1914), Matisse (his first *papier collé*, from 1937), Cézanne (*La Montagne Sainte-Victoire*), a Vuillard painting of the artist's mother and sister from 1890, but also works by Bonnard, Braque, Gainsborough, Munch, Delacroix, Klee, and the *Portrait de Madame de La Rue* by Ingres. Wherever one looked, there was something beautiful to see, even on the doors, where studies by Delacroix were discreetly hung. Everything was reflected in a large mirror. On the other side of the room, on an easel, was Goya's *L'Enfant Bleu*, a portrait of a child with a dog. Along with snakes (the chair with cobras by Eileen Gray) and birds, strange animals seemed to meet in the shadows of an opulent greenhouse with sofas upholstered in panther, obelisks made of rock crystal, and columns that were often grouped in pairs, like the two Nigerian dolls that were the bodyguards of an Etruscan vase. "Symmetry soothes me, and the lack of symmetry disturbs me," Yves said, as if the loneliness of an object was much more intolerable for him than the loneliness of a man. He liked to multiply fateful connections, placing, for instance, an enamel plate featuring Henri II with a fleur-de-lis on the spot of his fatal wound next to an enamel cup that belonged to Diane de Poitiers, Henri

II's mistress, with a fleur-de-lis painted on the bottom, humorously pre-empting Proust's judgment: "The more dubious the titles, the more space is given to crowns on the glasses, silver, stationery, and trunks."[25]

Here is the inventory of the décor at a dinner given by Yves Saint Laurent in honor of *Women's Wear Daily*: a 1930 Brandt marble table, eighteenth-century Compagnie des Indes plates, 1930 silver bread baskets and place settings, Napoleon III crystal glasses and carafes, silver cigarette cups, lily white linen napkins (Arène), a Sèvres porcelain centerpiece by François-Xavier Lalanne featuring water lilies and ducks, Vieux Paris knives, and more. On the console table, a rock crystal pyramid (Misia Sert collection). How distant the whole obsession with looking chic seemed from such profound moments, when his entire being was concentrated and he found the right lines.

And the abundance of articles about Yves Saint Laurent's houses in home decorating magazines, which proliferated during the 1980s, recalls the way that Swann with his overflowing of proper names and his habit of displaying the origins and references of every object publicized a high-society dinner, an invitation, a visit, the kind word of an acquaintance. Proust described this snobbery with a scathing sentence: "In this way, the Swanns' living room was like hotels in spa cities where telegrams are tacked up."

"Remembrance of Things Past. The First Look at Yves Saint Laurent's Proustian Fantasy." The first story—on four full pages—appeared in *Women's Wear Daily* on January 14, 1983. The house, designed by Ernest Saintin for an American client in 1874 and completed in 1883, was described as "distinctly unsocialistic" by the American magazine. Yves and Pierre purchased it in 1980. This neo-Gothic retreat was located in Bénerville, near Deauville; Proust was said to have met Gaston Gallimard there. But Proust's "little train," which went along the coast between Trouville and Houlgate, no longer stopped at Bénerville, so Pierre had a private landing strip built, enabling him to get there in twenty-five minutes in his white AS 342 helicopter. "He bought a jacket to pilot it in. Yves looked at him, always a little bit mocking," John Fairchild recalled. The house had a total of twenty rooms, twelve chimneys, a seventy-four-acre garden, and was maintained by six people year round. "This place is one of the craziest ideas I've ever had," Yves told *Women's Wear Daily*. The stone pediment had no coat of arms. What could they engrave on it? The incorrigible Jacques Chazot had an idea: "Oh, a thimble and needle!"

Everything modern was banned, except in the kitchen. Most of the fabrics, including yellow taffeta and red velvet, were produced in Lyon from Victorian-era cartoons. The ground floor had a dining room, two parlors, whose opulent Napoleon III atmosphere—with upholstered armchairs overflowing with silk and crystal chandeliers with pendants—recalled the set of Zeffirelli's *La Traviata*, as did the conservatory, where more than thirty varieties of green plants grew. It took Jacques Grange, Yves's decorator and friend, two years of searching to find all the furniture, most of which was from the nineteenth century. He stated, "I didn't want to reread Proust, so I wouldn't be influenced."

Yves asked him to design the rooms to evoke characters in *Remembrance of Things Past*. Engraved copper plates were screwed onto the doors: Swann (Yves's three-room suite), Charlus (Pierre's suite), and other characters including Elstir, the Guermantes, and Madeleine Lemaire. The Madeleine Lemaire door opened onto a room of roses—half a kilometer of woven silk hanging from the windows and walls—where the visitor seemed to hear Odette's perfumed words: "Look, they're princes, they've risen in rank." The guests were assigned rooms according to the roles that Swann and Charlus gave them. And as at the maison de couture, where an old tradition required that the most recent worker had to change her name if there was already someone with that name—being called Lucette during the day and going back to Isabelle at home—the game started. On a little card with Gothic lettering and the image of Château Gabriel, Yves Saint Laurent assigned rooms like roles. Charlotte Aillaud was Oriane de Guermantes, Anne-Marie Muñoz was Albertine, her husband José Muñoz was Elstir, Loulou and Thadée Klossowski were the Verdurins, Betty Catroux was Madeleine Lemaire, and Madison Cox was Morel.

Was it like the movies, where they say any resemblance to actual persons is purely coincidental? Was Pierre Bergé, like Charlus, really the kind of man who could let a queen die "rather than missing his appointment with the hairdresser who was to curl his hair"? The man whose "boundless chatter" was described by the narrator?[26] And was Madison Cox, like Morel, the man who "thrilled Baron de Charlus' senses"? In private, Yves called him "the Madonna." Was Yves Saint Laurent really Swann, who, after attaining "a prophet's age," saw everyone look at his face, "so finely carved by illness"?

There is certainly some affinity in appearance between Charlotte Aillaud, so long and slender in her Saint Laurent dresses that brushed her skin, and Oriane de Guermantes, described by Proust in this way: "Her neck and shoulders emerged from a snowy wave of mousseline, which was occasionally struck by a swan-feather fan." And there are other similarities to be found. It can be fun to search for the key, and to find random connections in an anecdote (true or false) or story about the habits of the little clan. But we pursue only phantoms. The only certainty is that the Saint Laurent clan certainly existed. It was a tribe, a chapel inside the world of fashion, which has its offshoots in the realms of politics, theater, and literature. "The left and the right don't exist. There are only human beings, who suffer just as much, rich or poor. Some are obliged to be privileged."[27]

But the question remains: how could this man, who ten years earlier had stripped naked, exhibit his mystery in this way? How could this man, whose job was to give life to something that was thought to be inanimate, choose to renounce his own life and take on another that was written, organized, and prepared in advance? There is a kind of doubling of Yves Saint Laurent: the man who aimed for what

Proust called "the suspected truth," and the other Yves Saint Laurent, who in life seemed to seek only the imitation of this truth. In Paris, he had to have a "frothy" fountain and a garden as "mysterious" as the one in Cocteau's *Beauty and the Beast*. In Deauville, he had to have the doors he saw in Visconti's *The Innocent*. A bedroom like that in *India Song*, the film by Marguerite Duras that he said he "adored." In the middle of Normandy, he planted pine trees, and dug a lake like Ludwig. He asked a painter named Mériguet to paint Monet's water lilies to give him "the impression of living in water." In front of the Monet-inspired frescoes in the large salon, he placed a painting by the pre-Raphaelite painter Burne-Jones, like a piece of the past—Talitha Getty, Marrakesh, the end of the 1960s—that had been turned into an image. According to Jacques Grange, "Yves has a very spontaneous and very funny nature. But money has separated him from daily life. He was taken care of, watched over by his chauffeur. He's King Tut buried in the tomb. You go off into his delusions. He chooses the place, the spirit, and I translate. It's very easy, because he is extremely clear in the definition of what he likes. There are always many references. To Coco Chanel, Art Deco, Pierre Loti. But everything is mixed together—it becomes a Saint Laurent sauce. He has this great tradition of quality. Pierre Bergé grumbles and he follows him. He trusts his aesthetic sense."

Roland Petit described Yves's residences in this way: "In Paris, you're at the Musée d'Art Moderne. At Deauville, you're with Proust. Yves loves to have shows around him. Now, what do you think he wanted to stage? A Visconti-style ballet? No. *Die Fledermaus*? Of course not. He told me one day what his dream was: a contemporary *Threepenny Opera* that would take place in the year 2000. I saw Pierre and talked to him about the project. He replied: 'Don't take it on.'" Roland Petit, who describes the 1950s and 1960s with nostalgia, got burned by the last show, in 1977: "The dresses arriving with pins, I think it was self-destruction."

He had that tough attitude that the most vulnerable sometimes employ to protect themselves from harm that they know they'll be exposed to first. "I don't fear death. I know that death can come at any moment, but it's strange and egotistical, I don't have the feeling that it would transform my life."[28]

He displayed a strange indifference to pain, especially that of others. "When you're sick, with Yves, it's better not to mention it," said someone who was close to him. But his hypersensitivity affected areas other than his heart. "He can be moved by a little wool muslin!" emphasizes Madame Felisa. But in there was no trace of condescension. "Except for Mademoiselle, it was the first time I had dinner at a couturier's house," said the hairdresser Alexandre. "But Chanel didn't invite me—she asked me to stay. As for the others, they didn't think of it." Paul, his chauffeur, went with him every morning to the maison de couture: "We came back home at lunchtime. Then we'd leave again. He always sat next to me, with his dog [Moujik II] in back. Except on days when he was with a guest."

Everything about his attitude proved that he was struggling, at the height of a position that seemed to establish him permanently in the media's eyes. The Americans called him "the Picasso of fashion," and the media considered him an artist, placing him in a privileged position. For a long time, there had, of course, been a special relationship between couturiers and art. Doucet had purchased Picasso's *Les Demoiselles d'Avignon.* Chanel, the first tradesperson to be received in high society, financed the Ballets Russes; Schiaparelli worked with Cocteau, Bérard, Vertès, and Man Ray. Dior had known the Paris of the Roaring Twenties—his friends at the time were Henri Sauguet, Max Jacob, and Erik Satie—before managing an art gallery. Each of them participated directly in the center of artistic movements of their era, like Saint Laurent during the time of Andy Warhol and Pop Art, in the early years of Rive Gauche. They made art without knowing it.

Yet Yves Saint Laurent acted as an artist in a deeper sense: by describing the movement of time, and making its passage look unforgettable. Once again, in discussing his work, he expressed most sincerely the qualities that he liked to find in writing and painting. He was a couturier who talked about "concentration" and "silence." "For in a dress, the most important thing is the material, that is, the fabric and the color. You can make a pretty design, you can put all the knowledge of your profession into a design—if you don't have the material, you lose your dress. The anxiety isn't about wondering about the placement of the pockets or the belt, the shape of the neckline, or the cut. It's about you facing the fabric and the color, since you have to tap into the material, just like the painter with his brushes or the sculptor with his clay. And it's the material you have to conquer, so that a dress will correspond to what you imagine."[29]

As an artist, he gave emotion the way others gave knowledge. He didn't teach anything beyond what people knew already. Many cultured people would be disappointed to hear him say "aerodrome" instead of airport, or to learn that he read *Paris Match,* loved chocolate, and made spelling errors. That when he said good night to his servants, Bernard, Boujemaa, and Albert, he would sometimes watch TV with them. That he still liked chicken, ham-and-butter sandwiches, and his dog Moujik II. As well as oompah bands, Charles Trenet, and Juliette Gréco singing about Paris. He always drew on a wooden board covered with good luck charms given to him by his models: a plastic Statue of Liberty, a porcelain Moujik. "All the designers have superb studios. Yves has a slummy side that you wouldn't expect. He draws. The dog pisses," Loulou said. "Disorder doesn't bother him at all. It's his Eastern side. He needs people close to him to whom he can say, 'My God, I've done nothing.' He's comfortable in this job with the people who do this job. He hates being harassed. What does he hate? Grotesque and forced things. Theater productions without updated settings. A self-satisfied attitude. When he doesn't like something, he says, 'It's trying too hard,' 'it's too fashionable,' 'too many details.'"

He had started writing again, working on "the story of a man and a woman who meet in a bar in Singapore. I love ports, because of the sea, I love the lights at night and the glimmer of the coasts. The night makes me think of black mousseline, one of my favorite materials." The announced collection of stories would never be published. "Writing? I dropped it. My head isn't in it. It will come back, full of dresses, I hope."[30]

He was forty-seven years old, and, someone close to him told me, dreaded the "fateful time of leaving for the maison de couture." However, that was where he seemed to experience his greatest happiness: "While you're working on it, a collection belongs to you, it's sacred." And this happiness he aimed for as he rose higher and higher was only a reason to come back down even lower each time: "As soon as the collection is given over to other people, you feel a violent feeling of frustration. You're dispossessed. Then depressed. Then it fades. Then comes the moment I love very much: you have the joy of having given, you see the women dressed, the dresses start to live. And life starts up again."[31]

Yet he experienced a torpor that seemed only to be interrupted—except for those moments of excitement—by the strident ringing of those pointless hours, those days when he wandered, a stranger to himself. Tormented by fear, taunted by doubt. All that for, as Pierre Bergé said, "a profession that doesn't require such high standards and such talent....Perhaps that is why he is unhappy."

His duty was dresses, which were also a vision of the world. Nothing small or sappy or insipid. A black line. Three spots of color. It vibrated. A large piece of jewelry. Eyes that shot flames. His dresses were a way of fighting another battle, a challenge that was a bit suicidal, but the only one that mattered. He could anticipate troubles, joys, desires, hell, and design them, making everyone think that all this was only about clothes. He could hold the room, charm it with springtime whites, and then, suddenly, a spot of lemon yellow appeared, his way of seeing Paris again, of saying, "Hello, old sun." He had skies of fog and others, blue-green, that were soaked in light.

There were other influences that were even stronger than that of Picasso. Delacroix wanted painters to go to Morocco to see "ready-made paintings." And if there is another artist to whom Yves Saint Laurent seemed linked by his sensibility, it was Matisse, in his treatment of Morocco, that "lion-colored" land, where he surprised women in green with yellow slippers, blue landscapes, and "interiors with eggplants." And we find there the same intensity of light.

On the runway, his colors stunned: a dress in purple taffeta shadowed with tulle, a bolero jacket of turquoise feathers. Why were his reds more red? His pinks more pink? His blacks more black? His blues so intense? How did he match porcelain blue with turquoise blue, strike orange against lemon yellow without leaving any acidic taste? Yves Saint Laurent, thanks to the palette of colors that he mastered, would avoid all the neons and metallic, urban blacks of the 1980s, just as he avoided the pearly hues and psychedelic shades of the 1960s, and the beiges and ugly browns of the 1970s.

*

By seeking his balance on the sharpest summits of sensation, he gave fabrics an expressive force that was unusual in haute couture. It was usually only in the theater that colors were described in this way: Titian, Veronese, and Matisse greens, Cranach red, Frans Hals black, Goya gray. But he added to this tradition a special connection with matter and attitude: his Van Dyck brown was very often attached to mousseline, where everything was draped, moving, dissolved, and his Velázquez green crackled and shone on the bodies of the great ladies of Spain. With colors from the cinema (black), literature (pink), tragedy (red), and his Mediterranean dreams (blues and greens), Yves Saint Laurent would restore something unique. A fleeting art that would be the sum of all the arts, glimpsed for a fraction of a second, the instant of a page in color, a sound painting, a piece of music to read, a woman who passes by.

Because everything he loved faded and disappeared, his only joy would be to encircle the body to learn all its secrets, carefully discovering the desire of all women, by offering the body a thousand masks to attach to a face. The design changed. It was necessary to have seen many women in order to be able to draw a single one that way. On the page, the line became more airy, more drawn out, followed the secret slopes of a body dressed in a gown that showed everything without letting anything be seen. But the face was empty. There were no more eyes, no mouth, no nose, just an oval, as if the name of the beloved had been erased.

He found his well-being in these quasi-aquatic universes: the room of mirrors in his apartment on Rue de Babylone, the pond with water lilies in Marrakesh that seemed to have come from a Virginia Woolf story, the lake in Deauville, which he enlarged, because he found it too small: "A lake isn't a puddle!" He had once lived on a barge, and even once talked about drowning himself in the Seine, with his neck weighed down by a bronze candelabrum. The waters seemed to hold all kinds of dreams, lamentations, secrets, voices rising up from the depths, which had always attracted him irresistibly: "If Narcissus drowned himself, it's because he glimpsed his soul. The mirror in which thought is reflected is sometimes more dangerous than the uncontrolled waters of a lake in a storm. It lets us see such terrible things that at every moment we risk death. By loving ourselves too much we end up perceiving in ourselves irrevocable things that are so terrible that the revelation kills us."

He distilled fragrances from his past life, as if these scents could conjure up the uninterrupted telling of an old story, real or imaginary. In 1971, he had caused a controversy by posing nude for Rive Gauche, a fragrance that reminded so many men of all those they had loved. Ten years later, he launched another men's cologne, Kouros, "the fragrance of the living gods." Through what alchemy did a long-ago vacation to the Aegean sea morph into a gay neo-antique ad, with a background of Greek columns and sensuous dives? The concept? The spirit of conquest. In the ad, a lithe young man displayed his muscles. More than 2,200 people were invited to a gala for the launch of the cologne on February 20, 1981 at the Opéra Comique, where Rudolf Nureyev would perform.

But the bigger launch was Paris, a fragrance for the lady in pink. Ever since his Impressionist collection (summer 1981), this new character strolled down the runway every season. She didn't wear a tuxedo, and she dreaded an offense that would break her heart—which was more delicate than Venetian glass—into a thousand sharp little pieces. She was adorable, and her battles were not the same as those of smart women; she wanted to please, while they wanted to convince. Her carnation-pink blouse enveloped her like a couturier's dream. This was the woman to whom he seemed to say, "You are too pretty to be mean."

He dedicated the haute couture show of summer 1983 to the lady in pink. He wrapped a rhinestone bracelet around her lithe ankle. A muse with violets, or a Sappho veiled with lace-embroidered tulle, this woman exuded nothing but a carefree spirit. For her he sewed onto his fabrics forget-me-nots, jasmine, pomegranate flowers, and zinnias, designing an organza blouse that looked like a bouquet of primroses. To her he offered polka-dots, straw hats that passed by to the tune of Charles Trenet's "Douce France." And crepe dresses, trembling with wisteria and violets, spreading around themselves the warm fragrance of a childhood: woman at her most capricious, fickle, flighty, greeting her admirers on an avenue with barely any sunlight. "I love pink accessories. Pink is beautiful with beige, brown, purple. It's a color that replaces white gloves."

She had a special way of wearing her suit, brightening it with a mousseline scarf. Pink lent a more light-filled and fragile effect than blue or yellow. With pink, Yves Saint Laurent suggested the sigh of a body shot through by fleeting desire, letting something tender and delicious be glimpsed. Like Madame Bovary, he colored all his dreams of love in rose. At the end of the haute couture show on July 28, 1983, Mounia, dressed as an island bride in white bird feathers, appeared under a veil like "the display of a swan-colored peacock." Her uplifted hands held a pink and black bottle. Josephine Baker sang, "J'ai deux amours, mon pays et Paris." Yves Saint Laurent proffered his farewell gift:

Paris. My new perfume. Paris, a gray-blue sky. The Eiffel Tower. A woman and a bouquet of roses. A crystal bottle. Who could better evoke the image of this impossible dream? How could anyone resist this woman's magic? In a single blow, she gave life to this fragrance. And suddenly, Paris without her. The Luxembourg Gardens in the early morning. All that was left were these two empty chairs that whisper stories, and the silent fountain. This woman who was glimpsed, was she unfaithful? Intoxicated by the scent of the roses, had we even agreed to a rendezvous? I am lost, abandoned. I see statues with their arms wrapped around each other, baroque stone decorations, and I find myself on Rue Saint Laurent. So there is a Rue Saint Laurent in Paris. A street where I could go for a walk with her, if I found her again.... I return to reality. I run onto the Pont Alexandre III, where, urged on by the legendary group of the Marly horses, I remain stunned by the flight of this heroic flag. But there are too many splendors, too many processions, too many glorious memories.... I prefer to fall back to earth. On this earth I must find this woman. Café de Flore. Garçon, coffee and hot croissants. Saint-Germain-des-Prés: outdoor cafés, a church tower, a few trees. A whole empire. And suddenly, I'm floating in a strange world. I see her, it's really her. I see her. I smell her perfume. The Eiffel Tower is a crest above her head. The street lamps cast a shadow on her and, mysteriously, she disappears into the Paris *métro*. I shout with all my strength. She vanishes into the crowd.[32]

Yves Saint Laurent was the only couturier who granted so much importance to his fragrances, which seemed to emanate from his dresses and his encounters. His temperament in this respect revealed him to be more sentimental than artistic. Paris was a potpourri of roses, violets, mimosas, and irises. It was as if he rediscovered his favorite heroine, Madame Bovary, at the point in the novel when "she wished she could stop living entirely, or sleep continuously."[33] In one of the great letters that he wrote at a time when, like her, he was more fatigued by "these great impulses of vague love" than by "great debauchery," he pursued his illusion: "Your scent nails me to a tree. I won't forget it. I will surely find you again one day. There exist a thousand places in Paris where I can see you again and crush your roses against my heart. Our roses. The most beautiful ones. Perhaps you were only an excuse to accomplish my dream: to give a fragrance to Paris. Prestigious Paris that dazzles. Your blazing, crackling fireworks make the world sparkle. For this new perfume, I chose your name because there is no more beautiful one. Because I love you. My Paris."[34]

An illusion? In February 1993, the fragrance's tenth anniversary, Paris was, along with Opium, one of the top fragrance lines sold in Europe, with a total of more than one billion francs in revenue (about 181,820,000 dollars in 1993). This single line contained twenty-one products. The fragrance had even become a color, Paris Pink. "One day, he came to the agency, all alone. He wanted the Eiffel Tower to be in the photo for the campaign," Denise Fayolle recalled sentimentally (along with Maïmé Arnodin, she headed Agence Mafia, which handled the advertising). Almost thirty years after his arrival in the capital, Yves had conquered the city to the point of having generated the fragrance that embodied it, its essence. Yves Saint Laurent was, along with Hubert de Givenchy, the last to defend haute couture, this matter of millimeters. But, like de Gaulle, Hubert de Givenchy defended *une certaine idée de la France* and recalled the women he had seen; Yves Saint Laurent added the fantasy of those in his dreams.

And his dreams had pursued him ever since Oran, where he wrote, in 1950:

You will run tenderly
To the home of your mistresses
With a bouquet of roses
A smile that is not at all morose
You will open the door,
"Léa, look what I've brought you!"

At age forty-seven, he had become a giant.

On December 5, 1983, a retrospective of twenty-five years of designs by Yves Saint Laurent opened at the Metropolitan Museum of Art. It was the first time that a living fashion designer was celebrated by the museum. The Costume Institute, which was headed by Diana Vreeland, had organized shows on themes such as the Belle Époque (1982), women in the eighteenth century (1981), traditional Russian costume, and deceased couturiers (including Balenciaga). At the same time, just down Fifth Avenue, the cultural services of the French Embassy held an exhibition of Yves Saint Laurent's designs for the theater. Diana Vreeland wrote the following to Yves by telegram: "Yves, you are the quicksilver and the touchstone of all current fashion. You are totally French, you are the most completely Parisian couturier. When I'm with you, I'm in Paris. You contain and you offer to all the wonder and magic of the most beautiful city in the world."[35] High praise from a woman whose judgment everyone feared. (In 1978, she had declared that Andy Warhol was no longer avant-garde.)

A great blue flag fluttered on the museum's façade: "Yves Saint Laurent: 25 Years of Design." "Nothing systematic, but a different setting in every room: one went from a couture house salon to a ballroom, from vivid lacquered colors to satiny shadows, from a botanical garden to a racecourse," the novelist Hervé Guibert wrote in *Le Monde*. It was the first time in the paper's history that it had run a story about a couturier on the front page: "The flowing gestures of the mannequins express his style. They walk on floors of daffodils, swoon to bursts of music: Josephine Baker, *Carmen*, Mozart, and the Beatles." This show would attract one million visitors between December 5, 1983 and September 2, 1984.

Guibert certainly wrote one of the most beautiful reviews of it, noting how it showed

that a couturier can and must be a geometrician, a passionate person who hasn't exhausted his abilities to love, an illusionist, a child, an astronomer, a naïf and a genius, a Sunday or nighttime writer, a copier, a tamer, a smooth-talker, and a clairvoyant. And that women don't want to resign themselves to being one thing, but all want to be saints and harpies, powerful forces and huntresses, virgins and courtesans, men, poor women and countesses, clowns and spies, calm young women under their gray wide-brimmed hats, and immobile world travelers. They travel into the history of painting, they become infantas, ladies-in-waiting, abstract; they travel into the history of theater, they slip into the skin of Shakespeare's heroines; they travel into the history of danger and blood, becoming toreadors who are toreadored. Yves Saint Laurent removes one foot from the Prado and projects it to the Hermitage, not the one in Leningrad but in Saint Petersburg. He lifts up a curtain from La Scala to hear Maria Callas sing one last time. He falls asleep on a luminous globe, and his Parisian women become illusions, they hunt elephants who look like Babar, they also travel inside his admirations, and acquire, from his pencil, heads that look as if they were drawn by Cocteau.[36]

The champagne flowed, and foie gras and salmon were served. His name was engraved on the 2,500 invitations that were sold starting May 15 (and sold out three days later, after the museum had turned down 800 people). They spared no expense for the gala evening held at the Met: after the sumptuous dinner, there was a ball in a room that the incomparable Jacques Grange had transformed into an emperor's garden with columns, a carpet of golden leaves, and tables draped with pink, red, and orange Abraham silk. "I worked from the cut-out cartoons of Matisse, which I adapted to the space. It's very simple, without details, like a Picasso drawing," he told *Women's Wear Daily*. On December 5, 1983, everyone who was anyone was there: Nancy Kissinger in a tunic dress with braided trim ("It was four years old," Janie Samet pointed out in *Le Figaro*); Jacqueline de Ribes, in a black velvet dress with rooster feathers. Yves Saint Laurent wrote, "She is the pearl set in the ear of the king of Poland, the cabochon emerald of the Queen of Sheba, the crescent of Diane de Poitiers, the ring of the Nibelungen. She's a castle in Bavaria, a great black swan, a royal orchid, an ivory unicorn. Her eyes are the reflection of the moon in the pools of Baden-Baden. She is the trembling feather that decorates the turban of a maharajah, the capricious and baroque curlicue. She is a Golconda diamond.... Above all, she is my friend and, on my knees, I kiss her hand." The countess was already a competitor, as she had opened her own maison de couture. Yet that night she honored the designer to whom she was most loyal. White lace for Marie-Hélène de Rothschild, black lamé for Paloma Picasso, black velvet with sky-blue flowers for Hélène Rochas, crushed velvet for Catherine Deneuve, velvet with gold details for Zizi, ruby red for Diana Vreeland. The festivities lasted a week. On December 3, Marie-Hélène de Rothschild had what she termed a "small and intimate" dinner: "Yves made a dress especially for me, it wouldn't be fair to reveal the surprise!" On December 4, Oscar de la Renta held a "very, very small" dinner in his apartment: twelve guests, "mainly Europeans," including Hélène Rochas, Alexis de Redé, Charlotte Aillaud, and Jacqueline de Ribes. On December 7, there was a lunch at Nan Kempner's with Annette and Sam Reed, Chessy and Bill Rayner, Jacqueline de Ribes, Loulou and Thadée Klossowski, Diana Vreeland, and Betty and François Catroux. On December 8, Jacqueline de Ribes invited forty people to Mortimer's. "This exhibition represents a very important date in my career," Yves had announced before leaving for New York. "Afterward, I will come back to work in my little atelier with Mounia, and a few meters of mousseline, to start my next collection."

In 1993, he talked about this show with particular emotion. "Diana Vreeland had special mannequins made for the dresses that went with them." He remembered their "special poses," which suggested the real-life movements of models. "Some looked abandoned. Others thrust into the air. There was also a big gallery of black dresses. It was splendid. And her that I love so much, that I've loved so much."

"Yves Saint Laurent is Paris, it's the *crème de la crème!*" his fans concluded. His American clients were the most numerous, but he seemed united to other women, who might never wear his clothes, by a connection that was more long-lasting and more invisible than a brand. He seemed to know these women without ever having met them. Like him, they believed in everything, in good luck charms, constellations, and bad angels. This woman hadn't learned the proper way to hold a knife and fork and went out to dinner without ever knowing if her bread plate was on her left or her right.

"I love lively, charming people, and the things of this world, the flame, the dancer and the dance. I'm thought to be hypersensitive, reclusive, and neurotic, which perhaps I am, but I hope that the year will not come, the moment when anxiety and fatigue will destroy my love for this life and all the things that inspire me: a line of music, a face by Vermeer, a character from opera, or a model born in Harlem. I love seeing how a model moves in my clothes, the way she gives them life, or, if they're bad, the way her life rejects them. A good model can advance fashion by ten years," he was quoted as saying in American *Vogue* in 1983.

The honors became obligatory over the years, as did the reasons to isolate himself with increasing solitude and invisibility. Journalists compensated for his physical absence by coming up with legends, describing the couturier in his library, listening to Maria Callas and reading Pierre Loti.

On May 3, 1984, Yves Saint Laurent and Pierre Bergé moved into their new house: they had bought the Villa Majorelle in Marrakesh, located in a palm grove. They gave it the name of a book by Eugène Dabit: Villa Oasis. The "House of Happiness in Serenity," the famous villa that was "pink like a woman's skin," became the villa of friends. There, under the trees, Moujik I, killed by a scorpion, was buried. Yves and Pierre had fallen "in love with a little mysterious garden, painted in the colors of Matisse, hidden in a forest of bamboo," Bergé recalled. So they purchased this house, which had been designed as a retreat by painter Jacques Majorelle.

Majorelle and Yves lived parallel lives. After all his travels in North Africa, the painter, for reasons of health (most likely tuberculosis), decided to settle in the villa in

1923. He gave up painting outside to paint in a studio. He built a house, Villa Bou Saf Saf. "He chose the soil of his existence outside the red walls of the west, at the place where the palm grove ends," wrote André Demaison. "It was an enclosed garden, he built a house there, by taking the best elements that both Moroccan architecture and the practical lines of modern comfort had to offer. Space and privacy, well-defined edges and suppleness, great tranquility of expression: these were all the signs of the country and the painter."[37] Was it chance that upon arriving in Morocco the painter also settled in a "little Arab box" located near the bazaar? "A mattress on a box spring on the ground will be our nuptial bed and we will live on rugs," he wrote to his wife at the time. He focused on painting genre scenes, Berber women with black turbans, Arab women in blue caftans, like those that Yves designed in the mid-1960s, because he saw them in the same way. "Imagine, my friend, what it's like to see Cato or Brutus walking in the streets at sunset, fixing shoes, and even having the same disdainful manner that masters of the world should have," the painter seemed to communicate to him. Yves Saint Laurent had seen and felt those blue-purple sunsets over the pink Kasbahs and this bustling of the city at twilight just as intensely, representing them in his Orientalist collections. But something had broken. "The 'house of the serpent' was small, and always full. This house was bigger, and usually empty," Betty Catroux said. She was his close friend and most regular guest, but she didn't stay in the Villa Oasis; instead she stayed in the Maison du Bonheur that had been added to the property. Architect Bill Willis explained in October 1992, "Over ten years separated the two houses. An eternity. That's the difference between the excitement of youth and the rest. I never saw him really live in the new house. . . . It's splendid. Every time, he brings wonderful things there. But what is there in this house?"

Heavy sandalwood doors opened onto a Moroccan salon with armchairs in dark wood from the Indies and cushions covered in cashmere. On the second floor, four corner rooms opened onto a little partially covered balcony that ran along the whole house. In the center, there was a little living room, the *minzah*, all in wood. There Yves Saint Laurent painted the ceiling beams in an astonishing range of shades of pink, ochre, and sea green, like a series of strips painted in watercolor. "I saw him take some boxer shorts and a page torn out of *Vogue* to discover the right shades," said Bill Willis, who, like others, noticed Yves's energy. Willis added, "Yves taught me about color."

The house had doors and lintels of sculpted cedar, coffered ceilings, and traditional Moroccan *zellige* (terra cotta tile work covered with enamel). Completed by the finest artisans in Fez, the massive project took four years: the entrance hall was painstakingly renovated to match the original design, and many rooms were entirely redesigned, including the dining room, the blue living room, and the library. One hundred people worked on the project. "With Pierre Bergé and Yves Saint Laurent, no detail is too small. When we showed Yves where the light switch went, he wanted to see a sample of the baseboard," recalled Bill Willis. It took nine months to get the perfect shades of blue and green for the traditional Moroccan painted flowers on a red background in the library, Yves's favorite room. An opulent coziness was created by paintings by Orientalist Théodore Frère (selected by Pierre Bergé), books by Nerval, Rilke, and Loti, and a chandelier of crystal and engraved bronze—from the Château de Grignan, dear to French author Madame de Sévigné. There was a tortoise clock (a nineteenth-century Chinese-inspired piece), two rock crystal candlesticks (also from the nineteenth century), and crystal palm trees bought at Maison Comoglio in Paris. The damask bench had belonged to a castle owned by the Rothschilds. In an alcove, a lantern from a thirteenth-century Syrian mosque illuminated Monvoisin's portrait of Ali Pasha of Ioannina and his last wife. "We redid everything, starting with the green *zellige* floors," explained Bill Willis. Water was once again the focus: Yves Saint Laurent asked Willis to create a blue bedroom where he would have "the feeling of being under the sea." Featuring a Syrian dresser inlaid with mother-of-pearl and striped silk curtains, the room, like a big aquarium, opened onto the garden with the water lilies. "He said to me, 'Bill, I see this house with the color of the water's reflections.'"

This cubist house built on a rectangular base released the heady scent of decadence. In colors of ochre, green, and blue, and topped with balconies and a pointed hat of tiles, the house was reflected in a great pool of papyrus sedge, bordered with golden bamboo and coconut palms. It was a Mediterranean garden: in the shade of the giant palm trees grew silver eucalyptus, red bougainvillea, and orange trees with shiny leaves, which contrasted with the green-gray of the cypress trees.

Majorelle had bought another plot of land in 1932. He brought in the rarest plant varieties, countless types of cacti, phoenix palms, banana trees, pink trumpet vines, blue geraniums, lemon trees, and bamboos. A great lover of gardens, Pierre Bergé would write sixty-two years later, in a very different style than that of his speeches: "Preparing the soil required great effort, plants were brought in from everywhere, springs were harnessed, waters were tamed. Pools imprisoned lotus flowers, water lilies, papyrus sedge, and elephant ears. A Moroccan pavilion was the starting point for a waterway that fed into a fountain. Pergolas held up bougainvillea of every color. A sun shelter protected the Lady Palms and the philodendrons....But however beautiful this may be, it could not be an ordinary garden. In the Orient, the English are the masters at the art of combining lawns and succulents, and all over the world, refined aesthetes prune plants with Latin names every morning. Just as periwinkle becomes beautiful and mysterious when it's called 'vinca major.'" Pierre Bergé praised Majorelle's genius at great length. "Indeed, he was the first to transform the landscape into a work of art....I said elsewhere that the garden married nature and painting, and I'd like to add that this is the first time we can apply this sentence by Nabokov to a landscape artist: 'We watch the artist build his castle of cards, and we watch the castle of cards become a castle of sparkling glass and steel.'"[38]

The former owner, "a bourgeois man from Casablanca," according to Mustapha, wanted to build a clinic and sell the garden to developers. "Then Monsieur Bergé got involved with the people he knew. A commission from the king came to see it," Mustapha said with a triumphal air. After restoring this part of the garden, Yves and Pierre decided to open it to the public. One hundred eighty thousand people visit it annually. At the entrance, a small sign indicates what is not allowed: "Dogs, cats, strollers, children who are under 12, or unaccompanied, unauthorized paintings and drawings. Fashion photos are not allowed."

Yves went to Marrakesh in a private plane about four times a year, after the shows. Up until 1978, he spent the month of August there, but afterward, he began going to Deauville. In Marrakesh, he would get up at 7:30, swim a few lengths in the morning—usually in the old pool—and walk in the Majorelle Garden between noon and 2:00 PM, when it was closed to tourists. Lovers had carved their names on the bamboo. He went out at twilight, when the sky became pink. He came back for dinner: "For Monsieur Bergé, it has to be fast and simple. As for Monsieur Saint Laurent, with scrambled eggs, a cold dish, or fillet of sole…he's happy." He received few guests. "Here, he doesn't read the newspaper, He comes here to forget it all, he's a family type," said Mustapha, who, having seen many people come through, took a moment to preach: "There are so many who hang around him for money. Flunkies. Manipulators. People who cause trouble. Before, when he was with a clan that had a lot of money, there was no jealousy or envy around him. If Monsieur Bergé set him free, he'd be ruined."

But the "Venice of the Orient," as Yves Saint Laurent called it, lost a bit of its magic every day. All his love for this "daughter of the desert" was coupled with the awareness of a world that was ending, this world that he knew intimately but which he was nevertheless not a part of. Boul de Breteuil didn't ask a designer to do her library. She didn't read Proust, but *Les Bonnes Fortunes* by Jean Orieux or *La Jeunesse d'Alexandre* by Roger Peyrefitte. There was a pleasant disarray at Boul's: stacks of letters, ballpoint pens in a silver christening mug, and a leather armchair with the patina of age. "I live in the country. I don't know what happens on the front lines," said this born comedian. Wealth that was even more recent than that of Yves Saint Laurent and Pierre Bergé had conquered the city. The energetic jet-set indulged in swimming pools with mosaic-tiled bottoms and other such extravagances. The men did business in their ultra-plush terrycloth bathrobes. They bought carved wood furniture with gold leaf details, feared antiques dealers, and slept on monogrammed pillowcases. The palm grove became "little Florida." The development of a huge tourist complex was announced for 1986. Pierre Bergé managed to torpedo the project. But tourism had become one of the city's main activities. Foreigners came to fill up on Vuitton mules and fake Cartier wallets. A Club Med opened just steps away from Djemaa El Fna square. On the way out, tour guides waited for the tourists: "A quick tour of the bazaar?" With Gucci t-shirts under their djellabas, women passed by on motor scooters. The luxury hotel La Mamounia was under construction. The Sahara Inn had grown like a bad dream. Meanwhile, Mustapha showed the house to journalists when Yves wasn't there. Yves's bedroom was wide open. On his bedside table was an old paperback copy of Cocteau's *Le Grand Écart*. But also *Queer* by William S. Burroughs. Also *Paris, Notre Siècle* by the actor couple of Jean-Louis Barrault and Madeleine Renaud, edited by Pierre Bergé. In the green marble bathroom were an exercise bike, a scale, an Evian water mister, a half-empty bottle of Rive Gauche cologne, Elnett hairspray, and a basket of medications. In the "siesta room" were some dog-eared books: *Villa Triste* by Modiano, *Le Puits de Solitude*, the lesbian novel by Radclyffe Hall, as well as *Un Siècle d'Elégance Française*, illustrated by Bérard.

Now he was doubly foreign, a mysterious billionaire whose house was protected by two entrances. He could give a five hundred franc bill just as easily as ten dirhams to a gardener who moved a pot. They were kings. All the drivers of the beige "little taxis" knew the Saint Laurent house, but it was silent there, as still as the stone Moor in a white mantle that he was fond of. And in the street, one encountered men who were as proud as desert warriors, whose pride sometimes rebelled. Their bodies gave themselves over to the steam of the hammam. The mystery of a likely accident that to this day has not been made public floated around this city, like the cruel memory of a wound that had never fully healed. In Marrakesh, Yves acknowledged that he relaxed "with a free mind." "I am a man of the hot climes, and there, I feel good, in this city which is to my eyes one of the last bastions of dignity."

He transformed Majorelle's studio into a museum of Islamic art, the only one in Marrakesh. It was a collection of anonymous treasures, magic lanterns, heavy carved Berber doors, ancient rugs, cedar wood chests, and Fez ceramics from the nineteenth century that shone under the flame of an impressive collection of daggers, including one with a scorpion on the handle. Yves's influence could be seen here, as it was in the salon where suddenly, on a table, the colors of objects that he had staged came to life: an amber necklace wrapped around a blue lamp like a snake, orange opaline glass, and stones. Mustapha described their decorative style in this way: "Monsieur Bergé loves paintings and auction houses. He brings something in and knows exactly where it should go. Monsieur Saint Laurent loves objects, he mixes them up. He has an uncanny gift. As we say in our country, he has six fingers."

16 / THE SOLITUDE OF HONORS

f the photographers will remove their cameras from the runway, the show will begin in a few minutes.

If you haven't heard this sentence, you've never been to a Saint Laurent show. This is Pierre Bergé's version of dimming the lights in the theater to signal the performance is about to begin. He has checked the seats of every person in the room, down to the very last invitation. When he was involved with the Théâtre de l'Athénée, he said, "Theater is an appointment. I prefer to choose my friends." On the day of the winter 1985–86 haute couture show, he welcomed everyone, with an eye on the regulars. "I like seeing the faces of the people I sell tickets to." The runway shows took place four times a year and were always on a Wednesday at eleven o'clock: two Rive Gauche shows (in March and October in the Louvre's Cour Carrée) and two haute couture shows (in January and July). According to Yves Saint Laurent, "Haute couture is a bunch of secrets that have been whispered for years. It's an open door to all possibilities. Achieving the greatest simplicity to achieve the greatest extravagance. If you don't have that strength of technique, you can do theater, but you can't make a dress."

At 10:50, in a gray suit, Pierre Bergé marched out onto the runway and greeted the guests in the first row with a quick wave, while the people in standing-room-only squeezed together behind the chairs. Hardly anyone came in late: in fact, Saint Laurent shows were the only ones for which the fashion writers showed up early. Alaïa didn't send invitations; but Yves Saint Laurent didn't send an RSVP card. In the splendor of the Imperial Salon at the Hotel Intercontinental, the tension rose bit by bit, though there was no bumping or shoving, just the quiet commotion of a theater premiere. Leaning on his cane, André Ostier, a short gentleman with gray hair, discreetly observed the audience. People came to greet him. How many were still around who had seen him dressed as the painter Le Douanier Rousseau at Marie-Laure de Noailles's Bal des Artistes? Now a cane had replaced his camera. "My legs are bad, but my head can wander!"

Starting in 1972, he documented a vanished world by photographing the descendants of the society figures who had inspired Proust's characters. For this chronicler of Parisian high society, the Saint Laurent runway show was the last one that was still faithful to the Dior tradition. The maison Saint Laurent, which had the largest ateliers in Paris, was also the one that had the most regular clients: about 250. In the order book for 1986, the names included Christina Onassis, Madame Khashoggi, Mrs. Henry Ford, Mrs. Gordon Getty, Nancy Kissinger, and the Queen of Jordan. The luxury sector was doing well. At Yves Saint Laurent, couture produced net profits of 56 million francs in 1985 (22 percent of revenue). In Paris, a thousand designs were shown in one week during 22 runway shows that were now conceived of as spectacles with themes. Comic opera at Jean Patou, Venetian Renaissance at Jean-Louis Scherrer, where, that year, the sales record was forty dresses for the wife of an African president whose name the label would not reveal. At Dior, a princess ordered her daughter a dollhouse with clockwork figures representing the saleswomen, the doorman, the delivery man, and the clients. But at Yves Saint Laurent, they said that these special orders were not frequent. To keep their distance from this "gala of frills and flounces," as described by *L'Express* in July 1985, Yves Saint Laurent had the models walk down the runway in silence.

On that day, many of the long-time employees from the Rue Spontini days were at the entrance ushering clients to their seats. Always in black, the saleswomen greeted their clients, who were in the habit of giving them the program after the show with the designs they wanted checked off. "Couture? It's very irritating, a little superficial. We all pull together so that it works," said Claire de Billy, a high-pitched little voice perched on long legs. She had been a model at Lelong. "We went to the races. At Auteuil. We were all thin and had no shoulders."

Gabrielle Buchaert, the press officer, passed out the programs: no introductory text—"couture poetry," Chanel called it—but a white folder with the famous YSL logo by Cassandre and a list of numbers followed by descriptions of the designs. Day ensembles, cocktail dresses, tuxedos, long evening ensembles. Since the Ballet Russes collection (fall/winter 1976), their number had noticeably risen, to 182 designs in 1984, and 151 for summer 1985, the 50th collection. Much time had passed since Yves Saint Laurent had held private fashion shows for his clients with 56 outfits in the salons on Rue Spontini. Now there were three shows each day, at 11:00 AM, 3:00 PM, and 5:00 PM, with 1,500 guests in all. A few gold chairs with cards that read "Reserved" strung across them were still empty. Hélène Rochas arrived in a camel day suit, never too much powder, never too many jewels, but outrageous crocodile pumps. "She's so Paris," the Americans said.

It was 10:55. In the first row, at the end of the runway, sat John Fairchild and one or two colleagues from *Women's Wear Daily*—the only member of the press to attain this honor. To him, Yves was all about strength. "He has consuming passions in his head. He has physical strength in his hands." John Fairchild was always seated next to Catherine Deneuve, who had a reserved seat at every show. "I've seen almost all his collections. I always watch them with a sense of wonder. I expect surprises, I'm just as demanding as the others. It's exactly like going to the movies. I'm a spectator." The photographers snapped away. On her left was Zizi Jeanmaire in a gray fox coat, with her eyebrows drawn in pencil, and legs that always seemed to be *en pointe* even when she was sitting down. On Deneuve's right, after John Fairchild, was Princess Firyal, Danielle Mitterrand and her sister, Christine Gouze-Rénal, along with Monique Lang, the wife of culture minister Jack Lang. Across from them was Betty Catroux, with straight blond hair, dark glasses, and a Rive Gauche peacoat. She was one of the only Saint Laurent women who didn't wear make-up (that day or any other). She was still Yves's best friend and one of his only close friends who didn't work for the company. They talked on the phone almost every day: "He sounds like he's dying, and then after two minutes I find him again, and we laugh." He was the godfather of her daughter Maxime. Next to her was Charlotte Aillaud, the sister of Juliette Gréco, "born on a trip to Ferney Voltaire, near Geneva," who remembered the "very Sarah Bernhardt" mousseline dresses that she ordered in the early 1970s. "Yves is very solitary, but he feels the need to see his dresses. His relationship to the world is very aesthetic. He loves special moments. Inviting people to spend a couple days at his house. He loves people to be beautiful; for him, it's a moment of happiness."

Sao Schlumberger and her diamonds were always in the front row. She acknowledged, "Life has changed a lot since 1981. There were three big parties per season. We were much more dressed up!" She hated shopping and boutiques, and had never taken the subway in her life. Her one principle: "Never overbuy." Every year, she sent a box of chocolates to the seamstresses of Madame Catherine, her "fitter." On her right was Gaby van Zuylen, who always gave her dresses names, such as Scarlett, Queen of the Night, and Siren. "But when I gain weight, I call it Sausage!" On her right was Marie-Hélène de Rothschild. And then there were the American women, who never wore boots in winter and always wore stockings in summer, often on their way back from a trip to Deer Valley or Nassau. Nan Kempner, in her sapphire suit and turquoise blouse, had never missed a Saint Laurent show. She had met the couturier at Dior in 1958. "It's an expensive habit! But it gives me false courage: I think I look beautiful in Saint Laurent. We were tall and thin. His drawings looked like me. With him, everything happens inside. You're never uncomfortable or too dressed up. When you're not twenty anymore, you have no excuse for being shy." She was Lady Saccharine. She was so thin that you always felt like she was shivering, when it was ninety degrees under the spotlights. She used to have too many feathers, too much lace. Later she stated, "I like to dress up, but in a simple way." The era of balls had passed. But she loved to host "little dinners of eight or ten people…with lots of conversation." Francine Weisweiller no longer arrived in a Bentley, but in a Renault 9. "She loves only her dog," said the saleswomen, whom she tormented. "My husband loves horses, that's all I can say.…I was very spoiled, now I have a fixed amount per month," said the former Elizabeth Arden beautician, who was born Francine Worms. Other guests there that day included Comtesse de Ravenel, Baronne de Waldner, and Carmen Rossi, Franco's granddaughter, who was more discreetly referred to as the Duchess of Cádiz. Paloma Picasso always sported bright colors. "Never any prints," she specified. "However I dress, people always think I'm wearing Saint Laurent. I live intimately with his style."

Lucienne Mathieu-Saint-Laurent was seated on the side. In the orchestra seats were the Lalannes, Jacques Grange, and Maxime de la Falaise, who now worked for the company, handling the baby clothes licenses in New York. "Saint Laurent is my second family," she said. But she was attached to nothing more than to her independence: "I've never belonged to something. I'm really a loose cannon." While others framed the Love posters that Yves drew and sent to about a thousand lucky friends to mark the new year, she used them as lampshades. She had always "had a colorful life" and chose the most dazzling and theatrical outfits by Yves. Didn't he make "the most beautiful togs in the world"? The American women were on the right. In back, behind the five rows, were Yves's servants, Bernard and Boujemaa (Mustapha's younger brother).

It was 11:03. The workers removed the transparent plastic that covered the runway, which was carpeted with ecru canvas. The journalists glanced over the program; they were overloaded with fashion shows that week, and that day they had all put on their Rive Gauche suits. The photographers, seated single-file along the runway, grunted like predators seeking their prey. The entrance was strictly watched by a man with a moustache, René Pittet, head of facilities, who blocked the entrance to the changing room. The company drivers, along with Yves's and Pierre's personal chauffeurs (the brawny and mustachioed Paul and the slender Alain) were working security. The whole studio team was backstage, as well as Monsieur Alexandre and his hairdressers and the make-up artists. A sound booth was also specially set up that day. At the mixing console was Joël Le Bon, a blond former model with muscles like Schwarzenegger who was the darling of the nightlife jet-set. He joined Yves Saint Laurent in 1978 after working for Pierre Bergé at the Théâtre de l'Athénée. Now he was in charge of the entire audiovisual department. Saint Laurent was the only one who didn't outsource the music on the day of the runway show. "We can't use reggae, rap, or anything too contemporary. Saint Laurent is jazz—Ella Fitzgerald, Cole Porter, Gershwin—and a range of French singers, including the trinity of Montand-Trenet-Piaf, or classical music. We avoid Schubert, it's too sad. For opera, we choose Mozart."

The dressers took care of the last details. Each one was responsible for one model. Amalia. Khadija. Mélanie. Ariane. Pat. Many Eurasian, mixed-race, and black women. Mounia described the work thusly: "Bracelet, necklace. Not one gesture too many or too few. It's somewhere in between playing with a Barbie doll and a surgical operation." Every outfit had its description written on a giant Bristol board, with the list of accessories: "hammered metal e.r. [earrings], fawn fedora, peccary leather gloves, gold suede boots." At the foot of each clothes rack were boxes of stockings. And then shoe in lizard skin and kid leather, as well as satin and shot silk for eveningwear, lying in big clumps of color on the garnet-colored carpet. "My first pair were white wedge sandals!" recalled Hélène Chenot, always impeccably dressed in YSL suits with big padded shoulders and crepe blouses, which gave her a very chic, retro look. On the day of the show, she worked as a dresser. But this Orthodox Russian seemed to prefer her regular job: at the company, her title was "Madame Hélène of the Packaging." With her auburn hair permed in front, she kept her cocky Parisian attitude and spoke to "her" drivers the way a lead dancer ordered around a male chorus line, in a sharp, no-nonsense style: "You got two sevenths and a first," she'd say, to indicate deliveries in the seventh and first arrondissements. "A beautiful package is fantastic. When the client opens the box, she has to discover something crisp, like a bouquet of flowers. Oh, I've seen such wonderful things." Like all the faithful of the maison Saint Laurent, she talked about fabric as if it were a living thing: "Feathers? You have to fight with them. They always stand up. Especially rooster feathers. Single-feather details, too, but they're more fragile. They break if you just look at them!"

Loulou was there, very pale, with lips like a long red line. She designed the hats and jewelry, including huge rhinestone crosses, gold butterflies, and ebony cuffs with inlaid stars. Yves described her as "a very rare woman. She is the essence of chic nonchalance. I love her gestures. Her attitude: the simplicity of her clothing, and the boldness of her accessories."

Behind his tortoiseshell glasses, Yves always seemed to be smoking the same cigarette. A stack of ash would suddenly fall. His assistants, such as Robert Merloz, bustled about without meeting his eyes and watched him. One didn't suspect all the concentration hidden under this face distorted by alcohol, this wrecked body in which he took refuge like a pearl at the bottom of the sea. "He has an amazing memory. He picks up on everything. If the dresser makes a mistake, he notices it immediately. No one can put one over on him," said Madame Felisa. Loulou called it "looking with his ears." He'd give free rein to the others to catch their weak point, their flaw—therein lay his power. "He'd give a masterful flick to the blazer. Adjust a red bow in a puff of fabric. Smooth away an imaginary crease. His long, beautiful hands flew like a blessing," observed Mounia. She added, "he had a gold chain bracelet on his wrist, like a very spoiled young man."

It was 11:10. The show started. Bénédicte de Ginestous, "The Voice," announced the outfits: "Numéro deux. *Number two.*" Day ensemble. Peacoat in saffron serge. Brown grain de poudre pants. Orange jersey sweater. Pierre Bergé sent out the collection. He and Yves were in direct contact with the sound team. There Pierre was in his shirtsleeves, holding the arm of a model who was a good foot taller than he was. The women walked onto the runway.

At Dior, elegance meant not disturbing the air, the kind of elegance that the Duchess of Windsor had. With Chanel, it consisted of moving naturally. She wanted to crush the old aristocracy of the Faubourg Saint-Germain by hiring young women from high society. As for Yves Saint Laurent, starting in 1985 he pursued a love story with his "ebony sirens." In July, he brought out Khadija, who was already called "the African Queen" in Paris. "She came from nowhere. She had won a Queen of Africa contest. Helmut Newton brought her to the maison. She was completely lost in the midst of this jungle of girls," recalled Nicole Dorier, who had become the modeling director. She describes an "epidermic affinity" between Yves and Khadija. "As soon as he loves someone, everyone is ready to give themselves over body and soul." So Khadija turned up in Paris, with a suitcase full of cotton scarves in her hand. She stayed with Nicole Dorier for a while. She would become the star model with "the appearance of a cheetah, the eyes of a gazelle," according to *Paris Match*. She dethroned Mounia. "How beautiful you are," Yves said to her, kissing her hand. "Don't change anything," the professional told his learned assembly.

"Black models have…always contributed tremendously to what I do. I love the light they give the fabrics. I think the depth of color of their skin makes the intensity of the colors come out better. They have never disappointed me. I love their expression, the sparkle of their eyes, their long lines and the irresistible suppleness of the way they move. To me, they have what is most magical in a woman. Mystery. Not the old mystery of *femmes fatales*, but the dynamic mystery of a woman of today."

The safari jacket was back, but in brown leather, with padded shoulders and a belt. A new palette colored this dark skin: all the rosewoods, saffrons, desert sands, and the raw fabrics that he favored: skirts in rope-colored linen canvas, terra cotta shantung dresses, and other dresses with brown snake or bush prints. They weren't 1950s stars posing in polka-dotted one-piece bathing suits, but "ebony sirens" like Amalia, gracefully draped in a panther-print satin crepe dress. The famous Saint Laurent panther, reworked in the colors of precious stones. "On very beautiful silks or on crushed velvet, it moves, it looks like a beast," said Loulou de la Falaise.

Yves once again aroused competition between all the longtime employees from the Rue Spontini, who were cold to these black models. The undercurrent of jealousy that always ran through their profession was exacerbated by the white models' discussion of black models as fundamentally different due to their race. The main target was Mounia, whose whims increased as her influence declined. She wrote her biography with the journalist Denise Dubois-Jallais and distributed Rive Gauche clothing in Fort-de-France. "I want to dazzle Martinique, and tell them all, 'Here's what white people in France say about me.'"[1] Even Felisa admits, "My Mounia had an amazing body. But she had a big butt. Kirat was a model. Actually, I've forgotten her face. She knew how to showcase everything I made, she could feel it. Without long legs, you can't do anything."

Yves Saint Laurent was definitely not English chic. Terry Cohen, who was hired as artistic director of Yves Saint Laurent perfumes in 1985, said, "I was immersed in this brand before coming to work here." She added: "I always wanted people to want to touch the color and to feel it." This Egyptian Jewish woman spoke in depth about "caftan pink" blushes and "Majorelle blue" mascaras. "Saint Laurent made color explode into the world of make-up." His line of lipsticks had the largest number of pinks on the market: about twenty per season, including the famous Pink 19, the most blue toned of all—created in 1978—which was a best seller. The lipsticks lasted, too, as if they contained concentrated pigments like the rouge of

Berber women that was sold in the bazaar in Marrakesh. As if he gave to his make-up the name that he kept for certain dresses: "Don't Touch."

Still, in 1986, the big news was elsewhere. Jean-Paul Gaultier caused a scandal with his men in skirts. The *enfant terrible* of fashion, who scandalized journalists by sending them live turkeys for Christmas, cut tank tops out of lace and turned couture conventions upside down by using nonstandard models in his fashion shows: "from the fat Algerian woman with Saint-Tropez-style bleached-blond hair, to the round little blonde to the tall intellectual brunette…Saint Laurent clothing is a provincial preppy cliché, kind of a small-town has-been look. Montana is the old rich cliché. Beretta is the cliché of simplicity. My inspiration is the street."[2] What was important for Gaultier at that time was to "demolish tradition and its overly strict rules a bit, shake it up to find new inspirations…."[3]

At the maison Saint Laurent on Avenue Marceau, outside information came through only in filtered form. In fact, they had difficulty imagining that the outside world still existed. Everything took place down to the millimeter, in the space between whisperings, silences, and scheming to match the intrigue of any palace. Hélène de Ludinghausen, the head of couture, dropped off a little package to be delivered to a client along with her card. It was a straw clutch embellished with blue stones. "She'll like it. She's very superstitious. It's against the evil eye. She's invited me to lunch three times. I'd like her to buy something this season."

These women defended their craft because they had put their whole lives and their whole hearts into it, with that displeased attitude of a tragic actress who always seems to say, "No, I definitely can't get used to this green." Here, women played with colors to announce their moods. Because she put on a big wool coat, one would say, "Oh, I'm all shriveled up today." And another woman, looking lively with several necklaces, a green t-shirt, and an orange cardigan, would say, "I feel very Marrakesh. Did you see it's the first day of spring?" For that kind of woman, getting dressed is always a celebration. A lemon yellow mousseline scarf stuck out from a mandarin orange bag.

In the cafeteria, which was located under the ateliers—a spacious room, with light wood tables and benches—Pierre Bergé's canaries seemed to watch this world of performers from their cages. The women from the studio were the only ones who wore pants. One could recognize the licensing people—who worked on Avenue George V—by their somewhat too-flashy way of mixing red and pink and their out-of-style clothes that seemed to have been purchased on the last day of the staff sales.

Paule de Mérindol, who was in charge of sales of couture accessories—jewelry, scarves, and bags—wore a black jersey dress to work. As if to remain loyal to Mademoiselle Chanel at Yves Saint Laurent. Her judgment was as merciless as her silhouette was straight: "She's not even vulgar, she's below that," she said as a strange character in heels walked by.

It may seem strange that so many different personalities could put up with one another. Only their attachment to Yves Saint Laurent kept them together. But each one seemed to hold a piece of the past, like the piece of a puzzle. Every decade had its own memories. The couture ladies pronounced Warhol as va-rol, the way François Mitterrand said ko-vayt for Kuwait. They had an old-fashioned vocabulary, saying that someone had "gumption" or that somebody was a "fussbudget." "Suzanne Luling? Monsieur Gaby tried on her dresses when she wasn't here. He was as big as she was!" said a former Dior employee.

The Rive Gauche staff always had a more hyperrealist vision: "Violeta Sanchez didn't shave under her arms. Helmut asked her to. She was thrilled," someone recalled. Some had had hard lives—they were always very pale, very powdered, with dark red lips and their bodies contained in subtle combinations of black and brown: "Oh, it's a relic of the couture world," said one, dipping her lips into her glass of red wine. Joan Crawford made people forget that her name had been Lucille LeSueur and that she was born in Texas. But whatever their paths, they all remembered that they owed something to the maison. Most had started off picking up pins, as the laws of couture demanded.

Less than a minute after finishing lunch, they all had the same reflex: touching up their lipstick. Red, of course. They felt naked without lipstick. It was as if this golden tube gave them extra strength to make men a bit paler. All the women seemed to say of managers in suits and ties, "Oh, they're jealous!"

It became harder and harder to get access to the master. One example: In 1986, Carlos Muñoz—the son of Anne-Marie Muñoz, the head of the couture studio— was making a film about the company. Despite his close connection, he did not get permission to film Yves Saint Laurent working. Was it because of this protection that Yves sometimes seemed like a child who'd been grounded? The new habits had taken over gradually. After the nighttime rivalries of the 1970s, which ended spectacularly with Visconti-style duels and glasses of champagne thrown in faces, a new, more rational and sober method of media warfare took over. The studio, with more than 1,000 CDs and cassettes, maintained the company's records and heritage. All the films (about 500) were managed by computer.

Since 1962, Gabrielle Buchaert had conscientiously archived articles and photos about Saint Laurent in big black folders. She was Mademoiselle Memory. So much so that all the events in her life seemed to be linked to the company. When she wanted to remember the date when she went into the hospital for an operation, she would say, "Oh, yes, it was before the Met show." A swarm of assistants bustled around her black desk. They cut out articles and sorted them with white gloves so their hands wouldn't get dirty. For important articles, they bought as many as twenty or thirty copies of certain newspapers. Everything was sorted, labeled, and put away with a sense of organization inherited from the Dior school. There was even a Saint Laurent library, two rooms located in the "peanut gallery" of the building, with shelves loaded with complete collections of *Vogue* and *Harper's Bazaar*. No couture house had such complete documentation on the history of fashion over the previous thirty years. The Love posters were stored in big boxes. The room was kept locked. People at the company never went there, as if by superstition. Only researchers and academics had access, but they had to be accompanied by someone from the company.

The "books" increased considerably, though, paradoxically, the best photos belonged to the past: Avedon, Horst, Bourdin, Sieff, Newton (who continued to work on advertising catalogues for Rive Gauche), and David Seidner, who staged big events at Yves Saint Laurent in painterly compositions—with decoupage, out-of-focus effects, and shadows. Photographing an Yves Saint Laurent tuxedo without knowing the ones that came before it was like walking into a movie theater in the middle of the film. But there was no changing of the guard at YSL, even as other designers were starting to publish prestigious catalogues and team up with a new generation of photographers: Rei Kawakubo and Peter Lindbergh, Yohji Yamamoto and Nick Knight, Sybilla and Javier Vallhonrat, Romeo Gigli and Paolo Roversi. Helmut Newton, who had followed all Yves Saint Laurent's collections since 1962, was the last one who was truly interested in fabric, the color black, and the cut, with a humility that was sometimes lacking in other photographers, who were more concerned about themselves than what they were showing. But he didn't escape the occasional blow-up at the couture house. He recalled with humor, "I remember one day when I found myself in the office of Francine Crescent, the editor-in-chief of *Vogue Paris*. Pierre had raised a big fuss because he didn't like my series. I grabbed the phone and yelled: 'Pierre, I don't tell you how to make clothes!'" He concluded, "I like him a lot. Pierre is a Scorpio like me. He's mean like me. We're very close friends!"

The Saint Laurent image got established: the photo by Irving Penn (which appeared on the cover of the 1986 catalogue for the show at Paris's Musée des Arts de la Mode) increased his mystery. The Queen in Cocteau's *The Eagle with Two Heads* used a fan to hide her face; Yves left the fan to Karl Lagerfeld, who could make it clack like a pair of castanets. With a Cartier watch on his wrist, Yves showed himself to the lens with his left hand placed on his face, revealing only one eye. In this position, his hand made a *Y*. He seemed to wear a safari jacket from the early days of Rive Gauche menswear. This photo definitively consecrated his mystery, a self-hatred that was as great as his narcissism.

Yves had become very isolated and protected within his own company, which recalled certain memories for one accessory maker: "Chanel was the same thing. When she left the Ritz, the maid called to say, 'Mademoiselle is coming.' She thought she would surprise everyone. He's a prisoner, like her. Except that he's not eighty years old. I'd very much like to talk with Monsieur Saint Laurent, as I did with Mademoiselle. But there's this constant barricade. They've turned him into a hermit, and some of them take advantage of it. Sometimes he gets angry. Just so he can say, 'I'm the boss.'"

His official biography was cleaned and purged. With humorous omissions: the first prize in the International Wool Secretariat contest appears, but not the third prize that preceded it. But there were shadowy areas that couldn't be touched. For instance, the three years between 1958 and 1961, contained in the gap that separated these two paragraphs: "In 1958, he showed his first collection and immediately became famous. Three years later, he founded his own maison de couture with Pierre Bergé." As if he hadn't existed before. And then 1978, which fell into a hole, the only year when no one received the traditional Love poster. Someone mysteriously pulled out the articles from 1962 from the folders. A year that disappeared, flew away, like that green dove, fleeing two birds gripping a branch, one innocently blue, the other frightening, a mean red thing with a pointed beak and a black eye (Love, 1979). When Yves was asked in 1983 which collections were his favorites, he said, "The first one, 1958, and my last one for Dior. And then summer 1978."

Always watchful, Pierre Bergé, who turned fifty-six in 1986, moved incredibly fast wherever he had to, with an eye on who did what, who came, and who left. The press department was next to his office. Only insiders could enter. The first test: good manners that hid many tensions and internal struggles. In the hallway that connected the studio to Pierre's office was his portrait by Andy Warhol. And in this somewhat "gypsy" atmosphere, as Loulou called it, one learned on the job what happened backstage: the great art of silence or the anger contained in a glance. Nothing seemed too important to be taken into consideration and nothing was insignificant enough to be ignored.

In front of the glass door to the secretaries' area, Ficelle, Pierre Bergé's dog, and Moujik II, Yves Saint Laurent's dog, played and chewed on a red plastic ball. Monsieur was there. "He has wide wings. He's here, he's present, constantly, even when he isn't," said Pierre. Never being the apparent source of authority, and yet having it entirely, pulling the strings, and never being considered responsible, always standing behind the one who holds the primary position—this gave Yves Saint Laurent extra strength. "The fashion designer is a sleepwalker who designs in his sleep," said Pierre.

At times Yves seemed to use his invisibility the way Deneuve said she used her dark glasses: "They let me watch people at my leisure. Illusory or not, they're there like a veil, a kind of screen, to protect me." He insisted on demanding nothing by his own authority, but through a silent understanding. "He has the power to astonish you," said Anne-Marie Muñoz. "It's his eye and his hand. There is no abuse. No desire for power. It doesn't happen through arguments but through high standards. We're together. The goal is to succeed. There is always a great deal of humility to reach the goal."

In Beijing, the National Art Museum of China held an exhibition of Yves's work in 1985. He had his picture taken there in a dark suit, walking with a cane.

He had wonderful memories of the trip: "The kids designed dresses for days." Pierre Bergé, who by then had definitively left their apartment on Rue de Babylone and moved into a suite in the Hôtel Lutetia, seemed to become younger every day. "We couldn't both sink!" He was also president of DEFI (the Committee for the Development and Promotion of French Clothing) and president of the Chambre Syndicale du Prêt-à-Porter, des Couturiers et des Créateurs de Mode, which he had founded in 1973. He was on the boards of several French and foreign companies and organizations: C. Mendès, Dollfuss-Mieg et Compagnie, Fondation Cartier, Parsons School of Design, and soon the France Libertés-Fondation Danielle Mitterrand. The first lady of France wore Yves Saint Laurent. Hélène de Ludinghausen, the head of couture, described her taste: "She likes red and navy blue. She has very simple tastes and can keep the same suits for two years. She trusts us. She is happy to let us guide her."

A believer in values such as immigrants' rights, culture, and honor, Pierre Bergé practiced humanism the way others did self-defense. While Yves Saint Laurent wasn't afraid of death, Pierre Bergé said he wasn't afraid of aging, and always quoted this phrase by Gide: "My old age will begin the day I stop being outraged." With typical conviction, he promised, "I love life. I'll never commit suicide!" He was just the opposite of Yves and his depression. While Yves had a chef to serve him a simple slice of ham, Pierre loved to cook. He enjoyed ortolans, cognac, gardens, and horse-drawn carriages. He had his picture taken sitting in a carriage in Deauville in a honey-colored cashmere sweater and a checkered shirt, with a Rhett Butler flair and a whip in his hand. On his left, Yves wore a white jacket and seemed to close his eyes. It looked as if he had staged the photo: wasn't this how he had depicted the mythical couple in *Gone with the Wind* when he was in Oran? Pierre subscribed to the journal *Aschenbach*, which regularly published the results of international draft horse and carriage horse competitions.

In Paris, Yves Saint Laurent's existence was constantly linked to rumors: "So, how is he doing?" In the press office, Gabrielle Buchaert answered in a flat voice: "Monsieur Saint Laurent doesn't like interviews. He gives them for certain occasions. When he's stuck and can't get out of it. He's very attached to the people he works with. So we don't disturb him."

In the ateliers with the *premières*, all these tensions finally loosened. These women had husbands and children. They seemed happy. Especially the ones in the *atelier flou*. Their faces were rounder, their bodies were plumper, and their soft hands picked up the fabric delicately. "It's through the touch." Madame Felisa said, "Of course Monsieur Saint Laurent laughs. His heart is bigger than his body. I don't know him outside of work. But I know that for him, the worst part is when he has finished. If he were as adorable with his friends as he is with his staff, they would surely help him. They would leave him alone!" But she left the company in 1986 to live a comfortable life, dividing her time between Deauville and Málaga, Spain. "I left because of him," she said, indicating her husband. She considered Balenciaga like a father and Saint Laurent like a mother: "I miss him. But my life is complete. I started with the best, and I finished with the best."

The more he gave to his craft, the more attention was paid to his health, at a time when being in shape was becoming a concern in France. Aerobics, vitamins, and superwomen: the American ideal had arrived. Some people reacted by becoming reclusive and seeking silence and solitude, perhaps to protect themselves. One way to find those conditions was to begin writing. In 1984 Françoise Sagan published *Avec mon Meilleur Souvenir* (With Fondest Regards), an autobiography in which she described staying up all night in Saint-Tropez, the wild Saint-Germain scene, and the people she had known, including Billie Holiday, Orson Welles, Jean-Paul Sartre, Carson McCullers, Marie Bell, Tennessee Williams, and Rudolf Nureyev, whom she called "the very reflection of virility and grace combined in one body."

Just three months after the French president presented him with the Cross of the Legion of Honor, Yves Saint Laurent, the most respected designer in France, was accused of plagiarism. On June 27, 1985, the Paris court issued its decision: "Design number 91 by Yves Saint Laurent, called Toreador (1979), is a copy of a design by Jacques Esterel. The Yves Saint Laurent company will pay the Jacques Esterel company the sum of 100,000 francs in damages." A vaudeville corrida? After five years of legal proceedings, Benoît Bartherotte, the young head of Esterel, revealed his "misfortunes" to the press. Since 1979, the Chambre Syndicale had forbidden him to hold a fashion show. "The journalists don't come to see me anymore for fear of being stigmatized. I was only able to hold on because of the Japanese, for whom I've been cleaning houses for five years."[4] Defending his protégé, Pierre Bergé thundered, "It's the victory of a legless cripple over Nureyev. One million Americans came to see Saint Laurent's clothes at the Metropolitan Museum in New York, and 7,000 Chinese look at his designs every day in Beijing. The public respects Saint Laurent. I don't give a damn about this thing. It's no more important than if I had broken my toothbrush."[5] However, Yves Saint Laurent filed a countersuit for 500 million in damages. Bartherotte couldn't contain his joy: "You rose up too high, Monsieur Saint Laurent. Come back down a notch!" As the couturier to the president's wife, Yves Saint Laurent inspired jealousy and backbiting. Without naming him directly, Bartherotte denounced "the speculation on temptation, the exploitation of human poverty by fashion designers: people spend money in advance to look successful. It's like putting on make-up before washing their faces. Yet what's more pleasant than buying a lightweight shirt when you have the first ray of sunlight on your skin?"[6]

With eighty boutiques worldwide, Rive Gauche celebrated its twentieth anniversary in 1986. The clients had aged, and the company discreetly expanded the waists by two centimeters, without changing the sizing. Hadn't Rive Gauche become slightly *Rive Droite*? The maison Saint Laurent made Saint Laurent clothes, without a true force inside preparing to face its era, to get out ahead of it, as the couturier had always done, following in Chanel's footsteps and giving a new twist to fabrics that were traditionally for men. At a time when the real innovation in fashion was less about shapes than about materials, Saint Laurent clothes looked more and more dressy and out of touch with the new interest in nature and sports. The public loved comfort and technical performance associated with leisure, and daily life now required mobility and a relaxed attitude. Hadn't Yves Saint Laurent been the first to foresee this development? "He invented the idea of sport in couture. The pea jacket was totally modern," said John Fairchild.

The era of the 1960s counterculture was in the past. Rive Gauche was turning toward luxury ready-to-wear that starting in 1985 was produced in the Mendès factory in Angers. Designed by Jean-François Bodin in collaboration with decorator Andrée Putman, it was spread out over 160,000 square feet. "We wanted this manufacturing unit to be a true extension of Yves Saint Laurent's design studio," said Léon Cligman, the CEO of Indreco and Mendès (in which Yves Saint Laurent held a 34 percent ownership stake at the time). Over 150,000 pieces were manufactured every year in this factory, which combined the most modern technology (computing and robotics) with hand-finishing. This represented 25 percent of its operations.

Yves Saint Laurent could get away with sending in his designs only three weeks before the fashion show. The factory accomplished his increasingly sophisticated visions: velvet patchwork, braided trim, dresses of mousseline and lace. That was his luxury: the factory could start producing a dress at the last minute, responding almost as flexibly as a couture atelier. But the prices kept climbing. A new line within Rive Gauche, Variation, was launched in 1984: the linings were glued (no interfacing), the pockets were false, and the fabrics were of lower quality. The couture staff was scornful of these low-end designs. Commercial success increased, distancing the couturier somewhat from all the bohemia of the 1970s. Rive Gauche meant clothing that the fashion journalists, now obsessed with low prices, refused to cover in their publications but never missed when there were sales for the press. "You see, Saint Laurent is good in real life, but not in photos," someone who ran in those circles remembered hearing. At 7 Avenue George V, the craziness began at 9:00 AM. Who hadn't dreamed of a Saint Laurent tuxedo or jacket, a nice classic for the coming season? The Saint Laurent suit, with bigger and bigger shoulders (that year their width reached its maximum, 52 centimeters or 20.5 inches), no longer represented the androgynous chameleon of the La Coupole years, but Woman, who referred to a model instead of inventing herself. "No one can say that I don't love bourgeois women," said Yves Saint Laurent, who never lost his sense of humor.

At this time, the Saint Laurent woman had a new ambassador: Catherine Deneuve became the official image of the maison. "Time has defined the reality and truth of our relationship: persistence. At first I was a special client. Today, I'm in between the world of friends and the professional world. Things have happened bit by bit: because I'm an actress, and I'm often at the shows, I'm often interviewed. There's nothing concrete. My relationship with Saint Laurent is about desires and responses. There's never been any problem." She recalled her first Saint Laurent dress: "It was embroidered white crepe, like a child's dress, very straight, very simple. Ordering it was totally unreasonable. But it had to be that one. That's what I wanted to wear to meet the Queen of England. I kept that dress for a long time. But at the time, clothes were still part of fashion: you gave them away, got rid of them, traded them. Today, everything is collected: clothing has become a work of art. I don't have the dress anymore. But I've never left Saint Laurent."

In a day suit and light-colored hose, Catherine Deneuve played Catherine Deneuve, the French Grace Kelly, a classical beauty with perfect features. Friendly, efficient, and direct, with beautifully styled hair, she could pick up her train of thought exactly where she left it before being interrupted by a phone call. Her emotions were under control. A few details betrayed her: her hands, which she moved nervously, the slightly authoritarian way she asked for the window to be closed or played the star at the moment she seemed to doubt it: "I'm the woman who gets the prettiest bouquets of flowers." She spoke precisely, with clear words that presented her as a free being, loyal in life to this "role of the responsible woman" that Truffaut spoke of regarding *The Last Metro*. She said, "I admire people who are persistent and who can define what they want to do. Yves has a style. A combination of simplicity and sophistication. I admire what he is and his kind of sacrifice. Especially from a king crowned during his lifetime. Public recognition is not a divine right."

There is certainly a parallel between Truffaut and Yves Saint Laurent. "They met each other once, during the filming of the 1969 film *Mississippi Mermaid*. But they didn't need to talk to each other a lot. There was such understanding. Yves could really feel Truffaut's universe. I played the role of a double-crossing woman in a *film noir*." She added, "Truffaut's demands regarding the clothes are very close to those of Saint Laurent, even if he didn't like pants. He always talked about women's legs. He only liked dresses that moved. Never anything stiff, straight, immobile." The director, the actress, and the couturier were linked by their love of cinema and their loyalty to the spirit of the masters. "She's a remarkable actress, capable of modesty, coldness, and dazzling generosity." Yves Saint Laurent dressed Deneuve the way François Truffaut looked at her behind his camera, having absorbed the lessons of Alfred Hitchcock: "If the sex is too flashy and obvious, there's no suspense. What dictates my choice of sophisticated blond actresses? We look for worldly women, real ladies who will become whores in the bedroom. Poor Marilyn Monroe had sex written all over her face, like Brigitte Bardot, it's not very subtle." Truffaut summed up: "Very reserved on the surface and very hot-blooded in private."[7] Deneuve represented fire under ice: "The only problem for total sensuality is that you can't be naked under Saint Laurent clothes. He is one of the only couturiers who still uses silk satin for the linings, which are never seen, but which you can feel."

She said that he was "quite solitary." They didn't see each other regularly. "Him for his reasons, and me for mine." They wrote to each other. He even dedicated a little prose poem to her, "The Child and the Kite." "For Catherine, whose hair of golden sand in the immensity of a summer day personifies gentleness and tenderness." "What does he like about me?" she asked. "My presence and my lightheartedness. I know he is a shy man, so I try to make him feel relaxed instead of asking him questions." He certainly recognized this consideration: "As a friend, she is the most exquisite, warmest, gentlest, and most protective person. When I go out with her or if we're having a photo shoot, she helps me to conquer my shyness and right away a delightful contact exists between us. She's a woman who makes me dream and dreams are so rare that she has a special place in my heart."

Their differences concealed many shared traits. Catherine Deneuve said, "At times a very bright light is shined on me. And when it's not, I go into the shadows, not to flee, but to get my strength back. I have the possibility of totally removing myself from my profession, because I don't have a company. I work a lot, but I'm a bird on a branch. No one depends on me. If I decide to stop working tomorrow, I only have to worry about myself. I don't have any factories, any artisans....I understand him. We're a bit similar. We're like snails. At certain times, we absolutely have to come out of our shells to do things. He hides. I show myself. It's a huge effort. He's lucky enough, or unlucky enough, not to have to do it. If Pierre Bergé hadn't been his guardian angel, I think he would have been more exposed. I think he still helped him. Pierre allowed him to flourish: what an artist needs is total protection. Otherwise, he pays with his life."

In the press office on Avenue Marceau, Dominique Deroche handled Catherine Deneuve's appointments with journalists. "I'm not like Loulou, his close friend. But I think that I'm not totally foreign to his universe. We have done several movies together. I was able to watch him work and he was able to see me in his clothes. This physical contact already creates a kind of knowledge. I can still see him very clearly in his lab coat and his big glasses, studying the image in the mirror. I think there must be a slightly narcissistic connection. But he is a man with very little vanity. If he were pretentious, it wouldn't be so easy for me to talk about him. I wouldn't want to be so close to his world. He's a man who really loves the women he loves."

Did Deneuve think Saint Laurent clothes had any flaws? "Perhaps their main quality: being immediately recognizable," she said, speaking in a faraway voice about "women who can't manage to exist on their own," who "let themselves be dominated by the clothing." She added, "I don't know if Saint Laurent clothes look good on me, but they've become very natural for me. I don't even ask myself the question anymore. I don't see myself posing in boxer shorts and a sweater. That wouldn't look very good on me. Oh, I forgot to tell you, I'm crazy about shoes. I should have been in *Diary of a Chambermaid*!" That was the most that she would reveal. She refused to answer any questions about money. He seemed to look at her the way all of France did.

Everyone played a role, adapted to the screenplay of the era: the fashion of culture. Yves agreed to be interviewed by Catherine Deneuve for *Globe*, a magazine financed by Pierre Bergé. "What other painters inspire you?" the actress asked him. "Oh, there are so many! Velázquez, for example, has dresses that look like oceans. In Manet, I admire the splendid whites, in different shades like the dress in *Le Balcon*, and his portrait of Berthe Morisot. I think the pre-Raphaelite women are sublime, very modern, and already liberated."[8]

Starting in the mid-1980s, his name was defended by a political and cultural caste that wanted to mark its passage into history with a heretofore unseen ambition: the restoration of historical sites and ambitious building projects, all known as François Mitterrand's Grands Travaux. Yves surely knew that "the more a man is a great artist, the more he must desire titles and decorations, like a shield."[9] Even if this recognition locked him into an image that wasn't his own. He was the leading misfit of couture, preferring to sit next to his chauffeur, "because it's bourgeois to sit in back." He became a revolutionary lavished with honors, someone about whom people said at dinners in Paris: "I don't understand it, he has everything, he's recognized during his lifetime, and he suffers as much as a starving artist."

For culture minister Jack Lang, Yves Saint Laurent embodied "the great classicism and art of Louis XIV. An intuition of time. Extreme kindness. Extreme subtlety. A great gentleman." Naughty Lulu would surely have displayed her derrière to the television, with *MERCI* painted on it in big black letters. While museums became cathedrals, his fashion shows had the reputation of a High Mass. Yves Saint Laurent was beyond criticism, surrounded with superlatives that flattered his ambition but also suffocated him in a way. He had always had contempt for grades and report cards issued by experts: he was the only couturier who refused to be examined every year by a committee of journalists who, under the leadership of Pierre-Yves Guillen, awarded the Golden Thimble. He wanted to reign alone and supreme, a demand that perhaps only people in the profession would and did understand. "He has this way of whispering about what he does, to never want to leave his footprint on the ground. He's like Buñuel or Truffaut. Everything they do is first of all to make people dream, to let them take off, and be led somewhere else, far from a rather irritating, painful reality. It's the opposite of banality," said Catherine Deneuve.

Yves Saint Laurent entered the Larousse dictionary in 1985, was the subject of a question in Trivial Pursuit ("Who designed Bianca Jagger's wedding dress?"), and became the first living couturier to have his work shown in a museum. He was canonized by history-making exhibitions: one million visitors in New York (1983), 600,000 in Beijing (1985), 260,000 in Moscow (1986), 132,000 in Paris (1986), 240,000 in Leningrad (1987), 100,000 in Sydney (1987), or a total of nearly two and a half million visitors between 1983 and 1987. Published on the occasion of his show at the Musée des Arts de la Mode, the book *Yves Saint Laurent et le Théâtre* had a preface by Edmonde Charles-Roux.

The book started and ended with a great stream of praise, from people including Françoise Sagan, Paloma Picasso, Françoise Giroud, Ricardo Bofill, John Fairchild, Rudolf Nureyev (the only one who used the word "man"), Alexander Liberman, Diana Vreeland, Catherine Deneuve, and François-Marie Banier. "His life is a legend. His name is an empire. His dresses, still with the scents of the women who loved them, have entered museums. And he goes through all this—all this glory, all these tributes, along with all this chaos and hullaballoo—with the distant silence of a great Proustian dandy."[10] Jack Lang was not one of the contributors; at that time, he was no longer culture minister, having been replaced by François Léotard in Jacques Chirac's coalition government. And Pierre Bergé added to his list of embattled opinions a different concept of fashion, which was more about defending skill and craftsmanship than about expressing designers' personal visions: "They have horrible shapes. They display their equations, but not the simple concept of proportionality. They invent third legs, a second collar. I tell them, 'Make me a blazer, perhaps you will find new proportions, new shapes.' Hats with flowerpots were wonderful when it was Schiaparelli, because she knew what she was doing." He added: "Not everyone is Karajan. We're missing first violins!" And he didn't hesitate to make political statements: "Fashion was fashion because of Jack Lang. It's in reference to him that it continues to be so. But I think the government hasn't yet understood its importance. We must defend our reputation: France has no rival in the field of fashion."

Pierre Bergé publicly supported François Mitterrand during the presidential campaign of March 1988. And Mitterrand was grateful. In the catalogue for the Yves Saint Laurent show, the longest contribution was by Mitterrand, the first French president to write about fashion: "Fashion, which inspires costume design and stages our daily lives, has now been fully recognized as an art. It is a dose of fantasy that modern life has for us. But this fantasy stimulates and supports a large market that is a powerful contributor to our industrial activity and to France's commercial influence. An alliance between creativity and business, fashion is a way forward for our country. For twenty-five years, Yves Saint Laurent invented shapes and colors that have entered the history of elegance. He is one of the ambassadors of French genius in the world. The Musée des Arts de la Mode lets us take stock of his talent, before we meet him once again, all around us, every season."[11]

On January 28, 1986, Mitterrand inaugurated the Musée des Arts de la Mode, located in the Pavillon de Marsan, part of the Louvre, at the end of the building of the Union des Arts Décoratifs, of which it was a part. The building was constructed in the seventeenth century, burned during the Commune, and then rebuilt between 1875 and 1904.

The Pavillon had been renovated starting in 1984 at the initiative of Jack Lang, who told me he wanted to make it "an impressive mirror of the history of customs and society." It was over 43,000 square feet and had 11 floors. But 15 months after it opened, only one quarter of the rooms were available for use, due to internal tensions, planning errors, and lack of funds. Projects that had been enthusiastically announced would never come to pass: this was the case with the work spaces (the documentation room and conference rooms) and the Institut de la Mode, which was originally planned for the underground level. After several studies, it turned out that this was too expensive, and the institute—which had been founded by Pierre Bergé—stayed in its 14,000-square-foot mansion on Rue Jean Goujon.

The museum was criticized by *L'Express-Paris* as "a gigantic farce." Had it been hastily thrown together? The interior designer was none other than Jacques Grange. Edmonde Charles-Roux was the curator of the first exhibition, *Moments de la Mode*, a compilation that was shown a few months before Saint Laurent's show, after his star turn in America. The government had established the Musée des Arts de la Mode thanks to an injection of sixty million francs but hadn't planned for an operating budget: for 1986 to 1987, grants of three million francs were made on a one-time basis. *Après Saint Laurent, le déluge?*

The Musée des Arts de la Mode was one of the symbols of the prevailing political tensions between the City of Paris—which had its own fashion museum, the Palais Galliera, opened in 1977—and the culture ministry. This was the kind of thing that could tarnish the image of an institution with foreign fashion and textile curators, especially when it had gotten off to a rocky start. Additionally, after all this hullaballoo, the location, which before its renovation was one of the biggest potential museum spaces in Paris, would become a shadow zone in the president's projects less than one year after its opening. The competition was fierce: in 1989, the Palais Galliera and the Musée des Arts de la Mode both had exhibitions about the French Revolution. Doubling up for the bicentennial!

Everything became complicated, but Pierre Bergé managed to emerge unscathed yet again. He escaped all the clans and sided with no one, even letting Guillaume Garnier, the curator at the Palais Galliera, buy an embroidered set of court clothes. "Pierre Bergé was always a thorn in the side of the old guard," Didier Grumbach summarized admiringly. Grumbach had become the CEO of Thierry Mugler, having left Mendès in 1978 and sold his stock. He recalled with emotion the beginnings of Rive Gauche—"People followed me in the street, trying to open boutiques!"—and lunches at Maxim's on the day of the collection show: "Everyone took the microphone and gave a little speech. People clapped and there were tears. Finally, there were too many people. We couldn't hear each other anymore. We had the last one at L'Alcazar!" Pierre Bergé amazed him. He said with a smile, "He's an angel compared to what he once was. In Lyon, in the mid-1960s, he almost knocked down a police officer!"

Did Pierre Bergé have a score to settle with Pierre Cardin? "Lucky Pierre" (as *Le Figaro* called Cardin) was a designer, a restaurateur (Maxim's), a hotel owner, and the president-owner of an empire that was built on selling his brand any way possible: "We won't have any macaroni, or, unlike what Cardin does, any chocolate," Bergé promised. Cardin pointed out that he didn't own a palace in Marrakesh or any racetracks, and that he wore nylon shirts instead of tailor-made ones. But nothing stopped Pierre Bergé, who wanted to make the name Yves Saint Laurent shine in lights, under the nose of his rival. For thirty-five million francs, he decided, through Cerus (Carlo de Benedetti's French holding company) to buy the Ledoyen restaurant, which was located across from the Espace Cardin on the Champs-Elysées. But the city of Paris, which owned the structure, opposed the sale. The reason: the leaseholder had sold his rights without letting the city know. A call for offers would be launched. The first setback for Yves Saint Laurent. Régine ended up taking over the luxury restaurant. Pierre Bergé raised a fuss. Once he stepped out of the shadows, he made up for lost time.

The 1980s truly marked the beginning of Pierre Bergé's public rise. Between 1985 and 1987, he received the same honors as Yves Saint Laurent: Cross of the Legion of Honor (1985), senior advisor to the Ministry of Light Industry and Textiles of the People's Republic of China (1986), an honorary degree and a gold medal from the Weizmann Institute of Science, the National Order of Merit of France. All honors except one: at the Palais Garnier, on October 23, 1985, Yves Saint Laurent received the "Oscar of Fashion" for his contribution to the history of fashion.[12] But Pierre Bergé organized this tailor-made event, of course.

Cardin conquered the markets, invested in real estate, owned apartment buildings and shops in all the world's great cities. Bergé defined himself as an "anti-business leader: I don't really like doing business. That's why I do it well. Because if you do it badly, you have to redo it." Their ambitions were at odds. As Cardin, who was once the accountant for the Red Cross, put it, "Why would I be aristocratic for selling perfume and despicable for designing and giving my name to a tin of sardines? In wartime, which one would you prefer?"

Cardin admitted to not having read a book since 1975. Pierre Bergé saw himself first and foremost as a man of culture. "A great business leader will have read Erasmus, Proust, Duras." Pierre Cardin did the accounts for his empire himself every evening in spiral notebooks and signed the checks for all his employees himself. Pierre Cardin spoke little. Pierre Bergé was interviewed more and more. Regarding revenue, he said, "It didn't go too badly with Saint Laurent. This fragile craft is practiced by fragile people, who mustn't be drowned in figures. I have total admiration for Yves. He had to express himself sheltered from contingencies."

Bergé headed the Chambre Syndicale du Prêt-à-Porter, des Couturiers et des Créateurs de Mode, leading the fashion industry and ruling over this elite club with an iron fist. It was said that during their meetings no one else dared speak. Ever since Ungaro (1968), whom he privately called "color-blind," the Chambre Syndicale hadn't authorized the establishment of any maisons de couture because of very outdated rules that hadn't been revised since 1945. The first would be Christian Lacroix, in 1987. Bergé's quick tongue and his scathing expressions hadn't yet reduced his popularity in the fashion world, even if, in the shadows, bitter feelings were growing. People thought he was angry and duplicitous. But even his enemies owed him something: it was thanks to him that designers had their shows in the Cour Carrée du Louvre since 1982, and that they were first received by the French president in 1985.

Everyone acknowledged it: "We need another Pierre Bergé." In lordly fashion, he stated, "I will pay a debt to this profession before I die." In 1985, he created the Institut Français de la Mode: "The manufacturers grumble. I want designers and managers to get along. We need to solidify the foundations of this profession. Currently there are schools, but they just teach pretense. What's interesting is to build a fortification that the designers can lean on to live their dreams."

Pierre Bergé was the first to make the role of manager something more than a number-cruncher. He was the only owner who rolled up his sleeves on the day of the fashion show. His strength lay in dropping the calculator and setting an overall course. He'd say, "Give me the numbers," and make fast and efficient decisions in a small group, avoiding the slow pace of marketing studies, even if they had a flashy appeal. However, a little advice could have helped him avoid some lawsuits, such as the one filed by the Fédération de la Parfumerie Sélective in 1983. Yves Saint Laurent had to change the labeling on the bottles by adding "YSL." The reason was that the name "Paris" could not be a registered trademark, since, according to French law, no one could exclusively use the name of a place. So the fragrance became "Paris d'Yves Saint Laurent." How many expenses of this kind did Pierre Bergé have to pay out, even though the maverick billionaire hated waste and the privileged classes?

As they say in the army, Bergé "had brass balls." He denounced racism, which he considered "the most disgusting thing in the world." He cracked the whip. He pushed forward. He asserted himself. He made mistakes. He yelled even louder when he figured out he was wrong. He didn't hesitate much. He was a player and a Pygmalion. Pierre Bergé held forth and lost his temper. Against French CEOs. Against fashion journalists. "In France they're the least serious. At least in the United States fashion has a status, they don't choose just anyone to talk about it. There's *Women's Wear Daily*. Here, the editors still think that fashion is something frivolous. They give the section to the woman who dresses a little better than the others. Her coverage is just about short or long hemlines, and her main adjective is 'delightful.' The fashion journalists treat the shows like a chess game. They forget that they're not the ones who are playing. I've always preferred designers to those who hang around them or try to make or break them."

Cardin said he was a capitalist. Pierre Bergé claimed the title of "leftist CEO," although there were not any union representatives in his company at the time and a workers' advisory committee wasn't established until 1989. That was the way of the maison. There was no "thirteenth month" at Saint Laurent (a standard end-of-year bonus calculated as one-twelfth of one's annual salary), but an identical bonus for everyone, "from the janitor to the boss." Paternalistic and attentive, Bergé made it a point of honor to listen to grievances and establish justice like the head of a household. He knew the first names of all his employees. Curious by nature, he liked to bet on winners with the energy of a racehorse trainer. After falling in love with the play *Equus*, he bought the rights in New York and produced it in Paris, with François Périer and a young Stéphane Jobert. He wasn't afraid of taking on responsibility. He flew his helicopter, played piano, spoke a little Arabic, knew how to buy flowers for men, "especially for the day of their funeral," as a female enemy said of him. He spent his time being available. In his office, instead of a fax machine and electronics, there were auction catalogues and piles of books. He had given up on learning how to use a personal computer. His favorite technology was the telephone. What other CEO could boast of being able to call Andy Warhol to ask for a portrait of Jean Cocteau that would be on the front page of a special issue of *Libération*? Who else went every October to the mass for the anniversary of Cocteau's death at the Église Saint-Roch? Or published a new edition, with a preface by Patrick Modiano, of a book of erotic drawings by Cocteau, *Le Livre Blanc*, which was published anonymously in 1928 with a run of twenty copies? Bergé announced his homosexuality loud and clear in the accompanying editor's note. He also put condom machines in the company bathrooms in 1986. "I have always fought for what is essential," he said.

His favorite book was *Madame Bovary*, and he had an original edition inscribed to Victor Hugo by Gustave Flaubert. He often said that "culture is the future." After all, he brought the writer and philosopher Bernard-Henri Lévy onto the board of directors of Yves Saint Laurent. He received visitors the way a doctor received patients, with an attitude of "Tell me what's going on." He had his guests sit on a big leather sofa while he sat in a slightly raised armchair. When people asked him about Saint Laurent, he praised his talent unstintingly. He wrote about Yves, and his emotion came through in loads of quotations and references.

This is how Pierre Bergé described a fashion show: "A dress comes out in a perfectly ordinary way, and all of a sudden, it's Proust's Duchesse de Guermantes. She turns around and meets Natasha Rostova from Tolstoy's *War and Peace*. In the distance, la Traviata faints in the arms of Germont *père*, and suddenly, for Ludwig II of Bavaria, seated all alone in an empty theater, Wagner has an English horn sound out....Marlon Brando's blue jeans get off the streetcar; Zizi's feathered headdress is wrapped around a *maja* by Goya, and Scarlett O'Hara borrows Rhett Butler's hat. Callas goes to stab Scarpia once more, while Matisse and Warhol do the boogie-woogie with Mondrian. Then Visconti is at the head of a funeral procession, etc."

*

They always had that way of exaggerating. None of them were fooled, by themselves or anyone else. "When you live too much in imagination, sometimes you regret not having been closer to reality," Yves Saint Laurent said. "Don't forget that in the expression *monstre sacré*, there's the word *monstre*." But they follow the party line. "Monsieur Saint Laurent's only family is Monsieur Bergé," said Mustapha. He enigmatically added, "We were educated there. We saw everything. The pages that turned and disappeared. The tempest when there was no storm."

Like Napoleon and Fouché, they both served, linked by the attraction of opposites. "He has accomplished what I never would have been able to accomplish: a business," said Yves Saint Laurent in New York in 1983. "He saved me from all kinds of financial trouble and let me be free to design what I wanted, when I wanted. He never asked me any questions about expenses: we've always had the best fabrics, the best assistants, the best materials. He's the kind of artistic director that other designers dream of having."

According to a close friend, "Yves is more of a strategist, he's more complicated. Pierre is the man who gets things done." They liked to test themselves, one through solitude, the other via power, which electrified their relationship and spurred their jealousy: "When you talk to Pierre, Yves gets suspicious. When you talk to Yves, Pierre goes crazy," said someone close to the couple. The second test: Pierre's anger. He shouted, his face turning white. Everyone had to face it at one time or another. It was no use losing your head over it. It was a sign that he knew you, that you were part of the clan. At YSL, everything happened instinctively: the important thing was to be in harmony. If not, forget about it! He waited, he demanded, he provoked, like a lover you can't resist caught up in wordless court intrigues.

It's certainly clear that, as a YSL employee said, "It's a very special company. You can't get in easily. And you don't get out in one piece." Mustapha confirmed, "After so many years, it has marked you. You're designated; you can't leave him." The maison Dior was a school. The maison Saint Laurent was a club whose members were sometimes chosen based on an interview that barely lasted five minutes, possibly launching someone on a brand new life. Christophe Girard was a student in Japan before being hired by Pierre Bergé in 1975. As chief administrative officer of the company, he sketched this portrait of Bergé: "People often say that Pierre Bergé is terribly insincere, but I don't think so. He has a determined sincerity about his choices. He's possessive and exclusive, he doesn't share his power (although he delegates it) or his friends. He is deeply generous and he likes people to need him. He is the perfect blend of tenderness and brutality." Some felt there was misogyny at the company. "We can have important positions. But we know we're always at the mercy of a male protégé," said one female employee. Pierre Bergé seemed scornful of women, while Yves Saint Laurent was scornful of men, saying, "I always found men less interesting than women."

Feared and stubborn, Pierre Bergé was more sentimental. He felt as a man the need reach out to others, even if, like Molière's Orgon, he seemed always to say, "No, I don't want to be loved." He would take a friend to the hospital at two in the morning, giving as much of himself as possible: his care, his generosity, his trust, his money. But when Yves Saint Laurent bought an object that once belonged to Chanel from his friend Jacques Chazot, he broadcast the news: "He doesn't have a cent!" "Pierre likes to care for others," said an acquaintance. The most important quality was certainly loyal friendship. He only got angry at those he loved. "For one day, two months, or a lifetime," said a friend. A question of honor. "In other times, this adventurous La Rochelle native could have been a conquistador, ruling over a court of artists and pleasant parasites," Matthieu Galey wrote.[13]

One day, one of his longtime colleagues calmly left his office while he had an angry outburst. He followed her. "How can I shout at anyone if there's no one there to listen?" His love of theater never left him. "I had no other training than that of my passions," said Pierre Bergé, who had his first taste of theater magic just after he'd moved to Paris, when he went to a production of *The Madwoman of Chaillot* by Jean Giraudoux. Yves and Pierre always admired Bérard and Jouvet. They learned everything by listening and looking. They had a way of rehearsing their roles, from season to season, as if they were on stage for the first time. It was as if they had made this saying by Jouvet their motto: "In the theater, there is nothing general: everything is individual, momentary, or ephemeral: everything has the character of fashion and everything is justified by success."[14]

Pierre Bergé and Yves Saint Laurent accomplished many things by watching. They both knew how to judge the men and women who would be useful to them. But each had his own way of seeing. One observer told me, "[Bergé] puts the brakes on Yves's over-the-top ideas, and he also stimulates Yves. He says, 'It's so beautiful!' Obviously, Yves doesn't always appreciate Pierre's taste. Sometimes he likes the one dress that Yves wasn't happy with."

They were both able to discuss a dress that a woman once wore many years later. But not in the same way. Pierre Bergé would sketch her in a precise, efficient, quick way. In context. Sometimes funny, always in colorful language, often a force to be reckoned with. Those around him became thick-skinned by necessity. Once, before a fashion show, he said to a rather plump colleague wearing yellow and green, "Gabrielle, you look like a hard-boiled egg on a lettuce leaf!"

More instinctive, Yves wasn't afraid of silence. It always felt as if he had you with his pencil. That he had identified the flaw. The button that wasn't straight. The blemish, the tiny mark. You thought you were observing him, but all along he was observing you. He would say, "Elegance is a way of smoking," while calmly lighting your cigarette. He talked about a face that had a "way of moving." His sentences extended into thousands of pointillist details. He could use a single word that seemed unimportant, but which would later open up like a bizarre flower, leaving behind a phosphorescent trail, a secret to be decoded. "He despises so many things," said Paule de Mérindol. "I see very few authentic things around him except for his sense of satire. Everything is simulated and everything is sincere. He's out of the ordinary. That's why he's so creative." "They're both made of steel," Roland Petit concluded. Catherine Deneuve expressed a more subtle sense of what was special about Yves: "Yves is someone exceptional because of his precision and his gifts. His strength lies in everything that's ambiguous and paradoxical. But this is also hard to live through, which obliges him to seek beauty in painful areas." Loulou summed up: "Pierre is obsessed with righteousness, Yves with aesthetics."

"The only thing Pierre has no control over is Yves's anxiety," said an acquaintance. Pierre acknowledged, "We can't both deal with anxiety. He'll die like that. I don't have a talent for that." He tamed his own anxiety through constant over-activity. He never dined at home, rushed to every premiere, and hated Sundays. Could he be more alone in his solitude than Saint Laurent, who made solitude his confidant? Yet it was Yves who stayed quiet. Pierre exploded, rushed into the arena. "He's a Scorpio, but for me, he's really Taurus the bull in all his forms," said Christophe Girard. After years working for the duo, Mustapha learned to respond to every situation: "Monsieur Bergé shouts, but then it's over. Monsieur Saint Laurent sees things, but does not react right away. He ruminates on the situation, before exploding."

Yves resisted, turning around in his cage and saying nothing. "When he doesn't like something, he shuts down," said Madame Felisa. Sometimes, in the studio, during a fitting, he would go to the back of the room and disappear. Everyone pretended not to notice. The more he hid, the more Bergé shone. Sometimes brutal with shy people, Pierre Bergé liked to be listened to. "He doesn't like flattery, he tries to identify it, but he endures it in spite of himself. He doesn't know how to say no. So that he doesn't have to say no, he protects himself behind his unpopularity."

Pierre had an opinion of people, and people had an opinion of him. He was passionate about men who made history, those who experienced their era, while Yves felt the same about those who transcended their era. Pierre Bergé liked "poetic" physiques: "He's the one who likes Proust!" joked a close friend. Ugliness repulsed him. Yves Saint Laurent, on the contrary, caught the flaw, the imbalance, as if the monstrous fortified him, helped him to live, to make beauty necessary. Which one was more vulnerable? "Yves is a diamond," said the decorator Isabelle Hebey. Perhaps that gem's dictionary definition can offer a path to understanding him: "Diamond: precious stone, the brightest and hardest of all, most often colorless. The diamond scratches all surfaces without being scratched," per the 1985 Petit Robert.

In the depths of his madness, Yves Saint Laurent was perhaps calmer, spending long afternoons alone in his "house of happiness" in Marrakesh, which had only a few guests passing through. It was always just as cheerful and light-filled, a real vacation home, with baskets of rushes and other objects that all seemed to have been bought after returning home from a stroll. Nothing had changed. Not Yves's room, with its good luck charms hanging from the wood openwork screen that served as his headboard: a cross, Muslim prayer beads, a Hand of Fatima, and a plastic swan on the mantel. Not the white salon, with its big sofas, its music corner, the Barbara 45s ("Ma Plus Belle Histoire d'Amour"), the cassettes of Amanda Lear, Otis Redding, and others, tapes with the handwriting of Pierre Bergé: "La Jeune Fille et la Mort— Schubert." On a cedar wood table lay a numbered copy of *Naughty Lulu*. There were still magazines from the 1970s around. A copy of the magazine *20 Ans* with the headline "What is Prince Charming's Sexuality?" was prominently displayed. The most recent magazine was a 1981 *Paris Match*, with a photo of Catherine Deneuve and Yves with his fists clenched. His drawings lined the shelves. One with snakes. Another of Loulou with her blue turban and Pierre Bergé when he was a blond young man with a beard and a cigarette. "In August 1976, it was so hot that no one could sleep," said Mustapha mysteriously.

Yves Saint Laurent seemed to stage memories on the shelves of his bookcases. Behind a postcard of Poseidon, five books were grouped together: an introduction to helicopters, another to gardening, and a third to haute cuisine. Then Aragon's *Le Paysan de Paris* and *The Solitude of Compassion* by Jean Giono, who was a friend of Pierre's.

Pierre wrote in a lively, tight style, always on the alert. After all, he cut his teeth in journalism, writing an article on Malaparte's adaptation of Proust, which Fresnay produced at the Théâtre de la Michodière. "No matter what you do, Monsieur Mauriac, this class that you're part of, this class you're so proud of, this class that accepted World War I and planned World War II, this class that killed Jaurès, Salengro, and Gandhi—this class disgusts us!"[15] Decades had passed, one administration had followed another, but Pierre Bergé had maintained his faith in struggle, summarized by this expression, which stood the test of time, like a Saint Laurent jacket: "The struggle that is beginning is unending. We may be defeated, but faced with the current state of things, I write and I shout: We're ready!"[16]

You remembered the way Pierre Bergé talked and the way Yves Saint Laurent looked at you. Pierre was very available, but he gave only very short interviews. (The longest, which he would interrupt by impatiently looking at his watch, lasted one hour.) The Proust Questionnaire? No way. Sometimes, he opened up, remembered the happy times and spoke like a young man: "Everything was cool, with no complications. Reading, listening to music. Walking through the bazaars. Cooking food… Oriental dishes…things like that. Yves made his clothing in peace and quiet. The collection was shown every day. That was the golden age." Yves Saint Laurent gave every journalist the feeling that he was making a confession. Pierre granted his time; Yves gave it, like a torn-up gift that came undone in the middle of the sea. "Yves cries like a child, Pierre like a man," said Isabelle Hebey. Admired, lauded, observed like a human specimen, Yves Saint Laurent, the "nut in the loony bin," as soldiers said, was more cutting, and could be merciless. "What is vulgarity? The tone of someone's voice." One suffered from never being able to love. The other suffered from never being loved enough. Pierre Bergé needed people. Yves needed mirrors. But he had to break them to see himself in them.

At Yves's apartment on Rue de Babylone, seven people worked for him personally: his driver, his chef, his servants Bernard and Boujemaa, and two cleaning ladies, as well as an ironer. Bernard, who was already seventy years old, was first employed by Pierre Bergé in 1950. In 1961, he started working for Yves and never left him. "He's the best gift I ever gave Yves!" said Pierre Bergé.

In the mid-1980s, Yves Saint Laurent reflected on his past, writing and drawing his memories of the years 1954 to 1955, when he arrived in Paris and went to work for Dior. He asked the press office to use the photo of him taken by André Ostier at Dior for photo requests. In his winter 1986–87 haute couture collection, he revisited the black dress that had won first prize in the International Wool Secretariat competition. But the movement was more loose, more theatrical, with draped flame-red satin and a huge velvet hat with a little veil. A manifestation of woman, as photographed by Horst. At a time when women were wearing opaque tights, Yves Saint Laurent became the last couturier to be fascinated by black stockings.

Mounia started the show in a white officer's suit wearing a fez. With Yves, spring started with a departure, the image of a woman boarding a ship, such as *Le France*. As in Dior's time, Yves Saint Laurent gave nicknames to his designs, as if he saw the film of his life taking place through his dresses: Demain Toujours, Petit Matin, Blazer My Love, Café de Flore, La Vie en Rose, Voulez-Vous Jouer Avec Moi?, Portier de Nuit, Pierrot la Tendresse, Oriane, Forever Black, Pont des Soupirs. One ensemble was called Moujik, after Yves's dog. Two designs followed each other single file, Je Ne Suis Pas Ce Que L'On Pense (I Am Not What You Think) and Je Suis Comme Je Suis (I Am the Way I Am). The last item was called Je Vivrai un Grand Amour (I Will Experience a Great Love Story). But that year, at the Hotel Intercontinental, the silence was a little too pious. "Mounia, you're the only one who can make them clap," the couturier said to his star model. "One hundred francs for you if you can meet the challenge." Yves was having fun. "I can tell, it's a game to loosen up the atmosphere: 'I want to win, I'll wiggle my behind in navy blue jersey.'"

But that year, the press didn't talk about Yves Saint Laurent's black dress, but Azzedine Alaïa's. Along with agnès b. and her famous cardigan with snaps, he became the latest designer to influence the street. "Fashion still generates interest and attraction, but from a distance, without unbridled magnetism. A cool attitude pervades the ideological space and the political society. Fashion has entered the relatively unpassionate era of consumption, an era of relaxed, amused curiosity," wrote Gilles Lipovetsky.[17] The latest fashion success story was an accessory, the Swatch watch—more than ten million sold in 1986.

Yet designers were at the peak of their influence in the media. "I don't work, you'll never see me drawing anything. I have fun!" said Philippe Starck, the designer of choice of the 1980s. In the various places where he did the décor—such as the hot nightclub Les Bains Douches and the Café Costes in Les Halles—and with his pared-down chairs, he celebrated the return of "less is more." Smooth, rectangular, and zipped up to the neck, fashion expressed itself in a big urban display, from Jean-Paul Gaultier's androgynous models in camouflage and lace to Thierry Mugler's Hollywood warrior women. But the more fashion turned into spectacle, the more it polished its reputation, and only the English made fun of it. In London, they created t-shirts reading "Azebeen Alaïa," "Claude Monotonn," "Yuppie Yamamoto," "Jean-Paul Goat Yeah," and even "Yves Saint Lawrent."

Yves Saint Laurent looked at the era with the feeling that it wasn't his type, even if he was its son. His taffeta and tulle dresses were admired at balls, along with Isabelle Adjani's costume for Luc Besson's *Subway*. He kept expanding the pool of artistic references that fashion could no longer do without. He still admired Vivien Leigh in *A Streetcar Named Desire*: "Her fragile character dressed in sublime old cast-off clothing fascinates me." He loved *Senso* and other Italian films, red velvet, dark jewels, and splendor, the "powerful luxury of the nineteenth century, of Fellini or Visconti, Callas, Verdi," these "fellow travelers" whom he often visited in order to escape from reality.

His designs were honored by retrospectives, but he had too much fury in him, too much life to be buried alive in his own legend, these myths that imprisoned him. "Elegance," he said again, "is totally forgetting what you are wearing. There are a thousand definitions, a thousand different possible versions. The personality counts above all. The elegance of the gesture, the elegance of the heart. It doesn't mean wearing very expensive clothing. If it were only that, that would be terrible." In December 1986, he was in Moscow for the Yves Saint Laurent retrospective at the Central House of Artist of the Soviet Union. He was asked once again to define elegance. He answered, "A happy woman is a woman with a black sweater. A black skirt. A big fake jewel. And a man alongside her."[18] That day, seeing bigwigs wearing very colorful Saint Laurent clothing with loads of jewelry, he said to Jacques Grange, "I think the KGB is very out of touch...."

Yves Saint Laurent spoke to women. And to them alone. Like them, he was able to hide the most serious things under the most carefree manner in the world, and vice versa. He was never more sincere than when he was playing around. "Oh, I love that image," said Catherine Deneuve. "A woman in love is not a woman covered in jewels. But a woman for whom everything becomes simple and natural again. It's true, what's more chic than a black sweater and a black skirt? If the sweater is very soft and the skirt has a great cut, especially. If her heels aren't worn down. If the man is attractive. Well...a woman in love isn't necessarily reasonable. You can make mistakes in love. But pleasure from any source is always welcome!"

He designed dresses as if writing letters to women who would carry this love, since he could not give it. And that's why he was Saint Laurent, rolling on the waves of his time, seeking the equilibrium that he rejected as soon as he attained it. Yet he was the one who threw himself into couture with a fierceness that men judged and women understood. It was a secret he whispered with his colors that then vanished, only to reappear the next season expressed in other words. Wasn't the first design of the summer 1986 collection called Rendez-Vous Avec Vous? But who were these women? What did they do?

In 1986, for the first time since 1963, the annual total of haute couture sales (clients and buyers combined) declined noticeably, dropping from 51 million francs to 38 million francs. A few factors partly explained this phenomenon: the fall of the dollar and the terrorist attacks of 1986 kept Americans away from Paris that year. But the reasons were also connected to changes in women's tastes. They no longer saw themselves in a sophisticated image.

A once loyal Rive Gauche customer admitted:, "Starting in 1985 to 1986, it's true, I started looking elsewhere. Looking all around. A little Montana, a little Mugler. A little bit nun in Japan. I dressed in black. Above all, I didn't want to be noticed. And then there was Marc Audibet's stretch fabric: you can't fight against elastic clothing." From then on, she did her "art gallery marathon" around the Pompidou Centre in black stretch pants with a big bottle of water and a green apple in her Hervé Chapelier nylon tote. André Ostier observed, "Street elegance no longer exists. It's very rare today to turn around and say, 'That woman looks chic.'" In the fashion shows, the trend was toward both ingénues and brazen women. "I'm sure the photographer is in love with me," said the model in the ad for Kookaï, the first ready-to-wear label that promoted its brand without showing the clothes. The young designer Christian Lacroix showed Creole women wearing African faille robes, and Karl Lagerfeld came up with the winged look of his Chantecler line. No one was worried about how they would live or even sit down in these clothes, as long as they twirled on the runway. The press praised Chanel's parodies on the muse Inès de La Fressange, the little neon tweed suits that would become the uniform of Anna Wintour, editor-in-chief of American *Vogue*.

A new era was beginning under the guise of a return to the 1950s. "Because the more people are worried about the future, the more fashion takes refuge in the attic," said Christian Lacroix. In Paris, the hip people whirled around to waltz tunes at the imperial ball at La Nouvelle Eve and the rose ball at Les Bains Douches for its thousand-and-first night of operation. Taffeta was wrapped up, frills and flounces came back, and the minimalist era was flooded with flirty ruffles. Fashion showed off—was put in the window—and haute couture dresses looked more and more like trinkets, celebrating an America where rich women hoped to become baby dolls.

The temples of the night were transformed now that sex was tinged with death. A club called Haute Tension was renamed Salon, and Le Palace broke up its space into cozier areas: a smoking room and bars. Fear lurked all around. The pop star Barbara sang a song called "Sid'Amour à Mort," a play on the words SIDA (French for AIDS) and amour. The risk wasn't creating life, but finding death. People hid behind coyness. Warhol was gone: the king of Pop Art died on February 22, 1987, at age fifty-eight. After undergoing routine gallbladder surgery, he died twenty-four hours later of a heart attack. His death would be his last work of art: a gold mine for publishers, gallerists, and auction houses, where prices of his work shot up. Art critic Otto Hahn called his Campbell's soup cans the "twentieth-century Mona Lisa." The Museum of Modern Art planned the largest traveling exhibition ever for a painter. The "paragon of the banal" had passed away, while his prophecies were coming to pass: "In the future, everyone will be world-famous for fifteen minutes."

American art collecting fever took over interior design and fashion. Culture became obligatory: "I have so many books to read, so much music to listen to," said Sao Schlumberger, who took the Concorde to Museum of Modern Art board meetings, determined to get rid of her eighteenth-century furniture collection. She bought Barceló. The media was obsessed with the figure of the artist, which crystallized all desires for permanence. Every art lover could have the feeling of participating in history by buying a unique piece—a chair or even a numbered edition of a dress—and stating, "I collect, therefore I am." Art became a safe investment, and, even more, a kind of salvation by which money itself became a work of art. In Paris, the Japanese invested millions in real estate, including art galleries. As for the financiers, they bought designers.

For the first time since Ungaro opened in 1968, a maison de couture was launched in February in Paris, on Rue du Faubourg Saint-Honoré, exactly forty years after Dior opened his own company. Christian Lacroix was thirty-six. On July 26, 1987, the Arles native had his first fashion show. With designs such as Lampion, Colomba, and Jules César, his meringues of taffeta, and his leather-skirted herdswomen, his dancing girl outfits with embroidery, overstitching, and quilting, Christian Lacroix created a sensation. It was a couture fireball. The images came to life on the runway, like memories of a southern French street festival. On that Sunday, the photographers were more nervous than bullfighters. The journalists fanned themselves with bright pink press folders, and the silk rustled to the strains of Spanish flamenco singer Camarón de la Isla and "Djobi Djoba" by the Gipsy Kings. "It's baroque," the journalists said. A dancing procession of trim, chenille, tassels, and bullfighting capes. "I'll never be a high-society couturier. My truth is in Camargue," said Lacroix, referring to the wetlands south of Arles. He became the new hero of Parisian fashion. His sponsor at the Chambre Syndicale was Pierre Bergé. He described himself as "more of a decorator than an architect." Bird wings and gold shrubs stuck up in the air from his hats. Couture wasn't a calling for Christian Lacroix: with an art history degree in hand, he had come to Paris to become a museum curator. "Fantastic, this is the new couture!" exclaimed John Fairchild of *Women's Wear Daily*. Christian

Lacroix made the cover of *Time* magazine, something that had never happened to Yves in his thirty-year career.

Haute couture would offer itself one last illusion of splendor, before the fall caused by the Gulf War: the skirts bubbled out, the hairstyles expanded into beehives, the breasts were filled out with silicone, the handbags shrank, and the pretty woman silhouette swelled like an ephemeral bubble of prosperity.

Yves Saint Laurent was once again alone. Trained in the school of artifice, he would find a way of redefining himself in simplicity, like women who were not born into high society but became its last ambassadors. He would emerge from his silence.

But how could a style, however modern, fight its era? Times were changing. Could Yves surpass himself once again? Could he continue to transform his company while preserving its intimate atmosphere as a "maison d'amour"? Like Scarlett taking down the green curtains to make a dress, he got ready to go into town.

Mergers, consolidations, expansion. The war for the Paris luxury market had begun. Pierre Bergé and Yves Saint Laurent jumped into the fray in December 1986, when they bought Charles of the Ritz perfumes from Squibb for 630 million dollars. The goal was to capitalize on the prestige of the Saint Laurent name and support the couture studio with a very profitable sector—perfumes and cosmetics. This sector was responsible for 2.2 billion out of 2.5 billion francs in revenue. Opium (38 percent) and Paris (18 percent) were responsible for most of the fragrance sales.

This was a decisive step in the company's history, as it took it from a prosperous business (339 million francs in 1987) to an international company. Of Yves Saint Laurent's 2,650 employees, 2,308 worked in fragrances and 342 in couture. The company had become a manufacturer whose cosmetics factory, located in Lassigny in the Oise department, employed 650 people. One hundred million francs would be invested to develop the cosmetics line. The headquarters were in Neuilly, just outside Paris, in the former Charles of the Ritz building. Eighty percent of Yves Saint Laurent's revenue came from abroad, and there were fourteen subsidiaries around the world.

For Pierre Bergé, who said he got into business "by chance," the goal was clear: to become the leading global luxury company in three years. In January 1987, he told the French magazine *L'Express*, "I prowled around Vuitton a lot a few years ago, so why not leather goods? But there are other interesting areas to explore by buying quality companies: wine, champagne, cognac…" That same year, LVMH (Louis Vuitton-Moët-Hennessy) was formed, becoming the number one luxury company in the world, and the one with the highest market capitalization on the Paris stock market.

While Cardin made it a point of honor to "never borrow a penny from a bank," Pierre Bergé and Yves Saint Laurent took on debt. Alain Minc, the head of Cerus, Carlo de Benedetti's French holding company, played a key role. Cerus purchased a stake in Yves Saint Laurent; as of December 31, 1986, Cerus owned 37 percent of the company and Pierre and Yves held 63 percent.

The financial adventure had begun with 2.8 billion francs of debt. After acquiring the YSL fragrances, Pierre Bergé quickly sold some of the brands in the Charles of the Ritz portfolio to Revlon in June 1987: Charles of the Ritz, Alexandra de Markoff, and the Bain de Soleil line of sun products. Debt was thus reduced to 1.9 billion francs.

The company was restructured in late 1987 and then again in June 1989, in order to be listed on the Paris stock market via a newly created entity that would be safe from a takeover: it was transformed into a joint-stock company managed by the limited liability company Yves Saint Laurent Management. Pierre Bergé announced the listing on the stock market, which provided more than one billion francs in capital. This move was delayed due to the stock market crash, but was completed in July 1989.

Pierre Bergé began his offensive, adopting a policy of high-end brand positioning. Regarding fragrances, he closed his accounts with "certain suspect clients," which translated into a "voluntary loss" of 50 million francs in revenue, the establishment of a U.S. distribution center, and a research center in La Celle-Saint-Cloud, near Paris. He also bought back Yves Saint Laurent Fashion B.V., which held the rights to the couture brands for North America and Australia. He took back control of furs, which had been licensed out. An accessories boutique was launched in Paris on Rue du Faubourg-Saint-Honoré (just steps from the Rive Gauche boutique, which was bought back in 1987) and another was relaunched in New York in great splendor.

Pierre Bergé was now the head of Yves Saint Laurent Management. He had his hands in all the company activities and put two men under forty years of age in high-ranking positions: Jean-Francis Bretelle and Pierre de Champfleury became the directors of the company in 1988. Bergé supported the development of new product lines: over 20 percent of revenue would be devoted to marketing and advertising for product launches. He decreed, "From now on, all activity is focused on the single name Yves Saint Laurent."

Communications became more structured with the creation of a department of art direction within the company. Its first big success was the launch of Jazz perfume in March 1988 with a film by Jean-Baptiste Mondino. Sales reached 169 million francs in the first year, surpassing estimates by 70 percent. The executives met in strategic committees. In their offices, there were no shelves filled with files, but photos of Yves hung up like icons. He was venerated. This was the only company that illustrated its luxurious annual reports with photos of the master arranging a hat on one of his muses.

However, connecting the fragrance sector to the maison de couture wasn't a seamless process. "They considered us poor relations. For them, we were just soap sellers," remembered Marie-Françoise Savary, director of international relations at Parfums Yves Saint Laurent from 1986 to 1992. Codes were established. There were those who called him "Yves Saint Laurent" or "Monsieur Saint Laurent" and others who referred to him as "Yves." Everything connected to design, the studio, and the ateliers was with Yves, and everything regarding management and image was with Pierre. There was hatred and love, there were spats and silence. But those who tried to organize cabals were quickly stymied. "Don't go talking behind people's backs! They'll trap you," someone recalled hearing said. This was the strength of the *grande famille*.

Yves Saint Laurent was in a situation that was paradoxical, to say the least: he was the only one since Dior and Chanel to create a name that was recognized all over the world and strong enough to give fragrances an image that they then lent to the women who wore them—bewitching Opium (the number one selling perfume in Europe) or charming flowery Paris (number six). The couturier continued to design for these women from one collection to the next, with great faithfulness.

Catherine Deneuve described Yves's work: "When I think of him, I think of couture in all its splendor and rigor, a skill practiced by extraordinary men and women. He is both the head and the hands, but there are many other hands needed behind him. His *maison de couture* is his *maison*. It has an incredible intimacy and warmth. It's surely the least snobby department in the company. The people are simple. Perhaps because they're closest to what he is, to his creativity, and they know the real labor hidden behind these wonders. They have no illusions; they can't be fooled by an appearance of luxury. There's too much work behind all that. This maison must bring him a lot of joy, and sometimes I imagine all this must weigh on him."

Would the man be swallowed up by his empire? The revenue from couture (including haute couture, licenses, and the boutiques) increased by 9 percent from 1987 to 1988, but it still amounted to only 370 million francs. That amount was broken down as follows: 278 million francs for licenses, 55 million francs for the boutiques that belonged to the company (the men's and women's boutiques on Place Saint-Sulpice, one boutique in Deauville, and another in New York, which was 50 percent owned by Léon Cligman). An additional 38 million francs in revenue came from haute couture itself (tailor-made). The figure reached 41 million in 1987, but with 25 million in losses. The number of regular clients was 150, and only about ten were French; Liliane Bettencourt, the richest woman in France, remained the most discreet and loyal client. In all, 500 pieces were sold per season. It was the smallest department in the company, represented by 250 seamstresses. But wasn't it the one that assured the company's fame? Profits from licenses (around 500 licensing agreements, including ties, bags, watches, belts, and slippers) were the lion's share. And they allowed Yves to construct his collections with no financial limitations. A haute couture show, including the runway and the models, cost an average of 4 to 10 million francs. At Yves Saint Laurent, it cost 15 million francs, or 30 million francs per year. "We have the luxury of not being able to resist their talent," Loulou said, referring to the accessory makers. In July 1987, Yves Saint Laurent let a "bride of paradise" take flight on the runway, which required the feathers of twenty birds. "The most expensive in the world," specified feather artist André Lemarié.

Inside his château, Yves Saint Laurent created another château. In 1987, he asked Jacques Grange to design his dream office in red and gold on Avenue Marceau. Thick cream wall hangings soaked up the light in silence. A chandelier with rock crystal pendants reflected sheaves of wheat that were placed on art books like good luck charms. In the library were a photo of Silvana Mangano and a portrait of Gustav Zumsteg (who, as head of Abraham, created exclusive fabrics for Yves

Saint Laurent) by Christian Bérard. Watercolors by Bérard for Louis Jouvet's theater productions were also on the walls. Above them was a discreetly hung drawing, *La Bohème* by Forain, which Yves had found in 1962 in the basement at 30 bis Rue Spontini alongside an overturned ten of clubs playing card. Facing it was the portrait of the Baron de Mauvière, which Lucienne Mathieu-Saint-Laurent had brought from Oran. She and her daughters were the only ones who called it "the David." The room had the peppery scent of lilies. A bouquet was permanently placed on Yves's father's Empire desk. As in his houses, which could be visited in his absence, one always had the feeling that Yves's shadow was there, watching. A pile of white papers, sharpened pencils—everything was placed and staged, in an obsessive and touching search for perfection.

Yves had told Jacques Grange what he wanted the design to be based on: "I would like Besteigui's modernist apartment on the Champs-Élysées" that was designed by Le Corbusier in 1935, a model combination of the old and the modern, with contrasts between the light colors and the ruby velvet on a Jean-Michel Frank bench. Yves was there without being there, for all the objects expressed his sensibility and his memory. But, as Loulou said while nonchalantly placing her Perrier on a sharkskin table by Jean-Michel Frank, "He never comes here, it's for interviews."

Yves Saint Laurent did not attend the opening of the Rive Gauche boutique in New York on September 14, 1987. "He'd promised me, but he didn't come," said Joy Hendericks, senior vice president of corporate image. Christophe Girard, who had personally handled all of Yves Saint Laurent's appearances since 1983, explained, "Pierre Bergé has never wanted to impose insurmountable travel on Yves Saint Laurent. We avoid dragging him all over, both for him, and in order not to trouble people who want to see him 'well.'" Wherever Yves Saint Laurent had to shake people's hands, Christophe Girard would smooth the way for him. A slender bodyguard with the physique of a seminarian, a guard with a boy scout's voice, he was the man of official communiqués and air kisses. His job was to be nice. It was quite an art. In his office, located halfway between Pierre Bergé's office and the studio, he had a framed quotation by Pascal, like an announcement: "The nature of power is to protect." To the right was a photo of Pierre Bergé with François Mitterrand.

Joy Hendericks remembers the Rive Gauche store opening. "Some people canceled when they found out that Yves Saint Laurent wasn't coming. In the U.S., Yves Saint Laurent is a star. Yves can say, 'It's nice out,' when it's raining. The Americans are under his spell." Pierre Bergé made it a memorable evening in New York. Mortimer's was entirely redecorated for the occasion. Bergé placed Pamela Harriman on his right. With the glaring exception of Yves, everyone was there: Faye Dunaway and her bodyguard, the Kissingers, Ann Getty with her triple row of emeralds, Kathleen Hearst, Louis Malle and Candice Bergen, Bianca Jagger, Basia Johnson (the billionaire who wanted to buy the construction sites of Gdansk), the Maharani of Jaipur, Pier Luigi Pizzi, and Plácido Domingo. "A time of a lot of hype, a lot of glamour," recalled Joy Hendericks. "Taxes had gone down, people made a lot of money. It was the 1980s. People spent 15,000 dollars on flowers for a dinner." Joy divided her time between Paris and New York. She always used English words when speaking French and French words when speaking English. Every season, the ateliers made four haute couture ensembles for her. This young blond woman made it a point of honor to choose what she would wear for lunch with a journalist at Le Cirque or to spend a weekend in Nassau at Nan Kempner's. Listed as one of the ten most elegant women in the world, she would attract twenty new couture clients during the 1980s. Her royal motto was "Never explain, never complain."

Pierre Bergé and Yves Saint Laurent began to reveal the extraordinary ambition they harbored. As great and prestigious French brands fought over worldwide stakes, they sharpened their weapons and prepared to duel, with the awareness that a new era was beginning.

Skyrocketing art prices, speculation, stock market madness, a gambling boom: the 1980s set wild records. Financial mercenaries built and destroyed empires at high speed. By age forty-two, Donald Trump had put his name on three hotels, and buildings all over Manhattan. He owned an airline and what was then one of the most famous casinos in the United States. Success belonged to golden boys who were brilliant at the swap market technique, which consisted of trading something for something else: currency, commodities, bonds, raw materials, real estate. At the time, Pierre Bergé said, "I've been diverted by destiny. I was made to be a politician or a writer. Life dragged me off elsewhere."

Pierre Bergé and Yves Saint Laurent found the energy to reject the era but still accomplish their dreams in it. Each in his own way went back to his youth. "For there are two solutions," said Pierre Bergé. "You project yourself into childhood and close yourself off. Or you continue to project yourself into the future, because the age of twenty is the only time in your life with the greatest hopes, the greatest desires, the greatest disappointment."

The United States had fashioned Paris in its own image. To keep its influence, Paris had to submit to the taste of these new billionaire women for whom appearance was only a business weapon in the pitiless world of the Dow Jones. That meant orange-pink, pollen yellow, and purples as phosphorescent as their fortunes were new. After a bad experience, the maison Saint Laurent started asking for deposits from new clients. In New York, the 1987 movie *Wall Street*, set in the pitiless world of brokers, showed that the little rich girl was no longer what she once had been. At the top of her game, with a muscular body, she dreamed of a yellow diamond and a penthouse with a roof deck, and she bought sofas that matched her contemporary art collection. Avenue Montaigne became the Valley of Luxury, and Paris was the capital of fashion spectacle: 950 models from 20 different countries paraded for 12,000 spectators at the Festival International dc la Mode, which was organized by professional fashion associations. Fireworks and spangles masked the growing disparity between Paris, where everything was shown, and Milan, where everything was sold. Between 1982 and 1988, the number of accredited journalists at the ready-to-wear shows at the Louvre's Cour Carrée grew from 1,200 to 2,000. These shows in March and October had many other impressive figures: 200 mirrors, 500 clothes racks, 4,500 chairs, 40,000 square meters of fabric for the runways, and 15 kilometers of cables.

Paris defended its role as a fashion showcase with panache. Openings and launches: everything and anything was an excuse for parties and celebrations. In Paris, the perfumers and couturiers were the latest patrons of the arts: Ricci called on Sol LeWitt for the packaging of its new perfume, Vuitton had scarves designed by Sandro Chia and Arman. Vuitton also financed the Canaletto exhibition at the Metropolitan Museum of Art, and Guerlain gave a Samsara ball in the Galerie des Batailles at Versailles. Dior's Poison ball was unforgettable. With a budget of five million francs, it was the most expensive perfume launch in history. Jacques Grange had decorated the Château de Vaux-le-Vicomte, and 220,000 leaves of ivy papered the walls for 800 guests. It was an era, declared André Ostier, ruled by people who didn't "know if they're in Hong Kong or Paris. These aren't the kind of people who make a society."

Pierre Bergé's rival was no longer Cardin—even businessmen who knew nothing about fashion said his stuff was junk. Bergé's rival was Bernard Arnault, who was already nicknamed "the young prince of Avenue Montaigne." With his victory in place, he was now focused on management. He was said to be secretive and a poor speaker. But he had enjoyed a meteoric rise. Born in Roubaix in 1949, he attended the prestigious École Polytechnique and early on had a few successes under his belt, including purchasing the Boussac textile company, which owned Christian Dior, in 1985. Although he initially invested only 90 million francs, he used leverage to coldly impose a strict recovery plan that cut back on the company's textile activities. Alliances, counter-alliances, takeover attempts: the Arnault method was established. With a global distribution agreement between Guinness and Moët-Hennessy in June 1987, Arnault strengthened his positions, obtaining the resignation of Alain Chevalier (head of Moët-Hennessy) and dragging seventy-five-year-old Henry Racamier to court to obtain ownership of Vuitton and to sideline Racamier as president. In March 1989, Arnault became the sole master of the company, which had 16.4 billion francs in revenue in 1988 and 22 billion in 1992 (to compare, Yves Saint Laurent's revenue was 2.6 billion in 1988 and 3 billion in 1992). In 1985, one of Arnault's first actions was to make himself president (PDG) of Christian Dior. Called by Le Nouvel Economiste a "self-controlled man with rather cold manners," Arnault belonged to the new generation of "eager bosses" in the luxury sector. He was convinced that a good manufacturer was first of all a good financier. He had the power to govern a company, although he actually owned only about 3 to 4 percent of its capital. He built his empire with the support of banks and, with American training in the field, he applied the formulas he had tested in construction and real estate to haute couture.

Dior opened specialty shops and rented Disneyland Tokyo to celebrate the maison's fortieth anniversary. In Paris, a retrospective was held at the Musée des Arts de la Mode and drew 80,000 visitors. A party was given for the staff at the Lido. They took no risks. The boutique on Avenue Montaigne was recreated identically in a slightly new style. When asked, "How much did you spend?" Bernard Arnault replied, "Much too much." In his corner, Jean-Pierre Frère reflected, "They buy a tree with fruit. They start by cutting the roots. The tree dies." Frère was one of the last pillars of the maison Dior. When he talked about its founder, he still referred to him as "Monsieur Dior." Built like a cartoon character, with two little legs under a big stomach, he was a rather bitter person who complained about "these fucking computers."

So, here were Bernard Arnault, the yuppie raider, and Pierre Bergé, the business artist—two different generations, two different styles, two different kinds of management. "I always thought that creators in general—let's say couturiers, to be more precise—were all megalomaniacs," Bergé told Sonia Rykiel in an interview published in the March 1988 *Femme*. "They all think they're the greatest. The difference between the real and the fake couturiers is that the real ones are unhappy megalomaniacs and the fake ones are happy megalomaniacs.…Couturiers, more than other artists, are afraid that their work will disappear, whereas painters, writers, and musicians can always cling to the judgment of eternity. So they need to be more encouraged and reassured."

Pierre Bergé was an entrepreneur and a leader, and, although he liked flying his helicopter, he was definitely a man of the nineteenth century, "the century of truth and jokes. Never were there more lies, or more quests for truth."[1] His principle was to teach others what he didn't know just yesterday, to remember that he started out "buying books along the Seine." At the end of an interview, he strategically mentioned, "My work in theater and publishing is a bit dormant…but I haven't said my last word. Maybe I'll get a bit involved in politics. 1988 is a good year."[2]

Bernard Arnault was first of all a financier, and he came from a world where the custom was to be discreet, combining French standards of polite behavior with the raiding techniques imported from Wall Street, i.e., discovering the other person's strategy while hiding your own. When he wasn't managing his company, he was playing tennis. His literary choices seemed more limited. He liked *A Brief History of Time* by Stephen Hawking and *The Nature of Managerial Work*, which he reviewed for the business magazine *Challenges*. Every season, wearing a dark suit, he sat in the front row for the fashion shows of the companies in his stable: Dior, Lacroix, and Givenchy (as of 1988). In a strange mirror effect, he was like another Marcel Boussac, who had funded Dior forty years earlier. In 1987, Arnault invested 50 million francs in Christian Lacroix.

Christian Lacroix was a media success, which was all the more astonishing, as it had nothing to sell but haute couture dresses: 96,000 francs for the Colomba dress, made of velvet with fishnet embroidery, and 188,000 francs for the Vaccares coat, made of pastel mink. This euphoria quickly led to a high-end ready-to-wear line and a rapidly launched fragrance, C'est la Vie! This high society glory plunged the couturier into the illusion of a triumph that was too quickly won: 39 million in losses for 89 million francs of revenue in 1992. Worried? "Yves Saint Laurent took fifteen years to get into the black," a source recalled hearing at the time.

But in 1988, Christian Lacroix was part of the excitement surrounding Spain's entry into the European common market. Not the Spain of Picasso and Goya, but that of street festivals, tapas, and generally a different South. The French cable channel Canal Plus broadcast bullfights live. *Actuel* accompanied the Gipsy Kings to a gypsy wedding. Seville vibrated at the Bastille. Women whirled around at Distrito and nibbled *gambas a la plancha*, while *Femme* had a ten-page spread on the "gypsy look": "Don't hesitate to try on the proud look of the people of Camargue." And the beautiful people discovered the *alegría de la Movida* ten years late. Fashion journalists put away the black dresses they'd bought from the Japanese, because with Christian, "design is youthful again." In New York, at charity galas, billionaires showed off their little embroidered suits. Even Sao Schlumberger played along. The next season she said, "Oh, yes, I love Lacroix! In fact, I gave a bubble dress to the Palais Galliera. I'm keeping the Saint Laurent tuxedos. I can't wear plunging necklines anymore."

Indeed, haute couture would rediscover everything that seemed to have definitively disappeared after the 1950s: Second Empire crinolines, fluffy lace jabots, skirts bursting with flares, torrents of duchesse satin, ruched taffeta ball gowns, and Winterhalter-style petticoats. Tassels, pompoms, ruffles, and lace trim were everywhere. It was the Musée d'Orsay effect, suggesting Napoleon III interiors. But instead of flipping through encyclopedias and art books, as in Dior's time, designers tore out pages from coffee table books. They juxtaposed, and they decorated, imitating an imitation. The spirit of the masters faded under the constantly cruder features of erudition. As of 1987, haute couture had rediscovered inlaid furniture, gilded wood, and bisque porcelain, in a quite spectacular return to tradition: 80,000 gold spangles and 700 hours of labor for the Atys ensemble from Chanel.

At the time, Pierre Bergé thundered, "Christian Lacroix didn't revive haute couture. He revived those who were asleep. Saint Laurent is at the cutting edge of contemporary, of boldness, of creativity. Saying that couture is anachronistic is a false debate, forgetting that it's about design, about a work of art. A haute couture dress is just about as rare and expensive as a valuable painting. Haute couture is here, we have to deal with it. Engravings and lithographs are our perfumes. Is it anachronistic to make paintings? Is a dress made to be sold? I have no idea. Did Picasso think about the price of his painting while he was painting it? Fashion is part of contemporary art." For Pierre Bergé, doing business was just a way of "working with the beautiful." He saw Saint Laurent as "a combination of Flaubert and Nerval."

The clothing wars had started. You were Lacroix. Or you were Saint Laurent. It was almost like a religion, like belonging to a clan. Paris against Arles. Lines versus decorations, which were intellectualized with the term "postmodern." One of the Saint Laurent faithful put it this way: "With a Lacroix jacket, I can do to a cocktail party at Maxim's. With a Saint Laurent jacket, I meet business leaders and artists. People who have a lot of money, and people who don't have any. I can dress up or dress down a Saint Laurent suit. I told my friend, 'You're a brunette, you're typical, you live in Toulouse. Lacroix is perfect for you.'"

For the first time since he started, Yves Saint Laurent did not make the front page of *Women's Wear Daily*—Lacroix did. So Yves Saint Laurent banned John Fairchild, the all-powerful head of the American paper, from his shows. As usual, Pierre Bergé had to man the battlements. "John Fairchild has been having duels with this profession for a long time. When Saint Laurent gets on his hobby horse, it makes noise, it will make noise. We like critics just fine, but you can't go that far. He's definitely no longer invited. Fashion journalists look at fashion shows like a game of chess. The problem is, they're not the ones who are playing. In a few years, no one will know who John Fairchild is. We're not here to be subjected to this guy's menopausal moods," he said in September 1987. Bergé's anger ran hot, but it only lasted for two seasons. "My best title is to be the friend of John Fairchild," he said in 1993. Fairchild had a polite and diplomatic way of describing the squabble: "We put Lacroix on the front page because we had found something new. We're journalists, right?" Some people in the industry said that America wanted to "make" Lacroix as it had "made" Dior forty years earlier. A failure?

In October 1987, Yves gave the press a big dose of showy theater, as if to recapture its attention. It was his tribute to Hockney: big Pierrot-style smocks belted with black satin, Harlequin blouses, ruffs, pointed hats, suits made of a heavy silk blend with big discs for buttons. The whole spirit of Ravel's opera *L'Enfant et les Sortilèges* burst out in a fantasy of roses and little soldiers with shoulders of red raffia. To return to his first love, Yves called on Madame Fougerolles, Roland Petit's costume designer, for these ballerina skirts sprinkled with roses. "Hockney meant *joie de vivre*. It was very tempting. Since I'm usually so severe, so sparse." For the first time in a long time, the runway featured men dressed like those that Yves drew in the Casino de Paris era, with their muscles protruding under their red, orange, and green pants.

After being invisible for four years, Yves started to go out again. "Baron and Baronne Guy de Rothschild have the illusion that you will come dance around Vanessa at their home on Friday, December 11, 1987 at 10:30. Enchanted dress." Printed on a white silk scarf, the invitation was slipped into a Magician's Cone shell. It was the first grand party given at the Hôtel Lambert since 1981. The guests had to get past the double barrier of photographers and security. The cobblestones in front of the mansion were sprinkled with silver dust. In the entrance, an immense mirror welcomed "people of fairies, princes, elves, and enchantresses," which thrilled Étienne de Montpezat, who wrote it up for *Vogue*. Powdery snow fell in sparkling clouds. Four ballerinas from the Ballet de l'Opéra de Paris did graceful arabesques, while others in romantic tutus and silver tiaras moved along the staircase. Yves Saint Laurent had designed Vanessa's dress. She appeared in white tulle with constellations of silver stars and crescent moons "like a guardian angel opening the gates of Paradise," *Vogue* noted. Everyone was arriving. A servant in Louis XVI–era garb announced the guests. Coincidentally, this was also Christian Lacroix's first big social appearance since his success. The clan was there: Pierre Bergé, Clara Saint, Charlotte Aillaud, Jacques Grange, and Betty Catroux, in a jacket embroidered with white mice. "You could tell the Saint Laurent women. In the midst of all those gigantic dresses, they had jackets and pants, they were straight lines," noted Colombe Pringle, editor-in-chief of *Vogue Paris*. On the dance floor, musicians wearing diamond bowler hats made magical music for the queens of the night, who had come "from the mists of the North and the sands of the desert": from Brazil, the Mayrink Veigas; from California, Gregory Peck and his wife in a pink dress with pink hair; from Florence, the Frescobaldis; from Italy and Paris, all the Brandolini d'Addas; from Greece, a squadron of Goulandrises; from Spain, the painter Rafael Cidoncha; from England, Sir James Goldsmith and his daughter Isabel all garbed in gold. "We noticed the absence of Caroline of Monaco, who had said she'd come as a sapphire fairy, and of Liz Taylor, who couldn't leave Los Angeles. Sons and granddaughters of French political stars appeared in the Galerie d'Hercule: Henri Giscard d'Estaing, Olivier Barre, Henri Balladur, Elisabeth d'Ornano, along with members of the Académie Française (Jean d'Ormesson, Maurice Rheims), researchers (Pierre Nora, Joël de Rosnay) and the eternal ballerina chasers: Jacques Chazot and Rudolf Nureyev. It was after midnight when Françoise Sagan made her appearance, in wonderful clouds with a Puss-in-Boots ruff: "a Saint Laurent in a Saint Laurent."[3]

That night, Marie-Hélène lost a jewel, creating ripples of panic among the guests the following days. But another incident happened toward the end of the night. It must have been about 3:00 AM. Yves Saint Laurent was at the same table as Françoise Lacroix, the wife of Christian Lacroix. Putting down her glass of wine, she said in a bitter voice, "This guy is not a genius at all. He's been doing the same thing for twenty years." Yves was eating his spaghetti, bent over his plate. "He was a little embarrassing to see," recalled one of those present. No one moved. "Who is this lady?" asked Yves. He extended his hand to her and said, "Hello, I'm Yves Saint Laurent." After a few minutes, he got up, staggering slightly. "This woman is too ill-mannered. I cannot stay at her table." The whole clan got up. The editor-in-chief of an important fashion magazine did the same: "Sorry, I wear the colors of

Yves Saint Laurent." In the room, they waltzed, the editor supporting Yves's weight. Christian Lacroix later denied that it ever happened.

"You must believe in fairies for them to appear," said Loulou. Five weeks later, Yves Saint Laurent showed Paris a spectacular collection, which put him on the cover of *Vogue* and *Femme* and garnered him great praise in *Paris Match* and a sensational comeback in the American press. "Marriage of Fashion and Art by Saint Laurent" (*New York Times*). "Love Takes Wing in Paris" (*New York Daily News*). "I have more than a new joy in life, I have a new joy in creating," he told Frédéric Marc of *Femme* by telephone. Created in three weeks, the Cubist collection was inspired by Braque. Doves made of embellished white gazar or feathers were attached to peacock blue or ibis pink dresses, perched in the hollows of the throats, with gray pearls in their beaks. Writing for the newspaper *L'Humanité*, Michel Boué said, "He's no longer Saint Laurent, he's Saint Francis, and we give him thanks." Yves Saint Laurent embroidered Braque's cubist violins on capes of ecru canvas. But the biggest attractions were two jackets embroidered to look like paintings by Van Gogh, *Sunflowers* and *Irises*, the latter of which was at the time the most expensive painting ever sold at auction, fetching 53.9 million dollars at Sotheby's on November 11, 1987. At a time when the art world was all about spiking prices, Yves Saint Laurent showed the most expensive jackets in the world (450,000 and 500,000 francs). Each jacket required 670 hours of labor. "To obtain this impression of being painted with a knife, tips of ribbons had to be added to the embroidery, which then had to be steamed with a special product to get the colors to blur on the canvas," explained embroiderer François Lesage. The Iris jacket required 250,000 sequins in 22 colors, 200,000 beads threaded with a crochet needle, and 250 meters of ribbon. The Sunflowers jacket had 350,000 sequins and 100,000 tiny porcelain tubes that were sewn on one by one. But nothing was too expensive for his clients: one of the six women who bought the jacket special-ordered a long version of it. It spotlighted the difference between a time when women were admired as works of art, made to bankrupt men, and the modern period, when women had a price based less on what they were worth and more on what they wore.

In retrospect, those items were problematic. First of all, in real life Yves dreaded birds more than anything. But perhaps more tellingly, the jacket-paintings obscured what was really special about Yves Saint Laurent—qualities that a press eager for spectacle was already aiming to overlook. "I really liked the 'day' portion of this collection," he said. His true development lay there. After the show he said calmly, "I started out more fanciful. For twenty years, I've sought an unchangeable wardrobe. A very fine suit. Beautiful skirts. Today it's extreme simplicity that brings me the greatest joy. Getting to the point where it is everything and nothing at the same time. I always think of the modern woman who is weighed down by nothing. The more the clothes are simple, the more the cut counts. Finally, couture is an act of love. Men hate women in costume. It's not enough to have a puffy red skirt and a tuft of feathers on your head to get noticed. Technique is what matters. Otherwise, you could just gather fabric, pin it with flowers, and put on green bird-of-paradise feathers."

These years were essential to Yves Saint Laurent's aesthetic: while other couturiers developed increasingly elaborate get-ups, he took a zen approach to the material. "Elegance is simplicity," he said. He attained this simplicity without leaving any traces of a struggle. In the nudity of his fabrics, he revealed himself as a being of a different species, leaving the memory of all women in a single one in the portrait of his heroines. His line became more supple, and his color combinations became more and more subtle. There was a new harmony in the design, the color (which was emphasized by the refining of the cut), and the construction. The ateliers were inseparable from him. All his sense of theater was concentrated in a search for effects that were less and less theatrical. He chose models with more regular features, beauties with light-colored eyes who bordered on coldness, such as Tatiana or Sylvie Gueguin, who embodied this new ideal of flawlessness and elegance. "I love camel, shades of beige, the colors of cashmere. The shoulders are very straight. To me, that's me," he said, referring to the image of a woman with white gloves moving down the runway, in a suit that she seemed to wear for herself and her friends, as naturally as possible.

The shadows became colors. They took on a range of shades, blended together, and enveloped the fabrics, resulting in havana whipcords, autumn leaves flannels, cream three-quarter-length cashmeres. The color of a duck blue mousseline or a pair of purple suede gloves awoke the fabrics with a vivid touch, as the frosty sun lights up the Seine on a winter day. And then something more tender, more overwhelming was felt. The "sharks of the Boulevards" with their fuchsia cheekbones and too-thin hips whom he had celebrated just two years earlier were no more. It's as if he got closer to women, to an image in movement, suggesting the portrait of a woman passing by. It was Naughty Lulu, "just a woman." The silence of a black dress. A naked back. A mane of hair. Legs. A light draped fabric, held by a single button, like putting the final dot on the "i" of fashion.

In 1988, it was his pleasure to "Revoir Paris," like a song someone hums. A reignited desire. A dance-hall tune. All these memories melted together. Memories of childhood, of a first painting at age eight. *A Village Wedding* by Rubens. Memories of Saint Laurent Swing, from the lighthearted early 1970s, intoxicating nights of gigolos and pink champagne. "I had no youth," he never stopped saying. On the contrary, he would prove that he never stopped being a child, this man with an image of "an overgrown teenager, thin as a rail, already hidden by huge glasses" (in Louis Malle's 1963 film *The Fire Within*) that was always distorted in the mirror. But this physical change only brought him closer to his childhood. He continued to dream when seeing a woman getting out of a taxi, like the hero of *The Fire Within*: "You see, you want to touch her. Paris is like her. Life is like her."

A tree had earned him a perfect score on the drawing portion of his *baccalau-réat* exam, and that remained the symbol of this quest, this imaginary rootedness. His memory continued to develop like living matter. Yves Saint Laurent didn't get stuck: it was as if in his work the images started moving again. When you see these women, you always think of Cukor's *The Women*, a movie without men that talked only of men. He spoke of the Parisian woman, with the goddesses of the silver screen before his eyes, the ones who made him dream when American movies and magazines only increased his desire for Paris. "Elegance is a charm in the face, a mystery. It's the way she holds her legs, puts her arms on a sofa, smokes a cigarette. I'm obsessed with women with cigarettes. I think it's ever since Marlene or Lauren."

In March 1988, the Rive Gauche show was once again a big event. While fashion was filled with back stories, decorative details, and excess, he stripped down his designs, and in sketches that were more and more focused, he gave expression to the fabric, the dress, and the woman who wore it. "He is incredibly close to his ateliers. It's a unique situation in the couture industry," said John Fairchild. Yves designed "melon" cuffs, indicated the color of the lipstick, "smoky stockings," in that way he had of again becoming Yves Mathieu-Saint-Laurent, the little boy who at age three, according to his mother Lucienne, cried "because he didn't like my dress." In 1988, he continued in that vein, saying, "She must have heels for evening." He still had that energetic line, with which he drew this "black crepe dress. Lining of enormous silk satin. Big jewelry." Of course, everything was perfectly arranged, even his handwriting, which was more and more impressive, with big thick lines and firmly marked accents, like drops of rain on a child's drawing. His imagination made the design real. He tamed the fabric, the sleeves flowed and stopped,. They were definitions of dresses, and in the plunging neckline whose delicate point seemed to continue all the way to the floor, he let his signature be seen once again, like a *Y* on the skin. At the end, Naomi Campbell came out in a black wrap-around skirt and a bolero tuxedo jacket with no shirt, holding a bottle of Jazz. There was a lunch for 1,500 people under a tent in the Louvre's Cour Carrée.

Yves Saint Laurent kept his lifelong weapons: "My glasses, my pencils." He always stayed true to his drawing pencils, Mars Lumograph 100 2B Staedtlers in blue and black. "They're the only ones that are good for drawing. The others don't have that strength." In a slightly mocking tone, he specified, "In Marrakesh I don't draw. But in Paris, yes. On a little desk by Jean-Michel Frank made of shagreen. It happens all by itself." Music inspired him: "I still haven't gotten out of all my problems with the outside world. I hate being recognized on the street," he said, surely realizing that he was recognized less and less because his body and appearance had changed. When he came out at the end of the show, some women started crying. Backstage, people rushed over to kiss him. Afterward, he left, with lipstick on his cheeks, a little bit out of it, led off by his staff. One day, he delayed, and was there, squatting down, drawing on the ground for a black woman in a lab coat. Like two crazy people, they were two quiet children crouching under the crowd that showered its compliments and judged behind one's back. "I thought he would age like an old young man, like Cocteau," said Claude Berthod, editor-in-chief of *Maison Française*, wearing all Alaïa, in her white and gray office. "The turning point wasn't handled well. I feel that he was seized by his handlers." She remembered with amusement the love letters that Yves Saint Laurent sent her after his interview on *Dim Dam Dom* twenty years earlier. "I almost could have used them to get a divorce!" In 1968, she had asked him to answer the Proust Questionnaire: "To what faults do you feel most indulgent?" "Betrayal."

Around this time, Pierre Bergé decided to test his wings. "As lucid and responsible men, let's try to seize this historic opportunity," he wrote in a March 1988 letter to five thousand French business owners, asking them to support François Mitterrand's re-election. "He seems to me to be the only one who can take us safely to the gates of the year 2000." Jacques Calvet, the CEO of Peugeot, immediately went on the offensive and told his staff to stop buying Saint Laurent products. Bergé retorted, "Unlike his cars, Calvet's opinions aren't very advanced." Bergé accompanied Mitterrand on his annual pilgrimage climb of the Rock of Solutré in Burgundy and believed him to be the only man "who can answer the big questions: the rights of man, immigration, inequality. Who else today among the candidates is moving in the direction of a better and more just humanity?"

Pierre Bergé was like a young man again. The more he showed himself, the more Yves hid himself, as far as the press was concerned, since they judged a couturier less for what he did than for what he said, outside of his collections. Some people said that the white salon that once held the Warhols had enveloped him completely. "I live in a vacuum. I'm lucky enough to have feelers. Sometimes, I only go out in a car. Sometimes, it's a way of walking, flowing hair, or a gesture that inspires me." Francine Weisweiller, one of his oldest clients, said: "He was even more shy than he is now. Ever since he's been called the greatest couturier in the world, I admire his modesty even more!" Charlotte Aillaud pointed out, "His dresses show up in homes where he never goes, and in these beloved streets where he hardly ever goes." However, he knew how to make an appearance when necessary. In March 1988, he was noticed at the club Les Bains Douches, posing next to Georges-Marc Benamou, the editor-in-chief of *Globe,* and Loulou, who wore a scarlet satin jacket. "That was the first time I had seen him again since Le Palace," said Guy Cuevas.

But he was so removed from what was happening at the time that he forgot to sign a letter dated April 6, 1988, supporting Françoise Sagan, who was charged with illegal drug use. Thirty-two prominent personalities signed the letter, including Barbara, Jane Birkin, Jean-Jacques Beineix, Inès de la Fressange, Jean-Paul Gaultier, and Sonia Rykiel. In the letter, they said that they were all guilty of "having smoked a joint or had a little too much to drink." Pierre Bergé, who didn't smoke and wasn't known for excessive drinking, signed the letter as well.

On August 31, 1988, Pierre Bergé was named president of the Paris opera houses by François Mitterrand, a post which he accepted without remuneration, like all of his other positions, except for that of CEO of the Saint Laurent company. At the time, Bergé was at the height of his popularity in cultural circles. He was an active supporter and president of the anti-AIDS organization ARCAT. Yet he said, "I had already chosen a position in the shadows when I founded the maison Yves Saint Laurent. I don't like making a spectacle of myself! People who have galas, who collect money that way to give to the poor and the sick, that's their problem. Personally, I find it a bit indecent for them to promote their own star status through philanthropy. I like discretion." Yet this didn't prevent him from being quoted more and more widely in the press, outside of his connection with the maison Saint Laurent. He was practically the sole financial backer of the monthly magazine *Globe*, which supported François Mitterrand (the March 1988 headline read, "Uncle, Don't Leave Us"). In addition to standing alongside Harlem Désir (one of the founders of SOS Racisme), whom he considered "one of the most important men of this time," and supporting researchers in the fight against AIDS, he now played a role in great humanitarian struggles. He helped researchers by making donations first to the most promising ones, and eventually to all of them—"He's the one who will find the vaccine!"—and he did so with an impatience evinced by few French business leaders. They were certainly less concerned by this scourge. "If you only knew how many doctors in the provinces confuse pneumocystis with pneumonia! There should be a campaign, we should open anti-AIDS centers all over France."[4]

He stood out as a patron of the arts thanks to a skilled ability to combine his generosity with media savvy: he signed a check for one million francs so that the painting *Saint Thomas* by Georges de La Tour could be purchased by the French government. Whatever he did, he never looked like a fighter. He decorated his suite in the Hôtel Lutetia like a cabinet of curiosities designed by Jacques Grange. There were drawings by Ingres and paintings by Braque hung on walls designed to look like parchment. He had an Augsburg dog-clock, a marble Apollo, a collection of *objets*, a terra-cotta Sun King placed in front of the library nook, twelve seventeenth-century busts of Caesar in gilded wood, and even a Degas hung over the bathtub. On his nightstand was a portrait of Virginia Woolf.

On Sundays, he liked to go to the bird market on Quai de la Mégisserie. "I have a great passion for birds. It dates to the time when an old doctor friend of mine showed me a sublime ornithology handbook that he wrote. The book never came out. I had canaries, and I also love cages. Cages by Madame Foix are the best in the world!" He liked to cross "a true goldfinch with a canary: it creates hybrids that are sterile." His ferocious yelling fits created greater and greater distance between the public man and the regular man every day. Wasn't he actually more secretive than Yves Saint Laurent, who exhibited his invisibility and his depression? Facing the media, he used as much skill to hide his origins as Proust's character Charlus did to hide his homosexuality. Deep down, who was this billionaire who admired heirloom varieties of roses, who showed up at his florist on the Rue de Grenelle, spoke with young Malika in Arabic, asked for a bouquet, and then went behind the counter and helped to pluck the leaves and even to remove the thorns? "He says it relaxes him!" When asked what quality affects him most in others, he didn't give "beauty" as an answer. "I like those who have a 'poetic' physique. The most important quality is faithfulness, not bedroom faithfulness, but true faithfulness—to oneself, to an idea of oneself, to someone else."

In July 1988, a few weeks before Pierre Bergé's appointment as head of the Paris opera houses, Yves Saint Laurent showed his winter collection, Les Raisins de la Colère, the French translation of *The Grapes of Wrath*. "Yves Saint Laurent gave me his pencils so I could be sure of the colors. That's the most wonderful memory of my whole career," said accessory maker François Lesage. It took 16,000 hours of labor, with 45 embroiderers working for three weeks to create a series of embroidered suits and capes. Absinthe satins with turquoise, rose, and black leaves. Colors of pure pigments. A yellow wool cape embroidered with gold and brown foliage on a dress of dove gray velvet. Sprayed with gold, the bunches of grapes didn't seem to be attached to the capes; they moved on "embedded moss" of buckskin, as if lifted by the wind. It was Yves Saint Laurent's tribute to Bonnard's sunny terraces: it was as if he had amassed stockpiles of light, as if he had plunged his hands into purple satin and chartreuse taffeta, for the fabrics were soaked in color. The line was more firm, drawn with a vigorous hand in oil pastel. As if, now, like Majorelle, who no longer painted outdoors, he had captured life. That day, I heard him say sadly backstage, "I'm a failed painter." Yet he told the magazine *Le Point*: "I don't consider what I do to be fashion."[5]

The maison Saint Laurent was living through the glasnost era: on September 8, 1988, Pierre Bergé put on a fashion show at the Fête de *L'Humanité*, the Communist newspaper's annual music festival, with the help of Michel Boué, a journalist there. The real show was in the room, or rather on the grass, while 130 designs came down a huge black runway. That night, the *gauche caviar*—"caviar left," the French equivalent of "limousine liberals"—soaked up some real left-wing populist atmosphere. The scent of Chanel No. 5 mingled with that of grilled merguez sausage. The whole seventh arrondissement was there. No one had ever seen so many limousines in the working-class Parisian suburb of La Courneuve. "I have a dress for Yves in the trunk," said Georges-Marc Benamou. "Come through, Comrade!" The maison Saint Laurent was the only one to receive a visit from Raisa Gorbachev. She looked at a few designs, and Yves came out to greet her. They offered her scarves, a bag, and a big bottle of Opium. The photographers took tons of pictures. "Save your film!" the wife of the head of the Soviet Union said humorously.

Hélène de Ludinghausen, director of haute couture, couldn't hide her joy: she could get back her family's palace in Leningrad—which would soon be renamed

Saint Petersburg. That family ("The Stroganoffs, the ones who gave Siberia to Ivan the Terrible") would turn it into a foundation. The palace was located on Nevsky Prospect. She used "the servants' quarters," an apartment that she had decorated by François Catroux, Betty's husband: "250 square meters, a maid, a car, and a garage." Later, on the foundation's opening day in April 1992, she would send "300 kilograms of clothing for the women curators. I wanted to give them the feeling that this city would discover its splendor again."

Paris, the capital of all excess, was thriving in the euphoria of flowing dollars. At Christmastime, Hermès sold a silk scarf every twenty seconds. Bernard Arnault sharpened his strategy: at a press conference at Paris's Hôtel de Crillon on May 12, 1989, he announced that Gianfranco Ferré would take Marc Bohan's place at Dior. With a beard sprinkled with gray and a silk pocket square that matched the polka-dots on his tie, this Italian couturier managed his career like a businessman. "I'll come to Paris every week," promised the Pavarotti of fashion, who was rich, famous, and loaded with honors. His Milan company, created in 1978, was a small empire. He designed ten collections per year. At Dior, "team initiatives" were underway: they were talking about "display" and "timing," while the company invested sixty million francs in design in 1989.

In 1989, the maison Saint Laurent had more than three billion francs in revenue. In November, a dazzling fashion show was held in Delhi and Bombay in India. *The Times of India* called it "a magical dream." The profit-sharing plan for the company's employees was at its peak (26 million francs in 1989, dropping to 24 million in 1992). Yves Saint Laurent could measure his success based on his clients' loyalty. The total for haute couture sales (clients and buyers) climbed from 37 million francs to 44 million francs from 1988 to 1989. It was a company record. Yet this success was not quite enough to fulfill him completely. "It wouldn't be very hard to make people elegant. It would only take a great company, that's my dream," he said at the time, as if he were making a list for Santa Claus.

Called "the couturier for the *gauche caviar*" and "the czar of couture," Yves Saint Laurent couldn't resist his own creative dreams. While he and Pierre funded a Paris exhibition of historical Russian costumes from the Hermitage Museum, in Deauville they built a dacha. In the shade of the birches, they reconstructed an *izba,* or Russian log cabin, like the one Peter the Great built in Karelia that had been preserved on Vasilyevsky Island in Saint Petersburg. Put together like a child's construction kit by a local carpenter, the structure was made of massive logs from Siberia. Eight nineteenth-century stained-glass windows from France made it radiant. Jacques Grange, the interior designer of Paris high society (who also worked for Paloma Picasso, Isabelle Adjani, Marisa Berenson, and Sylvia Vartan) had carte blanche once again, looking for antiques in the company of Pierre Passebon, his favorite antiques dealer. In fact, this dacha was almost like a Normandy branch of his Paris Gallery. It was extremely eclectic: sofas with gold-embroidered cushions and

Russian armchairs with feet made of animal horn were combined with an Oriental-style French fireplace and a chandelier by Serrurier-Bovy over a medieval-inspired table. But one piece of furniture stood out, perhaps because it was the least noticeable of all: a chaise longue by Mies van der Rohe, the MR20, which was designed in 1927. It was like a pure line in the midst of all this decorative splendor. It was a reminder of the modern spirit found in the apartment on Avenue de Breteuil, which he acquired in the late 1970s and where he wanted to write.

The house soon acquired a reputation as a model of cocooning and attracted reporters. Yves wasn't there. They took photos of his photograph in a frame inlaid with cabochon turquoise and rubies, between a silver cup, enameled tiles, and a book on Russian ascetics. Pierre Bergé was in that photo, too, in a big green and red cardigan, with a scarf tied around his neck, standing behind the seated Yves with his right hand on the designer's shoulder.

"I know Pierre Bergé and his astounding energy," Rudolf Nureyev told *Libération* on January 6, 1989, a few days after he was named artistic director of the Palais Garnier, the home of the Paris Opera Ballet. "When he walks, it's like you can hear his balls clanking against each other. We haven't yet had a real duet together, just a short recitation for him and a long monologue for me." One week later, the Barenboim affair exploded.[6] In the Saint Laurent press office, the black binders reserved for "the boss" would multiply, while a series of shocking resignations and firings guaranteed that these events would be a hotter topic in the media than all the Saint Laurent fashion shows.

While Parisians were saying, "The Bastille? A place that isn't really made for evening gowns," Yves Saint Laurent got totally immersed in his haute couture collections, even though he had previously announced the death of this profession and already claimed he wanted to stop doing it as early as 1971. He was like a dying man who put on a sublime act while people said every season, "This is the last one." He was called "beyond repair."[7] "Tranquilizers and alcohol don't make things any better." People started to poke around his life the way they did around his houses. An article about him was titled "The Agony of Saint Laurent."

He protected himself with his dreams, his whims, and his colors. Like Deneuve in *Peau d'Ane*: "I want a dress the color of the sun," he said. "I want a coat like a lion." Not only did he get it, through the sway he held over his ateliers, but the wild beast was suddenly on the stage. Katoucha moved forward, ready to leap. As accessory maker André Lemarié recalled, "Loulou de la Falaise gave me a fabric from Abraham, and we made a sample, and then another one. Agreed. We had the green light." The coat was made of vulture, pheasant, and rooster feathers. "Two hundred fifty hours of labor," said Lemarié. "We dyed natural feathers, which makes the colors blend together."

The intensity of Yves Saint Laurent's colors influenced the Rive Gauche collections as well as the cosmetics. Between 1987 and 1991, make-up sales doubled. In 1988 alone, they increased 24 percent. And all this happened without a marketing strategy directing the design process. Terry Cohen, the artistic director for Yves Saint Laurent Fragrances, which launches a make-up line every season, remained closely attuned to the spirit of the couture collections: starting in the late 1980s, she worked on colors inspired by the materials in order to re-create the effect of a fabric—the airiness of mousseline, the sheen of satin, or the matte texture of crepe. Asked about her relationship with Yves, she said, "I must have met him twice in my life. We never had any meetings." But they didn't need to know each other to understand each other.

The more Yves hid in real life, going by the name "Monsieur Swann" on the rare occasion when he traveled, the more he removed himself from his own legend, from all the myths that hindered him. And in this way, the man who seemed the most distant from his own time was actually the man who reflected it best, because he stripped it of everything random or incidental.

He returned to what he deemed a "classicism of the body and the clothes" that brought him ever closer to his role model, Coco Chanel. He seemed closer to the material, too: "I love wool capes for evening. The shoulder was put together very well, you couldn't see the seam. Couture is about directions. There's cutting on the true bias or obliquely. The simplification of the cut makes it modern."

With a multiplicity of references, fashion became more and more decorative, and home décor became more and more fashionable. The home got dresses, put on skirts, and uncovered itself, and it asked women every season, "Well, what color? What hemline?" At a time when his princesses looked like the bourgeois women he'd made fun of twenty years earlier "with smooth hair and always a brooch on the side," his queens—Mounia, Katoucha, Amalia—seemed much more elegant than the real queens photographed in the tabloids. Not because he dressed them as chic women, as in the early 1980s, but because, while others crushed them under fancy outfits, with Yves they didn't trip in their sheath dresses, drop their earrings down the front of their blouses, or bump into the chandelier with their hats. Yves Saint Laurent, the first couturier to evoke art, systematically would also be the only one who didn't keep women immobilized in a golden frame during the late 1980s.

Farewell to the operatic monsters, the tormented souls, the tragic reds, the divas, and other figures of narcissism, such as androgynous, angular creatures. The designs remained. But it was no longer Tosca singing to her torturer: "*Vissi d'arte, vissi d'amore*." It was Tatiana in the finale of *Eugene Onegin* who rejects passion and tries to resist its appeals: "You can't bring back the past."[8] It's Countess Serpieri in *Senso* who hopes to get another letter although she knows it will never come. It's love giving itself. The women of this new era would be all the stronger because they called for protection, because everything in their attitude, the suppleness of these large burnooses with rounded shoulders, these big, slightly pleated skirts, revealed him being true to himself: "To me, this is me." Fewer accessories. Just here and there, a nugget of quartz or hammered metal cuff bracelets. The colors attracted each other, gave each other character: ibis pink and chocolate silk satin, or ivory and pearl gray. And then suddenly, it happened, like a burst of laughter, with red rhinestone buttons on a pink jacket, bird-of-paradise or ostrich feathers that disrupted the naked skin: "Women aren't just about pared-down style or a rigorous line. You need some dreams, some sensuality. What could be more beautiful than to make them look like birds of paradise?"

He draped velvet like crepe, tossed a man's coat over a lacy evening gown, made navy the new black, and made pink the color of enchantment. In his hands, everything seemed easier, even though he embraced constraints: he avoided easy solutions, the conventionalism of couture. Pink mousseline that was too fluttery. Casanova red satin from a TV movie version of Venice. The organza that some designers put graffiti on to look young and hip.

Because he tamed the fabric, he could forget it and express himself more through it. He moved inside his own story and made the dreams of the Little Prince of Dior become visible. The designer who once announced cloud-colored silk organdy now showed straw flowers and black nights without naming them. Katoucha moved along like a ghost, her face veiled in mousseline.

In October 1988, the finale of his Rive Gauche show ended with fifteen women draped in white crepe, while Edith Piaf sang *"Non, je ne regrette rien."* "Neither do we," wrote *Libération*, praising the "radiance" and distinction of the "unchallenged master of perfect colors and cuts."[9] Even if that season the big event was Martin Margiela's first collection, which turned the fashion world upside down with its "reclaimed" clothing. In Paris, fashion victims started rejecting puffy skirts and rediscovered the underground virtues of the poverty-stricken look. "Be poor," they said. In New York, billionaires were troubled: "These homeless people break your heart. It's horrible. Before, there were a few bums on the Bowery, but we didn't see them," said Sao Schlumberger.

Yves Saint Laurent said that he didn't watch TV or read newspapers anymore. But the black birds were flying over his head, like dark omens of beauty. His father died on November 8, 1988. Separated from his wife, he had lived in Monaco since 1972 and lived "a retired life among friends." Brigitte, Yves's sister, said, "My father was my friend. By the end, he was my child." At noon, he had lunch in his "little restaurant," Sam's. In the afternoon, he often went to the Rive Gauche boutique, whose owner was Brigitte's godmother. He also liked La Maison du Caviar and the Café de Paris, where he told stories in an Algerian accent. After each fashion show, he sent a telegram. A heavy smoker, he died at age seventy-nine after a respiratory illness. He hadn't seen his son since 1985. "When he saw him, Yves cried out, 'Papa,' in such an extraordinary way, as if all his love went into this cry. He got down on his knees. He arranged his pocket handkerchief," said Brigitte, who recalled this "terrible moment" at the Monaco funeral home. "In his cry there was all the regret of not having known him. I can still hear it. I'll never forget it." His ashes were scattered in the harbor of Toulon, at the foot of Notre-Dame-de-Cap-Falcon, where there was a statue of the Virgin Mary that had been brought back from Oran by the *pied-noir* community after the Algerian War. In addition to their beach house in Trouville, the Mathieu-Saint-Laurents had a little cabin on Cap Falcon near Oran.

Yet three months later, Yves Saint Laurent showed an haute couture collection of exceptional flawlessness. "A happy woman is a woman with nothing weighing on her," he said. It was as if he had painted the air that blew over the water in Neptune and Ultramarine, capes of iridescent blue mousseline. His fabrics made waves; he was there in a pure blue immensity that purified and transported him, all bundled up in his gestures. "The body must breathe. Everything is in the cut, the movement. It's not possible to go any further."

Everything became movement and sensation. There was no longer any need, as in the early 1980s, to make references to Proust by showing a woman strolling through the Bois de Boulogne under her parasol in a polka-dotted dress. Forgetting the inspiration allowed him to draw out its intimate truth. Swann brought the image of Botticelli's Zipporah close to him to "hold Odette against his heart." Yves held that book against his heart, and it came to life in his eyes and hands. That was the source of his Aurore mousselines, caressing smooth skin as cold as alabaster, his contours of light indicating the fleeting appearance of the woman in pink. No longer the orange-shaded, flowery pink of Paris. But a pink that was more and more powdery, like the illusion of pink. Draped crepe fabric skimmed her skin as she passed by. "A charming, ephemeral dream," he said. No trace of violence, of sensual contact, of a bodily struggle with the fabric. Something troubling and indefinable floated in the air, in the atmospheric softness of these pinks, like vapors of pink, in a garden of bougainvillea. He walked with Gustav Zumsteg in his garden in Marrakesh. He picked a flower. A burst of organza brought it back to life. "The body of a naked woman, which I must dress without harming the freedom of her natural movements. Basically, my job is a loving dialogue with this naked woman, magically wrapping her in my fabric."

Ninety designs. On the way out, the street seemed fuzzy, shapeless. His silhouettes were sometimes so sparse that they looked like test garments, like designs that had just been born in the atelier. Few accessories, just the occasional mother-of-pearl earrings or caps made of gazar punctuating striped ensembles of white linen canvas or a French blue wool jersey dress. The fabric trembled, slid over the shoulders, in the breath of these draped garments that were like sketches, which seemed to say, "These are women who love love."[10]

Pierre Bergé was once again in the headlines. With the strategic aid of Alain Minc, he masterfully orchestrated Yves Saint Laurent's spectacular entrance onto the stock market. On June 4, 1989, at the Louvre, a brand became a stock. Several hundred golden boys and notables of Parisian finance thronged in front of I. M. Pei's pyramid, which had been inaugurated in October 1988. "In general, this happens in hotel basements, or at La Défense. Up until now, museums and monuments had avoided this kind of meeting," noted Philippe d'Abzac, the former chief administrative officer of Saint-Gobain, who was there. "All these people in gray suits were excited." The meeting took place in the auditorium. The financial data were shown on a screen while opera music played. The suspense had begun. Bergé appeared. Saint Laurent wasn't there, but a life-sized photo stood in for him. "Everyone understood that we had to settle for that," added Philippe d'Abzac. "It was like the crowning of the bust of Voltaire by the actors of the Comédie Française after the performance of *Zaïre*." A big cocktail party was given under the great stairs. Champagne flowed freely. Each guest left carrying a gift that was rather cumbersome compared to traditional company gifts: a limited-edition drawing of costumes by Yves Saint Laurent for *The Marriage of Figaro* (1965) in a black wooden frame. "Two young women portrayed American-style," Yves noted at the bottom of the sketch. On July 6, 1989, 400,000 shares (10.36 percent of the capital) were offered on the Paris stock market with a share price of 853 francs; applications to purchase 103 million shares came in, which was 260 times the number of shares offered to the public. In the six months after this ceremony, the shares were very successful, reaching their peak price of 1,200 francs in December 1989 and then beginning to decline.

Just before the bicentennial of the French Revolution, the maison Saint Laurent was in a state of grace. Pierre Bergé's actions on behalf of Chinese students after the Tiananmen Square massacre of June 4, 1989, attracted attention: on Rue de Tournon, he opened the Maison Chinoise de la Démocratie. This gesture occurred at a time when fashion people, cut off from the world, seemed more concerned with stories in the gossip columns. "They squeezed our Christian like a lemon," said the editors. Karl Lagerfeld saw his popularity decline: things were going badly with his muse Inès de la Fressange. In 1984, she had signed an exclusive seven-year contract with Chanel. Five years later, she was telling *Le Figaro*, "Karl is petty and he has absurd ideas. He wanted me to walk the runway in a dress with *fleurs de lys*. His 'Kaiser' side comes out a lot." In her interview, she gave up her chains for jeans and a blue shirt. The reason for the dispute was that she had agreed to be the face of the French national icon, Marianne, "the symbol of everything that is boring, bourgeois, and provincial," said Karl Lagerfeld. The break was permanent. And to top it all off, for her wedding, Inès chose a white suit made by Yves Saint Laurent. On July 24, 1989, for the first time, she didn't appear on the runway. The next day, Yves Saint Laurent finished his season beautifully. The public gave him a true ovation. "This collection is completely different. I hope people will see that. Otherwise, it's just like usual."

Backstage, people pushed one another, almost knocking one another down so they could approach the master. He only had eyes for a tea-rose mousseline dress. A butterfly in the midst of the crowd. As if he were afraid that it would get torn. Two minutes earlier, he moved a photographer out of the way as he was about to step on the bride's train, this madonna with her head encircled with a golden sheaf of wheat who appeared to the sounds of *Agnus Dei* sung by Barbara Hendricks. That was his only concession to lyricism. No decorations, nothing that was too much. It was the extreme point of the line on the page, the perfect note.

There was a new kind of ease, giving a dress of bronze buckskin the suppleness of a sweater that you would slip on with simply two ebony bracelets or a gilded pebble held by a leather string. Eveningwear was like a ritual, with grain de poudre tuxedos that were barely more curvy than before. For night, the brocades crackled and contrasted and the mousseline blazed forth, taking on a purplish, amaranthine, or golden sheen. Embroidery had almost disappeared. He had come back to the most intimate of his performances, that of lines and construction. "Managing to make dresses that seem to stand up all by themselves," said Madame Jacqueline, *première* of the *atelier flou*, who had replaced Madame Felisa, and who had also previously worked for Balenciaga. "You can't rush with mousseline, otherwise it slips through your hands." The crepe dresses seemed to quiver through and through, the skirts were draped like sarongs, the scarves rolled up and disappeared within the movement of the fabric that flowed over the skin. And one could make out the shadow of Odette Swann, receiving guests in her conservatory in a skimpy crepe de Chine dress: "The bending of a body that made silk quiver like a mermaid whisks the waves" (Marcel Proust).

Backstage, he took mischievous pleasure in answering, all smiles, a young woman who was doing her first interview for a radio station no one had ever heard of. When an old television hand spoke to him rather familiarly: "So, Yves, it's very classic this season," he replied, "Well, yes, otherwise I wouldn't be a great couturier."

In the fashion reviews in *Elle*, Yves Saint Laurent got four pages, while the other designers got only one or two. The magazine praised "the unrivaled pleasure of pink and black" and "the supreme example of colors": on a gray whipcord suit, and a glacier blue satin blouse, he had wrapped a fuchsia stole and added an emerald fedora and gloves to set it off.

A few days later, Yves went to Deauville by helicopter and Pierre headed to Ashford Castle in Ireland. "Everything would be fine if Yves's health were better. In that regard, there are more downs than ups," Pierre wrote to Dick Salomon.

In June 1989, Yves attended the funeral of his friend Patrick Thévenon, a journalist for *L'Express*. Some of those who were there had a poignant image of him: "I saw a different man. Fallen to pieces. He could hardly stand up," recalled Sylvie de Nussac. Yves Saint Laurent seemed to bear on his shoulders the sadness of a generation that counted its dead like war victims every day. "AIDS is a normal topic, unfortunately," said Christophe Girard, chief administrative officer of the company and co-vice-president of the AIDS organization ARCAT. "I went through my address book and removed 30 names. This is not a normal pace." "This terrible illness," said Yves Saint Laurent. "I'm losing more and more friends. In this company, many people are gone…" In the fashion industry, any absence became a cause for concern, as friends and colleagues worried that the missing person might have fallen ill.

The past was fraying: the billionaires enjoyed its splendor at charity galas that revived the illusion of café society balls for a short while. "You should see these American women with their old legs wobbling under their jewelry at 9 A.M.," said the pitiless Maxime de la Falaise. In New York, she designed china for Tiffany's and put together "surrealist coffins" lined with old fur coats. "You can use them as bars." On the door of her New York apartment, she put up a sign reading, "*Attention chien bizarre.*" Her living room, with painted trees on the walls, was furnished like an aristocratic trailer. Silverware lay alongside old pots and pans, in a jumble of colors and memories. Maxime dressed nonchalantly in a big black t-shirt and Rive Gauche harem pants. She was busy "sprucing up an old barn in the Pyrenees." "I'm not on the social lists. I knew Man Ray, Duchamp, Max Ernst, Jean Genet, Rauschenberg. So the hare-brained ideas of big shots don't interest me. Rich people don't make any waves." Yves reminded her of Matisse, Cocteau, and all her illustrator friends, "those who never put down their pencil. They can draw a vision with just one line. With no trouble. But getting down the person's essence—that is magical."

She stripped her own past of its mystique with humor, this existence that had made Yves dream in Oran. In 1948, she posed for *Vogue* in a ball gown, holding in her hands an infant in organdy named Louise (Loulou). "We were great bluffers! We lived at the Hôtel de Passy, then later in a sublet on Avenue Foch. We went to all the parties, at the Polignacs', the Noailles'. We borrowed money. All our money was spent on taxis. At 9 AM, we had to give the dresses back." She laughed, drinking her first Pernod of the spring. And looking at her full red lips and her worn hands it seemed that "the true stars of the world are tired of appearing in it."[11]

All around Yves, dreams were dissipating. The new America, which was no longer New World America, adjusted its dreams to the size of the TV screen and the presence of the ubiquitous woman. "I'm not nostalgic at all. Finally I'm having fun with fashion!" said Bettina Graziani, the former star model for Fath and Givenchy, who appeared at art openings in skin-tight dresses by Alaïa. "Now, I'm taking care of myself." The fifty million bottles of vitamins sold in France in 1988 proved the rise of the fitness woman, with her stretchy, skin-tight look including black tube top and multicolored leggings that made Joy Hendericks, representing the couture house in New York, say: "I'm ashamed to say that Yves Saint Laurent isn't part of the selection." While Tom Wolfe's best-selling novel *The Bonfire of the Vanities* was made into a movie, Karl Lagerfeld of Chanel got America excited about his more stereotypical visions of the Parisian woman, with camellias and little quilted purses, which gave money its arrogance. The Chanel suit became an external sign of wealth and social status. Suzy Menkes of the *Herald Tribune* described Lagerfeld as "the Salieri of fashion," as contrasted with Yves Saint Laurent, "the Mozart."[12]

Yves Saint Laurent had told women, "Seduction means loving yourself a little so that others will love you a lot." They forgot it, believing only in youth, buying new breasts, new legs, a new stretched face so they wouldn't have wrinkles. At the same time, a generation realized that it had aged prematurely. The publication of Andy Warhol's diaries in the U.S. in July 1989 was very revealing. Everyone had thought he was silent like "the eunuch in the harem." And now, in 20,000 pages, ten years of his observations flowed forth. Panic on Park Avenue: sex, cocaine, drinking sprees. None of the beautiful people was spared by the old magpie with the silver wig. "Such trash!" said Maxime de la Falaise. "Imagine Andy Warhol making a comeback! If I were rich, I'd have bought his diaries and printed them on toilet paper."[13] Warhol had coldly taped shameful details, secrets shared by Pierre Bergé and tales of how John McKendry, Maxime's husband, stole Loulou's boyfriends. Loulou recalled: "Andy was always a voyeur. He took his Polaroid. He always had his machine on. He was a shy person. He liked dumb stories. He was crazy about gossip. His diary is meaner than he was. Like all vampires, he distorted things...."[14]

But once more, Warhol had predicted correctly: "Everyone is scared to get the gay cancer. So now they're fucking with their big toes and competing to see who has the biggest toe," one source recalled him saying.

The dandies, barons, and muses of Le Sept and Le Palace found themselves condemned to being "back room" survivors. They no longer trusted anyone but their dogs. "The nights were full of available men. Now they're full of books," said Javier Arroyuello, with the image of Loulou bursting through his brain like a shooting star: "She's someone who sparkles. Sparkling and bubbling like champagne! Her desire to avoid boredom was theatrical and glamorous. We talked a lot. Sex was important. We were the artisans of a new attitude. When I get bored at a dinner, I make top ten lists, I try to find ten actresses who weren't blond and played the role of blonds. The important thing was to never be bored. It happened at the Club Sept. Now it happens by calling a friend on a phone between one and two in the morning." As Guy Cuevas explained, "Once there's no more mixing, there's no more fun. Back then, we forgot ourselves, we danced to anything. We were in a state of grace....Now going out to a club is like making love to somebody who's looking at their watch."

All the excitement of the time burned out in disillusionment, while the end of the 1980s reached back to reliable values: home, family, country. With AIDS, a world was ending, the one that Yves Saint Laurent had designed for: the sexual liberation of the '60s and '70s. In Rome, the Pope preached sexual abstinence. In France, Jean-Marie Le Pen, the leader of the far-right Front National party, talked about excluding people suffering from AIDS. In the U.S., intolerance made headway: the Mapplethorpe affair, Senator Jesse Helms's campaign in favor of restoring censorship, and the X-rating for Almodóvar's film *Tie Me Up Tie Me Down* all revealed the rise of a puritanical spirit.

The artificial and the exaggerated reigned, as avant-garde fashion started describing the new torments of virtue for a public that was more and more voyeuristic and conservative, women who loved a "trendy little suit for our best friends' wedding." On the runway, silicone-stuffed breasts were displayed, in fashion's way— because it doubted itself—of shouting louder and louder in order to be heard. "We weren't so filled-out," recalled Vesna, a former model for Yves Saint Laurent. Like TV announcers, professionals had to follow the law of the media in order to survive: increase viewership.

As in the time when queens required members of the court to shave their hairlines because they were losing their hair, designers imposed on women the kind of armor that was worn in the back rooms: the body was shielded with cups, corsets, and laces; it was shaped by latex tubes, an obsessive reference to condoms. Designs for women were suddenly all the same. The 1980s generation of designers celebrated the towering, cosmopolitan Parisian woman, but Thierry Mugler, with his squeaky metallic superwomen, and Claude Montana, with his icy beauties, belonged to a different world than Yves Saint Laurent. Claude Berthod had once asked Yves, "What is true unhappiness to you?" His answer was, "Loneliness." Now he said, "I refuse to answer."

What did he inflict on himself in order to never do his women harm, to be so in love with them, so tender, to caress them this way with his fabrics? Over the following three years, fashion would pull out its whole arsenal of leather underpants (Dior), chrome breasts (Mugler), and S&M harnesses (Gianni Versace). As all the professionals cheerfully chained up a rich, strapped-up body, he refused this vision of the forbidden woman. "Americans are such prudes," he said. It was true that topless beaches were still forbidden, especially where alcohol was served. Filmmakers asked actresses to "wear something to bed."

He hadn't given up his subversive spirit. In October 1989, he didn't show breasts, as everyone else did, but a single breast. It was his portrait of a free woman: Diana the huntress. The models went out, wearing their Moroccan crepe dresses draped across them like Amazons, his divinities of the wind. But was beauty the latest thing that scared people? In October 1989, the press called showing a breast in the summer 1989 Rive Gauche collection "provocative" (*Le Figaro*) or an example of "absurd gimmicks" (*Daily Mail*), and the *London Evening Standard* illustrated its article with off-color caricatures. Yet, this half-hidden nudity, this half-revealed clothing may have said more about Saint Laurent than all the raving about his colors and his suits. All Yves Saint Laurent's holy secrets, pinned in one drawing, on the bulletin board in his studio: a woman in black satin jeans with a nude golden-skinned bust, a drawing chosen by Loulou and Anne-Marie Muñoz, to dress Yves Saint Laurent's Statue of Liberty at the Musée des Arts de la Mode.

People were starting to say that Yves Saint Laurent was out of fashion, but wasn't he actually more cutting-edge than all the others? In May 1993, a design with an uncovered breast was shown in British *Vogue*. But for Yves Saint Laurent, it had been an action, a moment in time—it was just a piece of fabric that he had moved aside on the day of the show. But in the magazine, it was a design, sold as is, frozen in place as a media object. In 1993, Calvin Klein, Anne Klein, Zoran, and Karl Lagerfeld all featured transparent designs.

"He suffers in his body. But he is graced," said an admirer. But at what price? He would let himself age more, proving to *Le Figaro* that he was the last dandy, not Warhol. He seemed to identify with another character from *Remembrance of Things Past*, the painter Elstir, who, "lacking bearable company, lived in an unsociable isolation that society people called posing and bad upbringing, the authorities called a negative outlook, his neighbors called madness, and his family called selfishness and arrogance."[15] But Elstir had "a yen for violets," Yves Saint Laurent covered his house with flowers, just as Proust wallpapered his room in cork. Every week, the florist Arielle Lemercier from the Arène flower shop drove a little white truck to show him the new flowers. "There are still a few people in Paris who have kept up this tradition." Some of his favorites were Casablanca lilies, very large, star-shaped lilies that were some of the most expensive flowers, as well as freesias, daffodils, garden roses, armfuls of tulips, and cherry bushes. "He loves flowers so much! Sometimes I have to rein him in," she said. "Sometimes, when he's not there, his butler chooses. But sometimes I've had to replace a bouquet because he didn't like it. He hates marigolds and yellow roses, for example." Five minutes from his home, at Liliane François on Rue de Grenelle, where he was driven by his chauffeur, he chose himself the flowers he sent to his friends. "He is a bit lost in his own thoughts. But he knows what he wants. He can spend fifteen minutes just looking. He sees it and loves it." He had no money on him. But they were all under the spell of his charm, his "kindness," which his *premiers* and *premières* spoke of, and like the people who "waited on" him, without him needing to add any statement of authority to his power. "We see lots of couturiers. Some of them give orders in a very unpleasant way....But we can't disappoint Monsieur Saint Laurent." But outside of this realm, it was as if he were thrust into a pitiless arena of people who judged him, watched him, stared at him, clearly seeing him as an old man led around by a nurse with dirty fingernails.

They followed him with their eyes. On Rue Léonce-Paul Reynaud, he waited for his chauffeur with a sheaf of wheat in his hands, which, along with rock crystal, was one of his good luck charms. They watched him walk off, with a strange step, the weight of his body uneven, weak and swollen, always with those suits, which were like another challenge to the bourgeoisie, who only tolerated seeing this kind of thing in people who were poor and badly dressed. One day, he was at Caviar Kaspia on Place de la Madeleine. There was silence around him. His arm looked twisted, the fork stuck out at an awkward angle above his plate, he was leaned over the table with his full weight. Across from him was a big fellow bundled up in a suit, a knight who was serving him wordlessly. "He has his chauffeur and his dog. It's kind of like a nanny with a little kid," said Loulou.

He got up early. He usually spent the morning in his library, with its shelves lined with images and memories. A photo of Loulou in a black sweater smoking a cigarette. Another of Yves posing with Kirat. "He's very solitary. Sometimes he cries for help. He says, 'You didn't call me!' But he didn't call me either," says Jacques Grange. "We have lunch. He's on the verge of collapse. He takes a nap." In Deauville or Marrakesh, he liked to look in the antiques shops or the bazaar. Sometimes he said, "This very beautiful woman will come over, I think she looks like…" as if his sharpened nerves coincided with greater and greater isolation. In his living room, his only address book was a few speed-dial keys on the big gray telephone, with one written in red felt-tip pen: "Psychiatrist." Sometimes he left a message. Returning from their travels, his friends would question their housekeepers: "Are you sure it was him, and not the store?"

His quest for beauty became all-encompassing. "Things come to me, objects call to each other." In his library in Marrakesh, his favorite room, everything seemed to be an illusion. What if those gold-edged glass cases were only an effect of the light? Here, life outside the walls seemed more unreal. The windows with cast-iron arabesques made the garden seem as still as a painting, the gardeners looked like blue shadows. Nothing seemed to be left to chance, not even this postcard, a portrait of Rimbaud stuck to a wall like a Post-It note. On the shelves, the books and images seemed to be linked by strange connections: a photo of Jean Cocteau with his dog against Baudelaire's *Fleurs du Mal*. A photo of Moujik that hid the binding of *Madame de*, by Louise de Vilmorin. A drawing by Rossetti, "Joli Coeur," covered up *Le Rouge et le Noir* by Stendhal. The eye had no rest. Every object wished to be admired, like his women of yesterday. They looked at each other, prisoners of their reflections and all the spells cast back and forth by the chandelier and the saber, the silver table and the Chinese vase, whose red netted pattern was reflected in it so perfectly. But nothing moved because the tree was made of crystal and the dove of ivory. And there too was Yves, who sometimes destroyed everything in a rush of violence.

He came back. With this new collection in January 1990, Homages, with 119 designs that were created in two weeks. He took the microphone, and like the ringmaster backstage, announced the styles as they appeared. They were all tributes to various figures that were significant to him: Bernard Buffet, Christian Dior, Silvana Mangano, Louis Jouvet, Maria Callas, Marcel Proust, Françoise Sagan, Zizi Jeanmaire, Catherine Deneuve, Maria Casarès, Coco Chanel, and Marilyn Monroe. It was as if each had asked him to create something astonishing. The spirit of Paris was present in songs by Montand, Trenet, Gréco, Zizi, and Brel: "*Une lettre de toi, une lettre qui dit oui, et c'est Paris demain!*" It was as if he brought these idols back not to embalm them, but to give them life through the most marvelous image that they gave of themselves. Because in the Watteau dress (an homage to Dior), women showed their legs in black stockings. Because this Chanel suit in navy blue bouclé with white braiding had the Saint Laurent structure, shoulder, and line. But he withdrew again in order to have even more power of suggestion: How did he manage to describe Marilyn's vulnerability in a red-headed woman? To make Rita Hayworth appear without her red satin gloves or her Gilda sheath dress? But in a slightly transparent duffel coat that seemed made for her to sing, "Put the blame on me"? How was he able to evoke the memory of Marcel Proust in a mauve and yellow cloud? Could any other man dress this "magically-designed city" with his fabrics? Could anyone else describe springtime in Paris like this, with its gray-blue hail showers, its elegant ladies in navy blue with mother-of-pearl buttons, and its acid colors asserting themselves on the café terraces on the first sunny days?

Some saw this collection as Yves's last will and testament, but in fact it was perhaps the least nostalgic of them all. Surely because Yves Saint Laurent did more that day than go back over his past: that day, he told the story of his past as if it were before him, like a weightless morning, when everything seems new. For this collection, he asked his sister Michèle to come work secretly in one of the company's ateliers. "It's like a rebirth," he said backstage. He gave his sorrow and his tears, and the shade of Maria Casarès appeared in a long draped black crepe dress. The shade of Maria Callas was there in a Spanish dress of red and pink guipure lace. The famous red heart was sailing on a flood of black veils: the homage to Bernard Buffet.

Suddenly, the serious, melancholy voice of Louis Jouvet sounded out in the magnificent Imperial Salon: "The day of the third performance of *The Imaginary Invalid*, Molière was pained by his chest troubles much more than usual. So he decided to call his wife, to whom he said, in the presence of Baron, 'As long as my life was an equal combination of pains and pleasures, I believed myself happy, but today, when I am stricken with pain with no moments of satisfaction and sweetness, I see that I must quit the game. I cannot struggle against the pain and discontent that does not give me an instant's respite. But,' he added as he reflected, 'how much a man suffers before dying!'"

In the front row, some people could turn slightly and catch Yves's eye. He had barely opened a door on the left of the runway so that he could see and listen to the applause and the silence. The audience held its breath. And then a jacket with gold and sky-blue sequins appeared, embroidered with wisps of straw in honeyed tones, with glass mirrors, cabochons, and translucent drop-beads. It was "Homage to my company." It had required 700 hours of labor. "He asked me to make him blue-gray Paris reflected in the crystal chandelier in his office on the Avenue Marceau," recalls François Lesage. "'I'd like to make an evening dress out of this reflection of the sky and sun in the mirror,' he said." Worn over a white crepe sheath dress, the jacket's background music was Gainsbourg's "La Javanaise." Soon, rapturous applause drew him out and carried him to his beautiful models, whom he kissed, with his head in the clouds. It was as if he had attained the knowledge of fabrics that he had sought as early as 1950, when, at age fourteen, he started to speak of love, "this pink fog that commands us like a master."

The press noticed that he had lost twenty pounds. "Yves is in shape!" On that Wednesday, January 24, Gabrielle Buchaert called a few close friends of the maison Saint Laurent. "It was the first time in a very long time that they called us after a haute couture show to tell us that Yves was having a dinner that night," recalls Colombe Pringle. The whole clan was together again: the Lalannes, Charlotte Aillaud, Clara Saint, Philippe Collin, Marie-Hélène de Rothschild. Anna Wintour, the editor-in-chief of American *Vogue*, was also there. She was wearing a sleeveless mini sheath dress with a crewneck by Versace. "What is she wearing?" asked a guest. "She borrowed her daughter's dress," joked Pierre Bergé. There was a festive atmosphere. "Pierre was showing us the paintings and the first editions. Yves said he had stopped drinking. He was like never before. His lover was there. He was nice. We left at two in the morning," recalls Colombe Pringle. But that night, a circuit blew, and the second story caught on fire. Yves's room burned, reducing his memories, letters, and good luck charms to ash. "It was like fate," says Colombe, still feeling the impact. "Just when he was coming out of his gloominess, everything darkened once more. We didn't see him anymore after that."

18 / BABYLON: 1990 TO 1993

n January 1990, there was something prophetic about the Homages collection. Starting then, beauty became suspect. Recession, unemployment, environmental disasters. "High Anxiety" was the cover of *Time* on October 15, 1990. Art prices collapsed. Fashion now had to justify itself, to serve causes. And the 1990s began, under the dark gaze of guilt: as if the "healthy," the "pure," the "authentic" could cleanse the world of its plagues on their own. The time of reality shows had begun. The average Joe and Jane took their revenge. Difference frightened them. Being healthy became a must. Artists fell from their pedestals, people investigated their dubious morality, and criticism gave way to moral investigations, reducing artworks to news stories and aesthetic judgment to moral condemnation. Those who had dominated the scene had to fight with weapons other than their skill, giving way to dilettantes who were greedy for images, who knew everything without having learned anything. Female athletes put their names on clothing, and interior decorators took up architecture, "artists" said they were couturiers, couturiers called themselves photographers, photographers turned into filmmakers, fashion editors were now "stylists," and models were superstars. Yves Saint Laurent seemed to say "No, thank you" to all this with his natural fierceness, inflicting on his body the bruises of a world without guides or signposts. The cycle started again: in March 1990, in Marrakesh, the purple curtain rose. He drank two bottles of whisky a day. He painted on the walls. He wanted to look like a soldier and cut his hair close to his head. He met an antiques dealer who delivered in his little van pounds of trinkets for a hundred million cents. The servants said, "We have to talk to him like soldiers." "He was mentally ill," says his sister Brigitte, who came to take him back to Paris. He refused. Finally, he was brought back to Paris by plane, going through a hidden entrance at the airport. He was put "into a kind of clinic with bars," and called it "incarceration": "I shouted 'Murderers' in the hallways. I wanted to leave. I don't hold it against anyone. For everyone copped out. Who is responsible? Pierre? My mother? My sister? I think it's my sister. I sobbed when I saw Pierre. He said nothing, he was very uncomfortable. If he had taken care of it, I would have gotten out earlier."

Yves Saint Laurent was hospitalized for three weeks in a facility in Garches, about ten miles from Paris, for "rehab." "We dragged him off," Pierre Bergé says nonchalantly. "For the first two days, he was in the disturbed ward. The windows are permanently shut so people can't jump out. Then, he was completely free: there's a big pool table and a park, it's not at all like a prison!" Yves was hospitalized on a Saturday and unable to finish the collection, which was shown on the following Wednesday in the Cour Carrée of the Louvre. He wasn't there to take a bow. The collection was completed by Loulou de la Falaise and Anne-Marie Muñoz: "It was very pretty, I saw the photos." Six months later, while going to Tokyo for a retrospective of his work at the Sezon Museum, he added, "I'm lucky to have marvelous people who work with me, but not in the same way I do."

In Japan, Yves had to make an appearance. Negotiations were said to be planned with Seibu. In the hallways of the hotel, Alain Minc and some Japanese businessmen were seen walking by, and the businessmen left with Yves's drawing of the *Mariage de Figaro* in a YSL bag. At a press conference at the Budokan arena, Pierre Bergé had a surprise for the journalists, declaring, "And now here is the man you are all waiting for." He came through a little door and sat down at the desk covered with lilies, between Loulou and Pierre Bergé. "Hello!" he called out like a child to the frozen audience. He was asked strange questions about his future replacement. He answered calmly: "I maintained Dior's traditions. I struggled against Chanel and Balenciaga, but I don't want to be ossified like a legend." In 1990, haute couture sales dropped noticeably to 40 million francs. But a single German client purchased about thirty items. "She only wears them to have dinner with her husband," the saleswomen said.

1991 began in a climate of economic recession. At YSL, profits were down: 252 million francs in 1990, 233 million in 1991 (7.6 percent of revenue). In 1990, Yves Saint Laurent stock had begun its long decline. The company was still in debt to the tune of 1.9 billion francs, but had purchased, in May 1991, 14.5 percent of the capital from Cerus, which wanted to get out. In addition to the general crisis affecting the luxury industry, where investors who had paid for prestigious names realized that profitability didn't happen right away in this field, there were also the effects of the crisis: the Gulf War and the fall of the yen and the dollar. Balmain got out of haute couture: "Too expensive, too hard," said Alain Chevalier. Ricci laid off workers. Meanwhile, at Dior, the princesses were demanding dresses that were less ostentatious.

The champagne was no longer flowing. On December 28, 1990, *Le Nouvel Economiste* announced "the end of the crazy years: is the French luxury industry over-confident? Loaded with honors, stockpiling cash, rapidly expanding abroad, France may have been blinded by twenty years of easy street.... In 1975, France represented almost 75 percent of the global luxury market. In 1989, its share fell to 50 percent. And now, the challenge comes from Italy. Trussardi and Ferré, and especially Armani and Valentino."

Paris was losing its position, and Milan came up with the male-female version of the suit of the 1990s, designed by Armani, the maestro of modernity. Returning to the idea of "less is more," the suits were black, beige, and white, without padding or stiff backing. Basically, they were soft Saint Laurent combined with very efficient management of the image and the product. John Fairchild added a new name to his very limited list: "Chanel, Balenciaga, Saint Laurent, and Armani. They are the only ones who have been able to establish a style, meaning something that everyone knows about!" Meanwhile, the Rive Gauche style was losing ground to new synthetic materials, which were wrinkle-free and feather-light. And Saint Laurent worshippers had their sights on another couturier whose efforts with fabrics gave a new lightness to timeless shapes: Issey Miyake, who did technologically updated versions of dresses by Fortuny, the famous Albertine pleats that were described in great detail by Proust. But the surprise and radiance of the YSL haute couture collections remained. His January 1991 runway show, with ninety-four designs, which occurred in the unfavorable context of the Gulf War, was spot-on, with the clearest lines seen that week. Yves had once again simplified and condensed his style.

That same month there was a ruckus in the couture world. Pierre Bergé had publicly laid into the profession. On January 24, 1991, the newsmagazine *Le Nouvel Observateur* published a sidebar titled "Funeral Service: The Twilight of the Couture Designers." "I think haute couture is doomed. First of all, because most women, even very rich ones, prefer to wear ready-to-wear now. Not only are there no more clients, but there aren't any more couturiers, except for Givenchy and Saint Laurent." Who put this idea in his head? One month later, in the same magazine, journalist Katia D. Kaupp called it "Bergé's misstep": "By announcing the death of haute couture, the CEO of Yves Saint Laurent has launched an all-out war." Haute couture had revenue of 375 million in 1990. The journalist defended this profession, which provided, thanks to ready-to-wear and accessories, 40,000 jobs, "with most of them going to women." Three thousand seamstresses still worked in the ateliers. The couturiers were furious. "He insults us," said Cardin. "Ridiculous and shameful, he speaks only for himself," added Lagerfeld. Ungaro called it "a comical statement of truly ludicrous arrogance by someone who has never made a dress in his life," as readers learned in *Le Nouvel Observateur* one month later. In the *Daily Telegraph*, Pierre Bergé seemed to backpedal a bit, saying that "it will only last ten more years." In financial circles, people started saying that "the magic spell is broken." The stories of excessive spending at the Opéra were definitely making too many waves. The YSL affair was just as badly managed. "It has to do with two men. One of them is too old to act that way and the other is clinically depressed," an observer heard. It was true that Bergé's statements made people uneasy: "Couture is certainly a wonderful luxury that Yves can and should indulge in. But if he left, I would close the line immediately. I don't see myself hunting for designers from Italy or elsewhere in a media circus."

Had Pierre Bergé found a replacement? The fashion crowd was all astir. In March, 1991, Robert Merloz showed his second fur collection under the Yves Saint Laurent label in the Louvre's Cour Carrée. The company archives were moved in order to make room for the fur department. That day, Yves was seated in the last row, on the side, and was the first to applaud, despite having his hand in a cast. Whatever he thought about the situation, he even kissed Robert Merloz and posed for photos with him. In a photo published in *Vanity Fair*,[1] Yves looks lordly, holding a stunned Robert Merloz by the arm. On the way home in his car, he said to Christophe Girard, "It's crazy how much this young man has learned at my side."

An alumnus of the school of the Chambre Syndicale de la Couture, Merloz had been working as an assistant at the studio since 1985. Pierre Bergé decided that the maison Saint Laurent would back the opening of a ready-to-wear company that had its first show in July 1992, at the same time as the haute couture show. Yves signed a memo announcing the opening of this company to his staff and expressing his "delight." But in Paris, Pierre Bergé's "new protégé" was the subject of much gossip. "It's *All About Eve*!" said the film buffs. Pierre Bergé would turn a bedroom affair into a professional commitment. "The flesh is weak," said a close associate. Things seemed to be spiraling downhill. "I don't know what they're doing at Saint Laurent, but as long as I've still got couture…," Yves said to Jacques Grange. Pierre Bergé acknowledged the troubles: "The night of the fur show, Yves called me to say that he thought it was great. Later, he didn't like it so much. People muddied the waters, and Yves likes the waters crystal clear. But that's their problem." Surely, Pierre Bergé, at age sixty-one, was trying to rediscover his lost youth. His support of another man, one whose gestures and attitudes were a carbon copy of those of Yves Saint Laurent, could be seen as the last great proof of his love. But the past weighed on him. Just six months earlier, he was describing Yves's "narcissism." "He has no curiosity for anyone else. He's completely self-sufficient, he doesn't go out. Surrounded by luxury, he has combined ostentation with asceticism."[2]

Pierre Bergé was seen at Lipp or Loulou in Montparnasse. People still ran into him at the Café de Flore or in the antique shops along Rue Jacob or Rue de Grenelle in the afternoon with his dog Ficelle, looking for Renaissance bronzes. But he spent his weekends working on his book, *Liberté, J'écris Ton Nom*, about his ideology and politics.[3] He never directly mentioned Yves Saint Laurent, although he didn't hide the substance of his passion from anyone who could read between the lines: "Everyone who fervently celebrates today the birthdays of Mozart and Rimbaud would be quite surprised if someone told them who this anarchist musician and this homosexual poet really are. Artists produce bombs, which are sometimes time bombs, and toss them at the society of their time. Artists—the real ones—are not entirely of this world. They're not really among us. I know something about this. I've known a few artists." Loulou commented, "Yves only knows how to give love literally. His only love story is Pierre." She compared them to Vita Sackville-West and Harold Nicolson, "except that they invented a tradition all by themselves. Vita had a garden and ancestors. They're more fierce. Naturally, it doesn't go as well."

In 1991, no one could tell whether Pierre Bergé wanted to save Yves Saint Laurent by fleeing him, or he wanted to save himself. If he wanted to kill a horse to spare it the suffering. Because he knew that this time, the die had been cast. And that "you have to follow developments if you don't want to be a has-been." But it looked as if Yves Saint Laurent, who was irreplaceable and unbearable, no longer protected him, abandoning him to other victims. "They accuse me of making too many heads roll," he said about the Opéra Bastille. "They're right. If I could do it over again, I would. I'm not seeking any approval. I have a serious flaw: I have very solid disdain. Not for people in life. But for those who hold a position, who claim…." The more his popularity collapsed, the more he forged ahead. At a party, he caused a scandal when he called Marina de Brantes, the president of the Association pour le Rayonnement de l'Opéra de Paris a "pest."

Yves Saint Laurent played along with a time period that was eager for revelations, when, "honesty was the best policy." "Fight, you'll speak later," said Maria Casarès as Hélène in Bresson's *Les Dames du Bois de Boulogne*, one of his favorite films. After all, he redecorated his room like that of the heroine. He fought and he spoke. Two articles appeared on July 11 and 15, 1991, in *Le Figaro*. The headlines spread out over a full page: "An exclusive interview with the great couturier Yves Saint Laurent": "I Was Born with Nervous Depression." And four days later: "Yves Saint Laurent: 30 Years of Glory, 30 Years of Anxiety. The Most Secretive Living Legend Talks to *Le Figaro*." "For the first time, the great couturier tells all." In a long interview with Janie Samet and Franz-Olivier Giesbert, Yves Saint Laurent talked for the first time about his military service and 1960 at the Val-de-Grâce military hospital: "It was horrible. They wanted to keep me from leaving. So they knocked me out with medication. I was lying down in a room, alone, with people who came and went like crazy people. Real crazy people. Some of them touched me. I wouldn't let them. Others were screaming for no reason. There was everything that could make you anxious. In two and a half months I only went to the bathroom one time, I was so scared. At the end I must have weighed only eighty pounds and I was mentally disturbed. The doctor who was treating me said that he had given me the most powerful dose of tranquilizers that can be given. He said, 'You'll see, you'll be back on them.' That's just what happened. I ended up leaving when the military doctors signed a petition where they said that they wouldn't be responsible for me anymore." He added, "These last two years were so awful with the rehab that I lost my sight." He complained that he was "badly cared for." He concluded: "Surely Pierre Bergé is right when he says that I was born with nervous depression. I'm very strong and very fragile at the same time."

For the first time, Yves Saint Laurent exposed himself, now that he didn't take drugs or drink anymore and was under the spell of a decade that demanded confessions. Twenty years after posing nude for Jeanloup Sieff, he revealed something altogether unexpected: his own psyche, at the risk of sacrificing what he had always defended through his designs: "When a woman loses her mystery, she loses everything."

"Bad psychoanalysis! It's not even worthy of Woody Allen," said Loulou de la Falaise about these two interviews. But Janie Samet, the first journalist who ever interviewed Yves Saint Laurent, back in 1954, seemed to know her subject well: "I remember this great man who was so clever and shy in Oran. He was on his way to glory. That was my first article. He became stooped over. But he still has this whimsical spirit, these mischievous eyes looking through the window." That same month, July 1991, he found the name for his next women's fragrance. Patricia Turck-Paquelier, the new head of international marketing, who had previously worked for Procter & Gamble, told him about the concept: "A woman who is happy, who sparkles." He replied, "Champagne!"

Le Figaro published a piece by the couturier, titled "Glory." "I love glory. Glory is a celebration. I love celebrations. They're cheerful. They scintillate. They sparkle. A glass of champagne, the gold of a candelabra, the gold of wood paneling, the gold of ornamentations. Glory can only be imagined in gold. Gilded with gold leaf. It's old, it's ancient. It makes noise, lots of noise. It detonates. It strikes like lightning. It doesn't care about anything. It walks over the world. It disturbs. I wanted glory. It strengthens me. It cleanses, purifies, and perfumes me. I am an effigy crucified on the chest of this heroine, this demi-goddess, this quasi-queen called glory."[4]

In late July 1991, Yves Saint Laurent showed his 120th collection. For those who were expecting a settling of scores or an explosion, it was a disappointment. For the others, it was a lesson in fashion, which was felt as a humanist challenge to a time in crisis. A flowing show of 146 designs that returned to the sources of couture, in a new acknowledgement of Chanel. The designs were shown to variations by Bach. The clear desire for structure won out over instinct and sometimes over emotion. Catherine Deneuve praised the collection: "The culmination is a paring-down. The more you strip yourself down, the more you manage to let things go. It's the same thing with acting: the more you can drop your defenses, the more you can get rid of your tics, your last remaining armor."

Everything was more exact, even his whimsical evening designs, the dresses made of guipure lace and black Chantilly lace emphasizing the curves of Jacques Demy's *Lola*, which were delicately tied with black ribbons. Every bit of skin was a little glimpse of mystery. Newton noticed these dresses that were cut in the spirit of Rochas, the inventor of the corset. Anna Wintour of American *Vogue* refused to publish the images, deciding they were too daring, since you could see a nipple sticking out through the lace.

In 1968, Yves's answer to the question, "What is your greatest happiness?" had been, "Going to sleep with the people I love." In 1991 he said, "Good press!" What did he dread the most now? "The date." And in life? "Indifference."

For the first time since 1971, Yves Saint Laurent's collections were very harshly reviewed, especially by the *Herald Tribune*. Suzy Menkes wrote that the puffy pants seemed to have come from "the brochure of a low-cost tourist agency…Compared to the collections of Lacroix and Lagerfeld, Yves Saint Laurent's clothes are 'dead'…. He has nothing new to say." However, one of his summer 1991 designs, number 59—a coral shantung bolero jacket, a saffron crepe skirt, and a fuchsia crepe blouse—was the haute couture best seller of 1991: twenty clients ordered this evening ensemble, which cost 23,000 dollars. On the list, Versace and Emanuel Ungaro were right behind him. "I know almost everything that's happening at the company, it's diabolical," Yves said in January 1992. "Couture is not as much as in danger as people think! The women from Arabia didn't come for one season, because of this horrible war. But one of them came back. She ordered four million francs' worth. I know what works the best." Paradoxically, it was just when they said he was out of fashion that his style came back systematically into the fashion shows. Tuxedos, suits, transparent looks, colors. In a poor version (Helmut Lang) or rich version (Oscar de La Renta).

But he gave a more authoritarian image of himself. In an interview with Vanessa van Zuylen, who in a fairytale story became the editor of the magazine *L'Insensé*, a kind of seventh arrondissement remake of *Egoïste* and *Interview*, he was very blunt: "A void, I tell you. Since the time when Balenciaga and Chanel were head to head, there's nothing, really nothing, except Givenchy and me. People think there are still maisons de couture, but *I* know there aren't anymore. Yes, of course, you can mention some names that I won't even say. But these names don't exist. They're misunderstandings, they're not worth talking about." Journalists? "They need to believe their own lies and their own errors of taste. They have to fill up articles, cover the paper with print." The time period? It was "defective." "I'm nostalgic for the 1920s. Now it's like a void, a desert, boredom….Where is Jouvet? Where is Bérard? And, now that Warhol is gone, who has replaced him? Who, since he left us, can hold up the kind of mirror to society that it deserves? Yes, that's it: with Bérard and Warhol, something essential has died. They had the grace, the genius, the art of living. Who today shows us Madonna with as much power and truth as Warhol when he showed Marilyn?"[5] With great naïveté, Vanessa van Zuylen said that she "rewrote the interview, to beef it up a bit."

But the couturier closed himself off and brooded. "Four suitcases to go to Marrakesh! He wants us to wear evening dresses to dinner," said Loulou. Her daughter, who was Yves's goddaughter, turned six in 1992. Loulou spent her weekends gardening at her country house, which was "kind of under construction." At the traditional Sunday lunch, she served lamb with mint sauce under the weeping willow, which was named Halloween. Another life, another time: "I have lots of friends with only children." Loulou worked a lot, and even gave lectures to students. She was the head of accessories, and her name was now listed on the program at the haute couture shows. "She was once eccentric, but she isn't anymore," said Maxime, her mother. Yet Loulou could still astonish. And she continued to say, as if she were writing a love letter to Yves, "I never thought rich people were glamorous. Too much wealth kills eccentricity." She was one of the few fashion people who hadn't made black a constant part of her wardrobe. "I try not to be the girl who gets dressed without thinking." Yet every day she had to surprise Yves more. "He has standards that men don't have anymore," she said. In Marrakesh, he gave a party for Catherine

Deneuve. Her new look was in all the magazines. It was the new Deneuve, who said, "When I run my hand over the back of my neck, I feel like I'm touching a boy's neck." On the last day of filming of Régis Wargnier's *Indochine*, she had cut her blond waves and burned them in the fireplace of her house in the country. She cautioned, "Don't think this is an existential turning point in my life," as if she secretly suspected it was. For the first time in her life, she had signed a contract with Yves Saint Laurent to be the face of his new beauty line.

Women changed. Would they be less shy? Leaving behind implants and padding, they didn't want to hide behind their clothing anymore. Their make-up was lighter, their skin softer, their shoulders more natural, their heels lower. This comfort hid a few anxieties: the men who didn't look at them anymore, the rights that they had gained and had to defend once again, the seductiveness that had abandoned them. "Yves was unquestionable, but there's no more unquestionable," said Paloma Picasso, in black Dior boxer shorts, a black Hermès sweater, a Paloma Picasso silk scarf, and a bright pink Saint Laurent jacket. "I always mixed everything to be dressed as myself." A model wiped off her lipstick after the show: "It's too bourgeois!" They wanted to live, to breathe. Like him?

On November 25, 1991, Yves Saint Laurent came back from Marrakesh to celebrate Saint Catherine's Day, a traditional holiday for the Parisian couture industry. "Of course, my children, with you we can do anything, my rays of sunshine, my fairies, my troubadours, my queens, and my kings," Yves told them. "I feel thirty years younger and thanks to you, I want to make my most beautiful collection yet: a flawless jewel, a constellation. Those who bore us to death by saying haute couture will soon be over, let's kick them out with high heels into the underground parking lots of stupidity and wickedness where Madame Muñoz is waiting for them with a machine gun. There, I've said it all. Except thank you, but I never would have forgotten that. See you tomorrow, the next day, and for always." Yves then thanked the absent Pierre Bergé: "I thank the entire company. Monsieur Bergé." And, after listing a few more names, he ended by thanking the executives in general: "Thank you to all the perfectly ironed white collars who surround me." The room was in high spirits as Yves concluded, "There, that's everything. Time for joy, crazy laughter, and dancing. As Trenet sang, '*Il y a de la joie, les hirondelles partent en vacances.*' Happy Saint Catherine's Day!" Everyone clapped. He left, like a child, with traces of kisses on his cheeks.

January 1992. In the ateliers, the fabrics resisted under their hands. They had to iron them to flatten them out. A little cotton trapeze dress was pinked around the edges to improve its silhouette. Nothing was ever taken for granted here. Couture had evaded forecasting, profitability calculations, and career plans. Madame Renée became *première d'atelier* when her sister Esther retired. She had waited twenty-four years to fit clients herself, and discovered that she "lost some of them because they considered me a beginner." Her craft was a struggle with fabric. "The simpler it is, the harder it is to hold your own." In the *atelier flou*, they recognized the dominance of the Dior technique. A taffeta bustier dress with underwiring of feather and iron contained, under its butterfly-like exterior, a veritable system. "To make the *décolleté* round and thick, we add cotton. Otherwise, it collapses on your breasts," said Simone, one of the last women to still work in a lab coat. "His style hasn't aged a bit. That's the privilege of masterpieces," Pierre Bergé wrote in the introduction to a special catalogue published by the company, with texts by Françoise Sagan, Bernard-Henri Lévy, and Marguerite Duras that had been written three years earlier. "A woman. She is there. And him. He is here. He sketches. And the woman. Now she is dressed," wrote Duras. The book included photos of all those who had inspired him. The largest picture was of Jouvet. "Thirty years takes a lot of strength. Still here. Like a beginner. I'm petrified," said Yves Saint Laurent in his office on Avenue Marceau, although he acknowledged, "Today this profession is in decline. I can't understand. At Chanel, they put chains and leather straps everywhere. This poor woman must be rolling over in her grave. I see frightening, sado-masochistic things." Pierre Bergé said, "We've had a wonderful journey."

In January 1992, after thirty years, the estimated worth of the brand was 15 billion francs on the basis of international retail sales. Yves Saint Laurent was one of the very top names for luxury in the world. Eighty-two percent of revenue was produced by fragrances (2.5 billon francs) and 18 percent by couture (527 million francs). A significant portion of the couture revenue came from royalties paid by manufacturing partners that had licenses to produce and sell Yves Saint Laurent–branded products. The operating profit was 512 million francs, or 16.7 percent of revenue. Three-quarters of the company's sales came from abroad. The company had 2,993 employees: 2,430 for fragrances and 533 for couture. The equity was significant: Pierre Bergé and Yves Saint Laurent owned 43 percent of the capital through their Berlys company.

For the couture house's thirtieth anniversary, each of the old-timers (seamstresses, *premières*, saleswomen) was given a couture design by the company. For this anniversary, *Vogue* asked all the "pioneers" who had been with the company since 1962 to pose at the old location at 30 bis Rue Spontini. The building housed a technology company by then, and a few managers in shirt sleeves had slightly surprised looks on their faces as they watched the photo shoot. Sixteen women headed over in a small bus. "I remembered this staircase as much bigger!" They waited for Yves before taking the photo. He arrived, in a navy blue peacoat, just like in 1962. "Oh, how cute this house was!" Pierre Bergé exclaimed. "You remember?" January 29, 1992, came. There was no retrospective approach, just many airy dresses, with polka-dots and flowers, moving along the runway to youthful music. They flew, they moved. The thirty-year-anniversary Le Smoking had the number 67804. There was only one version of the signature tuxedo out of ninety-one designs in the collection. Yet it was, Yves said, his "favorite piece."

On February 3, 1992, the couture house celebrated its anniversary fashion show at the Opéra Bastille with 2,800 guests. "A simple evening like a family get-together," Pierre said to Yves. "You have led us like a Napoleonic general!" He appeared on stage, after a show of 130 designs. All the Yves Saint Laurent women were there: the felines, the water sprites, the "Oriental" women, the "Indian" women, the birds. It was a burst of colors out of darkness. He didn't see the show, since Pierre Bergé took him backstage. Catherine Deneuve, in a long green-sequined skirt and a Matisse blue jacket, kissed him. He spoke: "I wanted to thank you for coming tonight. Mademoiselle Deneuve was kind enough to accompany me. I'm falling flat on my face! It's a life of love in a company made from love. In my clothes, I manage to express what is the most precious to me: the love of a woman." During the dinner, photographers snapped away as Yves sat with Catherine Deneuve and Victoire, who had returned for this special occasion. She had written about her memories in *Paris Match*. At his table were Loulou and Thadée, Yvonne de Peyerimhoff, who was now in her eighties, and Rudolf Nureyev. The dancer would succumb to AIDS one year later. Also there was Jacques Chazot, who looked like a skeletal shadow. He would die in July 1993. Pierre Bergé strolled from table to table: "We're the only ones who can do this. And there will be no other."

The ceremony was called a "veterans' retreat in a devastated city" by the *Wall Street Journal Europe*. This judgment was too hasty, and surely didn't take into account the true decline of a world that this celebration symbolized. In New York, billionaires donated their dresses for tax deductions. In Paris, haute couture clothes set new records at auction. But did memory have a price?

In the newspapers, Yves Saint Laurent's name was not always associated with his work, but often with Pierre Bergé and his personal and political struggles. Right after the celebration at the Opéra Bastille, *L'Événement du Jeudi* published an article about Bergé titled "Portrait of a Presidential Insider." That same week, Bernard Tapie, the leader of the presidential majority in Provence-Côte d'Azur, settled a score with Bergé: "You gotta see these Le Pen meetings! There aren't a lot of poor unemployed people. Three-quarters of them have gold chain bracelets, Hermès bags, and Yves Saint Laurent shawls," he told *Libération*.[6]

In July 1992, in the midst of the couture season, Robert Merloz had his first ready-to-wear show at the École des Beaux-Arts. As she left, Lucienne Mathieu-Saint-Laurent, elegantly dressed in an ivory shantung dress, told *Le Figaro*: "My son is devastated. It wasn't worth causing him so much pain." A way of making her rivalry with Pierre Bergé official? Four days later, fashion journalists spread the word as they entered the Imperial Salon of the Hotel Intercontinental, where the Yves Saint Laurent show was taking place as usual: "We'll give him a standing ovation. He didn't deserve that!" There was a feverish atmosphere. "No one backstage," said René Pittet, with a moustache like an old Gaulish warrior, the man of delicate missions. There were fifty designs, and many references to the film *Les Dames du Bois de Boulogne*, with surprising Carmen Miranda–style turbans. The wedding dress was red, and the bride wore a black domino mask that hid her face. The show started twenty-five minutes late. At 11:00 AM, Yves was still in bed. But silence was golden. "We have suffered with him," said Marie-Thérèse Herzog, who had worked in the studio since the beginning. "But you can't achieve any more for beauty." They all knew they were a little bit possessed. And perhaps they had in mind the ghosts of those who left and never got over it: Madame Raymonde, riding the bus all over Paris without going anywhere. Madame Ida, who had passed away, and whose neighbor told me, "I think when she stopped working, she slowly went crazy."

But what demon had possessed Pierre Bergé? "A fatal accident during a performance in Seville. A series of resignations. A stream of defects. Flawed acoustics. A maestro playing diva. Is the ghost ship of the Opéra cursed?" asked *L'Express* on September 10, 1992. On September 18, Bergé announced to *Le Nouvel Observateur* that he was selling at least 14 percent of his capital in Yves Saint Laurent: "Yes, I'm negotiating the sale of Yves Saint Laurent."

October 1992. "After what I saw in the papers today, I can't speak. My mouth is burning. I have canker sores." Yves was beside himself. Because of "that crazy Gaultier" whose Los Angeles show had been covered by *Paris Match*. They said that "the undresser" had "blown Hollywood away." There were photos of Madonna with her breasts showing under the suspenders of her dress and Raquel Welch in a tuxedo jacket, fishnet stockings, and yellow feathers: "Jean-Paul Gaultier created a surprising show to fight against AIDS." "This made him crazy," said Loulou. In a smoky car, Paul, Yves's chauffeur, recalls the couturier's reaction: "He told me, 'This must have been bought in a sex shop. It can't be. It's from a brothel in Germany!'"

In the salon, which had been turned into a dressing room before the Rive Gauche show, Anne-Marie Muñoz, the high priestess of grain de poudre, watched over the lines, over everything that was subdued and embellished by the expert *tailleur* seamstresses. "These buttons are really cute," said Loulou, who was wearing satin jeans and a red roll-neck sweater. She pinned a heart onto a velvet sweater. "Very chic—photo!" A young woman with a Polaroid responded immediately. The models walked by. Yasmeen, Naomi, the prettiest girls in the world, took off their white lab coats. They were naked, made-up, with black pantyhose and heels. At that moment, it was as if they didn't exist. Suddenly, everything snapped into motion; everyone's eyes were focused on them. They became Saint Laurent, Parisian women playing at being from the East, Eastern women playing at being Parisian, in velvet pants with sandals with diamond buckles. A gold jacket slipped on over a jersey sweater. The dresses arrived like guests. Others were slow to arrive: "The embroidered jacket at 5:30," promised Madame Catherine. "And this dress. Madame Renée?" "It's almost done," replied a gentle voice. "Just a few last-minute touches." Loulou talked to Yves Saint Laurent, seated on the red sofa. "Do you want their hands bare? Do you want soft gloves?" On the black velvet trays, fake jewels sparkled: rhinestone stars, blue camellias, hammered gold necklaces. He answered with a wave of his hand. Diana put on a panther-printed coat: "Should we give her bug shoes?" He went to pick up a black satin ribbon under the trestle tables. Sometimes, he walked to the back of the room and disappeared. The tension dissipated, and the assistants would play client. "Do you happen to have a cigarette with refreshingly mild menthol?" Yves would have other angry crises, against his mother in particular. And then he would announce that he didn't want to see any women anymore. He ordered a new car, a Safrane. "Let pleasure drive," promised the ad. The chauffeur chose it. But Yves selected the color: twilight.

On December 2, 1992, Jean-François Dehecq, president of Sanofi, met with Pierre Bergé: "What if we went beyond 15 percent? What if we had a real merger?" They spent about a month going back and forth. Also on December 2—the anniversary of Napoleon's coronation as emperor—Pierre Cardin became the first couturier to be elected to the Académie des Beaux-Arts. He told *Le Figaro* that he would have "liked to hear from Yves Saint Laurent."

On January 3, 1993, Pierre Bergé returned from Latche, where he had spent New Year's Eve at François Mitterrand's house, and called some colleagues into his office, where he flew into a rage because all of Paris already knew the name of the fragrance that was going to be launched in June. "I'm sick of this! This profession is screwed. There's no more ethics in this industry. Anyway, I'm done with this shit." It was true that a new era had begun in couture: for example, Jean-Louis Scherrer was let go overnight by the owners of his company, thus losing the right to use his own name. Christian Lacroix complained that he had sold his. Claude Montana ended up doing only five collections at Lanvin before he was let go. He was said to be down in the dumps. Italian methods had arrived in France: in the magazines, the advertisers laid down the law, wielding their advertising budgets against editorial.

The latest stars were the models, who were asked for their autograph after the shows. The most popular supermodel was Claudia Schiffer, who was Karl Lagerfeld's muse and was on 450 magazine covers between 1988 and 1993. Nicole Dorier, the head of the modeling department at Yves Saint Laurent, said: "He doesn't go for luscious blondes. There has to be some mystery. If a model doesn't have a story to tell, nothing will happen."

On January 19, 1993, in the cellars of the Hôtel George V, which had aquarium blue paneled walls, a press conference was held to announce the purchase of Yves Saint Laurent by the state-controlled company Elf Sanofi. With legislative elections two months away, the news was harshly received in financial circles: "A coup for Bergé!" The significant boost to shares of Yves Saint Laurent (32 percent between mid-December and mid-January, while the market overall lost 2.96 percent) even led to rumors of insider trading. The day after the official announcement, the market inflicted a 10 percent drop on Elf Sanofi. The media had a field day: "Yves Saint Laurent, Speculators with a Keen Nose."[7]

"The rumors are swirling, the media is getting upset," *Le Monde* wrote one week later. The paper explored the political implications of " a friend of the French president getting helped out by someone who owed the president a favor. It seemed that Mr. Pierre Bergé, the head of a luxury company weighed down by debt, was bailed out by Mr. Loïk Le Floch-Prigent, president of a state-controlled company, just before upcoming elections."[8] Bergé's enemies didn't waste any time. On February 4, he lost his reelection bid to the presidency of the Chambre Syndicale de la Mode.[9]

With this merger/takeover, Elf-Sanofi—which made 30 percent of its revenue in cosmetics with its portfolio of Roger & Gallet, Stendhal, Van Cleef & Arpels, and Oscar de la Renta, as well as a 50 percent stake in Nina Ricci—became the third-largest international luxury fragrance group, behind L'Oréal and Estée Lauder. "With Sanofi, I'm sure that I've found a French solution. Handing over Yves Saint Laurent's destiny for the future was a way of continuing the policy of high standards Yves Saint Laurent has had for thirty years."[10] Thanks to this transaction, Pierre Bergé and Yves Saint Laurent would each see capital gains of 300 million francs before taxes. In addition to this sum, they would receive annual fees for fragrance development and marketing consulting. *Le Monde* reported that these fees were on the order of 10 million francs, a number that the company neither confirmed nor denied. Yves Saint Laurent and Pierre Bergé kept only a 10 percent stake in the company, which took the form of a 150-million-franc investment in the maison de couture. "My greatest ambition was to please Yves. Being a minister so I can come to the office at 8:00 AM and sign papers until midnight? No way. I have cars, chauffeurs, a helicopter. A fabulous art collection."

On May 17, 1993, the merger of Elf Sanofi and Yves Saint Laurent became official, after the shareholders of each company had approved. A press conference was held with Yves present. He had been in Deauville. "We put him in a helicopter," said Pierre Bergé with a laugh. At exactly 6:00 PM, Yves read the following statement:

"This is an important day, because it marks the merger of Yves Saint Laurent and Elf Sanofi. For over thirty years, I've done all I could to build a brand that was worthy of representing France around the world. I've done it without compromises, without concessions. I was the first couturier to have a show at the Metropolitan Museum of Art in New York, and I exhibited my work in Moscow, at the legendary Hermitage Museum in Saint Petersburg, in Beijing to amazed Chinese audiences, in Sydney, in Tokyo, and, of course, in Paris. I have tried to the best of my abilities to show that fashion is an art. In this regard, I followed the advice of my mentor

Christian Dior and the enduring lessons of Mademoiselle Chanel. I have designed for my era and I have tried to foresee what tomorrow will look like. I always kept my distance from tricks and gimmicks, and I always believed that style was more important than fashion. Those who have created a style are rare, but there are many makers of fashion. During all these years, and especially during recent years, I asked myself the question of the future of my company and my name. Today, I am happy that Yves Saint Laurent is passing into the hands of Elf Sanofi, which is a powerful company and especially a French company. That is what I wanted and I have faith in Mr. Dehecq to continue the work that I began with Pierre Bergé and myself.

"I'd like to add that for two years I have been working on a new fragrance, which I am proud to have brought to this wedding celebration. It will go on sale in September and will be presented to the press next month. But I'd like to tell you about it now. It's made for happy, cheerful, lighthearted women who sparkle. This is only natural, because it is called 'Champagne.' It's a fragrance, but it's more than that. It's a concept. It's a fragrance intended for celebrating happy occasions. Like the one that has brought us here today. This is what I wanted to tell you and I'm happy I could say it here. Thank you."

Above him was a screen with a dove, the symbol of Sanofi, whose slogan must have bruised his head: "Health is our goal." Dehecq thanked him. Yves left. "We made him go through this horrible exercise but I don't regret it."

An employee of Sanofi sat down in the seat that had just been occupied by Saint Laurent and moved the name card. "We'll have to take over the name," said Dehecq with a laugh. When he was asked if Yves Saint Laurent would continue to design the collections, the microphone crackled. He went off into a long speech describing Sanofi as "a company that is overinvested in high tech" and announced that the merger "will release significant synergies." Afterward, Loulou, all in red, said that it "put her totally to sleep." There were stacks of blue and white folders on the tables. Men in gray suits that were a bit wrinkled from the long day left with little gift bags containing Volupté perfume by Oscar de la Renta. On his way out, Pierre Bergé said he felt a little nostalgic, but "happy... In any case, I wouldn't have been able to keep on going. This profession is becoming awful. They make so many demands on you. The saleswomen. The decoration. The distributor sends the merchandise back to you.... I think we're stronger with several brands. That's why I had a long flirtation with L'Oréal." There was a sentimental gleam in his eyes. As if Pierre Bergé were drifting away. But he snapped back to attention: "Now I have more power than before."

But events soon spiraled out of his control. "The Yves Saint Laurent affair took an unexpected turn today," *Le Monde* wrote one month later.[11] "Although the January sale of the company is no longer a source of controversy, an investigation by the Commission des Opérations de Bourse [French Securities and Exchange Commission] has revealed a large sale of shares before the merger outside the Paris stock market but a few weeks before the stock price drastically fell. The date?

Summer 1992. The amount: 100 million francs. The place: Switzerland." On June 17, 1993, *Le Figaro* asserted that the sellers were none other than Pierre Bergé and Yves Saint Laurent. And, while scandals hit the political class, tarnished by trials involving financial corruption, *Le Monde* wondered, "Insider trading?" In an atmosphere of social, economic, and ethical collapse, Pierre Bergé hung on. For months, people had been whispering that he would be replaced as head of the Paris opera houses. Brilliantly, he held a press conference at the Opéra Bastille to announce the 1993–94 season. On June 7, at the Hotel Intercontinental, he clashed with champagne producers who had come to express their anger. They were suing to force Yves Saint Laurent to change the name of its new fragrance, Champagne. The company was said to have already invested 100 million francs in the new product. On June 7, Pierre Bergé spoke to one hundred journalists who covered fashion and perfume. "This day marks the end of one era and the beginning of another. That twilight moment when shadows turn violet." Yves was not there. On July 2, the maison Saint Laurent announced that Pierre Bergé had been named a goodwill ambassador by the director of UNESCO, Federico Mayor. He was the third Frenchman to receive this honor, after composer Jean-Michel Jarre and designer Pierre Cardin. On July 21, Yves Saint Laurent showed his 124th haute couture collection to the music of *The Merry Widow*. Two days later, it was revealed that Hugues Gall, the director of Geneva's Grand Théâtre, had been named as head of the Paris opera houses starting in 1995.

At the maison de couture, men with their brows furrowed by numbers seemed to be cowed by its women, who were less afraid of anger than of silence, which meant boredom: "Oh, there's no more clan!" said Paule de Mérindol in a tired voice. She reapplied powder before going to lunch: "I'm transparent today!" Madame Hélène from packaging climbed up the stairs heroically: "I'm old-fashioned. When these gentlemen can get a dress out of a computer, then we'll talk!"

Here, the art of hiding a secret counted more than the secret. What was said at the mysterious lunch that Lucienne Mathieu-Saint-Laurent had with the "old-timers" on February 17, 1993? The maison de couture had 13 ateliers, the most in Paris, and employed 194 workers (50 of whom had followed Yves from Dior). Back in 1962, there were 5 ateliers with 80 workers. The air was heavy with little dramas that resolved themselves silently. "Oh, the poor dear died!" said Maryse Agussol about a client. And, regarding another client: "She must be 100 years old!" Agussol had joined Yves Saint Laurent in 1962 and was responsible for updating the secret order book and keeping track of the development of couture sales. Here, there were no computers. She had used the same cardboard binder for 30 years, hiding it in her black desk. She opened it and took a look at winter 1963: "Liz Taylor, Dorchester Hotel, London. Suede jacket. 5,415 dollars. Niki de Saint Phalle, hat." She hastily read the name of Barbara Thurston: "The poor thing! She was found dead in the bathtub at the Plaza. She ordered six pieces per season!" As usual, at noon, as well as at 6:00 PM, a musical tone resounded in the ateliers. It wasn't strident, but sounded like the scale at the Paris airports that precedes announcement of departures or arrivals: "Flight such-and-such to such-and-such will depart." Gabrielle Buchaert explained the structure that was in place for the transition: "Pierre Bergé will remain president of Couture until 2001....In case of...It will prevent a horrendous battle." At 5 Avenue Marceau, the company stuck with typical bureaucrat-speak: "Monsieur Saint Laurent designs the collections."

For 1993, he didn't draw a Love card, the giant holiday card that he sent every year to 1,500 people. He didn't offer all his queens a heart, but a cross in rock crystal. He wasn't there for Saint Catherine's Day. The holiday cards sent by the maison Saint Laurent had the colors of his fragrance, Champagne. "Red and gold, that's me," he told Loulou.

Yves Saint Laurent had never visited the premises of Parfums Yves Saint Laurent. Yet, in December 1992, although he usually avoided all official events, he wanted to be present for the opening of the spa on Rue du Faubourg Saint-Honoré. Was it simply a way to show he was angry? His name was not on the invitations. The spa was an offshoot of the maison de couture, and Jacques Grange had done the décor. There was nothing clinical about it. A sofa in the shape of lips was a copy of one by Dalí, the screens were inspired by Jean-Michel Frank, and the details—the doors with knobs by Robert Goossens that looked like gilded shells, the rock crystal chandelier, and the console tables made of burnished bronze—recalled Yves's dream office on Avenue Marceau. The air that was breathed here was that of Paris. As if he had sprayed the perfume of the memories of the boutique where he had started off, arranging his mannequin heads in the windows of 30 Avenue Montaigne at Dior.

One of the estheticians was named Marlene, a brunette born in Oran. They all seemed to become actresses here. And he was the director. In this palace of frippery, all the Yves Saint Laurent accessories were also available. They included heart-shaped powder compacts and bracelets with a smattering of rhinestone stars. The reigning color was green, which was also used in the grand salon of the maison de couture when it was renovated in 1993. This was also the color of the company's thirtieth-anniversary fragrance, Love, which was surely the most elegant of his perfumes, along with Y, which had been created in 1963.

Green was considered a cursed color in couture. But what if it was, in fact, the ultimate Yves Saint Laurent color? The green of seascapes, of the Napoleonic empire, of lawyers' offices. Military green, Scarlett O'Hara green, romantic green, watery green. The green of childhood paradises and of Ludwig's forests and Ingres's *L'Odyssée*, the painting of which he had a postcard at the head of his bed for so long. Wasn't it in the work of this painter, who liked to think of himself as being "original while imitating," that he found the lines of an ideal beauty that he used to depict women, the same way this artist glorified heroes and gods?

Pierre Rivas, a classmate who sat next to him in history class at Lycée Lamoricière in 1953, remembered him as "a rare bird." Forty years had passed, but

Rivas remembered Yves as if it had been yesterday. "Promise me you'll give me back this photo, because it's a moment that is dead and will never come back again." Now a college professor, Rivas wondered how someone born in Oran could become a fashion designer. How did this man bring his dreams to life so powerfully in a town where some people said the soul was "fossilized"? The town was as if frozen in an oppressive life with no grandeur. Nevertheless it still shone like the sun inside all those who had left it. With some of his friends, such as François Catroux, Betty's husband, Yves explored his memories—"Do you remember Promé Couture?"—and laughed about them. He communicated with his sister by fax. "We always admired him," Brigitte said. Once a week, Lucienne Mathieu-Saint-Laurent and her daughters had lunch together and "talked about Yves." Brigitte, "two cats, two dogs, two marriages," maintained her southern cheerfulness, and recalled nostalgically the anise croquettes, *agua limón*, and the green velvet dress with a satin belt that Yves had made for her by Mathilde Montier, the seamstress "who sang operettas like crazy." Oran was still intact in their memories. Brigitte still wondered: "I think one of my father's movie theaters was called Le Pigalle, but I'm not sure."

Perhaps the secret shone in Lucienne Mathieu-Saint-Laurent's green eyes. The same green as the emeralds he gave her on New Year's, asking her the following day, "Did you put them on?" "He loves me, he showers me with such splendid gifts that I can't wear them, he calls me his 'Mamushka,'"[12] said Lucienne, who was so happy to go to the theater, even if all she remembered afterward was that she was there and wore a new dress. It was as if she came out of a box, always busy with mysterious appointments that kept her so occupied every day, like people who have never worked a day in their lives, and are tinged with regret about not sharing in close relationships with loved ones like the ones they maintain, due to self-interest or sincerity, with the hairdresser, the manicurist, the saleswoman in the boutique.

Madame Saint Laurent walked her dog, Nouba, who had a sapphire blue leash, the same color as the YSL towel that the animal sat on in the back seat of her Autobianchi. "Yves is happy when I go out. I don't ask him any questions. I know if he wants to talk to me. Or else I call his butler. I tell him I'm there, that's all. I ask how his dog, Moujik, is doing or I give a little note to his chauffeur. I'm easy. I'm not a mother who is going to annoy him. A little more champagne?" She rarely had lunch at home, but, like her daughter Brigitte, she always had bottles of Roederer Cristal chilling. In her apartment in the sixteenth arrondissement, Lucienne Mathieu-Saint-Laurent always had candy dishes with chocolates and gooey candied chestnuts wrapped in gold paper from the best shops in Paris. As soon as the sun came out in springtime, she brought out her black crepe de Chine dress printed with red and green sweet william: "This is all me, this is Oran," she said, while spraying a bit of Guerlain's Vol de Nuit perfume in the living room. She listened to classic French singers: Aznavour, Trenet, Joe Dassin: "*On ira où tu voudras quand tu voudras, et on s'aimera encore, lorsque l'amour sera mort.*" Leaving her apartment, you felt that life was so lighthearted, so intoxicating! "From time to time, he goes to say his prayers at Saint-François-Xavier, and say hello to Little Thérèse....We like [the church] a lot," said Lucienne Mathieu-Saint-Laurent over lunch at Port Alma, a restaurant overlooking the Seine designed to like a blue and white boat. Her eyebrows were two seagulls flying above her big green eyes, and her lips were delicately drawn in bright pink. Her apartment had been broken into. The thieves took jewelry and furs. But they left Yves's drawings and paintings. "I can't do anything. The police are overwhelmed!" she said, with the lack of concern of a young girl, cursing the problems and the recession that made people sad. "Oh, we need bubbles to get out of this stagnation!" she said in July 1993, after her son's runway show, during the traditional cocktail party held by the maison. Lucienne Mathieu-Saint-Laurent wore her emeralds and radiated youthfulness in her bright pink suit, as she continued to survey other women's clothing constantly. She could be sought but never found. She always came alive in a special way in front of her red and gold tube of lipstick. When asked, "What do you think makes him happiest?" she answered, "Oh, for me to look attractive!"

19 / WHAT IS SILENT AND WHAT FADES AWAY

Oh, to create joyful, lively dresses that make people turn and look, to imagine bold accessories, and couture jewels that are so much cleverer than real ones," Yves had said during his first interview in 1955. Time seemed to have no hold over this man, and his physical decline was perhaps only an additional illusion. After all, Mishima had been the first, in *The School of Flesh*, to note that this young man had "nerves of steel."

Just as Yves Saint Laurent was withdrawing from the fashion world, runway shows were becoming noisier and noisier and more distanced from reality. After ten years of trying to imitate the street, fashion seemed to have lost its last privilege: being copied. By fleeing its own legacy, fashion left the empty space occupied by dreadful shadows. After having been covered with gold and trinkets, the body became elongated and grouchy under big puritan nightshirts that seemed to be accepted like dictates from on high. What was left of those years of euphoria and excitement for luxury, supported by America and Japan? Fashion kept on apologizing for its existence, under a black coat of ennui, a random look with shreds and holes. Factories closed. The masters had no time to teach and the students were in too much of a hurry to succeed, without even taking the risk of exposing themselves, of going against the grain. Everyone wanted to be on stage, and the audience left, indifferent. Something was disappearing, with no noise, no shouting. Women didn't buy clothes anymore! The crisis had arrived: in France, in the first six months of 1993, ready-to-wear sales declined by 8 percent. But it wasn't only because of economic stagnation. Ugliness just didn't sell well.

Clumsy shoes replaced aristocratic mules, and coarse, fuzzy, and felted clothes reigned over a false elite that was determined to scorn what it once worshiped. Everything that hung down loosely was declared "authentic." At the end of a runway show, backstage, it was as if Yves Saint Laurent had to justify his profession: "I'm a couturier. My profession is to make clothes for women. We must idealize them and make them beautiful."

In 1993, he complained: "This morning, I met a very pretty girl who had a dress no bigger than sixteen inches. Her garters were showing. Be nude or wear clothes, but this? No! All this ugliness makes me progress." His supreme strength was moving forward by taking from reality everything that could distance him from it. He was elsewhere. Elusive. It was as if, out of his bed, he wobbled, like people who, when they're up, have only one desire: to go back to bed and sleep. He seemed to forever repeat, "I am horrified by what I see."

Although Yves Saint Laurent had aged, and at age fifty-seven talked like "an old patriarch," like Gabrielle Chanel saying "I have dressed the universe and it goes naked,"[1] he always managed to escape, to be elsewhere. Definitively against. Beyond the honors and tributes, his work was strong enough to condemn fakery all on its own. Whatever one said about his fashion—which some said was out of style—with him, you were always dealing on the runway with women, with women who were in love, lovers, friends, enemies. Nothing was more real for him than what he imagined. You strolled through his collections as if reading a book. Each one was the continuation of a story, brought to life by women who hated each other since the beginning of time, united in their rivalry for a man's attention.

He was the only one who could dare say about the contemporary woman: "I invented her past, I gave her her future, and this will last long after my death."

From what no longer existed, from what was silent, from what faded away, he made a world, his own world. He knew that a world had started with him, and that after him, it would be over. There were multiple honors, books, and retrospectives. The cult of restoration and heritage had revived Paris's title as the capital of fashion, without the present renewing this memory. He remained a master without a student. Even if all his contemporaries felt his influence.

Was he the "terrible dominating cobra" that Matthieu Galey wrote about? Did he cast spells? He put in drops of poison, like Lulu giving rotten eggs to children. Because of him, couturiers could no longer accept being just couturiers: they had to be "artists" or "anti-artists." Every two-bit designer wanted to have a retrospective or a book. Because of him, the adjective "Proustian" had become a sign of style, a way that fashion intellectuals had of putting their hand on their hearts in order to cover up the absence of a heart. "I loved this very Proustian passage." Because of him, couturiers felt they had to talk about their mothers when promoting a fragrance, and to turn dresses into literature. He broke the rules of the game, and he demanded to be buried with them.

Predatory, he was the sum of all the couturiers of the twentieth century: Poiret, Vionnet, Chanel, Balenciaga, Dior, Schiaparelli, and also Givenchy. "He took the best and he made something else out of it," said Robert Goossens, the accessory maker, who made costume jewelry for the maison Saint Laurent, one of his main clients. They all wanted to be the guardians of something. Lagerfeld, of the moment. Lacroix, of history. Cardin, of the future. An unmoving traveler, Yves Saint Laurent let time slip through his fingers. He captured the ephemeral with lines in order to let it be free, for he depicted nothing other than movement, escape, the story of women, of their moods, their love affairs, and, as Françoise Giroud wrote, "their talent for being several women in one, to wear many masks, to be a proper young lady in the morning and at night, a sultana, an androgynous creature, or a harlot."[2] He made many things unfashionable: indecent assault, prudishness, propriety, and gorgeous airheads.

He struggled against anything that was moralizing, small-thinking, overdone, pretty, twee, or overly decorative. He made tight outfits unfashionable, along with push-up bras, overt sex appeal, risqué and racy styles, nose jobs, and bleached blonds on ski slopes. He found beauty in flaws. Because with him, fashion stopped being about hemlines, colors, and age; he gave women back their power. How could he accept that they were slipping away from him? He had avoided baby doll looks, futurism, and now the grunge look. He dressed demons, those women to whom one says: "You're the man I would have liked to be." They recognized themselves in Le Smoking; it was a pact with the bizarre, lies, and doppelgängers, disguising reality, and everything that wasn't about order, conventionality, and stereotypes. It revealed the strength of women, which lies in knowing how to put on an act.

Because he worked with all the resources of his art, he was an artist, while others who tried to make art were just making fashion. His work remained the testimony of a painter depicting modern life, finding the unlimited nature of creativity in the fleeting, the bizarre, the fierce, the strange, and the individual. Because he obeyed the rules of the game—the science of proportions, the balance of the line and movement—he was able to attain great freedom. That alone made all his boldness possible. In the early 1990s, he had expressed the essence of his style in his collections: "The most beautiful adornment for a man or woman is love."[3] His women always seemed out of step with the clichés of chic, being by turns serious and lighthearted, able to move with ease in any world, for a date at the Palace Hotel or the Lux Bar in Montmartre. Wherever they went, they had a Saint Laurent aura, an elegance such as Baudelaire compared to "bohemians wandering on the edges of genteel society."[4]

He respected this craft so much that he considered it "an issue of millimeters," but he was the only one who was able to break the rules. Then the fabrics seemed to have been dyed in vermilion blood, satin was draped in lemon yellow, the skirt was pink, the belt raspberry, and the bolero jacket was lime green (summer 1992 haute couture collection). So shape became a color.

Saint Laurent was the school of the eye. In Marrakesh, when you walked in the medina at twilight, it was if these women in light robes had been brought together by Yves, like fabrics. One red, one pink, one orange. A yellow basket with a bundle of mint. It was him. His colors swallowed everything in a giant wave. The tragic events of his life could later reveal them, but never explain them. Nothing, no fact, could justify this mad flow of color.

In the Majorelle Garden at Yves's villa in Marrakesh, I had the impression that the mauve flowers and blue pottery had been dyed by his hand, that the pink bougainvillea flowers were printed silk. This jungle was his, with cacti that looked like candelabra full of spines, tentacled plants that had come out of *Suddenly, Last Summer*, and so many trees with strange names whose branches are still wound together in the sky.

If I had to come up with just one word to describe Yves Saint Laurent, it would be "strength." The strength of those who search for truth, and are only wary of those who have found it. Asked to define Yves, Catherine Deneuve chose Rilke's *Letters to a Young Poet*. She must have seen a similarity with the one who "confidently confronts the storms of springtime without worrying that no summer will follow them. Summer comes in spite of everything. But it only comes for the patient ones who are there, in their vast, untroubled peace. As if they had the summer before them."[5]

This man, who was afraid of a trinket seller whose store he didn't dare step into, this man full of phobias and superstitions, didn't fear death. It ultimately became harmless. He flirted with death with the formidable frivolity of those who don't believe in friendship or love, and he taunted it, seeming to say about it each day to his chauffeur, "Paul, drop off the lady wherever she would like." Always faithful to Cocteau, who depicted death as an elegant lady in *Le Testament d'Orphée*, hadn't he always imagined death "in a long dress"? The important thing for him seemed to be the way he would stage death, always in reference to his myths: dying on stage like Molière or Jouvet, committing suicide by a lake like Ludwig, drowning like Virginia Woolf, or swallowing poison like Emma Bovary?

He traced his life the way he designed women's bodies. He changed his physical appearance, the way Dior changed his line. But inside, he was sharp as a tack. A piercing eye. "He saw us and laughed. He made fun of the way we were overdressed," recalled his childhood friend Simone. Born one month apart, Yves and Simone had been "engaged" by their parents at the age of two. She became a humanities teacher in a high school in Paris. When she talked about Yves, she lost all her grown-up cool. Her voice became soft, full of emotion and fear. As if I had touched a painful scar. "I remember how he made fun of one of my dresses when I was eight. I had a ribbon in my hair. I had a very authoritarian mother who controlled that kind of thing and I was often pushed and pulled in different directions. As a result, I'm amazingly incompetent at clothes: I can never find anything that looks good on me."

He set traps, at the same time that he showed wonderful new directions: he transformed a world with this "constantly sharp" look that Simone talked about, which illuminated or burned those who came too close. For, as Loulou de la Falaise said, "He shines like a star and a lunar eclipse at the same time." He seemed to manipulate people from afar, without losing his bearings. Others got their feet caught in his traps, being against him or with him, but never indifferent. Plus, beauty for Yves Saint Laurent seemed always to be in danger, on the edge of the bizarre.

You couldn't escape Saint Laurent, even his absences. There were many people who took drugs or drank too much, who, like him, thought they were in love with handsome young men chosen for their resemblance to screen idols like Marlon Brando or James Dean. There were many people who sniffed a little loudly or stared at people's shoes, with their faces beset by odd tics. I met so many artistic types while writing this book who petted their dogs while listening to Maria Callas and telling me, "Oh, we all dream of having an empty apartment!" or "For your information, I took cocaine starting in 1964!" All along the Paris-Marrakesh-New York axis, there are so many living imitations of his personality: "No, I hardly ever go out in public anymore. When I have guests, I feel as if I have to entertain them!"

He managed to live alone and under observation, creating ghosts as he did when he ordered his sisters to dress in costume. Even if he said in 1993, "I'm done with my clothes," and mentioned "playing hooky" like a distant memory. He sought danger inside himself, mutilating himself to see his own blood flow, to remain a man, and to prove himself in a more superhuman way than others did. He came out of depression twice. Everything in him was exaggerated, contradictory, dramatized by his fear of ennui, which he dreaded more than anything else in the world. When interviewed by G. Y. Dryansky for the 1982 book *Bravo Yves*, he said, "I may have to stop one day because of this immense anxiety that prevents me from living. I don't live, I'm completely cloistered away. I don't go out at night. I have no relationship with outside life. I want to lead a normal life, but it seems that this is the life of great designers."

The more women wanted to look young, the closer he got to childhood, even if his body said the opposite, making him look like all the fathers in his life. He was both Emma and Charles Bovary. "He's thirty or forty pounds overweight because he let it happen. It's total anarchy in the bourgeois meaning of the term. He's always felt he was a victim. He was this curious, cheerful, very intelligent young man, with a sharp eye on the world, but with long periods of listlessness and depression. Back then, he controlled it," said Pierre Bergé. "Creative people are monsters before which all bends and must bend. He lives his life as a victim. It's true that he's a victim. That he's deeply unhappy. But his worst tormentor is himself. If you miss his sadomasochism, you miss everything."

It seemed as if he always needed to strengthen the bars of his prisons in order better to escape into his dreams. He admired Proust, whom he called a "man who sacrificed his life to his work." But did he really sacrifice it? "He had a hand in everything that happened. He resisted all the attacks that he made on his body," said Loulou de la Falaise. "In Proust, he found a nervous, cloistered figure like himself!" said Pierre Bergé, judging him with the severity that love makes possible when it knows that it is doomed. "His heart is crippled." In 1993, as he reflected on his past, Pierre said, "I got into fashion for Yves. Since I shared his life, I wanted to speak his language. I knew very well that he would never bother to learn mine. I'm the most important man in his life. Is it because he loves me the most in the world, or because he needs me? I don't know."

The mystery thickened around these two men, Yves Mathieu-Saint-Laurent, the teenager in the black suit who came to Paris with fifty drawings in a suitcase, and Pierre Bergé, born on the Île d'Oléron, this incredible couple who built an empire like a golden city on the ruins of a world in decline. Two men were united, bound to passions, hatreds, and interests that only history will reveal. They ruled over Paris to the point where the streets seemed to have been invented for them: one lived on Rue de Babylone and the other on Rue Bonaparte, where in 1993 he moved into an apartment after leaving the Hôtel Lutetia. But Pierre made their intimacy clear: "I'm at home on Rue de Babylone. I have the key in my pocket." Yves? "He has marvelous drawing skill, but he can't do perspective. Since I first met him, I've been telling him to take drawing classes. He never wanted to get into it. He has written with a lot of joy. It's sometimes a bit lyrical. But it's certainly not worthless. All this proves that he was trying to find a path," said Pierre Bergé, who didn't consider fashion to be a major art, even if he pretended to believe it. He still said about Yves, "He was much too talented for this profession. There is genius in him."

This man sought color deep inside himself. Like Gauguin continuing to paint orange rivers and red dogs, he dyed reality with his visions. He injected this continually dying world with a liquid that would make it beautiful and crazy, to keep it alive artificially, full of sirens who dreamed of being the most beautiful, the most fragrant, the most hated, while everything was slowly slipping away—beauty, desire, scandal, the voluntary servitude of women who were addicted to Saint Laurent. "You devil, you've forgotten me," he said to a faithful Rive Gauche client at the company's thirtieth-anniversary celebration. She was upset, and realized the next day, "Of course, it's because I wasn't wearing Yves Saint Laurent!"

He stole women's passions, and gave them back more beautiful, dipped in red and gold. He dyed the sky onto his fabrics and rolled himself up inside them, inside these houses filled with Casablanca lilies, which for Yves suggested both the flower of forbidden love and that of heraldic glory. And wasn't the French word for lily, *lys*, an anagram of YSL? "I'm ambitious," he said.

His colors rumbled and shivered. One day, we understood that they contained something besides color. I first attended an Yves Saint Laurent runway show in March 1987 in the Louvre's Cour Carrée. It was like a slap in the eyes. A purple taffeta dress shaded with tulle, a bolero jacket made of turquoise feathers, and the audience standing up, clapping, flooded with light. I especially remember a long dress like a black lily lined with bright pink satin that lit it up from the inside. Why were his pinks pinker? His reds redder?

We can chase down and delve into this mystery, but all attempts to grab hold of the man are in vain, or rather they push you farther away, make you lose your way: you can collect facts, but the enigma remains. He had a gift for wearing out his life until it was threadbare, destroying himself, letting himself sink, and then slipping into women's secrets, what makes them thinner and taller without deforming them. He issued an invitation—let them come to him—applied the rules of love to fashion. He asked for nothing, just observed and waited. He didn't make them pretty, but beautiful. And they spoke of him as they would a lover.

Yves Saint Laurent designed for couture's last golden age, the era when Madame Felisa would do a fitting for Madame Mellon or Countess Bismarck on Capri: "Felisa, how many suits have I ordered this season?" He was the first couturier to compare himself to a drug. With him, fashion followed the adventures of love. It was in life, in secret nooks, stolen instants. It talked about waiting, rendezvous, encounters, and passions. This was between 1968 and 1983, between the pill and AIDS. Love meant anytime, anywhere, anyone.

Observing his era without ever letting it control him, designing clothes that liberated women in the 1960s, embraced the nostalgia of the 1970s, and fled the eclecticism of the 1980s, he followed the curve of lasting time, just as he followed the bodies of his muses, and the lines of his fabrics. Yves Saint Laurent never imposed orders. His name is so linked to everything that happened over twenty-five years that in order to isolate him in the past one would need a museum that could contain an entire era. But fortunately life never stands still in a box.

He was the couturier whose work was most collected by museums, and he was the first one to open up his own museum (the couture house has 7,000 pieces). But these facts may omit what is most essential: his dresses always look bored when they're not on a woman. A megalomaniac? Others have become so for less: he simplified fashion to adapt it to new ways of life. Everything that happens in the street today has passed through his hands and in his drawings. "When I see the number of women who wear clothes that I designed, it moves me very much, because I haven't done my work for nothing. What gives me the most joy is to see a blazer or a Rive Gauche tuxedo move on a woman. These are timeless pieces."

He mourned himself, because he mourned a world that was disappearing. He talked about his life as if it were a fabric. And he talked about fabrics as if they were life. He compared his destiny to "a woman like any other."

He always received you with a mischievous smile. When it seemed as if his dog was about to tear your suit apart, he'd comment, "Moujik hates women in pants!" (This was Moujik III.) The king was available, but wouldn't answer questioning. He wounded you with his absences, his missed appointments, and his attitude of an old gentleman who has forgotten everything. He was well behaved enough to play at being crazy and exhibit his nervous depression like a shield that protected him. Would Saint Laurent outdo himself at playing Saint Laurent?

His artistic references, these intimate reflections that he used to make dresses, ended up engulfing him. His roles were stacked one inside another like matryoshka dolls. He embodied Swann with his mania for name-dropping, and, because he was Saint Laurent, he gave them imaginary accents: "Le Vicomte de Noailles always said: when you have very beautiful objects, if you want to keep on loving them, you have to move them around, because your eye gets used to them." He couldn't keep himself from playing. He pulled the strings of his life, just as he once pulled those of his Illustre

Théâtre. He talked about himself using stand-ins as if, through their movements, he had glimpsed a bit of himself, even though just yesterday he expressed these characters through his dresses. "Saint Laurent became Saint Laurent because he emerges from himself in order to make women happy," said Robert Goossens. He had an ability to make other people feel that he was inventing his memories while he was telling them. As if the memory lapses caused by the medications and the side effects of drugs had only developed his extraordinary imaginative abilities. Sometimes it seemed as if he were parodying Saint Laurent, and sometimes as if he wanted to take a vacation from himself. While he hid his impossibility of being alone, of facing himself, it seemed as if all his performances just revealed it all the more. He could only live through his dreams, which had always coincided with those of women. He couldn't write himself without these women; he was "the writer who no longer writes."

He caressed stories the way he caressed "the softness of a fabric." He mentioned Flaubert, wondering how this man, who was very withdrawn from the world, was able "to capture women so well." Wasn't the most famous one Madame Bovary, a current woman coming back to the present day? Yves talked about her as if he were discussing a real woman: "I remember the scene in the theater, this woman discovering sexuality, or rather sensitivity, thanks to a dancer." Where did fiction stop and reality start? His aunt seemed to have come out of an imaginary movie that was a mash-up of *Senso, Gone with the Wind*, and *The Eagle with Two Heads*, all mixed with an Yves Saint Laurent couture collection: "I flunked math. My aunt went to see the headmaster, with whom she had had an affair in the past. We dressed her up, we put her jewelry on, and black veils to hide her face."

He was a man of the theater. Who he was and who he was pretending to be seemed inseparable. Saint Laurent was women in pants, and women in black stockings. Lines and artifice. When you tried to define his fashion as pink, it had already become black. When you tried to capture it with words like "test garments," "cut," and "technique," it slipped away like mousseline in the breeze. But sometimes, his sentences were broken by silence. It was like the reply of the baron, Louis Jouvet, in Renoir's film *The Lower Depths*: "There's a kind of fog floating in my head, as if my life were just a series of costumes."

Sometimes he searched for words as if he were digging around in his pockets. "I'm sorry, all these medications make me lose my memory." And then, with a theatrical delivery, he would state, "I have been in two hospitals that I won't recommend to you." But there was his look. It could dismantle his entire face, wrecked by anger. Frighteningly hard eyes, ready to demolish everything. But, another day, they curled up in the midst of smiles, unbelievable sweetness, and armfuls of flowers that he sent that very evening with a love note saying, "I'm sorry. I'll call you tomorrow."

This game would mean nothing without the suffering that gave rise to it. For why so many identifications? Didn't they begin that day when, at age thirteen in Oran, he began writing "Pourquoi Parler d'Amour"? The author did his first pastiche:

an imitation of Molière's *The Imaginary Invalid* (Act II, Scene 9) when Egyptians disguised as Moors dance between two laments by Argan. He never referred directly to this play, except in January 1990, in his Homages collection, with this terrible sentence by Molière stated by Jouvet: "How a man suffers before dying!"

Yves had never revealed himself as much to the press as he did in the early 1990s. Yet surely he hid the essential, once again. The cry of a man? He hid his father's death, as if to survive him better, in a silent identification. He had his white salon redone: "I couldn't take it anymore!" The salon was redecorated by Jacques Grange and imitated that of the Noailles family in Fontainebleau, in the Pompadours' retreat. The dragonfly bar and the Lalanne sheep were stored elsewhere: "Moujik was eating all their wool!" A neo-Gothic tapestry by Burne-Jones depicting two madonnas replaced the Warhols. On the oak bookshelves, the decorative objects were gone. The photos had disappeared, as if erased from the room. "I like all these hardbound books. That's a good look for a bookcase."

The first time I went to his apartment, he showed me an extraordinary collection of ancient cameos and told me about the antiquarian who had devoted his whole life to collecting them. "Sometimes I'd like to touch them, but they're all behind glass!" Five years later, the exact same ritual took place. We went down the black staircase leading to the salon. He lit up the windows, but this time he said, "I have to lock everything up. I can't invite anyone. My servant steals from me!" According to Pierre Bergé, this was all in Yves's imagination. "The poor people!"

He would burst into laughter while watching his dog and stopped talking when Moujik left the room, announcing that his master was tired. One could never tell if he was a billionaire pretending to be a child, or a child pretending to be a billionaire. He believed in God: "But I offend Him so much!" He was able to keep that particular treasure intact. "He has faith in religion, any religion," said a friend. His good luck charms included wheat and lilies, "my favorite flower." Also, a bronze Venus, "the symbol of my profession." A seventeenth-century cross that had belonged to Mademoiselle Chanel. The ten of clubs. *Remembrance of Things Past* by Proust, though he said he had never read the last volume, *Time Regained*. "If I finish the book, something in me will be broken." The lion: "my astrological sign." A game: "solitaire." He added at the end of the Proust Questionnaire: "my pencils." "You can't kill the dream," he said in January 1992, in reference to a rebirth. A demon condemned him to repeat, "I am well," as if the rest he desired so much left him with only a feeling of emptiness. As if he suffered from no longer suffering. He fled like a snake, just as he had always fled himself in order to cheat this horrible ennui of living, even if this unceasing flight is life itself, for "childhood is still there, continuing inside me like a dream, and it doesn't want to die."

When I interviewed Yves on March 6, 1993, in his apartment on Rue de Babylone, he reflected on founding his company, the experience of haute couture design, and changes in fashion. By this point he was famously reclusive, yet he discussed with me candidly his childhood, his relationship with his parents, and his homosexuality. The following are excerpts from our conversation.

Health

I have changed a lot recently. I'm stronger, and in better health. I take less medication. I'm calmer. I've given up cocaine and alcohol. I see the world as it is. I've done this for seven years. It's fate. One day, I broke my arm. I didn't realize anything was wrong. It didn't even hurt. The wound was purple. My manservant Boujemaa said, "You can't stay like this!" They called an ambulance. A wonderful cardiologist looked after me. I was in rehab for two weeks. I came out of there totally happy.

Now I understand better what my earlier life was like. I reject it completely. Except for my teenage years and a few years of happiness, I prefer to forget it so I can live today.

Life seems different to me, much more joyful. I no longer have those times where I was helplessly unhappy for as long as three weeks, at the very bottom of a hole. I didn't know why because I loved my job. I saw a psychotherapist. I feel a great need for freedom, meaning not being compelled. The collections are one after the other. You end up unable to do it anymore. You can't ask someone to create constantly. It's too much. You have to work fast.

I took too much medication. I had a real life, I can see that now. And I don't regret anything. Everything is clear and everything is also in darkness. I've done this job for thirty-five years and that's why everything I see hurts me so much: this powerful ugliness, this determination to massacre everything that is beautiful. Ugliness is stronger than beauty. Now it's rather sad. It's like we have the sword of Damocles over our heads. Someone once wrote that "beauty kills." It's too fragile. I consider my profession to lie in clarity and simplicity. When you've seen beauty, when you've known beauty, you can disappear. But you have to reach that moment. I reached it very quickly.

Haute Couture

In the beginning, you're so happy, you have so many ideas and you don't think about women so much, you just think about fulfilling your creative gift, of showing off. The hardest part is finding the shape of a collection or a piece, not losing your way. To see how a fabric will fall without betraying women's bodies. The clothes must move on them. I had the precision of Dior, but Chanel's fluidity was hard for me. And then I met a former *première* at Balenciaga. Then, I dared to take any risk. I always work on a live model. Gradually, the suit changes, as we mark the lines and take the measurements. You see the light come forth. When you see a very beautiful woman, or a very beautiful dress, it's amazing how much progress you make. I can't decide on anything without models. Some of them come at the last minute, which torments me. But there's Suzanne, Natacha, and the cornerstone, Diana, because she has an extraordinary body that can wear anything. With her, I learn more every season.

I was made to make dresses like lines. The most beautiful thing for a couturier is to have a line and to never leave it. Doing this job means protecting yourself—protecting myself. If I didn't make dresses, I would die.

My Company
We started with five of us in a rented room on Rue La Boétie. We didn't even know who would finance us. Pierre happened upon an extraordinary American who wanted to invest in business. At our first show, only society women known for their elegance came. That wasn't enough....We needed more. They came with a collection of suits. The money came, you know how Americans are! Now I consider myself responsible for 250 seamstresses. I think there is great love between the ateliers and myself. Some of the old women have left. There are only smiles when I come through the ateliers. I was impressed the other day because all these girls were young and beautiful. I like things to develop. That's why we made the decision, Pierre Bergé and I, to sell the fragrances. It was an incredible moment. These investors—I don't remember their names—are really wonderful, admirably kind. They're buying it—to their minds—so that there will be a couturier still in France. So that, for me, this world will never be constrained.

Creating a Collection
I've been petrified all my life. I still am today. But when I did my first collection for Dior, I had no anxiety, because I knew that I could do it.

The hardest part is finding a starting point. On the one hand, there's this anxiety that I'm more and more familiar with, the anxiety of responding to women's joy. On the other hand, there's this confidence, this skill that I possess. The two end up meeting so that I can finish my collection. But the equilibrium doesn't happen right away. Once I've found it, I can work extraordinarily fast.

Fashion Shows
They're tiring. They're like a celebration. I go home. There are three showings. I come back fifteen minutes before it's over. The following days aren't very happy, even if the reviews are great. Because it has left me. I feel dispossessed.

Clients
It's ridiculous, but there will always be clients because they will never be able to see themselves in a mini-skirt with their garters sticking out!

Money
I don't know how much money I have. Anyway, it's nice always to be able to buy

what you like. I've never been poor. I'm not interested in money. The important thing is to have it.

Moujik

When I'm petrified, I look at Moujik, and since he wants to go to the studio so much, when I see him all sad after a long day because I didn't go to work, he twists my arm, and the next day I go! He always entertains me. When Moujik is here, no one can get near my bed. In Deauville, when I was sick one day, the only way they could give me my medicine was to put it on a shovel! These dogs are very close to their humans.

My Body

Yes, it's important. But with Coca-Cola as a replacement [for alcohol] I've gained so much weight! I'm sagging everywhere, I really have to do something about it. My body plays tricks on me. It's crazy how much alcohol can hurt you. I'd like to take a long vacation and go to the hammam every day.

Rest

It's Marrakesh…and also an empty place. I'm going to have that in Paris. With a Negro statue and a bar. I have another apartment on Avenue de Breteuil. A very beautiful place. It looks over all of Paris. You have a full view. You see the light, you see the monuments. It's a heady feeling to be able to breathe in a place with so little furniture. But in this new place, there will be nothing. I don't want to be hooked on a Picasso, a Goya, a Matisse.…I'll be able to have friends over.

What Makes Me Move Forward

Beauty. Not the beauty of the dresses. But the beauty of the models in the dresses. I'm very strict with myself. I caused a terrible scandal by showing a breast. People got used to my first black transparent blouse. This ugliness doesn't escape me. I can't get over it. But it always gives me something. It makes me move forward toward perfection.

The Women of Oran

They dressed up all the time. You can't imagine how attractive they were! My eyes were glued on my mother when she went out. I'll never forget when she went to a party at the tennis club. My mother was extraordinarily beautiful, with hair like Rita Hayworth's. She had a red satin suit. Wonderful legs. Red shoes. My father wore a tuxedo. These are memories that you can never tear away.

My grandmother was very funny. She had a way of saying about my two sisters, who went out and did awful things, I think, "Oh, Satan is possessing them!" She had a wonderful vocabulary. She had suffered a lot. She had been in love with a man, an orchestra conductor who had come for two days to the local opera on tour. He disappeared. She wanted to be buried with her love letters. They think he was my mother's father. She was very unhappy, that's why I try to spoil her every way possible. My mother grew up in the shadow of a dreary little town surrounded by a family who didn't want to see the truth. My mother has a hidden side, which is her childhood. My aunt took charge of her and raised her like a daughter: the night-mare disappeared. I get very emotional when I think about what it must have been like when she met my father. Marrying him meant joining the upper-middle class, marrying into a very well-known Oran family, because of my grandfather. It was revenge for her life. Well, I can say that she was very happy starting at age fifteen. My aunt did everything to get her out of the dump where they hid her. She visited Paris with my two cousins, who were incredibly attractive.

Adolescence
Just imagine, I had two lives. In class, I was the one who was teased. My father, no one knows why, got it into his head that I should go to this religious school. Maybe he thought it was more reserved, or closer to heaven. I had a terrible life in class, and in the evening, when I got home, I had pure freedom. Nothing weighed on me any-more. I only thought about my puppets, my marionettes, which I dressed according to the plays I had seen, such as *The Eagle with Two Heads*.

And then, for my *baccalauréat* exam, I went to the *lycée* in town. Then the nightmare was over. I had wonderful friends. The horror was gone. It was dramatic to go to the parties, to pretend. We went to all the parties in town, and we had a lot of fun.

My Childhood Friend Simone
I was very much in love. Even though I was gay, I loved her. I was fiercely jealous. From the beginning, I knew she was my prisoner, that she was in my control. And when I tried to kiss her, she slapped me.

Women
I try to fulfill all the beings who are around me, to extract beauty while respecting the bodies that I dress, so that all these women, even the least beautiful ones, can still be the most beautiful. This love is always in me. And this impossibility of loving them. I know only one thing: they're always right.

Love?
Yes, I've experienced passion. Where anything is possible, and everything's impossible....

I must have been fifteen and I had the incredible opportunity of discovering *The School for Wives*. At an age when I was still unsure of myself, when the curtain went up on this wonderful set, my first passion became real. That's when I first experienced Bérard, or rather, when I first entered his world. In the theater, you can't act like a couturier. I learned the profession inside out with Madame Karinska's daughter. The real difference with couture has to do with the material. A red curtain on a black background is enough to create an atmosphere. Like a big Chinese vase with paper chrysanthemums.

Being Gay

I hung on to this female friend; with her, I could go out, accompanied by other friends, boys and girls. This group of friends didn't want to know that I was gay, out of respect. But once again, I had two sides. I went with strangers. Arabs. That was all hidden. I was ashamed. It all happened in fear and misgiving. A terrible fear that remained with me for a long time. Being gay in Oran was like being a murderer. I never said anything to my parents. Finally I knew that they knew who I was, my mother before my father. The day when I received the Legion of Honor, my father was very overwhelmed. I had my beautiful red ribbon, and I don't know why but I ended up alone with him, and I cried. I said, "Papa, you know what I am. Perhaps you would have wanted me to be a real boy who could carry on the family name." He said, "That's not important at all, sweetheart." This was in 1985. We had never talked about it before.

My Father

He was an exceptional person. He always managed it so that we had a good connection with him. He was very happy in his little principality of Monaco, because he could only live near his Mediterranean, "my sea," as he said. In 1962, he stayed out on the boat the whole time, to watch what used to be his life disappear. I could tell he felt very abandoned then, during the Algerian War, when all those people were dispossessed of their property. But ultimately he was very happy in Marr…in Monte Carlo. Fashion wasn't his thing. But he was so proud of me. I was like God to him. There was a truly rare tenderness. And you know, what touched me the most was seeing him in his coffin. He was so elegant, so slim! His hands were especially beautiful, like in an El Greco painting. After his ashes were scattered, I didn't want everyone to start crying, as in those situations.…But I wanted it to be like people who see death as a journey and not as a morass. People who want people to enjoy themselves after a death. You drink, you have cocktails, and you end up carrying off your love hidden deep in your heart. My father was a man of immense tenderness. His friends robbed him all the time. He was described when he was alive as the son of an exceptional man, who was my grandfather. This family was always something joyful. I always called my father "the cockatoo." He had such a laugh! He was a beautiful macaw with amazing colors who loved life.

My Mother
It was very painful when I left her, I always picture her on the street corner. She was crying and I was too. We almost didn't say goodbye because we had to keep on going. I watched her from afar, and it was very poignant for me. She told me goodbye. At that time, people wore hats, and she had a single feather, like a dagger.

On Birds
I hate birds. This is a fear that has stayed with me. When I was four, I went to an estate with my parents one Sunday. At this wonderful house, while I was visiting the yard—the animals roamed free—a male goose chased me and bit my behind. (*laughs*) I can't tell you how scared I was of its claws. In art I love birds, but in real life, they scare me. My Senufo bird was the first thing I purchased.

This Crisis That Lives Inside Me
I was a student at the school of the Chambre Syndicale, where I stayed for three months. I must admit that I was very wild at the time. I had a wonderful bunch of friends at Dior. You can't imagine what Paris was like back then. I loved my first years at school. But later I was so bullied by other children that it had become hell to go there. My classmates treated me very badly. I stayed in the bathroom during recess because I was afraid, or sometimes they locked me in the dark, and suddenly they'd open the door. Everyone can be cruel, but taking it that far....When I had to do my military service, I was in a state of terror, because I was afraid that these annoyances would start up again. All that suffering is rooted in me for life. But I feel so much freer. Because I'm someone who has completely fulfilled himself.

What I Don't Know How to Do
Everything.

20 / SEARCHING FOR THE ABSOLUTE: 1993 TO 1998

Black clouds gathered and cast a shadow on the Sun King of fashion. On October 8, 1993, for the first time ever, Yves Saint Laurent's Rive Gauche show didn't close Paris Fashion Week. This absence was symbolic enough that Suzy Menkes of the *Herald Tribune* called it the victory of "minimalists" and "deconstructionists" over the "Old Regime." The title of her article was "A New Order, Plain and Simple." After having been celebrated, idolized, and exhibited, the French fashion of which Yves Saint Laurent was the ambassador was suffering from a serious identity crisis. The conventions of elegance had collapsed. The rules of the game had changed. Under the influence of Belgian designers, fog-gray mousseline skirts floated above work boots. Yet Paris remained the guardian of the notion of chic, and, in 1993, Paris and Opium were still number five and number seven respectively on the French fragrance market, with Chanel No. 5 still the perennial number one. Yet around Yves Saint Laurent, the fortress walls had cracks. Even leaving aside Pierre Bergé's angry tirades (he was nicknamed "the pit bull of French fashion" by *Women's Wear Daily*), the malaise was deep enough to reveal that the seemingly mighty empire of YSL was in fact very vulnerable, particularly due to the emotional relationship between two men, Yves Saint Laurent and Pierre Bergé.

Bergé had been betrayed by his peers: in a memorable vote on April 4, 1993, he was deposed as president of the Chambre Syndicale de la Haute Couture, an organization that he himself had founded. The reason, someone in attendance reported, was his rather "dictatorial" character, especially his refusal to move forward the dates of the fashion shows under pressure from Milan. "They want to make creativity subservient to financial imperatives. They expelled Jean-Louis Scherrer from his company, and Givenchy and Lacroix are run by LVMH," Bergé roared. In his eyes, Armani was "merely a commercial success." Surrounded by Procter & Gamble directors and other CEOs who had trained at the soap companies that now ran the bastions of the luxury industry, Bergé admitted, "I don't do business because I like it, but because it benefits something I like. If I could do it over again, I would write! That was my real passion."

The company was now divided into two separate entities: Parfums Yves Saint Laurent, 100 percent owned by Elf Sanofi, and Yves Saint Laurent Couture, 80 percent owned by Elf Sanofi and managed by Pierre Bergé. In 1993, for the first time in its history, the company had to downsize. "You went to work for Yves Saint Laurent for life," said an old-timer, who added, "Never in any couture house was the personnel treated so highly." In 1993, about thirty people took early retirement. Yet tensions remained. Yves Saint Laurent, who envied Proust "for having been able to indulge in the luxury of his isolation," found himself pulled into a world whose rules he could no longer control. "Retiring is a very great luxury," he said. "I have to produce four collections per year." The clothes hadn't aged, but the management of their image was out-of-date, along with the Variation line, the décor of the Rive Gauche stores, and a system that confused loyalty with inaction, while graphic artists and designers were busy stripping the gilded surface of a vocation in fashion. The world of fashion was shattering into a thousand pieces of broken mirrors. With piercings, tattoos, and dyed hair, the spectacle of the new urban tribes was a real gift for trend forecasters, who were becoming increasingly important, carried along by trendy concepts such as cross-cultural influences, hippie chic, and so forth. Plus, Yves Saint Laurent, who, according to Pierre Bergé was the first to have "moved fashion from the aesthetic realm and into social territory," found himself in competition with corporate functionaries on his home turf. Using his imagination, he had turned the world into an immense space with no borders, but it would be shrunk down by the relentless hammering of business magnates, the new financial controllers of the WASP universe.

Style, products, merchandising: the 1990s saw a whole series of labels emerging, giving a new sheen to the American fashion industry, which had an inferiority complex after almost half a century of Parisian supremacy. In New York, Nike and Levi's opened stores near Fifth Avenue. From Donna Karan to Calvin Klein, the new global brands bought large-scale real estate, massive stores that transformed cities into shopping malls, while a new generation of brand-crazy women emerged in Asia, eager for all the colors and sequins that were rejected by upscale Western women with beige lips and flat shoes. Yves Saint Laurent, who, after Pierre Cardin, had been the next couturier to be recognized in China and Japan, missed this new opportunity in Asia, where his brand was widely represented by a flood of licenses (167 in all) that harmed his image and isolated the man from his logo. His brand had extensive sales volume—40 percent of his revenue in Asia was from licensing contracts—but its reputation for quality had suffered. "We just let it happen," said an employee. An internal report on the decline of the Saint Laurent empire was casually ignored by Pierre Bergé. "He didn't want to hear about it. Monsieur Bergé isn't an executive. He's a prince. He has a court, or perhaps an army. He's impulsive, not strategic. Monsieur Bergé likes money. He has exceptional financial skill. But he doesn't like business," an insider told me.

In his artistic home on Rue de Babylone, was Yves Saint Laurent aware that his name was used to sell bath mats, cheap pens, watches made by Citizen, cigarettes by R. J. Reynolds, and even oilcloth print fabrics that the Dutch designers Viktor & Rolf put a humorous twist on in a parody fashion show? "The company was headed for trouble. The shareholders wanted results. Our problem was the licenses. They still brought in money, but the company hadn't invested in oversight," said a longtime employee. "The license holders had lots of freedom with few obligations. By launching jackets or baseball caps, they were responding to the demands of local markets and didn't give a damn about the image of Yves Saint Laurent. It was a terrible setback."

Now commonplace, the Saint Laurent product became less and less identifiable on the luxury market, which had been magnified by the success of Prada, with 100 stores opened between 1987 and 1998. Yves Saint Laurent had to face an offensive by companies whose runway shows enhanced the brand awareness of their accessories. In the oppressive rhythm of the collections that followed one on the next, the moment became absolute and the advertiser was the supreme authority. Subject to financial imperatives, fashion would establish a new value system (the brand instead of the name, the designer instead of the couturier, Milan and New York instead of Paris), leaving Yves Saint Laurent and Pierre Bergé behind, orphans of an *art de vivre* that was shared by skilled artisans, such as landscape artists, antiques dealers, florists, upholsterers, and restaurateurs. In his mansion on Rue Bonaparte, where he moved after two years of renovations, Pierre Bergé collected items such as ivory skulls and miniature busts of Julius Caesar. While tending his "bird-infested" garden, he watched the decline of the Parisian salons. While Yves Saint Laurent seemed unaware that one of his best friends didn't have enough money to take a taxi, Pierre Bergé was grateful to his friends and was a generous tyrant, sometimes writing a big check "from his own pocket" to a friend in trouble. Paternalistic, he also let little feudal systems spring up inside his business, where some employees with vague titles earned salaries just for showing up. Some found the company structure "outlandish," and sometimes the press office, in order to hold the Rive Gauche show, had to ask the manufacturer Mendès, which produced the ready-to-wear line, for money. Located at 7 Avenue George V, the licensing departments seemed completely separate from the "château" at 5 Avenue Marceau, where some would certainly have had a heart attack if they had seen the designs that were being sold under the name Yves Saint Laurent. Was love blind? According to some people, the management was faulty. "Clients had access to the sales for employees!" said a longtime Rive Gauche employee. Starting in 1993, Pierre Bergé began thinking about the public legacy of the company that he had built, announcing the future establishment of an Yves Saint Laurent foundation: "All our property, absolutely everything we own, will go to this foundation."[1]

At the fashion shows in January and July, Pierre Bergé and Yves Saint Laurent reserved special seats every season for friends of the maison de couture. But new networks of influence were being established between couturiers and fashion magazines, which were more and more dependent on advertisers. Fashion flirted with the codes of money and power, and the scene devolved into a pitiless war between labels, against a backdrop of media lynching and changes in ownership. For example, journalists such as Suzy Menkes would be banned from Dior shows for a while for having dared to criticize them. Haute couture was no longer a profession, but a never-ending sales demonstration where people threw their weight around.

In this way, the separation between the world of Yves Saint Laurent and Pierre Bergé and that of the logo managers continued to grow. The most famous of them was Bernard Arnault, president of LVMH: during the 1990s, the "raider of Roubaix" became the global leader in luxury, with revenue of 55 billion francs (8.38 billion euros) in 2000. The luxury industry was now led by consumer goods experts and aspired more to establishing globalized behaviors than to creating an art of distinctive style. Of course, they still called Yves Saint Laurent "the Saint." The fashion capital would still kneel down before him. In New York, athletic-inspired fashion was all the rage, but Yves Saint Laurent persisted with his own vision. "They say that fashion should constantly change, but when it finds itself, it doesn't need to change anymore: it's become a style. What is important to me is refining this style, not changing for the sake of change."[2] In a shocking move, an Yves Saint Laurent dress was photographed in American *Vogue* on a model shod in Adidas mules. It was true that with a white stripe on a black background, the shoe was one of the most stylish of the season. Yet America imposed its socially correct rituals, and its images of women with their foreheads as smooth as silicon breasts, these new "pretty women" were the opposite of the sparkling, irregular beauties Yves Saint Laurent was crazy about. *Time* had a nine-page article on what it called "A New Touch of Class." And in an era rife with fear of sexual harassment, which could start with a look in the elevator, this hybrid style avoided all the pitfalls of seduction; black was stripped of its intrigue. This was a very different animal from Yves Saint Laurent's chameleon black, the black of extreme temptation and raw sensuality.

He still had his loyal supporters. In January 1994, for the opening of the guest house of the Château de Blérancourt, Pamela Harriman, the U.S. ambassador, symbolically wore Saint Laurent couture pants. She would later die of a cerebral hemorrhage that struck her in the Ritz swimming pool. But in hip Parisian circles, where what was ordinary became a must, and heroin chic was a photography standard, the couturier seemed to be less celebrated than in London and New York: in those cities, social representation still required a sense of performance. "In Italy and New York, the street is more attractive, you notice the women more. They're simpler. In France, the colored parkas, the big shoes...There's something shapeless in the air," said Yves Saint Laurent. "In New York, the influence of sports is better understood and interpreted, in the movement of the city. I think athletic clothes are wonderful. In Paris, the streets in general signify a sad kind of clothing. Energy and newness means very simple clothing with clean lines." For all the women who didn't want to dress like their daughters, Yves Saint Laurent was there, with his navy blue blazer and his pantsuit, his good luxury classics every season.

Yet a veil of sadness fell over the Saint Laurent family, in mourning for all those night owls who had been seen one last time, their faces ravaged by illness. AIDS continued its devastation. "Now on the runways, in photos, and in real life, seduction tends to be erased. People have toned down temptation. The profession has quieted down. Attitudes have become hardened. Smiles and languid bodies have disappeared. The atmosphere has become radical. Maybe it reflects our time. We've gone from selling dreams to selling reality. The atmosphere is disoriented," lamented a former regular of Le Sept and Le Palace. While history was speeding up, with one event erasing another, Saint Laurent time had shifted into an era of Parisian memory flowered by one of the splendid bouquets of lilies that the couturier sent to the Palais Garnier for the official memorial service for Rudolf Nureyev, who died on January 6, 1993. Yves had honored the dancer in his summer 1993 haute couture show, and like Nureyev, he could have said, "I only live, I only exist on stage." That day, young ballet students had placed eighty bouquets of white chrysanthemums before his coffin. Betty Catroux, hidden behind her dark glasses, Charlotte Aillaud swathed in mink, and Zizi Jeanmaire, a bird of prey in black stockings and a panther stole, had come to celebrate the man whose physical strength Yves had once envied. That year, the couturier, who like Proust seemed to be surrounded by "monsters and Gods,"[3] fell sick with pneumonia and took several months to recover.

"One must always shock with a beautiful thing, never with an exhibition of monsters," he said. In late 1993, five months after Sanofi's purchase of Yves Saint Laurent, a new affair isolated the couturier in his dreams and fantasies once more, which some thought were those of a prima donna. The field of scandals seemed now to be controlled by powerful lobbies who codified the rules of marketing and put forward their own interests. The man who was amused to see one of his branded towels in a porn movie, or who still declared, "Women love what's forbidden," had to confront the wrath of those who didn't all share his sense of celebration. Inside the company itself, there was already disagreement: between the "oil men" (Sanofi) and the leadership of Parfums Yves Saint Laurent, the atmosphere was tense. Many on the perfume side already felt abandoned by Pierre Bergé at the time of the sale. "We already had a complex. We were the soap makers in comparison to the artists on Avenue Marceau. So then we just totally shut ourselves away. For the Sanofi people, everything was always too beautiful and too expensive. They called us 'luxury chicks,'" an insider told me. Between 1993 and 1998, there were four different heads of fragrances. The first, Claude Saujet, expanded the sale of YSL fragrances to American big-box stores. "A high-volume policy that really harmed the prestige of the brand," said a company executive, revealing that some of these wholesalers were said to have resold their perfume to drug traffickers who needed to launder money. The management of Sanofi Beauté crossed a line in 1996. The following anecdote, reported to me by an employee, shows what a wide gap there was between the liberated world of Saint Laurent and that of the typical French company with its mundane sexism: an angry Sanofi executive went so far as to scornfully lift up the long linen skirt of a colleague who usually wore pants and cry out, "Look, there are actually women's legs under here." Franz Lehár's "The Merry Widow," which was heard at the YSL winter 1993–94 haute couture show, became the telephone hold music for 5 Avenue Marceau.

The press launch for the Champagne fragrance took place in a turbulent atmosphere. Despite legal threats against it, the perfume had been brought to market in September. But the Institut National de l'Origine et de la Qualité (formerly the Institut National des Appellations d'Origine) and the champagne producers sued, and on October 28, 1993, the court ruled in their favor, declaring that all the packaging and marketing materials with the name Champagne had to be destroyed. An era was ending: on October 31, Federico Fellini passed away, leaving behind dreams of splendor, madness, and seduction that were foreign to the new frantic, multimedia era. The bubbles would sparkle no more. Letters of support for Yves Saint Laurent didn't make any difference, and neither did the millions of francs that had been spent on the launch of this fragrance whose name had been chosen by Yves himself in 1991. The press criticized the company for having gotten involved in "a risky venture."[4] The French state-owned tobacco company Seita had lost in court in 1984 after launching a cigarette also called Champagne. Yet the situation was ambiguous: Parfums Caron still had the right to sell Bain de Champagne, which had been launched in 1943. On December 15, 1993, the Paris appeals court held up the previous ruling, forbidding YSL to sell its fragrance under the name Champagne. The company had to withdraw all the bottles of perfume from sale or face a fine of 3,000 francs (457 euros) for each violation. In this affair, some saw the influence of Bernard Arnault, the owner of the champagne company Moët et Chandon, which joined the lawsuit. "He could have dropped it, but he likes that kind of thing," said friends of Pierre Bergé. "Maybe if Dior had come out with a fragrance called Champagne, there wouldn't have been a lawsuit." Yves Saint Laurent said he was "deeply hurt." He said, "I thought, perhaps immodestly, that my name attached to that of champagne symbolized the union of luxury and quality.... If I displeased the champagne growers, I am sorry, for that was not my intention."[5] Something had been broken. There would be no new name, for now at least. That was what the couturier had decided. The company developed its fallback strategy. There was no love lost between Jean-François Dehecq, the president of Sanofi, and Pierre Bergé. As one source recalled, "The 'oil men' had a complex about this quick-tempered empire builder, this man of principle who could casually say outrageous things and who snubbed the company's apparatchiks." Additionally, the positions taken by Bergé, who was president of the anti-AIDS organization ARCAT and who said that "to me, being gay is as natural as being left- or right-handed," shocked heteronormative propriety.

Despite what Yves had previously decided, on January 4, 1994, the name Champagne disappeared, and the fragrance became known as "Yves Saint Laurent," with the same bottle and packaging—a solution that the company had already tried out in Saudi Arabia with the perfume Opium. But the situations were very different: "Opium was a scandalous perfume, connected to a scandalous time. In the case of Champagne, it was a war of economic interests that initiated a big struggle between finance tycoons," said an observer. Once again, the company had cashed in on a scandal: Champagne, with a fruity, citrus, woody, flowery bouquet, had brought in revenue of 200 million francs (30.49 million euros) in three months. Over 350,000 bottles had been sold. This didn't keep the couturier from taking his revenge. In January 1994, he opened his summer 1994 haute couture show with the song "Paris, C'est du Champagne," sung by Luis Mariano, announcing a *grand cru* season. Forget-me-not crepe, cloud printed russet mousseline, embroideries with crystal fringe—a new suppleness swept away what had come before. His blouses had become t-shirts worn with rock crystal necklaces. "A cardigan made of bird-of-paradise feathers worn over a long champagne-colored mousseline dress is a wonder," wrote *Elle*[6] about number 50, which instantly became the favorite of Yves's clients for their informal evenings. "There were only sixty-one designs, in an YSL compilation where each piece looked like the essence of his style," wrote *Libération*.[7] Detecting Chanel's influence, the paper praised "three charleston dresses flowing with teardrops." Suzy Menkes of the *Herald Tribune* was just as excited about Yves Saint Laurent as back in the old days. "In the same way as when his shows closed the season, he set the course."[8]

On January 19, 1994, André Ostier breathed his last. In the salons of the Hotel Intercontinental, leaning on his cane, the elegant gentleman photographer had continued to murmur, "Elegance means making women beautiful. Making them look better than they are." The magazines rapidly prepared their special couture issues. For Italian *Vogue*, a young woman with peach-hued skin posed in an Yves Saint Laurent ball gown, a long damask evening gown with short flared sleeves and a large bow on the *décolleté* that were reminiscent of an outdoor eighteenth-century scene. At age fifteen, the luscious brunette Laetitia Casta made her debut that year for Jean-Paul Gaultier. It would be another five years before she modeled for Yves Saint Laurent. "When I knew her, she was like a baby. And then she exploded," said Yves.

Starting in February 1994, the perfume with the name that was forbidden in France (and also in Switzerland) was sold exclusively by Saks Fifth Avenue in New York. The official launch took place in September with a memorable celebration at the Statue of Liberty—the first and only one of its kind. "The sun was setting over Manhattan. We had put down red carpets on the docks of Battery Park. Boats took us there. It was complete happiness. There were women in evening gowns and champagne. And 20,000 white candles to mark the way. It was Saint Laurent magic," remembered Marianne Honvault, who was a press attaché for Parfums Yves Saint Laurent. "We could already feel that it was anachronistic. That the world was changing. It was Hollywood, a movie in the city." There were 2,000 beautiful people there, including clients such as Nan Kempner and Lynn Wyatt and couturiers such as Bill Blass and Oscar de la Renta. There were three orchestras and six buffets, and 3,000 tailor-made red velvet cushions were set up along the walls by the water. Amid scents of musk and nectarine, the night vibrated, along with a thousand bottles of Bollinger champagne. Pierre Bergé, who had at first been so impudent as to suggest California champagne, ended up being magnanimous. "I quashed my intense urge to be insolent in order to express my French point of view."[9] The city had YSL fever: there was a huge ad in the *New York Times* that showed Yves hugging the Statue of Liberty, and YSL windows paying tribute to the couturier at Saks. Champagne went to the heads of the happy few whose latest thing was cross-dressing. For the occasion, Yves Saint Laurent had gone to New York, a "city that sparkles like champagne," after a ten-year absence. He posed, radiant, with a perfume bottle like a trophy of gold and crystal in his hands. He felt renewed by Manhattan, where he saw an exhibition of pre-Colombian jewels and went twice to the retrospective of the couturier Madame Grès, whom he admired so much. "Things are born here, there's a creative atmosphere. Actually, all of America is becoming exciting. I'm always surprised by our condescension toward their culture, toward Hollywood in particular. Maybe it's their space that makes them so dynamic."[10]

That night, Yves wore a starry tie. He continued to have an ambiguous relationship with the United States, where the brand's revenue was then fifty million dollars according to *Women's Wear Daily*. Why was he in such a bad mood the day after the celebration? Supposedly, he was furious after the cocktail party in the Rive Gauche boutique on Madison Avenue. "There were only old female friends there," recalled an observer. It was as if he had caught sight of a terrible reality in the mirror. The man with the relentless gaze who admitted to being a "megalomaniac" already knew he was doomed. He had his absences, his awful moments, when he fell into that black hole surrounded by the ghosts of a declining kingdom. "It's not that people don't understand me, it's that I'm withdrawing from the world bit by bit. I struggle with solitude because I love life. Perhaps life doesn't love me!" he later said.

But the lion who often complained of "not having the strength anymore" continued to roar. Worn by the seventeen-year-old Israeli model Maayan Keret, the winter 1994 Yves Saint Laurent Rive Gauche wedding dress was scarlet. The entire show was inspired, he said mysteriously, by a bouquet of red roses that he had received. As soon as his perfume was on the market, he broke a diplomatic taboo by suing Ralph Lauren. The American designer had shown a tuxedo that Yves believed was too similar to the one in his fall/winter 1991–92 haute couture show. In May 1994, a Paris court ruled in Yves's favor and ordered Ralph Lauren to pay the couturier 395,000 dollars for violating his intellectual property rights. Six months earlier, when the powerful *Women's Wear Daily*[11] asked Pierre Bergé whether American designers were influential, he had answered, "No…What's the name of the one whose name I can never remember? Oh, yes, Ralph Lauren." At Parisian dinner parties, Pierre Bergé's theatrical tirades amused other businessmen. But some were worried about them. Was this a threat to the image of France? Certainly, in fall 1994, the revenue from Champagne was already one million dollars. A flash in the pan? Champagne would have competition from other fragrances. It would definitely not be a new Opium.

The French fashion industry took a hard blow when in September 1994 the Galeries Lafayette department store closed its New York branch. Saks had devoted all its windows to Yves Saint Laurent for the launch of Champagne, but he was no longer one of the top three highest-selling ready-to-wear brands, which were now Armani, Chanel, and Ungaro. There had been a sea change. Madison Avenue was becoming Milan's Via Montenapoleone, a luxurious hub of Italian and American fashion. The misfits of the Big Apple were on their way out as the city became Disneyfied. The couturier who smoked three packs of Stuyvesant cigarettes a day didn't really fit into this "light" era, which required designers to be as tan and surgically lifted as their clients. While supermodels were the new marketing magic, Yves Saint Laurent was a lone wolf. At the time, the star of the runway was Claudia Schiffer, Karl Lagerfeld's muse, the Lolita of Düsseldorf, who held the record for the most magazine covers. The supermodels were "overpaid, overexposed, and over-protected" according to Pierre Bergé's news magazine *Globe*. But they had managed to make fashion in their own image, and perhaps even to erase the clothes that they once made shine. Yves Saint Laurent found top models' manners "abominable" and refused to give in to the pressure. Yet he was the first to hire Stella Tennant, who aristocratically embodied his style, walking the runway in black dresses with her pale skin, dark lips, and slightly stooped shoulders. Others wouldn't get that privilege. Yves's judgment could be very harsh. To Anne-Marie Muñoz and Loulou de la Falaise, he would make comments such as "Who on earth is this Gorgon?" and "Looking at her is like watching paint dry." Usually shy, he could be overcome by anger. Sometimes he would slam the door of the grand salon violently. "We had to say no to many top models because he didn't like them." He had such high standards that he was the last to hire a hairdresser and make-up artist during the ten days preceding the fashion show. The models had to be able to embody luxury. It was out of the question that one of them appear before him with her hair a mess.

Yves Saint Laurent also continued to hire many black models. At first he selected them in the United States in response to the market, and then because of his own particular sensibility. The most loyal and longest-serving was Amalia, who was first hired in 1980, and who described Yves as "a father, a brother, a virtual lover." Even with nothing on but a lab coat, she seemed to be wearing Saint Laurent, with the lines of her shoulder, neck, and legs stepping straight out of the couturier's sketches. One day, he threw a tantrum because Amalia wasn't listed at the beginning of the fashion show with the top models. "I'm very unhappy." Around him, people tried to defuse the situation, as if they all dreaded his foul mood, which seemed so out of proportion to the incident. He began to sulk, letting his head hang, as if he were crying without tears, despondent. As Jean-Pierre Derbord, technical director for the haute couture ateliers, described it: "His collections are one collection that never ends. He tells a story with his clothes. He wants to find the expression of his design on the model. Otherwise he feels betrayed. It's as if his lines were off."

While the brand was worth 15 billion francs (2.29 billion euros), the company's image had been harmed by its legal battles and other affairs. On May 30, 1994, a formal investigation of Pierre Bergé was launched for insider trading and selling shares outside the Paris stock market. He was suspected of having sold 120,000 shares of the haute couture company in the summer of 1992 at a high price (100 million francs or 15.24 million euros) just before the announcement of bad news concerning the company: a loss of 26.8 million francs (4.09 million euros) during the first half of the year. The case was ultimately dismissed on October 16, 1995. But the rumors remained: the help that François Mitterrand allegedly gave Pierre Bergé in thanks for his support by arranging for the company's purchase by Sanofi, a subsidiary of state-owned Elf Aquitaine. The rumor was powerful enough that the *New Yorker* discussed it in a long article (the longest ever to focus on Pierre Bergé) titled "The Impresario's Last Act."[12] In 1994, Bergé's term as president of the Paris Opéra ended, after five years of a media firestorm. "I had a very ambitious plan," he told *Le Figaro*.[13]

It was a time of numerous public and political embarrassments for Pierre Bergé. But Yves Saint Laurent kept his title of untouchable angel. Wasn't his main personality trait, as he said himself, "indulgence"? The more reality caught up with him, the more he fled, insisting that the most beautiful journey is the one "you go on around your room." Underneath the look of a student-patriarch in a duffle coat, he was still a relentless observer, criticizing the French school system: "It's very sad. The schools do their job very badly. We bore so many children stiff with subjects they don't like and we don't teach art history. Nothing about architecture, painting, or fashion. What a waste! How irresponsible! How can we prepare for the beauty of the future if we carelessly erase the beauty of the past?"[14]

In July 1994, with his fall/winter 1994 haute couture collection, he proved once more that great art means turning all you can imagine into reality. His show was the only one to receive a standing ovation. "YSL is Once Again King," read Suzy Menkes's headline for the *Herald Tribune*. "This is my son's most beautiful collection in seven years," Lucienne Mathieu-Saint-Laurent said with tears in her eyes. From his patent crocodile leather coat, worn with a black velvet tunic dress and thigh boots, to his brocade coats, the eighty-nine designs moved down the runway with the ease that was his secret. The iris velvet and pink lace had intimate meetings, the golden gauze and the midnight blue mousseline seemed to call out for burning caresses under the moon. "Have you ever noticed his shadow? You'd be surprised to see how tall and strong he is," Catherine Deneuve said about Yves Saint Laurent, who was watching a world fall apart. In December 1994, Paris learned that Madame Grès, the grande dame of haute couture, had died a year earlier. They said she had withdrawn from society and gone mad after the abrupt closing of her maison de couture, after her wooden mannequins were chopped up with a hatchet and her dresses were thrown into garbage bags. Her daughter had kept her death a secret in revenge on the industry that had not supported her. Yves was alone, more alone than ever, reflecting on the declaration of faith of this priestess of draped fabrics: "I always thought that life was an endless struggle and I was convinced that if I abandoned this struggle, life would abandon me."

Yves Saint Laurent got up early and arrived at the maison de couture around 10:30 or 11:00 AM. He left at 1:00 PM to have lunch at home. Sometimes he fell asleep in his solitude. Because of cigarette holes on the sleeves, some of his custom-made suits from Charvet had to be returned almost immediately to the company's ateliers on Rue de la Paix for repair. "I'm all alone with my books and paintings, Matisse, Cézanne, Picasso, Braque. Unfortunately I can't buy anything anymore because my rooms are bursting with paintings, sculptures, and objects. It's as if I live in a museum, all alone." He also said, "I'm incredibly bored. My health is very delicate and I must live in a very disciplined manner."

Around him, around a life that he described as a torn fabric, the world was changing. The apprentices at Dior began to weep when they were asked to tear the clothes for John Galliano's runway show in his destructive style. The number of haute couture artisans had dropped from 35,000 in the 1940s to 4,500 in the 1990s. "The artisans are used like a showcase for financier-managers. Today the couturiers work under pressure: they have to be accountable," said embroiderer François Lesage. Yves Saint Laurent was one of the last couturiers to ask Lesage to design samples. The models continued to inspire him with their gestures and their bodies, and he seemed to dress their souls. In January 1995, his fashion show was set to Gershwin music and had an almost austere simplicity. A white linen canvas suit. A navy blue crepe dress. A suit of black wool crepe and a blouse of black satin and white organza. But the night was sketched out in a flight of gold and silver, pink, or blue and black butterflies, embroidered on a gazar jacket. The beetle, which he had made the symbol of depression in *Naughty Lulu*, returned to haunt these styles in black tulle. The magic was there, illustrated once again by the technical performance of new tuxedo dresses that were worn like inside-out jackets with silk satin trim having become pockets. This "Venus Emerging from a Tuxedo" (*Herald Tribune*) made him even more inimitable.

"Out of these young women, I chose Nadja because I thought she represented today's modernity, which is both sweet and provocative," he said about Nadja Auermann, a model from Berlin with a boyish neck, who struck a flamboyant pose in *Elle* in a pantsuit with tennis stripes from the spring/summer 1995 Rive Gauche collection.[15] He stayed true to "noble" materials, excluding all the new synthetic fabrics. The gap between his work and that of other designers was growing. From his words and his work, one could tell that all his efforts were focused on haute couture: "Women are tired of the crazy ideas in ready-to-wear. Designers today act like directors. They don't make collections anymore but spectacles. I have distanced myself from the world because this kind of fashion doesn't belong to me. There is something so terrifying that I can't help but exclude myself from this group, from all these people. For me, the starting point and goal of couture is a woman's body."[16]

Couturiers now had significant adversaries: plastic surgeons who could slim the body and give it a youthful shape, skills that were previously the domain of tailor-made clothing. The waiting room had replaced the fitting room. Now, new techniques, gold threads and plastic strips under the skin to prevent cracks and wrinkles on the face, were developed and copied as quickly as clothing designs. Two face-lifts for the price of one dress—who could beat that? In March 1995, Yves's winter 1995–96 ready-to-wear collection was all black and contrasted with other designers' clothes that season. Yves Saint Laurent, who was famous for his way of bringing three colors together in the same look, managed, according to Suzy Menkes, "to give a breath of fresh air to these familiar shapes by using a darker palette."[17]

What bad omen was haunting him now? In July 1995, Hubert de Givenchy had his last fashion show before retiring. His brand had been obliged to lay off thirty workers in one year. His final show was like a warning. He was one of the last ones who could say, from his height of six feet, six inches, "The important thing is that the dresses look like they're floating while being very constructed." He had designed for Gloria Guinness and the Duchess of Windsor. He was a survivor of that world where American women ordered several of the same design, where Rose Kennedy, for her son's funeral, had asked to have her pearls sewn on to the neckline of her dress so that they wouldn't bump against the coffin. As Yves wrote, "He is one of the last stars of our profession and his retirement will be a hard blow to all those who admire him. I will never forget what he meant to me during my adolescence and with all my heart I wish him a happy life. He has chosen the time when he is ready to leave and whatever we think, we must respect his decision."[18] Hubert de Givenchy was a model for couture in his own way. A high point of French elegance: skillful technique, crisp suits, and chic crepe dresses.

Hubert de Givenchy had his memories of the women he had known. Yves Saint Laurent kept alive the memory of the women he still dreamed of. Inspired by paintings by Goya and traditional images of Spain and its matadors, his line became more and more sensual. With his Spanish-influenced collection of winter 1995–96, he distanced himself from illustration in order to bring together the simple and the superb in one style. Black became a material in a velvet bolero jacket and a wool cape, supple lines that glided along together. Never had a long lead-colored satin evening gown seemed so light. It was pure contour and movement. Never had shapes appeared so close to gestures: the cut of Seville pants, jackets with the slightly skewed waists, and the dark shadow of a tuxedo expressed communion with the bodies they dressed. The colors rubbed against one another. Raspberry lace and bright pink faille. A cloud blue wool cape over a storm blue satin dress. "Sometimes I create with fabric. At times it happens that I haven't made a drawing, and the flow of a fabric inspires me. I've made dresses with big mousseline scarves. I also like duchesse satin which has flair, and grain de poudre, which is as sharp and clear as an outline."[19]

In terms of fragrances, these were the final hours of Saint Laurent luxury. The couturier who was the first to give colors to make-up launched some star products, such as Rouge Definition, a lipstick that looked like a mascara applicator; the shades, from ruby to deep brown, emphasized the allure of the kind of woman who was still addicted to Saint Laurent and wore a black sweater, a big lapis lazuli and turquoise necklace with Chinese beads, an amber pashmina, and leather gloves in the colors of precious stones. At 34 Rue du Faubourg-Saint-Honoré, the spa, which was entirely decorated by Jacques Grange, became a kind of annex to the maison de couture, and many friends and celebrities stopped by, from Catherine Deneuve to Jeanne Moreau. They were die-hard fans of treatments by Marlène, shiatsu massage by Sendi, who used to work at Carita and was booked two months in advance, and the exceptional pedicures of Monsieur Ho. Even Hillary Clinton, when she was in Paris, came to buy lipstick that couldn't be found elsewhere, since it was the only location in the world that had every item in the line. There were limited series that became collector's items, such as heart-shaped powder compacts, make-up brushes with gilded handles, and especially the famous Love perfume in its crystal bottle. The heavy door with its bronze doorknob sculpted by Robert Goossens made an impression, and, inside, the atmosphere of a white and emerald green velvet salon with rock crystal and gold was equally unforgettable. "When important people came, there was an X in the appointment book. Three minutes beforehand, we still didn't know who it was. That was for security reasons," said physical therapist Odile. Men such as Hubert de Givenchy and Yves Saint Laurent also came to the spa, where Agathe, a certified esthetician, took care of the gentlemen. "He never came into the spa like the clients. He came through the boutique first." He was still shy, and remained as he was on his very first day, submitting the world to the authority of his gaze, which sometimes seemed capable of killing its prey. Very distant from "tricks and gimmicks," as he himself said, Yves Saint Laurent pursued his craft, attentive to celebrating "the love of a woman."

Lucienne was still in the front row. He posed with her for photographer Françoise Huguier and *Marie-Claire*. In his apartment on Rue de Babylone, the day of the shoot, the atmosphere was electric in a chilly spring. Boujemaa, one of his servants, slipped in a puddle and was immediately taken to the hospital. Lucienne, who had had shoes made for her by Massaro, looked anxiously at the gray sky. It was raining. Suddenly, for a few minutes, the rain miraculously stopped. "For the photo, he told me to wear white. So I put on this suit, with a ring that he gave me, which was a gift from the Aga Khan to Rita Hayworth," she said. That day, Moujik, Yves's French bulldog, was furious. There were too many people around his master. He bit the visitors who got too close. "I can never go to Yves's house with my little dog Nouba. He would bite her. He's very jealous. He's stuck to me. This dog wasn't trained," said Lucienne.[20]

*

While the pressure from Milan and New York grew, designers such as Jean-Paul Gaultier created colorful, hybrid designs that contrasted with the straight, sleeveless dresses of yesteryear. Christian Lacroix came up with a cheeky portrait of a pop woman from Arles who came out of a cyber version of his native Camargue region. All on its own, the world of Yves Saint Laurent was a vast enough land for the imagination to wander in it, leaving the body in Paris without costuming it or weighing it down: an ease that could be seen in the summer 1996 Rive Gauche collection, with safari jackets, a fresh white piqué sheath dress, and bright Indian pinks and oranges with gold sequins. Two or three dresses were like women in love who remembered the man who had loved them so much, and who returned, alone, to his silence. Accomplished women were disappearing, among them Denise Fayolle, who, along with Maïmé Arnodin, was the director of Agence Mafia, which was inseparable from the aesthetic of manners that was the great strength of the Saint Laurent style. The voluptuous black of large frock coats, velvet black, tuxedo black, rhinestone platform shoes, the days and nights of Yves Saint Laurent strode through the real world, adding a dose of fanciful style that resisted classification. While fashion seemed increasingly cut-and-pasted, and designers' inspirations were more and more abstract, he was like the storyteller who could make the last flames of a European golden age shine. Backstage, when the TV cameras tried to get a comment from him about the trends this season, he spoke last, and was the only one to express the following wish: "May women be happy!"

Two leading houses seemed to be fighting over his legacy. Two looks of the moment were both influenced in their own way by Yves Saint Laurent: the new Belle de Jour by Miuccia Prada (a passionate collector of vintage Rive Gauche clothes, her revenue had increased by 50 percent between 1996 and 1997) and Gucci's international spy by Tom Ford, who worshiped the androgynous Rive Gauche woman of the 1970s. While Miuccia Prada dug through fashion's flea markets, Tom Ford accumulated images in a kind of fashion hard drive that he made into his war chest. Born in Austin, Texas, in 1961, the year that Yves Saint Laurent launched his maison de couture, he went to New York and experienced Studio 54 in the 1970s. The American press was charmed by this former student of the Parsons School of Design who once starred in a McDonald's ad, an unfettered spirit of the runway who was politically incorrect and expressed the new giddiness of rediscovered prosperity: sex, power, logos, and the jet-set. At Gucci, his bags were a huge hit. He had found the business formula: consolidating the unity of a brand by totally controlling its image and its production. From the bag with the bamboo handle to the moccasins with the famous gold horse-bits, Gucci mania took hold of the fashion world just as easy listening had grabbed the airwaves. Thanks to Tom Ford, between 1994 and 2000, Gucci's revenue climbed from 262 million to 2.2 billion dollars. How far could he take the company? In this battle for attention, Yves Saint Laurent used his latest weapons: the love of a public that acclaimed him and worshiped a man whose products were nevertheless less and less identifiable. When asked, "How do you choose your colors?" he answered enigmatically, "I listen to a Mozart symphony and dream." This was very far from the Tom Ford techniques that resulted in "must-haves" worn by Gwyneth Paltrow or Madonna. He had chosen the exile of creativity, a kind of imaginary Eden, where all his beautiful dreams could flourish.

While Hollywood cheered its new idols, Yves Saint Laurent became the first couturier to have a runway show live-streamed on the Internet. "Another one of P.B.'s ideas," said a friend, who was rather annoyed by the excited young people whom the boss couldn't resist. Yves Saint Laurent was more and more alone. The king was naked. "Paris looks like one of those stars that shine long after they're dead," said the fashion designer Marc Audibet, who viewed French fashion as incapable of solidifying its economic position and doomed to become the "dancing girl" of financiers. With all the strength of his accomplishments, Yves Saint Laurent resisted the grandstanding of the moment. He still showed a simple black cashmere sweater in his haute couture collection, aristocratically defying all the pretentious trendsetters. When wearing his clothes, the models had an aura of distance that wasn't felt elsewhere, as if his clothes expressed strength and intelligence. On March 3, 1996, Marguerite Duras, one of Yves Saint Laurent's favorite writers, died. Described by Jean-Marie Rouart as "the explorer of the abyss," she had been able, with her pen, to undress the couturier: "He sees with his eyes closed," she wrote. "I can't help but think that Yves Saint Laurent's real sleep is the work of creating.…He sees in you what you don't know you are. He doesn't look at what you thought you were, he dismantles you. He puts you back into your mortality."[21]

The haute couture collections of the "white-skinned man from Oran," as he had been called at Dior, were more and more divided in two: during the day, he met his clients' expectations, offering them impeccably cut suits. In the front row, the journalists fanned themselves with their programs. "What's new?" asked Suzy Menkes in July 1996. "Saint Laurent just did what he does exceptionally."[22] Eveningwear was still his specialty, as his tuxedos, like dark messengers, announced. His lacy dresses like his airy mousseline saris were "liquid architecture" according to Suzy Menkes, magnifying the body that obsessed him, while the contrasting colors, the lamé and iridescent fabrics celebrated perfectly subtle nuances, with colors like misty pink, Oriental blue, butterfly wing, flame, and sun. "I created my era and I tried to predict what tomorrow will be," said the man, whose collections some American editors skipped, won over by the more conventional refinement of Karl Lagerfeld for Chanel, Oscar de la Renta for Balmain, or Valentino. His haute couture collections were reviewed less and less frequently. Although he had once been omnipresent on magazine covers, his media appearances could now be counted on one hand. His dresses didn't fit into themes (neo-symbolism or neo-fetishism); they were just Saint Laurent.

*

He admitted, "I was an emotional and passionate man. Now I live like a recluse and my social life no longer exists." But he found in his work the wings of desire. He described women as "untouchable celestial birds," whose cardigans made of feathers and airy mousselines caressed a body that elsewhere was submitted to spectacles that were more and more fetishistic. In January 1997, a season of big news with the arrival of Alexander McQueen at Givenchy and the announcement of John Galliano's move to Dior. The fashion shows of Thierry Mugler and Yves Saint Laurent were two extremes: Mugler manufactured a body, but Saint Laurent gave it movement. One started with a shape, but the other started from women. The two brides were both green, one in a nun's mantle and the other like Madame de Pompadour in a gold damask coat. Beyond their fashion differences, they expressed two different visions of the world. At the Palais de Chaillot, Thierry Mugler brought out demon women sheathed in Neoprene. It was a bizarre rite of spring, where childhood nightmares and latex slugs moved in monitored freedom, along with jackets with flying saucer-like tailcoats and a skirt with vinyl wing sleeves. It looked like the "life teeming inside a wound" Kafka described in *The Metamorphosis*. Yves Saint Laurent was definitely elsewhere. From his very first silhouette, a rose-petal grain de poudre pantsuit with a mauve crepe blouse, he invited the public to a most intimate spectacle. The immaculate trim and ivory blouses were a new reference to Mademoiselle Chanel, and to all the women who kissed him and whispered, "Thank you for looking out for us." But Chanel, as I once heard Edmonde Charles-Roux explain, "took her revenge through her models. They were younger than she was. They still had success with men. These women had to represent her. Yves doesn't settle any scores in his career. Women are still a dream for him. Love is there, along with respect and wonder. He's the most romantic of our couturiers."

All influences melted under his gaze, from Christian Dior, to whom he paid homage with a Bar suit made of shantung, to Hubert de Givenchy, whose clients he knew would now come to him. Night fell in the quiet of stole-dresses that were airily enveloping, made for humming "Just You, Just Me." Everything moved, everything breathed, within a silence that was the ultimate provocation. The models moved along the runway with lines, waves, promises intact, in the smoothness of draped fabrics with supple open backs. There were delicate dresses, mousselines printed with pink, aquamarine, or alexandrite roses. There were feathery shawls caressed until late into the night by hands of love. This was another difference from Chanel, according to Edmonde Charles-Roux: "Chanel worked by starting with the fabrics. Then with the braiding of her suits. She expected them to be brought to her all put together. Then she attacked the completed design. She pulled out the threads and completely took apart the clothes to improve them and give it the equilibrium that she demanded. With Yves Saint Laurent, the approach is completely different. The test garment they bring to him is as precise as a model car. Looking at the designs, he has objections related to proportion and lightness. You hear him say, 'It has to fly, it has to float away.' His concentration is extraordinary. There is reciprocal admiration, between the man saying, 'It's beautiful' and the model who replies, "Thank you, Monsieur.'" For Charles-Roux, this "Thank you, Monsieur" was "overwhelming." She noted, "It's closer to painting than haute couture....The atmosphere in his studio reminds me of the studios of certain painters, such as Derain, and especially Balthus." The magic was there. As Madame Georgette, the *première* of the *atelier flou* for Yves Saint Laurent, once explained, "Movement has to be supported, allowed to open up, otherwise it breaks down. A dress must hold together without looking sewn."

This lightness was also expressed in his suits and Le Smoking, the company's best seller. Why did Yves's faithful clients want nothing but Yves Saint Laurent? They had to go through three fittings and a month of waiting to slip on the skin of this eternally unmatched style and pay close to 140,000 francs (28,000 euros) for the privilege. Over time, he streamlined his designs. The ribbons on the edges of the lapels had disappeared, along with the interfacing to stiffen the fabric at the waist, which now moved supply. With hourglass-inspired padding and the insides of the pockets lined with bias-cut fabric, the androgynous silhouette had become feminized without betraying itself. "Other people notice it, you forget it," said Jean-Pierre Derbord, the technical director of the haute couture ateliers at Avenue Marceau, which still had the look of a green and gold temple where one was escorted by saleswomen in black. Whether flannel, grain de poudre, or gabardine, the fabric of an Yves Saint Laurent couture suit was the material that made the process worthwhile: "Here, we like fabrics that hold up. We want them to be strong, but not like cardboard. Supple. When they fall well, you can tell, from the first effect on the test garment, that you won't be betrayed." Five meters of fabric required ninety hours of labor for a jacket, or forty for pants. The padding was one of the essential ingredients, the one that held the jacket in a straight line down the back. Shaped with an iron for hours, the padding fit the shape of the shoulder, whose secret lay in a combination of right angles and ease. Silk linings were finely stitched and folded over, and buttonholes were embroidered by hand. All the work in the atelier responded to a particular technical outlook, the Saint Laurent hand, that wanted fabric to be controlled while remaining alive. Everything was very ordered from the beginning. Everything fit with one piece inside the other, like a child's toy. There was no suffering in the sleeves. They said that Yves Saint Laurent was inspired by men's suits: "He added additional comfort," said a fascinated young man who entered the atelier of Monsieur Jean-Pierre. The pants obeyed the same strictness. The darts were pressed with an iron. There was bias-cut organza under the edge of the pocket to prevent it from getting stretched out, and the belt was reinforced with a grosgrain ribbon. The crotch was smoothed out with an iron; everything was an issue of millimeters. "What's important," specified Jean-Pierre Derbord, "is the vertical line and the way the fabric falls when the body moves. If the crotch is too short, the pants will pull, and if it's too long, they hang down."

The more his work disrupted the clouds and floated off toward serenity, the more the man seemed broken, petrified by the spectacle of his isolation. He expressed fierce opinions to the German magazine *Focus*: "I'm horrified by what I see. It's a laughable spectacle that would look better in a cabaret. I think the direction couture may be taking today is dangerous. People who don't want to sell couture but perfumes and licenses went to get Galliano. They don't sell dresses anymore. The clients come to me. But I fear that dozens of workers will be let go at these maisons." His judgment was merciless: "In haute couture, after Coco Chanel and me, there will be nothing more."[23]

In January 1997, the Yvon Lambert Gallery was hung with Bérard-style trompe l'oeil panoramic images, and Jean-Paul Gaultier designs appeared in tribute to the master. Tuxedo dressing gowns, a feathered bolero jacket over bare skin: there was a little something of Saint Laurent there, which could be felt through a retro, melodramatic, and dark vision of Paris. One could recognize the guitar dress photographed by Jean-Loup Sieff in 1971. It wasn't worn by a woman, but by a man. Show after show, the rumors grew, until one day in 1998, when Pierre Bergé issued an official denial: "No, Jean-Paul Gaultier is not Yves Saint Laurent's successor."[24] Until then, Yves had frequently criticized Gaultier, but his remarks became gentler. "I like Jean-Paul Gaultier very much. He has an outlandish side, but he has a sense of the cut." he said of the designer, whose men's raincoats and pantsuits were constant tributes to YSL—a master without a student who, in turn, never stopping speaking about his own master, Christian Dior.

In Paris, the all-powerful Bernard Arnault led the media dance. Pierre Bergé expressed his rivalry with LVMH by criticizing corporate sponsorship of the arts. "We must never confuse support with sponsorship. I never tried to get results, as they say, from anything I did. I'm altruistic.… I don't believe in business leaders who support the arts. Sometimes they'd do better to support Camembert than works of art: in order to support something, you have to love it. Supporting something doesn't mean making a trade. Support for the arts doesn't exist, it means letting artists work.…Today many people selling clothes or perfumes call themselves patrons of the arts and want to publicize their names and make trades. It suits them like a fish with a bicycle. When I see a leather goods brand sponsoring a Gauguin show, I don't see what connection there is to the leather goods brand, unless it's that Gauguin had skin as thick as leather."

Was the calendar of the Chambre Syndicale de la Haute Couture mainly controlled by LVMH? People whispered that the choice of John Galliano and Alexander McQueen was linked to the influence of certain big names in American media, such as Anna Wintour of *Vogue*, who saw Paris haute couture as a reservoir of entertaining images. Yves Saint Laurent didn't yield to the pressure. "I was the first one to show a woman's chest, but now they're on the runway nude, which is vile on the part of the couturier," Yves said. He was more and more neglected by the press. Although his collections were the most praised, they were photographed less and less. Galliano, McQueen? "I'm not at all in that atmosphere." Nothing was more unacceptable to him than "frills and flounces, too many ideas in one dress, too many colors, too much fabric, and ridiculous feathered hats." Only Karl Lagerfeld was spared: "He did a good job with Chanel, but I don't like the others." That didn't prevent him from criticizing his old friend through a description of the 1997 bourgeois woman: "Her hair is blond, actually yellow because it's dyed. She wears pink jackets, badly-cut pants, hideous shoes and carries a Chanel bag. This bag, which was a wonderful bag, has become the symbol of the bourgeoisie."[25] He also said, "I dreamed the other night that Mademoiselle Chanel and I were going to have dinner at the Ritz and as we walked by the windows of her maison on the Rue de Cambon we both started to cry."[26] The height of his joyful provocation: the appearance of Claudia Schiffer in his Pompadour wedding dress in the YSL haute couture spring/ summer 1997 show.

From March 1996 to March 1997, YSL haute couture orders were said to have tripled. "There is a Saint Laurent school. To be serious, not boring. To emphasize the line above all. To try to learn about the human body. To love women like crazy. I love them because they make me suffer," said the couturier. But was Yves Saint Laurent once again the victim of Parisian rivalries? What strange fate did history have in store for the man who had built his life's work on memory, and who was pushed out by memory? The Musée de la Mode, whose new location opened in January 1997, revealed the wars between clans that had started when it was founded back in 1982: except for a pair of Salomé shoes from the 1970s and a dress designed for Dior in 1958, there wasn't a single item by Yves Saint Laurent. Pierre Bergé, who was president of the fashion department of the Union Centrale des Arts Décoratifs, was said to be "shocked." Yves Saint Laurent's isolation was also expressed in the way the fashion magazines covered ready-to-wear collections in New York, Milan, and Paris. With the specter of the year 2000 rising up like a fearful barrier, the designers had erected another barrier, a barrier of images that drove one crazy. It was like being in a bus with no brakes, pounded by techno music. Heads grew on top of other heads, with Afro helmets, volcanoes of flaming hair, and spiky rocker hairdos. In the crowd, a transvestite's face was wrapped in a bandage with glasses on top. The fashion victims had gotten out their No Future t-shirts. The poisonous flowers were on the runway, with crazed looks, and sometimes with heroin injected between their toes. The front rows seemed to have been struck with amnesia. They applauded the return of "power suits" and a more aggressive femininity. The runway shows felt like boxing matches. Who fell, who got back up, who will win? Reality had tossed out imagination. Its only refuge was the world of the theater, where John Galliano took inspiration for his costume balls and illusions. His ladies of Shanghai, like his silk

Nefertitis, gave artificial sustenance to haute couture, which, for the needs of model-ing, had become a huge time machine.

Between 1990 and 1996, the number of haute couture workers dropped by 35 percent. The gap was widening between Paris, the city that reigned in name only, and Milan, where Gucci and Prada revealed the rise in power of brands. Gray and black uniformity gained ground. Yves Saint Laurent's suffering was more and more acute, and he could neither confront nor flee his isolation. "I'm more and more alone. I can't go out. I'm afraid of the outside world, the street, the crowds. I'm only all right at home with my dog, my pencils, and my papers." There was a new break with tradi-tion: thirty years after starting Rive Gauche, Yves Saint Laurent withdrew from the calendar of the Chambre Syndicale. He began showing his ready-to-wear collection privately in his salons. Thirty-one designs worn by nine models. "I would be unable to put on a show. I'm out of breath before all this mayhem." Amy Spindler of the *New York Times* acknowledged Yves Saint Laurent's "effect" on fashion even if his shows "have lost their influence." But the classic silhouettes that he always updated every season were praised: the slimmer officer's jacket, the lengthened suede coats, the peasant blouse that was so frequently copied that season. "The public sees what is new on the fashion runways. At Yves Saint Laurent's shows, they simply see what will last."[27]

Yet it was clear that things had changed; as the *Herald Tribune* put it, "YSL Withdrawal is End of an Era." With ninety shows in one week, Paris was mad with fashion. Black fabric spread out like puddles on the runways. With remakes of Visconti's *The Damned* and hunting scenes in a Berlin brothel, things were dark and furious. Degradation became a stylistic effect. Disheveled blond hair, mascara bleeding from their eyes, bony frames, and nude torsos under men's coats—the 1997 bat-cave look was quite different from the supple-bodied divinities of Yves Saint Laurent. Martin Margiela, who would later be hired by Hermès, let some girls slip out of a tourist bus in "unfinished" suits with pins still sticking out of the shoul-der pads. As one designer said, "The problem is that we don't have time to dream anymore." Jean-Charles de Castelbajac designed clothes for the Pope. Jean Louis, the Hollywood costume designer, passed away. "Everyone still wonders how a dress can stay in place on her body while she sings and dances," said Jean Louis about Rita Hayworth, whom he dressed in *Gilda*. Everyone except perhaps Yves Saint Laurent. He was the only one who knew those invisible tricks that made a dress a display and gave the body its supreme strength, even when it was almost naked. The man who suffered from the fashion world's noise was also made vulnerable by silence. "He was furious," an observer recalled. "He wanted his runway, his lights, his room. Yves likes the stage." Where is the truth? It must lie somewhere within the contradictions of the man Pierre Bergé defined as "a conventional revolutionary" and a "firestarter."

In July 1997, preparations for the winter 1997–98 haute couture collection took place in a euphoric atmosphere. The hip magazine *Dutch* had decided to bring out a special issue on Yves Saint Laurent. The press office was all astir, gathering photos and the collection of Love holiday cards. Studio assistants passed by with treasures in their hands, such as a gold helmet with embroidery by Lesage. "Black is a color, black is the stroke that draws the line on the white page," he had written in his July 1997 runway show program. His Renaissance collection focused on ladies who were dear to the School of Fontainebleau painting style of the Renaissance, which included Fouquet portraits of Gabrielle d'Estrées and Agnès Sorel. Berets edged with feathers seemed to have come straight out of a Holbein painting. It was a new ode to black that made velvet, grain de poudre, and gazar gleam. "I love colors. I love gold, a magic color, for the sheen of a woman, it's the color of the sun. I love red, which is aggressive and wild, and the tawny colors of the desert. But to me black is a refuge because it expresses what I want. With it everything becomes simpler, more linear, and more dramatic," he said.

Katoucha, "the Peul princess," became his muse again for a season, haughty in the Le Smoking pantsuit that was a YSL signature style. After arriving in the studio with her long hair with blond highlights, she appeared on the runway with short hair, as he wanted to see her, like a figure from his sketches. Yves Saint Laurent was the first designer to hire her as a runway model in 1984. She described him this way: "You can't confine him to a single continent. Deep inside, I dare to think that he's a little bit African. The way he looks at you imposes self-restraint." The reviews were mixed. In the *New York Times*, Amy Spindler remarked a bit mean-spiritedly that each shoulder weighed about twenty pounds less. She omitted Yves Saint Laurent from her top three list of Gaultier, Lagerfeld, and Lacroix. But for Suzy Menkes, the collection was "exceptional, pure, harmonious. A moment of grace."[28]

Once again, guests left the show happy, as if released from a fashion week of tormented appearances. Yves seemed more and more blasé. Only visual grandstanding could grab the fashion editors, who were more and more afraid of aging and sought by any means necessary to hang onto an era that taunted them with images. Never had the female body seemed so tormented. Was hell this "continuation of the extravagant life" that Thomas Mann loved? With anguished presences, angular silhouettes, and heads with snake-like hair, thinness was worshiped, establishing all the fears of the "lost civilization" described by Paco Rabanne, a preacher of the apocalypse. Tarnished by the heinous rumor that he used human remains in his collection, Alexander McQueen looked like the devil at the helm of Givenchy, the black sheep of LVMH's luxury holdings. Pierre Bergé added fuel to the fire by saying that Alexander McQueen and John Galliano had a "ridiculous starlet side." In the midst of this hubbub, Paris celebrated the tragic love affair of rage and opulence. A few days after fashion week, everyone learned Versace had been murdered in Miami.

Finally, three years after its launch, Yves Saint Laurent's newest fragrance received the name Yvresse (a play on the word *ivresse*, meaning drunkenness, intoxication). The man who said he no longer drank a drop of whisky or wine seemed to be returning from a long trip. "I went very far into alcohol, and it played nasty tricks on me. I think it didn't mix with the antidepressants." He himself compared it to drugs: "I felt its absence less, but it's still something that hooks a human being. It makes you euphoric, it removes your inhibitions. Alcohol is more harmful." Giving up drinking was an ordeal. Yves Saint Laurent had permanently lost his artificial paradise. "You get used to drugs, they're like miracle medicine. And afterwards you come down and that's very serious for a human being's equilibrium." He said he felt "more lucid about people and work." But reality broke in abruptly and was hard to deal with. The world around him sent him back to his aesthetic fantasies, which became more and more obsessive. "The older I get, the more haunted I am by the urge for perfection and that's why it's hard—I didn't have this feeling when I was young." He guzzled Coke and complained of stomachaches. The star was faced with reality and made other people feel it. "He's against everything," said Pierre Bergé. Something still devoured him. Another drug, one that was much more unshakeable. The only one he seemed unable to give up: "Success."

1958 to 1998. The decades blended together. Since the height of misfortune was time passing by, he appeared to try to abolish it. His bedside reading was Pietro Citati's literary biography of Proust, who "one day understood that he had to explore that cavern of shadows that was inside him."[29] Yves Saint Laurent was surely also someone who, through subtle shades, was in the process of attaining, toward the end of a tireless and passionate career, "smooth perfection, vibrating with echoes, of his delicately blended style."[30] But Yves was surrounded by too many chasms of despair. The place where he had grown up, which he had built himself, was fading away under his feet, leaving him only the certainty of suffering that consumed and regenerated him. He liked to quote one of his favorite sentences from Proust: "Sorrows are dark and hated servants, against whom we struggle, under whose empire we fall more and more, abhorrent servants, impossible to replace and through whom subterranean paths lead us to truth and death." The couturier who defined himself as a "manufacturer of happiness" knew that he would never find happiness again, unless it was through a ray of sunlight, the scent of a flower, or the smile of a woman. Despair could seem like a role he played. One day, Yves Saint Laurent was climbing the stairs normally. Realizing that he could be seen in the mirror, recalled Christophe Girard, "he started to bend over and slowed down, as if overcome by terrible fatigue."

On the fashion runways, London had found its swing. Meanwhile, Paris was about to become a city-museum, crowned by the president's big construction projects (the expansion of the Bibliothèque Nationale de France by architect Dominique Perrault, opened to the public in March 1995). London was competing with Paris and had a flurry of creative achievements in art, music, and fashion. The press focused on London's buzz, covering the fusion cuisine served in chic restaurants like Nobu, the new zen-style hotels (the Hempel), and the hip new neighborhoods (Notting Hill).

The gray years of Thatcherism seemed to be a thing of the past, to the great delight of brokers in the city, whose total bonuses were 1.5 billion euros in 2000. Pierre Bergé, always in touch with the spirit of the times, made a donation of more than one million pounds (1.5 million euros) to the National Gallery. The gift was to renovate the French painting rooms, which were graced by a portrait of Cardinal de Richelieu by Philippe de Champaigne and one of the Marquise de Seignelay by Mignard. "It's easier to work with English museums," said Bergé, provoking the wrath of French museum curators.

In Paris, designers drew freely from the work of others—with results including Eric Bergère's jumpsuits and Isabel Marant's androgynous pants—and Yves Saint Laurent was the most fashionable myth of the moment. For *Dutch*, Jean-Baptiste Mondino photographed bodybuilders in branded swimsuits, and Mario Testino photographed "mischyves," models seemingly gagged by belts, shoelaces, and even the tie of a mousseline blouse. Steven Klein shot the Lalanne dress on a model with her face painted red, as part of a series of "provocatyves." But Yves once again opted for privacy, presenting his Capsule collection in October 1997 in the salons of Avenue Marceau. It featured delicate silhouettes, including reed-like silk dresses and flowing pants that seemed to have stepped out of an Eden of the 1930s for a spring holiday.

The unadorned look of these new beauties hinted at a secret, something inadmissible. A column of navy blue crepe, side-button pants that were worthy of Jacques-Henri Lartigue's elegant ladies, and a pleated Marilyn dress blew airily past. But this spare sophistication had to confront a human and economic reality that was increasingly tough. "Right now, it's not the collection that scares me. It's me. I feel I'm in danger." He added, "Fashion is beyond me. My imagination goes beyond the normal limits and takes me where I don't want to go."[31] In one of his rare interviews, he explained that everything was "gray and gloomy" and that he wanted to live in Marrakesh. Did he want to forget everything, and then come back again? He felt increasingly distant from the fashion world, but wasn't it "an incurable virus"?

The situation became oppressive. "Watching yourself live makes you dizzy, but through this dizziness we reach equilibrium."[32] Yves Saint Laurent wrote aphorisms that were published by *Madame Figaro*. He said that he couldn't go out, that he was afraid of the outside world, the streets, the crowds. Pierre Bergé made a decision: having gotten himself invited to the Guy Laroche runway show in October 1997, he chose a new heir apparent for Yves Saint Laurent: Alber Elbaz, a thirty-seven-year-old Israeli who had defected from Geoffrey Beene in New York and who, chosen by Ralph Toledano, had managed in less than two years to give new brilliance to Guy Laroche, a brand whose identity had been forgotten. The designer's style clashed with the politically correct restraint of the time. Born in Casablanca, he grew up in Tel Aviv and then moved to New York with 800 dollars in his pocket. A hypochondriac, he was faithful to colorful Comme des Garçons shirts. At Guy Laroche, he was immediately nicknamed Coluche after an irreverent French comedian, while the American press fondly called him the Woody Allen of fashion.[33] "When someone tells me, 'I don't like your dress,' I think this person doesn't like me," he said.

In October 1997, two hours after the Guy Laroche show ended, Bergé called Elbaz to offer him the job. "Is this your choice, or Monsieur Saint Laurent's?" he asked. "Both," Bergé answered laconically. Elbaz would only meet Yves some time later. The news was not officially announced until June 1998. "For a long time, Yves wanted to be released from ready-to-wear. He was having less fun with it, and it was wearing him out," stated Pierre Bergé, happy to have selected a designer who worked for only one fashion house. "Not like these delusional doubles who spread themselves out between several brands. Alber is very touching and his blended background certainly has something to do with it. And Alber isn't a faker. He doesn't think he has to dye his hair green and wave a fan around and announce 'Fashion designer alert!' But I'm not naming any names."[34]

Elbaz signed a three-year contract that would take him through 2001, the year that Bergé was contractually obligated to leave the maison de couture. "Coming into this fashion house, I knew this would all be temporary," said Elbaz, who, when he arrived on November 1, discovered the twists and turns of a system that was unsuited to his practical visions of the profession. "There were lots of banana peels waiting for him," recalled an insider. Up until then, the ready-to-wear designs had been handled by Yves's haute couture ateliers. They were driven by loyalty to Yves, and it was difficult to transfer their affection to someone else. So a new atelier was established for Elbaz at 7 Rue Léonce Raynaud. He changed the sacrosanct house rules by choosing to cut leather with sharp edges, by making jackets without collars, and by choosing zippers over buttons. At the same time, Hedi Slimane was hired to design men's ready-to-wear. His arrival was more low-key than that of Elbaz, since YSL men's ready-to-wear had lost its prestige and Pierre Bergé had less to say about Slimane and, in fact, seemed not to like him very much. Someone told me about witnessing this scene during that time: "Attention, men's campaign. I want someone direct. Art for taking photos. I don't think this is true of Hedi," Bergé wrote in hasty script on a white piece of paper. He underlined it twice, added the word, "Essential," and gave it to one of his coworkers.

Bergé decided that 1998, the fortieth anniversary of Yves Saint Laurent's career as a designer, would be spectacular. "For him, it was really the year that would mark the end and the conclusion of haute couture," said a coworker. The calendar was full of media and sales events, including the launch of In Love Again, a temporary fragrance and make-up line, a photography show at the International Festival of Fashion Photography in New York in March, and the opening of the renovated Yves Saint Laurent and Pierre Bergé rooms at the National Gallery in May. "He thought he was the artistic director," said some annoyed employees. Pierre Bergé couldn't help giving his opinion on the model casting for the Opium for men campaign, photographed by Jean-Baptiste Mondino with Linda Evangelista and Rupert Everett, who had a very feminine physique. A glossy booklet was printed for the occasion, and these words by Yves were printed in gold lettering: "Almost twenty years ago, I created Opium. I wanted to offer women a journey into dreams, poetry, and the Orient. Today, I'm thinking of men. Opium for men will become their world of imagination, excitement, and certainty. Between Chinese lacquer and Macassar ebony, Opium for men will take the time to reveal its secrets to them." Pierre Bergé had never seemed so excited about a fragrance. In Paris, the media launch was held at C. J. Loo's pagoda, which was built in the 1920s by a Chinese art-lover in the seventeenth arrondissement. The walls were entirely covered with lacquer screens and fantastic landscapes, and journalists were invited to smell the notes that composed this fragrance of "absolute sensuality:" blackcurrant, star anise, Chinese galangal, fresh Bourbon vanilla, Sichuan peppercorns, tolu balsam, and Atlas cedar. They left with lacquer writing cases filled with vellum envelopes lined with purple silk, which would become Lucienne Mathieu-Saint-Laurent's signature stationery. For the winter 1998–99 Rive Gauche ad campaign, Pierre Bergé asked the Wolkoff et Arnodin agency for "something original and a bit disturbing." The result was a series of photos by Mario Sorrenti that were take-offs on famous paintings. Like a new Gabrielle d'Estrées, Kate Moss pinched the left nipple of a man. The nude figure in Manet's *Le Déjeuner sur l'Herbe* was dressed, and was now a man. Bergé loved the campaign so much that he decided to expand it to posters as well as print media ads. This shows how much the company responded to passion, to sudden impulses and excited urges that could change everything and reverse decisions from one day to the next. Everything was determined by a barometer taking emotional readings. Some days they happened, and some days they didn't, and Bergé's coworkers lived in the intense ups and downs of these enthusiastic urges, which were wonderfully spontaneous, but could also be exhausting.

The maison seemed to have a new focus on youth. Yves had repeated many times that he hadn't had a real childhood, and the events of 1998 took a rather artificial turn. Make-up cases in neon candy colors and a black-and-white video for Live Jazz (YSL's new fragrance for men) by two young graphic artists summed up this crowd-pleasing youthful style. In February, the press presentation for Live Jazz included a party with 2,000 guests with Dimitri From Paris as deejay. Pierre Bergé's imperial touch could be seen in a different project that was very dear to him: the spectacular parade at the Stade de France for the soccer World Cup. "A tall order, a challenge" was how Bergé saw it when World Cup co-organizer Michel Platini discussed the idea with him.[35] "In terms of art, what France does best is fashion. And in terms of fashion, the best is Saint Laurent. If we were in America, we'd have majorettes. But we're in France. There's a meaning to all this—it isn't random."[36]

Pierre Bergé always charmed journalists with his bons mots. "I'd rather buy my baguette from a gay baker than from a National Front baker," he once quipped.

But some days, he didn't feel witty. His office colleagues knew this. When he got to Avenue Marceau with a grumpy look, they knew a difficult conversation with Yves had irritated him. Pierre, who was more easily influenced than people thought, would then become meaner to serve his king, whose talent he would support to the end. To him, the work of Galliano and McQueen was "an idiotic, out-of-date, fascist image."[37] He was impulsive, and began to be seen everywhere with a young man, Marc Gusils, who had the ravishing beauty of Alain Delon in *Rocco and His Brothers*. Introduced to Pierre by Robert Merloz in 1994, Gusils was a self-taught ex-model. After selling "Alaska gold nugget" bracelets on the beach at Saint-Tropez, then t-shirts printed with photos, and after launching a women's lingerie brand, Gusils became Pierre's advisor and then received the title of director of strategy tasked with "encouraging change and modernizing the company." Starting in 1997, observation of events such as the "weakening of creative legitimacy, the loss of control of the brand and products to the license holders, etc." was used to justify Gusils's establishment of a unit that produced analyses and studies at a cost of approximately 610,000 euros per year.

"Monsieur Bergé feared abuses," said Marc Gusils. "He had kept control of marketing so that he could check the product and communication strategy." Marc Gusils was enthusiastic, but he wasn't universally liked. "He went to all the meetings. When Monsieur Bergé said something he didn't like, he would kick him under the table. It was sad," recalled a colleague. But Pierre Bergé was on cloud nine. He was excited about the 1998 film *Zelda,* a portrait that young Olivier Meyrou, a friend of Christophe Girard, made of Connie Uzzo, the head of YSL's New York office. Bergé organized a private showing of *Zelda* at the Pompidou Centre. At the same time, he opened the maison de couture up for a thirty-minute "making of" film on the life of the ateliers, the special atmosphere of the studio, and the maison de couture as a whole. Titled *5 Marceau*, it was made available on videocassette, and many of the seamstresses purchased it. However, the film was not stored in the company archives. The reason for this absence is surely connected to the arguments between Pierre Bergé and Christophe Girard, who left YSL on February 19, 1999. He went to work for Bernard Arnault as a fashion advisor in September, and then was elected deputy mayor for culture under Mayor Bertrand Delanoë in 2001.

In January 1998, Yves Saint Laurent dyed his hair black. "I was losing it." He seemed to have regained the figure of the young man he was at Dior. He lost thirty-five pounds. The merciless portraits by Cometti in *Dutch* revealed an empty face with terrible eyes imprisoned by tortoiseshell glasses. He wasn't happy with the photos. The magazine spread had been anticipated as a big event, but it practically went unmentioned at the company. From then on, the press office only gave out official portraits (by André Rau or Carlos Muñoz Yagüe) and other favorite photos taken between 1958 and 1971. "He looks like a young doctor," said Pierre Bergé. "That looks good on you," said Edmonde Charles-Roux, one of the only people to use the familiar *tu* form with him. She was there when he arrived at the offices of *Vogue* in 1955. "Yves," she said, "is an inspired reed....From the first day, he was a prisoner of his shyness and his fragility, which jumped out at you, but which must have escaped the notice of the army bureaucrats who called him up for service." In one writer's eyes, Yves Saint Laurent had a "devastating angel in him....Deep inside him, he's still the teenager he was when he arrived from Oran. He shut himself up in his problems, his creativity, his suffering. He's not a joyful designer, like Fath was. But at the same time, he's not only a tortured genius. In his suffering, he remains joyful, with an incredible childishness."[38] He seemed relieved. "One shouldn't get too attached to fashions and believe in them too much, getting caught up in them. One should look at each style with humor, go beyond it, believe in it enough to give the impression of experiencing it but not too much, in order to be able to keep one's freedom."[39]

The forty-year anniversary collection had only fifty-six designs. Unusually, the cover of the program, which looked like an opera program held by a red satin string, was printed with a photo by Pierre Boulat—an image of Yves in 1961, writing by hand the initials that would later become some of the most famous initials in the world. Inside, sketches were reproduced on a red background. The Paris dress, Yves's portrait by Warhol, and drawings from his six collections for Dior. Next to a red heart, it read, "Finding oneself is the most difficult search one can take on. Finding oneself without compromise, with honesty and integrity. It took me forty years to find myself and sometimes I'm still looking. Yves Saint Laurent." Excess of fear, media pressure? Despite the wonderful finale with Laetitia Casta, the collection did not get the expected praise. It seemed that the images from Yves's youth looked too much like relics of the past. Even though, like the teenager who lived on inside him who was happy to look at the sea, lie naked on the golden sand, and feel the transparent play of the wind on his skin, he seemed to have put his whole heart into the mousseline dress shadowed with green and a shell pink silk crepe sheath dress. A sky blue gabardine suit with a primrose green silk crepe blouse still breathed the eternal glory of a spring Sunday in Oran. People felt the collection was too conventional. Too sappy for Saint Laurent, as if, abandoning the thrills that were sacred to the enchantment of his Dior years, he had disavowed himself. "Yves Saint Laurent Celebrates 40 Years in a Minor Key" was Suzy Menkes's headline in the *Herald Tribune*. The piece made ironic reference to the A-line shape for women "who have lost their waist but not their appetite for couture."[40]

Pierre Bergé, who claimed he hated "gossip and cliques," couldn't sit still. He needed to find additional outlets outside the fashion industry for his boundless energy. He got into more terrestrial passions: he bought a 49 percent share in the Estudor company, a sturgeon-farming concern in the Dordogne region that also produced caviar. This gave new drive to a company with six employees and annual revenue of 2 million francs (300,000 euros). He also signed a 99-year lease on the Maison Zola. But the Saint Laurent demon ate away at him to the point of ecstasy. "In the stadium, for the World Cup final, there will be a winner. But this winner will have been preceded by another winner: Yves Saint Laurent. That is our history. An ancient scene: the 300 most beautiful women in the world sheathed in gold, silk, and light, dressed by Saint Laurent, will be with the gods of the stadium, looking like ancient warriors."[41] Two billion people watched the fashion show on television. It cost about 30 million francs (4.57 million euros), including the official uniforms for World Cup personnel, which were all produced by YSL. The maison Yves Saint Laurent had invested about 10 million francs (1.5 million euros) in the 12-minute show.

On July 12, the grass of the Stade de France was covered with a sky-colored canvas. The models wore shoes that were specially made for the event. At 7:30 PM, to the roar of the 100 percussionists in Metal Voice, fashion prepared to dance on the clouds. Eight hundred people were backstage. "Seen from the top of the bleachers, miniature giants, as Cocteau would have said, the most beautiful women in the world glided by in a multi-color kaleidoscope to the sounds of Ravel's *Bolero*," Janie Samet wrote in *Le Figaro*.[42] A true flow of silk and gold. "The red and gold Oriental fabrics set aglow the Russia of the czars and the China of the mandarins."[43] In box number twelve, Yves Saint Laurent, in a navy blue suit and a starry tie for great occasions, gazed on the spectacle. Next to him were Catherine Deneuve, Jack and Monique Lang, Isabelle Huppert, Erik Orsenna, and Jean-François Dehecq.

The winter 1998 haute couture collection was a triumph. Laetitia Casta, the "bird of paradise" who had made her first appearance in January, was by then part of the exclusive club. Yves Saint Laurent had first taken notice of her after photos of her by Dominique Issermann appeared in *Elle*. "Sublime!" exclaimed Jean-Paul Gaultier, seated next to Catherine Deneuve. Seventy-one designs, the biggest collection of the week. A winter that was almost exclusively black, for which Yves Saint Laurent strove to express atmospheric definitions of himself as close as possible to the body. It was as if he shook everything up, sweeping away with a look whatever weighed down the eye, anything that was too much, the details, the ennui that others hid underneath mountains of fabric. A model seemed to wear a Barguzin sable jacket like a simple knit vest. Mousseline became a breeze of sapphire or iris air, the dresses reflected an intimate knowledge of nature and vision, suggesting an iridescent wave under the moon, the white foam breaking into a multitude of trembling pleats that flowed over the body. A star in the night, a twin set embroidered with gold beads on a black skirt. A black satin sheath dress disappeared under a ball of white ostrich feathers. Nothing was compact. Everything was enveloping, draped, fleeing into the mysterious small of the back or the hips, to come back as naturally as could be, magnifying supple shoulders and legs that were skimmed by the shadow of silk crépon or the sheen of shifting mousseline. As if, through his dresses, Yves Saint Laurent was indicating the laws of the clouds, lights, and sea, celestial refuges where he no longer felt alone, without a nest, lair, or cushion for his head. Ovation. Kisses. The curtain fell. His demons were waiting.

The day before, Christian Lacroix had presented his Nocturne collection celebrating a world that was being born…or breaking apart. That season also saw the discovery of Viktor & Rolf, with their "atomic bomb tuxedo," whose white blouse rising out of a black column suggested a mushroom cloud. That fall, rumors started swirling. People said that Yves Saint Laurent's couture house and fragrances were going to leave Sanofi, which was about to merge with Synthélabo on December 3, and be purchased by LVMH. Saint Laurent bought by Arnault? Meaning bought by Dior, where he had been let go in 1960? It was a shock. The figure of 5 billion francs (760 million euros) was mentioned for all of Sanofi Beauté, which included, in addition to Saint Laurent, the brands Oscar de la Renta, Roger & Gallet, Van Cleef & Arpels perfumes, and the fragrances of the Italian companies Krizia and Fendi. Yves Saint Laurent had produced revenue of 2.6 billion francs in 1997 (400 million euros), including 2 billion (300 million euros) from fragrances and beauty products. Opium and Paris were still among the top ten best-selling perfumes in the world. There was a veritable duel between LVMH and L'Oréal for the company. The pressure was intense. Deadlines loomed, and the financiers seemed to be growing impatient. In January 1999, the summer haute couture shows seemed to reveal, perhaps at the dawn of a new romanticism, the charms of a world that was being fought over, as in Musset's *Confessions d'un Enfant du Siècle*, by "the expansive souls" who had "a need for the infinite" and the "inflexible men of the flesh." The former were shrouded in "obsessive dreams," while the latter had "no other concern than to count their money."[44]

The American press criticized Yves Saint Laurent for not using lighter, more unexpected fabrics. But in his designs, nighttime spread its black and navy blue vapors, with Parthenon draped fabrics in homage to Madame Grès, while the colors, from the sand whipcord to the Macassar ebony silk crepe, along with savannah mousseline, marked a new palette from elsewhere, a dream of flight with shades of an imaginary Africa, enhanced by the presence of Naomi Campbell in a silk cigaline and lace blouse and black wool crepe shorts. The end of the show was illuminated by the almost dancing appearance of Laetitia Casta, her body haloed in roses, an eternal Eve in an ephemeral dress. Alber Elbaz was in the front row. Two months later, on March 8, he showed his first ready-to-wear collection. "I don't want to do Alber Elbaz for Yves Saint Laurent, but Yves Saint Laurent by Alber Elbaz," he announced. At the Carrousel du Louvre, Catherine Deneuve had attached her YSL heart like a brooch. The first design was an apparition: black pants, black sweater, the waist strapped with a leather tie and a large man's hat, as if better to say, "I love you." Nevertheless, the *Herald Tribune*'s response was withering: "Seven years at Geoffrey Beene haven't given Alber Elbaz the mastery of technique." Although the man in the "knickers he found in his mom's closet" had his collection panned, some of his pieces were still the most frequently photographed of the season, including the Belle de Jour ballerina heels in crocodile, which were soon sold out in the Rive Gauche boutiques.

But inside the company itself, the arrival of Elbaz was eclipsed by other events. Pierre Bergé had stolen his thunder: after criticizing three years earlier "all-powerful curators who looked down on the rest of the world" and their "unbearable bureaucracy," he did an about-face, announcing that he and Yves Saint Laurent would finance the renovations of the permanent collection rooms at the Musée National d'Art Moderne. But what did it matter? The die was cast. Ten days later, the ax fell: on March 19, the retail group Pinault-Printemps-Redoute (PPR, which would change its name to Kering in 2013) and François Pinault's holding company (Groupe Artémis) announced that they were buying Yves Saint Laurent and Gucci. The cost of the investment was 3.5 billion euros. "Bernard Arnault—who owns 34.4 percent of Gucci—is stunned," *Le Monde* reported. The president of LVMH, who was getting ready to spend the weekend at Disneyland with 450 of his executives, had to change his calendar. The counter-attack against PPR had begun. "Monsieur Pinault may be the richest man in France, but he's also the most in debt," said someone close to Bernard Arnault. Arnault had been interested in Yves Saint Laurent, but hadn't he decided it was a rotten deal? Too expensive? François Pinault had set the price for Sanofi Beauté: 6 billion francs (910 million euros). At a press conference at 11:30 AM, one man had a big smile on his face: Tom Ford, more seductive than ever, couldn't stop repeating, "It's a dream." His eyes shone with a promise that would fulfill his ambition, and he was ready to seize his prey: Yves Saint Laurent.

21 / THE END OF A DREAM: 1999 TO 2002

On Monday, January 7, 2002, Yves Saint Laurent gave his first-ever press conference to announce that he was retiring and closing the maison de couture that he had founded with Pierre Bergé in 1961. The whole world was shocked. That day would remain a historical date in the hearts of those who listened at 5 Avenue Marceau as, wearing a dark suit, he withdrew four white pieces of paper from a Majorelle blue folder and gave this speech to stony silence: "I have invited you here today to announce important news concerning my personal and professional life. I was lucky enough to become Christian Dior's assistant at age eighteen, to succeed him at age twenty-one, and to meet success starting with my first collection in 1958. That was almost forty-four years ago. Since then, I've lived for my profession and through my profession."

Reaction from the press was immediate and spectacular. Headlines, special features, special shows on Canal Plus…Yves Saint Laurent, the first couturier to have a museum show during his lifetime, was indulging in a supreme luxury: attending his own funeral. By speaking of the "great movement of liberation that the last century experienced," the magician of so many revelations placed himself squarely in the past. Ten years earlier, he had said that life was "a temperature chart with joy and happiness at the highest degrees, and suffering and misfortune at the lowest. Through these constant fluctuations, a heart struggles."[1]

In January 2002, the man "with the unbearable gaze of kindness and sadness" described by Marguerite Duras designed his departure the way he would create a fine tailor-made suit.[2] Balenciaga had closed his company in 1968, saying that the new era was no longer his. "I don't understand my era, but I feel it," said Yves Saint Laurent. He was the first couturier to quit rather than waiting to be pushed out by a financier, or death. According to his contract with François Pinault, he would continue to design his collections until 2006. For the forty-year anniversary of his maison de couture, the eternally sad young man had moved up his meeting with history, moving off the beaten path like the free spirit he was. "It's an act of freedom," said Maïmé Arnodin, who, along with the late Denise Fayolle, was one of the high priestesses of Yves Saint Laurent's image, especially through her work on the famous Opium ad campaign shot by Helmut Newton. A few minutes before the press conference began, people were whispering the most far-fetched rumors, such as "Bernard Arnault is going to open a little maison de couture for him under the name Yves Mathieu Saint Laurent." Then the invisible curtain fell. When he left the room, the *premières d'ateliers* were waiting for him in tears. "We kissed him. We didn't say anything. Everything was inside."

It was unusual to see Pierre Bergé with tears in his eyes. "Yves Saint Laurent was less and less comfortable in this profession, which is now haute couture in name only.…It's not fun to play tennis when no one hits the ball back to you. It's better to put away your racket." Bergé said that the motive was not weariness, but "lucidity." "Designing and marketing don't work well together. This era is no longer ours." Speaking after Yves, Bergé made sure to clarify one point: "It would be an insult to François Pinault to think that he could have broken our agreement." On the morning of January 7, the meeting of the workers' advisory committee had been followed by a meeting with all the staff. One saleswoman said regretfully, "We didn't get to have Monsieur Saint Laurent there." But observing the couture motto of "never complain, never explain," each one resisted with the weapons that had always been used at Yves Saint Laurent. "There's nothing worse than stopping when things are on the way down. He's leaving on a high note, still in his prime," said Monsieur Jean-Pierre with flair. They all seemed to be on the same page. Many of them wore black or purple. Outside, a freezing wind blew. A saleswoman in black looked at a huge pot of red amaryllis that had been sent by an admirer. "Look, there are also rhododendrons. I don't know if they'll bloom."

One minute after the end of his speech, Yves Saint Laurent had already disappeared. That day, multiple voices seemed to speak in him, for him, through him. That of Betty Catroux, his androgynous double, blond in black pants, his faithful friend since the 1960s: "I get to play the hero. I don't believe in nostalgia. We'll finally be able to party more together." That of Loulou de la Falaise, his muse with green eyes faded by tears and a smile of poppy red lipstick: "It'll be hard. He is saying goodbye to a family, a world. But it's better to go our separate ways like this, when everyone is still energetic." The third voice was that of his mother, Lucienne Mathieu-Saint-Laurent, reached by telephone a few hours before her son's press conference: "I had lunch with him on Sunday. I felt that he was extremely calm and certain. You know, he has incredible strength. You can't go against him." She continued, "This was his decision. Because recently, everything has deteriorated. He couldn't take it anymore. This mixing with Gucci, this Pinault in the middle of things.…It was awful. Today, I feel a great deal of sorrow, but I know that if he's taking this action, it's because he has decided it of his own free will. He's been wounded. He's ending on a high note. He will continue to astonish us." Many people had explanations for his farewell. Yves Saint Laurent's strength was to foresee an impossible future. His technical director, Jean-Pierre Derbord, had announced his intention to retire in 2002. Yves had met him at Dior in 1957, and he joined the company in 1965. Anne-Marie Muñoz, his studio director whom he also met at Dior, was planning to retire as well. These were two pillars of his life, intimately connected to a profession to which he had once more proven his attachment, in this samurai gesture, which tore him apart and revealed his strength. "He made this decision because he had no choice," said an informed observer of the fashion world. The tale of these events surely allowed each person to interpret this decision as they saw fit, and the truth is probably nothing more than the perceptible sum of objective events, with all of those involved keeping hold of secrets that time perhaps will reveal one day. The mystery deepened around this man whose maison de couture would officially close on July 31, 2002, the day before his sixty-sixth birthday.

On March 19, 1999, Pierre Bergé had said he was "very happy" with the sale of Yves Saint Laurent to François Pinault. But a legal battle was going full throttle. The sale of Yves Saint Laurent had revealed the pitiless financial war between Bernard Arnault and François Pinault. Tom Ford would say, "I do not think I will stay at Gucci if Mr. Arnault wins the final victory."[3] At Gucci, in Milan, Ford chiseled a portrait of a snake-woman for winter 1999–2000, a Russian rock star with swaying hips in puffy velvet pleats and anaconda boots with twenty-two-inch heels. Leopard-print goatskin coats and Davy Crockett jeans with sable tails seemed to express signs of immediate assurance for people all over the world seeking an identity. For Tom Ford, it was clear that sex and power were the same. This was very far from the aristocratic nonchalance of Yves Saint Laurent women. But after all, this was still just Gucci. Why would anyone confuse the world of intimate dinners with the chaotic world of partygoers? The time of statements with that of dreams?

In May 1999, Tom Ford announced loud and clear his intention to support the Pinault group. The idea of his taking over Yves Saint Laurent, "a fabulous brand," lurked in the background: "I have immense respect for Monsieur Saint Laurent and Monsieur Bergé. They are models to me." He added, "Saint Laurent doesn't need a soul. It already has one: Monsieur Saint Laurent himself. I could bring my experience in many areas: setting up stores, brand image, advertising, accessories…and even the manufacturing aspects. To be sure that the right product is delivered at the right moment to the right place and the right people. That's the key to success in fashion."[4] Bernard Arnault suffered defeat: On May 28, 1999, an Amsterdam court approved the alliance between PPR and Gucci. LVMH found itself reduced to the rank of powerless shareholder.

In July 1999, Yves Saint Laurent, stimulated by an award he received from the Council of Fashion Designers of America on June 5 in New York, put on a splendid runway show. The presence of one VIP overshadowed that of celebrities such as Catherine Deneuve and Lauren Bacall, and even that of François Pinault who was there with his wife: Tom Ford in person, who described the show as "perfect." The same adjective was used by the *New York Times*: "Saint Laurent's Perfect Score."[5] Tom Ford made another statement that set off alarm bells at Avenue Marceau: "I'd like to do haute couture." The height of provocation: according to Suzy Menkes, Yves Saint Laurent showed a collection that was just like ready-to-wear. What had more simple elegance than an amethyst wool sweater? Or a camelhair coat? Or a heather wool jacket? It was the new easy look that had remarkably supple tweed pants, jersey tunics, and a series of five peasant blouses embroidered with gold, jet, or nasturtiums by Lesage. A sublime velvet dress was worn by Esther Cañadas, who, according to Yves Saint Laurent, walked "like a goddess." Faithful to the color black, he said he was "in love" with his models. There were eighty-one designs in a flowing display with mousseline blouses in emerald colors, blends of tawny colors from red fox to Van Dyck brown velvet, and velvety gestures under cashmere capes that gave this winter season the shades of an imaginary forest, on the edge of enchantment. Through dresses that quivered with secrets and abandon, he expressed an inexpressible expectation, in a sort of hymn to light, a supreme song of the sky and wind. His goals seemed increasingly mystical: "Designing a collection means rediscovering my childhood," said the man who also told me each Sunday he went to "pray to the Virgin Mary" at Saint-François-Xavier, his neighborhood church.

This was all quite far from the fierceness that animated the predatory ritual of the runway shows. In March, 2,000 journalists and photographers in Paris witnessed a new battle between wild-rustic-hairy-frizzy chic and vivid lines, Prozac white, and market-crash black accessorized with dog collars and stiletto heels. A fairy tale versus the mistresses of the corporate raiders: a fiery war had been declared, in the image of a late-century world order that opposed unbridled free-market capitalism and communitarian utopias.

Far from the dark finery of a raider's mistress, Yves Saint Laurent's black was a caress on the skin and calligraphy in motion. The models looked like great black birds, skimming the air with their magic. The dresses, like mascara on the eyelashes, dressed the intimate flutterings of a gaze. He hated black cats because they clawed him and his worst nightmare seemed to come from Hitchcock's *The Birds*—"If you want to kill me, lock me in a room with a crow, I won't survive the night"—and he saw the shadows approaching. Puritan black was knocking on his door: the stiffer, colder black, the metallic black of men in black, like predators around the château. A witness told me that when Pierre Bergé had his first meetings with Tom Ford and Domenico De Sole, they described his personality as "interesting." Was this a polite description for a troublemaker? Yves stopped by the office for a few moments, before flying to Tangier, a city that was less sweltering than Marrakesh in the summer. His summer reading was Rabindranath Tagore.

All seemed for the best in the best of all possible worlds. Pierre Bergé said that he could work with Tom Ford and Domenico De Sole because they shared the "same approach, the same strategy on what a luxury brand in general should be, and what Yves Saint Laurent in particular should be": reducing the licenses, "investing a lot" to open "real boutiques" that were entirely controlled by the brand. "I'm eager to work with real professionals," Bergé even said, referring to six years of appalling relations with Jean-François Dehecq, head of Sanofi. The most destabilized was Alber Elbaz, who had to design his spring/summer 2000 Rive Gauche collection under psychologically difficult conditions, though, as Maryvonne Numata, who was then a press attachée with Rive Gauche, acknowledged, "We worked without anyone coming to tell us anything." Something new: Rive Gauche designs such as transparent blouses were photographed in very hip magazines like *Dazed & Confused*, *The Face*, or *Citizen K*. However, Paris was already set to welcome the new guard. In October 1999, an editor-in-chief in the front row asked Maryvonne Numata, "So, when are you leaving?" In Paris and New York, the only topic on everyone's lips was Tom Ford's arrival at Yves Saint Laurent.

With lines that were extremely sharp and geometrical dresses with torn arms, Tom Ford's spring/summer 2000 collection for Gucci didn't please everyone. The so-called "stud of the runway" seemed more concerned with Yves Saint Laurent, whom he couldn't stop praising. According to Ford, Yves embodied the law of fashion and "invented a modern uniform and a way of dressing adopted by all women." This was surely a way of dreaming out loud about what Domenico De Sole called the "brand potential" of YSL. In its red box, the Gucci fragrance that Tom Ford launched that fall could have been a personal advertisement: Rush. He didn't hide his impatience. He knelt at the altar of genius. "In my childhood, like most designers of my generation, Saint Laurent was a god. He still is. I have immense respect for Monsieur Saint Laurent." Tensions rose, and it started to seem as if the visions of the two clans were split. On October 8, Gucci's board could not come to a decision on the purchase of Sanofi Beauté. It asked the leaders to "quickly resolve some outstanding problems." And for a good reason: no agreement had been reached on Pierre Bergé's role. The gnashing of teeth began. "Monsieur Bergé Blocks Gucci's Purchase of Yves Saint Laurent," read the headline in *Le Monde* the next day. Pierre Bergé clearly made a distinction between François Pinault "who is a personal friend" and "the great work of Tom Ford and Domenico De Sole" in which he had always "shown a great interest," but, he specified, "Gucci is Gucci, and I'm me. Each has his own method and sensibility."[6] These sentences were spoken with great firmness, given that letting him go would cost, according to Reuters, the tidy sum of 76.2 million euros. He didn't imagine for a second that Tom Ford and Domenico De Sole would come work in his office some day. For Pierre Bergé, "It's unthinkable. This place, this building are untouchable territory. It's the territory of haute couture, pure and untouchable." Bergé also told the press, "I don't want money. I ask for nothing.... My only life's goal has been to protect the integrity, autonomy, and independence of Yves Saint Laurent."[7] He made it clear that control of haute couture was what was at stake in the deal for him. Was this a way of signaling François Pinault to get him out of Gucci's clutches? It worried financial analysts, who saw Bergé as the primary cause for the delay in signing the deal. On November 15, 1999, Gucci Group announced that it had struck an agreement with Artémis, Pinault's holding company, allowing it to acquire Sanofi Beauté for one billion dollars. "A major strategic step forward" that would let Gucci position itself "as a multi-brand luxury group."[8]

Yves Saint Laurent would sell his company but keep haute couture. After a separate transaction, Pierre Bergé, received, along with Yves Saint Laurent, a nice gift for his sixty-ninth birthday: 68.8 million euros paid by François Pinault in exchange for the intellectual property of the famous brand. The press noted, ironically, that the snub had paid off, although the deal had almost been scuttled. The jackpot also came with security for Bergé and Saint Laurent because Artémis remained the owner of YSL couture, their fiefdom. The shareholders would have to be patient. The new bosses of Yves Saint Laurent would have to struggle against competing sales in fragrances. Prune back the licensing agreements. Open new stores. The cleanup would impact profitability. As for Yves, he was saved. Now he was under the protection of François Pinault, who, as specified in a Gucci statement dated November 15, wanted to retain this area "in order to allow Yves Saint Laurent to pursue his creative calling." That was how people talked about madmen, or those sentenced to death, granting them a few moments of reprieve.

Yves Saint Laurent haute couture, which employed 158 people, had revenue of just over 6 million euros per year, and ran a large deficit, despite the influx of orders. By comparison, YSL ready-to-wear and accessories brought in revenue of 94 million euros, while YSL Beauté had annual revenue of about 488 million euros. It was clear that, starting on this date, in the United States, the flowers sent to Yves Saint Laurent certainly looked like media-friendly chrysanthemums: "For some time, *Vogue* and Yves Saint Laurent—probably the greatest designer of the century—have experienced enmity....I would like Monsieur Saint Laurent to know that for many years, I could only wear Saint Laurent, and that I remain a great admirer of everything he has done for fashion and his influence on young designers," wrote Anna Wintour, who was in some respects considered exasperating by the company.[9] Faithful to the front row, the whole team of American *Vogue* had even been physically excluded from the couture shows from 1995 to 1998 and replaced by clients. Indeed, on the occasions that Anna Wintour did appear, she sat with her dark glasses, looking as if she was not paying attention, almost bored. Hadn't she been the first to say that the CFDA Fashion Awards ceremony in New York was "too long"? The message was clear: "Yves Saint Laurent has marked twentieth-century fashion with his signature. Gucci will ensure the brand's development in the twenty-first century," said the November 15 press release.

Yves Saint Laurent, who had turned fashion into gold, was an embalmed alchemist: in France, his face was engraved on the last franc coins of the millennium, available in a limited series. Heads was his image from a Pierre Boulat photo, while tails was the heart, which he had made his symbol. As one journalist commented, Yves Saint Laurent had never been in the headlines so much as when he stopped designing his ready-to-wear. References, tributes. "For three seasons, we've seen Saint Laurent-style designs at all the women's runway shows," wrote *Elle*. "The spring/summer

2000 collections are rife with new versions of the key elements of his style. Helmut Lang revisits his mousseline blouses. Miuccia Prada pays tribute to 1970s YSL chic, and everyone has done a tie-neck blouse and a pantsuit, a belted trench coat, and heaps of bracelets. So, thank you, Monsieur."[10]

Yves Saint Laurent's world was breaking up into several stories, including that of the master and that of Alber Elbaz, from whom the wiry and photogenic Hedi Slimane would soon steal the media's favor. At the MTV Awards, Madonna was a sensation in her Rive Gauche tuxedo...for men. Hedi had his fans: Brad Pitt, George Michael, Robbie Williams, and Keith Richards, and his very androgynous style even found an influential fan: the enthusiastic octogenarian Maïmé Arnodin, who wore his slender black suits with immaculate tae kwon do shoes. Hedi Slimane, who said he was inspired by icons such as David Bowie and Mikhail Baryshnikov, borrowed certain coded signifiers from 1970s Rive Gauche style. His slim suits, his exact lines, and his ultra-long trench coats made him the mascot of the English-speaking press, who nicknamed him "Saint Slimane," "The House Master," and "Mr. Big Stuff." The magazine *Technikart* was charmed by his "hypnotic" eye. Amnesia would do the rest: "Though Yves Saint Laurent liberated women, he didn't do much for men. Until a new designer from elsewhere opened the door of the old house. The name of this magician: Hedi Slimane."[11] When he arrived in 1997, the men's department had been reduced to "a seller of shirts and ties with two of its own stores," according to an observer. In three years, sales increased by 20 percent and points of sale jumped from five to seventy-five, including Colette in Paris, Barneys in New York, and Joseph in London. In November 1999, the reopening of the men's store on Place Saint-Sulpice in Paris, with a very pared-down décor, was one of the hip events of the season. It contrasted with the more opulent atmosphere of Rive Gauche points of sale for women in Paris. American *Vogue* ran an eight-page spread on Hedi Slimane's men's clothes being worn by women.

Yves Saint Laurent was now part of Artémis. At Parisian dinners, people were astounded by Pierre Bergé's performance, saying that he was able to sell his company twice, or even three times. In 1993, when it was sold to Sanofi, Yves Saint Laurent and Pierre Bergé pocketed 340 million francs (51.83 million euros), according to *Le Monde*. This time, according to the terms of the contract with François Pinault, which was valid through December 31, 2006 and renewable for two successive five-year terms, Parfums Yves Saint Laurent would pay Berlys (Pierre Bergé and Yves Saint Laurent's company) 0.4 percent of the revenue produced by its brands. This payment was capped at four million dollars annually. In its article "Un Parfum de Stock-Options," *Le Monde* did the following calculation: a theoretical maximum total of 64 million dollars over 16 years. The foundation that Pierre Bergé and Yves Saint Laurent were planning to "preserve the designs, garments, and sketchbooks" of the couturier also received a cut: it would be partly funded by a payment of 0.25

percent of the revenue of Parfums Yves Saint Laurent, capped at 1.875 million dollars annually. Basically, it was becoming clear that the "fabulous legacy" that Tom Ford talked about didn't come cheap. And other problems were on the horizon. With variations on the theme of "Tom Ford killed me," Yves Saint Laurent was poised to turn himself into a victim once more.

Yves Saint Laurent considered the people who worked for him his children, and never in the two years that followed had he felt the heart of his company beat so strongly. The head of the press office, Dominique Deroche, remained an affectionate and devoted presence, making appointments for him not just with journalists, but also with his pedicurist and his tailor. This "maison d'amour," the first in the industry to start negotiating a thirty-five-hour work week, would experience the last hours of a very paternalistic system. Pierre Bergé, a member of the friends of *L'Humanité*, got close to Robert Hue, the leader of the Communist party—who supported his candidacy in Paris's sixth arrondissement. The company was experiencing a progressive mood in labor relations. "We were more good-natured. They're stricter and more about numbers," said Jean-Luc Le François, the CGT union rep at Yves Saint Laurent. The Gucci Group managers were called "our friends from across the way." Yves Saint Laurent would never mention Tom Ford by name, calling him "that person," as in, "I hope that person will be able to take inspiration from my work. Otherwise this won't work."[12]

The spring/summer 2000 haute couture collection, which Yves Saint Laurent showed in January, was marked by these rifts but rose above them: it was simple but exceptional. It spoke to all women in order to have a better conversation with one woman alone, and responded to the completely contradictory demands of the clients and the press, going beyond the everyday and the unreal into the world that he made so familiar—the world of dreams. Compared to his designs, the others appeared too basic or too spectacular. At age sixty-three, here he was, much like the young man that he had been in the early Rive Gauche era: his look was the continuation of a story instead of its nostalgic reflection. On the program the following was written in capital letters: "Daytime in a safari jacket, nighttime as a gypsy." Wisteria and sand gabardine, a dress of organza, tulle, and lace. The hours of the day alternated, as if he projected onto the designs the early glow of dawn, that of twilight, and then the night, avoiding what all Mediterranean people flee behind their closed shutters: the full sun.

Meanwhile, the big spring cleaning had started: at 7 Avenue George V, where anthracite gray sofas with matching carpet now presided, the team of Mark Lee, the president of Yves Saint Laurent Rive Gauche, had gotten to work. Between January 2000 and January 2001, the number of licensing agreements was reduced from 167 to 62 and then dropped all the way to 15 in January 2002. There was a corresponding drop in revenue from royalties: from 67 million dollars in 1999 to 13 million dollars for the first nine months of 2001. There were 15 Rive Gauche stores in 2000, and that number was doubled in one year. Then, in January 2002 there were 43, with a goal of 55 in 2003. The house architect, Bill Sofield, had the mission of giving a unified style to all the locations, whether commercial or administrative. The company offices in Milan, Paris, and London had the same bouquets of flowers, the same fig tree candles by Diptyque, the same ashtrays, and the same Eames sofas. Receptionists in black sat behind counters that blocked their vision, gray carpeting, and white walls: it was a sterile atmosphere.

Each clan seemed to construct its own fortress of silence. In January 2002, the luxurious headquarters of the Association pour le Rayonnement de l'Oeuvre de Monsieur Saint Laurent were inaugurated at La Villette. They featured glass arches and paneling with gold leaf that provided an antique patina for a tailor-made museum that held 5,000 pieces of clothing and 15,000 accessories. The green of the reading room was inspired by one of the rooms in Yves's Villa Majorelle. On the second floor, sketches and clothes were preserved. They were all stored in white metallic cabinets that looked like safes, in a space almost 10,000 square feet in size, with a temperature maintained at 59 degrees. Hector Pascual, the director, and his assistant were the only ones permitted near the clothes, which were meticulously cleaned and restored by white-gloved hands. The doors opened, revealing a white silhouette worn by Grace Kelly. A dress for the Duchess of Windsor. Sunflowers like balls of fire under glass. The sleeves stuffed with tissue paper seemed to hold thousands of secrets. Life was there, spurting forth in a flood of colors, and withdrawing into its minimalist igloo after the visit ended. The inaugural exhibition focused on the test garment or toile, which, according to Yves Saint Laurent, "has the magic of a drawing. You must pay close attention to the toile before choosing the fabric that it will be made of in order to maintain the mystery of the sketch," he wrote. In his text, Pierre Bergé compared the toile to a "chrysalis that, before our eyes, will transform into a butterfly."[13] Also in January, the new 1900–1945 rooms of the Musée National d'Art Moderne were opened, after being renovated using a gift of 10 million francs (1.52 million euros) from Yves Saint Laurent and Pierre Bergé.

Yet, in the arms of history, Yves Saint Laurent seemed even more naked and more alone than when facing the dreaded fact of mortality. It was a moment that thrilled him nevertheless, giving him the strength to combat, to continue to fight, to struggle always against his demons, to take on challenges. "What I miss the most is not having anymore giants to fight. Facing Givenchy, Balenciaga, and Chanel, I transcended myself," he said.[14] Journalists wanted to see him. He hid in his maison de couture, where the workers in the atelier watched him through a small window. He was both so close and so far away, both a child and a monument. There were two sides to him, just like his refuges at 5 Avenue Marceau: one was a red and gold dream office like a cavern of glory filled with the scent of lilies, with watercolors by Christian Bérard, Monsieur Dior's cane, and Silvana Mangano's photo. The other was the design studio, where a young man in a trench coat seemed to have forgotten his scarf on a Swedish wood chair from the Rue Spontini years. While the celebrity-focused media reigned supreme, it took an average of a year's wait to obtain an interview with YSL. With him, though, everything could happen due to a chance encounter, because, as those around him said, he didn't function with dates, but with emotions. "I know, I know, he may not come down. That's his privilege," said a journalist who was trying to be understanding. But unlike other couturiers, Yves wouldn't first be clearing it with his communications department.

On May 4, 2000, Alber Elbaz left Saint Laurent, and Tom Ford officially became the company's creative director. A few weeks later, Yves Saint Laurent spoke openly to the press, by turns playful, defeated, splendid, broken. "I'm a failed artist. All I had going for me was my mad love of painting and theater. But all that was just intuition. I don't know any of their rules. I settled for stealing from Braque, Matisse, Picasso, Andy Warhol, Wesselmann." His soul was tormented, but he knew his strength: "I seek to capture the human. That's my passion. I want to reveal the best in a woman, her body, her heart…this state of grace."[15]

Yves Saint Laurent, nicknamed "the dictator of velvet" by a Belgian newspaper, had always emphasized intuition over analysis. He had urges, desires, regrets. He wondered aloud whether he should have abandoned haute couture to focus on ready-to-wear. "Fashion touches the most people possible. And then, you can express your modernity." The idea of never again seeing women wearing him was hard to accept. "But I couldn't resign myself to part with my ateliers and the wonderful people who have supported me for so long." His successors were struck by the sentimental atmosphere that Yves Saint Laurent had created around his brand. Nothing seemed to have changed in this Napoleon III–era mansion with its staircase shaded on either side by kentia palms, where a receptionist wore the same smile to greet society women and other visitors, such as a young man who came humbly seeking an invitation to the runway show with a bouquet of roses in his hand. A labyrinth with its three staircases, its bathrooms tiled in black that would fit in at a nightclub, its unwritten rules, and its women with red lips. The more the media put the couturier on a pedestal, fixing him on a stone throne, the more he infused the entire company with his presence, giving every detail—Joanna's finger-waved hair, the diamond buckle on a black satin shoe—special resonance. Everything pulsed around him. That is why his last runway shows reached an extreme clarity, giving the exceptional the generous scent of the ordinary. "The show is going to start. Please turn off your cell phones." Pierre Bergé's ritual words, as he stood on the runway of the Imperial Salon of the Hotel Intercontinental, sounded out again on July 12, 2001.

Ninety-two designs by Yves Saint Laurent were shown, with Tom Ford in the audience. The powerful entertainer didn't yet know that he was attending a fashion show by the master for the last time. "Everything terribly," read the program, quoting the poet Apollinaire. Anthracite chevrons, tobacco cashmere, and the astonishing green loden coat maintained, under their Irish intonations, a strictly "client" line, stretched to the extreme, cinched at the waist and square at the shoulders. Starting with number 58, the intoxication was there, the fabric surrendered, in an almost sacred game, as if the darts, by disappearing, revealed the entire soul of a body given back to its secrets that were enveloped, without being betrayed, by brown, purple, and gray-green crepe virginal dresses. Then came gold and pecan damask dresses with the sheen of bronze statues, black rumblings of taffeta, whisperings of sequined lace and black bird of paradise feathers. No *décolletés*, but lines under the shoulders or bare breasts. The brilliance of a cape of bright pink satin with tulle embroidered with stars over a long iris crepe skirt. The infinite line of an extremely sharpened black dress, like the essence of passion.

Pierre Bergé's legendary anger and Yves Saint Laurent's whispers had filled the space At 5 Avenue Marceau, which constantly adjusted itself according to the time, the air, the rain, the sun, the little nothings that ended up becoming everything, without anyone holding the key to this capricious barometer. There were sacks of toys brought back from New York by Connie Uzzo for Yves's French bulldog, the black-and-white ballet of the chauffeurs, the powdered laughter of the saleswomen, always wearing black skirts "so as not to overshadow the clients," they told me. It was like being inside a living body whose nerve endings were rooms, doors that closed or slammed, or were left ajar to allow the light in, a mousseline sheath dress like an apparition, a mauve cloud of happiness. And then silence. Sometimes heavy with tension, sometimes light as a butterfly. The room across from the design studio was a kind of antechamber with mirrors where the models rehearsed before going on stage. Their beauty was concentrated in the expressions they wore during their brief time in the garments. The story of a gaze, of the shoulders, of the attitude. For him. In his studio, the fabrics gave off their pink and orange light. The chaos of life was there, with his whimsy, his kitschy good luck charms, his holiday cards pinned to the bulletin board, the soccer ball signed by Michel Platini that Moujik liked to chew.

Rational and obsessive, Tom Ford hated chaos. He himself admitted, "I don't keep anything." His calendar consisted of large sheets of paper carefully annotated in black ink. When he changed a date, he didn't erase it, but used white-out. Janie Samet of *Le Figaro*, to whom Yves Saint Laurent gave his first-ever interview in 1955, described the American designer as "thin as a sharp scalpel. A perfect profile, a dark look in his eyes. He oozes seduction."[16] Even though he worked out with a personal trainer every day, Tom Ford was a little edgy. In March 2000, the third and last runway show by Alber Elbaz for Yves Saint Laurent was not just a success, but "a triumph," as Suzy Menkes put it.[17] Elbaz left with a big check and the additional accomplishment of having been chosen for his job without having to buy his way into it. The incorrigible Pierre Bergé couldn't help stirring the pot with one of his casual remarks: "When you buy a Porsche, you don't buy the driver who goes with it."

Hedi Slimane, who designed the menswear collection, said he would be leaving Yves Saint Laurent. As of June 29, 2000, LVMH announced that he would become the creative director for Dior's men's line. For the press, Hedi was immediately described as the new "little prince of the new look." Bernard Arnault rolled out the red carpet for him, offering him a haute couture atelier for designing his ready-to-wear. "Tom Ford has a very imperial side to him. It was impossible to have two very strong personalities like that at the same company," a colleague reportedly said. People around Paris were already saying that when he arrived, Tom Ford didn't want anyone to be in the hallways. It was rumored that Ford had 457 million euros in stock options. He had a gift for turning concepts into products. He would only spend two months a year in Paris, supported by an inner circle of creative types, to whom he repeated tirelessly: "I hate, I love, I hate, I love," like a fashion version of *The Night of the Hunter*. The important thing was to eliminate each time whatever didn't fit with the image he sought. This could be the pattern on a blouse or even the color of an ashtray. "Shock Treatment for the King of Chic," was the headline in *Le Nouvel Observateur*. No visitor could be spared from the image. Everything had to be done as cleanly as possible. Even the downsizing. The Variation line was eliminated, the ready-to-wear would be produced in Gucci factories, and the shoes would be manufactured by Sergio Rossi (which had just been acquired by the company). Three hundred ten out of 622 jobs would be eliminated, but there would be only seven layoffs: "Gucci has imposed a new discipline on us and we are having a hard time getting used to it. But you'd have to be blind not to see that the company had to evolve. We expected restructuring for a long time and we agree with what Gucci is doing: we have to start fresh," explained Jean-Luc Le François. In his atelier on Rue Magellan in the eighth arrondissement, where the prototypes for Rive Gauche ready-to-wear were produced, he hung up Tom Ford's portrait next to Yves Saint Laurent's. The prototypes had previously been produced in the haute couture ateliers. "We loved our designs so much that we didn't want to leave them. Today, it's so fast we don't even see them go," someone said.

Luxury was experiencing the end of an age of excess, and fashion was flashier than ever. Diamonds and furs accessorized a solid-gold silhouette that was made to shine from Paris to New York and Milan. The war between the giants LVMH and Gucci was called a "luxury battle" by the American press. Bernard Arnault's empire had 40 percent growth in net earnings. Gucci anticipated revenue approaching 2.6 billion euros. Everything was selling, and everything was for sale. From a cell phone studded with diamonds to a new pair of silicone breasts. Opulence was flowing over the fashion world, and Tom Ford—young, handsome, and rich—embodied this ideal of success perfectly. That was why his first Rive Gauche show, announced on Friday, October 13, was the most anticipated event of the season. "If I redo Saint Laurent, people will accuse me of copying. But if I distance myself from it, they'll say it's a betrayal. What I want to do is to immerse myself in his spirit so that I can design for our time. The world is so different now. If Grace Kelly were thirty years old today, she would've dropped her string of pearls for a piercing, like Stella Tennant. Rich people today are so rich and so young." His ready-made formulas were pure candy for journalists: "The Gucci girl is a rock star who drives a Maserati. She's provocative and up for anything, anytime. The Saint Laurent woman is a star. A seductress who knows how to wait. She rides a limousine, and she's less flashy and more chic." He also said, "Gucci is more Los Angeles, and YSL is more Paris."[18]

To hear Tom Ford tell it, he seemed to have entered an archaic system: "There weren't even any buttonhole machines!" Everything went very fast. Through video-conferencing, Ford could be in London or Los Angeles and still handle a fitting in Paris. He slept only four hours a night and was very, very rich. "But not as rich as Yves Saint Laurent or Giorgio Armani," he admitted with a smile. "Though it's true I'm younger." He could easily have lived extremely well for the rest of his life on the fortune he had made during five successful years at Gucci. But he had ambition. What drove him? "The desire to reinvent myself. I was afraid of getting bored once Gucci was back in orbit. I needed a new challenge. I want Monsieur Bergé and Yves to be proud of me."[19] The last sentence was a little too much.

The Texan had never been so tense. His arrival in Paris was not exactly a walk in the park. LVMH continued its legal battle against Gucci and was preparing to file another suit demanding the cancelation of the three-billion euro reserved capital increase that PPR benefited from in 1999. On October 11, Gucci filed a counter-suit in Amsterdam district court demanding that LVMH cede its minority share, which it was allegedly misusing to "exert an influence on Gucci's activities that was contrary to fair competitive practices." "The situation is tragic, but it isn't serious," said Domenico De Sole,[20] who told me that he was tailed by private detectives hired by LVMH.

What else? In Milan, Tom Ford had his first real flop. His spring/summer 2000 collection for Gucci, shown in October, provoked malaise. The American press didn't like his combat corset-pants, which it found too macho. Finally, Tom Ford had good reason to see red: at Avenue Marceau, the announced launch in the couture boutique of new versions of key designs such as the tuxedo suit, the first pants, and the safari jacket was seen by the Gucci clan as a slap in the face. Hadn't they generously paid for the rights of reproduction? "It's just a flea on the back of a herd of elephants," Loulou de la Falaise said ironically.[21] The cardigans embellished with flowers and arabesques by the talented hands at Avenue Marceau were a challenge. Nearby, the cherished colors and accessories of Loulou de la Falaise clashed with the first clothes designed by Tom Ford in the Rive Gauche boutique on Rue du Faubourg Saint-Honoré, where he had already pared down the décor. It was his cruise collection, with white jackets and black tuxedo suits hanging in a stony silence. It was as if the new team, by trying to reassure others, was trying to reassure itself. Mark Lee, now president of Yves Saint Laurent, even sent a memo to all the staff to announce "the clients' excitement about the new products designed by Tom Ford in his cruise collection with results that were up 100 percent over several days."[22] To top it all off, let's not forget Pierre Bergé's devastating quote in *Libération*: asked about the new fashion investors, he answered, "They want to make money right away. As with racehorses, they have set up stables, buying Galliano, Marc Jacobs, or Italian-American livestock like Tom Ford at Gucci. In music, singing, and dance, you find these products of American schools. They're extremely gifted, and their touchstone is integrated marketing. They're just missing one thing: a soul."[23]

Friday the thirteenth arrived. The place was none other than the Musée Rodin, transformed with a black box décor. At the entrance thirty women and men in black were lined up to welcome the guests. Inside, a garden of black orchids and smoky incense. On Plexiglas trays, flowers with petals like crimson droplets accessorized this décor of silence and overly asserted power. On black cushions, there were black cards that read, in white lettering, "Today, it is important to go toward the essential. To make choices. To avoid excess. To purify and clarify. To decide: black or white." The public, seated on gray flannel sofas (with satin pillows for the front rows) took its seats. Backstage, his eyes shining and his jaw clenched, Tom Ford made strategic decisions. Orlando Pita did the models' hair Betty Catroux-style, cutting strands of hair with a razor. Tom Ford had thought about a bun and red lipstick, but feared, he said, that the American magazine *Harper's Bazaar* would say that "looked old." And he hated red lips, "not sensual, not kissable." So make-up artist Pat McGrath made the lips subtle. One week before the show, Tom Ford changed all the shoes. He called in milliner Philip Treacy to ask him to make hats. Every model had her instructions: "R Hand in pocket."

The show began. A white suit on a blond woman. Pants with darts and tank tops cut like men's vests. The army of shadows moved onto the stage. Nothing quivered, everything held together. Systematized, paralyzed by ambition, Saint Laurent black had lost its magic. In trying too hard to clone an idea, Tom Ford seemed to have forgotten the resolute strength of the man whose dresses had made love to the women who wore them. The man who made classicism a fringe version of extravagance. Yves Saint Laurent had exposed himself each time. Tom Ford gave the impression of having set up his studio in an armored limousine. He protected himself with signs, with cut-and-pasted references to Betty Catroux, trying to make his muse, Carine Roitfeld, into her double. That day, the sun did not get through. What could have been a sincere expression of his admiration was reduced to a cold line-up of silhouettes cut out with a scalpel. Yves Saint Laurent was in Marrakesh and hadn't made the trip. But he was seen a week later in Paris, dining at the Hôtel Costes restaurant with Catherine Deneuve. "It was clean," said Loulou de la Falaise politely. "Citizen Bergé," as the *New York Times* had dubbed Pierre in a long article, refused to comment. He called Yves from his car. "He wanted to know my opinion. I give it to him. I don't give it to you," he told American journalist Cathy Horyn.[24] Except for the *Herald Tribune*, which described Tom Ford's début at YSL as "tepid," the American press praised his performance, but in cool tones. J. P. Morgan analysts even called the collection "smart," "safe," and "hyper-modern," predicting, "it should sell well."

In fact, the couture clan was furious. The events that followed increased the tension. The first ad campaign for Rive Gauche ready-to-wear, and especially the campaign for Opium, photographed by Steven Meisel, set off a veritable battle of nerves. As the press kit said, "the bottle stands out by its absence." It added that "omission" was always stronger than demonstration. "Great artists know this. Tom Ford has understood it too." The image of a naked Sophie Dahl, which was censored in Great Britain, was fiercely criticized by Yves Saint Laurent. "He sent me three handwritten letters about Opium and my first collection," Tom Ford said when I met him in London in February 2002. He added, "I think this image is less scandalous than the fact of calling a perfume Opium!" He also acknowledged, "I think it must be very difficult to accept having someone do things in your name."

Chantal Roos, who spent fifteen years at Parfums Yves Saint Laurent before founding Beauté Prestige International, was called on by Domenico De Sole and Tom Ford to take back the reins of this sector. A marketing genius, she had to make tough decisions, starting with the closure of the Yves Saint Laurent spa on December 23, 2000. "The clients were furious, and they even talked about holding a protest," one of the estheticians recalled. "They canceled all the appointments and closed the doors one week before the scheduled date. We knew about it since June. They told us that the spa wasn't profitable, that the rent had gone up. But everything happened in a very shocking way. The furniture was auctioned off. The terrycloth towels were destroyed and the staff's clothing was thrown out. They let us take home the leftover products in garbage bags."

In January 2001, Yves Saint Laurent had his summer 2001 haute couture show. Toned-down bright colors, powdery yellows, chalk blues, gray whipcord with a mother-of-pearl sheen, the master of the "Now Look" tossed out the colors he had perceived under a veil, or in the mist, for a silhouette that was incredibly delineated and precise. His suit had become more supple, with a cinched waist, gracefully belted, in a nod to his years at Dior, evoked with an inspired, weightless line. It looked as if his ateliers had worked outdoors. The dresses seemed to float in a light wind, gardens of silk that quivered under a rain shower, airy blouses of white organdy, like featherweight fabrics that aerated the body while delicately emphasizing its contours, shoulders, wrists haloed with flared sleeves. A white gazar coat with playful ostrich feathers passed by. A white that was both fresh and sensual, neither minimalistic nor priestly, moved past, lighter than a cloud. To the tune of "Teach Me Tonight" and "Call Me Irresponsible," the voices of Nancy Wilson, Sarah Vaughan, and Diana Washington caressed the 105 designs, in a breeze of distant shores and happiness. At the end, Laetitia Casta appeared in a beige suit with her hair in finger-waves and her lips red, looking like classic Hollywood, on the arm of Yves Saint Laurent, as if on the cusp of a honeymoon in Marrakesh. Applause.

A few days later, there was a scandal during Hedi Slimane's first show for Dior. It was Sunday, January 28. Was he really there? It was 3:30 PM. In the black-haloed twilight of the botanical garden, Janie Samet recognized him. It was Yves Saint Laurent in person, with Pierre Bergé and the clan (Catherine Deneuve, Betty Catroux, and Maïmé Arnodin). The photographers rushed over, under the cunning eye of Bernard Arnault, who seemed to be on cloud nine. Hedi's show even received a standing ovation. It was much more successful than Tom Ford's first Rive Gauche show, which had taken place the day before and which Yves hadn't deigned to attend. Tom Ford thought it was a good idea to have his models in striped suits wear tortoiseshell glasses inspired by Yves's own glasses. "He's great, great. What a shame he didn't stay at Yves Saint Laurent," said the master of Hedi Slimane. With this, Yves Saint Laurent and Pierre Bergé openly declared war, causing real shock waves in the fashion world, and drawing the wrath of the Gucci Group, which was furious at being betrayed in this way.

"Political intrigue. Suspense. Emotion," *Women's Wear Daily* wrote about the most electric fashion week Paris had experienced in years. "Ford Shines, But Stars Come Out for Slimane" was the big headline in the January 30 issue of the *Herald Tribune*. "Hedi had told me that he had never met Yves Saint Laurent. I was amused to see them kiss that day. It was clear that Yves wasn't happy," Tom Ford said, adding, "After that day, I stopped calling him and sending him my ad campaigns ahead of time." Subtle but persistent irritation pierced Tom Ford's ever-controlled words. "When we bought the company, all the businessmen said we had to stop doing haute couture. It was thanks to me, Domenico, and François that he was able to keep going." Starting at that time, the Gucci Group launched its own Operation Desert Storm, according to a member of the company. Employees who had gone to Slimane's Dior menswear show received a warning letter and were called in by the administration. Relations between the two clans became frosty. Tom Ford had only dined once with Yves Saint Laurent. It was in Paris, at Le Grand Véfour. "I remember when I showed him my first cruise collection, he said, 'I'm happy that you are doing Yves Saint Laurent.' He would deny it today," said Tom Ford in February 2002.

An even more serious event took place: a conversation between Yves Saint Laurent and Bernard Arnault that was secretly recorded by Canal Plus on January 28. "You know that I'm going through agony," said Yves. "Yes," replied Arnault. "If you could get us out of these shenanigans…," Yves then said to the head of LVMH. Sitting next to Arnault, Pierre Bergé smelled a trap. "Careful, there are microphones everywhere, don't say anything." Too late. The conversation would be related on TV: "Yves Saint Laurent, the godfather of French fashion and an ally of PPR and the

Gucci Group, causes a scandal by getting cozy with the enemy Bernard Arnault, and their mysterious conversation won't calm down the paranoiacs in the industry," said Canal Plus.

An irreversible step had been taken. There was no more communication between the salespeople at the Yves Saint Laurent Rive Gauche boutique on Rue du Faubourg Saint-Honoré and those at the accessories store. Their faces were smooth and their lips were sealed. Inside the company, corporate rigidity took over. An insider told me the primary goal was spelled out for them: "to elevate YSL among" the greatest names in the luxury industry by applying a business model "based on clear and consistent brand positioning and total control of the image, of design, of production, and of distribution." A former employee observed, "There was more of an outcry with Alber Elbaz than with Tom Ford because with him, people are afraid of losing their positions." But outside, voices were heard. In the words of *Libération*, the inventor of the pantsuit and his "Lord High Chancellor" couldn't stand seeing themselves "pushed out by a duo in their image but in a marketing-shark version."[25]

America, however, was unanimously won over. Boosted by an impressive advertising push (Gucci's ad budget was said to have climbed to more than 16 million euros between 2000 and 2001), the American fashion press worshiped Tom Ford. The man who had the last name of a former president, a filmmaker, and an automobile maker stimulated nationalistic fervor with the scent of revenge. Carine Roitfeld had become the editorial director of *Vogue Paris*, and the magazine saw him as the "pop model." International, open, loving art and artists, he embodied the "cool" style of the twenty-first century, sponsoring the pop art exhibition *Les Années Pop* at the Pompidou Centre, as well as sculptor Richard Serra's show at the Venice Biennale. On June 8, at a gala dinner on the terrace of the building housing the Collezione Peggy Guggenheim, Tom Ford gathered a host of beautiful people, including Bianca Jagger, Nan Kempner, Princess Gloria von Thurn und Taxis, and gallerists such as Larry Gagosian and Thaddaeus Ropac. In New York, thanks to his second collection for Yves Saint Laurent Rive Gauche, he received the Womenswear Designer of the Year Award. Forty-four magazine covers, 88 articles, 2,292 product mentions: Tom Ford's media score at YSL surpassed all hopes. Some even said that Yves was jealous of the man who was also voted best designer of 2001 by *Time* magazine as well as by the Fashion Editors Club of Japan. In July 2001, Tom Ford presented Nu, the new YSL fragrance, at a historic building that once housed the Paris stock market, as if to point out even more clearly to the financial markets that Gucci had heard their warnings: on June 19, Gucci stock had fallen 5.2 percent on the Amsterdam stock market and 3.1 percent on the New York exchange. In the midst of the great hall where investors once roamed, 40 nearly naked dancers moved on satin cushions in an enclosure of transparent Plexiglas. However, the perfume was not as successful as expected. The luxury market had entered a phase of uncertainty, due to an economic slowdown in the United States. In the case of the Yves Saint Laurent brand, the slowdown was due to investments made by the group and losses connected to the elimination of licensing agreements. "Are Designers Out of Fashion?" asked the *Wall Street Journal* in 2001, placing Yves Saint Laurent, John Galliano, and Tom Ford all in the category of "endangered species." Meanwhile, LVMH and PPR seemed to have buried the hatchet.

On July 12, 2001, Yves Saint Laurent showed his winter haute couture collection. Did he know that it would be the last one in that location? Seventy-seven designs were shown in an ode to color, with princely faille dresses, the brilliance of cherry red and glacier blue satin, and emerald velvet, all inspired by the painters of the Italian Renaissance. To strains of Verdi, from *Il Trovatore* to *Rigoletto*, he celebrated rich velvet, shot silk, and Barguzin sable in a combination of splendor and severity. It was a moonlit invitation to a last ball where the divine women had their faces veiled with black tulle or rhinestone netting. Black was elongated, slender in grain de poudre, intense, silky, and liquid like the lining of a cashmere coat, as fiery as the velvet heart of Visconti's Countess Serpieri. With lyricism, the couturier rediscovered his Viscontian loves. His dresses, which evoked passion and drama, hid the excitement of the hand that designed them on the edge of a bowl-shaped décolleté, or of a Carosse pump, or of a belt with a crinkled gold buckle. This hand found once again, going through its sketches, the Dovima dress designed for Dior in 1955 and the scenes from *Madame Bovary* that he illustrated as a teenager in Oran. In a daffodil and lavender satin sheath dress, the body both curled up and took flight.

In August, for the first time in a long time, Pierre Bergé took a three-week vacation. The author of the book *Inventaire Mitterrand* put the finishing touches on his plans for the fall. He had bought a restaurant, Prunier, and in the fall he announced, "Drouot [the Paris auction house, which he meant to buy] will be my last adventure." Auctioneers who were in favor of his purchase offer told me they saw him as "a charismatic figure, a great collector, a fighter, and a breath of fresh air" who could save the auction house from the "tanks of the multinational corporations." Yet that autumn turned out to be a difficult time. "Yves Saint Laurent, Not So Flamboyant As All That," was the headline in *Capital*, under the section, "Successes and Slip-Ups."[26] "François Pinault should have been more careful," claimed the magazine. "His eagerness to get into this sector at any cost blinded him," said a consultant from Media Invest, a consulting company for mergers and acquisitions.

Then on September 11 came the attacks on the World Trade Center. It was the day that Tom Ford had chosen to launch the new Yves Saint Laurent Rive Gauche boutique on Madison Avenue. Despite 5 million dollars in losses in 2011, he was showered with praise: "It has only taken three collections for Tom Ford to make a name for himself at Yves Saint Laurent," wrote Suzy Menkes. "He has a gift for turning the name of an artistic expression into a brand image."[27] The American press also gave a warm reception to Tom Ford's spring/summer 2002 collection for Rive Gauche with the theme Safari Uptown.

As for Yves Saint Laurent, he seemed more and more alone. In December 2001, he had made his decision. The wheels were in motion. On January 7, 2002, the news was announced, at the same time as the announcement of the retrospective show held three weeks later at the Pompidou Centre. Two thousand people were invited to this event, which caused real madness around the world. Sixty technicians worked at the Pompidou Centre for over a week. At 5 Avenue Marceau, which the maison de couture had called home since 1974, there was excitement about serving the man of their lives. "We're like chickens whose heads have been cut off but who still move," said one. "It's like we've been dumped, like the end of a love affair," another told me the day after the press conference. "The Last Emperor of haute couture must ensure his legacy.... Based on what objective criteria can one decide to destroy a world-renowned company with 158 employees?" An open letter from the workers' advisory committee was hung up in the hallways. The committee had office hours every Monday in a new office located along the small staircase that led from the floor of Yves's and Pierre's offices to the ateliers.

"Everything will move around now," some predicted, but in January 2002, no one had tackled the problem of transferring employees to other positions. Haute couture was an ivory tower. Ready-to-wear? "It's a different craft," one insider told me. What would happen to the space? Would the famous foundation take it over? What if Gucci arrived with men in black and white room dividers? Questions hung in the air, unanswered, like the smoke rings from Monsieur Saint Laurent's gold Stuyvesants. Preparing for the show demanded everyone's energy. A show with two sides: the retrospective was on the ground floor, while the second floor, where the design studio was, held the secrets shared by the workers of the company—the secrets that made it so different from the others, a place where everything was felt before being said.

"I'm petrified," he repeated. Saint Laurent time would be nothing without these hours washed clear by waiting. While the deadlines loomed, anxiety wafted like a perfume, between bursts of laughter and dark circles under the eyes, wordless looks and tears shining in the dark eyes of Amalia, among others. "I feel as if I'm going through the desert with a canteen with a hole in it," she said, opening her cigarette case *Sunset Boulevard*–style. "The closer the show is, the more scared I am of dying of thirst." She came to work at YSL in 1980 and was the star model. The previous three years, she had come to pose every day. "Close to him," she said of Yves, "are vibrations and feelings. I recognize myself in the lines of his drawings. I try to bring them to life." The models arrived, with their long necks, endless legs, and busts chiseled from ebony or alabaster. They slipped into these bits of wind that each required one hundred hours of labor. A silver and gold lamé sheath dress for Amalia, a mousseline blouse like a blue gleam on nude skin for Kate, the ambitious Moldavian, who, trembling at first, came out again radiant, escorted by Georgette, the *première* of the *atelier flou*, whom Kate seemed to have made into her infanta. Seated behind his desk, the master noticed a slight frizziness. "We need to work more on our neck-lines," announced Georgette to her *seconde*, before going back upstairs to her atelier. One last design, a blouse like a shadow on the skin. Once out of the Holy of Holies, the models seemed stripped of their magic. One was sad. Another, an angel in blue silk cigaline, strutted around in rather vulgar fashion in front of the mirror. An easy kind of seduction for a different man, surely less refined, whose heart she had captured in her Nokia Mini. The assistants bustled about, using hairspray to shine the soles of shoes with names like Bornéo, Java, Malte, and Saint-Barth, a beige croc-odile pump with four-inch heels. A receptionist, who, unusually, was wearing pants (it was the weekend) wrote the names of the outfits in careful script: "Dawn mous-seline dress, earrings of topaz and white rhinestones with pink drops…"

In the grand salon, Yves Saint Laurent continued going through the clothes from the museum to which he was so attached. Audrey Marnay, the Amélie Poulain of the runway, was going to wear Yves's first peacoat from 1962. She also donned the cocoon wedding dress in Irish wool from 1967. Nicole Dorier, head of the modeling office and grand priestess of this retrospective show, pinned the names of the models to the items of clothing. Marie N'Dao, Alimata, and Shirley would wear the dresses with embroidered beads from the Bambara collection (summer 1967). Ivanova, Tania, and the others would don the designs from winter 1976. On the models' bodies, the past regained its modernity. "In July 1998, at the World Cup, all the girls went out at the same time and the show lasted sixteen minutes. We had to be expansive, fill up the space. We had six themes with fifty dresses for each. Here, we want to show the best," explained Nicole Dorier, who had to juggle time constraints, sizes, and styles. "She would even be beautiful in governess' clothes," she said about a beautiful Portuguese woman with black hair who came to try something on. But there were some difficul-ties. Since 1998, some models had grown! Each dress had the demands of its decade. For the draped clothing, "you need a body," for the Mondrian dresses of 1965, "skinny legs" with an androgynous shape. But Saint Laurent magic carried the day. Every design, while reflecting its era, didn't seem to be held hostage to it.

The ateliers were shrouded in a strange silence. While sadness at this end of an era could be read on everyone's faces, draped mousseline fabric, placed like a pink cloud on the work table, spread a sensation of dawn around it, like all the begin-nings of the world. The astounded workers stopped sewing when Joanna put on a mauve sheath dress. When she took it off, it was as if her body shrank into the background, and the dress floated off once more. The great art of YSL was to make clothes "that didn't seem to have been touched." In the *atelier flou*, Colette and Georgette strove for "chic, dexterous" work, "the way we feel it." Their plump fingers with gold rings caressed black satin so fragile it frayed. Their hands were so sensi-tive that they seemed to drain the fabric's lymphatic system. "If there's a flaw, the *atelier tailleur* can just press it out with an iron, but we have to undo everything," they explained. There was a different atmosphere in the *atelier tailleur* of Monsieur

Jean-Pierre, where there were many men. Turkish men energetically pressed grain de poudre. The women were more velvety. On a table, they had made a wall of brown paper so that a black wool crepe wouldn't dirty a beige gabardine by pilling. Chance was their enemy. "Everything hangs on technique. It's as if everything were written out," said Hervé Antoine Mayer, who was hired in December 2001 to help with the show. "Everything is well adjusted from the beginning. Everything fits together with everything else. There is no discomfort in the sleeves....Although he was inspired by men's suits, Yves Saint Laurent made them more comfortable." Monsieur Jean-Pierre, technical director of the ateliers, took out Yves's sketches for summer 2002 from a folder. "Strength is there, but it's gentle. When you touch the other side, you don't feel the seams. In his sketches, there's everything—movement, the way the fabric hangs, the dimensions. It's almost a story without words."

Never had so many celebrities been seen at the Pompidou Centre, including Catherine Deneuve, Bianca Jagger, and Jerry Hall, who was wearing a white satin Marilyn dress. Lauren Bacall made a special trip from the United States for the show and sat in the front row with Jeanne Moreau and Paloma Picasso. "When it's pants, it's Yves," she had said at the opening of the first Rive Gauche boutique in New York in 1968. At twilight, the plaza in front of the Pompidou Centre looked like the red carpet for the Cannes Film Festival. Jeanne Moreau arrived with her lucky YSL heart; the same heart was also hanging from the neck of Lucienne Mathieu-Saint-Laurent.

"Please sit down, the show is about to start." This was the last time Pierre Bergé was going to make an announcement backstage. Was it the last time Yves Saint Laurent would come out to greet the crowd? Shows come and go, but emotion remains. *"Ma plus belle histoire d'amour c'est vous."* Everyone would remember Catherine Deneuve singing a song made famous by Barbara. She was soon joined on the runway by Laetitia Casta, also wearing Le Smoking. There were more than eighty women in black on the stage around the couturier. He came on stage after an hour of the show, with a slightly lost look in his eyes, as if stunned by the flash, like the young man who told Claude Berthod in 1968, "What would I like to do? Go away for a very long time, forget everything, see everything, and see if I still want to make dresses." From the 1965 Mondrian dresses to the 1976 Ballets Russes collection, the decades intermingled, like the places, from the Pop New York of Warhol to the Morocco of Delacroix. Yves Saint Laurent's summer 2002 collection was even bold enough to slip in, with very haute couture discretion, among the designs from the 1970s and 1980s.

One hundred forty attendants and 200 security guards were there. "He controlled everything," recalled his friend Martine Barrat, who was backstage. Yet one could tell, here and there, that a reduced staff had been rushed for time. Eighty people dressed 120 models, and things did not always go smoothly. As if due to haughtiness, the designs seemed sometimes to resist the constraints of cut-and-paste, the sometimes badly run staging and presentation. The work found all its strength and intensity in the constellations of colors, the embroidered capes, and on the bodies of the black models wearing the beaded dresses from 1967 with aristocratic nonchalance. And especially, with the airy mousselines. Clients had come from as far away as Australia to see this historic show. It was exceptional to see so many fashion-world figures, including Sonia Rykiel, Yohji Yamamoto, Alber Elbaz, and Jean-Paul Gaultier coming together to see the work of a single designer. Paul Smith said that his wife had already made an appointment with the company to place an order. "True haute couture is ending tonight with him. Afterwards, there will be just couture," said Hubert de Givenchy. "A breeze passes," said Anouk Aimée, surrounded by apprentices, accessory makers, and clients, all caught up in a crush of people when the show ended. "A bit of time has ended," she said. "Nostalgia helps us move toward the future." At Le Georges, the restaurant on the sixth floor of the Pompidou Center, the kaleidoscope of the YSL era shone forth with all its brilliance in a mixing of genres, with pearl necklaces alongside Studio 54–style outfits, with Grace Jones sparkling in her ruby-red hood and a woman in black passed out next to her champagne glass. The Gatsby of couture, Yves Saint Laurent had already left to meet his close friends for dinner at the Ritz.

Every party may be different, but the next morning is always the same. At a dinner in Paris, François Pinault's son complained that he and his mother had had a bad seat. "With all the money we gave them…" "You can't do business with those people," his father reportedly said. In the following days, the maison de couture seemed to be turned upside down. In the heart of the grand salon, the hanging dresses looked tired. They wanted to go back to their silent boxes, kind of like Yves telling Dominique Issermann backstage after the show, "I want to go home." There were drawstring bags full of hats, accessories that couldn't be tracked down. Clothes that couldn't be identified because they were missing their runway numbers. After the post-show lunch, the workers, a bit tipsy from champagne, staged a protest of sorts. They banged their chairs loudly on the floor. They wanted to see Monsieur Saint Laurent. He finally came upstairs. The next day. Interviewed by Kathleen Evin of France Inter radio, Pierre Bergé compared Yves Saint Laurent to a widower who had just lost his wife. "The grieving period will be hard."

Pierre Bergé did not manage to buy Drouot, the auction house that he had openly pursued since December 2001. The duo of Yves and Pierre, one of the most elusive of the twentieth century, was still full of mysteries. "Yves only met one person in his lifetime, and that was himself," Pierre once said. "And he is bored with this person, but his narcissism, his megalomania meant that he couldn't choose anyone else." Fernando Sanchez said, "Never forget they are a couple, and they are two accomplices who will grab each other's throat, and neither of them will ever let go. They will die with their hands on the other's throat. They would like to be each other's victim, but there is no victim here—and I would tell it to their faces: 'You're both two monsters.'"[28] Surely a sad end for a maison de couture sold on March 18,

2002, by François Pinault to Patrice Bouygues, whose company produced clothing for French haute couture and ready-to-wear brands. The price was one symbolic euro, for 158 employees (including 110 seamstresses and tailors) to create "a kind of platform for designers in which Patrice Bouygues would own a stake."[29] Was Bouygues, who seemed to share nothing more than his initials with Pierre Bergé, really a "luxury incubator," as some saw him, or, as others in financial circles claimed, a "butcher" responsible for doing the "dirty work" that François Pinault—concerned with salary issues at retailer FNAC—preferred to stay out of?

Mystery also surrounded the hands that were so magnificently filmed from 1998 to 2000 by Olivier Meyrou for *Célébration*, a film Pierre Bergé refused to distribute, even though he had not seen it. Hands that saw. Hands that reflected and whose fingers caressed the shadow of everything. Of a voice. Of a smile. Of a heard melody. Rossini's *Petite Messe Solennelle*. To Bergé it is "strange. It may be the most beautiful music in the world. He was an atheist, but he wrote religious music." The camera focused on the Mercedes with license plate 388MCJ75 that stopped at Rue Léonce-Reynaud, with Yves Saint Laurent stepping out of it, like an actor from the French New Wave. A man whose cigarette ash will no longer fall onto his fashion sketches. "As far as you may go, we will be there, we'll help you, we'll be at your side," said Bergé in 1998, when Yves celebrated forty years of his design career at the Ritz. "Don't slouch over the microphone, stand up straight," Bergé is heard saying in Olivier Meyrou's film, when Yves is practicing his acceptance speech for receiving an award in New York. According to Bergé, "Yves is like a somnambulist. You must not wake him up. I try to see to it that this somnambulist can walk across the roofs without slipping or falling." The Imperial Salon of the Hotel Intercontinental remained filled with this splendor, with his dresses that had whirled under the gold chandeliers, with his perfumes mixed with lilies and jasmine. "I start with a woman's face. And suddenly the dress follows," Yves told David Teboul.[30] Was it a dream? The runway was once again a buffet for weddings, bar mitzvahs, birthdays, and anniversaries. On Sundays, a clown named Rainbow came to entertain children. He told them about loving fairies wearing dresses with all the colors in the world. In his colorful costume, he repeated, "A little stardust, a little moon dust, a little love dust, and the magic will come back."

YVES SAINT LAURENT STATEMENT AT PRESS CONFERENCE
JANUARY 7, 2002

Ladies and gentlemen,

I have invited you here today to announce important news regarding my personal life and my career.

I was lucky enough to become Christian Dior's assistant at age eighteen, to succeed him at age twenty-one, and to meet with success starting with my first collection in 1958. In a few days, it will be the forty-fourth anniversary of my first collection.

Since then, I have lived for my profession and through my profession.

I want to pay tribute to those who influenced me, who guided my way, and were models for me.

First of all, Christian Dior, who was my master and the first one to show me the secrets and mysteries of haute couture.

Balenciaga, Schiaparelli, and Chanel, of course. Chanel gave me so much and, as we all know, liberated women. This allowed me, years later, to give them power and, in a certain way, to liberate fashion.

By opening the first ready-to-wear boutique in the world under the name of a grand couturier in 1966 and by designing without referring to haute couture, I am aware that I have made the fashion of my time move forward and let women have access to a universe that was previously forbidden.

Like Chanel, I always accepted copies, and I am very proud that women all over the world wear pantsuits, tuxedos, peacoats, and trench coats. I tell myself that I have created the wardrobe of the contemporary woman and participated in the transformation of my era. I have done it with clothes, which is surely less important than music, architecture, painting, and many other arts, but, in any case, I did it.

I hope it will not seem too conceited to say that, for some time now, I have believed that fashion is here not only to make women beautiful, but also to reassure them, give them confidence, and let them accept themselves.

I always objected to the fantasies of some people who satisfy their egos through fashion. On the contrary, I have tried to be at women's service. Meaning that I serve them.

Serving their bodies, their movements, their attitudes, their lives. I wanted to support them in that great movement of liberation in the last century.

I was lucky enough to found my own maison de couture in 1962. That was forty years ago.

I want to thank those who believed in me from the beginning.

Michel de Brunhoff who introduced me to Christian Dior. Mack Robinson who believed in my destiny and allowed me to start my company. Richard Salomon to whom I owe so much.

How could I forget journalists such as John Fairchild, Carmel Snow, Diana Vreeland, Nancy White, Eugenia Sheppard, Edmonde Charles-Roux, Françoise Giroud, and Roger Thérond?

Closer to me, I want to thank Pierre Bergé, of course, but do I even need to say it? Anne-Marie Muñoz and Loulou de la Falaise as well.

I cannot list all the *premiers* and *premières* who have been with me from the beginning. Yet what could I have done without them? Without their great talent that I gladly recognize?

All the seamstresses and tailors whose admirable devotion has helped me so much and to whom I wish to express my deep gratitude, as I do to everyone at the maison de couture.

I want to thank the women who wore my clothes, the famous ones and the unknown ones, who were so loyal to me and have given me so much joy.

I am aware of having accomplished my work during these long years with rigor and high standards. Without compromise. I always held this profession in highest esteem. It is not exactly an art, but it needs an artist in order to exist.

I think I haven't betrayed the teenager who showed his first sketches to Christian Dior with unshakeable faith and belief. This faith and belief have never left me. I've battled for elegance and beauty.

In order to live, every man needs aesthetic phantoms. I have followed them, sought them, tracked them. I went through much anxiety and many hells. I knew fear and terrible isolation. The fake friends of tranquilizers and narcotics. The prison of depression and the prison of hospitals. From all that, one day I emerged, overwhelmed but sobered. Marcel Proust had taught me that "the magnificent and pitiful family of neurotics is the salt of the earth."

I want to cite this passage in its entirety: "Neurotics—and no one else—are the ones who founded religions and wrote masterpieces. The world will never know all it owes them and especially what they went through in order to create. We could almost say that works of art, like artesian wells, rise even higher when suffering has dug deeper into the heart."

Without knowing it, I was part of that family. It's mine. I didn't choose this fateful line, but because of it I rose into the skies of creation, I stood alongside the makers of fire mentioned by Rimbaud, I found myself, and I understood that the most important encounter in life is the encounter with oneself.

Yet I have chosen today to bid farewell to this profession that I have loved so much.

I also bid farewell to my aesthetic phantoms. I have known them since my childhood, and I chose this marvelous profession in order to find them again.

Thanks to them, I gathered a family around me that helped, protected, and loved me very much.

This family is mine and you can imagine that it is heartbreaking to leave them, for I know that the most beautiful paradises are the ones you have lost. I want my family to know that they will be in my heart always. My heart, which, for forty years has beaten in time with that of my company.

The next fashion show I am inviting you to on Tuesday, January 22, at 6:00 PM at the Pompidou Centre will be primarily a retrospective of my work.

Many of you already know the designs that will be shown. I'm naïve enough to believe that they will withstand the attacks of time and keep their place in today's world. They have already proven it. Other designs from this season will be with them. I also want to thank Mr. François Pinault and express my gratitude to him for allowing me to bring this marvelous adventure to a close harmoniously. Like me, he believed that this company's haute couture should end with my departure.

Finally, I want to thank you who are here, and those who are not here, for having been there faithfully for me for so many years. For having supported, understood, and loved me.

I won't forget you.

Yves Saint Laurent

MY DIALOGUE WITH WOMEN IS NOT OVER

In his red and gold office at 5 Avenue Marceau, Yves Saint Laurent spoke about his last collection, the meaning of his profession, and also his dreams colored with *douceur de vivre*.

What does the summer 2002 collection represent for you?
In these 40 designs, I tried to express the essence of haute couture, of what it should be: lightness, clarity, and lines. I end the show with mousseline dresses because no one knows how to make mousseline dresses. It's the hardest thing. It's about how the fabric falls with utter fluidity. It's getting a sense of the body under transparent color. It's the femininity of the fabric. It's flight. Something that makes you tremble. There are also tuxedos and spencer jackets with very flowing and linear pants. The linings of the jackets are thinner. The pants are much wider and looser. I think I have feminized them, by giving them more fluidity. Basically, it's a very sensual collection, not based on sex, which is mundane. It's a breath. Porno-chic is disgraceful, it's the worst. Horrible things spread by a little clique, a little circle in fashion that gets a lot of attention, but is removed from real life.

You have often created shocking designs yourself.
I don't deny the shock I've caused. But I was younger. And now there's no more haute couture. No company can attain that level of elegance. I've worked with transparent looks for a long time. The important thing with them is to keep the mystery.

What motivated the announcement that you are giving up haute couture?
We are in a world of disorder and decadence. The struggle for elegance and beauty caused me a lot of sadness. I didn't feel that I belonged to a world anymore....I felt marginal, and alone. More alone than ever. That's partly what motivated my decision.

In your ateliers, there is much sadness and emotion.
It's a company of love, based on love. I only had one model, Monsieur Dior's company. With him, I learned not only how to make dresses, but how to understand the extraordinarily high standards that he had for a company founded on respect and love. I'm sad. I tell myself that we'll continue until June with the clientele. The company won't close suddenly, that's impossible. We will still have much love. It's a profession that causes a lot of hurt, but also offers you a lot of joy.

What's next?
I will try to write again. I wrote a lot for five or six years. It was a real passion. It was prose poems, more like *Les Chants de Maldoror* than a novel. I must find this style again. For ten years now I have been writing less and less. In fact, one of my friends, François-Marie Banier, encouraged me to write. He showed some of my pieces to Nathalie Sarraute. She said, "If you keep on writing like this every day, you will be more famous than as a couturier."

How do you see yourself?
I can no longer express what I want to say through my profession. That is something very important. It's a discipline in clothing that would be compatible with the future. Of course, I've already launched lines. I think I've done the most possible for women's liberation. I designed clothes that can enter the 21st century totally comfortably. I don't think there will be a big revolution. The revolution happened in the 20th century. It started with the idea of freedom. That is when I knew Andy Warhol, a one-man band, an extraordinary phenomenon for me. He left his mark on the life we're living. Today I'm seeking something in addition to what I do. If I knew what, I would tell you. For a few seasons now, it's a feeling that has haunted me each time I designed a collection.

What do you fear the most?
Solitude. I would like to continue being stable, and not lost.

People say you are inaccessible.
That's not true. I'm open. My dream is to be open to everything that can bring me tranquility and *douceur de vivre*.

Is there a final message you'd like to send to women?
First I'd tell them "count on your seductiveness above all." But I think that my dialogue with them is not over. My life is a love story with women. I hope this story won't end here. When I think of all the people that I'm going to leave, it will be very painful. They are all my children. I would like to keep this skill. I'll keep on surprising you. Who knows? Mademoiselle Chanel started up again at 70.

Interview conducted on January 12, 2002

TIMELINE

August 1, 1936: Yves Henri Donat Mathieu-Saint-Laurent is born at the Jarsaillon Clinic in Oran, Algeria, the son of Lucienne and Charles Mathieu-Saint-Laurent. The eldest of three, he will be joined by sisters Michèle in 1942 and Brigitte in 1945. The family lives in a mansion at 11 Rue Stora, on the edge of the Arab neighborhood.

September 1942: Yves attends a Catholic school. "At age six, I became someone else."

September 1948: He attends the Collège du Sacré-Coeur. He begins designing dresses, costumes for paper dolls, and characters for his Illustre Théâtre. He puts on shows for his sisters. He develops a passion for *The Eagle with Two Heads* by Jean Cocteau and Scarlett O'Hara in *Gone with the Wind*. He buys American magazines at the Manès bookstore.

February 23, 1949: Yves begins writing *Pourquoi Parler d'Amour?* He designs his first dresses for his mother and sisters, and they are made by a seamstress. He draws in the style of Jean-Gabriel Domergue.

May 9, 1950: He sees a production of Molière's *The School for Wives* in Oran, directed by Louis Jouvet, who also plays Arnolphe, with sets by Christian Bérard. Yves draws theater sets and fashion sketches in the style of Bérard, Gruau, Dior, Balenciaga, and Givenchy. He creates illustrations for Musset's *Les Caprices de Marianne* and Flaubert's *Madame Bovary*.

Summer 1951: "Underground jazz" in the garage of the Mathieu-Saint-Laurents' house in Trouville, where Yves hosts existentialist parties.

June 1952: His first mention in the press. In *L'Echo d'Oran*, an anonymous journalist praises the "magnificent costumes designed by fifteen-year-old Yves Mathieu-Saint-Laurent" for a children's performance at the Municipal Opera.

December 1953: Yves goes to Paris with his mother to receive third prize in the International Wool Secretariat contest. Jacqueline Delubac awards him the prize at the Théâtre des Ambassadeurs. He meets *Vogue* editor-in-chief Michel de Brunhoff, who tells him to retake his *baccalauréat* exam. He returns to Oran and retakes his philosophy class at Lycée Lamoricière.

February 1954: He begins corresponding with Michel de Brunhoff. They continue writing letters until February 1955, and Yves sends him sketches for theater sets and fashion designs.

June 1954: He passes his *baccalauréat* exam at Lycée Lamoricière. He is on the honor roll. He wins second prize for his philosophy essay and receives a perfect score on his drawing exam.

September 1954: Yves moves to Paris. His father enrolls him at the school of the Chambre Syndicale de la Haute Couture, where he will stay only three months. He lives in a room at 209 Boulevard Pereire in the seventeenth arrondissement. He meets Fernando Sanchez, who will remain a close friend.

November 25, 1954: He wins the first and third prizes in the dress category of the International Wool Secretariat contest. His sketches are chosen from 6,000 entries. The winning design, a cocktail dress in black crepe, is made by the ateliers of Hubert de Givenchy.

December 1954: Yves receives the prizes at Maxim's. The first prize in the coat category goes to twenty-one-year-old Karl Lagerfeld from Hamburg. Yves shows fifty new sketches to Michel de Brunhoff, who immediately shows them to his best friend, Christian Dior.

June 20, 1955: Yves Mathieu-Saint-Laurent goes to work for Dior as a design assistant in the studio. First photo of his first dress: "Dovima and the Elephants" (Avedon, 1955). Yves's father writes to Michel de Brunhoff.

1956: Yves makes his first appearance in society at a ball given by the Baron de Rédé at the Hôtel Lambert. He meets Zizi Jeanmaire and Roland Petit.

October 24, 1957: Christian Dior dies of a heart attack in Montecatini, Italy, at age fifty-two.

November 15, 1957: Yves Mathieu-Saint-Laurent is named Christian Dior's successor. He becomes Yves Saint Laurent, the youngest couturier in the world (age twenty-one). He obtains a deferment for his military service. He moves into a large studio at Square Pétrarque in the sixteenth arrondissement.

January 30, 1958: Yves shows his first collection and triumphs with the Trapeze line, which wins him the Neiman Marcus Fashion Award. He is nicknamed "Christian II" and "the sad young man."

February 3, 1958: He meets Pierre Bergé for the second time (Bergé had congratulated him after his fashion show a few days earlier). Marie-Laure Bousquet hosts a dinner at La Cloche d'Or. At the time, Pierre Bergé, who was born in 1930 on the Île d'Oléron and came to Paris in 1948, is the partner and manager of the successful painter Bernard Buffet.

January 1958–July 1960: Yves designs six collections at Dior. He designs the first couture leather jackets (in crocodile). He is influenced by Chanel: "The line fades as style takes over" (Natural line, summer 1959). Dresses inspired by Goya and the Infantes of Aragon. The scandal of the "barrel" line.

September 1960: Yves Saint Laurent is drafted. Marc Bohan replaces him at Dior.

October–November 1960: Yves is hospitalized at the Val-de-Grâce military hospital for six weeks. He is kept in isolation and treated for nervous depression. He is discharged on November 14. Pierre Bergé celebrates his thirtieth birthday. They travel to the Canary Islands.

January 1961: Yves begins living with Pierre Bergé, and they move into an apartment on Place Vauban across from Les Invalides in the seventh arrondissement. He sues Dior for breach of contract.

July 1961: Yves decides to start his own couture house. He and Pierre rent a three-room apartment for this purpose on Rue La Boétie in the seventh arrondissement. Three colleagues from Dior join them: the model Victoire, Claude Licard, and Gabrielle Buchaert.

November 14, 1961: Yves signs a contract with J. Mack Robinson, an Atlanta businessman, who becomes the first American to invest in a Parisian couture house. His name will not be publicly revealed until 1963.

December 1961: His first dress, with the number 00001, for Patricia Lopez-Willshaw. Yves also designs costumes (the "feather thing" and the little black sweater) for Zizi Jeanmaire's performance at the Alhambra and for *Les Forains*, choreographed by Roland Petit. Graphic artist Cassandre creates the YSL logo. The ateliers are set up at 30 bis Rue Spontini in the sixteenth arrondissement in the former mansion of the painter Forain. Half of the seamstresses come from Dior.

December 4, 1961: Official opening of the Maison Saint Laurent.

January 29, 1962: First fashion show under his own name. "The best suits since Chanel" (*Life*). The "now look" or the foundations of the Saint Laurent style are present: the blouse, the peacoat, the striped sailor shirt, the coat. "Yves Saint Laurent's great talent is to give an aristocratic look to the idiosyncrasies of his time" (Lucien François, *Combat*, February 23, 1962).

July 1962: After Algeria declares its independence, Yves's parents and sister move to Paris.

1963: In April, he makes his first trip to Japan and signs a contract with Seibu. His collection is shown in Osaka and Tokyo. In *The School of Flesh*, Mishima describes him as a child "with nerves of steel."

1964: The fragrance Y is launched to bad reviews. The press talks only about the Courrèges bombshell. "That's the only time I made a mistake. That season, I had bad models," he later says of the winter 1963–64 collection.

July 1965: Triumph of the Mondrian collection (haute couture, winter 1965–66). "The best collection," according to the *New York Times*. For *Women's Wear Daily*, Yves Saint Laurent is "the king of Paris": "I had had enough of making dresses for blasé billionaires." His first trip to New York. The company is sold to Richard Salomon (Charles of the Ritz). Beginning of a long friendship with Rudolf Nureyev and Margot Fonteyn, for whom he made both regular clothes and costumes. Costumes for *Notre-Dame de Paris* (Roland Petit, Théâtre National Populaire).

January 1966: First tuxedo (haute couture, summer 1966), which will be part of every subsequent collection and hence becoming, in the couturier's words, the Yves Saint Laurent "label." First transparent clothing. The MMM MMM dress. The nude look.

July 1966: Pop Art collection (haute couture, winter 1966–67). Meets Andy Warhol.

September 26, 1966: Opening of the first Rive Gauche boutique at 21 Rue de Tournon in the sixth arrondissement. Catherine Deneuve is there; Yves designs her clothing for *Belle de Jour*, a film by Luis Buñuel based on a novel by Joseph Kessel. The same year, Yves receives the *Harper's Bazaar* award.

January 1967: Bambara dresses, a collection inspired by African tribal art (haute couture, summer 1967). Publishes a comic book, *La Vilaine Lulu* (Naughty Lulu), which he started when he went to work for Dior in 1955. The same year, Yves and Pierre discover Marrakesh and buy "the house of the serpent" in the medina. He meets Talitha Getty, the bohemian billionaire.

January 1968: First safari jacket and the safari look. First jumpsuit. The color black and costume jewelry. The Bermuda shorts tuxedo and silk cigaline see-through blouse. "I became suddenly aware of the female body. I started to dialogue with women and understand who modern women are." Becomes close friends with Betty Catroux. The Il (He) style.

February 11, 1968: Gabrielle Chanel designates Yves Saint Laurent as her spiritual successor on the television show *Dim Dam Dom*, "since one day or another someone will have to carry on what I do."

September 1968: Opening of the first Rive Gauche boutique in New York. "Yves's Name is Magic" (*Time*, September 27, 1968). "When it's pants, it's Yves," says Lauren Bacall. First evening mini-dresses and men's suits. Influence of Marlene Dietrich.

1969: Yves meets François Truffaut when he designs costumes for Catherine Deneuve in *Mississippi Mermaid*. Lalanne dresses. First Rive Gauche men's boutique. He meets Loulou de la Falaise.

1971: On January 10, Gabrielle Chanel dies at age seventy-eight. Three weeks later, Yves Saint Laurent, inspired by Paloma Picasso, who buys clothes at the flea market, shows his Liberation collection. "Yves Saint Debacle" (*Time*). The scandal of the "retro style." Yves wants to give up haute couture, which he calls an "old lady." He launches Rive Gauche, "not a perfume for unassuming women." He poses nude for Jeanloup Sieff to advertise his first men's fragrance: "I'm up for anything to sell myself." Costumes for the Casino de Paris: Zizi and the dancer Jorge Lago. And for the Proust Ball at the Château de Ferrières (December 2).

1972: Yves Saint Laurent and Pierre Bergé buy the maison de couture, and Richard Furlaud (Squibb Pharmaceuticals) acquires the fragrances. Growth of licensing agreements. Yves and Pierre move into an apartment on Rue de Babylone in the seventh arrondissement, a duplex measuring over 8,500 square feet with a garden. They collect many Impressionist and modern works of art, as well as furniture from the 1930s. Warhol does a series of paintings of Yves. Loulou joins the studio, becoming Yves's muse. "Yves Saint Laurent has changed the face and perhaps the future of fashion," Nina Hyde writes in the *Washington Post*. On March 24, 1972, Cristobal Balenciaga dies at age seventy-seven. On November 13, 1973, Elsa Schiaparelli dies at age eighty-three. Yves Saint Laurent is the "last living king" according to Pierre Bergé.

July 14, 1974: The company moves into a Second Empire mansion at 5 Avenue Marceau in the sixteenth arrondissement. "Haute couture has only seven years to live." In Marrakesh, Pierre and Yves buy "the house of happiness in serenity."

1975: The "lean look." The height of the androgynous style. Black lines. Launch of the fragrance Eau Libre.

July 1976: Ballet Russes collection (haute couture winter 1976–77), of which Yves later says, "I don't know if it's the best, but it's the most beautiful." International success and a cover story in the *New York Times* for a collection "that will change the course of fashion around the world" (Bernadine Morris). "It's not nostalgia for the past, but for the eternal present that is on the other side of the past," Pierre Schneider writes in American *Vogue*. Yves Saint Laurent turns forty in August.

March 1977–1978: Rumors of Yves Saint Laurent's death. Revelation of color. Red and pink. Imaginary journeys. The great exotic collections: The Spain of Velázquez, the Morocco of Delacroix, and China, with the launch of the fragrance Opium on October 12, 1977. The "end of a dream": Maria Callas dies on September 16, 1977, and Yves writes a tribute to her two days later in *Le Monde*. He writes in his "refuge," an apartment on Avenue de Breteuil in the seventh arrondissement.

July 1979: Homages to Picasso, Aragon, Apollinaire ("Everything terribly"), Cocteau's broken mirror, the Shakespeare collection (haute couture winter 1979–80).

1980: In Marrakesh, Pierre and Yves buy the Majorelle Garden and the Oasis villa that belonged to the painter Jacques Majorelle; they will move in after the renovations are completed four years later.

1981: Yves designs the ceremonial robe for Marguerite Yourcenar, the first woman admitted to the Académie Française. Homage to Matisse.

January 29, 1982: The twentieth anniversary of the Yves Saint Laurent label, celebrated at the Lido, where he receives the International Award of the Council of Fashion Designers of America.

January 1983: Black and Pink collection and launch of the fragrance Paris. Pierre and Yves buy Château Gabriel in Bénerville in Normandy, where Proust is said to have met the editor Gallimard.

December 5, 1983: The exhibition *Yves Saint Laurent: 25 Years of Design*, organized by Diana Vreeland, opens at the Metropolitan Museum of Art in New York. It is the most widely seen retrospective ever devoted to a living couturier (one million visitors). Yves Saint Laurent is listed in the Larousse dictionary. He withdraws from the world like Marcel Proust.

March 12, 1985: French president François Mitterrand honors Yves by making him a Chevalier de la Légion d'Honneur at the Élysée Palace. Yves sees his father, who has been living in Monaco since 1972, for the last time.

May 6, 1985: First trip to China for the exhibition of his work at the National Art Museum of China in Beijing (600,000 visitors).

October 23, 1985: At the Opéra de Paris, Yves is recognized as the greatest couturier for his body of work.

May 1986: Exhibition at the Musée des Arts de la Mode in Paris.

November 1986: Yves and Pierre, in collaboration with the Cerus holding company, buy Charles of the Ritz, which includes Yves Saint Laurent's fragrances. Pierre lives in a suite at the Hôtel Lutetia, while Yves remains on Rue de Babylone.

1987: Yves Saint Laurent exhibitions in Moscow (Central House of Artists), Leningrad (the Hermitage Museum), and Sydney. In February, Christian Lacroix opens his couture house. Andy Warhol dies (February 22). In October, Yves pays tribute to David Hockney in his Rive Gauche collection.

December 1987: Yves returns to Parisian society at the Fairy Ball given by Marie-Hélène de Rothschild at Hôtel Lambert.

January 1988: The most expensive jackets in the world, embroidered with designs inspired by Van Gogh's sunflowers and irises. Homage to cubism. "Making static things move on a woman's body" (*Paris Match*, February 1988).

July 1988: The Grapes of Wrath collection.

August 31, 1988: François Mitterrand names Pierre Bergé head of the Paris opera houses.

September 9, 1988: Yves Saint Laurent is the first couturier to have a fashion show at La Courneuve for the Fête de *L'Humanité* organized by the French Communist party.

November 8, 1988: Yves's father dies at age seventy-nine after a respiratory illness.

1989: On July 6, shares of Yves Saint Laurent are offered on the Paris stock market. Yves and Pierre have a dacha built on the grounds of Château Gabriel.

January 1990: Homages collection (Bernard Buffet, Zizi Jeanmaire, Marcel Proust, Catherine Deneuve). That night, there is a fire in Yves's room.

March 1990: Yves spends three weeks at a hospital near Paris for rehab.

January 1991: "Haute couture is doomed," Pierre Bergé says in *Le Nouvel Observateur* (January 24). Six months earlier, Saddam Hussein invaded Kuwait. The Gulf War has a negative impact on the luxury market.

July 1991: "For the first time, the great couturier reveals all." In an interview with Janie Samet and Franz-Olivier Giesbert (*Le Figaro*, July 11 and 15), Yves Saint Laurent discusses drugs, homosexuality, alcohol, and depression.

January 29, 1992: Yves Saint Laurent shows his 121st collection. "A renaissance." The colors of Matisse in Morocco. The bubble shapes of the first collection (January 1958) reappear.

February 3, 1992: Yves Saint Laurent celebrates his company's thirtieth anniversary with 2,800 guests at the Opéra Bastille. The empire has three billion francs in revenue, with 82 percent coming from fragrances. The company employs 2,993 people—including 2,430 in fragrances.

September 1992: In *Le Nouvel Economiste*, Pierre Bergé announces his intention to sell the 15 percent ownership stake sold back to the company by Cerus (*Le Nouvel Economiste*, September 18).

January 19, 1993: Yves Saint Laurent will remain a French company. After a month and a half of negotiations between Pierre Bergé and Jean-François Dehecq, YSL and Elf Sanofi announce their merger-takeover at a press conference at Hôtel George V. Yves Saint Laurent and Pierre Bergé sell the fragrances but keep the maison de couture.

May 17, 1993: The plan is approved by the shareholders of both companies. By acquiring Yves Saint Laurent, Sanofi becomes the third largest international luxury fragrance and cosmetics brand, after L'Oréal and Estée Lauder. At 6:00 PM, Yves Saint Laurent reads his speech: "I designed for my era and I tried to predict what tomorrow will be." He brought as a "dowry" a new fragrance: Champagne, "for happy, lighthearted women who sparkle."

June 1993: The *Commission des Opérations de Bourse* (the French equivalent of the Securities and Exchange Commission) investigates a sale of 100 million francs' worth of YSL stock in Switzerland in summer 1992, a few weeks before the stock price tumbled. *Le Figaro* writes that the sellers were Pierre Bergé and Yves Saint Laurent. There is a press conference to launch the fragrance Champagne at the Hotel InterContinental. The champagne growers' association files a lawsuit to prevent the sale of the fragrance, which is scheduled to go on the market in September.

July 1993: Yves Saint Laurent announces that Pierre Bergé has been named a goodwill ambassador for UNESCO on July 2. On July 21, Yves presents his 124th haute couture collection, set to the music of *The Merry Widow*.

August 1, 1993: Yves celebrates his birthday at home on Rue de Babylone with his mother, Lucienne Mathieu-Saint-Laurent, and his sister Brigitte. He is fifty-seven.

September 27, 1993: Yves Saint Laurent's new fragrance Champagne enters the European market.

October 28, 1993: Following a lawsuit by the Institut National des Appellations d'Origine, the Comité Interprofessionnel du Vin de Champagne, and Moët et Chandon, a Paris court rules that the fragrance Champagne must be taken off the market.

December 10, 1993–March 27, 1994: The exhibition *Yves Saint Laurent: Exotismes* is shown in the Espace Mode Méditerranée at Marseille's Musée de la Mode.

December 15, 1993: A Paris appeals court upholds the ruling against the fragrance Champagne. Yves Saint Laurent must take all the bottles labeled Champagne off the market by midnight December 30 or face a fine of 3,000 francs per bottle.

January 1994: Yves Saint Laurent shows his 125th haute couture collection with sixty-one designs: forget-me-not crepe, dresses with crystal fringe, mousseline with cloud or nasturtium prints are the "essence of the Saint Laurent style" according to *Libération*. For UNESCO, Yves designs a white dress decorated with doves worn by Iman, David Bowie's wife.

February 1994: In New York, the fragrance is sold exclusively at Saks. The official launch takes place in September with an unforgettable celebration at the Statue of Liberty—the only one of its kind. Yves makes his first trip to New York since 1983.

May 18, 1994: A Paris court rules that Ralph Lauren must pay 395,000 dollars to Yves Saint Laurent for violating his intellectual property rights. Ralph Lauren was accused of having copied one of his tuxedo dresses.

May 30, 1994: Pierre Bergé is investigated for insider trading and selling shares outside the Paris stock market. The case is dismissed on October 16, 1995.

February 16, 1995: In late 1998, Yves Saint Laurent will give up on selling a fragrance called Champagne. After eighteen months of court battles, a "global, balanced agreement" is announced between the Sanofi subsidiary Parfums Yves Saint Laurent and the Institut National des Appellations d'Origine and the Comité Interprofessionnel du Vin de Champagne. Until the Champagne brand is definitively withdrawn from the market, it will still be sold under this name, except in France, Switzerland, and Germany, where the use of the brand name has been prohibited by the courts. Yves Saint Laurent launches his fourth men's fragrance, Opium Pour Homme.

March 1996: Yves Saint Laurent's influence is strongly felt in the ready-to-wear collections in Milan, New York, and Paris. Marie-Hélène de Rothschild, the magician of Ferrières, the queen of Parisian balls, and a loyal client of Yves Saint Laurent's couture house, passes away.

May 1996: Yves Saint Laurent is the guest of the season at La Redoute. For the fall/winter 1996–97 mail-order catalogue, he presents his tuxedo, "a little sonata from an international champion of elegance," according to *Elle. L'Express* asks, "Is luxury still luxury when it is affordable to any budget?" For Maïmé Arnodin, who was the first one to invite designers into the catalogue (Marc Audibet, Issey Miyake), this is a victory in a long battle. She has finally succeeded in convincing the manufacturer, Mendès. To her, the YSL tuxedo is the most attractive proof that a product can change while remaining the same. She deems it the ideal expression of the "beautiful and useful." A few months after the launch, 20,000 tuxedos have been ordered.

July 10, 1996: Yves Saint Laurent's fall/winter 1996–97 haute couture collection is transmitted live over the Internet, a worldwide first. "People copy everything, except soul and talent. We're not hunkering down into protectionist positions. We're not scared of the Internet and we can't turn our backs on our time," says Pierre Bergé, who also observes, "Haute couture is an activity that tends to become obsolete....Monsieur Saint Laurent does haute couture today because he likes it, because it's his job, and because, in the end, it's what he does best and he is the greatest. The day he wants to stop, we will immediately end haute couture and his work will remain intact." (*Air France Madame*, October–November 1996)

October 27, 1996: Yves Saint Laurent receives small groups of fashion journalists in the salons on Avenue Marceau to show his summer 1997 Rive Gauche ready-to-wear collection.
　　Pierre Bergé, who, with Yves Saint Laurent, contributed to the purchase of a painting of *Saint Thomas* by Georges de la Tour, criticizes French museums' attitude toward collectors and announces a gift of one million pounds to the National Gallery of London. "As long as we have museum curators and directors or perhaps ministers who consider that owning a work of art is strange, if not outright suspect, and that inheritance has no raison d'être, there will be a problem....The government is like death who waits for each person and knows he will get him. He will get his paintings, his artworks, either by donation, or through the estate tax, or by not allowing an artwork to leave the country. That way seems a bit scandalous and even contemptible to me." He concludes, "France is a backwards country." (*Connaissance des Arts*, May 1997) He promises the head of the editorial committee of the gay monthly magazine *Têtu*, which he finances, "In 2002, there will be a gay vote." (*Evenement Du Jeudi*, June 20, 1996)

November 1996: Pierre Bergé and ten other defendants are charged with involuntary homicide following the collapse of an opera set in Seville.

August 1, 1996: Yves turns sixty.

January 1997: At the end of the summer 1997 haute couture show, Claudia Schiffer appears in the Pompadour wedding dress of sea-green taffeta. Fashion celebrates the fortieth anniversary of the New Look. Yves Saint Laurent expresses his desire to "remove all the details, to show a pure, fluid, and simple line." Pierre Bergé attends Jean-Paul Gaultier's haute couture show. Earliest rumors about the possibility of Yves Saint Laurent's successor. The Saint Laurent empire, with total sales of 7 billion francs (1.07 billion euros), employs 20,000 people directly and indirectly throughout the world. Controversy regarding the reopening of the Musée de la Mode. Pierre Bergé, vice president of the Union des Arts Décoratifs and president of the Union Française des Arts du Costume (UFAC), says he is shocked: "To my great amazement, in a museum that is kind of like our home, UFAC was totally forgotten. We weren't consulted regarding this exhibition or regarding the museum design." (*Le Journal des Arts*, March 1997)

February 3, 1997: In an interview in the German magazine *Focus*, Yves Saint Laurent says, "I'm horrified by what I see.… There will be nothing left after Coco Chanel and me. I don't see a single talent." Yves Saint Laurent also reveals that he feels "old as the hills" and is terribly bored after having given up "alcohol, drugs, doing stupid things, and chocolate."

"Of course, he has sometimes disappointed us, but doesn't that happen in the best relationships? That doesn't stop them from growing old together. That's what we have done for fourteen years," Pierre Bergé says about François Mitterrand, who has shared with him "many hopes, many plans, many dreams." (*Le Nouvel Economiste*, May 7, 1997)

March 19, 1997: In London, the French painting wing opens in the National Gallery. The names of Yves Saint Laurent and Pierre Bergé are engraved at the entrance. Bergé gives 250,000 pounds to renovate a room with works by Lorrain and Turner. "The twentieth century belongs to Saint Laurent," *The Guardian* writes on September 27, 1997. "Great artists don't need new ideas, after all, they have a vision instead."

July 1997: For the winter 1997–98 haute couture collection, Katoucha models for Yves Saint Laurent again: "I was in Tokyo when he asked me to show his new collection. I couldn't turn him down. It was such an honor."

September 26, 1997: First Rive Gauche boutique in Moscow opens.

November 1997: Launch of the Opium Pour Homme ad campaign with Rupert Everett, a gay icon. YSL contributes to the costs of holiday lighting on Regent Street in London starting on November 10 (250,000 pounds).

October 1997: First contacts between Yves Saint Laurent, Pierre Bergé, and Alber Elbaz, who is a designer at Guy Laroche. Paris à la Mode-Haute Couture, a Christian Dior cocktail ensemble designed by Yves Saint Laurent in 1958, sets an auction record at Sotheby's New York, fetching 17,250 dollars.

January 1998: Yves Saint Laurent, the "lone fighter" according to Edmonde Charles-Roux, celebrates his fortieth anniversary designing haute couture. "One shouldn't get too attached to fashions and believe in them too much, getting caught up in them. One should look at each style with humor, go beyond it, believe in it enough to give the impression of experiencing it but not too much, in order to be able to keep one's freedom," he says. Launch of Live Jazz, "the fragrance of youth," in the Salle Wagram, which is transformed into a concert space with deejay Dimitri From Paris. Creation of the temporary fragrance In Love Again; the good luck heart of rhinestones, crystal, and beads, which has been hung on Yves's favorite design each season since 1962, is produced. The spring/summer 1998 haute couture collection contains only fifty-six designs and receives mixed reviews. Announcement of a 100 percent increase in haute couture revenue since the previous year.

May 14, 1998: Unveiling of the obelisk at the Place de la Concorde, renovated with the support of Pierre Bergé and Yves Saint Laurent.

June 1998: Yves Saint Laurent hands over the Rive Gauche ready-to-wear line to Alber Elbaz. Hedi Slimane becomes artistic director of the men's Rive Gauche line. Pierre Bergé denies that Jean-Paul Gaultier will be Yves Saint Laurent's successor. Yves Saint Laurent show at Colette, the first Parisian concept store (photos and drawings, including Yves's 1968 drawings for *La Vilaine Lulu* [Naughty Lulu]).

July 12, 1998: Spectacular show with 300 Yves Saint Laurent designs on the field of the Stade de France before the World Cup final.

September 1998: Pierre Bergé buys a 49 percent stake in a sturgeon farming and caviar producing company called Estudor. September: A CD-ROM about Yves Saint Laurent's forty years of design is launched, the first of its type devoted to a couturier.

October 1998: Bergé signs a ninety-nine-year lease for the Maison Zola.

December 3, 1998: Merger of Sanofi and Synthélabo, making the cosmetics group co-owner of the prestigious couturier through Sanofi Beauté.

January 1999: Laetitia Casta appears at the end of the summer 1999 haute couture show, and becomes the symbol of Yves Saint Laurent's new fragrance, Baby Doll, "a fun, chic perfume."

March 2, 1999: Pierre Bergé announces that he and Yves Saint Laurent will finance the renovation of the rooms housing the permanent collection at the Pompidou Centre.

March 8, 1999: Alber Elbaz's first Rive Gauche show. Yves Saint Laurent does not attend.

March 19, 1999: At 11:30 AM, the Pinault-Printemps-Redoute (PPR) Group holds a press conference announcing the purchase of Sanofi and Sanofi Beauté (Yves Saint Laurent, Oscar de La Renta, Van Cleef & Arpels, Yves Rocher). Pierre Bergé says he is very happy with the sale to the group and agrees to PPR head François Pinault's personal holding company, Artémis, purchasing the couture house, on the condition that it will still be run by Bergé and Saint Laurent. The contract signed with Pinault keeps Bergé in his current position until 2006 and Saint Laurent as couturier until 2016. The pair maintain a majority on the board of the maison de couture and have veto power over the use of the name and the development of new fragrances. At 4:22 PM, LVMH's response arrives: a takeover bid for Gucci. The showdown has started: Gucci finds its white knight (in Amsterdam and New York). The PPR Group decides to invest 2.9 billion euros through a capital increase that will give it 40 percent of the Italian company. PPR becomes the largest shareholder in Gucci, ahead of LVMH.

June 2, 1999: In New York, Yves Saint Laurent receives an award for his career from the profession as a whole. "The designer seems as frozen as the bronze statuette that he just received for his body of work." (*Challenges*, June 1999) At his side is his new muse, Laetitia Casta, the inspiration for Baby Doll, "a lovely perfume for the prettiest girl in Paris," "a youthful beauty who makes heads turn."

October 1999: Alber Elbaz's second Rive Gauche show.

November 15, 1999: Gucci, a subsidiary 42 percent owned by PPR, confirms that Artémis, Pinault's personal holding company, has purchased Sanofi Beauté. Gucci becomes the owner of the Yves Saint Laurent brand, including "rights of control and certain other rights" of the two founders, Yves Saint Laurent and Pierre Bergé.

December 20, 1999: The Paris Mint issues a collectors' series of 100,000 five-franc coins and 1,000 5,000-franc coins containing an ounce of gold, both featuring Yves Saint Laurent.

January 2000: Pompidou Centre reopens after being closed two years for renovations. Yves Saint Laurent and his couture house are among the donors. The gift supported the historical section devoted to the great masters of modern art. Pierre Bergé is on the Pompidou Centre's advisory board. He is also on the board of the Cartier Foundation for Contemporary Art. Launch of Body Kouros. After his fall/winter 2000–01 Black Tie collection, Hedi Slimane leaves Yves Saint Laurent.

March 2000: Alber Elbaz's third and last Rive Gauche show.

May 2000: The head designer for Gucci, Tom Ford, officially becomes artistic director at Yves Saint Laurent in order, according to official statements, to "completely relaunch the brand" with a "new business model based on direct control of distribution and production."

July 12, 2000: Fall/winter 2000–01 haute couture show. In the front row, Tom Ford attends an Yves Saint Laurent show for the second and last time. Hedi Slimane becomes the designer for Dior menswear.

October 13, 2000: Tom Ford's first Rive Gauche show. New ad campaign for Opium with nude photos of Sophie Dahl by Steven Meisel. Yves Saint Laurent writes a letter to express his displeasure to Tom Ford. The novel *Ingrid Caven* by Jean-Jacques Schuhl (Gallimard) wins the Goncourt Prize. The novel features long descriptions of Yves Saint Laurent working in his design studio. "Magician Yves opens and unfurls the fabric over the body, like a paper doll game for children or Japanese origami: a paper flower that opens up and unrolls into the water."

January 19, 2001: Party to honor Yves Saint Laurent and Pierre Bergé for their donation of 10 million francs (1.52 million euros) to renovate the historical rooms (1900–45) of the Pompidou Centre.

January 28, 2001: Yves Saint Laurent and Pierre Bergé cause a scandal by attending Hedi Slimane's first menswear show for Dior after skipping Tom Ford's Rive Gauche show. "I consider it a little irresponsible and inappropriate to support a rival label. But people who worked for and with Yves at Yves Saint Laurent were hurt and even shocked, especially since he didn't even come to our own menswear show." (Tom Ford in *Le Vif L'Express*, March 30, 2001)

March 14, 2001: Tom Ford's second Rive Gauche collection. March 15–June 18, 2001: *Les Années Pop* exhibition sponsored by Gucci at the Pompidou Centre.

March 24, 2001: In Palermo, Yves Saint Laurent receives La Rosa d'Oro, an award established in 1984 and given to a cultural figure. Previous winners include Henri Cartier-Bresson, Pierre Boulez, Peter Stein, I. M. Pei, and Eduardo Chillida.

May 2001: Pierre Bergé publishes *Inventaire Mitterrand* (Stock) and hosts a party at the Bastille for the twenty-year-anniversary of May 10, Mitterand's election to the presidency.

July 9, 2001: Tom Ford launches the new Yves Saint Laurent woman's fragrance Nu at the Palais Brongniart. A few days later, Yves Saint Laurent shows his winter 2001–02 haute couture collection under the title Tout Terriblement, borrowed from Apollinaire.

September 2001: Pierre Bergé buys the restaurant Prunier and produces *Le Voyage d'Hiver*, a performance of Schubert songs directed by Bob Wilson at the Théâtre du Châtelet, with Jessye Norman, who wears a dress by Yves Saint Laurent.

January 7, 2002: Yves Saint Laurent announces his retirement from haute couture and the closing of his couture house. Pierre Bergé announces his intention to buy the auction house Drouot.

At 5 Avenue Marceau in Paris, the Pierre Bergé-Yves Saint Laurent Foundation opens its doors, with a collection of 5,000 garments and 15,000 haute couture objects.

January 22, 2002: Yves Saint Laurent fashion retrospective opens at the Pompidou Centre.

March 18, 2002: François Pinault sells Yves Saint Laurent Haute Couture to Patrice Bouygues for one symbolic euro.

July 8, 2002: Colette sells a limited edition of 500 copies of *La Vilaine Lulu* (Naughty Lulu), the 1967 comic written and illustrated by YSL. The books are sold in a special format box set with a cover and cost 550 euros each (Editions Tchou).

July 31, 2002: Official closing of Yves Saint Laurent Haute Couture.

October 7, 2002: Tom Ford's spring/summer 2003 women's fashion show for YSL Rive Gauche.

December 5, 2002: The Pierre Bergé-Yves Saint Laurent Foundation receives official non-profit status.

January 2003: Tom Ford's YSL Rive Gauche menswear show. "I wished to evoke a kind of outdated elegance," he says of the collection. In print, Tom Ford's name is mentioned in every edition, as YSL Rive Gauche by Tom Ford.

March 10, 2003: Rive Gauche show. Tribute to Diana Ross and the Supremes.

July 2003: YSL Rive Gauche menswear show by Tom Ford.

Fall 2003: New edition of *La Vilaine Lulu* (Naughty Lulu) in its original 1967 version (Editions Tchou).

October 12, 2003: Tom Ford's YSL Rive Gauche show.

January 23, 2004: Helmut Newton dies in Hollywood behind the wheel of his Cadillac.

2004: Launch of the fragrance In Love Again. In Love Again is promoted as "the unforgettable fragrance of love" and a new tribute to women, "to colors, and to life, to celebrate forty years of Yves Saint Laurent fragrances."

January 2004: Tom Ford's last menswear show for YSL. Models with a 1970s dandy look, wearing black glasses, cinched-waist velvet jackets, bowties, and very colorful high-necked sweaters, accompanied by specially trained standard poodles.

March 7, 2004: Tom Ford's last YSL Rive Gauche show. Standing ovation from the American press.

March 10, 2004: Fondation Pierre Bergé - Yves Saint Laurent opens its doors to the public with the exhibition *Yves Saint Laurent, Dialogue avec l'Art*. Between 2004 and 2016 about twenty more exhibitions will follow, dedicated to art, fashion, and design.

March 28, 2004: Tom Ford receives the Rodeo Drive Walk of Style Award in Los Angeles for his contribution to the fashion world.

Late April 2004: Tom Ford leaves as head of design. After four years designing at Yves Saint Laurent, he says he wants to make movies.

At age thirty-eight, Stefano Pilati succeeds Tom Ford as artistic director for Yves Saint Laurent. Originally from Milan, he began his career at Giorgio Armani as a ready-to-wear design assistant in 1993. He then went to Prada, where he stayed for five years. In June 2000, Tom Ford offered him a job as design director for YSL ready-to-wear. In 2002, he was promoted to the position of design director for the entire line of YSL Rive Gauche products and accessories. "When I fell in love with fashion for the first time, it was clear that Monsieur Saint Laurent was the master. He brought the sensibility of a great couturier to ready-to-wear while making it perfectly accessible."

October 10, 2004: Stefano Pilati's first show for Yves Saint Laurent. The name Rive Gauche has disappeared from the invitations. The maison de couture's logo is used. "This collection is a wardrobe dedicated to women and their desire to seduce, to convince, to be loved, to experience luxury like an everyday adventure," reads a sign on the gilded chairs at the Palais Brongniart. "Pilati avoids memorials at all costs, even if all his designs have a big black patent belt." (*Le Figaro*, October 12, 2004) Critics call the collection "very Saint Laurent," and Pierre Bergé congratulates him in person for a collection that he calls "great."

2004: Launch of the fragrance Cinéma. (The book *Tom Ford* by Tom Ford is published by Assouline with prefaces by Anna Wintour and Graydon Carter. Interviews by Bridget Foley.)

January 29, 2005: Stefano Pilati's first show for Yves Saint Laurent men's ready-to-wear.

March 7, 2005: Stefano Pilati's second show for Yves Saint Laurent women's ready-to-wear. "Inspired by Philippe de Champaigne and the Calvinist paintings of the seventeenth century, Pilati combines elements of ecclesiastical garments with loose shapes.... A unique voice for Yves Saint Laurent." (*Le Figaro*, March 8, 2005)

April 2005: Launch of the fragrance Opium Fleur de Shanghaï.

May 2005: Launch of the fragrance Paris Roses Enchantées.

July 5, 2005: Stefano Pilati's second show for Yves Saint Laurent men's ready-to-wear.

September 2005: PPR and Yves Saint Laurent sponsor the Dada exhibition at the Pompidou Centre.

October 10, 2005: Stefano Pilati's third show for Yves Saint Laurent women's ready-to-wear, on the theme of the Spanish Imagination. *Vogue* calls the collection "superb, at the boundaries of couture."

January 29, 2006: Stefano Pilati's third show for Yves Saint Laurent men's ready-to-wear.

February 25 and 27, 2006: For the fortieth anniversary of YSL, an auction is held at Drouot-Richelieu by the auction house Cornette de Saint Cyr and the experts Dominique Chombert and Françoise Sternbach. Over 400 lots of clothing, jewelry, and accessories are sold with a selection of pieces from the 1970s and 1980s. The sale is originally intended to last one day, but is extended over two days due to the increasing number of lots put up for sale. The highlight is a necklace with balls made of lace. Estimated at 300 euros, it fetches 4,000 euros.

March 2006: At the Pompidou Centre, there is a Shocking Pink background for the Yves Saint Laurent winter 2006 womenswear show: "At Saint Laurent, a Blueprint for the Future." (*New York Times*, March 4, 2006)

July 2006: Event organized by the Yves Saint Laurent company at London's Serpentine Gallery.

July 2, 2006: Stefano Pilati's menswear show for Yves Saint Laurent.

August 1, 2006: Yves Saint Laurent turns seventy.

October 2006: Stefano Pilati's womenswear show for Yves Saint Laurent. The show takes place at the Grand Palais with the runway transformed into a field of violets, "the symbol of femininity, virginity, and humility." Four themes: urban power, peaceful woman warrior, monochromatic cocktail, and flower woman.

Launch of the Yves Saint Laurent fragrance L'HOMME. The actor Olivier Martinez is chosen as the model for the campaign.

Launch of the Yves Saint Laurent fragrance Young Sexy Lovely.

Introduced at the cruise collection show the prior year, the Muse bag is a new Yves Saint Laurent icon, the prelude to a whole series of cult accessories, from Tribute sandals to Downtown bags and the Saddlebag. "Yves Saint Laurent had made it the only bag 'one' of his women would ever carry."

2007: Launch of the Yves Saint Laurent fragrance Elle, "a floral harmony with wood notes in perpetual movement." Coco Rocha is the face of the fragrance, in a film made by Michael Haussman at the Institut du Monde Arabe. The photographer is Mark Segal. Launched with a lot of buzz involving the Internet game Second Life, the campaign initially hides Coco Rocha's identity, showing just her back.

March 2007: Stefano Pilati's womenswear show for Yves Saint Laurent. "This collection is a break. A break in 'blacks,' with the color in the plural." "YSL's Big Black Magic" is the headline of the *International Herald Tribune*. For Suzy Menkes, the "contrast with the tortured early collections is clear."

May 2007: The Yves Saint Laurent company sponsors the premiere of *Paris, Je t'Aime* at the Paris Theater in New York.

July 10, 2007: Val Garland becomes the new artistic advisor for Yves Saint Laurent cosmetics.

September 2007: Stefano Pilati's womenswear show for Yves Saint Laurent, "a treatise of post-minimal elegance that is gentle and discreet." The brand's logo, designed by Cassandre in 1963, appears on jacquard jackets, blending almost invisibly into the texture of the clothing. Elsewhere it is used as part of an abstract pattern.

December 6, 2007: French president Nicolas Sarkozy awards Yves Saint Laurent the title of Grand Officier de la Légion d'Honneur. The ceremony takes place with a few close friends at the couturier's house.

January 2008: L'Oréal offers 1.15 billion euros to PPR to buy YSL Beauté. YSL Beauté had revenue of approximately 630 million euros in 2006, with the brands Yves Saint Laurent, Roger & Gallet, Boucheron, Stella McCartney, Oscar de la Renta, and Ermenegildo Zegna.

According to Jean-Paul Agon, CEO of L'Oréal, "This planned agreement is a wonderful opportunity for L'Oréal and its luxury products division. Yves Saint Laurent is a mythic French luxury brand, it has great international presence, and it complements our brands very well. We are convinced that its integration into our luxury products division will accelerate its development. This strategic agreement will strengthen our position on the luxury cosmetics markets." François-Henri Pinault, CEO of PPR, states, "Through this strategic planned agreement with the number one international cosmetics company, Gucci Group chooses to give YSL Beauté the means to fully achieve its growth potential and allows the YSL brand to benefit, in the cosmetics field, from an ambitious plan to match its worldwide presence. In this way, Yves Saint Laurent would strengthen its position as a great luxury brand."

Kate Moss, the superstar model with an estimated net worth of sixty million euros, is the new face of Yves Saint Laurent for the spring/summer 2008 ready-to-wear collection. The campaign by Inez & Vinoodh is photographed at the Fondation Pierre Bergé - Yves Saint Laurent. In the photos, Kate Moss always appears on the other side of glass, as if outside an impenetrable world.

January 16, 2008: Video presentation of Stefano Pilati's fall/winter menswear collection for Yves Saint Laurent. Shown on a triptych of three LCD screens, it features British actor Simon Woods, and is then broadcast worldwide on the Yves Saint Laurent site.

Yves Saint Laurent Beauté celebrates its thirty-year anniversary.

February 4, 2008: The line Elle Plaisirs Cosmopolites. Fragrance, body spray, perfumed deodorant for the body.

February 25, 2008: Reopening of the YSL boutique at Place Saint Sulpice. The store is entirely redecorated by Stefano Pilati with architects Alain Moatti and Henri Rivière. Yves Saint Laurent opened this boutique for the first time in 1979.

February 27, 2008: Stefano Pilati's *Il Manifesto* is distributed on the streets of Paris (especially in front of the Pompidou Centre). Inside this newspaper are photos of the new campaign with Kate Moss.

February 28, 2008: Death of Katoucha Niane, one of Yves Saint Laurent's star models in the 1980s.

February 29, 2008: Stefano Pilati's fall/winter 2008–09 womenswear collection is shown at the Grand Palais. Cathy Horyn writes on the *New York Times* fashion blog that "The Chic Is Real," and the *International Herald Tribune* describes it as "Tough Chic."

March 3, 2008: Relaunch of the fragrance L'Homme in a limited series of 100,000. The design of the bottle by architect Jean Nouvel is in the shape of a sex toy with a little luminous float to indicate the level. It can also be used as a cigar case.

April 1, 2008: Launch of the fragrance Cinéma Scénario d'Été in a limited edition.

Spring 2008: To celebrate the thirty-year anniversary of Yves Saint Laurent Beauté, the company brings out a special-edition sun powder, Soleil d'Afrique, inside a compact that can be worn like tribal jewelry.

June 1, 2008: Yves Saint Laurent dies at home at age seventy-one.

June 5, 2008: His funeral is held at the Church of Saint-Roch in Paris.

June 11, 2008: Yves Saint Laurent's ashes are scattered in the rose garden of Villa Oasis in Marrakech. A stele is erected in his memory in the Majorelle garden.

November 5–7, 2008: A selection of lots from the sale of the Yves Saint Laurent and Pierre Bergé collection is exhibited at Christie's in New York.

January 31–February 3, 2009: A selection of lots from the sale of the Yves Saint Laurent and Pierre Bergé collection is exhibited at Christie's in London.

February 23–25, 2009: Sale of the Collection Yves Saint Laurent and Pierre Bergé. Seven hundred thirty-three masterpieces are on display at the Grand Palais, where more than 30,000 visitors come to admire them in three days, often lining up for four hours. The catalog, consisting of five volumes and weighing 22 pounds, has become a collector's item. The set is sold for 375.3 million euros by Christie's France and Pierre Bergé & Associés, a record for a single collection. From the first evening, record bids are made, notably for James Ensor's *The Despair of Pierrot*, which sells for 4,993,000 euros. *Les Coucous, tapis bleu et rose* by Henri Matisse sells for 35.9 million euros, while *Madame. L.R.*, a sculpture by Constantin Brancusi, sells for 29.18 million euros. Eileen Gray's famous armchair sells for 21.9 million euros, a record for a piece of twentieth-century furniture. Emperor Qialong's rat and rabbit heads, two bronze statuettes, are among the biggest successes of this sale: each one estimated at between 8 million and 10 million euros, these pieces, carved in the eighteenth century to decorate the zodiacal fountain of the Summer Palace of Emperor Qialong, sell for 15.74 million euros each. *L'Oiseau Sénoufo*, the first piece bought by Yves Saint Laurent and Pierre Bergé, is not part of the sale.

March 2009: Launch of La Nuit de L'Homme perfume. Vincent Cassel stars in a film advertisement shot by Gaspard Noé and a photo campaign by Mert & Marcus.

October 27, 2009: Creation of the Pierre Bergé endowment fund for the fight against AIDS.

November 12–16, 2009: Exhibition at Christie's France of a selection of lots from the second sale of the Collection Pierre Bergé–Yves Saint Laurent. The sale is comprised of 1,185 lots coming partly from the Chateau Benerville in Normandy.

November 17–20, 2009: Second sale of the Collection Pierre Bergé - Yves Saint Laurent by Christie's Paris in association with Pierre Bergé & Associés, at the Marigny Theater. A large nineteenth-century Dutch chandelier sells for 37,000 euros. A Napoleon III work table by Alphonse Giroux finds a taker at 49,000 euros (it was appraised at between 2,000 and 3,000 euros). The total proceeds of this second sale reach 89.99 million euros.

March 11–August 22, 2010: Retrospective is held at the Petit Palais, with more than three hundred designs. Two years after the death of the designer, nearly 300,000 visitors are immersed in more than forty years of Yves Saint Laurent's creations, from the Dior years to his last collection in 2002.

June 2010: Pierre Bergé joins forces with Xavier Niel and Matthieu Pigasse to take a majority stake in the group La Vie -Le Monde. On December 15, 2010, he becomes Chairman of the Supervisory Board of Monde SA and SEM (Société Éditrice du Monde).

June 29, 2010: The death of Lucienne-Andrée Mathieu Saint Laurent at the age of ninety-six in Neuilly-sur-Seine.

March 5, 2011: Opening of the *Saint Laurent Rive Gauche* exhibition, at the Fondation Pierre Bergé - Yves Saint Laurent. Nearly seventy designs are presented in a scene inspired by the decor of the first Rive Gauche boutique on Rue Tournon.

April 2011: Christian Louboutin files a complaint with the Manhattan Federal Court against Yves Saint Laurent, accusing the brand of "trademark infringement" and "unfair competition" for designing the Tribtoo shoes with red soles.

August 6, 2011: The death of Hélène Rochas at the age of eighty-four in Paris. She was the one who introduced Pierre Dinand, the creator of many bottles of perfumes (including Yves Saint Laurent Rive Gauche and Opium) to Yves Saint Laurent, in 1961.

November 5, 2011: The death of Loulou de la Falaise at the age of sixty-three, in her home in Oise. A memorial service is held at the Church of Saint-Roch in Paris.

December 3, 2011: Opening of the Berber Museum in place of the Museum of Islamic Art, in the old painting workshop of Jacques Majorelle, in Marrakesh, with more than six hundred works collected by Pierre Bergé and Yves Saint Laurent.

March 2012: Hedi Slimane, forty-three, is appointed artistic director of Yves Saint Laurent, in charge of women's and men's collections. He does not design collections from Paris but from his studio in Los Angeles.

June 2012: Hedi Slimane chooses to rename the brand "Saint Laurent Paris," a decision supported by Pierre Bergé himself. The perfumes preserve the logo created by Cassandre in 1961.

July 21, 2012: The brand reveals its new logo on its Facebook page. In the photograph, a black case, resting on a piece of marble, bears the words "Saint Laurent" in Helvetica typeface.

August 22, 2012: Twenty years after the creation of Touche Éclat by Terry de Gunzburg, the launch of Teint Touche Éclat, inspired by the illuminating pen and offered in twenty-two shades.

September 10, 2012: Release of Manifesto perfume. The bottle, reminiscent of a woman's silhouette with an amethyst belt at its center, is created by Yves Saint-Laurent couture studios. The TV spot stars Jessica Chastain, and was directed by Nicolas Winding Refn.

October 1, 2012: Hedi Slimane presents his first collection for Saint Laurent, at the Grand Palais. Among the four hundred guests are Jessica Chastain, Valerie Trierweiller, Kate Moss, Salma Hayek, and Marc Jacobs. The show is dedicated to Pierre Bergé.

October 16, 2012: The PPR Group, which owns the Saint Laurent brand, announces in a statement that it wants to put an end to the proceedings that pit it against shoe designer Christian Louboutin. An American appeals court recognized that red soles could be a registered trademark unless the rest of the shoe was the same color.

March 2013: The PPR group changes its name to Kering.

July 2013: Francesca Bellettini (formerly of Gucci and Bottega Veneta) is appointed general manager of Saint Laurent, instead of Paul Deneuve.

October 2013: In an article in *WWD*, the Parisian concept store Colette reveals that it has received a cease-and-desist letter from Saint Laurent, for selling a parody t-shirt by the American brand What About Yves with the saying "Ain't Laurent Without Yves." Believing the product to be detrimental to the brand, Kering's management filed suit against What About Yves (eventually settling out of court) and withdrew the entire Saint Laurent collection from Colette for carrying the t-shirt.

October 14, 2013: Auction of Yves Saint Laurent's model and muse Danielle Luquet de Saint Germain's private haute couture and ready-to-wear collection. Among the three hundred lots, an Yves Saint Laurent gown in transparent black chiffon decorated with ostrich feathers, created in 1968, and estimated between 13,000 and 15,000 euros, is sold for 118,750 euros (including fees).

January 8, 2014: The biopic *Yves Saint Laurent* by Jalil Lespert, adapted from the biography by Laurence Benaïm, is released, starring Pierre Niney as Yves Saint Laurent (winner of the César Award for Best Actor in 2015), Guillaume Gallienne as Pierre Bergé, Charlotte Le Bon as Victoire Doutreleau, and Laura Smet as Loulou de la Falaise.

April 8, 2014: Olivier Chatenet exhibits at the Convention Center in Dinan, for one month, forty silhouettes selected from his personal collection of Yves Saint Laurent Rive Gauche archival drawings from 1969 and 1978.

August 26, 2014: Release of Fusion Ink Foundation, offered in sixteen shades, and Black Opium perfume, a sensual, rock-and-roll version of the original Opium fragrance, launched in 1977.

September 24, 2014: Release of Bertrand Bonello's feature film *Saint Laurent*, with Gaspard Ulliel as Yves Saint Laurent, Jérémie Régnier as Pierre Bergé, Léa Seydoux as Loulou de la Falaise, Louis Garrel as Jacques de Bascher, Aymeline Valade as Betty Catroux, and Helmut Berger as Yves Saint Laurent in 1989. The film, which did not receive the endorsement of Pierre Bergé, wins the César Award for Best Costumes (designed by Anaïs Romand).

2015: Construction begins on the Yves Saint Laurent Marrakesh museum, for a projected cost of 15 million euros, by the French studio Studio KO, founded by Olivier Marty and Karl Fournier. Composed of terracotta, concrete, earth-stained terrazzo, and stone fragments from Morocco, the building is intended to fit harmoniously into its environment. The bricks made of Moroccan soil are manufactured by a local supplier. "Yves Saint Laurent and I discovered Marrakesh in 1966, and have never left. This city had an influence on Saint Laurent and his work, and allowed him to discover color. The Studio KO architects share this passion. Their admiration for the region and its culture as well as their intellectual and artistic rigor make them the ideal architects for this museum," said Pierre Bergé in an official statement.

March 19, 2015: The exhibition *Yves Saint Laurent, la collection du scandale* opens at the Fondation Pierre Bergé - Yves Saint Laurent, about the collection from January 29, 1971. Called "Forty," it was violently criticized by the press at the time, and marked a break in the fashion designer's career.

July 28, 2015: The house returns to couture, under the artistic direction of Hedi Slimane. The ateliers (Flou and Tailleur) are located in the Hôtel de Sénecterre, a recently renovated seventeenth-century town house at 24 Rue de l'Université in the seventh arrondissement. Special orders are created for clients in music and cinema, and marked with a label "Yves Saint Laurent."

October 2015: Launch of the "Vestiaire des Parfums." Tuxedo, Caban, Saharienne, Trench, and Caftan, five historically emblematic Yves Saint Laurent pieces, become the key fragrances of a new perfume collection under Yves Saint Laurent Beauté.

December 11, 2015: Opening of the sale of Pierre Bergé's personal library, made up of some 1,600 works, books, and manuscripts. Among these jewels of literature, the manuscript of Flaubert's *Sentimental Education* (470,000 euros), Louise Labé's works (430,000 euros), and a drawing by Victor Hugo (400,000 euros) were the most successful. In total, the sale, organized at Drouot by Pierre Bergé & Associés in collaboration with Sotheby's, yielded more than 11.68 million euros, more than the high estimate. Among the surprises of the sale, the original edition of *Les Fleurs du Mal* by Baudelaire, estimated between 40,000 and 60,000 euros, sold for 225,000 euros.

February 1, 2016: Release of Black Opium Nuit Blanche, designed by four master perfumers, Nathalie Lorson, Marie Salamagne, Honorine Blanc, and Olivier Cresp.

February 10, 2016: Hedi Slimane presents his fall 2016 (men's) and pre-fall 2016 (women's) collections at the legendary Los Angeles Concert Hall, attended by Lady Gaga, Jane Fonda, Sylvester Stallone, Lenny Kravitz, Demi Moore, and Justin Bieber, who arrived on his skateboard.

March 7, 2016: Hedi Slimane presents the Saint Laurent fall/winter 2016–17 show, which celebrates fifty years of ready-to-wear Rive Gauche, in the new couture salons of the house. Pierre Bergé makes his announcement at the microphone the beginning of the show. The forty-two designs of this "Collection de Paris" are honored by Bénédicte de Ginestous, who had done so at Yves Saint Laurent fashion shows between 1977 and 2002. "Fashion is a punctuation of the time, a way to document it. . . . Everything is intuitive, I do not want to dissect, to break down. Saint Laurent is first and foremost an energy," writes Hedi Slimane in the press kit.

April 1, 2016: Hedi Slimane leaves his position as artistic director of Saint Laurent. In four years, the brand has tripled its sales.

April 5, 2016: Anthony Vaccarello, thirty-six, is appointed artistic director. Winner of the Hyères Festival (2006) and Andam Grand Prix de mode (2011), he created his brand in 2009, before joining Fendi alongside Karl Lagerfeld, and Versace in 2015. The brand removes all the photos from its Instagram account except for one, Anthony Vaccarello's portrait in black and white.

May 2016: Launch of Vinyl Couture Mascara in Los Angeles, with Yves Saint Laurent Beauté's new face, Zoë Kravitz.

June 2016: Launch of the perfume Mon Paris, in tribute to Yves Saint Laurent's attachment to the City of Light. The fragrance combines the sensuality of white musk, the hypnotic harmony of the datura flower, and the intensity of patchouli, in a bottle surrounded by a black lavallière.

August 25, 2016: Launch of Y, a new men's fragrance, featuring three men with very different profiles: rapper Loyle Carner, artificial intelligence researcher Alexandre Robicquet, and artist-sculptor David Alexander Flinn.

September 27, 2016: Anthony Vaccarello's first show for Saint Laurent (spring/summer 2018 collection), the first day of Paris Fashion Week. The event is held in Rue de Bellechasse in Paris, in the old Cistercian abbey of Penthemont which is undergoing restoration to become the future headquarters and showrooms of Saint Laurent.

November 8-9, 2016: Second sale of Pierre Bergé's personal library, under the hammer of Pierre Bergé & Associés in collaboration with Sotheby's, for a total auction amount of more than four million euros. Two manuscripts won the highest bids: *The Wedding of Herodias* by Stéphane Mallarmé (587,720 euros) and *Over Strand and Field* by Gustave Flaubert (537,880 euros).

December 22, 2016: Pierre Bergé is decorated, by King Mohammed VI of Morocco, with the Grand Cordon Wissam Alaouite, a Moroccan honorary order created in 1913, distinguishing foreign personalities who have rendered outstanding services to the Kingdom.

January 26, 2017: Makeup artist Tom Pecheux is named international beauty director Yves Saint Laurent Beauté.

February 2017: Aurélie Samuel becomes Director of Collections of the Fondation Pierre Bergé Yves Saint Laurent Museum (with 5,000 pieces of haute couture clothing and 15,000 accessories), with a view to the inauguration of the Yves Saint Laurent Museum in autumn 2017, the first dedicated to a designer in his home of origin.

March 10, 2017: Two posters of the Saint Laurent campaign, visible in Paris, are considered "degrading" and withdrawn at the request of Laurence Rossignol, Minister of Women's Rights.

March 31, 2017: Pierre Bergé marries Madison Cox, vice-president of the Pierre Bergé - Yves Saint Laurent Foundation. Born September 23, 1958, in San Francisco, the landscape gardener, historian of the art of gardens, and expert in botany oversaw the restoration of the Majorelle Garden of Marrakesh, which earned him the praise of Claude Lalanne.

June 8, 2017: Pierre Bergé's last public appearance at the Cité de la Mode, on the occasion of the press conference organized to announce the opening of the two Yves Saint Laurent museums in Paris and Marrakesh: "We must transform the memories into projects."

July 5, 2017: Opening of the exhibition *Christian Dior, Designer of Dreams*, designed by Olivier Gabet and Florence Müller at the Musée des Arts Décoratifs in Paris. For six months, more than 700,000 visitors admired the room dedicated to the creations of Yves Saint Laurent, the very first successor of Dior.

September 8, 2017: Pierre Bergé dies at Saint-Rémy-de-Provence, at the age of eighty-six. He outlived Yves Saint Laurent by nine years, just missing the opening of the two museums in Paris and Marrakesh. Madison Cox, his husband, becomes president of the Fondation Pierre Bergé - Yves Saint Laurent.

September 12, 2017: Funeral of Pierre Bergé. His ashes are scattered with those of Yves Saint Laurent in their garden of Marrakesh. At the heart of the garden, the stele "Yves Saint Laurent couturier Français" is modified to read "Yves Saint Laurent and Pierre Bergé."

September 28, 2017: Anthony Vaccarello presents the Saint Laurent spring/summer 2018 collection at the Trocadéro fountain. In the background, the Eiffel Tower flickers exceptionally throughout the show. In attendance are Catherine Deneuve, Kate Moss, Lenny Kravitz, Charlotte Gainsbourg, and Courtney Love. "My Saint Laurent is that of the night," says Anthony Vaccarello in *Le Figaro*, October 2017.

October 3, 2017: Inauguration of the Yves Saint Laurent Museum, in the former fashion house at 5 Avenue Marceau. In its 450 square meters, designed by Nathalie Crinière and Jacques Grange, it reveals the salons formerly open to customers, Yves Saint Laurent's studio, and around fifty designs, sketches, photographs, and videos. Since its opening, an average of 700 people visit the museum every day.

October 14, 2017: Inauguration of the Museum Yves Saint Laurent Marrakesh (mYSLm), near the Majorelle Garden, in a building of four thousand square meters designed by the studio KO, including a permanent exhibition space of 400 square meters, a hall for temporary exhibitions, a library of more than 5,000 books, an auditorium, a bookstore with décor inspired by the first ready-to-wear boutique opened in 1966, and a café. Bjorn Dahlstrom is in charge. The permanent exhibition room presents a "corridor of time" with high-fashion collection boards, and fifty designs chosen by Laurence Benaïm and Dominique Deroche, scientific advisors, articulated around themes dear to Yves Saint Laurent (such as extraordinary gardens, art in life, black, and imaginary journeys). Seven hundred square meters are dedicated to the actual conservation of the collections: the Fondation Pierre Bergé - Yves Saint Laurent lent 1,000 objects, housed under optimal conditions of conservation. Every year a gallery dedicates a photographer to the world of Yves Saint Laurent; the inaugural exhibition presents the work of André Rau. Princess Lalla Salma of Morocco, wife of King Mohammed VI, cuts the ribbon, dressed in Yves Saint Laurent Rive Gauche from spring/summer 1983 (Olivier Chatenet collection). Also present are Catherine Deneuve, Marisa Berenson, Jack Lang, and Betty Catroux.

October 19, 2017: Opening of the Yves Saint Laurent Museum Marrakesh.

November 2017: Launch of three new couture fragrances, olfactory transcriptions of addresses related to the house: 24 Rue de l'Université refers to the mansion where the workshops are, 37 Rue de Bellechasse evokes the new headquarters, and 6 Place Saint-Sulpice one of the older shops.

November 21–22, 2017: Sale of the Jacques Grange collection at Sotheby's, in Paris, for a total result of 28.4 million euros. Two woolen sheep by François-Xavier Lalanne (1969), having belonged to Yves Saint Laurent, are sold for 1,569,000 euros.

December 20, 2017: Colette, in Paris, permanently closes its doors. The space is taken over by Saint Laurent; the company planned to install a shop there. During the month before closing, the brand invests the first floor of the store with collector's items: t-shirts and hoodies, a vintage Polaroid SX-70, makeup palettes, lighters, a vinyl compilation, a Baccarat crystal heart, ruby helmets and an all-black signed Saint Laurent Vespa.

January 2018: Opening for four days of the YSL Beauty Hotel in Paris, the first "pop-up" hotel entirely dedicated to beauty, where each suite offers an exclusive experience: Powder Room, YSL Beauty Bar, photo shoots, and master classes.
   La Blouse joins the Vestiaire des Parfums, launched by Yves Saint Laurent Beauté in October 2015.

January 11, 2018: The Yves Saint Laurent Museum in Marrakesh wins the Best New Public Building prize, awarded by the English magazine *Wallpaper*.

October 2018–January 2019: First thematic temporary exhibition organized at the Yves Saint Laurent Museum in Paris, dedicated to "Yves Saint Laurent's Imaginary Asia."

NOTES

PREFACE

1 Théophile Gautier, *Mademoiselle de Maupin* , trans. B. Rascoe (New York: Alfred A. Knopf, 1920).

2 Susan Sontag, "Notes on 'Camp.'" In *A Susan Sontag Reader* (New York: Farrar, Straus & Giroux, 1982), p. 115.

CHAPTER 1 / BITTERSWEET ORAN

1 *Le Monde*, "Portrait de l'Artiste," December 8, 1983.

2 *Vogue Paris,* 1950.

3 Albert Camus, "The Minotaur" in *The Myth of Sisyphus and Other Essays*, trans. Justin O'Brien (New York: Knopf Doubleday, 2012).

4 Ibid.

5 At that age, Yves had already removed the hyphens from his name. He would do so definitively in 1958 when he became Yves Saint Laurent, after the media mistook Mathieu for a middle name and omitted it.

6 Franz-Olivier Giesbert and Janie Samet, "Yves Saint Laurent: 'Je Suis Né Avec Une Dépression Nerveuse.'" *Le Figaro* July 11, 1991.

7 Gustave Flaubert, *Madame Bovary*, trans. W. Blades (New York: P.F. Collier and Son, 1902).

8 Gérard-Louis Soyer, *Jean-Gabriel Domergue: L'Art et la Mode* (Paris: Ed. Sous le Vent/ Vilo, 1984).

9 Ibid.

CHAPTER 2 / A PARISIAN EDUCATION

1 Honoré de Balzac, *Lost Illusions (1837–1843)*.

2 Violette Leduc, *Vogue Paris*, 1953

3 Jean Cocteau, *Le Passé défini* (Paris: Gallimard, 2011).

4 Christian Dior, *Dior et Moi* (Paris: Amiot-Dumont, 1956).

5 These statistics can be found here: http://fresques.ina.fr/jalons/fiche-media /InaEdu01235/la-retransmission-televisee-aux-parisiens-du-couronnement-d-elizabeth-ii-muet.html

6 Edmonde Charles-Roux, *Le Figaro Littéraire*, February 12, 1968.

7 Dior, *Dior et Moi.*

8 Yvonne Deslandres, *Poiret* (Paris: Editions du Regard, 1986).

9 Maurice Sachs, *Au Temps du Boeuf sur le Toit* (Paris: Grasset, 2005).

10 William Parker, *Dessins de Mode: Vogue* (Paris: Thames & Hudson, 2010), 109.

11 *Vogue Paris,* 1950s.

12 Dior, *Dior et Moi.*

13 "The Strong Ones," *The New Yorker,* September 28, 1957.

14 Ibid.

15   Dior, *Dior et Moi.*
16   Jean Giradoux, *Pour Lucrèce* (*Duel of Angels*, trans. by C. Fry)
17   Janie Samet, *L'Echo d'Oran*, January 7, 1955.
18   Ibid.
19   Archives Fondation Pierre Bergé Yves Saint Laurent
20   Dior, *Dior et moi.*
21   Ibid.
22   Ibid.
23   Ibid.
24   This image set an auction record for an Avedon photo when it was sold by Christie's Paris in November 2010 to Maison Christian Dior for 1.2 million dollars. It was a seven-foot-high print, the largest of the image, that was made in 1978 for Avedon's retrospective at the Metropolitan Museum of Art.
25   Dior, *Dior et Moi.*
26   Ibid.
27   Ibid.
28   Dior, *Dior et Moi.*
29   Ibid.
30   Ibid
31   Ibid.
32   Matthieu Galey, *Journal 1953-1973* (Paris: Grasset, 1987).
33   *Elle*, August 27, 1956.
34   Gustave Flaubert, *Madame Bovary.*
35   Sachs, *Au Temps du Bœuf sur le Toit.*
36   Dior, *Dior et Moi.*
37   Sachs, *Au Temps du Bœuf sur le Toit.*
38   Dior, *Dior et Moi.*

CHAPTER 3 / A YOUNG KING AT DIOR

1   Dior, *Dior et Moi.*
2   *Hommage à Christian Dior, 1947-1957* in *Yves Saint Laurent, 28 Années de Creation.* (Musée des Arts de la Mode, Paris, 1986).
3   *L'Express*, December 19, 1957.
4   François Mauriac in *L'Express*, 1957.
5   The March 1958 issue of *Vogue Paris* published large excerpts of this essay.
6   Dior, *Dior et Moi.*
7   Galey, *Journal,* September 22, 1957 entry.
8   Ibid.
9   Galey, *Journal*, March 30,1959 entry.
10   "La Ligne Saint Laurent Vue par Bernard Buffet," *L'Express*, February 6, 1958.
11   *Vogue Paris*, February 1958.
12   Kathleen Winsor, *Forever Amber* (New York: Macmillan Publishers, 1944).
13   Dior, *Dior et Moi.*
14   Galey, *Journal*, n.d.
15   "La Ligne Saint Laurent Vue par Bernard Buffet," *L'Express*, February 6, 1958.
16   "Yves Saint Laurent, le nouvel enfant triste," *L'Express*, February 6, 1958.
17   Fondation Pierre Bergé - Yves Saint Laurent archives.

CHAPTER 4 / THE DRAFT, THE PRINCESS, AND THE ALGERIAN WAR

1   Dior, *Dior et Moi.*
2   Marie-France Pochna, *Bonjour Monsieur Boussac* (Paris: Laffont, 1980).
3   Hélène Cingria, "De Carpaccio à Ingres, le Panorama de la Mode d'Automne." *Les Lettres Françaises*, July 7, 1958.
4   Hélène Cingria, *Les Lettres Françaises*, February 11, 1959.
5   *L'Express*, March 3, 1960.
6   *L'Express*, August 6, 1959.
7   M. A. Souza, "La Silhouette de Demain," *Le Figaro*, January 28, 1960.
8   Lucien François, "Le Style Libre de la Mode," *Combat*, January 29, 1960.
9   *L'Express*, March 3, 1960.
10 *L'Aurore*, November 20, 1959.
11 Hélène Lazareff, *Elle*, February 12, 1960.
12 *L'Aurore*, November 20, 1959.
13 Program for spring/summer 1959 collection.
14 Pierre Galante, *Les années Chanel* (Paris: Editions Mercure de France, 1972), 234.
15 *Le Figaro*, July 27, 1960.
16 Lucien François in *Combat*, July 1960.

CHAPTER 5 / A MAN DISAPPEARS

1   Galey, *Journal* August 30, 1959 entry.
2   "Catherine Deneuve Pose Pour Fêter ses 30 Ans de Chefs-d'oeuvre. Victoire, son Egérie, Raconte les Terribles Débuts qui ont Précédé la Gloire," *Paris Match*, February 6, 1992.
3   Ibid.
4   "Le Retour d'Yves Saint Laurent," *Paris-Presse l'Intransigeant,* April 18, 1961.
5   Dior, *Dior et Moi.*
6   Pochna, *Bonjour Monsieur Boussac.*
7   Ibid.
8   Ibid.
9   Ibid.
10 Honoré de Balzac, *Splendeurs et misères des courtisanes*, 1838–1847.
11 Pochna, *Bonjour Monsieur Boussac.*
12 "Catherine Deneuve," *Paris Match.*
13 *Le Journal d'Alger*, November 27, 1961.
14 Franz-Olivier Giesbert and Janie Samet, "Yves Saint Laurent: 'Je Suis Né Avec une Dépression Nerveuse,'" *Le Figaro*, July 11, 1991.
15 Fondation Pierre Bergé - Yves Saint Laurent archives.
16 Jean Freustié, "Le Show de Zizi," *France Observateur*, December 21, 1961.
17 Galey, *Journal*, January 27, 1962 entry.
18 Albert Camus, *L'Exil et le Royaume* (Paris: Gallimard, 1957).
19 "Catherine Deneuve," *Paris Match.*

CHAPTER 6 / THE CHILD WITH NERVES OF STEEL

1   *Paris-Presse*, January 31, 1962.
2   *Women's Wear Europe*, January 1992.

3   *Elle*, March 1962.
4   Dino Buzzati, "Le Solo de Saint Laurent," *Corriere della Sera*, January 30, 1962.
5   Lucien François, *Combat*, February 23, 1962.
6   Lucien François, *Comment un Nom Devient une Griffe* (Paris: Gallimard, 1962).
7   *Bravo Yves* (Paris: Maison Yves Saint Laurent, 1982).
8   Nadine Liber, "The Comeback of Yves Saint Laurent," *Life,* April 9, 1962.
9   *Vogue*, March 1962.
10   Hélène Cingria, "Architecte de la Mode," *Les Lettres Françaises*, February 14, 1962.
11   *Bravo Yves.*
12   Buzzati, "Le Solo."
13   Dior, *Dior et Moi.*
14   *Elle,* January 12, 1962.
15   Yukio Mishima, *L'Ecole de la Chair* (Paris: Gallimard, 1963).
16   Michel Winock, *Chronique des Années Soixante* (Paris: Le Seuil 1990).
17   *Vogue Paris*, November 1963.
18   Fondation Pierre Bergé - Yves Saint Laurent archives.
19   Paul Morand, *L'Allure de Chanel* (Paris: Hermann, 1976).
20   François, "Le Poète de la mode," *Combat*, July 31, 1962.

CHAPTER 7 / THE BEATLE ON RUE SPONTINI

1   Patrick Thévenon, "Le Couturier Qui a Pensé aux Femmes d'Aujourd'hui," *Candide*, August 9, 1965.
2   Ibid.
3   Piet Mondrian and Theo Van Doesburg, *De Stijl*, 1918.
4   Thévenon, "Le Couturier."
5   *Le Figaro*, January 26, 1966.
6   Thévenon, "Le Couturier."
7   *Vogue*, 1960
8   Ibid.
9   A makeup line by Charles of the Ritz. Its slogan was "baby-face make-up for grown-up girls."
10   A reference to Givenchy's clothes being expensive.

CHAPTER 8 / THE RIVE GAUCHE SPIRIT, FROM *BELLE DE JOUR* TO ANDROGYNY

1   *Belle de Jour* screenplay.
2   Marcel Proust, *On Reading Ruskin* (New Haven: Yale University Press, 1989).
3   Marcel Proust, *The Prisoner*, in *Remembrance of Things Past*.
4   Fondation Pierre Bergé - Yves Saint Laurent archives, 1967 notes.
5   Claude Berthod, "Saint Laurent Coupez Pour Nous!" *Elle*, March 7, 1968.
6   *Dim Dam Dom*, March 10, 1968.
7   "Fashion should be a game": http://www.azquotes.com/author/11962-Mary_Quant.
8   *Dim Dam Dom.*
9   Ibid.
10   Berthod, "Saint Laurent Coupez Pour Nous!"
11   Galey, *Journal*, October 21, 1967 entry.

12   *Elle*, August 26, 1968.
13   Berthod, "Saint Laurent Coupez Pour Nous!"
14   Ibid.
15   Ibid.
16   *Elle*, March 5, 1969.

CHAPTER 9 / YVES, LOULOU, AND THE SERPENTS
1   *Exposition Bakst des Ballets Russes à la Haute Couture*, Opéra de Paris, 2016.
2   Fondation Pierre Bergé-Yves Saint Laurent archives.
3   Theophile Gautier, *Mademoiselle de Maupin*, trans. B. Rascoe (New York: Alfred A. Knopf, 1920).
4   *Vogue*, 1970.
5   The Doors promotional materials.
6   "La Féminité est dans la Femme, Pas dans ce qu'elle Porte," *L'Express*, August 3, 1970.
7   Galante, *Les années Chanel*, 234.
8   *Paris Match,* 1970.
9   "La Féminité," *L'Express*, 1970.
10   Fondation Pierre Bergé - Yves Saint Laurent archives.
11   Marcel Proust, *The Fugitive*, in *Remembrance of Things Past*.

CHAPTER 10 / THE RETRO BOMBSHELL
1   Claude Berthod, "La Libération de la Femme Selon Saint Laurent," *Elle*, February 15, 1971.
2   Balzac, *Lost Illusions.*
3   Pierre-Yves Guillen, "Saint Laurent: L'Apprenti Sorcier," *Combat*, February 1, 1971.
4   Nathalie Mont-Servan, "Yves Saint Laurent Vient d'Annoncer qu'il Renonçait à la Haute Couture pour le Prêt-à-Porter," *Le Monde*, February 1971.
5   *Time*, February 19, 1971.
6   "I Want to Free Women from the Tyranny of Hemlines," *Vanity Fair*, February 1971.
7   Dior, *Dior et Moi.*
8   Berthod, "La Libération de la Femme Selon Saint Laurent," *Elle.*
9   Ibid.
10   Dior, *Dior et Moi.*
11   Berthod,"La Libération de la Femme Selon Saint Laurent," *Elle.*
12   Ibid.
13   From the preface of 1867 exposition catalogue.
14   "Cette Fois, les Hommes Seront Contents," *Paris Match*, February 6, 1971.
15   Susan Sontag, *Against Interpretation* (New York: Doubleday/Anchor 1990).
16   Ibid.
17   *Exposition Bakst*, 2016.
18   Edmonde Charles-Roux, "Le Music-hall, Aujourd'hui," *Les Lettres Françaises*, March 8, 1972.
19   Louis Aragon, *Les Lettres Françaises*, March 1972.
20   Ibid.
21   Philippe Bouvard, *Le Figaro*, January 12–30, 1972.
22   *Le Figaro*, January 30, 1972.

CHAPTER 11 / A PASSION FOR THE THIRTIES

1   Dior, *Dior et Moi*.
2   Ibid.
3   "Les Modes Passent. Le Style est Eternel…Dior m'a Appris mon Métier, Grâce à Chanel, j'ai Trouvé mon Style," *Vogue Paris*, March 1973.
4   Ibid.
5   Ibid.
6   Fondation Pierre Bergé - Yves Saint Laurent archives.
7   Joan Buck, "Rue de Babylone," *Vogue Décoration*, June 1986.
8   Danièle Heymann and Jean-Claude Loiseau, "La France Découvre la Mode Rétro," *L'Express*, March 4, 1974.
9   Translator's Note: Yves would pin a heart to his favorite design for every season's fashion show, and presumably his favorite model would get to wear that piece.
10 Michel Foucault, "Anti-Rétro," *Les Cahiers du Cinéma*, July–August 1974.
11 Peter Handke, *The Ride Across Lake Constance* (New York: Farrar, Straus, and Giroux, 1976).
12 Maria Riva, *Marlene Dietrich* (Paris: Flammarion, 1993).
13 Ibid.
14 Ibid.
15 Ibid.
16 *Le Monde*, 1974.
17 *Elle*, March 25, 1974.

CHAPTER 12 / THE MOVE TO FABULOUS AVENUE MARCEAU

1   Pauline Newman-Gordon, *Dictionary of Ideas in Marcel Proust* (Berlin: De Gruyter, 1968).
2   "Saint Laurent, the Romance That Shook the World," *Vogue*, October 1976.

CHAPTER 13 / BLACK IS A COLOR

1   Ernest Renan, *The Life of Jesus*. Dedication. Marcel Proust, *Les Plaisirs et les Jours* (Paris: Gallimard, 1993).
2   Charles Baudelaire, *Les Fleurs du mal*, 1857.
3   Baudelaire, "L'Exposition Universelle," in *Oeuvres Complètes*, II (Paris: Gallimard, 1975)
4   Yves Saint Laurent preface to Palmer White, *Elsa Schiaparelli: Empress of Paris Fashion* (London: Aurum Press, 1986).
5   Yvonne Baby, "Portrait de l'Artiste," *Le Monde*, December 8, 1983.
6   "The New New Look," *Time*, August 9, 1976.
7   François, *Comment un Nom Devient une Griffe*.

CHAPTER 14 / THE OPIUM YEARS

1   Yves Mathieu-Saint-Laurent, *Parlez-Moi d'Amour*, 1950.
2   Fondation Pierre Bergé - Yves Saint Laurent archives.
3   Barbara Schwarm and Martine Leventer, *Le Point,* July 31, 1977.
4   Ibid.
5   Ibid.

6   *Cinq Colonnes à la Une*, February 6, 1959.

7   Schwarm and Leventer.

8   Ibid.

9   "Comme un Débutant," in *Bravo Yves*.

10   Anthony Burgess, "All About Yves," *New York Times Magazine*, September 11, 1977.

11   Louis Jouvet, *Écoute mon ami* (Paris: Flammarion, 2001).

12   John Heilpern, "Saint Laurent Lives," *Observer Magazine,* June 5, 1977.

13   Jean-Pierre de Lucovich, "Yves Saint Laurent," *Saga*, February 1978.

14   *The Andy Warhol Diaries*, ed. Pat Hackett (New York: Twelve [reprint], 2014).

15   Ibid.

16   *Yves Saint Laurent* (London: Thames and Hudson, 1983).

17   Fondation Pierre Bergé - Yves Saint Laurent archives, press dossier.

18   Guillemette de Sairigné, "Style: Drôles de Dames," *Le Point*, March 23, 1987.

19   *The Andy Warhol Diaries*.

20   Fondation Pierre Bergé - Yves Saint Laurent archives, press dossier.

21   Ibid.

22   Alain Pacadis, *Un Jeune Homme Chic* (Paris: Sagittaire, 1978).

23   *The Andy Warhol Diaries*.

24   Robert Hossein, *Elle*, 1977.

25   Jean Cau, *Vogue Homme*, 1977.

26   Fondation Pierre Bergé - Yves Saint Laurent archives.

27   Elsa Schiaparelli, *Shocking Life* (London: Victoria & Albert Museum, 2007).

28   Françoise Giroud, "Les Vingt Ans du Petit Prince," *Vogue Paris,* April 1978.

29   Yves Saint Laurent preface to Jean Cocteau, *L'Aigle à Deux Têtes* (Paris: Gallimard, 1946).

CHAPTER 15 / WORKING IN RED

1   Fondation Pierre Bergé - Yves Saint Laurent archives.

2   "Saint Laurent par Françoise Sagan," *Elle*, March 3, 1980.

3   *Le Monde*, September 18, 1977.

4   *Le Monde*, December 6, 1983.

5   Fondation Pierre Bergé - Yves Saint Laurent archives.

6   Ibid.

7   "Saint Laurent par Françoise Sagan."

8   Dior, *Dior et Moi*.

9   Mounia and Denise Dubois Jallais, *Princesse Mounia* (Paris: Robert Laffont, 1987).

10   "Saint Laurent par Françoise Sagan."

11   Anthony Burgess, "All About Yves," *New York Times Magazine*, September 11, 1977.

12   Fondation Pierre Bergé - Yves Saint Laurent archives.

13   "Catherine Deneuve Passe avec Helmut Newton la Grande Revue des 20 Ans de Saint Laurent," *Paris Match*, December 4, 1981.

14   *Le Monde*, January 1, 1981.

15   "Yves Saint Laurent par François-Marie Banier," *Vogue*, March 1982.

16   *Le Monde*, December 6, 1983.

17   Lucien François, *Comment un Nom Devient une Griffe*.

18   "Hommage à Maria Callas, la Fin d'un Rêve." *Le Monde*, September 18, 1977.

19   *Elle*, March 5, 1980.

20   Martha Duffy, "The King of Fashion," *Time*, December 12, 1983.

21   Marcel Proust, *La Prisonnière*.

22   *Le Monde*, December 6, 1983.

23   Marcel Proust, *A l'Ombre des Jeunes Filles en Fleurs* (Paris, Gallimard, 1919).

24   Ibid.

25   Marcel Proust, *Sodome et Gomorrhe* (Paris, Gallimard, 1922) .

26   Ibid.

27   Michel Cressole, "Yves Saint Laurent, les Divinités Intimes, la Bibliothèque d'Yves Saint Laurent," *Libération*, July 24, 1982.

28   *Le Monde*, December 8, 1983.

29   Ibid.

30   Interview with G.-Y. Dryansky, 1982, Fondation Pierre Bergé - Yves Saint Laurent archives.

31   *Le Monde*, December 8, 1983.

32   Fondation Pierre Bergé - Yves Saint Laurent archives, press kit.

33   Gustave Flaubert, *Madame Bovary*, trans. Lowell Bair (New York: Alfred A. Knopf, 1993).

34   Ibid.

35   Fondation Pierre Bergé - Yves Saint Laurent archives

36   Hervé Guibert, "Yves Saint Laurent au Metropolitan. Aux Couleurs des Saisons, les Toiles Peintes d'un Voyant Charmeur," *Le Monde*, December 8, 1983.

37   André Demaison, Jacques Majorelle and Maroc, "La Renaissance de l'art français et étranger," *Revue L'Art vivant*, November 1930.

38   *Maison et Jardin*, February 1984.

CHAPTER 16 / THE SOLITUDE OF HONORS

1   Mounia, *Princesse Mounia*.

2   *L'Hebdo*, October 26, 1984.

3   Ibid.

4   *Le Monde*, January 1, 1981.

5   Ibid.

6   *Le Monde*, December 27, 1986.

7   François Truffaut, *Hitchcock* (Paris: Ramsay/Poche Cinéma, 1986).

8   Catherine Deneuve, "Je Suis un Homme Scandaleux, Finalement. Saint Laurent le Magnifique," *Globe*, May 1986.

9   Stendhal, *De l'Amour*.

10   Bernard-Henri Lévy in *Yves Saint Laurent par Yves Saint Laurent* (Paris: Herscher, 1986.)

11   François Mitterrand in *Yves Saint Laurent par Yves Saint Laurent*.

12   Bernadine Morris, "French Fashion Saultes Itself with Oscars," *New York Times*, October 25, 1985.

13   Galey, *Journal*.

14   Louis Jouvet, *Découverte de Sabbatini*. 1941.

15   *La Patrie Mondiale*, February 1949.

16   Ibid.

17 *L'Empire de l'Ephémère* (Paris: Gallimard/Bibliothèque des Sciences Humaines, 1987).
18 Fondation Pierre Bergé - Yves Saint Laurent archives.

CHAPTER 17 / THE SAINT LAURENT EMPIRE

1 Edmond and Jules de Goncourt, *Journal des Goncourt, 1851–1896.*
2 Frédéric Marc and Nicolas Weil, "Saint Laurent Exclusif par Pierre Bergé," *Femme*, March 1988.
3 *Vogue Paris*, February 1988.
4 *Gai Pied*, March 1988.
5 André-Jean Lafaurie, "Les Affres d'Yves Saint Laurent," *Le Point*, August 8, 1988.
6 Translator's note: After becoming director of the Paris opera houses, Pierre Bergé fired Daniel Barenboim from his position as music director of the Opéra Bastille because the conductor refused to accept a much-reduced salary.
7 Lafaurie, "Les Affres."
8 Tchaikovsky, *Eugene Onegin.*
9 *Libération*, October 28, 1988.
10 François Truffaut, *La Peau Douce.*
11 Marcel Proust, *Le Temps Retrouvé.*
12 *International Herald Tribune*, May 28, 1990.
13 Ibid.
14 Ibid.
15 Marcel Proust, *A l'Ombre des Jeunes Filles en Fleurs.*

CHAPTER 18 / BABYLON: 1990 TO 1993

1 Bryan Burrough, "Couture Clash: Saint Laurent Sale of a Lifetime," *Vanity Fair*, April 1993.
2 Michel Legris, "Saint Laurent en Mode Majeur," *L'Express*, October 25, 1990.
3 Pierre Bergé, *Liberté, J'écris Ton Nom* (Paris: Grasset, 1991).
4 Giesbert and Samet, "Yves Saint Laurent: 'Je Suis Né Avec une Dépression Nerveuse.'"
5 "La Passion Selon Saint Laurent," *L'Insensé*, November 1991.
6 *Libération*, February 3, 1992.
7 *Libération*, January 21, 1993.
8 François Bosnavaron and Pierre-Angel Gay, "Saint Laurent à Tout Prix, Controverse sur la Vente du Groupe de Luxe à Elf-Sanofi," *Le Monde*, January 27, 1993.
9 "Pourquoi Ils M'Ont Viré!", *Le Figaro*, February 11, 1993.
10 Fondation Pierre Bergé - Yves Saint Laurent archives.
11 Pierre-Angel Gay, "Après la Transmission du Dossier au Parquet, les Inconnues Juridiques de l'Affaire Saint Laurent," *Le Monde*, June 22, 1993.
12 Michèle Sider, "'Yves, mon Fils,' la Première Interview de la Mère du Grand Couturier," *Femme*, February 1992.

CHAPTER 19 / WHAT IS SILENT AND WHAT FADES AWAY

1 Paul Morand, *L'Allure de Chanel* (Paris: Hermann, 1976).
2 Giroud, "Les Vingt Ans."
3 Fondation Pierre Bergé - Yves Saint Laurent archives.

4   Beaudelaire, *Constantin Guys, Le Peintre de la vie moderne* (1943).
5   Rainer Maria Rilke, *Letters to a Young Poet*

CHAPTER 20 / SEARCHING FOR THE ABSOLUTE: 1993 TO 1998

1   Isabel Elsen, "Chez Pierre Bergé," *Journal du Dimanche*, November 28, 1993.
2   Lesley White, "The Saint," *British Vogue,* January 1994.
3   Proust, *A l'Ombre des Jeunes Filles en Fleur.*
4   Pierre-Angel Gay, "La Guerre des 'Champagne': Approche du Dénouement," *Le Monde*, November 30, 1993.
5   Yves Saint Laurent archives, official communiqué.
6   *Elle*, January 31, 1994.
7   Gérard Lefort, "Avis de Tempête dans le Taffetas," *Libération*, January 20, 1994.
8   Suzy Menkes, "Sober YSL, Naughty Valentino," *International Herald Tribune*, January 20, 1994.
9   Janie Samet, "Saint Laurent a Choisi la Liberté," *Le Figaro*, September 15, 1994.
10 *Paris Match*, September 29, 1994.
11 *Women's Wear Daily*, March 29, 1993.
12 Jane Kramer, "The Impresario's Last Act," *New Yorker*, November 21, 1994.
13 *Le Figaro*, February 10, 1994.
14 Catherine Schwaab, "Pierre Bergé Met les Pieds dans le Plat," *Paris Match*, April 1, 1993.
15 Fabrice Gaignault, "La Reine Nadja," *Elle*, January 2, 1995.
16 *Paris Match*, September 29, 1994.
17 *International Herald Tribune*, March 22, 1995.
18 Yves Saint Laurent archives, 1995.
19 Baudot, "La Passion."
20 Laurence Benaïm, "Cinq Couturiers et leur Mère," *Marie Claire,* November 1995.
21 Marguerite Duras in preface to *Yves Saint Laurent et la Photographie de Mode* (Paris: Albin Michel, 1989).
22 *International Herald Tribune*, July 1996.
23 Marika Schaertl, "Entre Ivresse et Solitude, Interview," *Focus*, April [February] 3, 1997.
24 Fondation Pierre Bergé - Yves Saint Laurent archives.
25 *Le Figaro*, September 25, 1994.
26 Ibid.
27 Amy M. Spindler, "There's Life in Couture's Old Guard Yet," *New York Times*, July 13, 1995.
28 *International Herald Tribune*, July 1997
29 Piero Citati, *La Colombe poignardée, Proust et La Recherche* (Paris:Gallimard, 1997).
30 Ibid.
31 Michèle Manceaux, "Yves Saint Laurent, le Génie et la Douleur," *Marie Claire*, March 1998.
32 *Le Figaro*, April 1998.
33 Mariella Righini, "Elbaz, le Woody Allen de YSL," *Le Nouvel Observateur*, March 4-10, 1998.
34 Ibid.
35 "Le Face-à-Face Bergé-Platini," *Journal du Dimanche*, July 12, 1998.
36 Ibid.

37 *Ex Aequo*, October 1998.

38 Laurence Benaïm, "Nos Années Saint Laurent," *Le Monde*, January 23, 2002.

39 "YSL: 40 Ans d'Elégance," *Madame Figaro*, January 21, 1998.

40 *International Herald Tribune*, January 1998.

41 *Paris Match*, July 6, 1998.

42 Valérie Duponchelle, "Pierre Bergé: 'Participer à un Patrimoine Collectif,'" *Le Figaro*, March 2, 1999.

43 Ibid.

44 Albert de Musset, *The Confession of a Child of the Century*, trans. by David Coward (New York: Penguin Classics, 2014).

CHAPTER 21 / THE END OF A DREAM: 1999 TO 2002

1 Sider, "'Yves, mon Fils.'"

2 Duras, *Yves Saint Laurent et la Photographie de Mode*.

3 Tom McGhie, "Man in black 'will leave Gucci' if LVMH wins," *The Guardian*, May 26, 1999.

4 *Le Monde*, May 27, 1999.

5 *New York Times*, July 1999.

6 Nadège Forestie, "Bergé: 'La Haute Couture Continuera sous ma Direction,'" *Le Figaro*, October 8, 1999.

7 Fondation Pierre Bergé - Yves Saint Laurent archives, 1999.

8 Gucci Group press release, November 15 , 1999.

9 *Vogue Paris*, August 1999.

10 *Elle*, November 1, 1999.

11 *Technikart*, February 2000.

12 Florence de Monza, "Je Suis un Artiste Raté," *Journal du Dimanche*, June 4, 2000.

13 Fondation Pierre Bergé - Yves Saint Laurent archives, 2000.

14 Ibid.

15 Monza, "Je Suis un Artiste Raté."

16 Janie Samet, "Tom Ford, l'Homme qui Pilote l'Avenir de Saint Laurent," *Le Figaro*, June 29, 2000.

17 *International Herald Tribune*, March, 2000.

18 Samet, "Tom Ford."

19 Ibid.

20 *Le Monde*, October 14, 2000.

21 *International Herald Tribune*, October 3, 2000.

22 Internal memo, reported to author.

23 Paquita Paquin and Cédric Saint André Perrin, "OPA sur la Mode et l'Art," *Libération*, October 7, 2000.

24 *New York Times Magazine*, December 24, 2000.

25 Luc Le Vaillant, "Ami Très Cher," *Libération*, May 9, 2001.

26 *Capital*, October 2001.

27 *International Herald Tribune*, October 12, 2001.

28 Cathy Horyn, "Yves of Destruction," *New York Times Magazine*, December 24, 2000.

29 *Libération*, March 19, 2002.

30 David Teboul, *Yves Saint Laurent* (Paris: La Martinière, 2002).

SOURCES AND BIBLIOGRAPHY

AUTHOR INTERVIEWS

Unless otherwise cited, all quotes are from interviews conducted by the author. Below is a partial list of interview subjects; some chose to remain anonymous:

Maryse Agussol, Charlotte Aillaud, Anouk Aimée, Alexandre, Fernand Baron, Brigitte Bastian, Pierre Bergé, Claude Berthod, Claire de Billy, Pierre Boulat, James W. Brady, Serge Bramly, Boul de Breteuil, Michael Brodsky, Gabrielle Buchaert, Pierre Cardin, Betty Catroux, François Catroux, Edmonde Charles-Roux, Hélène Chenot, Léon Cligman, Jean Cohen, Terry Cohen, Philippe Collin, Guy Cuevas, Philippe d'Abzac, Josiane Dacquet, Françoise Darmon, Baronne Geoffroy de Courcel, Hélène de Fougerolles, Bénédicte de Ginestous, Loulou de la Falaise, Maxime de la Falaise, Denise Barry de Longchamp, Hélène de Ludinghausen, Paule de Mérindol, Catherine Deneuve, Yvonne de Peyerimhoff, Jean-Pierre Derbord, Catherine Devoulon, Nicole Dorier, Frédéric Edelmann, Alber Elbaz, John Fairchild, Jean-Marie Farthouat, Jean-Pierre Frère, Jean-Paul Gaultier, Christophe Girard, Robert Goossens, Jacques Grange, Didier Grumbach, Isabelle Hebey, Joy Hendericks, Sylvianne Hodgkinson, Esther Jadot, Zizi Jeanmaire, Nan Kempner, Christian Lacroix, Mustapha Lahbali, Claude Lalanne, François-Xavier Lalanne, Simone Lamy (Tronc), Jack Lang, Vesna Laufer, André Lemarié, Corinne Le Ralle, François Lesage, Michèle Levasseur, Claude Licard, Rafael Lopez Sanchez, José Luis, Suzanne Luling, Madame Catherine Devoulon, Madame Esther Jadot, Madame Felisa Salvagnac, Madame Hélène Chenot, Madame Renée Cassart, Madame Jacqueline, Lucienne Mathieu-Saint-Laurent, Hervé Antoine Mayer, Bernard Minoret, Monette, Monsieur Jean-Pierre Derbord, Mounia Osmane, Albert Mulphin, Anne-Marie Munoz, Helmut Newton, Jérôme Nicollin, Katoucha Niane, André Ostier, Paquita Paquin, Hector Pascual, Paul the chauffeur, Anna Pavlowski, Elsa Peretti, Roland Petit, Paloma Picasso, Colombe Pringle, Andrée Putman, John Richardson, Hélène Rochas, Jean-Claude Rossignol, Jacques Rouet, Mercedes Rubirosa, Yves Saint Laurent, Felisa Salvagnac, Janie Samet, Fernando Sanchez, Comtesse San Just, Marie-Françoise Savary, Marina Schiano, Sao Schlumberger, Jeanloup Sieff, Étienne Tiffou, Brigitte Tortet, Susan Train, Patricia Turck-Paquelier, Gaby van Zuylen, Danielle Varenne, Victoire Doutreleau, Yves Vié-Le Sage, Roger Vivier, Francine Weisweiller, Bill Willis, Micheline Ziegler, Marie-Thérèse Herzog, Kenzo Takada, Javier Arroyuello, Marc Audibet, Maryvonne Numata, Amalia Vairelli.

BOOKS AND CATALOGUES

Yves Saint Laurent. Catalogue of the exhibition at the Metropolitan Museum of Art. London: Thames and Hudson, 1983.

Yves Saint Laurent par Yves Saint Laurent. Preface by Bernard-Henri Lévy. Catalogue of the exhibition at the Musée des Arts de la Mode. Paris: Herscher, 1986.

Yves Saint Laurent et le Théâtre. Preface by Edmonde Charles-Roux. Catalogue of the exhibition at the Musée des Arts de la Mode. Paris: Herscher, 1986.

Yves Saint Laurent Rétrospective. Catalogue of the exhibition at the Art Gallery of New South Wales. Sydney: Beaver Press, 1987.

Yves Saint Laurent et la Photographie de Mode. Paris: Albin Michel, 1989. Preface by Marguerite Duras, "Le Bruit et le Silence."

Mode 1958–1990. Catalogue of the exhibition at the Sezon Museum of Art, Tokyo. Tokyo: Ed. Yves Saint Laurent/Seibu, 1990. Preface by Kuniko Tsutsumi. Text by Laurence Benaïm.

Yves Saint Laurent Exotismes. Catalogue of the exhibition at the Musée de la Mode. Marseille: Réunion des Musées Nationaux, 1994.

Yves Saint Laurent, 5 Avenue Marceau 75116 Paris. Ed. David Teboul. Paris: La Martinière, 2002.

Yves Saint Laurent: Naissance d'une Légende. Paris: La Martinière, 2002. Photographs by Pierre Boulat, introduction by Laurence Benaïm.

Yves Saint Laurent by David Teboul. Paris: La Martinière, 2002.

Love by Marie-Claude Pellé. Paris: Assouline, 2005.

The Beautiful Fall: Lagerfeld, Saint Laurent, and Glorious Excess in 1970s Paris by Alice Drake. New York: Little, Brown, 2007.

This is the book that has currently gotten the fashion circus excited, as they migrate between New York and Milan, and will bring their crocodile suitcases to Paris next week. It has brought its author, Alice Drake, her fifteen minutes of fame. Everyone, especially those who haven't read it, is thrilled about the venomous anecdotes that are said to make it so interesting (the book hasn't yet been translated into French). People are whispering bad words like "lawsuit," "libel," and "censorship," although no legal action has yet been taken. Behind a rather foggy title, *The Beautiful Fall*, the journalist has the goal of telling the story of the definitive changes that fashion underwent in the 1970s. She has identified Yves Saint Laurent and Karl Lagerfeld as the two people responsible for this aesthetic revolution. Drake paints a portrait of two warring brothers at a time when their attitude had little to do with their current image or behavior. She logically dates their rivalry to 1954, when they both won prizes from the textile federation, which could not decide between the two apprentice designers. Their careers took off after 1968. Drake describes them going through a frenetic phase at the same time: exotic Marrakesh was already a refuge for Yves Saint Laurent, while Karl Lagerfeld, who still had poor control of his relationship to fame, unlike today, enjoyed wild, lavish nights in Paris or Saint-Tropez. Each had financial support (Pierre Bergé for Saint Laurent and Jacques de Bascher for Karl Lagerfeld) and both sought inspiration by meeting new people. Their "muses" of the time were not young Hollywood actresses who cashed in on their looks and image for millions of dollars. Female friends, lovers, girlfriends…their involvement went way beyond simple advertising. Especially since the all-night parties quickly wiped away any commercial relationship. Thadée Klossowski, the husband of Loulou de la Falaise, Yves Saint Laurent's almost-official muse, sums up the atmosphere of the time in one sentence: "I don't think any of us was especially interested in reality."

Suzy Menkes, the tireless and merciless journalist for the *Herald Tribune*, has issued her verdict. By losing her way in celebrity micro-revelations, Alice Drake has "forgotten something crucial: fashion….Some readers may wonder what these two people spent all day doing." (Olivier Wicker, *Libération*).

Quinze Hommes Splendides by Yvonne Baby. Paris: Gallimard, 2008.

Style by Yves Saint Laurent. Paris: La Martinière, 2008.

Histoire de notre collection de tableaux by Laure Adler. Paris: Actes Sud, 2009.

La Collection Yves Saint Laurent et Pierre Bergé: La Vente du siècle by Christianc de Nicolay-Mazery. Paris: Flammarion, 2009.

Les Paradis secrets d'Yves Saint Laurent et Pierre Bergé by Robert Murphy and Ivan Terestchenko. Paris: Albin Michel, 2009.

L'œuvre intégral: 1962–2002. Paris: La Martinière, 2010.

Requiem pour Yves Saint Laurent by Laurence Benaïm. Paris: Grasset, 2010.

Yves Saint Laurent. Catalogue of the exhibition at the Petit Palais. Paris: La Martinière, 2010.

Yves Saint Laurent mis à nu by Jeanloup Sieff. Paris: Albin Michel, 2010.

Yves Saint Laurent: Une Passion marocaine by Pierre Bergé. Paris: La Martinière, 2010.

Bill Willis by Marian McEvoy. Marrakesh: Jardin Majorelle, 2011.

Pierre Bergé, le faiseur d'étoiles by Béatrice Peyrani. Paris: Pygmalion, 2011.

Saint Laurent Rive Gauche. Catalogue of the exhibition. Fondation Pierre Bergé - Yves Saint Laurent. Jeromine Savignon, La Martinière, 2011.

Le Studio d'Yves Saint Laurent: Miroirs et secrets by Jérômine Savignon. Paris: Actes Sud, 2013.

Yves Saint Laurent: Les derniers jours de Babylone by Luc Castel. Paris: Editions du Regard, 2013.

Yves Saint Laurent Visionnaire. Catalogue of the exhibition at ING, Brussels. Ed. Florence Müller. Brussels: ING, 2013.

Femmes berbères du Maroc. Paris: Artlys, 2014.

Loulou de la Falaise by Natasha Fraser and Ariel de Ravenel. New York: Rizzoli International Publications, 2014.

Yves Saint Laurent by Roxanne Lowit. London: Thames & Hudson, 2014.

Yves Saint Laurent par les plus grands photographes. Text by Marguerite Duras. Munich: Schirmer/Mosel, 2014.

Jacques Doucet - Yves Saint Laurent: Vivre pour l'art. Paris: Flammarion, 2015.

Loves Yves Saint Laurent by Patrick Mauriès. Paris: La Martinière, 2015.

Vogue on Yves Saint Laurent by Natasha Fraser-Cavassoni. New York: Abrams Image, 2015.

Yves Saint Laurent, 1971, la collection du scandale. Paris: Flammarion, 2015.

Yves Saint Laurent: Style Is Eternal. Catalogue from the exhibition at the Bowes Museum. Barnard Castle: The Bowes Museum/Fondation Pierre Bergé - Yves Saint Laurent, 2015.

All About Yves by Catherine Ormen. Paris: Larousse, 2016.

Yves Saint Laurent. Ed. Florence Müller. Catalogue from the exhibition at the Seattle Art Museum. New York: Rizzoli International Publications, 2016.

Les Musées Yves Saint Laurent, Paris / Marrakech, collectifs. New York: Assouline, 2017.

Jacques de Bascher: Dandy de l'ombre by Marie Ottavie. Paris: Séguier, 2017.

Saint Laurent et moi, une histoire intime by Fabrice Thomas, with Aline Apostolska. Paris: Hugo Document, 2017.

Studio KO by Karl Fournier and Olivier Marty. Foreword by Pierre Bergé. New York: Rizzoli International Publications, 2017.

Yves Saint Laurent: La Folie de l'accessoire by Patrick Mauriès. New York: Phaidon, 2017.

Yves Saint Laurent: L'Album. Paris: Musée YSL Paris, 2017.

Published by the Yves Saint Laurent company

Bravo Yves (1982). *Yves Saint Laurent, 25 Years of Design* (press excerpts that were published during the Metropolitan Museum of Art exhibition in December 1983).
L'Esprit du Temps (1992).

Texts by Yves Saint Laurent

La Vilaine Lulu (Naughty Lulu). Paris: Claude Tchou, 1967. Out of print. Reissued, La Martinière, 2010.

"La Fin d'un Rêve. Hommage à Maria Callas." (*Le Monde*, September 18, 1977).

Preface to *L'Histoire de la Photographie de Mode* by Nancy Hall Duncan (Paris: Ed. Le Chêne, 1978.)

Correspondence between Yves Mathieu-Saint-Laurent and Michel de Brunhoff. Charles Mathieu-Saint-Laurent and Michel de Brunhoff (February 1954–June 1955). Published in *Jardin des Modes*, February 1982.

"Yves Saint Laurent," in *Yves Saint Laurent*, the Metropolitan Museum of Art catalogue (London: Thames and Hudson, 1983.)

"Madame Schiaparelli," in *Schiaparelli* by Palmer White (Paris: Ed. Le Chêne, 1986).

Preface to *L'Histoire Technique et Morale du Vêtement* by Maguelone-Toussaint Samat (Paris: Bordas Culture, 1990).

Texts written for the fragrances Opium (1977), Kouros (1981), and Paris (1983) published by the Saint Laurent company.

Texts by Pierre Bergé

L'Art de la préface. Paris: Gallimard, 2008.
Lettres à Yves. Paris: Gallimard, 2010.
Lettres à Yves. Paris: Gallimard Folio, 2011.

SELECTED ARTICLES AND INTERVIEWS

1955. "Parce qu'il ne Voulait pas être Notaire, l'Oranais Yves Mathieu-Saint-Laurent Sera (Peut-être) un Grand Couturier" (*L'Echo d'Oran*, Janie Samet, January 7, 1955).

1958. "La France Applaudit. L'Etranger Aussi. Vive la Femme Trapèze!" (*L'Aurore*, January 31, 1958). "Le Petit Roi de la Haute Couture a Passé le Bachot de la Gloire avec Mention Très Bien" (*Paris Presse-L'Intransigeant*, Merry Bromberger, February 1, 1958). "Un Timide Jeune Homme au Grand Destin" (*Arts*, Bernard Buffet, February 5, 1958). "La Ligne Saint Laurent Vue par Bernard Buffet" (*L'Express*, February 6, 1958). "Paris Couronne le Dauphin de Dior" (*Jours de France*,, Jean-François Bergery, February 8, 1958). "Dior sans Dior. Le Rideau se Lève" (*Paris Match*, Odette Valéri, March 1, 1958). "Le Phénomène Saint Laurent Succède au Phénomène Christian Dior" (*Vogue Paris*, March 1958). " Yves Mathieu-Saint-Laurent Dirige à 21 Ans la Plus Grande Maison de Couture du Monde" (*Arts*, André Parinaud, April 9, 1958). "De Carpaccio à Ingres, le Panorama de la Mode d'Automne" (*Les Lettres Françaises*, Hélène Cingria, August 7, 1958).

1959. "Yves Saint Laurent Sera l'An Prochain Habillé par un Grand Couturier: l'Intendance." (*Le Figaro*, Hélène de Turckheim, November 28, 1959).

1960. "La Silhouette de Demain" (*Le Figaro*, M. A. Souza, January 28, 1960). "Le Style Libre de la Mode" (*Combat*, Lucien François, January 29, 1960). "Saint Laurent est un Décorateur" (*Combat*, Lucien François, August 1, 1960).

1961. "Le Retour d'Yves Saint Laurent" (*Paris Presse-L'Intransigeant*, April 18, 1961). "Deux Parisiennes Semblent Porter du Saint Laurent (*Paris Match*, Henri Bostel, August 5, 1961). "Eye on Market" (*Women's Wear Daily*, December 12, 1961). "Zizi à l'Alhambra" (*L'Express*, Christine de Rivoyre, December 14, 1961). "Le Show de Zizi" (*France Observateur*, Jean Freustié, December 21, 1961).

1962. "Avec son Truc en Plumes, Elle a Reconquis Paris" (*Jours de France*, January 6, 1962)."Le Solo de Saint Laurent" (*Corriere della Sera*, Dino Buzzati, January 30, 1962). "Architecte de la Mode" (*Les Lettres Françaises*, Hélène Cingria, February 14, 1962). "The Comeback of Yves Saint Laurent" (*Life*, Nadine Liber, April 9, 1962). "Le Poète de la Mode" (*Combat*, Lucien François, July 31, 1962).

1964. "I Don't Design for Ordinary Women" (*New York Herald Tribune*, Hebe Dorsey, January 23, 1964).

1965. "Saint Laurent, la Tradition Fantastique" (*Vogue Paris*, Isabelle Hebey, July 1965). "Le Couturier Qui a Pensé aux Femmes d'Aujourd'hui" (*Candide*, Patrick Thévenon, August 9, 1965). "Yves's Métier Perfection" (*Women's Wear Daily*, August 9, 1965). "Saint Laurent Offers Best Art Show in Paris" (*Herald Tribune*, Carol Cutler, August 10, 1965).

1966. "Le Nombril de la Mode" (*Vogue*, March 1966). "Le Smoking Called Feminine, Even with Cigar" (*Herald Tribune*, Eugenia Sheppard, December 9, 1966).

1967. "Pierre Dumayet Met Saint Laurent Sur le Gril" (*Elle*, March 22, 1967).

1968. "Back to Eve" (*Evening News*, Penny Graham, January 29, 1968). "Yves Saint Laurent, Ce Petit Lycéen Qui Nous Vient d'Oran" (*Le Figaro Littéraire*, Edmonde Charles-Roux, February 12, 1968). "Saint Laurent Coupez Pour Nous!" (*Elle*, Claude Berthod, March 7, 1968). "L'Esprit de la Mode a Changé" (*Elle*, Hélène G. Lazareff, June 26, 1968).

1969. "Le Vénus à Deux Faces" (*L'Express*, Franka de Mailly, February 3, 1969). "Saint Laurent, le Style Direct" (*Marie Claire*, March 1969). "Louise Fitzgerald de la Falaise" (*Vogue Paris*, March 1969). "Les Hommes Nouveaux Que Nous Prépare Saint Laurent" (*Elle*, Claude Berthod, May 5, 1969). "Ne Soyez Pas Passive, Inventez-Vous Vous-Même (*Vogue Paris*, June 1969). "Yves's Other Eden. Saint Laurent in Marrakesh" (Patrick Lichfield, *Vogue*, July 1969). "Juliette et Messaline" (*L'Express*,

Françoise Giroud, August 4, 1969). "Zizi Jeanmaire, Première Girl de France" (*L'Express*, Guy Monréal, August 11, 1969).

1970. "La Féminité est dans la Femme, Pas dans ce qu'elle Porte" (*L'Express*, August 3, 1970).

1971. "I Want to Free Women from the Tyranny of Hemlines" (*Vanity Fair*, February 1971). "Saint Laurent: L'Apprenti Sorcier" (*Combat*, Pierre-Yves Guillen, February 1, 1971). "Cette Fois, les Hommes Seront Contents" (*Paris Match*, February 6, 1971). "Yves Saint Debacle" (*Time*, February 15, 1971). "La Libération de la Femme Selon Saint Laurent" (*Elle*, Claude Berthod, February 15, 1971). "Ce que je Veux: Choquer les Gens, les Forcer à Réfléchir" (*Vogue Paris*, March 1971). "Comme Chanel Faisait ses Tailleurs pour Elle, je Fais ma Collection Masculine pour moi" (*Le Figaro*, Hélène de Turckheim, April 6, 1971). "Yves Saint Laurent Vient d'Annoncer qu'il Renonçait à la Haute Couture pour le Prêt-à-Porter" (*Le Monde*, Nathalie Mont-Servan, February 1971).

1972. "Exhibitionnisme et Voyeurisme Font Tomber un Nouveau Tabou" (*Le Figaro*, Bernard Pivot, January 30, 1972). "Zizi au Casino de Paris, des Jambes qui ont de la Tête" (*France-Soir*, Pierre Marcabru, February 23, 1972). "Saint Laurent, la Collection que Seules ses Clientes Ont Pu Voir" (*Paris Match*, Gérald Asaria, February 28, 1972). "Les Paradis de Saint Laurent pour la Gloire de Zizi" (*Elle*, Fanny Deschamps, February 28, 1972). "De Zizi Jeanmaire à Alfred de Musset" (*Les Lettres Françaises*, March 1, 1972). "Le Music-hall, Aujourd'hui" (*Les Lettres Françaises*, Edmonde Charles-Roux, March 8, 1972). "Con i Costumi di Yves Saint Laurent, Jorge Lago, Nuovo Nurejev" (*Vogue Italia*, June 1972).

1973. "Les Modes Passent. Le Style est Eternel…Dior m'a Appris mon Métier, Grâce à Chanel, j'ai Trouvé mon Style" (*Vogue Paris*, March 1973). "Yves Saint Laurent Parle de la Mode, de sa Mode, de la Vie" (*20 Ans*, Sylvie Charier, April 20, 1973). "YSL: A 50-Million-Dollar Label" (*Women's Wear Daily*, September 26, 1973).

1974. "Saint Laurent Réinvente les Années 30" (*Elle*, Claude Berthod, February 18, 1974). "Anny Duperey dans *L'Affaire Stavisky*. C'est aussi l'Affaire Saint Laurent" (*Elle*, March 25, 1974). "Not Just an Ordinary Happening" (*New York Post*, Eugenia Sheppard, July 28, 1974). "I Sell Happiness, Not 1500-Dollar Dresses" (*People*, Rudolph Chelminski, September 9, 1974). "The King of Couture" (*Newsweek*, Lynn Young, November 18, 1974).

1975. "Here Come the Sirens" (*Women's Wear Daily*, January 23, 1975). "Le Raffinement de la Simplicité" (*Le Figaro*, Hélène de Turckheim, July 31, 1975).

1976. "I Did an Era in Which We Live" (*Newsweek*, Jane Friedman, June 7, 1976). "YSL Says Big Shapes" (*Women's Wear Daily*, July 29, 1976). "A Revolutionary Collection" (*New York Times*, Bernadine Morris, July 29, 1976). "YSL Has Discovered the Female Shape" (*Herald Tribune*, Eugenia Sheppard, July 29, 1976). "Americans Hail

YSL's Fantasy" (*Women's Wear Daily*, July 30, 1976). "C'était Donc Vrai, la Femme Existait" (*Le Journal du Dimanche*, René Barjavel, August 1, 1976). "The New New Look" (*Time*, August 9, 1976). "Rags to Riches" (*Newsweek*, Linda Bird Francke, Elizabeth Peer, August 9, 1976). "Le Roi Solitaire de Paris" (*Stern*, Marie-Louise Van Der Leyen, September 16, 1976). "Saint Laurent, the Romance That Shook the World" (*Vogue*, October 1976). "The Assurance of Dreams" (*Vogue*, Pierre Schneider, December 1976).

1977. "Je Veux Donner aux Femmes une Garde-Robe Universelle" (*Elle*, Claude Ferbos, January 24, 1977). "Saint Laurent Lives" (*Observer Magazine*, John Heilpern, June 5, 1977). "Yves Saint Laurent, Roi de la Mode" (*Le Point*, Barbara Schwarm and Martine Leventer, July 25, 1977). "Saint Laurent Verdict: China is in, Russia is out" (*Herald Tribune*, Eugenia Sheppard, July 28, 1977). "Et Puis Vint Saint Laurent Superstar" (*Le Figaro*, Hélène de Turckheim, July 28, 1977). "Loulou et Thadée Klossowski Ont Fait la Fête" (*Vogue Paris*, Hebe Dorsey, August 1977). "Who Choreographs the Best Follies and Fantasy?" (*British Vogue*, September 1977). "All About Yves" (*New York Times Magazine*, Anthony Burgess, September 11, 1977). "Yves Saint Laurent Vu par Joseph Losey" (*Vogue*, December 1977).

1978. "Mesdames, Attention à la Laideur!" (*JDD*, René Barjavel, January 29, 1978). "Yves Saint Laurent" (*Saga*, Jean-Pierre de Lucovich, February 1, 1978). "*L'Aigle à Deux Têtes* de Jean Cocteau" (*Le Figaro*, François Chalais, February 12, 1978). "*L'Aigle à Deux Têtes* de Jean Cocteau" (*Le Monde*, Michel Cournot, February 14, 1978). "Les Vingt Ans du Petit Prince" (*Vogue Paris*, Françoise Giroud, April 1978). "High Chic" (*Women's Wear Daily*, July 21, 1978). "On the Yves Change" (*Women's Wear Daily*, André Leon Talley, July 21, 1978).

1979. "La Naissance Secrète du Modèle Numéro 1043" (*JDD*, Simone Baron, January 30, 1979). "Chinese Americans Against Opium Perfume" (*New York Times*, April 24, 1979). "Saint Laurent, from Picasso to the Ballets Russes" (*Women's Wear Daily*, Patrick MacCarthy, July 20, 1979). "Saint Laurent: 'Couture is a Dream, like Opera or the Ballet'" (*New York Times*, Bernadine Morris, August 4, 1979). "Le Soir le Plus Grand" (*Vogue Paris*, September 1979). "The Opium War Part II" (*Women's Wear Daily*, September 22, 1979). "Dreams and Nightmares" (*Women's Wear Daily*, October 13, 1979).

1980. "Saint Laurent par Françoise Sagan" (*Elle*, March 3, 1980).

1981. "Catherine Deneuve Passe avec Helmut Newton la Grande Revue des 20 Ans de Saint Laurent" (*Paris Match*, Irène Vacher, December 4, 1981).

1982. "Yves Saint Laurent, 20 Ans de Succès" (*Elle*, Colombe Pringle, February 1, 1982). "Le Classique de l'Ephémère" (*L'Express*, Jean Pierrard, February 26, 1982). "Yves Saint Laurent par François-Marie Banier" (*Vogue*, March 1982). "Les Divinités Intimes, la Bibliothèque d'Yves Saint Laurent" (*Libération*, Michel Cressole, July 24, 1982).

1983. "Remembrance of Things Past. Château Gabriel" (*Women's Wear Daily*, January 14, 1983). "Saint Laurent Introspective" (*Women's Wear Daily*, Patrick MacCarthy and Christa Worthington, November 27, 1983). "All About Yves: Why Saint Laurent is Still in Fashion" (*Sunday News Magazine*, New York, Marian MacEvoy Brandsma, November 27, 1983). "A Salute to Yves Saint Laurent: The Man Behind the Mystique" (*New York Times Magazine*, E.J. Dionne Jr., December 4, 1983). "Yves Saint Laurent au Metropolitan. Aux Couleurs des Saisons, les Toiles Peintes d'un Voyant Charmeur" (*Le Monde*, Hervé Guibert, December 8, 1983). "Portrait de l'Artiste" (*Le Monde*, Yvonne Baby, December 8, 1983). "The King of Fashion" (*Time*, Martha Duffy, December 12, 1983). "Les Années Saint Laurent" (*Le Nouvel Observateur*, Jean-François Josselin, December 23, 1983). "Diana Vreeland Expose un Quart de Siècle d'Y.S.L." (*Libération*, December 27, 1983). "Des Robes de Maître" (*L'Express*, Patrick Thévenon, December 30, 1983).

1984. "Marrakech, Life in the Shade: YSL and Bergé's Moroccan Palace" (*Women's Wear Daily*, Ben Brantley, Christa Worthington, May 18, 1984). "Wall Street Fashion Empire: Haute Couture Means High Finance" (*Wall Street Journal*, John Kron, September 10, 1984).

1986. "Vingt-huit Années de Création" (*Libération*, Gérard Lefort, Saturday, May 31 and Sunday, July 1, 1986). "Je Suis un Homme Scandaleux, Finalement. Saint Laurent le Magnifique" (*Globe*, Catherine Deneuve, May 1986). "Rue de Babylone" (*Vogue Décoration*, Joan Buck, September 1986).

1987. "Yves Only: Loulou de la Falaise, Paloma Picasso, Tina Chow" (*Vogue* GB, September 1987). "Les Marginaux Milliardaires" (*Globe*, Patrick Thévenon, November 1987).

1988. "En Quelques Mois, Il a Reconquis un Royaume qui Eblouit le Monde Entier" (*Paris Match*, Katherine Pancol, February 12, 1988). "Le Choc Saint Laurent" (*Paris Match*, Patrick Thévenon, February 12, 1988). "Yves Saint Laurent et l'Art" (*Air France Madame*, Olivier Séguret, March 1988). "Saint Laurent Exclusif par Pierre Bergé" (*Femme*, Frédéric Marc and Nicolas Weil, March 1988). "Le Roi Yves a Décliné la Palette de ses Amours d'un Trait de Génie" (*Vogue Paris*, March 1988). "The Art of Fashion" (*Tatler*, Marian MacEvoy, April 1988). "La Vengeance" (*JDD*, Simone Baron, July 31, 1988). "Les Affres d'Yves Saint Laurent" (*Le Point*, André-Jean Lafaurie, August 8, 1988). "Yves Saint Laurent: Art and Drama Reign in His Paris Residence" (*Architectural Digest*, Charlotte Aillaud, September 1988). "The Yves Factor" (*Sunday Express Magazine*, Suzy Menkes, September 1988). "La Grâce et les Larmes. Le Triomphe Populaire des Modèles du Couturier" (*L'Humanité*, Michel Boué, September 12, 1988).

1989. "Yves Seins Laurent de nos Amours" (*Le Figaro*, Janie Samet, October 28, 1989). "Une Mode pour l'Intelligence" (*Le Figaro*, Renaud Matignon, October 28, 1989). "YSL Show: A Magical Dream" (*Times of India*, November 12, 1989).

1990. "Yves Saint Laurent, Designer of the Half Century" (*Connoisseur*, Diane Rafferty, February 1990). "Un Sein d'Esprit" (*Vogue Paris*, Laurence Benaïm, February 1990). "Le Coup d'Eclat d'Yves Saint Laurent: les Accessoires de Loulou de la Falaise" (*Elle*, Francine Vormese, March 26, 1990). "La 'Datcha' d'Yves Saint Laurent" (*Elle Décoration*, Gérard Puissey, July 1990). "Saint Laurent en Mode Majeur" (*L'Express*, Michel Legris, October 25, 1990). (*Glamour*, Dominique Dupuich, November 1990). "L'As de Coeur" (*Vogue Paris*, Laurence Benaïm, November 1990).

1991. "Crépuscule des Griffes" (*Le Nouvel Observateur*, January 24, 1991). "Le Couac de Bergé" (*Le Nouvel Observateur*, Katia D. Kaupp, February 21, 1991). "Yves Saint Laurent: 'Je Suis Né Avec une Dépression Nerveuse'" (*Le Figaro*, Franz-Olivier Giesbert and Janie Samet, July 11, 1991). "Trente Ans de Gloire, Trente Ans d'Angoisse" (*Le Figaro*, Franz-Olivier Giesbert and Janie Samet, July 15, 1991). "La Passion Selon Saint Laurent" (*L'Insensé*, November 1991).

1992. "La Haute Couture n'a pas d'Avenir" (*Le Figaro*, Pierre Bergé, January 24, 1992). "Identification d'un Homme" (*Le Monde*, Laurence Benaïm, January 29, 1992). "Il y a Trente Ans. Saint Laurent." (*W Europe*, February 1992). "'Yves, mon Fils,' la Première Interview de la Mère du Grand Couturier" (*Femme*, Michèle Sider, February 1992). "Saint Laurent: Ma Renaissance" (*JDD*, Michèle Stouvenot, February 6, 1992). "Catherine Deneuve Pose Pour Fêter ses 30 Ans de Chefs-d'oeuvre. Victoire, son Egérie, Raconte les Terribles Débuts qui ont Précédé la Gloire" (*Paris Match*, February 6, 1992). "Pierre Bergé: Oui, Je Négocie la Vente de Saint Laurent" (*Le Nouvel Economiste*, Béatrice Peyran, September 18, 1992).

1993. "YSL dans l'Orbite de Sanofi" (*Les Echos*, Valérie Leboucq, January 19, 1993). "YSL: Une Reprise Menacée de Retouches" (*Libération*, Renaud de la Baume and Sylvaine Villeneuve, January 25, 1993). "Saint Laurent à Tout Prix, Controverse sur la Vente du Groupe de Luxe à Elf-Sanofi" (*Le Monde*, François Bosnavaron and Pierre-Angel Gay, January 27, 1993). "Tribute to Yves" (*Vogue Italia*, Javier Arroyuello, March 1993). "L'Univers Secret de Saint Laurent" (*JDD*, Michèle Stouvenot, March 17, 1993). "YSL, The Great Wide Way" (*Women's Wear Daily*, John Fairchild, March 18, 1993). "Couture Clash: Saint Laurent Sale of a Lifetime" (*Vanity Fair*, Bryan Burrough, April 1993). "Pierre Bergé Met les Pieds dans le Plat" (*Paris Match*, Catherine Schwaab, April 1, 1993). "Saint Laurent Embourbé en Champagne: Les Viticulteurs Ont Décidé de Porter Plainte" (*Libération*, Sylvaine Villeneuve, June 9, 1993). "Après la Transmission du Dossier au Parquet, les Inconnues Juridiques de l'Affaire Saint Laurent" (*Le Monde*, Pierre-Angel Gay, June 22, 1993). "La Guerre des 'Champagne': Approche du Dénouement" (*Le Monde*, Pierre-Angel Gay, November 30, 1993). "Champagne: Qui Perd Gagne" (*Le Nouvel Observateur*, Emmanuelle Bosco, December 2, 1993). "Saint Laurent Privé de 'Champagne' en France" (*Le Figaro*, Janie Samet, December 16, 1993). "Le Parfum Prendra le Nom d'Yves Saint Laurent 'Champagne' Sera Interdit en France le 30 Décembre" (*Le Monde*, Pierre-Angel Gay, December 17, 1993).

1994. "The Saint" (*British Vogue*, Lesley White, January 1994). "Avis de Tempête dans le Taffetas" (*Libération*, Gérard Lefort, January 20, 1994). "Sober YSL, Naughty Valentino" (*International Herald Tribune*, Suzy Menkes, January 20, 1994). "Pierre Bergé Epinglé pour ses Discrets Bénéfices" (*Libération*, Renaud Lecadre, May 31, 1994). "Présidentielle: l'Indécence de Pierre Bergé" (*Le Monde*, Guy Carcassonne, June 10, 1994). "YSL is Once Again King" (*International Herald Tribune*, Suzy Menkes, July 21, 1994). "Uptown Shoot-Out in N.Y. Store War" (*International Herald Tribune*, Suzy Menkes, September 13, 1994). "Saint Laurent a Choisi la Liberté" (*Le Figaro*, Janie Samet, September 15, 1994). "YSL Sabre Le Champagne à New York" (*Elle*, Sylvie de Chirée, September 19, 1994). "Somebody from Paris Says He Loves New York" (*New York Times*, Bernadine Morris, September 20, 1994). "The Impresario's Last Act" (*New Yorker*, Jane Kramer, November 21, 1994).

1995. "La Reine Nadja" (*Elle*, Fabrice Gaignault, January 2, 1995). "Le Choléra, la Peste et la Lèpre" (*Le Monde*, Pierre Bergé, March 11, 1995). "L'Agneau Chirac et son Bergé" (*Le Monde*, Claude Allègre, March 15, 1995). "Monsieur le Président" (*Out*, Edward M. Gomez, April 1995). "There's Life in Couture's Old Guard Yet" (*New York Times*, Amy M. Spindler, July 13, 1995). "Cinq Couturiers et leur Mère" (*Marie Claire*, Laurence Benaïm, November 1995).

1996. "Arcat: Double Démission Annoncée" (*Le Figaro*, Armelle Héliot, January 16, 1996). "Haute Couture, l'Eclat du Crépuscule" (*Le Monde*, Laurence Benaïm, January 22, 1996). "Smoking pour Tout le Monde" (*Elle*, François Baudot, May 27, 1996). "Londres, Capitale de la Mode 'Politiquement Incorrecte'" (*Le Monde*, Laurence Benaïm, October 2, 1996). "YSL Withdrawal Is End of an Era" (*International Herald Tribune*, Suzy Menkes, October 8, 1996). "Paris, Capitale Assiégée du Prêt-à-Porter Féminin" (*Le Monde*, Laurence Benaïm, October 8, 1996).

1997. "Entre Ivresse et Solitude, Interview" (*Focus*, Marika Schaertl, February 3, 1997). "Des Américains à Paris" (*Le Figaro*, Janie Samet, February 20, 1997). "Haute Simplicité Selon Saint Laurent" (*Le Monde*, Laurence Benaïm, March 17, 1997). "Saint Laurent à Londres" (*Connaissance des Arts*, Philip Jodidio, May 1997). "Pierre Bergé Attaque les Musées Français" (*Le Figaro*, Valérie Duponchelle, October 20, 1997). "Mon Plus Grand Défaut, C'est Moi-Même" (*Dutch*, Laurence Benaïm, Winter 1997).

1998. "Yves Saint Laurent, 40 Ans de Règne sur la Mode" (*Madame Figaro*, Guillemette de Sairigné, February 14, 1998). "Yves Saint Laurent, la Mode et l'Art" (*Le Figaro*, Janie Samet, April 23, 1998). "Yves Saint Laurent, le Génie et la Douleur" (*Marie Claire*, Michèle Manceaux, March 1998). "Yves Saint Laurent et la Coupe du Monde" (*Le Figaro*, Janie Samet, May 21, 1998). "Yves Saint Laurent Désigne son Dauphin" (*Le Figaro*, Janie Samet, June 8, 1998). "Yves Saint Laurent Confie la Création de son Prêt-à-Porter à Alber Elbaz" (*Le Monde*, Laurence Benaïm, June 9, 1998). "Saint Laurent, le Dieu de la Mode pour les Dieux du Stade" (*Paris Match*, Jean-Claude Zana, July 16, 1998). "YSL's Mastery in Black and White" (*International Herald Tribune*, Suzy Menkes, July 23, 1998). "Le Mode Entre Toiles du Maître et Maîtresses Femmes" (*Paris Match*, October 1, 1998). "The Woody Allen of Fashion Joins the

Club at Saint Laurent" (*New York Times*, Elizabeth Hayt, November 8, 1998). "Duel LVMH-L'Oréal pour Conquérir le Monde de la Beauté" (*Le Monde*, Pascal Galinier, December 16, 1998).

1999. "Pierre Bergé: 'Participer à un Patrimoine Collectif'" (*Le Figaro*, Valérie Duponchelle, March 2, 1999). "Alber Elbaz, le Woody Allen de YSL" (*Le Nouvel Observateur*, Mariella Righini, March 4, 1999). "Taking on the Legacy of Yves Saint Laurent" (*International Herald Tribune*, Suzy Menkes, March 9, 1999). "François Pinault Prend 40% de Gucci et Achète Saint Laurent" (*Le Monde*, Pascal Galinier, March 20, 1999). "LVMH Prêt à Payer 30 Milliards de Francs pour Récupérer Gucci" (*Le Monde*, Pascal Galinier, March 22, 1999). "Le Temps de la Mondialisation" (*Challenges*, Jean-Pierre de la Rocque, September 1999). "Bergé: 'La Haute Couture Continuera sous ma Direction'" (*Le Figaro*, Nadège Forestier, October 8, 1999). "Gucci Moving to Buy Yves Saint Laurent, Fashion's Biggest Prize" (*International Herald Tribune*, Suzy Menkes, October 9, 1999). "Saint Laurent Vend sa Marque Mais Garde la Haute Couture" (*Le Monde*, Pascal Galinier, October 17, 1999). "Gucci Buys House of YSL for $1 Billion" "Yves Saint Laurent, un Parfum de Stock-Options" (*Le Monde*, Pascal Galinier, October 20, 1999). (*International Herald Tribune*, Suzy Menkes, November 16, 1999). "Yves Saint Laurent, C'est Cinq Francs" (*Le Figaro*, Dominique Savidan, December 7, 1999).

2000. "His Last Collection for Saint Laurent Is a Smash" (*International Herald Tribune*, Suzy Menkes, February 29, 2000)"Le Paris d'Hedi Slimane" (*Le Monde*, Jacques Brunel, March 11, 2000). "Musée Saint Laurent, un Hymne à l'Elégance" (*Le Figaro Madame*, Laurence Mouillefarine, April 15, 2000). "Wanted" (*Self Service*, Ezra Petronio, Summer 2000). "Je Suis un Artiste Raté" (*Journal du Dimanche*, Florence de Monza, June 4, 2000). "Couture Days: Saint Laurent's Perfect Score" (*New York Times*, Cathy Horyn, July 16, 2000). "OPA sur la Mode et l'Art" (*Libération*, Paquita Paquin and Cédric Saint André Perrin, October 7, 2000). "Yves Saint Laurent à l'Epreuve de Gucci" (*Le Monde*, Pascal Galinier, October 14, 2000).

2001. "Le Coup de Théâtre de Bernard Arnault" (*Le Figaro*, Martine Henno, January 29, 2001). "Tom Ford, un Style Sensuel, Sexy et Intellectuel" (*Le Figaro*, Martine Henno, January 26, 2001). "Ford Shines, But Stars Come Out for Slimane" (*New York Times*, Cathy Horyn, January 30, 2001). "The Return of Roos" (*Women's Wear Daily Beauty Biz*, Pete Born, February 2001). "La Guerre des Podiums" (*Le Monde*, Jacques Brunel, February 3, 2001). "El Rey de los Excesos" (*El País*, Cathy Horyn, February 25, 2001). "Ami Très Cher" (*Libération*, Luc Le Vaillant, May 9, 2001). "Légende" (*Numéro*, Philip Utz, July-August 2001). "La Bourse S'Interroge sur les Stratégies Croisées de LVMH et de PPR" (*Le Monde*, Pascal Galinier, July 11, 2001).

2002. "L'Adieu d'Yves Saint Laurent" (*Le Monde*, Laurence Benaïm, January 6, 2002). "Yves Saint Laurent Prêt-à-Partir" (*Libération*, Nicole Pénicaut, Gérard Lefort, Ondine Millot, January 7, 2002). "Yves Saint Laurent Quitte la Scène de la Mode dans l'Emotion" (*Le Monde*, Laurence Benaïm, January 9, 2002). "Prince Saint Laurent" (*Le Monde*, Laurence Benaïm, January 12, 2002). "Drouot: Pierre Bergé

Déclare Forfait" (*Le Figaro*, Valérie Duponchelle and Béatrice de Rochebouët, January 2002). "L'Uomo che Amava le Donne" (*L'Espresso*, Ulderico Munzi, January 17, 2002). "Yves Saint Laurent Retire son Epingle du Jeu" (*Paris Match*, Catherine Schwaab, Jérôme Béglé, and Elisabeth Chavelet, January 17, 2002). "Saint Laurent's Finale Shows Why He Is an Icon" (*International Herald Tribune*, Suzy Menkes, January 23, 2002). "Les Adieux d'Yves Saint Laurent" (*Le Figaro*, Janie Samet, January 23, 2002). "Per l'Addio di Saint Laurent Sfilano 40 Anni di Storia" (*Il Giornale*, Daniela Fedi, January 23, 2002). "Amid Tears, 40 Saint Laurent Years Pass in Review" (*New York Times*, Gina Bellafante, January 23, 2002). "Nos Années Saint Laurent" (*Le Monde*, Laurence Benaïm, January 23, 2002). "Saint Laurent: the Final Bow" (*Women's Wear Daily*, Robert Murphy, Miles Socha, and Samantha Conti, January 23, 2002). "Le Dernier Défilé d'Yves Saint Laurent, un Sentiment d'Eternité" (*Elle*, Marie-Pierre Lannelongue, January 28, 2002). "1962-2002 Yves Saint Laurent" (*Paris Match*, Edmonde Charles-Roux, January 31, 2002). "L'Adieu d'un Prince" (*Le Monde*, Laurence Benaïm, February 2002). "La Robe la plus Immatérielle d'Yves Saint Laurent" (*L'Officiel*, March 2002). "Yves Saint Laurent 1962–2002" (*L'Officiel "1001 Modèles Yves Saint Laurent,"* special issue no. 1, March 2002). "Swann Song" (*The New Yorker*, Judith Thurman, March 18, 2002). "Yves Saint Laurent 1962–2002" (*Mode et Mode*, Asako Turengin, April 2002).

2008. "Une Passion Marocaine, Caftans, Broderies, Bijoux" (*Connaissance des Arts*, March 3, 2008). "La Mort du Génial Créateur Yves Saint Laurent" (*Le Figaro*, June 1, 2008). "Le Couturier Français Yves Saint Laurent est Mort" (*Le Monde*, June 2, 2008). "La Mort d'Yves Saint Laurent, le plus Grand Couturier du Monde" (*Le Figaro*, June 2, 2008). "YSL 1936–2008" (*Libération*, June 3, 2008). "Saint Laurent Forever" (*L'Express*, June 5, 2008). "YSL Reflets Éternels" (*Les Inrockuptibles*, June 10, 2008). "Et Yves Saint Laurent Créa la Nouvelle Femme" (*Le Figaro Magazine*, June 14, 2008). "Yves Saint Laurent, le Maître de l'Élégance" (*Le Monde*, June 14, 2008). "Bergé, Saint Laurent: La vente du siècle" (*Le Figaro*, July 23, 2008). "The Spirit of YSL" (*New York Times*, September 12, 2009). "Cette Vente va Transformer des Souvenirs en Projets" (*Beaux Arts*, November 1, 2008).

2009. "Avec Pierre Bergé, dans les Coulisses de la Vente du Siècle" (*Le Figaro Magazine*, January 31, 2009). "Le Grand Goût Français de Bergé et Saint Laurent à Livre Ouvert" (*Le Figaro*, February 5, 2009). "Yves Saint Laurent, Son Histoire de l'Art" (*Le Figaro Madame*, February 7, 2009). "The Last Collection" (*New York Times*, February 12, 2009). "Les Secrets d'Une Collection" (*Le Nouvel Observateur*, February 12, 2009). "YSL/Bergé, la Vente du Siècle" (*Journal des Arts*, February 20, 2009). "Saint Laurent-Bergé, la Vente d'Une Vie" (*Libération*, February 23, 2009). "La Vente du Siècle: Les Confidences du Commissaire-Priseur" (*Le Figaro*, February 23, 2009). "YSL-Bergé: Ruée sur les Classiques et l'Art Déco" (*Le Figaro*, February 25, 2009). "Les Records Tombent Lors de la Vente Saint Laurent-Bergé" (*Le Monde*, February 25, 2009). "Les Records et les Leçons de la Vente Bergé-Saint Laurent" (*Le Monde*, March 1, 2009). "Coup de Frais chez Yves Saint Laurent" (*Le Monde*, October 6, 2009). "Pierre Bergé, Mécène et Entrepreneur des Bonnes Causes" (*Le Figaro Economie*, October 30, 2009). "Baisser de Rideau sur la Collection Saint Laurent-Bergé"

(*Le Figaro*, November 10, 2009). "Saint Laurent Auction Rich in Sentimental Value" (*New York Times*, November 13, 2009). "YSL, l'Ultime Triomphe" (*Le Figaro*, November 21, 2009).

2010. "Yves Saint Laurent, le Point Inal" (*Libération*, January 30, 2010). "Yves Saint Laurent a Fait de Son Métier Une Oeuvre" (*Le Monde*, February 27, 2010). "Saint Laurent Revolutionary Romantic" (*New York Times*, March 9, 2010). "Pleins Feux sur Saint Laurent" (*Les Inrockuptibles*, March 10, 2010). "Yves, Tout Simplement" (*Le Figaro*, March 11, 2010). "All Over Yves" (*Elle*, March 12, 2010). "Les Blessures *Fécondes d'Yves Saint Laurent*" (*Le Monde*, March 13, 2010). "YSL, à la Vie à l'Amour" (*Libération*, March 20, 2010). "YSL, Une Excellence en Son Palais" (*Libération*, March 20, 2010). "Saint Laurent au Firmamant" (*Le Figaro Magazine*, April 2, 2010). "Bergé, d'Autorité" (*Magazine Littéraire*, May 1, 2010). "Le Retour de la Sulfureuse Lulu" (*Le Figaro*, May 14, 2010). "Les Trophées pas si Vains de Pierre Bergé" (*Le Figaro*, August 20, 2010). "L'Amour Fou" (*Les Inrockuptibles*, September 22, 2010). "Yves Saint Laurent & Pierre Bergé, des Amours Haute Couture" (*Le Figaro*, September 22, 2010).

2011. "YSL's Stefano Pilati" (*W Magazine*, February 1, 2011). "Rive Gauche, Retour vers le Futur" (*Le Figaro*, February 23, 2011). "Stefano Pilati, Enfin Libre chez Yves Saint Laurent" (*L'Express*, March 15, 2011). "Yves Saint Laurent Poursuivi par Christian Louboutin" (*Elle*, April 12, 2011). "Loulou de la Falaise, l'Élégance Spirituelle" (*Le Figaro*, November 7, 2011).

2012. "Stefano Pilati to Exit YSL Next Week" (*Elle*, February 26, 2012). "Stefano Pilati Quitte Yves Saint Laurent" (*L'Express*, February 27, 2012). "HedYSLimane" (*Libération*, February 27, 2012). "Hedi Slimane chez Saint Laurent" (*Le Point*, March 1, 2012). "Hedi Slimane Officiellement chez YSL" (*Le Figaro*, March 7, 2012). "Hedi Saint Laurent ?" (*Le Figaro*, June 21, 2012). "Yves Saint Laurent sans Yves: Pierre Bergé Approuve" (*Elle*, June 21, 2012). "Yves Saint Laurent Change de Nom" (*L'Express*, June 29, 2012). "Channeling the Codes of Saint Laurent" (*New York Times*, October 1, 2012). "Saint Laurent: Back at the Château Marmont" (*New York Times*, October 2, 2012).

2013. "Yves Saint Laurent: les Deux Visages de Pierre Bergé" (*Le Figaro*, February 7, 2013). "Yves Saint Laurent Retrouve sa Ligne d'Antant" (*Challenges*, February 15, 2013). "Yves Saint Laurent entre Quatre Yeux" (*Le Monde*, February 26, 2013). "La Guerre des Deux Saint Laurent" (*Libération*, April 5, 2013). "Hedi Slimane Étend Son Pouvoir chez Yves Saint Laurent" (*Les Echos*, July 2, 2013). "Yves Saint Laurent Revit au Cinéma" (*Paris Match*, September 1, 2013). "Yves Saint Laurent, dans les Coulisses du film de Jalil Lespert" (*Elle*, September 2, 2013). "Une Robe Yves Saint Laurent S'Envole aux Enchères" (*Le Monde*, October 14, 2013). "Pierre Bergé, Éternel Compagnon d'Yves Saint Laurent (*L'Express*, December 31, 2013).

2014. "YSL, le B*âton de Bergé*" (*Libération*, January 7, 2014). "Quand Pierre Bergé se confiait à Match" (*Paris Match*, January 7, 2014). "Saint Laurent: Schizo haute couture" (*Libération*, May 19, 2014). "Gaspard Ulliel, Pierre Niney: Le match des Saint Laurent" (*Le Figaro*, September 24, 2014). "A Look inside Yves Saint Laurent's final home in Tangier" (*T Magazine*, October 14, 2014).

2015. "Yves Saint Laurent, le Retour Rive Gauche" (*Vogue*, March 2015). "Yves Saint Laurent: Anatomie d'un Scandale" (*Madame Figaro*, March 13, 2015). "Les Raisons du Succès Commercial de Saint Laurent" (*Le Monde*, March 16, 2015). "Yves Saint Laurent, la Collection du Scandale Exposée" (*L'Express*, March 20, 2015). "Saint Laurent Reprend ses Quartier Rive Gauche (*Marie Claire*, March 25, 2015). "Pierre Bergé vend sa Bibliothèque aux Enchères" (*Le Figaro*, April 25, 2015). "Hedi Slimane Lève le Voile sur Ses Inspirations" (*Vanity Fair France*, August 13, 2015).

2016. "Hedi Slimane & Saint Laurent: Les Dessous d'un *Départ*" (*Gala*, January 19, 2016). "Yves Saint Laurent: Deux Musées pour l'Automne 2017" (*Elle*, January 28, 2016). "Yves Saint Laurent, Deux Musées pour un Couturier" (*Le Monde*, January 29, 2016). "Pierre Bergé, Sorcerer of Yves Saint Laurent" (Suzy Menkes, Vogue.co.uk, February 2016). "Saint's Day: Hedi Slimane's LA Extravaganza" (*Financial Times*, February 11, 2016). "Love Story" (*Numéro*, February 28, 2016). "L'Hymne Glam de Slimane à Yves Saint Laurent" (*Next*, March 8, 2016). "Pourquoi Yves Saint Laurent a Perdu Son Créateur" (*Les Echos*, April 1, 2016). "YSL Picks Vaccarello as Creative Director" (*Financial Times*, April 5, 2016)."Anthony Vaccarello, le Nouveau Visage d'Yves Saint Laurent" (*Le Monde*, April 6, 2016). "Pierre Bergé, Partner of the Late Yves Saint Laurent" (*Financial Times*, April 7, 2016). "Marrakech et Yves Saint Laurent: De la Muse au Musée" (*Le Figaro*, May 2016). "Saint Laurent CEO Francesca Bellettini on the Making of a $1bn Brand" (*Financial Times*, May 26, 2016). "Avec Yves, le Coup de Foudre Fut Total" (*Grazia*, July 11, 2016). "A voix nue, Pierre Bergé" (*France Culture*, August 2016). "Le Saint des des Saints" (*Grazia*, September 2016). "Anthony Vaccarello: Le Lisse, ce N'est pas Saint Laurent" (*Le Monde*, September 28, 2016). "Saint Laurent: Le Sexy Selon Vaccarello" (*Le Figaro*, September 28, 2016). "Bernard Buffet, les Années 1950. Entretien avec Pierre Bergé" (*Connaissance des Arts*, October 18, 2016). "Succès pour le Deuxième Volet de la Bibliothèque Pierre Bergé à Drouot" (*Le Figaro*, November 11, 2016). "Le Cabinet de Curiosités de Pierre Bergé" (*Le Figaro*, November 28, 2016). "Yves Saint Laurent's Jardin Majorelle" (*Financial Times*, December 6, 2016). "Le Roi Mohammed VI du Maroc *Décore Pierre Bergé*" (*Paris Match*, December 28, 2016).

2017. "Aurélie Samuel, du Kimono au Smoking" (*Le Figaro*, February 21, 2017). "Anthony Vaccarello, Disciple de Son Temps et de Saint Laurent" (*Le Figaro*, March 1, 2017). "Pierre Bergé S'est Marié avec le Jardinier des Milliardaires" (*Le Figaro*, May 4, 2017). "Madison Cox, le Dernier amour de Pierre Bergé" (*Têtu*, May 9, 2017). "Anthony Vaccarello, dans les pas d'Yves Saint Laurent" (*Le Monde*, May 26, 2017). "Yves Saint Laurent va Avoir deux Musées" (*L'Obs*, June 8, 2017). "Catherine Deneuve et Yves Saint Laurent: Une Alliance Éternelle" (*Grazia*, September 4, 2017). "French Industrialist Pierre Bergé Dies Aged 86" (*Financial Times*, September 8, 2017). "L'Homme d'Affaires et Mécène Pierre Bergé est Mort" (*Le Figaro*, September 8, 2017). "Pierre Bergé, une Vie Haute Couture" (*Le Parisien*, September 8, 2017). "Pierre Bergé et

Yves Saint Laurent, Cinquante ans d'Amour et de Mode" (*Elle*, September 8, 2017). "Pierre Bergé, homme d'affaires et mécène" (*Les Echos*, September 10, 2017). "Pierre Bergé: Un Engagement Politique Tardif Mais Passionné" (*Libération*, September 8, 2017). "Pierre Bergé, une Vie d'Engagements" (*L'Obs*, September 13, 2017). "Pierre Bergé, avec son meilleur souvenir" (*Le Point*, September 13, 2017). "Celebrating Yves Saint Laurent" (*New York Times* International Edition, September 27, 2017). "Deux Musées pour une Icône" (*Le Figaro*, September 29, 2017). "The Future for Fashion in the Post-YSL-Pierre Bergé Era" (*Forbes*, September 29, 2017). "Style Is Eternal: A Designer Tale of Two Fashion Cities" (*The Telegraph*, September 29, 2017). "The Legacy of Yves Saint Laurent: Two New Museums Celebrate the Designer" (*Financial Times*, September 30, 2017). "YSL, la Cérémonie des Adieux" (*M le magazine du Monde*, September 30, 2017). "Musée Yves Saint Laurent: Dans le Saint des Saints" (*Le Figaro*, October 2, 2017). "Marrakech, un Abri de Lumière pour Saint Laurent" (*Libération*, October 5, 2017). "Yves Saint Laurent, de la Maison de Couture au Musée" (*Le Journal des Arts*, October 6, 2017). "Retour à Marrakech" (*Les Echos*, October 8, 2017). "Les plus Beaux Projets de Studio KO" (*AD Magazine*, October 10, 2017). "Le Musée Yves Saint Laurent Marrakech Inauguré ce Week-end" (*Le Figaro*, October 13, 2017). "Saint Laurent sous le Soleil de Marrakech" (*Le Figaro*, October 15, 2017). "YSL, d'Oran à Marrakech" (*Les Inrockuptibles*, October 18, 2017). "Yves Saint Laurent Marrakech, un Musée en Terre Promise" (*Le Temps*, October 28, 2017). "Saint Laurent For Ever" (*Le Point*, November 16, 2017). "Le Magasin Colette Ferme dans un Mois et Sera Repris par Saint Laurent" (*Le Parisien*, November 20, 2017). "Fantasia Yves Saint Laurent dans la Ville Rose" (*Almaviva*, November 28, 2017).

2018.   "Le Beau Succès du Studio KO" (*Connaissance des Arts*, January 11, 2018). "Yves Saint Laurent, l'Aura et les Icônes" (*Revue des Deux Mondes*, February 2018).

VIDEOS

"Yves Mathieu-Saint-Laurent, Lauréat du Concours de Dessin de Mode" (Actua-Gaumont, 1954). "Yves Saint Laurent Présente sa Collection (Dior) à la Princesse Margaret au Château de Blenheim (Grande-Bretagne)" (Actua-Gaumont, 1958). "Yves Saint Laurent Interviewé par Micheline Sandrel" (INA, 1958). "Yves Saint Laurent Répond à Claude Berthod." *Dim Dam Dom* episode 38 (INA, 1967). *Woman Is Sweeter*, Martine Barrat, 1971. "A Propos de L'Aigle à Deux Têtes" (INA, 1978). "Yves Saint Laurent Interviewé par Catherine Deneuve" (Globe TV, 1986). Videotapes of haute couture and Rive Gauche runway shows starting in 1978 (Musée Saint Laurent archives).

FILMS

1962.   *Le Business de la Mode* by William Klein, Cinq Colonnes à la Une, ORTF, INA.

1994.   *Tout Terriblement* by Jérôme Missolz, Lieurac Production.

1998.   *Les Couleurs du Monde*. Retrospective fashion show on July 12 at the Stade de France.

2001.   *5 Avenue Marceau* by David Teboul, Movimiento.

2001.   *Le Temps Retrouvé* by David Teboul, Movimiento.

2001.   *Célébration* by Olivier Meyrou.

2011. *L'Amour fou* by Pierre Thorreton, Les Films du lendemain.
Yves Saint Laurent, le dernier défilé, by Loïc Prigent, Arte / Story Box Press.

2014. *Yves Saint Laurent* by Jalil Lespert, M6 Vidéo.
Saint Laurent by Bertrand Bonello.

2016. "Le Divan de Marc-Olivier Fogiel, avec Pierre Bergé." February 2016, France 3.

2017. *Les Dessins d'Yves Saint Laurent*, by Loïc Prigent, Arte / Bangumi.
À Voix Nue, interview with Pierre Bergé by Joëlle Gayot, Radio France.
Yves Saint Laurent, Pierre Bergé, Un Aigle à Deux Têtes, by Edoardo Cecchin, Musée YSL Paris.
Célébration, by Olivier Meyrou.

COSTUMES BY YVES SAINT LAURENT FOR THE CINEMA

1960. *Les Collants Noirs* by Terence Young. Choreography by Roland Petit. Costumes for Moira Shearer.

1963. *The Pink Panther* by Blake Edwards. Costumes for Claudia Cardinale.

1966. *Arabesque* by Stanley Donen. Costumes for Sophia Loren.

1967. *Belle de Jour* by Luis Buñuel. Costumes for Catherine Deneuve.

1968. *Heartbeat* (*La Chamade*) by Alain Cavalier. Costumes for Catherine Deneuve.

1974. *Stavisky* by Alain Resnais. Costumes for Anny Duperey.

1975. *The Romantic Englishwoman* (*Une Anglaise Romantique*) by Joseph Losey. Costumes for Helmut Berger.

1977. *Providence* by Alain Resnais. Costumes for Ellen Burstyn.

SETS AND COSTUMES BY YVES SAINT LAURENT FOR THEATER AND DANCE

1959. *Cyrano de Bergerac*. Choreography by Roland Petit, based on the book by Edmond Rostand. Music by Marius Constant. Théâtre de l'Alhambra, Paris.

1961. *Les Forains*. Choreography by Roland Petit. Synopsis by Boris Kochno. Music by Henri Sauguet. French television. *La Chaloupée*. Choreography by Roland Petit. Book by M. Aymé. Music by M. Thiriet. Copenhagen Opera. Revue by Zizi Jeanmaire, *Le Truc en Plumes* (music by J. Constantin), choreography by Roland Petit. *España* (E. Chabrier), *Scaramouche* (Darius Milhaud), *Tarentelle* (Rossini), *Pas de Trois* (Marius Constant). Théâtre de l'Alhambra, Paris.

1962. *Les Chants de Maldoror*, choreography by Roland Petit. Théâtre Nationale Populaire, Paris. *Rhapsodie Espagnole* (Maurice Ravel). *Le Violon* (Paganini, M. Constant).

Choreography by Roland Petit. Sets and costumes by Yves Saint Laurent. Théâtre Nationale Populaire, Paris. (Staged at La Scala in Milan in 1963.)

1963. *La Silla, Gourmandises*. (M. Mention). Choreography by Roland Petit. Ballet show by P. Italie.

1964. *Le Mariage de Figaro* by Beaumarchais. Directed by Jean-Louis Barrault. Renaud-Barrault Company. Odéon-Théâtre de France, Paris. *Il Faut Passer par les Nuages*, by François Billetdoux. Directed by Jean-Louis Barrault. Renaud-Barrault Company. Odéon-Théâtre de France, Paris.

1965. *Adage et Variations*. Music by François Poulenc. Choreography by Roland Petit. Théâtre National Populaire, Paris. *Notre-Dame de Paris*. Choreography by Roland Petit, based on the book by Victor Hugo. Music by Maurice Jarre. Costumes for Claire Motte, Cyril Atanassoff, J.P. Bonnefous, Roland Petit. Théâtre National Populaire, Paris. *Des Journées Entières dans les Arbres* by Marguerite Duras. Renaud-Barrault Company. Odéon-Théâtre de France, Paris.

1966. *Les Monstres Sacré*s by Jean Cocteau. Costumes for Arletty. Théâtre des Ambassadeurs.

1967. *A Delicate Balance* by Edward Albee. Renaud-Barrault Company. Odéon-Théâtre de France, Paris. *Paradis Perdu*. Music by Marius Constant. Choreography by Roland Petit. Costumes for Margot Fonteyn and Rudolf Nureyev. Royal Ballet, London, February. Royal Opera House, London. (In Paris in October 1967.)

1968. *L'Amante Anglaise* by Marguerite Duras. Directed by Claude Régy. Costumes for Madeleine Renaud. Théâtre National Populaire, Paris, Gémier Theater. Zizi Jeanmaire's show. Music by E. Robrecht. Choreography by Roland Petit. Théâtre de l'Olympia, Paris.

1970. Zizi Jeanmaire's revue. Sets and costumes by Yves Saint Laurent. Casino de Paris. Show by Sylvie Vartan. Théâtre de l'Olympia, Paris.

1971. Johnny Hallyday's show. Palais des Sports, Paris.

1972. *Zizi Je T'Aime: La Veuve Rusée*. Music by Drigo and Kreisler. Casino de Paris. Sylvie Vartan's show. Théâtre de l'Olympia, Paris.

1973. *La Rose Malade*. Music by Gustav Mahler. Choreography by Roland Petit. Palais des Sports, Paris. *Harold et Maude* by Colin Higgins. Directed by Jean-Louis Barrault. Costumes for Madeleine Renaud. Renaud-Barrault Company. Théâtre Récamier, Paris. *La Chevauchée sur le Lac de Constance* by Peter Handke. Directed by Claude Régy. Costumes for Jeanne Moreau and Delphine Seyrig. Espace Pierre Cardin, Paris. *Shéhérazade*. Music by Maurice Ravel. Choreography by Roland Petit. Costumes for Michael Denard and Ghislaine Thesmar. Théâtre National Populaire, Paris.

1977. Zizi Jeanmaire's revue. Directed by Roland Petit. Théâtre Bobino, Paris.

1978. *L'Aigle à Deux Têtes* (*The Eagle with Two Heads*) by Jean Cocteau. With Edwige Feuillère and Martine Chevalier. Directed by Jean-Louis Dusséaux. Sets and costumes by Yves Saint Laurent. Théâtre de l'Athénée-Louis Jouvet, Paris. Ingrid Caven's show. Le Pigall's Cabaret, Paris.

1980. *Cher Menteur* by Jérôme Kilty. Based on a work by Jean Cocteau. Sets and costumes by Yves Saint Laurent. Théâtre de l'Athénée-Louis Jouvet, Paris. *Wings* by Arthur Kopit. Based on a work by Matthieu Galey. Directed by Claude Régy. Théâtre d'Orsay, Paris.

1983. *Savannah Bay* by Marguerite Duras. Directed by Marguerite Duras. Costumes for Miou-Miou and Madeleine Renaud. Théâtre du Rond-Point, Paris.

1993. *Marcel et la Belle Excentrique* by Jean-Pierre Grédy. Directed by Roland Petit. Costumes for Zizi Jeanmaire. Théâtre Montparnasse.

EXHIBITIONS AND PUBLIC FASHION SHOWS

1974. Exhibition of designs for costumes and stage sets at the Galerie Proscénium, Paris.

1978. Exhibition of designs for costumes and stage sets at the Galerie Proscénium, Paris.

1983. First retrospective: *Yves Saint Laurent: 25 Years of Design*. Metropolitan Museum of Art, New York (December 5, 1983–September 2, 1984).

1985. National Art Museum of China, Beijing (May 6–July).

1986. *Yves Saint Laurent, 28 Années de Création*. Musée des Arts de la Mode, Paris (May 26–October). Central House of Artist of the Soviet Union, Moscow (December 2, 1986–January 1987).

1987. Hermitage Museum, Saint Petersburg (February 3–March). Art Gallery of New South Wales, Sydney (May 19–July).

1988. Fashion show at the Fête de *L'Humanité*, La Courneuve, France (September 9).

1989. Yves Saint Laurent curates an exhibition of historical Russian costumes from the Hermitage Museum in Leningrad. Musée Jacquemart-André, Paris (March 1–May). *Yves Saint Laurent and Fashion Photography*. Pompidou Center, Paris (April–June). For the Year of France in India, fashion show at Sher Shah Gate, Delhi (November 9). Gateway of India, Mumbai (November 12 and 19).

1990. Fashion show at Budokan, Tokyo (November 20). *Fashion 1958-1990*. Sezon Museum of Modern Art, Tokyo (November–December).

1991. Yves Saint Laurent curates the exhibition *L'Art du Ballet en Russie, 1740-1940*. Palais Garnier, Paris (September–December).

1992. Fashion show in the French pavilion of the World's Fair. Seville, Spain (July 14).

1993. *Yves Saint Laurent: Exotismes*. Musée de la Mode, Marseille (December 10, 1993– March 27, 1994.

1998. Fashion show at the World Cup with 300 designs. Stade de France, Paris (July 12).

2002. Display of Yves Saint Laurent haute couture ateliers. Windows of the Galeries Lafayette, Paris (January 21–February 28). Exhibition of photographs by Pierre Boulat. FNAC Étoile, Paris (January 15–29). Retrospective show of forty years of the Maison Saint Laurent. Pompidou Centre, Paris (January 22). *40 Ans de Création en Dentelle: Yves Saint Laurent Haute Couture*. Musée des Beaux Arts et de la Dentelle d'Alençon, Alençon, France (June 8–September 29).

2004. *Dialogue avec l'Art*. Fondation Pierre Bergé-Yves Saint Laurent, Paris (September 1– October 21). *Les Fables de La Fontaine,* an exhibition by Robert Wilson. Fondation Pierre Bergé - Yves Saint Laurent, Paris (November 24, 2004–July 24, 2005).

2005. Exhibition of designs and dresses by Yves Saint Laurent. Broadbent Gallery, London (March 3–October 16).

2006. *Photographies*, by André Ostier. Fondation Pierre Bergé - Yves Saint Laurent, Paris (May 18–July 28). *Smoking Forever*. Fondation Pierre Bergé - Yves Saint Laurent, Paris (October 5, 2006–April 23, 2007) *Voyages Extraordinaries*. Fondation Pierre Bergé - Yves Saint Laurent, Paris (November 4, 2006–April 15, 2007).

2007. *Nan Kempner, une Américaine à Paris*. Fondation Pierre Bergé - Yves Saint Laurent, Paris (May 16–July 29). *Yves Saint Laurent, Théâtre, Cinéma, Music Hall, Ballet*. Fondation Pierre Bergé - Yves Saint Laurent, Paris (October 4, 2007–January 27, 2008).

2008. *Une Passion Marocaine, Caftans, Broderies, Bijoux*. Fondation Pierre Bergé - Yves Saint Laurent, Paris (March 14–August 31). *Yves Saint Laurent, Dialogue avec l'art*. Caixa Galicia Foundation, A Coruña, Spain (April 12–May 4). *Yves Saint Laurent, Style*. Musée des Beaux-Arts de Montréal, Canada (May 29–September 28).*Yves Saint Laurent*. De Young Museum, San Francisco (November 1–April 5, 2009).

2009. *Yves Saint Laurent, Voyages Extraordinaires*, Banco do Brasil Cultural Center, Rio de Janeiro. (June 1–July 20). *Jean-Michel Frank, Un décorateur dans le Paris des années 30*. Fondation Pierre Bergé - Yves Saint Laurent. (October 2–January 3, 2010).

2010. Retrospective at the Petit Palais, featuring more than three hundred designs and more than forty years of d'Yves Saint Laurent's creativity, from the Dior years to his last collection in 2002 (March 11–August 22). *Yves Saint Laurent, Archives de la création, 1962–2002,* IMEC, Caen, France (June 8–October 31).

2011. *Saint Laurent Rive Gauche.* Fondation Pierre Bergé - Yves Saint Laurent (March 5– July 17). *Yves Saint Laurent et le Maroc.* Villa des Arts, ONA Foundation, Casablanca (April 13–July 17). Retrospective at the Fondación MAPFRE, Madrid (October 5– January 8, 2012). Gisèle Freund, L'œil frontière, Paris 1933 – 1940. Fondation Pierre Bergé - Yves Saint Laurent. (October 14–January 29, 2012).

2012. *Kabuki, Costumes du théâtre japonais.* Fondation Pierre Bergé - Yves Saint Laurent (March 7–July 15). *Du côté de chez Jacques-Émile Blanche, Un salon à la Belle Époque.* Fondation Pierre Bergé - Yves Saint Laurent (October 11–January 27, 2013).

2013. *Yves Saint Laurent Visionnaire.* ING Cultural Space, Brussels (January 30–May 5). *Paris Haute Couture.* Exhibition at l'Hôtel de Ville in Paris, of the most beautiful pieces from the Palais Galliera's collections, among which were several Yves Saint Laurent designs (March 2–July 6).

2014. *Femmes berbères du Maroc.* Fondation Pierre Bergé - Yves Saint Laurent (March 21– July 20). *Crazy About Yves: Olivier Chatenet's Collection Pays Tribute to YSL.* Le French May Festival, Hong Kong (May 19–June 11). *Hedi Slimane, Sonic.* Photography exhibition at Fondation Pierre Bergé - Yves Saint Laurent. (September 18–January 11, 2015). *40 silhouettes composées d'archives Yves Saint Laurent.* Olivier Chatenet, Galerie 7.5, Paris (October).

2015. *Yves Saint Laurent 1971: La collection du scandale.* Fondation Pierre Bergé - Yves Saint Laurent (March 19–July 19). *Yves Saint–Laurent Style is Eternal.* Bowes Museum, Barnard Castle, Durham (July 11– October 25). *Jacques Doucet–Yves Saint Laurent.* Fondation Pierre Bergé - Yves Saint Laurent (October 15–February 14, 2016).

2016. *Paris Haute Couture.* Mitsubishi Ichigokan Museum, Tokyo.(March 3–July 7). *Yves Saint Laurent: The Perfection of Style.* Seattle Art Museum. (October 11–January 8, 2017).

2017. *Un regard sur Yves Saint Laurent, Dans la collection d'Olivier Chatenet.* Centre des Congrès, Dinan (April 8–May 14). *Yves Saint Laurent: The Perfection of Style.* Virginia Museum of Fine Arts, Richmond (May 6–August 28). *Dior, Couturier du Rêve.* Musée des Arts Décoratifs, Paris (July 5–January 7, 2018).

2018. *Saint Laurent by Laurent Goumarre.* Exhibition at Alain Gutharc Gallery, Paris (January 27–February 24).

ACKNOWLEDGMENTS

In this list dating back to 1993, updated in 2002, 2012, and again in 2018, the living and the dead are kept together, united by their shared passion. I didn't want to touch them, to separate them.

Naturally, my great thanks go to Yves Saint Laurent and Pierre Bergé. I must thank Olivier Nora, Christophe Bataille, Léa Laügt, Agnès Nivière, Muguette Vivian (Grasset), as well as Madison Cox, Bjorn Dalhström, Zohra El Hajji, Quito Fierro (Mysl), Olivier Flaviano, Aurélie Samuel, Domitille Eblé, Alice Coulon-Saillard (Musée Yves Saint Laurent, Paris); Pierre Scherrer, Jérôme Gautier, Frédéric Bourdelier, Olivier Bialobos (Dior); Karine Porret for her invaluable help in rereading this work, and Christophe Renard.

I would like to thank my parents, Paul and Nicole Benaïm, my husband, Bruno Krief, and all those who supported me throughout this project: Manuel Carcassonne, Jacques Brunel, Jeanine Attal, Fanny and Jean-Claude Chouchan. I am grateful for the help of Marc Audibet and Colombe Pringle, Jean Poniatowski, Antoine Kieffer, Karen Lombard, and Susan Train, in memory of years spent at *Vogue*. Warm thanks to Dominique Deroche, and also to Anne-Marie Muñoz, Betty Catroux, Philippe Mugnier, Fernando Sanchez, Brigitte Bastian, Michèle Levasseur, and Simone Lamy.

This book would not have been possible without the stories of those who *are* the memory of haute couture. I am very grateful to all the people who shared with me their memories and their affectionate loyalty to their profession and their years at Saint Laurent: Maryse Agussol, Amalia Vairelli, Denise Barry de Longchamp, Gabrielle Buchaert, Claire de Billy, Georgette Capelli, Renée Cassart, Laurent Chapus, Hélène Chenot, Terry de Gunzburg, Victoire de Courrèges, Josiane Dacquet, Jean-Pierre Derbord, Catherine Devoulon, Nicole Dorier, Jérôme Fayant-Dumas, Jean Marie Farthouat, Isabelle Gérin, Bénédicte de Ginestous, Christophe Girard, Joy Corinne Guillaud, Joy Hendericks, Marianne Honvault, Sylviane Hodgkinson, Esther Jadot, Reale de Haut de Sigy, Marie Thérèse Herzog, Simone Jacob, Danièle Leclercq, Raymonde Lelay, Vesna Laufer, Claude Licard, Hélène de Ludinghausen, Colette Maciet, Paule de Mérindol, Eléonore de Musset, Hector Pascual, Anna Pavlowski, Corinne Le Ralle, Ariel de Ravenel, Marie-Françoise Savary, Marie-Agnès Renault, Patricia Turcq Paquelier, Mercedès Rubirosa, Felisa Salvagnac, Marina Schiano, Danièle Varenne, Romain Verdure, and Micheline Ziegler. And those who we lost early: Pierre Barlat, Jacques Chazot, Loulou de la Falaise, Lucienne Mathieu-Saint-Laurent, Katoucha Niane, Hélène Rochas, Jean-Luc Rossignol, Stephen de Pietri, Madame Yvonne de Peyerimhoff, André Ostier, Jeanloup Sieff, and Roger Vivier.

My thanks go out as well to all the people who contributed to the writing of this book through their presence or their memories: Philippe d'Abzac, Charlotte Aillaud, Alexandre de Paris, Maïmé Arnodin, Claude Asnar, Yves Attal, Claude Aurensan, Javier Arroyuelo, Martine Barrat, Fernand Baron, Simone Baron, Gérard Benoit, Annie Boulat (Cosmos), Antoine Bourseiller, James Brady, Serge Bramly, Marcial Berro, Claude Berthod, Marguerite Bins, Michel Brodsky, Jackie Budin, Pierre Cardin, François Catroux, Edmonde Charles-Roux, Jean Cohen, Philippe Collin, Baroness Geoffroy de Courcel, Guy Cuevas, Roger Dadoun, Jacques and Françoise Darmon, Mademoiselle Catherine Deneuve, Jacques and Rolande Dijan, Victoire Doutreleau, Simon Dupuis, Frédéric Edelmann, Joe Eula, John Evans, John Fairchild, Denise Fayolle, Maxime de la Falaise, Jacques Fieschi, Jean-Pierre Frère, Countess de Gastines, Sylvie Grumbach, Jean-Paul Gaultier, Sophie Gins and Brigitte Torlet (Association des Anciens de Dior), Robert Goossens, Jacques Grange, François Heuzé, Zizi Jeanmaire, Alex and Yvonne Karsenti, Nan Kempner, Kenzo, Antoine Kieffer, Mustapha Labhali, Claude and François-Xavier Lalanne, Jack Lang, André Lemarié, Marielle Lemercier, François Lesage, André Levi, Patrick Lienhart, José Luis, Robert Malek, Bernard Minoret, Albert Mulphin, Carlos Muñoz, Jérôme Nicollin, Helmut Newton, Sylvie de Nussac, Mounia Orosemane, Paquita Paquin, Pierre Passebon, Irving Penn, Elsa Peretti, Roland Petit, Paloma Picasso, J. Mack Robinson, John Richardson, Pierre Rivas, Serge Roumegous, Jacques Rouet, Janie Samet, Olga Saurat, Jacques Siclier, Richard Salomon, Rafael Lopez Sanchez, Countess San Just, Sao Schlumberger, Étienne Tiffou, Yves Vié Le Sage, Baroness van Zuylen, Gaby van Zuylen, Bill Willis, Carole and Francine Weisweiller, Patricia Lopez-Willshaw, and Zkhiri (Le Yacout, Marrakesh). And great thanks to Jenny Capitain, Dominique Issermann, and Martine de Menthon.

I am also grateful for access to archives, libraries, and records, and would like to thank the following individuals and organizations: the archives of the Maison Yves Saint Laurent Haute Couture, the Fondation pour le Rayonnement de l'Oeuvre d'Yves Saint Laurent, the Bibliothèque Nationale de France (Paris-Versailles), the Bibliothèque de l'Arsenal, the Bibliothèque Forney, the Bibliothèque des Régisseurs de Théâtre, the research department of the Hôtel Drouot, the archives of the Maison Dior, Denise Dubois and Didier Grumbach (Chambre Syndicale de la Haute Couture et du Prêt-à-Porter des Couturiers et des Créateurs de Mode), Alberto de Fabro (Cinémathèque Robert-Lynen de la Ville de Paris), Sophie Gallouédec (Johnny Hallyday), Emmanuelle Montet (UFAC, Musée des Arts de la Mode), Lydie Nenirn (LVMH), Claude Visdomine (Association des Anciens du Lycée Lamoricière, Oran), Maison Renoma, Société d'Histoire du Théâtre, the research departments of Le Figaro, Elle, L'Express, Marie Claire, Le Monde, and Vogue, with special thanks to Anne-Céline Auché, Véronique Damagnez, Corinne Pineau, Ursula Redski, and Mary Stephen.

I'd also like to thank Françoise Chautemps, Claude Dalla Torre, Jean-Pierre Decaens, Ariane Fasquelle, Eliane Mounier, Jean-Pierre Pouchet, Marie-Laurence Roblin (Grasset), Georges Dersy, Marie-Jeanne Marcilly, and Muguette Vivian.

Sincere thanks to Céline Bokobsa, and also Anne d'Armagnac, Jean-Pierre Baux, Charles Bibas, Laure de Carrière, Olivier Chatenet, Caroline Deroche, Karl Fournier and Olivier Marty (Studio KO), Marianne Honvault, Elsa Gribinski, Laurence Kleinknecht, Jean-Luc Le François, Pascale Leautey, Cristina Malgara, Hervé-Antoine Mayer, Olivier Meyrou, Maryvonne Numata, Jean-Philippe Pons, Elie Romero, Olivier Segot, Lizza Schiek, Pascal Sittler, Odile Vilain.

PLAYLIST

Songs, arias, melodies, jazz, the voices of women…The maison Yves Saint Laurent was the first to give music a prominent role, even integrating a sound library at 5 Avenue Marceau in Paris. Often the name of a musician would be printed on the program of each haute couture collection. From the Ballet Russes collection in July 1956 to the launch of the perfume Jazz in 1988, music was an integral part of the aesthetic world of Yves Saint Laurent: "And suddenly, surging from the deep, a burning, deep, high, strident, supernatural, baroque voice, a voice unlike any other, tried to fight death," he wrote in *Le Monde* on September 16, 1977, on the occasion of the death of Maria Callas, whom he deeply admired. I chose to pay homage to the fashion designer with a journey through music, which in its own way extends the house of Saint Laurent.

Tino Rossi Méditerranée
Yvonne Printemps Je t'aime
Charles Trenet Revoir Paris / La mer / Le soleil et la lune / Que reste-t-il de nos amours
Yves Montand Sous le ciel de Paris / A Paris
Billie Holiday My Man
Marilyn Monroe Diamonds Are a Girl's Best Friend / I Wanna Be Loved by You
The Beatles Revolution / Here Comes the Sun
The Rolling Stones (I Can't Get No) Satisfaction / You Can't Always Get What You Want
Lou Reed Walk on the Wild Side
Johann Sebastian Bach Goldberg Variations / Prelude, Suite no. 1 in G Major
Vincenzo Bellini *Norma* (Aria: Casta Diva, Maria Callas)
Alfredo Catalani *La Wally* (Maria Callas)
Gaetano Donizetti Amore e morte
Wolfgang Amadeus Mozart Requiem / *The Magic Flute* / *The Marriage of Figaro* / *Così fan tutte* / *Don Giovanni* / Great Mass in C Minor
Giuseppe Verdi *La Traviata* / *Rigoletto* / *Il trovatore* / *Don Carlos* / *Otello* / *Stabat Mater*
Giacomo Puccini *Madame Butterfly* / *Tosca* (Aria: Vissi d'arte, la Callas)
Johannes Brahms Piano Concerto no. 1 / Danses hongroises
Serge Gainsbourg Bonnie and Clyde
Gustav Malher Symphony no. 5 in C sharp minor
Franz Schubert *Des Mädchens Klage* / String Quartet no. 14 in D Minor
Richard Wagner *Parsifal* / Prelude, *Lohengrin* / *Tannhäuser*
Zizi Jeanmaire Mon truc en plumes
Marlene Dietrich Lili Marlene / Falling in Love Again
Anton Bruckner Symphony no. 7 in E Major
Gluck Che farò senza Euridice from *Orfeo ed Euridice*, in *L'innocent* by Luchino Visconti
Maurice Ravel *Boléro*

Josephine Baker La vie en rose
César Franck Sonata in A Major for Violin and Piano
Gabriel Fauré Ballade, Op. 19
Henri Sauguet Les forains
The Velvet Underground Venus in Furs
Queen Don't Stop Me Now
The Weather Girls It's Raining Men
Gloria Gaynor I Will Survive
Carte de séjour Douce France
Barbara Le mal de vivre / Ma plus belle histoire d'amour / La solitude / L'aigle noir / Göttingen
Johnny Hallyday Allumer le feu / Quelque chose de Tennessee / Que je t'aime / Le pénitencier / Gabrielle / Ma gueule
Juliette Gréco Parlez-moi d'amour / Je hais les dimanches / Déshabillez-moi / Jolie Môme / Je suis comme je suis
Jeanne Moreau India Song
Camille Saint-Saëns Violin Sonata no.1, Op. 75
George Gershwin *Porgy and Bess*, especially Summertime / Rhapsody in Blue
Franz Lehár The Merry Widow
Ella Fitzgerald Summertime / The Lady Is a Tramp / A-Tisket A-Tasket
Louis Armstrong A Kiss to Build a Dream On / Summertime / C'est si bon
Henri Salvador Jazz Méditerranée / Syracuse
Catherine Deneuve Ma plus belle histoire d'amour
Jacques Brel La chanson des vieux amants / Les prénoms de Paris
Charlotte Gainsbourg Trick Pony
Selah Sue Just Because I do
Norah Jones Carry On / Don't Know Why
Diana Krall Just the Way You Are / Let's Fall in Love
Daft Punk Saint Laurent Music Project
SebastiAN Soundtracks to Saint Laurent Winter 2017 and Winter 2018 collections

INDEX